The Plays of Aristophanes

The Plays of Aristophanes

Aristophanes

MINT EDITIONS

The Plays of Aristophanes were first published between 423 B.C. and 411 B.C.

This edition published by Mint Editions 2021.

ISBN 9781513218601 | E-ISBN 9781513217604

Published by Mint Editions®

MINT
EDITIONS

minteditionbooks.com

Publishing Director: Jennifer Newens
Design & Production: Rachel Lopez Metzger
Project Manager: Micaela Clark
Typesetting: Westchester Publishing Services

Contents

THE KNIGHTS

INTRODUCTION

This was the fourth play in order of time produced by Aristophanes on the Athenian stage; it was brought out at the Lenaean Festival, in January, 424 B.C. Of the author's previous efforts, two, 'The Revellers' and 'The Babylonians,' were apparently youthful essays, and are both lost. The other, 'The Acharnians,' forms the first of the three Comedies dealing directly with the War and its disastrous effects and urging the conclusion of Peace; for this reason it is better ranged along with its sequels, the 'Peace' and the 'Lysistrata,' and considered in conjunction with them.

In many respects 'The Knights' may be reckoned the great Comedian's masterpiece, the direct personal attack on the then all-powerful Cleon, with its scathing satire and tremendous invective, being one of the most vigorous and startling things in literature. Already in 'The Acharnians' he had threatened to "cut up Cleon the Tanner into shoe-leather for the Knights," and he now proceeds to carry his menace into execution, "concentrating the whole force of his wit in the most unscrupulous and merciless fashion against his personal enemy." In the first-mentioned play Aristophanes had attacked and satirized the whole general policy of the democratic party—and incidentally Cleon, its leading spirit and mouthpiece since the death of Pericles; he had painted the miseries of war and invasion arising from this mistaken and mischievous line of action, as he regarded it, and had dwelt on the urgent necessity of peace in the interests of an exhausted country and ruined agriculture. Now he turns upon Cleon personally, and pays him back a hundredfold for the attacks the demagogue had made in the Public Assembly on the daring critic, and the abortive charge which the same unscrupulous enemy had brought against him in the Courts of having "slandered the city in the presence of foreigners." "In this bitterness of spirit the play stands in strong contrast with the good-humoured burlesque of 'The Acharnians' and the 'Peace,' or, indeed, with any other of the author's productions which has reached us."

The characters are five only. First and foremost comes Demos, 'The People,' typifying the Athenian democracy, a rich householder—a self-indulgent, superstitious, weak creature. He has had several overseers or factors in succession, to look after his estate and manage his slaves. The present one is known as 'the Paphlagonian,' or sometimes as 'the

Tanner,' an unprincipled, lying, cheating, pilfering scoundrel, fawning and obsequious to his master, insolent towards his subordinates. Two of these are Nicias and Demosthenes. Here we have real names. Nicias was High Admiral of the Athenian navy at the time, and Demosthenes one of his Vice-Admirals; both held still more important commands later in connection with the Sicilian Expedition of 415-413 B.C. Fear of consequences apparently prevented the poet from doing the same in the case of Cleon, who is, of course, intended under the names of 'the Paphlagonian' and 'the Tanner.' Indeed, so great was the terror inspired by the great man that no artist was found bold enough to risk his powerful vengeance by caricaturing his features, and no actor dared to represent him on the stage. Aristophanes is said to have played the part himself, with his face, in the absence of a mask, smeared with wine-lees, roughly mimicking the purple and bloated visage of the demagogue. The remaining character is 'the Sausage-seller,' who is egged on by Nicias and Demosthenes to oust 'the Paphlagonian' from Demos' favour by outvying him in his own arts of impudent flattery, noisy boasting and unscrupulous allurement. After a fierce and stubbornly contested trial of wits and interchange of 'Billingsgate,' 'the Sausage-seller' beats his rival at his own weapons and gains his object; he supplants the disgraced favourite, who is driven out of the house with ignominy.

The Comedy takes its title, as was often the case, from the Chorus, which is composed of Knights—the order of citizens next to the highest at Athens, and embodying many of the old aristocratic preferences and prejudices.

The drama was adjudged the first prize—the 'Satyrs' of Cratinus being placed second—by acclamation, as such a masterpiece of wit and intrepidity certainly deserved to be; but, as usual, the political result was nil. The piece was applauded in the most enthusiastic manner, the satire on the sovereign multitude was forgiven, and—Cleon remained in as much favour as ever.[1]

---

1. Mitchell's "Aristophanes." Preface to "The Knights."

Dramatis Personae

Demosthenes.
Nicias.
Agoracritus, a Sausage-seller.
Cleon.
Demos, an old man, typifying the Athenian people.
Chorus of Knights.

Scene: *In front of Demos' house at Athens.*

DEMOSTHENES: Oh! alas! alas! Oh! woe! oh! woe! Miserable
Paphlagonian![2] may the gods destroy both him and his cursed
advice! Since that evil day when this new slave entered the house
he has never ceased belabouring us with blows.

NICIAS: May the plague seize him, the arch-fiend—him and his lying
tales!

DEMOSTHENES: Hah! my poor fellow, what is your condition?

NICIAS: Very wretched, just like your own.

DEMOSTHENES: Then come, let us sing a duet of groans in the style of
Olympus.[3]

DEMOSTHENES AND NICIAS: Boo, hoo! boo, hoo! boo, hoo! boo, hoo!
boo, hoo! boo, hoo!!

DEMOSTHENES: Bah! 'tis lost labour to weep! Enough of groaning! Let
us consider how to save our pelts.

NICIAS: But how to do it! Can you suggest anything?

DEMOSTHENES: Nay! you begin. I cede you the honour.

NICIAS: By Apollo! no, not I. Come, have courage! Speak, and then
I will say what I think.

DEMOSTHENES: "Ah! would you but tell me what I should tell you!"[4]

NICIAS: I dare not. How could I express my thoughts with the pomp
of Euripides?

DEMOSTHENES: Oh! prithee, spare me! Do not pelt me with those
vegetables,[5] but find some way of leaving our master.

NICIAS: Well, then! Say "Let-us-bolt," like this, in one breath.

DEMOSTHENES: I follow you—"Let-us-bolt."

NICIAS: Now after "Let-us-bolt" say "at-top-speed!"

DEMOSTHENES: "At-top-speed!"

NICIAS: Splendid! Just as if you were masturbating yourself; first
slowly, "Let-us-bolt"; then quick and firmly, "at-top-speed!"

DEMOSTHENES: Let-us-bolt, let-us-bolt-at-top-speed![6]

NICIAS: Hah! does that not please you?

---

2. A generic name, used to denote a slave, because great numbers came from Paphlagonia,
a country in Asia Minor. Aristophanes also plays upon the word, (Greek: Paphlag on),
Paphlagonian, and the verb, (Greek: pathlazein), to boil noisily, thus alluding to Cleon's
violence and bluster when speaking.

3. A musician, belonging to Phrygia, who had composed melodies intended to describe pain.

4. Line 323 of the 'Hyppolytus,' by Euripides.

5. Euripides' mother was said to have sold vegetables on the market.

6. The whole of this passage seems a satire on the want of courage shown by these two
generals. History, however, speaks of Nicias as a brave soldier.

DEMOSTHENES: I' faith, yes! yet I fear me your omen bodes no good to my hide.

NICIAS: How so?

DEMOSTHENES: Because hard rubbing abrades the skin when folk masturbate themselves.

NICIAS: The best thing we can do for the moment is to throw ourselves at the feet of the statue of some god.

DEMOSTHENES: Of which statue? Any statue? Do you then believe there are gods?

NICIAS: Certainly.

DEMOSTHENES: What proof have you?

NICIAS: The proof that they have taken a grudge against me. Is that not enough?

DEMOSTHENES: I'm convinced it is. But to pass on. Do you consent to my telling the spectators of our troubles?

NICIAS: 'Twould not be amiss, and we might ask them to show us by their manner, whether our facts and actions are to their liking.

DEMOSTHENES: I will begin then. We have a very brutal master, a perfect glutton for beans,[7] and most bad-tempered; 'tis Demos of the Pnyx,[8] an intolerable old man and half deaf. The beginning of last month he bought a slave, a Paphlagonian tanner, an arrant rogue, the incarnation of calumny. This man of leather knows his old master thoroughly; he plays the fawning cur, flatters, cajoles; wheedles, and dupes him at will with little scraps of leavings, which he allows him to get. "Dear Demos," he will say, "try a single case and you will have done enough; then take your bath, eat, swallow and devour; here are three obols."[9] Then the Paphlagonian filches from one of us what we have prepared and makes a present of it to our old man. T'other day I had just kneaded a Spartan cake at Pylos;[10] the cunning rogue came behind my back, sneaked it and offered the cake, which was my invention, in his own name.

---

7. I.e. living on his salary as a judge. The Athenians used beans for recording their votes.

8. Place where the Public Assembly of Athens, the (Greek: ekkl esia), was held.

9. This was the salary paid to the Ecclesiasts, the jury of citizens who tried cases. It was one obol at first, but Cleon had raised it to three.

10. A town in Messina, opposite the little island of Sphacteria; Demosthenes had seized it, and the Spartans had vainly tried to retake it, having even been obliged to leave four hundred soldiers shut up in Sphacteria. Cleon, sent out with additional forces, had forced the Spartans to capitulate and had thus robbed Demosthenes of the glory of the capture. (*See* Introduction.)

He keeps us at a distance and suffers none but himself to wait upon the master; when Demos is dining, he keeps close to his side with a thong in his hand and puts the orators to flight. He keeps singing oracles to him, so that the old man now thinks of nothing but the Sibyl. Then, when he sees him thoroughly obfuscated, he uses all his cunning and piles up lies and calumnies against the household; then we are scourged and the Paphlagonian runs about among the slaves to demand contributions with threats and gathers 'em in with both hands. He will say, "You see how I have had Hylas beaten! Either content me or die at once!" We are forced to give, for else the old man tramples on us and makes us spew forth all our body contains. There must be an end to it, friend. Let us see! what can be done? Who will get us out of this mess?

NICIAS: The best thing, chum, is our famous "Let-us-bolt!"

DEMOSTHENES: But none can escape the Paphlagonian, his eye is everywhere. And what a stride! He has one leg on Pylos and the other in the Assembly; his rump is exactly over the land of the Chaonians, his hands are with the Aetolians and his mind with the Clopidians.[11]

NICIAS: 'Tis best then to die; but let us seek the most heroic death.

DEMOSTHENES: Let me bethink me, what is the most heroic?

NICIAS: Let us drink the blood of a bull; 'tis the death which Themistocles chose.[12]

DEMOSTHENES: No, not that, but a bumper of good unmixed wine in honour of the Good Genius;[13] perchance we may stumble on a happy thought.

NICIAS: Look at him! "Unmixed wine!" Your mind is on drink intent? Can a man strike out a brilliant thought when drunk?

DEMOSTHENES: Without question. Go, ninny, blow yourself out with water; do you dare to accuse wine of clouding the reason? Quote me more marvellous effects than those of wine. Look! when a man

---

11. Literally, his rump is among the Chaonians ([Greek: chain o], to gape open), because his anus is distended by pederastic practices; his hands with the Aetolians ([Greek: aite o], to ask, to beg); his mind with the Clopidians ([Greek: klept o], to steal).

12. The versions of his death vary. He is said to have taken poison in order to avoid fighting against Athens.

13. A minor god, supposed by the ancients to preside over the life of each man; each empire, each province, each town had its titular Genius. Everyone offered sacrifice to his Genius on each anniversary of his birth with wine, flowers and incense.

drinks, he is rich, everything he touches succeeds, he gains lawsuits, is happy and helps his friends. Come, bring hither quick a flagon of wine, that I may soak my brain and get an ingenious idea.

NICIAS: Eh, my god! What can your drinking do to help us?

DEMOSTHENES: Much. But bring it to me, while I take my seat. Once drunk, I shall strew little ideas, little phrases, little reasonings everywhere.

NICIAS (*returning with a flagon*): It is lucky I was not caught in the house stealing the wine.

DEMOSTHENES: Tell me, what is the Paphlagonian doing now?

NICIAS: The wretch has just gobbled up some confiscated cakes; he is drunk and lies at full-length a-snoring on his hides.

DEMOSTHENES: Very well, come along, pour me out wine and plenty of it.

NICIAS: Take it and offer a libation to your Good Genius; taste, taste the liquor of the genial soil of Pramnium.[14]

DEMOSTHENES: Oh, Good Genius! 'Tis thy will, not mine.

NICIAS: Prithee, tell me, what is it?

DEMOSTHENES: Run indoors quick and steal the oracles of the Paphlagonian, while he is asleep.[15]

NICIAS: Bless me! I fear this Good Genius will be but a very Bad Genius for me.

DEMOSTHENES: And set the flagon near me, that I may moisten my wit to invent some brilliant notion.

NICIAS (*enters the house and returns at once*): How the Paphlagonian grunts and snores! I was able to seize the sacred oracle, which he was guarding with the greatest care, without his seeing me.

DEMOSTHENES: Oh! clever fellow! Hand it here, that I may read. Come, pour me out some drink, bestir yourself! Let me see what there is in it. Oh! prophecy! Some drink! some drink! Quick!

NICIAS: Well! what says the oracle?

DEMOSTHENES: Pour again.

NICIAS: Is "pour again" in the oracle?

DEMOSTHENES: Oh, Bacis![16]

---

14. A hill in Asia Minor, near Smyrna. Homer mentions the wine of Pramnium.

15. The common people, who at Athens were as superstitious as everywhere else, took delight in oracles, especially when they were favourable, and Cleon served them up to suit their taste and to advance his own ambition.

16. Famous seer of Boeotia.

ARISTOPHANES

NICIAS: But what is in it?

DEMOSTHENES: Quick! some drink!

NICIAS: Bacis is very dry!

DEMOSTHENES: Oh! miserable Paphlagonian! This then is why you have so long taken such precautions; your horoscope gave you qualms of terror.

NICIAS: What does it say?

DEMOSTHENES: It says here how he must end.

NICIAS: And how?

DEMOSTHENES: How? the oracle announces clearly that a dealer in oakum must first govern the city.[17]

NICIAS: First dealer. And after him, who?

DEMOSTHENES: After him, a sheep-dealer.[18]

NICIAS: Two dealers, eh? And what is this one's fate?

DEMOSTHENES: To reign until a greater scoundrel than he arises; then he perishes and in his place the leather-seller appears, the Paphlagonian robber, the bawler, who roars like a torrent.[19]

NICIAS: And the leather-seller must destroy the sheep-seller?

DEMOSTHENES: Yes.

NICIAS: Oh! woe is me! Where can another seller be found, is there ever a one left?

DEMOSTHENES: There is yet one, who plies a firstrate trade.

NICIAS: Tell me, pray, what is that?

DEMOSTHENES: You really want to know?

NICIAS: Yes.

DEMOSTHENES: Well then! 'tis a sausage-seller who must overthrow him.

NICIAS: A sausage-seller! Ah! by Posidon! what a fine trade! But where can this man be found?

DEMOSTHENES: Let us seek him.

NICIAS: Lo! there he is, going towards the market-place; 'tis the gods, the gods who send him!

DEMOSTHENES: This way, this way, oh, lucky sausage-seller, come forward, dear friend, our saviour, the saviour of our city.

SAUSAGE-SELLER: What is it? Why do you call me?

---

17. Eucrates, who was the leading statesman at Athens after Pericles.

18. Lysicles, who married the courtesan Aspasia.

19. Literally, like Cycloborus, a torrent in Attica.

DEMOSTHENES: Come here, come and learn about your good luck, you who are Fortune's favourite!

NICIAS: Come! Relieve him of his basket-tray and tell him the oracle of the god; I will go and look after the Paphlagonian.

DEMOSTHENES: First put down all your gear, then worship the earth and the gods.

SAUSAGE-SELLER: 'Tis done. What is the matter?

DEMOSTHENES: Happiness, riches, power; to-day you have nothing, to-morrow you will have all, oh! chief of happy Athens.

SAUSAGE-SELLER: Why not leave me to wash my tripe and to sell my sausages instead of making game of me?

DEMOSTHENES: Oh! the fool! Your tripe! Do you see these tiers of people?[20]

SAUSAGE-SELLER: Yes.

DEMOSTHENES: You shall be master to them all, governor of the market, of the harbours, of the Pnyx; you shall trample the Senate under foot, be able to cashier the generals, load them with fetters, throw them into gaol, and you will play the debauchee in the Prytaneum.[21]

SAUSAGE-SELLER: What! I?

DEMOSTHENES: You, without a doubt. But you do not yet see all the glory awaiting you. Stand on your basket and look at all the islands that surround Athens.[22]

SAUSAGE-SELLER: I see them. What then?

DEMOSTHENES: Look at the storehouses and the shipping.

SAUSAGE-SELLER: Yes, I am looking.

DEMOSTHENES: Exists there a mortal more blest than you? Furthermore, turn your right eye towards Caria and your left towards Chalcedon.[23]

SAUSAGE-SELLER: 'Tis then a blessing to squint!

DEMOSTHENES: No, but 'tis you who are going to trade away all this. According to the oracle you must become the greatest of men.

---

20. He points to the spectators.

21. The public meals were given in the Prytaneum; to these were admitted those whose services merited that they should be fed at the cost of the State. This distinction depended on the popular vote, and was very often bestowed on demagogues very unworthy of the privilege.

22. Islands of the Aegaean, subject to Athens, which paid considerable tributes.

23. Caria and Chalcedon were at the two extremities of Asia Minor; the former being at the southern, the latter at the northern end of that extensive coast.

SAUSAGE-SELLER: Just tell me how a sausage-seller can become a great man.

DEMOSTHENES: That is precisely why you will be great, because you are a sad rascal without shame, no better than a common market rogue.

SAUSAGE-SELLER: I do not hold myself worthy of wielding power.

DEMOSTHENES: Oh! by the gods! Why do you not hold yourself worthy? Have you then such a good opinion of yourself? Come, are you of honest parentage?

SAUSAGE-SELLER: By the gods! No! of very bad indeed.

DEMOSTHENES: Spoilt child of fortune, everything fits together to ensure your greatness.

SAUSAGE-SELLER: But I have not had the least education. I can only read, and that very badly.

DEMOSTHENES: That is what may stand in your way, almost knowing how to read. The demagogues will neither have an educated nor an honest man; they require an ignoramus and a rogue. But do not, do not let go this gift, which the oracle promises.

SAUSAGE-SELLER: But what does the oracle say?

DEMOSTHENES: Faith! it is put together in very fine enigmatical style, as elegant as it is clear: "When the eagle-tanner with the hooked claws shall seize a stupid dragon, a blood-sucker, it will be an end to the hot Paphlagonian pickled garlic. The god grants great glory to the sausage-sellers unless they prefer to sell their wares."

SAUSAGE-SELLER: In what way does this concern me? Pray instruct my ignorance.

DEMOSTHENES: The eagle-tanner is the Paphlagonian.

SAUSAGE-SELLER: What do the hooked claws mean?

DEMOSTHENES: It means to say, that he robs and pillages us with his claw-like hands.

SAUSAGE-SELLER: And the dragon?

DEMOSTHENES: That is quite clear. The dragon is long and so also is the sausage; the sausage like the dragon is a drinker of blood. Therefore the oracle says, that the dragon will triumph over the eagle-tanner, if he does not let himself be cajoled with words.

SAUSAGE-SELLER: The oracles of the gods summon me! Faith! I do not at all understand how I can be capable of governing the people.

DEMOSTHENES: Nothing simpler. Continue your trade. Mix and knead together all the state business as you do for your sausages.

To win the people, always cook them some savoury that pleases them. Besides, you possess all the attributes of a demagogue; a screeching, horrible voice, a perverse, cross-grained nature and the language of the market-place. In you all is united which is needful for governing. The oracles are in your favour, even including that of Delphi. Come, take a chaplet, offer a libation to the god of Stupidity[24] and take care to fight vigorously.

SAUSAGE-SELLER: Who will be my ally? for the rich fear the Paphlagonian and the poor shudder at the sight of him.

DEMOSTHENES: You will have a thousand brave Knights,[25] who detest him, on your side; also the honest citizens amongst the spectators, those who are men of brave hearts, and finally myself and the god. Fear not, you will not see his features, for none have dared to make a mask resembling him. But the public have wit enough to recognize him.[26]

NICIAS: Oh! mercy! here is the Paphlagonian!

CLEON: By the twelve gods! Woe betide you, who have too long been conspiring against Demos. What means this Chalcidian cup? No doubt you are provoking the Chalcidians to revolt. You shall be killed, butchered, you brace of rogues.

DEMOSTHENES: What! are you for running away? Come, come, stand firm, bold Sausage-seller, do not betray us. To the rescue, oh! Knights. Now is the time. Simon, Panaetius,[27] get you to the right wing; they are coming on; hold tight and return to the charge. I can see the dust of their horses' hoofs; they are galloping to our aid. Courage! Repel, attack them, put them to flight.

CHORUS: Strike, strike the villain, who has spread confusion amongst the ranks of the Knights, this public robber, this yawning gulf of plunder, this devouring Charybdis,[28] this villain, this villain, this villain! I cannot say the word too often, for he *is* a villain a

---

24. As though stupidity were an essential of good government.

25. The Athenian citizens were divided into four classes—the Pentacosiomedimni, who possessed five hundred minae; the Knights, who had three hundred and were obliged to maintain a charger (hence their name); the Zeugitae and the Thetes. In Athens, the Knights never had the high consideration and the share in the magistracy which they enjoyed at Rome.

26. It is said that Aristophanes played the part of Cleon himself, as no one dared to assume the role. (*See* Introduction.)

27. They were two leaders of the knightly order.

28. The famous whirlpool, near Sicily.

thousand times a day. Come, strike, drive, hurl him over and crush him to pieces; hate him as we hate him; stun him with your blows and your shouts. And beware lest he escape you; he knows the way Eucrates[29] took straight to a bran sack for concealment.

CLEON: Oh! veteran Heliasts,[30] brotherhood of the three obols,[31] whom I fostered by bawling at random, help me; I am being beaten to death by rebels.

CHORUS: And 'tis justice; you devour the public funds that all should share in; you treat the officers answerable for the revenue like the fruit of the fig tree, squeezing them to find which are still green or more or less ripe; and, when you find one simple and timid, you force him to come from the Chersonese,[32] then you seize him by the middle, throttle him by the neck, while you twist his shoulder back; he falls and you devour him.[33] Besides, you know very well how to select from among the citizens those who are as meek as lambs, rich, without guile and loathers of lawsuits.

CLEON: Eh! what! Knights, are you helping them? But, if I am beaten, 'tis in your cause, for I was going to propose to erect you a statue in the city in memory of your bravery.

CHORUS: Oh! the impostor! the dull varlet! See! he treats us like old dotards and crawls at our feet to deceive us; but the cunning wherein lies his power shall this time recoil on himself; he trips up himself by resorting to such artifices.

CLEON: Oh Citizens! oh people! see how these brutes are bursting my belly.

CHORUS: What shouts! but 'tis this very bawling that incessantly upsets the city!

SAUSAGE-SELLER: I can shout too—and so loud that you will flee with fear.

---

29. Eucrates, the oakum-seller, already mentioned, when the object of a riot, took refuge in a mill and there hid himself in a sack of bran.

30. The chief Athenian tribunal only next in dignity to the Areopagus; it generally consisted of two hundred members; it tried civil cases of the greatest importance and some crimes beyond the competence of other courts, e.g. rape, adultery, extortion. The sittings were in the open air, hence the name ([Greek: Elios], the sun).

31. The Heliasts' salary. (*See* above.)

32. Tributary to Athens; Olynthus and Potidaea were the chief towns of this important Peninsula.

33. Meaning he frightens him with the menace of judicial prosecution forces him to purchase silence.

CHORUS: If you shout louder than he does, I will strike up the triumphal hymn; if you surpass him in impudence, the cake is ours.

CLEON: I denounce this fellow; he has had tasty stews exported from Athens for the Spartan fleet.

SAUSAGE-SELLER: And I denounce him, who runs into the Prytaneum with empty belly and comes out with it full.

DEMOSTHENES: And by Zeus! he carries off bread, meat, and fish, which is forbidden. Pericles himself never had this right.

CLEON: You are travelling the right road to get killed.

SAUSAGE-SELLER: I'll bawl three times as loud as you.

CLEON: I will deafen you with my yells.

SAUSAGE-SELLER: And I you with my bellowing.

CLEON: I shall calumniate you, if you become a Strategus.[34]

SAUSAGE-SELLER: Dog, I will lay your back open with the lash.

CLEON: I will make you drop your arrogance.

SAUSAGE-SELLER: I will baffle your machinations.

CLEON: Dare to look me in the face!

SAUSAGE-SELLER: I too was brought up in the market-place.

CLEON: I will cut you to shreds if you whisper a word.

SAUSAGE-SELLER: I will daub you with dung if you open your mouth.

CLEON: I own I am a thief; do you admit yourself another.

SAUSAGE-SELLER: By our Hermes of the market-place, if caught in the act, why, I perjure myself before those who saw me.

CLEON: These are my own special tricks. I will denounce you to the Prytanes[35] as the owner of sacred tripe, that has not paid tithe.

CHORUS: Oh! you scoundrel! you impudent bawler! everything is filled with your daring, all Attica, the Assembly, the Treasury, the decrees, the tribunals. As a furious torrent you have overthrown our city; your outcries have deafened Athens and, posted upon a high rock, you have lain in wait for the tribute moneys as the fisherman does for the tunny-fish.

CLEON: I know your tricks; 'tis an old plot resoled.[36]

SAUSAGE-SELLER: If you know naught of soling, I understand nothing of sausages; you, who cut bad leather on the slant to make it look

---

34. The strategi were the heads of the military forces.

35. They presided at the Public Assemblies; they were also empowered to try the most important cases.

36. An allusion to Cleon's former calling.

stout and deceive the country yokels. They had not worn it a day before it had stretched some two spans.

DEMOSTHENES: 'Tis the very trick he served me; both my neighbours and my friends laughed heartily at me, and before I reached Pergasae[37] I was swimming in my shoes.

CHORUS: Have you not always shown that blatant impudence, which is the sole strength of our orators? You push it so far, that you, the head of the State, dare to milk the purses of the opulent aliens and, at sight of you, the son of Hippodamus[38] melts into tears. But here is another man, who gives me pleasure, for he is a much greater rascal than you; he will overthrow you; 'tis easy to see, that he will beat you in roguery, in brazenness and in clever turns. Come, you, who have been brought up among the class which to-day gives us all our great men, show us that a liberal education is mere tomfoolery.

SAUSAGE-SELLER: Just hear what sort of fellow that fine citizen is.

CLEON: Will you not let me speak?

SAUSAGE-SELLER: Assuredly not, for I also am a sad rascal.

CHORUS: If he does not give in at that, tell him your parents were sad rascals too.

CLEON: Once more, will you not let me speak?

SAUSAGE-SELLER: No, by Zeus!

CLEON: Yes, by Zeus, but you shall!

SAUSAGE-SELLER: No, by Posidon! We will fight first to see who shall speak first.

CLEON: I will die sooner.

SAUSAGE-SELLER: I will not let you. . .

CHORUS: Let him, in the name of the gods, let him die.

CLEON: What makes you so bold as to dare to speak to my face?

SAUSAGE-SELLER: 'Tis that I know both how to speak and how to cook.

CLEON: Hah! the fine speaker! Truly, if some business matter fell your way, you would know thoroughly well how to attack it, to carve it up alive! Shall I tell you what has happened to you? Like so many others, you have gained some petty lawsuit against some

---

37. A country deme of Attica.
38. Archeptolemus, a resident alien, who lived in Piraeus. He had loaded Athens with gifts and was nevertheless maltreated by Cleon.

alien.[39] Did you drink enough water to inspire you? Did you mutter over the thing sufficiently through the night, spout it along the street, recite it to all you met? Have you bored your friends enough with it? 'Tis then for this you deem yourself an orator. Ah! poor fool!

SAUSAGE-SELLER: And what do you drink yourself then, to be able all alone by yourself to dumbfound and stupefy the city so with your clamour?

CLEON: Can you match me with a rival? Me! When I have devoured a good hot tunny-fish and drunk on top of it a great jar of unmixed wine, I hold up the Generals of Pylos to public scorn.

SAUSAGE-SELLER: And I, when I have bolted the tripe of an ox together with a sow's belly and swallowed the broth as well, I am fit, though slobbering with grease, to bellow louder than all orators and to terrify Nicias.

CHORUS: I admire your language so much; the only thing I do not approve is that you swallow all the broth yourself.

CLEON: E'en though you gorged yourself on sea-dogs, you would not beat the Milesians.

SAUSAGE-SELLER: Give me a bullock's breast to devour, and I am a man to traffic in mines.[40]

CLEON: I will rush into the Senate and set them all by the ears.

SAUSAGE-SELLER: And I will lug out your gut to stuff like a sausage.

CLEON: As for me, I will seize you by the rump and hurl you head foremost through the door.

CHORUS: In any case, by Posidon, 'twill only be when you have thrown *me* there first.[41]

CLEON: Beware of the carcan![42]

SAUSAGE-SELLER: I denounce you for cowardice.

CLEON: I will tan your hide.

SAUSAGE-SELLER: I will flay you and make a thief's pouch with the skin.

CLEON: I will peg you out on the ground.

---

39. This was easier than against a citizen because of the inferiority, in which the pride of the Athenian held those born on other soil.

40. When drunk he conceives himself rich and the man to buy up the rich silver mines of Laurium, in south-east Attica.

41. The Chorus throws itself between Cleon and Agoracritus to protect the latter.

42. An iron collar, an instrument of torture and of punishment.

SAUSAGE-SELLER: I will slice you into mince-meat.

CLEON: I will tear out your eyelashes.

SAUSAGE-SELLER: I will slit your gullet.

DEMOSTHENES: We will set his mouth open with a wooden stick as the cooks do with pigs; we will tear out his tongue, and, looking down his gaping throat, will see whether his inside has any pimples.[43]

CHORUS: Thus then at Athens we have something more fiery than fire, more impudent than impudence itself! 'Tis a grave matter; come, we will push and jostle him without mercy. There, you grip him tightly under the arms; if he gives way at the onset, you will find him nothing but a craven; I know my man.

SAUSAGE-SELLER: That he has been all his life and he has only made himself a name by reaping another's harvest; and now he has tied up the ears he gathered over there, he lets them dry and seeks to sell them.[44]

CLEON: I do not fear you as long as there is a Senate and a people which stands like a fool, gaping in the air.

CHORUS: What unparalleled impudence! 'Tis ever the same brazen front. If I don't hate you, why, I'm ready to take the place of the one blanket Cratinus wets;[45] I'll offer to play a tragedy by Morsimus.[46] Oh! you cheat! who turn all into money, who flutter from one extortion to another; may you disgorge as quickly as you have crammed yourself! Then only would I sing, "Let us drink, let us drink to this happy event!"[47] Then even the son of Iulius,[48] the old niggard, would empty his cup with transports of joy, crying, "Io, Paean! Io, Bacchus!"

CLEON: By Posidon! You! would you beat me in impudence! If you succeed, may I no longer have my share of the victims offered to Zeus on the city altar.

SAUSAGE-SELLER: And I, I swear by the blows that have so oft rained upon my shoulders since infancy, and by the knives that have cut me, that I will show more effrontery than you; as sure as I have

---

43. A disease among swine.
44. Cleon wanted the Spartans to purchase the prisoners of Sphacteria from him.
45. With piss—the result of his drunken habits.
46. A tragic poet, apparently proverbial for feebleness of style.
47. Beginning of a song of Simonides.
48. A miser.

rounded this fine stomach by feeding on the pieces of bread that had cleansed other folk's greasy fingers.[49]

CLEON: On pieces of bread, like a dog! Ah! wretch! you have the nature of a dog and you dare to fight a cynecephalus?[50]

SAUSAGE-SELLER: I have many another trick in my sack, memories of my childhood's days. I used to linger around the cooks and say to them, "Look, friends, don't you see a swallow? 'tis the herald of springtime." And while they stood, their noses in the air, I made off with a piece of meat.

CHORUS: Oh! most clever man! How well thought out! You did as the eaters of artichokes, you gathered them before the return of the swallows.[51]

SAUSAGE-SELLER: They could make nothing of it; or, if they suspected a trick, I hid the meat in my breeches and denied the thing by all the gods; so that an orator, seeing me at the game, cried, "This child will get on; he has the mettle that makes a statesman."

CHORUS: He argued rightly; to steal, perjure yourself and make a receiver of your rump[52] are three essentials for climbing high.

CLEON: I will stop your insolence, or rather the insolence of both of you. I will throw myself upon you like a terrible hurricane ravaging both land and sea at the will of its fury.

SAUSAGE-SELLER: Then I will gather up my sausages and entrust myself to the kindly waves of fortune so as to make you all the more enraged.

DEMOSTHENES: And I will watch in the bilges in case the boat should make water.

CLEON: No, by Demeter! I swear, 'twill not be with impunity that you have thieved so many talents from the Athenians.[53]

CHORUS (*to the Sausage-seller*): Oh! oh! reef your sail a bit! Here is Boreas blowing calumniously.

CLEON: I know that you got ten talents out of Potidaea.[54]

---

49. Guests used pieces of bread to wipe their fingers at table.

50. 'Dog's head,' a vicious species of ape.

51. They were allowed to remain in the ground throughout the winter so that they might grow tender.

52. An allusion to the pederastic habits ascribed to some of the orators by popular rumour.

53. He imputes the crime to Agoracritus of which he is guilty himself.

54. A town in Thrace and subject to Athens. It therefore paid tribute to the latter. It often happened that the demagogues extracted considerable sums from the tributaries by threats or promises.

SAUSAGE-SELLER: Hold! I will give you one; but keep it dark!

CHORUS: Hah! that will please him mightily; now you can travel under full sail.

SAUSAGE-SELLER: Yes, the wind has lost its violence.

CLEON: I will bring four suits against you, each of one hundred talents.[55]

SAUSAGE-SELLER: And I twenty against you for shirking duty and more than a thousand for robbery.

CLEON: I maintain that your parents were guilty of sacrilege against the goddess.[56]

SAUSAGE-SELLER: And I, that one of your grandfathers was a satellite. . .

CLEON: To whom? Explain!

SAUSAGE-SELLER: To Byrsina, the mother of Hippias.[57]

CLEON: You are an impostor.

SAUSAGE-SELLER: And you are a rogue.

CHORUS: Hit him hard.

CLEON: Oh, oh, dear! The conspirators are murdering me!

CHORUS: Strike, strike with all your might; bruise his belly, lashing him with your guts and your tripe; punish him with both arms! Oh! vigorous assailant and intrepid heart! Have you not routed him totally in this duel of abuse? how shall I give tongue to my joy and sufficiently praise you?

CLEON: Ah! by Demeter! I was not ignorant of this plot against me; I knew it was forming, that the chariot of war was being put together.[58]

CHORUS (to Sausage-seller): Look out, look out! Come, outfence him with some wheelwright slang?

SAUSAGE-SELLER: His tricks at Argos do not escape me. Under pretence of forming an alliance with the Argives, he is hatching a plot with the Lacedaemonians there; and I know why the bellows

---

55. It was customary in Athens for the plaintiff himself to fix the fine to be paid by the defendant.

56. Athené, the tutelary divinity of Athens.

57. And wife of Pisistratus. Anything belonging to the ancient tyrants was hateful to the Athenians.

58. An allusion to the language used by the democratic orators, who, to be better understood by the people, constantly affected the use of terms belonging to the different trades.

are blowing and the metal that is on the anvil; 'tis the question of the prisoners.

CHORUS: Well done! Forge on, if he be a wheelwright.

SAUSAGE-SELLER: And there are men at Sparta[59] who are hammering the iron with you; but neither gold nor silver nor prayers nor anything else shall impede my denouncing your trickery to the Athenians.

CLEON: As for me, I hasten to the Senate to reveal your plotting, your nightly gatherings in the city, your trafficking with the Medes and with the Great King, and all you are foraging for in Boeotia.[60]

SAUSAGE-SELLER: What price then is paid for forage by Boeotians?

CLEON: Oh! by Heracles! I will tan your hide.

CHORUS: Come, if you have both wit and heart, now is the time to show it, as on the day when you hid the meat in your breeches, as you say. Hasten to the Senate, for he will rush there like a tornado to calumniate us all and give vent to his fearful bellowings.

SAUSAGE-SELLER: I am going, but first I must rid myself of my tripe and my knives; I will leave them here.

CHORUS: Stay! rub your neck with lard; in this way you will slip between the fingers of calumny.

SAUSAGE-SELLER: Spoken like a finished master of fence.

CHORUS: Now, bolt down these cloves of garlic.

SAUSAGE-SELLER: Pray, what for?

CHORUS: Well primed with garlic, you will have greater mettle for the fight. But hurry, hurry, bestir yourself!

SAUSAGE-SELLER: That's just what I am doing.

CHORUS: And, above all, bite your foe, rend him to atoms, tear off his comb[61] and do not return until you have devoured his wattles. Go! make your attack with a light heart, avenge me and may Zeus guard you! I burn to see you return the victor and laden with chaplets of glory. And you, spectators, enlightened critics of all kinds of poetry, lend an ear to my anapaests.[62]

CHORUS: Had one of the old authors asked to mount this stage to recite his verses, he would not have found it hard to persuade me. But our poet of to-day is likewise worthy of this favour; he

---

59. He accuses Cleon of collusion with the enemy.
60. Cleon retorts upon his adversary the charge brought against himself. The Boeotians were the allies of Sparta.
61. Allusion to cock-fighting.
62. The tripping metre usually employed in the *parabasis*.

shares our hatred, he dares to tell the truth, he boldly braves both waterspouts and hurricanes. Many among you, he tells us, have expressed wonder, that he has not long since had a piece presented in his own name, and have asked the reason why.[63] This is what he bids us say in reply to your questions; 'tis not without grounds that he has courted the shade, for, in his opinion, nothing is more difficult than to cultivate the comic Muse; many court her, but very few secure her favours. Moreover, he knows that you are fickle by nature and betray your poets when they grow old. What fate befell Magnes,[64] when his hair went white? Often enough has he triumphed over his rivals; he has sung in all keys, played the lyre and fluttered wings; he turned into a Lydian and even into a gnat, daubed himself with green to become a frog.[65] All in vain! When young, you applauded him; in his old age you hooted and mocked him, because his genius for raillery had gone. Cratinus[66] again was like a torrent of glory rushing across the plain, uprooting oak, plane tree and rivals and bearing them pell-mell in its wake. The only songs at the banquet were, 'Doro, shod with lying tales' and 'Adepts of the Lyric Muse';[67] so great was his renown. Look at him now! he drivels, his lyre has neither strings nor keys, his voice quivers, but you have no pity for him, and you let him wander about as he can, like Connas,[68] his temples circled with a withered chaplet; the poor old fellow is dying of thirst; he who, in honour of his glorious past, should be in the Prytaneum drinking at his ease, and instead of trudging the country should be sitting amongst the first row of the spectators, close to the statue of Dionysus[69] and loaded with perfumes. Crates,[70] again, have you done hounding him with your rage and your hisses? True, 'twas but meagre fare that his sterile Muse could offer you; a few ingenious fancies

---

63. Hitherto Aristophanes had presented his pieces under an assumed name.
64. A comic poet, who had carried off the prize eleven times; not a fragment of his works remains to us.
65. An allusion to the titles of some of his pieces, viz. "the Flute Players, the Birds, the Lydians, the Gnats, the Frogs."
66. The Comic Poet, rival of Aristophanes, several times referred to above.
67. These were the opening lines of poems by Cratinus, often sung at festivities.
68. A poet, successful at the Olympic games, and in old age reduced to extreme misery.
69. The place of honour in the Dionysiac Theatre, reserved for distinguished citizens.
70. A Comic Poet, who was elegant but cold; he had at first played as an actor in the pieces of Cratinus.

formed the sole ingredients, but nevertheless he knew how to stand firm and to recover from his falls. 'Tis such examples that frighten our poet; in addition, he would tell himself, that before being a pilot, he must first know how to row, then to keep watch at the prow, after that how to gauge the winds, and that only then would he be able to command his vessel.[71] If then you approve this wise caution and his resolve that he would not bore you with foolish nonsense, raise loud waves of applause in his favour this day, so that, at this Lenaean feast, the breath of your favour may swell the sails of his trumphant galley and the poet may withdraw proud of his success, with head erect and his face beaming with delight.

Posidon, god of the racing steed, I salute you, you who delight in their neighing and in the resounding clatter of their brass-shod hoofs, god of the swift galleys, which, loaded with mercenaries, cleave the seas with their azure beaks, god of the equestrian contests, in which young rivals, eager for glory, ruin themselves for the sake of distinction with their chariots in the arena, come and direct our chorus; Posidon with the trident of gold, you, who reign over the dolphins, who are worshipped at Sunium and at Geraestus[72] beloved of Phormio,[73] and dear to the whole city above all the immortals, I salute you!

Let us sing the glory of our forefathers; ever victors, both on land and sea, they merit that Athens, rendered famous by these, her worthy sons, should write their deeds upon the sacred peplus.[74] As soon as they saw the enemy, they at once sprang at him without ever counting his strength. Should one of them fall in the conflict, he would shake off the dust, deny his mishap and begin the struggle anew. Not one of these Generals of old time would have

---

71. Besides the oarsmen and the pilot, there was on the Grecian vessels a sailor, who stood at the prow to look out for rocks, and another, who observed the direction of the wind.

72. Two promontories, one in Attica, the other in Euboea, on which temples to Posidon were erected.

73. An Athenian general, who had gained several naval victories. He had contributed to the success of the expedition to Samos (Thucydides, Book I), and had recently beaten a Peloponnesian fleet (Thucydides, Book II).

74. At the Panathenaea, a festival held every fourth year, a peplus, or sail, was carried with pomp to the Acropolis. On this various mythological scenes, having reference to Athené, were embroidered—her exploits against the giants, her fight with Posidon concerning the name to be given to Athens, etc. It had also become customary to add the names and the deeds of such citizens as had deserved well of their country.

ARISTOPHANES

asked Cleaenetus[75] to be fed at the cost of the state; but our present men refuse to fight, unless they get the honours of the Prytaneum and precedence in their seats. As for us, we place our valour gratuitously at the service of Athens and of her gods; our only hope is, that, should peace ever put a term to our toils, you will not grudge us our long, scented hair nor our delicate care for our toilet.

Oh! Pallas, guardian of Athens, you, who reign over the most pious city, the most powerful, the richest in warriors and in poets, hasten to my call, bringing in your train our faithful ally in all our expeditions and combats, Victory, who smiles on our choruses and fights with us against our rivals. Oh! goddess! manifest yourself to our sight; this day more than ever we deserve that you should ensure our triumph.

We will sing likewise the exploits of our steeds! they are worthy of our praises;[76] in what invasions, what fights have I not seen them helping us! But especially admirable were they, when they bravely leapt upon the galleys, taking nothing with them but a coarse wine, some cloves of garlic and onions; despite this, they nevertheless seized the sweeps just like men, curved their backs over the thwarts and shouted, "Hippopopoh! Give way! Come, all pull together! Come, come! How! Samphoras![77] Are you not rowing?" They rushed down upon the coast of Corinth, and the youngest hollowed out beds in the sand with their hoofs or went to fetch coverings; instead of luzern, they had no food but crabs, which they caught on the strand and even in the sea; so that Theorus causes a Corinthian[78] crab to say, "'Tis a cruel fate, oh Posidon! neither my deep hiding-places, whether on land or at sea, can help me to escape the Knights."

Welcome, oh, dearest and bravest of men! How distracted I have been during your absence! But here you are back, safe and sound. Tell us about the fight you have had.

---

75. Cleaenetus had passed a law to limit the number of citizens to be fed at the Prytaneum; it may be supposed, that those, who aspired to this distinction, sought to conciliate Cleaenetus in their favour.

76. The Chorus of Knights, not being able to sing their own praises, feign to divert these to their chargers.

77. A horse branded with the obsolete letter (Greek: sán)—(Symbol: Letter 'san'), as a mark of breed or high quality.

78. Crab was no doubt a nickname given to the Corinthians on account of the position of their city on an isthmus between two seas. In the 'Acharnians' Theorus is mentioned as an ambassador, who had returned from the King of Persia.

SAUSAGE-SELLER: The important thing is that I have beaten the Senate.[79]

CHORUS: All glory to you! Let us burst into shouts of joy! You speak well, but your deeds are even better. Come, tell me everything in detail; what a long journey would I not be ready to take to hear your tale! Come, dear friend, speak with full confidence to your admirers.

SAUSAGE-SELLER: The story is worth hearing. Listen! From here I rushed straight to the Senate, right in the track of this man; he was already letting loose the storm, unchaining the lightning, crushing the Knights beneath huge mountains of calumnies heaped together and having all the air of truth; he called you conspirators and his lies caught root like weeds in every mind; dark were the looks on every side and brows were knitted. When I saw that the Senate listened to him favourably and was being tricked by his imposture, I said to myself, "Come, gods of rascals and braggarts, gods of all fools, toad-eaters and braggarts and thou, market-place, where I was bred from my earliest days, give me unbridled audacity, an untiring chatter and a shameless voice." No sooner had I ended this prayer than a lewd man broke wind on my right. "Hah! 'tis a good omen," said I, and prostrated myself; then I burst open the door by a vigorous push with my back, and, opening my mouth to the utmost, shouted, "Senators, I wanted you to be the first to hear the good news; since the War broke out, I have never seen anchovies at a lower price!" All faces brightened at once and I was voted a chaplet for my good tidings; and I added, "With a couple of words I will reveal to you, how you can have quantities of anchovies for an obol; 'tis to seize on all the dishes the merchants have." With mouths gaping with admiration, they applauded me. However, the Paphlagonian winded the matter and, well knowing the sort of language which pleases the Senate best, said, "Friends, I am resolved to offer one hundred oxen to the goddess in recognition of this happy event." The Senate at once veered to his side. So when I saw myself defeated by this ox filth, I outbade the fellow, crying, "Two hundred!" And beyond this

---

79. The Senate was a body composed of five hundred members, elected annually like the magistrates from the three first classes to the exclusion of the fourth, the Thetes, which was composed of the poorest citizens.

I moved, that a vow be made to Diana of a thousand goats if the next day anchovies should only be worth an obol a hundred. And the Senate looked towards me again. The other, stunned with the blow, grew delirious in his speech, and at last the Prytanes and the guards dragged him out. The Senators then stood talking noisily about the anchovies. Cleon, however, begged them to listen to the Lacedaemonian envoy, who had come to make proposals of peace; but all with one accord, cried, "'Tis certainly not the moment to think of peace now! If anchovies are so cheap, what need have we of peace? Let the war take its course!" And with loud shouts they demanded that the Prytanes should close the sitting and then leapt over the rails in all directions. As for me, I slipped away to buy all the coriander seed and leeks there were on the market and gave it to them gratis as seasoning for their anchovies. 'Twas marvellous! They loaded me with praises and caresses; thus I conquered the Senate with an obol's worth of leeks, and here I am.

CHORUS: Bravo! you are the spoilt child of Fortune. Ah! our knave has found his match in another, who has far better tricks in his sack, a thousand kinds of knaveries and of wily words. But the fight begins afresh; take care not to weaken; you know that I have long been your most faithful ally.

SAUSAGE-SELLER: Ah! ah! here comes the Paphlagonian! One would say, 'twas a hurricane lashing the sea and rolling the waves before it in its fury. He looks as if he wanted to swallow me up alive! Ye gods! what an impudent knave!

CLEON: To my aid, my beloved lies! I am going to destroy you, or my name is lost.

SAUSAGE-SELLER: Oh! how he diverts me with his threats! His bluster makes me laugh! And I dance the *mothon* for joy,[80] and sing at the top of my voice, cuckoo!

CLEON: Ah! by Demeter! if I do not kill and devour you, may I die!

SAUSAGE-SELLER: If you do not devour me? and I, if I do not drink your blood to the last drop, and then burst with indigestion.

CLEON: I, I will strangle you, I swear it by the precedence which Pylos gained me.

SAUSAGE-SELLER: By the precedence! Ah! might I see you fall from your precedence into the hindmost seat!

---

80. The (Greek: moth on), a rough, boisterous, obscene dance.

CLEON: By heaven! I will put you to the torture.

SAUSAGE-SELLER: What a lively wit! Come, what's the best to give you to eat? What do you prefer? A purse?

CLEON: I will tear out your inside with my nails.

SAUSAGE-SELLER: And I will cut off your victuals at the Prytaneum.

CLEON: I will haul you before Demos, who will mete out justice to you.

SAUSAGE-SELLER: And I too will drag you before him and belch forth more calumnies than you.

CLEON: Why, poor fool, he does not believe you, whereas I play with him at will.

SAUSAGE-SELLER: So that Demos is your property, your contemptible creature.

CLEON: 'Tis because I know the dishes that please him.

SAUSAGE-SELLER: And these are little mouthfuls, which you serve to him like a clever nurse. You chew the pieces and place some in small quantities in his mouth, while you swallow three parts yourself.

CLEON: Thanks to my skill, I know exactly how to enlarge or contract this gullet.

SAUSAGE-SELLER: I can do as much with my rump.

CLEON: Hah! my friend, you tricked me at the Senate, but have a care! Let us go before Demos.

SAUSAGE-SELLER: That's easily done; come, let's along without delay.

CLEON: Oh, Demos! Come, I adjure you to help me, my father!

SAUSAGE-SELLER: Come, oh, my dear little Demos; come and see how I am insulted.

DEMOS: What a hubbub! To the Devil with you, bawlers! alas! my olive branch, which they have torn down![81] Ah! 'tis you, Paphlagonian. And who, pray, has been maltreating you?

CLEON: You are the cause of this man and these young people having covered me with blows.

DEMOS: And why?

CLEON: Because you love me passionately, Demos.

DEMOS: And you, who are you?

---

81. At the festival of the Pyanepsia, held in honour of Athené as the protectress of Theseus in his fight with the Minotaur, the children carried olive branches in procession, round which strips of linen were wound; they were then fastened up over the entrances of each house.

SAUSAGE-SELLER: His rival. For many a long year have I loved you, have I wished to do you honour, I and a crowd of other men of means. But this rascal here has prevented us. You resemble those young men who do not know where to choose their lovers; you repulse honest folk; to earn your favours, one has to be a lamp-seller, a cobbler, a tanner or a currier.

CLEON: I am the benefactor of the people.

SAUSAGE-SELLER: In what way, an it please you?

CLEON: In what way? I supplanted the Generals at Pylos, I hurried thither and I brought back the Laconian captives.

SAUSAGE-SELLER: And I, whilst simply loitering, cleared off with a pot from a shop, which another fellow had been boiling.

CLEON: Demos, convene the assembly at once to decide which of us two loves you best and most merits your favour.

SAUSAGE-SELLER: Yes, yes, provided it be not at the Pnyx.

DEMOS: I could not sit elsewhere; 'tis at the Pnyx, that you must appear before me.

SAUSAGE-SELLER: Ah! great gods! I am undone! At home this old fellow is the most sensible of men, but the instant he is seated on those cursed stone seats,[82] he is there with mouth agape as if he were hanging up figs by their stems to dry.

CHORUS: Come, loose all sail. Be bold, skilful in attack and entangle him in arguments which admit of no reply. It is difficult to beat him, for he is full of craft and pulls himself out of the worst corners. Collect all your forces to come forth from this fight covered with glory, but take care! Let him not assume the attack, get ready your grapples and advance with your vessel to board him!

CLEON: Oh! guardian goddess of our city! oh! Athené! if it be true that next to Lysicles, Cynna and Salabaccha[83] none have done so much good for the Athenian people as I, suffer me to continue to be fed at the Prytaneum without working; but if I hate you, if I am not ready to fight in your defence alone and against all, may I perish, be sawn to bits alive and my skin be cut up into thongs.

---

82. On which the citizens sat in the Public Assembly in the Pnyx to hear the orators. In the centre of the semicircular space the tribune stood, a square block of stone, (Greek: Bema), and from this the people were addressed.

83. Lysicles was a dealer in sheep, who had wielded great power in Athens after the death of Pericles. Cynna and Salabaccha were two celebrated courtesans.

SAUSAGE-SELLER: And I, Demos, if it be not true, that I love and cherish you, may I be cooked in a stew; and if that is not saying enough, may I be grated on this table with some cheese and then hashed, may a hook be passed through my testicles and let me be dragged thus to the Ceramicus![84]

CLEON: Is it possible, Demos, to love you more than I do? And firstly, as long as you have governed with my consent, have I not filled your treasury, putting pressure on some, torturing others or begging of them, indifferent to the opinion of private individuals, and solely anxious to please you?

SAUSAGE-SELLER: There is nothing so wonderful in all that, Demos; I will do as much; I will thieve the bread of others to serve up to you. No, he has neither love for you nor kindly feeling; his only care is to warm himself with your wood, and I will prove it. You, who, sword in hand, saved Attica from the Median yoke at Marathon; you, whose glorious triumphs we love to extol unceasingly, look, he cares little whether he sees you seated uncomfortably upon a stone; whereas I, I bring you this cushion, which I have sewn with my own hands. Rise and try this nice soft seat. Did you not put enough strain on your breeches at Salamis?[85]

DEMOS: Who are you then? Can you be of the race of Harmodius?[86] Upon my faith, 'tis nobly done and like a true friend of Demos.

CLEON: Petty flattery to prove him your goodwill!

SAUSAGE-SELLER: But you have caught him with even smaller baits!

CLEON: Never had Demos a defender or a friend more devoted than myself; on my head, on my life, I swear it!

SAUSAGE-SELLER: You pretend to love him and for eight years you have seen him housed in casks, in crevices and dovecots,[87] where he is blinded with the smoke, and you lock him in without pity; Archeptolemus brought peace and you tore it to ribbons; the envoys who come to propose a truce you drive from the city with kicks in their backsides.

---

84. Place of interment for those who died for the country.

85. Seated on the banks for the rowers.

86. Assassin of the tyrant Hippias, the son of Pisistratus. His memory was held in great honour at Athens.

87. Driven out by the invasions of the Peloponnesians, the people of the outlying districts had been obliged to seek refuge within the walls of Athens, where they were lodged wherever they could find room.

CLEON: This is that Demos may rule over all the Greeks; for the oracles predict that, if he is patient, he must one day sit as judge in Arcadia at five obols per day. Meanwhile, I will nourish him, look after him and, above all, I will ensure to him his three obols.

SAUSAGE-SELLER: No, little you care for his reigning in Arcadia, 'tis to pillage and impose on the allies at will that you reckon; you wish the War to conceal your rogueries as in a mist, that Demos may see nothing of them, and harassed by cares, may only depend on yourself for his bread. But if ever peace is restored to him, if ever he returns to his lands to comfort himself once more with good cakes, to greet his cherished olives, he will know the blessings you have kept him out of, even though paying him a salary; and, filled with hatred and rage, he will rise, burning with desire to vote against you. You know this only too well; 'tis for this you rock him to sleep with your lies.

CLEON: Is it not shameful, that you should dare thus to calumniate me before Demos, me, to whom Athens, I swear it by Demeter, already owes more than it ever did to Themistocles?

SAUSAGE-SELLER: Oh! citizens of Argos, do you hear what he says?[88] You dare to compare yourself to Themistocles, who found our city half empty and left it full to overflowing, who one day gave us the Piraeus for dinner,[89] and added fresh fish to all our usual meals.[90] You, on the contrary, you, who compare yourself with Themistocles, have only sought to reduce our city in size, to shut it within its walls, to chant oracles to us. And Themistocles goes into exile, while you gorge yourself on the most excellent fare.

CLEON: Oh! Demos! Am I compelled to hear myself thus abused, and merely because I love you?

DEMOS: Silence! stop your abuse! All too long have I been your tool.

SAUSAGE-SELLER: Ah! my dear little Demos, he is a rogue, who has played you many a scurvy trick; when your back is turned, he taps at the root the lawsuits initiated by the peculators, swallows the proceeds wholesale and helps himself with both hands from the public funds.

CLEON: Tremble, knave; I will convict you of having stolen thirty thousand drachmae.

---

88. A verse borrowed from Euripides' lost play of 'Telephus.'
89. Themistocles joined the Piraeus to Athens by the construction of the Long Walls.
90. Which were caught off the Piraeus.

SAUSAGE-SELLER: For a rascal of your kidney, you shout rarely! Well! I am ready to die if I do not prove that you have accepted more than forty minae from the Mitylenaeans.[91]

CHORUS: This indeed may be termed talking. Oh, benefactor of the human race, proceed and you will be the most illustrious of the Greeks. You alone shall have sway in Athens, the allies will obey you, and, trident in hand, you will go about shaking and overturning everything to enrich yourself. But, stick to your man, let him not go; with lungs like yours you will soon have him finished.

CLEON: No, my brave friends, no, you are running too fast; I have done a sufficiently brilliant deed to shut the mouth of all enemies, so long as one of the bucklers of Pylos remains.

SAUSAGE-SELLER: Of the bucklers! Hold! I stop you there and I hold you fast. For if it be true, that you love the people, you would not allow these to be hung up with their rings;[92] but 'tis with an intent you have done this. Demos, take knowledge of his guilty purpose; in this way you no longer can punish him at your pleasure. Note the swarm of young tanners, who really surround him, and close to them the sellers of honey and cheese; all these are at one with him. Very well! you have but to frown, to speak of ostracism and they will rush at night to these bucklers, take them down and seize our granaries.

DEMOS: Great gods! what! the bucklers retain their rings! Scoundrel! ah! too long have you had me for your tool, cheated and played with me!

CLEON: But, dear sir, never you believe all he tells you. Oh! never will you find a more devoted friend than me; unaided, I have known how to put down the conspiracies; nothing that is a-hatching in the city escapes me, and I hasten to proclaim it loudly.

SAUSAGE-SELLER: You are like the fishers for eels; in still waters they catch nothing, but if they thoroughly stir up the slime, their fishing is good; in the same way 'tis only in troublous times that you line your pockets. But come, tell me, you, who sell so many skins, have

---

91. Mitylené, chief city of the Island of Lesbos, rebelled against the Athenians and was retaken by Chares. By a popular decree the whole manhood of the town was to suffer death, but this decree was withdrawn the next day. Aristophanes insinuates that Cleon, bought over with Mitylenaean gold, brought about this change of opinion. On the contrary, Thucydides says that the decree was revoked in spite of Cleon's opposition.
92. When bucklers were hung up as trophies, it was usual to detach the ring or brace, so as to render them useless for warlike purposes.

you ever made him a present of a pair of soles for his slippers? and
you pretend to love him!

DEMOS: No, he has never given me any.

SAUSAGE-SELLER: That alone shows up the man; but I, I have bought
you this pair of shoes; accept them.

DEMOS: None ever, to my knowledge, has merited so much from the
people; you are the most zealous of all men for your country and
for my toes.

CLEON: Can a wretched pair of slippers make you forget all that you
owe me? Is it not I who curbed Gryttus,[93] the filthiest of the lewd,
by depriving him of his citizen rights?

SAUSAGE-SELLER: Ah! noble inspector of back passages, let me
congratulate you. Moreover, if you set yourself against this form
of lewdness, this pederasty, 'twas for sheer jealousy, knowing it to
be the school for orators.[94] But you see this poor Demos without a
cloak and that at his age too! so little do you care for him, that in
mid-winter you have not given him a garment with sleeves. Here,
Demos, here is one, take it!

DEMOS: This even Themistocles never thought of; the Piraeus was no
doubt a happy idea, but meseems this tunic is quite as fine an invention.

CLEON: Must you have recourse to such jackanapes' tricks to supplant
me?

SAUSAGE-SELLER: No, 'tis your own tricks that I am borrowing, just as
a guest, driven by urgent need, seizes some other man's shoes.[95]

CLEON: Oh! you shall not outdo me in flattery! I am going to hand
Demos this garment; all that remains to you, you rogue, is to go
and hang yourself.

DEMOS: Faugh! may the plague seize you! You stink of leather horribly.[96]

SAUSAGE-SELLER: Why, 'tis to smother you that he has thrown this
cloak around you on top of the other; and it is not the first plot
he has planned against you. Do you remember the time when
silphium[97] was so cheap?

---

93. An orator of debauched habits.
94. An accusation frequently hurled at the orators.
95. Guests took off their shoes before entering the festal hall.
96. An allusion to Cleon's former calling of a tanner.
97. A plant from Cyrenaïca, which was imported into Athens in large quantities after the
conclusion of a treaty of navigation, which Cleon made with this country. It was a very
highly valued flavouring for sauces.

DEMOS: Aye, to be sure I do!

SAUSAGE-SELLER: Very well! it was Cleon who had caused the price to fall so low so that all could eat it and the jurymen in the Courts were almost poisoned with farting in each others' faces.

DEMOS: Hah! why, indeed, a scavenger told me the same thing.

SAUSAGE-SELLER: Were you not yourself in those days quite red in the gills with farting?

DEMOS: Why, 'twas a trick worthy of Pyrrandrus![98]

CLEON: With what other idle trash will you seek to ruin me, you wretch!

SAUSAGE-SELLER: Oh! I shall be more brazen than you, for 'tis the goddess who has commanded me.[99]

CLEON: No, on my honour, you will not! Here, Demos, feast on this dish; it is your salary as a dicast, which you gain through me for doing naught.

SAUSAGE-SELLER: Hold! here is a little box of ointment to rub into the sores on your legs.

CLEON: I will pluck out your white hairs and make you young again.

SAUSAGE-SELLER: Take this hare's scut to wipe the rheum from your eyes.

CLEON: When you wipe your nose, clean your fingers on my head.

SAUSAGE-SELLER: No, on mine.

CLEON: On mine. (*To the Sausage-seller*) I will have you made a trierarch[100] and you will get ruined through it; I will arrange that you are given an old vessel with rotten sails, which you will have to repair constantly and at great cost.

CHORUS: Our man is on the boil; enough, enough, he is boiling over; remove some of the embers from under him and skim off his threats.

---

98. The name of a supposed informer. The adjective, (Greek: pyrrhos), yellow, the colour of ordure, is contained in the construction of this name; thus a most disgusting piece of word-play is intended.

99. The orators were for ever claiming the protection of Athené.

100. A very expensive burden, which was imposed upon the rich citizen. The trierarchs had to furnish both the equipment of the triremes or war-galleys and their upkeep. They varied considerably in number and ended in reaching a total of 1200; the most opulent found the money, and were later repaid partly and little by little by those not so well circumstanced. Later it was permissible for anyone, appointed as a trierarch, to point out someone richer than himself and to ask to have him take his place with the condition that if the other preferred, he should exchange fortunes with him and continue his office of trierarch.

CLEON: I will punish your self-importance; I will crush you with imposts; I will have you inscribed on the list of the rich.

SAUSAGE-SELLER: For me no threats—only one simple wish. That you may be having some cuttle-fish fried on the stove just as you are going to set forth to plead the cause of the Milesians,[101] which, if you gain, means a talent in your pocket; that you hurry over devouring the fish to rush off to the Assembly; suddenly you are called and run off with your mouth full so as not to lose the talent and choke yourself. There! that is my wish.

CHORUS: Splendid! by Zeus, Apollo and Demeter!

DEMOS: Faith! here is an excellent citizen indeed, such as has not been seen for a long time. 'Tis truly a man of the lowest scum! As for you, Paphlagonian, who pretend to love me, you only feed me on garlic. Return me my ring, for you cease to be my steward.

CLEON: Here it is, but be assured, that if you bereave me of my power, my successor will be worse than I am.

DEMOS: This cannot be my ring; I see another device, unless I am going purblind.

SAUSAGE-SELLER: What was your device?

DEMOS: A fig-leaf, stuffed with bullock's fat.[102]

SAUSAGE-SELLER: No, that is not it.

DEMOS: What is it then?

SAUSAGE-SELLER: 'Tis a gull with beak wide open, haranguing from the top of a stone.[103]

DEMOS: Ah! great gods!

SAUSAGE-SELLER: What is the matter?

DEMOS: Away! away out of my sight! 'Tis not my ring he had, 'twas that of Cleonymus. (*To the Sausage-seller*) Hold, I give you this one; you shall be my steward.

CLEON: Master, I adjure you, decide nothing till you have heard my oracles.[104]

SAUSAGE-SELLER: And mine.

CLEON: If you believe him, you will have to suck his tool for him.

---

101. This is an allusion to some extortion of Cleon's.
102. The Greek word (Greek: d emos) means both "The People" and fat, grease. The pun cannot well be kept in English.
103. A voracious bird—in allusion to Cleon's rapacity and to his loquacity in the Assembly.
104. The orators were fond of supporting their arguments with imaginary oracles—and Cleon was an especial adept at this dodge.

SAUSAGE-SELLER: If you listen to him, you'll have to let him skin your penis to the very stump.

CLEON: My oracles say that you are to reign over the whole earth, crowned with chaplets.

SAUSAGE-SELLER: And mine say that, clothed in an embroidered purple robe, you shall pursue Smicythes and her spouse,[105] standing in a chariot of gold and with a crown on your head.

DEMOS: Go, fetch me your oracles, that the Paphlagonian may hear them.

SAUSAGE-SELLER: Willingly.

DEMOS: And you yours.

CLEON: I run.

SAUSAGE-SELLER: And I run too; nothing could suit me better!

CHORUS: Oh! happy day for us and for our children, if Cleon perish. Yet just now I heard some old cross-grained pleaders on the market-place who hold not this opinion discoursing together. Said they, "If Cleon had not had the power we should have lacked two most useful tools, the pestle and the soup-ladle."[106] You also know what a pig's education he has had; his school-fellows can recall that he only liked the Dorian style and would study no other; his music-master in displeasure sent him away, saying: "This youth in matters of harmony, will only learn the Dorian style because 'tis akin to bribery."[107]

CLEON: There, behold and look at this heap; and yet I do not bring all.

SAUSAGE-SELLER: Ugh! I pant and puff under the weight and yet I do not bring all.

DEMOS: What are these?

CLEON: Oracles.

DEMOS: All these?

CLEON: Does that astonish you? Why, I have another whole boxful of them.

---

105. Smicythes, King of Thrace, spoken of in the oracle as a woman, doubtless on account of his cowardice. The word pursue is here used in a double sense, viz. in battle and in law. It is on account of this latter meaning, that Aristophanes adds "and her spouse," because in cases in which women were sued at law, their husbands were summoned as conjointly liable.

106. Because he had smashed up and turned upside down the fortunes of Athens.

107. The pun—rather a far-fetched one—is between the words (Greek: D orh osti) (in the Dorian mode) and (Greek: d orhon) (a bribe).

SAUSAGE-SELLER: And I the whole of my attics and two rooms besides.

DEMOS: Come, let us see, whose are these oracles?

CLEON: Mine are those of Bacis.[108]

DEMOS (*to the Sausage-seller*): And whose are yours?

SAUSAGE-SELLER: Glanis's, the elder brother of Bacis.[109]

DEMOS: And of what do they speak?

CLEON: Of Athens, of Pylos, of you, of me, of all.

DEMOS: And yours?

SAUSAGE-SELLER: Of Athens, of lentils, of Lacedaemonians, of fresh mackerel, of scoundrelly flour-sellers, of you, of me. Ah! ha! now let him gnaw his own penis with chagrin!

DEMOS: Come, read them out to me and especially that one I like so much, which says that I shall become an eagle and soar among the clouds.

CLEON: Then listen and be attentive! "Son of Erectheus,[110] understand the meaning of the words, which the sacred tripods set resounding in the sanctuary of Apollo. Preserve the sacred dog with the jagged teeth, that barks and howls in your defence; he will ensure you a salary and, if he fails, will perish as the victim of the swarms of jays that hunt him down with their screams."

DEMOS: By Demeter! I do not understand a word of it. What connection is there between Erectheus, the jays and the dog?

CLEON: 'Tis I who am the dog, since I bark in your defence. Well! Phoebus commands you to keep and cherish your dog.

SAUSAGE-SELLER: 'Tis not so spoken by the god; this dog seems to me to gnaw at the oracles as others gnaw at doorposts. Here is exactly what Apollo says of the dog.

DEMOS: Let us hear, but I must first pick up a stone; an oracle which speaks of a dog might bite me.

SAUSAGE-SELLER: "Son of Erectheus, beware of this Cerberus that enslaves freemen; he fawns upon you with his tail, when you are dining, but he is lying in wait to devour your dishes, should you turn your head an instant; at night he sneaks into the kitchen and,

---

108. A Boeotian soothsayer.
109. A name invented by the Sausage-seller on the spur of the moment, to cap Cleon's boast.
110. That is, Athenian; Erectheus was an ancient mythical King of Athens.

true dog that he is, licks up with one lap of his tongue both your dishes and. . . the islands."[111]

DEMOS: Faith, Glanis, you speak better than your brother.

CLEON: Condescend again to hear me and then judge: "A woman in sacred Athens will be delivered of a lion, who shall fight for the people against clouds of gnats with the same ferocity as if he were defending his whelps; care ye for him, erect wooden walls around him and towers of brass." Do you understand that?

DEMOS: Not the least bit in the world.

CLEON: The god tells you here to look after me, for, 'tis I who am your lion.

DEMOS: How! You have become a lion and I never knew a thing about it?

SAUSAGE-SELLER: There is only one thing which he purposely keeps from you; he does not say what this wall of wood and brass is in which Apollo warns you to keep and guard him.

DEMOS: What does the god mean, then?

SAUSAGE-SELLER: He advises you to fit him into a five-holed wooden collar.

DEMOS: Hah! I think that oracle is about to be fulfilled.

CLEON: Do not believe it; these are but jealous crows, that caw against me; but never cease to cherish your good hawk; never forget that he brought you those Lacedaemonian fish, loaded with chains.[112]

SAUSAGE-SELLER: Ah! if the Paphlagonian ran any risk that day, 'twas because he was drunk. Oh, too credulous son of Cecrops,[113] do you accept that as a glorious exploit? A woman would carry a heavy burden if only a man had put it on her shoulders. But to fight! Go to! he would shit himself, if ever it came to a tussle.

CLEON: Note this Pylos in front of Pylos, of which the oracle speaks, "Pylos is before Pylos."[114]

DEMOS: How "in front of Pylos"? What does he mean by that?

SAUSAGE-SELLER: He says he will seize upon your bath-tubs.[115]

---

111. That is, the tributes paid to Athens by the Aegaean Islands, whether allies or subjects.
112. The Lacedaemonian prisoners from Sphacteria, so often referred to.
113. That is, Athenian; Cecrops was the first King of Athens, according to the legends.
114. There were three towns of this name in different parts of Greece.
115. There is a pun here which it is impossible to render in English; the Greek (Greek: Pylos)(Pylos) differs by only one letter from the word meaning a bath-tub ([Greek: Pyelos]).

ARISTOPHANES

DEMOS: Then I shall not bathe to-day.

SAUSAGE-SELLER: No, as he has stolen our baths. But here is an oracle about the fleet, to which I beg your best attention.

DEMOS: Read on! I am listening; let us first see how we are to pay our sailors.[116]

SAUSAGE-SELLER: "Son of Aegeus,[117] beware of the tricks of the dog-fox,[118] he bites from the rear and rushes off at full speed; he is nothing but cunning and perfidy." Do you know what the oracle intends to say?

DEMOS: The dog-fox is Philostratus.[119]

SAUSAGE-SELLER: No, no, 'tis Cleon; he is incessantly asking you for light vessels to go and collect the tributes, and Apollo advises you not to grant them.

DEMOS: What connection is there between a galley and a dog-fox?

SAUSAGE-SELLER: What connection? Why, 'tis quite plain—a galley travels as fast as a dog.

DEMOS: Why, then, does the oracle not say dog instead of dog-fox?

SAUSAGE-SELLER: Because he compares the soldiers to young foxes, who, like them, eat the grapes in the fields.

DEMOS: Good! Well then! how am I to pay the wages of my young foxes?

SAUSAGE-SELLER: I will undertake that, and in three days too! But listen to this further oracle, by which Apollo puts you on your guard against the snares of the greedy fist.

DEMOS: Of what greedy fist?

SAUSAGE-SELLER: The god in this oracle very clearly points to the hand of Cleon, who incessantly holds his out, saying, "Fill it."

CLEON: 'Tis false! Phoebus means the hand of Diopithes.[120] But here I have a winged oracle, which promises you shall become an eagle and rule over all the earth.

---

116. Cleon was reproached by his enemies with paying small attention to the regular payment of the sailors.

117. Another poetical term to signify Athenian; Aegeus, an ancient mythical King of Athens, father of Theseus.

118. Impudent as a dog and cunning as a fox.

119. An orator and statesman of the day; practically nothing is known about him.

120. Another orator and statesman, accused apparently of taking bribes.

SAUSAGE-SELLER: I have one, which says that you shall be King of the Earth and of the Sea, and that you shall administer justice in Ecbatana, eating fine rich stews the while.

CLEON: I have seen Athené[121] in a dream, pouring out full vials of riches and health over the people.

SAUSAGE-SELLER: I too have seen the goddess, descending from the Acropolis with an owl perched upon her helmet; on your head she was pouring out ambrosia, on that of Cleon garlic pickle.

DEMOS: Truly Glanis is the wisest of men. I shall yield myself to you; guide me in my old age and educate me anew.

CLEON: Ah! I adjure you! not yet; wait a little; I will promise to distribute barley every day.

DEMOS: Ah! I will not hear another word about barley; you have cheated me too often already, both you and Theophanes.[122]

CLEON: Well then! you shall have flour-cakes all piping hot.

SAUSAGE-SELLER: I will give you cakes too, and nice cooked fish; you will only have to eat.

DEMOS: Very well, mind you keep your promises. To whichever of you twain shall treat me best I hand over the reins of state.

CLEON: I will be first.

SAUSAGE-SELLER: No, no, *I* will.

CHORUS: Demos, you are our all-powerful sovereign lord; all tremble before you, yet you are led by the nose. You love to be flattered and fooled; you listen to the orators with gaping mouth and your mind is led astray.

DEMOS: 'Tis rather you who have no brains, if you think me so foolish as all that; it is with a purpose that I play this idiot's role, for I love to drink the lifelong day, and so it pleases me to keep a thief for my minister. When he has thoroughly gorged himself, then I overthrow and crush him.

CHORUS: What profound wisdom! If it be really so, why! all is for the best. Your ministers, then, are your victims, whom you nourish and feed up expressly in the Pnyx, so that, the day your dinner is ready, you may immolate the fattest and eat him.

---

121. As pointed out before, the orators were fond of dragging Athené continually into their speeches.

122. One of Cleon's protégés and flatterers. The scholiasts say he was his secretary.

DEMOS: Look, see how I play with them, while all the time they think themselves such adepts at cheating me. I have my eye on them when they thieve, but I do not appear to be seeing them; then I thrust a judgment down their throat as it were a feather, and force them to vomit up all they have robbed from me.

CLEON: Oh! the rascal!

SAUSAGE-SELLER: Oh! the scoundrel!

CLEON: Demos, all is ready these three hours; I await your orders and I burn with desire to load you with benefits.

SAUSAGE-SELLER: And I ten, twelve, a thousand hours, a long, long while, an infinitely long while.

DEMOS: As for me, 'tis thirty thousand hours that I have been impatient; very long, infinitely long that I have cursed you.

SAUSAGE-SELLER: Do you know what you had best do?

DEMOS: If I do not, tell me.

SAUSAGE-SELLER: Declare the lists open[123] and we will contend abreast to determine who shall treat you the best.

DEMOS: Splendid! Draw back in line!

CLEON: I am ready.

DEMOS: Off you go!

SAUSAGE-SELLER (to Cleon): I shall not let you get to the tape.

DEMOS: What fervent lovers! If I am not to-day the happiest of men, 'tis because I shall be the most disgusted.

CLEON: Look! 'tis I who am the first to bring you a seat.

SAUSAGE-SELLER: And I a table.

CLEON: Hold, here is a cake kneaded of Pylos barley.[124]

SAUSAGE-SELLER: Here are crusts, which the ivory hand of the goddess has hallowed.[125]

DEMOS: Oh! Mighty Athené! How large are your fingers!

CLEON: This is pea-soup, as exquisite as it is fine; 'tis Pallas the victorious goddess at Pylos who crushed the peas herself.

SAUSAGE-SELLER: Oh, Demos! the goddess watches over you; she is stretching forth over your head. . . a stew-pan full of broth.

DEMOS: And should we still be dwelling in this city without this protecting stew-pan?

---

123. Terms borrowed from the circus races.
124. That is, at the expense of other folk.
125. Pieces of bread, hollowed out, which were filled with mincemeat or soup.

CLEON: Here are some fish, given to you by her who is the terror of our foes.

SAUSAGE-SELLER: The daughter of the mightiest of the gods sends you this meat cooked in its own gravy, along with this dish of tripe and some paunch.

DEMOS: 'Tis to thank me for the Peplos I offered to her; 'tis well.

CLEON: The goddess with the terrible plume invites you to eat this long cake; you will row the harder on it.

SAUSAGE-SELLER: Take this also.

DEMOS: And what shall I do with this tripe?

SAUSAGE-SELLER: She sends it you to belly out your galleys, for she is always showing her kindly anxiety for our fleet. Now drink this beverage composed of three parts of water to two of wine.

DEMOS: Ah! what delicious wine, and how well it stands the water.[126]

SAUSAGE-SELLER: 'Twas the goddess who came from the head of Zeus that mixed this liquor with her own hands.

CLEON: Hold, here is a piece of good rich cake.

SAUSAGE-SELLER: But I offer you an entire cake.

CLEON: But you cannot offer him stewed hare as I do.

SAUSAGE-SELLER: Ah! great gods! stewed hare! where shall I find it? Oh! brain of mine, devise some trick!

CLEON: Do you see this, poor fellow?

SAUSAGE-SELLER: A fig for that! Here are folk coming to seek me.

CLEON: Who are they?

SAUSAGE-SELLER: Envoys, bearing sacks bulging with money.

CLEON: (*Hearing money mentioned Clean turns his head, and Agoracritus seizes the opportunity to snatch away the stewed hare*) Where, where, I say?

SAUSAGE-SELLER: Bah! What's that to you? Will you not even now let the strangers alone? Demos, do you see this stewed hare which I bring you?

CLEON: Ah! rascal! you have shamelessly robbed me.

SAUSAGE-SELLER: You have robbed too, you robbed the Laconians at Pylos.

DEMOS: An you pity me, tell me, how did you get the idea to filch it from him?

---

126. Both Greeks and Romans drank their wine mixed with water.

SAUSAGE-SELLER: The idea comes from the goddess; the theft is all my own.

CLEON: And I had taken such trouble to catch this hare.

SAUSAGE-SELLER: But 'twas I who had it cooked.

DEMOS (*to Cleon*): Get you gone! My thanks are only for him who served it.

CLEON: Ah! wretch! have you beaten me in impudence!

SAUSAGE-SELLER: Well then, Demos, say now, who has treated you best, you and your stomach? Decide!

DEMOS: How shall I act here so that the spectators shall approve my judgment?

SAUSAGE-SELLER: I will tell you. Without saying anything, go and rummage through my basket, and then through the Paphlagonian's, and see what is in them; that's the best way to judge.

DEMOS: Let us see then, what is there in yours?

SAUSAGE-SELLER: Why, 'tis empty, dear little father; I have brought everything to you.

DEMOS: This is a basket devoted to the people.

SAUSAGE-SELLER: Now hunt through the Paphlagonian's. Well?

DEMOS: Oh! what a lot of good things! Why! 'tis quite full! Oh! what a huge great part of this cake he kept for himself! He had only cut off the least little tiny piece for me.

SAUSAGE-SELLER: But this is what he has always done. Of everything he took, he only gave you the crumbs, and kept the bulk.

DEMOS: Oh! rascal! was this the way you robbed me? And I was loading you with chaplets and gifts!

CLEON: 'Twas for the public weal I robbed.

DEMOS (*to Cleon*): Give me back that crown;[127] I will give it to him.

SAUSAGE-SELLER: Return it quick, quick, you gallows-bird.

CLEON: No, for the Pythian oracle has revealed to me the name of him who shall overthrow me.

SAUSAGE-SELLER: And that name was mine, nothing can be clearer.

CLEON: Reply and I shall soon see whether you are indeed the man whom the god intended. Firstly, what school did you attend when a child?

---

127. After his success in the Sphacteria affair Cleon induced the people to vote him a chaplet of gold.

SAUSAGE-SELLER: 'Twas in the kitchens I was taught with cuffs and blows.

CLEON: What's that you say? Ah! this is truly what the oracle said. And what did you learn from the master of exercises?

SAUSAGE-SELLER: I learnt to take a false oath without a smile, when I had stolen something.

CLEON: Oh! Phoebus Apollo, god of Lycia! I am undone! And when you had become a man, what trade did you follow?

SAUSAGE-SELLER: I sold sausages and did a bit of fornication.

CLEON: Oh! my god! I am a lost man! Ah! still one slender hope remains. Tell me, was it on the market-place or near the gates that you sold your sausages?

SAUSAGE-SELLER: Near the gates, in the market for salted goods.

CLEON: Alas! I see the prophecy of the god is verily come true. Alas! roll me home.[128] I am a miserable, ruined man. Farewell, my chaplet! 'Tis death to me to part with you. So you are to belong to another; 'tis certain he cannot be a greater thief, but perhaps he may be a luckier one.[129]

SAUSAGE-SELLER: Oh! Zeus, the protector of Greece! 'tis to you I owe this victory!

DEMOSTHENES: Hail! illustrious conqueror, but forget not, that if you have become a great man, 'tis thanks to me; I ask but a little thing; appoint me secretary of the law-court in the room of Phanus.

DEMOS (to the Sausage-seller): But what is your name then? Tell me.

SAUSAGE-SELLER: My name is Agoracritus, because I have always lived on the market-place in the midst of lawsuits.[130]

DEMOS: Well then, Agoracritus, I stand by you; as for the Paphlagonian, I hand him over to your mercy.

AGORACRITUS: Demos, I will care for you to the best of my power, and all shall admit that no citizen is more devoted than I to this city of simpletons.

CHORUS: What fitter theme for our Muse, at the close as at the beginning of his work, than this, to sing the hero who drives his swift steeds down the arena? Why afflict Lysistratus with our

---

128. That is, by means of the mechanical device of the Greek stage known as the (Greek: ekkukl ema).

129. Parody of a well-known verse from Euripides' 'Alcestis.'

130. The name Agoracritus is compounded: cf. (Greek: agora), a market-place, and (Greek: krinein), to judge.

satires on his poverty,[131] and Thumantis,[132] who has not so much as a lodging? He is dying of hunger and can be seen at Delphi, his face bathed in tears, clinging to your quiver, oh, Apollo! and supplicating you to take him out of his misery.

An insult directed at the wicked is not to be censured; on the contrary, the honest man, if he has sense, can only applaud. Him, whom I wish to brand with infamy, is little known himself; 'tis the brother of Arignotus.[133] I regret to quote this name which is so dear to me, but whoever can distinguish black from white, or the Orthian mode of music from others, knows the virtues of Arignotus, whom his brother, Ariphrades,[134] in no way resembles. He gloats in vice, is not merely a dissolute man and utterly debauched—but he has actually invented a new form of vice; for he pollutes his tongue with abominable pleasures in brothels licking up that nauseous moisture and befouling his beard as he tickles the lips of lewd women's private parts.[135] Whoever is not horrified at such a monster shall never drink from the same cup with me.

At times a thought weighs on me at night; I wonder whence comes this fearful voracity of Cleonymus.[136] 'Tis said, that when dining with a rich host, he springs at the dishes with the gluttony of a wild beast and never leaves the bread-bin until his host seizes him round the knees, exclaiming, "Go, go, good gentleman, in mercy go, and spare my poor table!"

'Tis said that the triremes assembled in council and that the oldest spoke in these terms, "Are you ignorant, my sisters, of what is plotting in Athens? They say, that a certain Hyperbolus,[137] a bad citizen and an infamous scoundrel, asks for a hundred of us to take them to sea against Chalcedon."[138] All were indignant, and

---

131. This grandiloquent opening is borrowed from Pindar.

132. Mentioned in the 'Acharnians.'

133. A soothsayer.

134. A flute-player.

135. An allusion to the vice of the 'cunnilingue,' apparently a novel form of naughtiness at Athens in Aristophanes' day.

136. As well known for his gluttony as for his cowardice.

137. One of the most noisy demagogues of Cleon's party; he succeeded him, but was later condemned to ostracism.

138. A town in Bithynia, situated at the entrance of the Bosphorus and nearly opposite Byzantium. It was one of the most important towns in Asia Minor. Doubtless Hyperbolus only demanded so large a fleet to terrorize the towns and oppress them at will.

one of them, as yet a virgin, cried, "May god forbid that I should ever obey him! I would prefer to grow old in the harbour and be gnawed by worms. No! by the gods I swear it, Nauphanté, daughter of Nauson, shall never bend to his law; 'tis as true as I am made of wood and pitch. If the Athenians vote for the proposal of Hyperbolus, let them! we will hoist full sail and seek refuge by the temple of Theseus or the shrine of the Euminides.[139] No! he shall not command us! No! he shall not play with the city to this extent! Let him sail by himself for Tartarus, if such please him, launching the boats in which he used to sell his lamps."

AGORACRITUS: Maintain a holy silence! Keep your mouths from utterance! call no more witnesses; close these tribunals, which are the delight of this city, and gather at the theatre to chant the Paean of thanksgiving to the gods for a fresh favour.

CHORUS: Oh! torch of sacred Athens, saviour of the Islands, what good tidings are we to celebrate by letting the blood of the victims flow in our market-places?

AGORACRITUS: I have freshened Demos up somewhat on the stove and have turned his ugliness into beauty.

CHORUS: I admire your inventive genius; but, where is he?

AGORACRITUS: He is living in ancient Athens, the city of the garlands of violets.

CHORUS: How I should like to see him! What is his dress like, what his manner?

AGORACRITUS: He has once more become as he was in the days when he lived with Aristides and Miltiades. But you will judge for yourselves, for I hear the vestibule doors opening. Hail with your shouts of gladness the Athens of old, which now doth reappear to your gaze, admirable, worthy of the songs of the poets and the home of the illustrious Demos.

CHORUS: Oh! noble, brilliant Athens, whose brow is wreathed with violets, show us the sovereign master of this land and of all Greece.

AGORACRITUS: Lo! here he is coming with his hair held in place with a golden band and in all the glory of his old-world dress; perfumed with myrrh, he spreads around him not the odour of lawsuits, but of peace.

---

139. These temples were inviolable places of refuge, where even slaves were secure.

ARISTOPHANES

CHORUS: Hail! King of Greece, we congratulate you upon the happiness you enjoy; it is worthy of this city, worthy of the glory of Marathon.

DEMOS: Come, Agoracritus, come, my best friend; see the service you have done me by freshening me up on your stove.

AGORACRITUS: Ah! if you but remembered what you were formerly and what you did, you would for a certainty believe me to be a god.

DEMOS: But what did I? and how was I then?

AGORACRITUS: Firstly, so soon as ever an orator declared in the assembly "Demos, I love you ardently; 'tis I alone, who dream of you and watch over your interests"; at such an exordium you would look like a cock flapping his wings or a bull tossing his horns.

DEMOS: What, I?

AGORACRITUS: Then, after he had fooled you to the hilt, he would go.

DEMOS: What! they would treat me so, and I never saw it!

AGORACRITUS: You knew only how to open and close your ears like a sunshade.

DEMOS: Was I then so stupid and such a dotard?

AGORACRITUS: Worse than that; if one of two orators proposed to equip a fleet for war and the other suggested the use of the same sum for paying out to the citizens, 'twas the latter who always carried the day. Well! you droop your head! you turn away your face?

DEMOS: I redden at my past errors.

AGORACRITUS: Think no more of them; 'tis not you who are to blame, but those who cheated you in this sorry fashion. But, come, if some impudent lawyer dared to say, "Dicasts, you shall have no wheat unless you convict this accused man!" what would you do? Tell me.

DEMOS: I would have him removed from the bar, I would bind Hyperbolus about his neck like a stone and would fling him into the Barathrum.[140]

AGORACRITUS: Well spoken! but what other measures do you wish to take?

DEMOS: First, as soon as ever a fleet returns to the harbour, I shall pay up the rowers in full.

AGORACRITUS: That will soothe many a worn and chafed bottom.

---

140. A rocky cleft at the back of the Acropolis into which criminals were hurled.

DEMOS: Further, the hoplite enrolled for military service shall not get transferred to another service through favour, but shall stick to that given him at the outset.

AGORACRITUS: This will strike the buckler of Cleonymus full in the centre.

DEMOS: None shall ascend the rostrum, unless their chins are bearded.

AGORACRITUS: What then will become of Clisthenes and of Strato?[141]

DEMOS: I wish only to refer to those youths, who loll about the perfume shops, babbling at random, "What a clever fellow is Pheax![142] How cleverly he escaped death! how concise and convincing is his style! what phrases! how clear and to the point! how well he knows how to quell an interruption!"

AGORACRITUS: I thought you were the lover of those pathic minions.

DEMOS: The gods forefend it! and I will force all such fellows to go a-hunting instead of proposing decrees.

AGORACRITUS: In that case, accept this folding-stool, and to carry it this well-grown, big-testicled slave lad. Besides, you may put him to any other purpose you please.

DEMOS: Oh! I am happy indeed to find myself as I was of old!

AGORACRITUS: Aye, you deem yourself happy, when I shall have handed you the truces of thirty years. Truces! step forward![143]

DEMOS: Great gods! how charming they are! Can I do with them as I wish? where did you discover them, pray?

AGORACRITUS: 'Twas that Paphlagonian who kept them locked up in his house, so that you might not enjoy them. As for myself, I give them to you; take them with you into the country.

DEMOS: And what punishment will you inflict upon this Paphlagonian, the cause of all my troubles?

AGORACRITUS: 'Twill not be over-terrible. I condemn him to follow my old trade; posted near the gates, he must sell sausages of asses' and dogs'-meat; perpetually drunk, he will exchange foul language with prostitutes and will drink nothing but the dirty water from the baths.

DEMOS: Well conceived! he is indeed fit to wrangle with harlots and bathmen; as for you, in return for so many blessings, I invite you

---

141. Young and effeminate orators of licentious habits.
142. By adroit special pleading he had contrived to get his acquittal, when charged with a capital offence.
143. They were personified on the stage as pretty little *filles de joie*.

to take the place at the Prytaneum which this rogue once occupied. Put on this frog-green mantle and follow me. As for the other, let 'em take him away; let him go sell his sausages in full view of the foreigners, whom he used formerly so wantonly to insult.

FINIS OF "THE KNIGHTS"

THE CLOUDS

Introduction

The satire in this, one of the best known of all Aristophanes' comedies, is directed against the new schools of philosophy, or perhaps we should rather say dialectic, which had lately been introduced, mostly from abroad, at Athens. The doctrines held up to ridicule are those of the 'Sophists'—such men as Thrasymachus from Chalcedon in Bithynia, Gorgias from Leontini in Sicily, Protagoras from Abdera in Thrace, and other foreign scholars and rhetoricians who had flocked to Athens as the intellectual centre of the Hellenic world. Strange to say, Socrates of all people, the avowed enemy and merciless critic of these men and their methods, is taken as their representative, and personally attacked with pitiless raillery. Presumably this was merely because he was the most prominent and noteworthy teacher and thinker of the day, while his grotesque personal appearance and startling eccentricities of behaviour gave a ready handle to caricature. Neither the author nor his audience took the trouble, or were likely to take the trouble, to discriminate nicely; there was, of course, a general resemblance between the Socratic 'elenchos' and the methods of the new practitioners of dialectic; and this was enough for stage purposes. However unjustly, Socrates is taken as typical of the newfangled sophistical teachers, just as in 'The Acharnians' Lamachus, with his Gorgon shield, is introduced as representative of the War party, though that general was not specially responsible for the continuance of hostilities more than anybody else.

Aristophanes' point of view, as a member of the aristocratical party and a fine old Conservative, is that these Sophists, as the professors of the new education had come to be called, and Socrates as their protagonist, were insincere and dangerous innovators, corrupting morals, persuading young men to despise the old-fashioned, home-grown virtues of the State and teaching a system of false and pernicious tricks of verbal fence whereby anything whatever could be proved, and the worse be made to seem the better—provided always sufficient payment were forthcoming. True, Socrates refused to take money from his pupils, and made it his chief reproach against the lecturing Sophists that they received fees; but what of that? The Comedian cannot pay heed to such fine distinctions, but belabours the whole tribe with indiscriminate raillery and scurrility.

The play was produced at the Great Dionysia in 423 B.C., but proved unsuccessful, Cratinus and Amipsias being awarded first and second prize. This is said to have been due to the intrigues and influence of Alcibiades, who resented the caricature of himself presented in the sporting Phidippides. A second edition of the drama was apparently produced some years later, to which the 'Parabasis' of the play as we possess it must belong, as it refers to events subsequent to the date named.

The plot is briefly as follows: Strepsiades, a wealthy country gentleman, has been brought to penury and deeply involved in debt by the extravagance and horsy tastes of his son Phidippides. Having heard of the wonderful new art of argument, the royal road to success in litigation, discovered by the Sophists, he hopes that, if only he can enter the 'Phrontisterion,' or Thinking-Shop, of Socrates, he will learn how to turn the tables on his creditors and avoid paying the debts which are dragging him down. He joins the school accordingly, but is found too old and stupid to profit by the lessons. So his son Phidippides is substituted as a more promising pupil. The latter takes to the new learning like a duck to water, and soon shows what progress he has made by beating his father and demonstrating that he is justified by all laws, divine and human, in what he is doing. This opens the old man's eyes, who sets fire to the 'Phrontisterion,' and the play ends in a great conflagration of this home of humbug.

Dramatis Personae

Strepsiades.
Phidippides.
Servant of Strepsiades.
Socrates.
Disciples of Socrates.
Just Discourse.
Unjust Discourse.
Pasias, a Money-lender.
Pasias' Witness.
Amynias, another Money-lender.
Chaerephon.
Chorus of Clouds.

Scene: *A sleeping-room in Strepsiades' house; then in front of Socrates' house.*

STREPSIADES:[1] Great gods! will these nights never end? will daylight
never come? I heard the cock crow long ago and my slaves are
snoring still! Ah! 'twas not so formerly. Curses on the War! has it
not done me ills enough? Now I may not even chastise my own
slaves.[2] Again there's this brave lad, who never wakes the whole
long night, but, wrapped in his five coverlets, farts away to his
heart's content. Come! let me nestle in well and snore too, if it
be possible. . . oh! misery, 'tis vain to think of sleep with all these
expenses, this stable, these debts, which are devouring me, thanks
to this fine cavalier, who only knows how to look after his long
locks, to show himself off in his chariot and to dream of horses!
And I, I am nearly dead, when I see the moon bringing the third
decade in her train[3] and my liability falling due. . . Slave! light the
lamp and bring me my tablets. Who are all my creditors? Let me
see and reckon up the interest. What is it I owe? . . . Twelve minae
to Pasias. . . What! twelve minae to Pasias? . . . Why did I borrow
these? Ah! I know! 'Twas to buy that thoroughbred, which cost me
so dear.[4] How I should have prized the stone that had blinded him!
PHIDIPPIDES (*in his sleep*): That's not fair, Philo! Drive your chariot
straight,[5] I say.
STREPSIADES: 'Tis this that is destroying me. He raves about horses,
even in his sleep.
PHIDIPPIDES (*still sleeping*): How many times round the track is the
race for the chariots of war?[6]

---

1. He is in one bed and his son is in another; slaves are sleeping near them. It is night-time.
2. The punishment most frequently inflicted upon slaves in the towns was to send them into the country to work in the fields, but at the period when the 'Clouds' was presented, 424 B.C., the invasions of the Peloponnesians forbade the pursuit of agriculture. Moreover, there existed the fear, that if the slaves were punished too harshly, they might go over to the enemy.
3. Among the Greeks, each month was divided into three decades. The last of the month was called (Greek: en e kai nea), the day of the old and the new or the day of the new moon, and on that day interest, which it was customary to pay monthly, became due.
4. Literally, the horse marked with the (Greek: koppa) (ϙ), a letter of the older Greek alphabet, afterwards disused, which distinguished the thoroughbreds.
5. Phidippides dreams that he is driving in a chariot race, and that an opponent is trying to cut into his track.
6. There was a prize specially reserved for war-chariots in the games of the Athenian hippodrome; being heavier than the chariots generally used, they doubtless had to cover a lesser number of laps, which explains Phidippides' question.

STREPSIADES: 'Tis your own father you are driving to death. . . to ruin. Come! what debt comes next, after that of Pasias? . . . Three minae to Amynias for a chariot and its two wheels.

PHIDIPPIDES (*still asleep*): Give the horse a good roll in the dust and lead him home.

STREPSIADES: Ah! wretched boy! 'tis my money that you are making roll. My creditors have distrained on my goods, and here are others again, who demand security for their interest.

PHIDIPPIDES (*awaking*): What is the matter with you, father, that you groan and turn about the whole night through?

STREPSIADES: I have a bum-bailiff in the bedclothes biting me.

PHIDIPPIDES: For pity's sake, let me have a little sleep.

STREPSIADES: Very well, sleep on! but remember that all these debts will fall back on your shoulders. Oh! curses on the go-between who made me marry your mother! I lived so happily in the country, a commonplace, everyday life, but a good and easy one—had not a trouble, not a care, was rich in bees, in sheep and in olives. Then forsooth I must marry the niece of Megacles, the son of Megacles; I belonged to the country, she was from the town; she was a haughty, extravagant woman, a true Coesyra.[7] On the nuptial day, when I lay beside her, I was reeking of the dregs of the wine-cup, of cheese and of wool; she was redolent with essences, saffron, tender kisses, the love of spending, of good cheer and of wanton delights. I will not say she did nothing; no, she worked hard. . . to ruin me, and pretending all the while merely to be showing her the cloak she had woven for me, I said, "Wife, you go too fast about your work, your threads are too closely woven and you use far too much wool."

A SLAVE: There is no more oil in the lamp.

STREPSIADES: Why then did you light such a guzzling lamp? Come here, I am going to beat you!

SLAVE: What for?

STREPSIADES: Because you have put in too thick a wick. . . Later, when we had this boy, what was to be his name? 'Twas the cause of much quarrelling with my loving wife. She insisted on having

---

7. The wife of Alcmaeon, a descendant of Nestor, who, driven from Messenia by the Heraclidae, came to settle in Athens in the twelfth century, and was the ancestor of the great family of the Alcmaeonidae, Pericles and Alcibiades belonged to it.

some reference to a horse in his name, that he should be called Xanthippus, Charippus or Callippides.[8] I wanted to name him Phidonides after his grandfather.[9] We disputed long, and finally agreed to style him Phidippides. . .[10] She used to fondle and coax him, saying, "Oh! what a joy it will be to me when you have grown up, to see you, like my father, Megacles,[11] clothed in purple and standing up straight in your chariot driving your steeds toward the town." And I would say to him, "When, like your father, you will go, dressed in a skin, to fetch back your goats from Phelleus."[12] Alas! he never listened to me and his madness for horses has shattered my fortune. But by dint of thinking the livelong night, I have discovered a road to salvation, both miraculous and divine. If he will but follow it, I shall be out of my trouble! First, however, he must be awakened, but let it be done as gently as possible. How shall I manage it? Phidippides! my little Phidippides!

PHIDIPPIDES: What is it, father!

STREPSIADES: Kiss me and give me your hand.

PHIDIPPIDES: There! What's it all about?

STREPSIADES: Tell me! do you love me?

PHIDIPPIDES: By Posidon, the equestrian Posidon! yes, I swear I do.

STREPSIADES: Oh, do not, I pray you, invoke this god of horses; 'tis he who is the cause of all my cares. But if you really love me, and with your whole heart, my boy, believe me.

PHIDIPPIDES: Believe you? about what?

STREPSIADES: Alter your habits forthwith and go and learn what I tell you.

PHIDIPPIDES: Say on, what are your orders?

STREPSIADES: Will you obey me ever so little?

PHIDIPPIDES: By Bacchus, I will obey you.

STREPSIADES: Very well then! Look this way. Do you see that little door and that little house?[13]

---

8. The Greek word for horse is (Greek: hippos).

9. Derived from (Greek: pheidesthai), to save.

10. The name Phidippides contains both words, (Greek: hippos), horse, and (Greek: pheidesthai), to save, and was therefore a compromise arrived at between the two parents.

11. The heads of the family of the Alcmaeonidae bore the name of Megacles from generation to generation.

12. A mountain in Attica.

13. Aristophanes represents everything belonging to Socrates as being mean, even down to his dwelling.

PHIDIPPIDES: Yes, father. But what are you driving at?

STREPSIADES: That is the school of wisdom. There, they prove that we are coals enclosed on all sides under a vast extinguisher, which is the sky.[14] If well paid,[15] these men also teach one how to gain law-suits, whether they be just or not.

PHIDIPPIDES: What do they call themselves?

STREPSIADES: I do not know exactly, but they are deep thinkers and most admirable people.

PHIDIPPIDES: Bah! the wretches! I know them; you mean those quacks with livid faces,[16] those barefoot fellows, such as that miserable Socrates and Chaerephon.[17]

STREPSIADES: Silence! say nothing foolish! If you desire your father not to die of hunger, join their company and let your horses go.

PHIDIPPIDES: No, by Bacchus! even though you gave me the pheasants that Leogoras rears.

STREPSIADES: Oh! my beloved son, I beseech you, go and follow their teachings.

PHIDIPPIDES: And what is it I should learn?

STREPSIADES: 'Twould seem they have two courses of reasoning, the true and the false, and that, thanks to the false, the worst law-suits can be gained. If then you learn this science, which is false, I shall not pay an obolus of all the debts I have contracted on your account.

PHIDIPPIDES: No, I will not do it. I should no longer dare to look at our gallant horsemen, when I had so tarnished my fair hue of honour.

STREPSIADES: Well then, by Demeter! I will no longer support you, neither you, nor your team, nor your saddle-horse. Go and hang yourself, I turn you out of house and home.

PHIDIPPIDES: My uncle Megacles will not leave me without horses; I shall go to him and laugh at your anger.

STREPSIADES: One rebuff shall not dishearten me. With the help of the gods I will enter this school and learn myself. But at my age, memory has gone and the mind is slow to grasp things. How can

---

14. Crates ascribes the same doctrine in one of his plays to the Pythagorean Hippo, of Samos.

15. This is pure calumny. Socrates accepted no payment.

16. Here the poet confounds Socrates' disciples with the Stoics. Contrary to the text, Socrates held that a man should care for his bodily health.

17. One of Socrates' pupils.

all these fine distinctions, these subtleties be learned? Bah! why should I dally thus instead of rapping at the door? Slave, slave! (*He knocks and calls*)

A DISCIPLE: A plague on you! Who are you?

STREPSIADES: Strepsiades, the son of Phido, of the deme of Cicynna.

DISCIPLE: 'Tis for sure only an ignorant and illiterate fellow who lets drive at the door with such kicks. You have brought on a miscarriage—of an idea!

STREPSIADES: Pardon me, pray; for I live far away from here in the country. But tell me, what was the idea that miscarried?

DISCIPLE: I may not tell it to any but a disciple.

STREPSIADES: Then tell me without fear, for I have come to study among you.

DISCIPLE: Very well then, but reflect, that these are mysteries. Lately, a flea bit Chaerephon on the brow and then from there sprang on to the head of Socrates. Socrates asked Chaerephon, "How many times the length of its legs does a flea jump?"

STREPSIADES: And how ever did he set about measuring it?

DISCIPLE: Oh! 'twas most ingenious! He melted some wax, seized the flea and dipped its two feet in the wax, which, when cooled, left them shod with true Persian buskins.[18] These he slipped off and with them measured the distance.

STREPSIADES: Ah! great Zeus! what a brain! what subtlety!

DISCIPLE: I wonder what then would you say, if you knew another of Socrates' contrivances?

STREPSIADES: What is it? Pray tell me.

DISCIPLE: Chaerephon of the deme of Sphettia asked him whether he thought a gnat buzzed through its proboscis or through its rear.

STREPSIADES: And what did he say about the gnat?

DISCIPLE: He said that the gut of the gnat was narrow, and that, in passing through this tiny passage, the air is driven with force towards the breech; then after this slender channel, it encountered the rump, which was distended like a trumpet, and there it resounded sonorously.

STREPSIADES: So the rear of a gnat is a trumpet. Oh! what a splendid discovery! Thrice happy Socrates! 'Twould not be difficult to succeed in a law-suit, knowing so much about the gut of a gnat!

---

18. Female footwear. They were a sort of light slipper and white in colour.

DISCIPLE: Not long ago a lizard caused him the loss of a sublime thought.

STREPSIADES: In what way, an it please you?

DISCIPLE: One night, when he was studying the course of the moon and its revolutions and was gazing open-mouthed at the heavens, a lizard shitted upon him from the top of the roof.

STREPSIADES: This lizard, that relieved itself over Socrates, tickles me.

DISCIPLE: Yesternight we had nothing to eat.

STREPSIADES: Well! What did he contrive, to secure you some supper?

DISCIPLE: He spread over the table a light layer of cinders, bending an iron rod the while; then he took up a pair of compasses and at the same moment unhooked a piece of the victim which was hanging in the palaestra.[19]

STREPSIADES: And we still dare to admire Thales![20] Open, open this home of knowledge to me quickly! Haste, haste to show me Socrates; I long to become his disciple. But do, do open the door. (*The disciple admits Strepsiades*) Ah! by Heracles! what country are those animals from?

DISCIPLE: Why, what are you astonished at? What do you think they resemble?

STREPSIADES: The captives of Pylos.[21] But why do they look so fixedly on the ground?

DISCIPLE: They are seeking for what is below the ground.

STREPSIADES: Ah! 'tis onions they are seeking. Do not give yourselves so much trouble; I know where there are some, fine and large ones. But what are those fellows doing, who are bent all double?

DISCIPLE: They are sounding the abysses of Tartarus.[22]

STREPSIADES: And what is their rump looking at in the heavens?

---

19. He calls off their attention by pretending to show them a geometrical problem and seizes the opportunity to steal something for supper. The young men who gathered together in the palaestra, or gymnastic school, were wont there to offer sacrifices to the gods before beginning the exercises. The offerings consisted of smaller victims, such as lambs, fowl, geese, etc., and the flesh afterwards was used for their meal (*vide* Plato in the 'Lysias'). It is known that Socrates taught wherever he might happen to be, in the palaestra as well as elsewhere.

20. The first of the seven sages, born at Miletus.

21. Because of their wretched appearance. The Laconians, blockaded in Sphacteria, had suffered sorely from famine.

22. In fact, this was one of the chief accusations brought against Socrates by Miletus and Anytus; he was reproached for probing into the mysteries of nature.

DISCIPLE: It is studying astronomy on its own account. But come in; so that the master may not find us here.

STREPSIADES: Not yet, not yet; let them not change their position. I want to tell them my own little matter.

DISCIPLE: But they may not stay too long in the open air and away from school.

STREPSIADES: In the name of all the gods, what is that? Tell me. (*Pointing to a celestial globe*)

DISCIPLE: That is astronomy.

STREPSIADES: And that? (*Pointing to a map*)

DISCIPLE: Geometry.

STREPSIADES: What is that used for?

DISCIPLE: To measure the land.

STREPSIADES: But that is apportioned by lot.[23]

DISCIPLE: No, no, I mean the entire earth.

STREPSIADES: Ah! what a funny thing! How generally useful indeed is this invention!

DISCIPLE: There is the whole surface of the earth. Look! Here is Athens.

STREPSIADES: Athens! you are mistaken; I see no courts sitting.[24]

DISCIPLE: Nevertheless it is really and truly the Attic territory.

STREPSIADES: And where are my neighbours of Cicynna?

DISCIPLE: They live here. This is Euboea; you see this island, that is so long and narrow.

STREPSIADES: I know. 'Tis we and Pericles, who have stretched it by dint of squeezing it.[25] And where is Lacedaemon?

DISCIPLE: Lacedaemon? Why, here it is, look.

STREPSIADES: How near it is to us! Think it well over, it must be removed to a greater distance.

DISCIPLE: But, by Zeus, that is not possible.

STREPSIADES: Then, woe to you! And who is this man suspended up in a basket?

DISCIPLE: 'Tis *he himself*.

STREPSIADES: Who himself?

---

23. When the Athenians captured a town, they divided its lands by lot among the poorer Athenian citizens.

24. An allusion to the Athenian love of law-suits and litigation.

25. When originally conquered by Pericles, the island of Euboea, off the coasts of Boeotia and Attica, had been treated with extreme harshness.

DISCIPLE: Socrates.

STREPSIADES: Socrates! Oh! I pray you, call him right loudly for me.

DISCIPLE: Call him yourself; I have no time to waste.

STREPSIADES: Socrates! my little Socrates!

SOCRATES: Mortal, what do you want with me?

STREPSIADES: First, what are you doing up there? Tell me, I beseech you.

SOCRATES: I traverse the air and contemplate the sun.

STREPSIADES: Thus 'tis not on the solid ground, but from the height of this basket, that you slight the gods, if indeed. . .[26]

SOCRATES: I have to suspend my brain and mingle the subtle essence of my mind with this air, which is of the like nature, in order to clearly penetrate the things of heaven.[27] I should have discovered nothing, had I remained on the ground to consider from below the things that are above; for the earth by its force attracts the sap of the mind to itself. 'Tis just the same with the water-cress.[28]

STREPSIADES: What? Does the mind attract the sap of the water-cress? Ah! my dear little Socrates, come down to me! I have come to ask you for lessons.

SOCRATES: And for what lessons?

STREPSIADES: I want to learn how to speak. I have borrowed money, and my merciless creditors do not leave me a moment's peace; all my goods are at stake.

SOCRATES: And how was it you did not see that you were getting so much into debt?

STREPSIADES: My ruin has been the madness for horses, a most rapacious evil; but teach me one of your two methods of reasoning, the one whose object is not to repay anything, and, may the gods bear witness, that I am ready to pay any fee you may name.

SOCRATES: By which gods will you swear? To begin with, the gods are not a coin current with us.

STREPSIADES: But what do you swear by then? By the iron money of Byzantium?[29]

SOCRATES: Do you really wish to know the truth of celestial matters?

---

26. Is about to add, "you believe in them at all," but checks himself.

27. This was the doctrine of Anaximenes.

28. The scholiast explains that water-cress robs all plants that grow in its vicinity of their moisture and that they consequently soon wither and die.

29. In the other Greek towns, the smaller coins were of copper.

STREPSIADES: Why, truly, if 'tis possible.

SOCRATES: . . . and to converse with the clouds, who are our genii?

STREPSIADES: Without a doubt.

SOCRATES: Then be seated on this sacred couch.

STREPSIADES: I am seated.

SOCRATES: Now take this chaplet.

STREPSIADES: Why a chaplet? Alas! Socrates, would you sacrifice me, like Athamas?[30]

SOCRATES: No, these are the rites of initiation.

STREPSIADES: And what is it I am to gain?

SOCRATES: You will become a thorough rattle-pate, a hardened old stager, the fine flour of the talkers. . . But come, keep quiet.

STREPSIADES: By Zeus! You lie not! Soon I shall be nothing but wheat-flour, if you powder me in this fashion.[31]

SOCRATES: Silence, old man, give heed to the prayers. . . Oh! most mighty king, the boundless air, that keepest the earth suspended in space, thou bright Aether and ye venerable goddesses, the Clouds, who carry in your loins the thunder and the lightning, arise, ye sovereign powers and manifest yourselves in the celestial spheres to the eyes of the sage.

STREPSIADES: Not yet! Wait a bit, till I fold my mantle double, so as not to get wet. And to think that I did not even bring my travelling cap! What a misfortune!

SOCRATES: Come, oh! Clouds, whom I adore, come and show yourselves to this man, whether you be resting on the sacred summits of Olympus, crowned with hoar-frost, or tarrying in the gardens of Ocean, your father, forming sacred choruses with the Nymphs; whether you be gathering the waves of the Nile in golden vases or dwelling in the Maeotic marsh or on the snowy rocks of Mimas, hearken to my prayer and accept my offering. May these sacrifices be pleasing to you.

CHORUS: Eternal Clouds, let us appear, let us arise from the roaring depths of Ocean, our father; let us fly towards the lofty mountains, spread our damp wings over their forest-laden summits, whence

---

30. Athamas, King of Thebes. An allusion to a tragedy by Sophocles, in which Athamas is dragged before the altar of Zeus with his head circled with a chaplet, to be there sacrificed; he is, however, saved by Heracles.

31. No doubt Socrates sprinkled flour over the head of Strepsiades in the same manner as was done with the sacrificial victims.

we will dominate the distant valleys, the harvest fed by the sacred earth, the murmur of the divine streams and the resounding waves of the sea, which the unwearying orb lights up with its glittering beams. But let us shake off the rainy fogs, which hide our immortal beauty and sweep the earth from afar with our gaze.

SOCRATES: Oh, venerated goddesses, yes, you are answering my call! (*To Strepsiades*) Did you hear their voices mingling with the awful growling of the thunder?

STREPSIADES: Oh! adorable Clouds, I revere you and I too am going to let off *my* thunder, so greatly has your own affrighted me. Faith! whether permitted or not, I must, I must shit!

SOCRATES: No scoffing; do not copy those accursed comic poets. Come, silence! a numerous host of goddesses approaches with songs.

CHORUS: Virgins, who pour forth the rains, let us move toward Attica, the rich country of Pallas, the home of the brave; let us visit the dear land of Cecrops, where the secret rites[32] are celebrated, where the mysterious sanctuary flies open to the initiate. . . What victims are offered there to the deities of heaven! What glorious temples! What statues! What holy prayers to the rulers of Olympus! At every season nothing but sacred festivals, garlanded victims, are to be seen. Then Spring brings round again the joyous feasts of Dionysus, the harmonious contests of the choruses and the serious melodies of the flute.

STREPSIADES: By Zeus! Tell me, Socrates, I pray you, who are these women, whose language is so solemn; can they be demigoddesses?

SOCRATES: Not at all. They are the Clouds of heaven, great goddesses for the lazy; to them we owe all, thoughts, speeches, trickery, roguery, boasting, lies, sagacity.

STREPSIADES: Ah! that was why, as I listened to them, my mind spread out its wings; it burns to babble about trifles, to maintain worthless arguments, to voice its petty reasons, to contradict, to tease some opponent. But are they not going to show themselves? I should like to see them, were it possible.

SOCRATES: Well, look this way in the direction of Parnes;[33] I already see those who are slowly descending.

---

32. The mysteries of Eleusis celebrated in the Temple of Demeter.
33. A mountain of Attica, north of Athens.

STREPSIADES: But where, where? Show them to me.

SOCRATES: They are advancing in a throng, following an oblique path across the dales and thickets.

STREPSIADES: 'Tis strange! I can see nothing.

SOCRATES: There, close to the entrance.

STREPSIADES: Hardly, if at all, can I distinguish them.

SOCRATES: You *must* see them clearly now, unless your eyes are filled with gum as thick as pumpkins.

STREPSIADES: Aye, undoubtedly! Oh! the venerable goddesses! Why, they fill up the entire stage.

SOCRATES: And you did not know, you never suspected, that they were goddesses?

STREPSIADES: No, indeed; methought the Clouds were only fog, dew and vapour.

SOCRATES: But what you certainly do not know is that they are the support of a crowd of quacks, both the diviners, who were sent to Thurium,[34] the notorious physicians, the well-combed fops, who load their fingers with rings down to the nails, and the baggarts, who write dithyrambic verses, all these are idlers whom the Clouds provide a living for, because they sing them in their verses.

STREPSIADES: 'Tis then for this that they praise "the rapid flight of the moist clouds, which veil the brightness of day" and "the waving locks of the hundred-headed Typho" and "the impetuous tempests, which float through the heavens, like birds of prey with aerial wings, loaded with mists" and "the rains, the dew, which the clouds outpour."[35] As a reward for these fine phrases they bolt well-grown, tasty mullet and delicate thrushes.

SOCRATES: Yes, thanks to these. And is it not right and meet?

STREPSIADES: Tell me then why, if these really are the Clouds, they so very much resemble mortals. This is not their usual form.

SOCRATES: What are they like then?

STREPSIADES: I don't know exactly; well, they are like great packs of wool, but not like women—no, not in the least. . . And these have noses.

SOCRATES: Answer my questions.

---

34. Sybaris, a town of Magna Graecia (Lucania), destroyed by the Crotoniates in 709 B.C., was rebuilt by the Athenians under the name of Thurium in 444 B.C. Ten diviners had been sent with the Athenian settlers.

35. A parody of the dithyrambic style.

STREPSIADES: Willingly! Go on, I am listening.

SOCRATES: Have you not sometimes seen clouds in the sky like a centaur, a leopard, a wolf or a bull?

STREPSIADES: Why, certainly I have, but what then?

SOCRATES: They take what metamorphosis they like. If they see a debauchee with long flowing locks and hairy as a beast, like the son of Xenophantes,[36] they take the form of a Centaur[37] in derision of his shameful passion.

STREPSIADES: And when they see Simon, that thiever of public money, what do they do then?

SOCRATES: To picture him to the life, they turn at once into wolves.

STREPSIADES: So that was why yesterday, when they saw Cleonymus,[38] who cast away his buckler because he is the veriest poltroon amongst men, they changed into deer.

SOCRATES: And to-day they have seen Clisthenes;[39] you see. . . they are women.

STREPSIADES: Hail, sovereign goddesses, and if ever you have let your celestial voice be heard by mortal ears, speak to me, oh! speak to me, ye all-powerful queens.

CHORUS: Hail! veteran of the ancient times, you who burn to instruct yourself in fine language. And you, great high-priest of subtle nonsense, tell us your desire. To you and Prodicus[40] alone of all the hollow orationers of to-day have we lent an ear—to Prodicus, because of his knowledge and his great wisdom, and to you, because you walk with head erect, a confident look, barefooted, resigned to everything and proud of our protection.

STREPSIADES: Oh! Earth! What august utterances! how sacred! how wondrous!

---

36. Hieronymus, a dithyrambic poet and reputed an infamous pederast.

37. When guests at the nuptials of Pirithous, King of the Lapithae, and Hippodamia, they wanted to carry off and violate the bride. That, according to legend, was the origin of their war against the Lapithae. Hieronymus is likened to the Centaurs on account of his bestial passion.

38. A general, incessantly scoffed at by Aristophanes because of his cowardice.

39. Aristophanes frequently mentions him as an effeminate and debauched character.

40. A celebrated sophist, born at Ceos, and a disciple of Protagoras. When sent on an embassy by his compatriots to Athens, he there publicly preached on eloquence, and had for his disciples Euripides, Isocrates and even Socrates. His "fifty drachmae lecture" has been much spoken of; that sum had to be paid to hear it.

SOCRATES: That is because these are the only goddesses; all the rest are pure myth.

STREPSIADES: But by the Earth! is our Father, Zeus, the Olympian, not a god?

SOCRATES: Zeus! what Zeus? Are you mad? There is no Zeus.

STREPSIADES: What are you saying now? Who causes the rain to fall? Answer me that!

SOCRATES: Why, 'tis these, and I will prove it. Have you ever seen it raining without clouds? Let Zeus then cause rain with a clear sky and without their presence!

STREPSIADES: By Apollo! that is powerfully argued! For my own part, I always thought it was Zeus pissing into a sieve. But tell me, who is it makes the thunder, which I so much dread?

SOCRATES: 'Tis these, when they roll one over the other.

STREPSIADES: But how can that be? you most daring among men!

SOCRATES: Being full of water, and forced to move along, they are of necessity precipitated in rain, being fully distended with moisture from the regions where they have been floating; hence they bump each other heavily and burst with great noise.

STREPSIADES: But is it not Zeus who forces them to move?

SOCRATES: Not at all; 'tis aerial Whirlwind.

STREPSIADES: The Whirlwind! ah! I did not know that. So Zeus, it seems, has no existence, and 'tis the Whirlwind that reigns in his stead? But you have not yet told me what makes the roll of the thunder?

SOCRATES: Have you not understood me then? I tell you, that the Clouds, when full of rain, bump against one another, and that, being inordinately swollen out, they burst with a great noise.

STREPSIADES: How can you make me credit that?

SOCRATES: Take yourself as an example. When you have heartily gorged on stew at the Panathenaea, you get throes of stomach-ache and then suddenly your belly resounds with prolonged growling.

STREPSIADES: Yes, yes, by Apollo! I suffer, I get colic, then the stew sets a-growling like thunder and finally bursts forth with a terrific noise. At first, 'tis but a little gurgling *pappax, pappax!* then it increases, *papapappax!* and when I seek relief, why, 'tis thunder indeed, *papapappax! pappax!! papapappax!!!* just like the clouds.

SOCRATES: Well then, reflect what a noise is produced by your belly, which is but small. Shall not the air, which is boundless, produce these mighty claps of thunder?

STREPSIADES: But tell me this. Whence comes the lightning, the dazzling flame, which at times consumes the man it strikes, at others hardly singes him. Is it not plain, that 'tis Zeus hurling it at the perjurers?

SOCRATES: Out upon the fool! the driveller! he still savours of the golden age! If Zeus strikes at the perjurers, why has he not blasted Simon, Cleonymus and Theorus?[41] Of a surety, greater perjurers cannot exist. No, he strikes his own Temple, and Sunium, the promontory of Athens,[42] and the towering oaks. Now, why should he do that? An oak is no perjurer.

STREPSIADES: I cannot tell, but it seems to me well argued. What is the thunder then?

SOCRATES: When a dry wind ascends to the Clouds and gets shut into them, it blows them out like a bladder; finally, being too confined, it bursts them, escapes with fierce violence and a roar to flash into flame by reason of its own impetuosity.

STREPSIADES: Forsooth, 'tis just what happened to me one day. 'Twas at the feast of Zeus! I was cooking a sow's belly for my family and I had forgotten to slit it open. It swelled out and, suddenly bursting, discharged itself right into my eyes and burnt my face.

CHORUS: Oh, mortal! you, who desire to instruct yourself in our great wisdom, the Athenians, the Greeks will envy you your good fortune. Only you must have the memory and ardour for study, you must know how to stand the tests, hold your own, go forward without feeling fatigue, caring but little for food, abstaining from wine, gymnastic exercises and other similar follies, in fact, you must believe as every man of intellect should, that the greatest of all blessings is to live and think more clearly than the vulgar herd, to shine in the contests of words.

STREPSIADES: If it be a question of hardiness for labour, of spending whole nights at work, of living sparingly, of fighting my stomach and only eating chick-pease, rest assured, I am as hard as an anvil.

SOCRATES: Henceforward, following our example, you will recognize no other gods but Chaos, the Clouds and the Tongue, these three alone.

---

41. These three men have already been referred to.
42. A promontory of Attica (the modern Cape Colonna) about fifty miles from the Piraeus. Here stood a magnificent Temple, dedicated to Athené.

STREPSIADES: I would not speak to the others, even if I should meet them in the street; not a single sacrifice, not a libation, not a grain of incense for them!

CHORUS: Tell us boldly then what you want of us; you cannot fail to succeed, if you honour and revere us and if you are resolved to become a clever man.

STREPSIADES: Oh, sovereign goddesses, 'tis but a very small favour that I ask of you; grant that I may distance all the Greeks by a hundred stadia in the art of speaking.

CHORUS: We grant you this, and henceforward no eloquence shall more often succeed with the people than your own.

STREPSIADES: May the god shield me from possessing great eloquence! 'Tis not what I want. I want to be able to turn bad lawsuits to my own advantage and to slip through the fingers of my creditors.

CHORUS: It shall be as you wish, for your ambitions are modest. Commit yourself fearlessly to our ministers, the sophists.

STREPSIADES: This will I do, for I trust in you. Moreover there is no drawing back, what with these cursed horses and this marriage, which has eaten up my vitals. So let them do with me as they will; I yield my body to them. Come blows, come hunger, thirst, heat or cold, little matters it to me; they may flay me, if I only escape my debts, if only I win the reputation of being a bold rascal, a fine speaker, impudent, shameless, a braggart, and adept at stringing lies, an old stager at quibbles, a complete table of the laws, a thorough rattle, a fox to slip through any hole; supple as a leathern strap, slippery as an eel, an artful fellow, a blusterer, a villain; a knave with a hundred faces, cunning, intolerable, a gluttonous dog. With such epithets do I seek to be greeted; on these terms, they can treat me as they choose, and, if they wish, by Demeter! they can turn me into sausages and serve me up to the philosophers.

CHORUS: Here have we a bold and well-disposed pupil indeed. When we shall have taught you, your glory among the mortals will reach even to the skies.

STREPSIADES: Wherein will that profit me?

CHORUS: You will pass your whole life among us and will be the most envied of men.

STREPSIADES: Shall I really ever see such happiness?

CHORUS: Clients will be everlastingly besieging your door in crowds, burning to get at you, to explain their business to you and to consult you about their suits, which, in return for your ability, will bring you in great sums. But, Socrates, begin the lessons you want to teach this old man; rouse his mind, try the strength of his intelligence.

SOCRATES: Come, tell me the kind of mind you have; 'tis important I know this, that I may order my batteries against you in a new fashion.

STREPSIADES: Eh, what! in the name of the gods, are you purposing to assault me then?

SOCRATES: No. I only wish to ask you some questions. Have you any memory?

STREPSIADES: That depends: if anything is owed me, my memory is excellent, but if I owe, alas! I have none whatever.

SOCRATES: Have you a natural gift for speaking?

STREPSIADES: For speaking, no; for cheating, yes.

SOCRATES: How will you be able to learn then?

STREPSIADES: Very easily, have no fear.

SOCRATES: Thus, when I throw forth some philosophical thought anent things celestial, you will seize it in its very flight?

STREPSIADES: Then I am to snap up wisdom much as a dog snaps up a morsel?

SOCRATES: Oh! the ignoramus! the barbarian! I greatly fear, old man, 'twill be needful for me to have recourse to blows. Now, let me hear what you do when you are beaten.

STREPSIADES: I receive the blow, then wait a moment, take my witnesses and finally summon my assailant at law.

SOCRATES: Come, take off your cloak.

STREPSIADES: Have I robbed you of anything?

SOCRATES: No, but 'tis usual to enter the school without your cloak.

STREPSIADES: But I am not come here to look for stolen goods.

SOCRATES: Off with it, fool!

STREPSIADES: Tell me, if I prove thoroughly attentive and learn with zeal, which of your disciples shall I resemble, do you think?

SOCRATES: You will be the image of Chaerephon.

STREPSIADES: Ah! unhappy me! I shall then be but half alive?

SOCRATES: A truce to this chatter! follow me and no more of it.

STREPSIADES: First give me a honey-cake, for to descend down there sets me all a-tremble; meseems 'tis the cave of Trophonius.

SOCRATES: But get in with you! What reason have you for thus dallying at the door?

CHORUS: Good luck! you have courage; may you succeed, you, who, though already so advanced in years, wish to instruct your mind with new studies and practise it in wisdom!

CHORUS (*Parabasis*): Spectators! By Bacchus, whose servant I am, I will frankly tell you the truth. May I secure both victory and renown as certainly as I hold you for adept critics and as I regard this comedy as my best. I wished to give you the first view of a work, which had cost me much trouble, but I withdrew, unjustly beaten by unskilful rivals.[43] 'Tis you, oh, enlightened public, for whom I have prepared my piece, that I reproach with this. Nevertheless I shall never willingly cease to seek the approval of the discerning. I have not forgotten the day, when men, whom one is happy to have for an audience, received my 'Young Man' and my 'Debauchee'[44] with so much favour in this very place. Then as yet virgin, my Muse had not attained the legal age for maternity;[45] she had to expose her first-born for another to adopt, and it has since grown up under your generous patronage. Ever since you have as good as sworn me your faithful alliance. Thus, like Electra[46] of the poets, my comedy has come to seek you to-day, hoping again to encounter such enlightened spectators. As far away as she can discern her Orestes, she will be able to recognize him by his curly head. And note her modest demeanour! She has not sewn on a piece of hanging leather, thick and reddened at the end,[47] to cause laughter among the children; she does not rail at the bald, neither does she dance the cordax;[48] no old man is seen, who, while uttering his lines, batters his questioner with a stick to make

43. The opening portion of the parabasis belongs to a second edition of the 'Clouds.' Aristophanes had been defeated by Cratinus and Amipsias, whose pieces, called the 'Bottle' and 'Connus,' had been crowned in preference to the 'Clouds,' which, it is said, was not received any better at its second representation.

44. Two characters introduced into the 'Daedalians' by Aristophanes in strong contrast to each other. Some fragments only of this piece remain to us.

45. It was only at the age of thirty, according to some, of forty, according to others, that a man could present a piece in his own name. The 'Daedalians' had appeared under the auspices of Cleonides and Chalistrates, whom we find again later as actors in Aristophanes' pieces.

46. Allusion to the recognition of Orestes by Electra at her brother's tomb. (*See* the 'Choëphorae' of Aeschylus.)

47. An image of the penis, drooping in this case, instead of standing, carried as a phallic emblem in the Dionysiac processions.

48. A licentious dance.

his poor jests pass muster.[49] She does not rush upon the scene carrying a torch and screaming, 'La, la! la, la!' No, she relies upon herself and her verses. . . My value is so well known, that I take no further pride in it. I do not seek to deceive you, by reproducing the same subjects two or three times; I always invent fresh themes to present before you, themes that have no relation to each other and that are all clever. I attacked Cleon[50] to his face and when he was all-powerful; but he has fallen, and now I have no desire to kick him when he is down. My rivals, on the contrary, once that this wretched Hyperbolus has given them the cue, have never ceased setting upon both him and his mother. First Eupolis presented his 'Maricas';[51] this was simply my 'Knights,' whom this plagiarist had clumsily furbished up again by adding to the piece an old drunken woman, so that she might dance the cordax. 'Twas an old idea, taken from Phrynichus, who caused his old hag to be devoured by a monster of the deep.[52] Then Hermippus[53] fell foul of Hyperbolus and now all the others fall upon him and repeat my comparison of the eels. May those who find amusement in their pieces not be pleased with mine, but as for you, who love and applaud my inventions, why, posterity will praise your good taste.

Oh, ruler of Olympus, all-powerful king of the gods, great Zeus, it is thou whom I first invoke; protect this chorus; and thou too, Posidon, whose dread trident upheaves at the will of thy anger both the bowels of the earth and the salty waves of the ocean. I invoke my illustrious father, the divine Aether, the universal sustainer of life, and Phoebus, who, from the summit of his chariot, sets the world aflame with his dazzling rays, Phoebus, a mighty deity amongst the gods and adored amongst mortals.

Most wise spectators, lend us all your attention. Give heed to our just reproaches. There exist no gods to whom this city owes more than it does to us, whom alone you forget. Not a sacrifice,

---

49. This coarse way of exciting laughter, says the scholiast, had been used by Eupolis, the comic writer, a rival of Aristophanes.
50. In the 'Knights.'
51. Presented in 421 B.C. The 'Clouds' having been played a second time in 419 B.C., one may conclude that this piece had appeared a third time on the Athenian stage.
52. Doubtless a parody of the legend of Andromeda.
53. A poet of the older comedy, who had written forty plays. It is said that he dared to accuse Aspasia, the mistress of Pericles, of impiety and the practice of prostitution.

not a libation is there for those who protect you! Have you decreed some mad expedition? Well! we thunder or we fall down in rain. When you chose that enemy of heaven, the Paphlagonian tanner,[54] for a general, we knitted our brow, we caused our wrath to break out; the lightning shot forth, the thunder pealed, the moon deserted her course and the sun at once veiled his beam threatening no longer to give you light, if Cleon became general. Nevertheless you elected him; 'tis said, Athens never resolves upon some fatal step but the gods turn these errors into her greatest gain. Do you wish that this election should even now be a success for you? 'Tis a very simple thing to do; condemn this rapacious gull named Cleon[55] for bribery and extortion, fit a wooden collar tight round his neck, and your error will be rectified and the commonweal will at once regain its old prosperity.

Aid me also, Phoebus, god of Delos, who reignest on the cragged peaks of Cynthia;[56] and thou, happy virgin,[57] to whom the Lydian damsels offer pompous sacrifice in a temple of gold; and thou, goddess of our country, Athené, armed with the aegis, the protectress of Athens; and thou, who, surrounded by the Bacchanals of Delphi, roamest over the rocks of Parnassus shaking the flame of thy resinous torch, thou, Bacchus, the god of revel and joy.

As we were preparing to come here, we were hailed by the Moon and were charged to wish joy and happiness both to the Athenians and to their allies; further, she said that she was enraged and that you treated her very shamefully, her, who does not pay you in words alone, but who renders you all real benefits. Firstly, thanks to her, you save at least a drachma each month for lights, for each, as he is leaving home at night, says, "Slave, buy no torches, for the moonlight is beautiful,"—not to name a thousand other benefits. Nevertheless you do not reckon the days correctly and your calendar is naught but confusion.[58] Consequently the

---

54. Cleon.
55. This part of the parabasis belongs to the first edition of the 'Clouds,' since Aristophanes here speaks of Cleon as alive.
56. A mountain in Delos, dedicated to Apollo and Diana.
57. Artemis.
58. An allusion to the reform, which the astronomer Meton had wanted to introduce into the calendar. Cleostratus of Tenedos, at the beginning of the fifth century, had devised the *octaeteris*, or cycle of eight years, and this had been generally adopted. This is how this system arrived at an agreement between the solar and the lunar periods: 8 solar years

gods load her with threats each time they get home and are disappointed of their meal, because the festival has not been kept in the regular order of time. When you should be sacrificing, you are putting to the torture or administering justice. And often, we others, the gods, are fasting in token of mourning for the death of Memnon or Sarpedon,[59] while you are devoting yourselves to joyous libations. 'Tis for this, that last year, when the lot would have invested Hyperbolus[60] with the duty of Amphictyon, we took his crown from him, to teach him that time must be divided according to the phases of the moon.

SOCRATES: By Respiration, the Breath of Life! By Chaos! By the Air! I have never seen a man so gross, so inept, so stupid, so forgetful. All the little quibbles, which I teach him, he forgets even before he has learnt them. Yet I will not give it up, I will make him come out here into the open air. Where are you, Strepsiades? Come, bring your couch out here.

STREPSIADES: But the bugs will not allow me to bring it.

SOCRATES: Have done with such nonsense! place it there and pay attention.

STREPSIADES: Well, here I am.

SOCRATES: Good! Which science of all those you have never been taught, do you wish to learn first? The measures, the rhythms or the verses?

STREPSIADES: Why, the measures; the flour dealer cheated me out of two *choenixes* the other day.

---

containing 2922 days, while 8 lunar years only contain 2832 days, there was a difference of 90 days, for which Cleostratus compensated by intercalating 3 months of 30 days each, which were placed after the third, fifth and eighth year of the cycle. Hence these years had an extra month each. But in this system, the lunar months had been reckoned as 354 days, whereas they are really 354 days, 8 hours, 48 minutes. To rectify this minor error Meton invented a cycle of 19 years, which bears his name. This new system which he tried to introduce naturally caused some disturbance in the order of the festivals, and for this or some other reason his system was not adopted. The octaeteris continued to be used for all public purposes, the only correction being, that three extra days were added to every second octaeteris.

59. Both sons of Zeus.

60. Hyperbolus had supported Meton in his desire for reform. Having been sent as the Athenian deputy to the council of the Amphictyons, he should, like his colleagues, have returned to Athens with his head wreathed with laurel. It is said the wind took this from him; the Clouds boast of the achievement.

SOCRATES: 'Tis not about that I ask you, but which, according to you, is the best measure, the trimeter or the tetrameter?[61]

STREPSIADES: The one I prefer is the semisextarius.

SOCRATES: You talk nonsense, my good fellow.

STREPSIADES: I will wager your tetrameter is the semisextarius.[62]

SOCRATES: Plague seize the dunce and the fool! Come, perchance you will learn the rhythms quicker.

STREPSIADES: Will the rhythms supply me with food?

SOCRATES: First they will help you to be pleasant in company, then to know what is meant by oenoplian rhythm[63] and what by the dactylic.[64]

STREPSIADES: Of the dactyl? I know that quite well.

SOCRATES: What is it then?

STREPSIADES: Why, 'tis this finger; formerly, when a child, I used this one.[65]

SOCRATES: You are as low-minded as you are stupid.

STREPSIADES: But, wretched man, I do not want to learn all this.

SOCRATES: Then what *do* you want to know?

STREPSIADES: Not that, not that, but the art of false reasoning.

SOCRATES: But you must first learn other things. Come, what are the male quadrupeds?

STREPSIADES: Oh! I know the males thoroughly. Do you take me for a fool then? The ram, the buck, the bull, the dog, the pigeon.

SOCRATES: Do you see what you are doing; is not the female pigeon called the same as the male?

STREPSIADES: How else? Come now?

SOCRATES: How else? With you then 'tis pigeon and pigeon!

STREPSIADES: 'Tis true, by Posidon! but what names do you want me to give them?

SOCRATES: Term the female pigeonnette and the male pigeon.

---

61. These are poetical measures; Strepsiades thinks measures of capacity are meant.

62. Containing four *choenixes*.

63. So called from its stirring, warlike character; it was composed of two dactyls and a spondee, followed again by two dactyls and a spondee.

64. Composed of dactyls and anapaests.

65. (Greek: Daktylos) means, of course, both *dactyl*, name of a metrical foot, and finger. Strepsiades presents his middle finger, with the other fingers and thumb bent under in an indecent gesture meant to suggest the penis and testicles. The Romans for this reason called the middle finger 'digitus infamis,' the *unseemly finger*. The Emperor Nero is said to have offered his hand to courtiers to kiss sometimes in this indecent way.

STREPSIADES: Pigeonnette! hah! by the Air! That's splendid! for that lesson bring out your kneading-trough and I will fill him with flour to the brim.

SOCRATES: There you are wrong again; you make *trough* masculine and it should be feminine.

STREPSIADES: What? if I say *him*, do I make the *trough* masculine?

SOCRATES: Assuredly! would you not say him for Cleonymus?

STREPSIADES: Well?

SOCRATES: Then trough is of the same gender as Cleonymus?

STREPSIADES: Oh! good sir! Cleonymus never had a kneading-trough;[66] he used a round mortar for the purpose. But come, tell me what I *should* say?

SOCRATES: For trough you should say *her* as you would for Sostraté.[67]

STREPSIADES: *Her*?

SOCRATES: In this manner you make it truly female.

STREPSIADES: That's it! *Her* for trough and *her* for Cleonymus.[68]

SOCRATES: Now I must teach you to distinguish the masculine proper names from those that are feminine.

STREPSIADES: Ah! I know the female names well.

SOCRATES: Name some then.

STREPSIADES: Lysilla, Philinna, Clitagora, Demetria.

SOCRATES: And what are masculine names?

STREPSIADES: They are countless—Philoxenus, Melesias, Amynias.

SOCRATES: But, wretched man, the last two are not masculine.

STREPSIADES: You do not reckon them masculine?

SOCRATES: Not at all. If you met Amynias, how would you hail him?

STREPSIADES: How? Why, I should shout, "Hi! hither, Amyni*a*!"[69]

SOCRATES: Do you see? 'tis a female name that you give him.

STREPSIADES: And is it not rightly done, since he refuses military service? But what use is there in learning what we all know?

SOCRATES: You know nothing about it. Come, lie down there.

STREPSIADES: What for?

SOCRATES: Ponder awhile over matters that interest you.

STREPSIADES: Oh! I pray you, not there! but, if I must lie down and ponder, let me lie on the ground.

---

66. Meaning he was too poor, Aristophanes represents him as a glutton and a parasite.
67. A woman's name.
68. He is classed as a woman because of his cowardice and effeminacy.
69. In Greek, the vocative of Amynias is Amynia; thus it has a feminine termination.

SOCRATES: 'Tis out of the question. Come! on to the couch!

STREPSIADES: What cruel fate! What a torture the bugs will this day put me to!

SOCRATES: Ponder and examine closely, gather your thoughts together, let your mind turn to every side of things; if you meet with a difficulty, spring quickly to some other idea; above all, keep your eyes away from all gentle sleep.

STREPSIADES: Oh, woe, woe! oh, woe, woe!

SOCRATES: What ails you? why do you cry so?

STREPSIADES: Oh! I am a dead man! Here are these cursed Corinthians[70] advancing upon me from all corners of the couch; they are biting me, they are gnawing at my sides, they are drinking all my blood, they are twitching off my testicles, they are exploring all up my back, they are killing me!

SOCRATES: Not so much wailing and clamour, if you please.

STREPSIADES: How can I obey? I have lost my money and my complexion, my blood and my slippers, and to cap my misery, I must keep awake on this couch, when scarce a breath of life is left in me.

SOCRATES: Well now! what are you doing? are you reflecting?

STREPSIADES: Yes, by Posidon!

SOCRATES: What about?

STREPSIADES: Whether the bugs will not entirely devour me.

SOCRATES: May death seize you, accursed man!

STREPSIADES: Ah! it has already.

SOCRATES: Come, no giving way! Cover up your head; the thing to do is to find an ingenious alternative.

STREPSIADES: An alternative! ah! I only wish one would come to me from within these coverlets!

SOCRATES: Hold! let us see what our fellow is doing. Ho! you! are you asleep?

STREPSIADES: No, by Apollo!

SOCRATES: Have you got hold of anything?

STREPSIADES: No, nothing whatever.

SOCRATES: Nothing at all!

STREPSIADES: No, nothing but my tool, which I've got in my hand.

---

70. The Corinthians, the allies of Sparta, ravaged Attica. (Greek: Kor), the first portion of the Greek word, is the root of the word which means a bug in the same language.

SOCRATES: Are you not going to cover your head immediately and ponder?

STREPSIADES: Over what? Come, Socrates, tell me.

SOCRATES: Think first what you want, and then tell me.

STREPSIADES: But I have told you a thousand times what I want. 'Tis not to pay any of my creditors.

SOCRATES: Come, wrap yourself up; concentrate your mind, which wanders too lightly, study every detail, scheme and examine thoroughly.

STREPSIADES: Oh, woe! woe! oh dear! oh dear!

SOCRATES: Keep yourself quiet, and if any notion troubles you, put it quickly aside, then resume it and think over it again.

STREPSIADES: My dear little Socrates!

SOCRATES: What is it, old greybeard?

STREPSIADES: I have a scheme for not paying my debts.

SOCRATES: Let us hear it.

STREPSIADES: Tell me, if I purchased a Thessalian witch, I could make the moon descend during the night and shut it, like a mirror, into a round box and there keep it carefully. . .

SOCRATES: How would you gain by that?

STREPSIADES: How? Why, if the moon did not rise, I would have no interest to pay.

SOCRATES: Why so?

STREPSIADES: Because money is lent by the month.

SOCRATES: Good! but I am going to propose another trick to you. If you were condemned to pay five talents, how would you manage to quash that verdict? Tell me.

STREPSIADES: How? how? I don't know, I must think.

SOCRATES: Do you always shut your thoughts within yourself. Let your ideas fly in the air, like a may-bug, tied by the foot with a thread.

STREPSIADES: I have found a very clever way to annul that conviction; you will admit that much yourself.

SOCRATES: What is it?

STREPSIADES: Have you ever seen a beautiful, transparent stone at the druggists, with which you may kindle fire?

SOCRATES: You mean a crystal lens.[71]

---

71. Mirrors, or burning glasses, are meant, such as those used by Archimedes two centuries later at the siege of Syracuse, when he set the Roman fleet on fire from the walls of the city.

ARISTOPHANES

STREPSIADES: Yes.

SOCRATES: Well, what then?

STREPSIADES: If I placed myself with this stone in the sun and a long way off from the clerk, while he was writing out the conviction, I could make all the wax, upon which the words were written, melt.

SOCRATES: Well thought out, by the Graces!

STREPSIADES: Ah! I am delighted to have annulled the decree that was to cost me five talents.

SOCRATES: Come, take up this next question quickly.

STREPSIADES: Which?

SOCRATES: If, when summoned to court, you were in danger of losing your case for want of witnesses, how would you make the conviction fall upon your opponent?

STREPSIADES: 'Tis very simple and most easy.

SOCRATES: Let me hear.

STREPSIADES: This way. If another case had to be pleaded before mine was called, I should run and hang myself.

SOCRATES: You talk rubbish!

STREPSIADES: Not so, by the gods! if I was dead, no action could lie against me.

SOCRATES: You are merely beating the air. Begone! I will give you no more lessons.

STREPSIADES: Why not? Oh! Socrates! in the name of the gods!

SOCRATES: But you forget as fast as you learn. Come, what was the thing I taught you first? Tell me.

STREPSIADES: Ah! let me see. What was the first thing? What was it then? Ah! that thing in which we knead the bread, oh! my god! what do you call it?

SOCRATES: Plague take the most forgetful and silliest of old addlepates!

STREPSIADES: Alas! what a calamity! what will become of me? I am undone if I do not learn how to ply my tongue. Oh! Clouds! give me good advice.

CHORUS: Old man, we counsel you, if you have brought up a son, to send him to learn in your stead.

STREPSIADES: Undoubtedly I have a son, as well endowed as the best, but he is unwilling to learn. What will become of me?

CHORUS: And you don't make him obey you?

STREPSIADES: You see, he is big and strong; moreover, through his mother he is a descendant of those fine birds, the race of Coesyra.[72] Nevertheless, I will go and find him, and if he refuses, I will turn him out of the house. Go in, Socrates, and wait for me awhile.

CHORUS (*to Socrates*): Do you understand, that, thanks to us, you will be loaded with benefits? Here is a man, ready to obey you in all things. You see how he is carried away with admiration and enthusiasm. Profit by it to clip him as short as possible; fine chances are all too quickly gone.

STREPSIADES: No, by the Clouds! you stay no longer here; go and devour the ruins of your uncle Megacles' fortune.

PHIDIPPIDES: Oh! my poor father! what has happened to you? By the Olympian Zeus! you are no longer in your senses!

STREPSIADES: See! see! "the Olympian Zeus." Oh! the fool! to believe in Zeus at your age!

PHIDIPPIDES: What is there in that to make you laugh?

STREPSIADES: You are then a tiny little child, if you credit such antiquated rubbish! But come here, that I may teach you; I will tell you something very necessary to know to be a man; but you will not repeat it to anybody.

PHIDIPPIDES: Come, what is it?

STREPSIADES: Just now you swore by Zeus.

PHIDIPPIDES: Aye, that I did.

STREPSIADES: Do you see how good it is to learn? Phidippides, there is no Zeus.

PHIDIPPIDES: What is there then?

STREPSIADES: 'Tis the Whirlwind, that has driven out Jupiter and is King now.

PHIDIPPIDES: Go to! what drivel!

STREPSIADES: Know it to be the truth.

PHIDIPPIDES: And who says so?

STREPSIADES: 'Tis Socrates, the Melian,[73] and Chaerephon, who knows how to measure the jump of a flea.

PHIDIPPIDES: Have you reached such a pitch of madness that you believe those bilious fellows?

---

72. That is, the family of the Alcmaeonidae; Coesyra was wife of Alcmaeon.
73. Socrates was an Athenian; but the atheist Diagoras, known as 'the enemy of the gods' hailed from the island of Melos. Strepsiades, crediting Socrates with the same incredulity, assigns him the same birthplace.

STREPSIADES: Use better language, and do not insult men who are clever and full of wisdom, who, to economize, are never shaved, shun the gymnasia and never go to the baths, while you, you only await my death to eat up my wealth. But come, come as quickly as you can to learn in my stead.

PHIDIPPIDES: And what good can be learnt of them?

STREPSIADES: What good indeed? Why, all human knowledge. Firstly, you will know yourself grossly ignorant. But await me here awhile.

PHIDIPPIDES: Alas! what is to be done? My father has lost his wits. Must I have him certificated for lunacy, or must I order his coffin?

STREPSIADES: Come! what kind of bird is this? tell me.

PHIDIPPIDES: A pigeon.

STREPSIADES: Good! And this female?

PHIDIPPIDES: A pigeon.

STREPSIADES: The same for both? You make me laugh! For the future you will call this one a pigeonnette and the other a pigeon.

PHIDIPPIDES: A pigeonnette! These then are the fine things you have just learnt at the school of these sons of the Earth![74]

STREPSIADES: And many others; but what I learnt I forgot at once, because I am too old.

PHIDIPPIDES: So this is why you have lost your cloak?

STREPSIADES: I have not lost it, I have consecrated it to Philosophy.

PHIDIPPIDES: And what have you done with your sandals, you poor fool?

STREPSIADES: If I have lost them, it is for what was necessary, just as Pericles did.[75] But come, move yourself, let us go in; if necessary, do wrong to obey your father. When you were six years old and still lisped, 'twas I who obeyed you. I remember at the feasts of Zeus you had a consuming wish for a little chariot and I bought it

---

74. I.e. the enemies of the gods. An allusion to the giants, the sons of Earth, who had endeavoured to scale heaven.

75. Pericles had squandered all the wealth accumulated in the Acropolis upon the War. When he handed in his accounts, he refused to explain the use of a certain twenty talents and simply said, "*I spent them on what was necessary.*" Upon hearing of this reply, the Lacedaemonians, who were already discontented with their kings, Cleandrides and Plistoanax, whom they accused of carrying on the war in Attica with laxness, exiled the first-named and condemned the second to payment of a fine of fifteen talents for treachery. In fact, the Spartans were convinced that Pericles had kept silent as to what he had done with the twenty talents, because he did not want to say openly, "*I gave this sum to the Kings of Lacedaemon.*"

for you with the first obolus which I received as a juryman in the Courts.

PHIDIPPIDES: You will soon repent of what you ask me to do.

STREPSIADES: Oh! now I am happy! He obeys. Here, Socrates, here! Come out quick! Here I am bringing you my son; he refused, but I have persuaded him.

SOCRATES: Why, he is but a child yet. He is not used to these baskets, in which we suspend our minds.[76]

PHIDIPPIDES: To make you better used to them, I would you were hung.

STREPSIADES: A curse upon you! you insult your master!

SOCRATES: "I would you were hung!" What a stupid speech! and so emphatically spoken! How can one ever get out of an accusation with such a tone, summon witnesses or touch or convince? And yet when we think, Hyperbolus learnt all this for one talent!

STREPSIADES: Rest undisturbed and teach him. 'Tis a most intelligent nature. Even when quite little he amused himself at home with making houses, carving boats, constructing little chariots of leather, and understood wonderfully how to make frogs out of pomegranate rinds. Teach him both methods of reasoning, the strong and also the weak, which by false arguments triumphs over the strong; if not the two, at least the false, and that in every possible way.

SOCRATES: 'Tis Just and Unjust Discourse themselves that shall instruct him.[77]

STREPSIADES: I go, but forget it not, he must always, always be able to confound the true.

JUST DISCOURSE: Come here! Shameless as you may be, will you dare to show your face to the spectators?

UNJUST DISCOURSE: Take me where you list. I seek a throng, so that I may the better annihilate you.

JUST DISCOURSE: Annihilate me! Do you forget who you are?

UNJUST DISCOURSE: I am Reasoning.

---

76. The basket in which Aristophanes shows us Socrates suspended to bring his mind nearer to the subtle regions of air.

77. The scholiast tells us that Just Discourse and Unjust Discourse were brought upon the stage in cages, like cocks that are going to fight. Perhaps they were even dressed up as cocks, or at all events wore cocks' heads as their masks.

JUST DISCOURSE: Yes, the weaker Reasoning.[78]

UNJUST DISCOURSE: But I triumph over you, who claim to be the stronger.

JUST DISCOURSE: By what cunning shifts, pray?

UNJUST DISCOURSE: By the invention of new maxims.

JUST DISCOURSE: . . . which are received with favour by these fools.

UNJUST DISCOURSE: Say rather, by these wiseacres.

JUST DISCOURSE: I am going to destroy you mercilessly.

UNJUST DISCOURSE: How pray? Let us see you do it.

JUST DISCOURSE: By saying what is true.

UNJUST DISCOURSE: I shall retort and shall very soon have the better of you. First, I maintain that justice has no existence.

JUST DISCOURSE: Has no existence?

UNJUST DISCOURSE: No existence! Why, where are they?

JUST DISCOURSE: With the gods.

UNJUST DISCOURSE: How then, if justice exists, was Zeus not put to death for having put his father in chains?

JUST DISCOURSE: Bah! this is enough to turn my stomach! A basin, quick!

UNJUST DISCOURSE: You are an old driveller and stupid withal.

JUST DISCOURSE: And you a debauchee and a shameless fellow.

UNJUST DISCOURSE: Hah! What sweet expressions!

JUST DISCOURSE: An impious buffoon!

UNJUST DISCOURSE: You crown me with roses and with lilies.

JUST DISCOURSE: A parricide.

UNJUST DISCOURSE: Why, you shower gold upon me.

JUST DISCOURSE: Formerly, 'twas a hailstorm of blows.

UNJUST DISCOURSE: I deck myself with your abuse.

JUST DISCOURSE: What impudence!

UNJUST DISCOURSE: What tomfoolery!

JUST DISCOURSE: 'Tis because of you that the youth no longer attends the schools. The Athenians will soon recognize what lessons you teach those who are fools enough to believe you.

UNJUST DISCOURSE: You are overwhelmed with wretchedness.

---

78. In the language of the schools of philosophy just reasoning was called 'the stronger'— (Greek: ho kreitt on logos), unjust reasoning, 'the weaker'—(Greek: ho h ett on logos).

JUST DISCOURSE: And you, you prosper. Yet you were poor when you said, "I am the Mysian Telephus,"[79] and used to stuff your wallet with maxims of Pandeletus[80] to nibble at.

UNJUST DISCOURSE: Oh! the beautiful wisdom, of which you are now boasting!

JUST DISCOURSE: Madman! But yet madder the city that keeps you, you, the corrupter of its youth!

UNJUST DISCOURSE: 'Tis not you who will teach this young man; you are as old and out of date as Saturn.

JUST DISCOURSE: Nay, it will certainly be I, if he does not wish to be lost and to practise verbosity only.

UNJUST DISCOURSE (*to Phidippides*): Come hither and leave him to beat the air.

JUST DISCOURSE (*to Unjust Discourse*): Evil be unto you, if you touch him.

CHORUS: A truce to your quarrellings and abuse! But expound, you, what you taught us formerly, and you, your new doctrine. Thus, after hearing each of you argue, he will be able to choose betwixt the two schools.

JUST DISCOURSE: I am quite agreeable.

UNJUST DISCOURSE: And I too.

CHORUS: Who is to speak first?

UNJUST DISCOURSE: Let it be my opponent, he has my full consent; then I will follow upon the very ground he shall have chosen and shall shatter him with a hail of new ideas and subtle fancies; if after that he dares to breathe another word, I shall sting him in the face and in the eyes with our maxims, which are as keen as the sting of a wasp, and he will die.

CHORUS: Here are two rivals confident in their powers of oratory and in the thoughts over which they have pondered so long. Let us see which will come triumphant out of the contest. This wisdom, for which my friends maintain such a persistent fight, is in great danger. Come then, you, who crowned men of other days with so many virtues, plead the cause dear to you, make yourself known to us.

---

79. A character in one of the tragedies of Aeschylus, a beggar and a clever, plausible speaker.

80. A sycophant and a quibbler, renowned for his unparalleled bad faith in the law-suits he was perpetually bringing forward.

JUST DISCOURSE: Very well, I will tell you what was the old education, when I used to teach justice with so much success and when modesty was held in veneration. Firstly, it was required of a child, that it should not utter a word. In the street, when they went to the music-school, all the youths of the same district marched lightly clad and ranged in good order, even when the snow was falling in great flakes. At the master's house they had to stand, their legs apart, and they were taught to sing either, "Pallas, the Terrible, who overturneth cities," or "A noise resounded from afar"[81] in the solemn tones of the ancient harmony. If anyone indulged in buffoonery or lent his voice any of the soft inflexions, like those which to-day the disciples of Phrynis[82] take so much pains to form, he was treated as an enemy of the Muses and belaboured with blows. In the wrestling school they would sit with outstretched legs and without display of any indecency to the curious. When they rose, they would smooth over the sand, so as to leave no trace to excite obscene thoughts. Never was a child rubbed with oil below the belt; the rest of their bodies thus retained its fresh bloom and down, like a velvety peach. They were not to be seen approaching a lover and themselves rousing his passion by soft modulation of the voice and lustful gaze. At table, they would not have dared, before those older than themselves, to have taken a radish, an aniseed or a leaf of parsley, and much less eat fish or thrushes or cross their legs.

UNJUST DISCOURSE: What antiquated rubbish! Have we got back to the days of the festivals of Zeus Polieus,[83] to the Buphonia, to the time of the poet Cecydes[84] and the golden cicadas?[85]

---

81. The opening words of two hymns, attributed to Lamprocles, an ancient lyric poet, the son or the pupil of Medon.

82. A poet and musician of Mitylené, who gained the prize of the lyre at the Panathenaea in 457 B.C. He lived at the Court of Hiero, where, Suidas says, he was at first a slave and the cook. He added two strings to the lyre, which hitherto had had only seven. He composed effeminate airs of a style unknown before his day.

83. Zeus had a temple in the citadel of Athens under the name of Polieus or protector of the city; bullocks were sacrificed to him (Buphonia). In the days of Aristophanes, these feasts had become neglected.

84. One of the oldest of the dithyrambic poets.

85. Used by the ancient Athenians to keep their hair in place. The custom was said to have a threefold significance; by it the Athenians wanted to show that they were musicians, autochthons (i.e. indigenous to the country) and worshippers of Apollo. Indeed,

JUST DISCOURSE: 'Tis nevertheless by suchlike teaching I built up the men of Marathon. But you, you teach the children of to-day to bundle themselves quickly into their clothes, and I am enraged when I see them at the Panathenaea forgetting Athené while they dance, and covering themselves with their bucklers. Hence, young man, dare to range yourself beside me, who follow justice and truth; you will then be able to shun the public place, to refrain from the baths, to blush at all that is shameful, to fire up if your virtue is mocked at, to give place to your elders, to honour your parents, in short, to avoid all that is evil. Be modesty itself, and do not run to applaud the dancing girls; if you delight in such scenes, some courtesan will cast you her apple and your reputation will be done for. Do not bandy words with your father, nor treat him as a dotard, nor reproach the old man, who has cherished you, with his age.

UNJUST DISCOURSE: If you listen to him, by Bacchus! you will be the image of the sons of Hippocrates[86] and will be called *mother's great ninny*.

JUST DISCOURSE: No, but you will pass your days at the gymnasia, glowing with strength and health; you will not go to the public place to cackle and wrangle as is done nowadays; you will not live in fear that you may be dragged before the courts for some trifle exaggerated by quibbling. But you will go down to the Academy[87] to run beneath the sacred olives with some virtuous friend of your own age, your head encircled with the white reed, enjoying your ease and breathing the perfume of the yew and of the fresh sprouts of the poplar, rejoicing in the return of springtide and gladly listening to the gentle rustle of the plane-tree and the elm. If you devote yourself to practising my precepts, your chest will be stout, your colour glowing, your shoulders broad, your tongue short, your hips muscular, but your penis small. But if you follow the fashions of the day, you will be pallid in hue, have narrow shoulders, a narrow chest, a long tongue, small hips and a big tool; you will

---

grasshoppers were considered to sing with harmony; they swarmed on Attic soil and were sacred to Phoebus, the god of music.

86. Telesippus, Demophon and Pericles by name; they were a byword at Athens for their stupidity. Hippocrates was a general.

87. The famous gardens of the Academia, just outside the walls of Athens; they included gymnasia, lecture halls, libraries and picture galleries. Near by was a wood of sacred olives.

know how to spin forth long-winded arguments on law. You will be persuaded also to regard as splendid everything that is shameful and as shameful everything that is honourable; in a word, you will wallow in debauchery like Antimachus.[88]

CHORUS: How beautiful, high-souled, brilliant is this wisdom that you practise! What a sweet odour of honesty is emitted by your discourse! Happy were those men of other days who lived when you were honoured! And you, seductive talker, come, find some fresh arguments, for your rival has done wonders. Bring out against him all the battery of your wit, if you desire to beat him and not to be laughed out of court.

UNJUST DISCOURSE: At last! I was choking with impatience, I was burning to upset all his arguments! If I am called the Weaker Reasoning in the schools, 'tis precisely because I was the first before all others to discover the means to confute the laws and the decrees of justice. To invoke solely the weaker arguments and yet triumph is a talent worth more than a hundred thousand drachmae. But see how I shall batter down the sort of education of which he is so proud. Firstly, he forbids you to bathe in hot water. What grounds have you for condemning hot baths?

JUST DISCOURSE: Because they are baneful and enervate men.

UNJUST DISCOURSE: Enough said! Oh! you poor wrestler! From the very outset I have seized you and hold you round the middle; you cannot escape me. Tell me, of all the sons of Zeus, who had the stoutest heart, who performed the most doughty deeds?

JUST DISCOURSE: None, in my opinion, surpassed Heracles.

UNJUST DISCOURSE: Where have you ever seen cold baths called 'Baths of Heracles'?[89] And yet who was braver than he?

JUST DISCOURSE: 'Tis because of such quibbles, that the baths are seen crowded with young folk, who chatter there the livelong day while the gymnasia remain empty.

UNJUST DISCOURSE: Next you condemn the habit of frequenting the market-place, while I approve this. If it were wrong Homer would

---

88. Apparently the historian of that name is meant; in any case it cannot refer to the celebrated epic poet, author of the 'Thebaïs.'
89. Among the Greeks, hot springs bore the generic name of 'Baths of Heracles.' A legend existed that these had gushed forth spontaneously beneath the tread of the hero, who would plunge into them and there regain fresh strength to continue his labours.

never have made Nestor[90] speak in public as well as all his wise heroes. As for the art of speaking, he tells you, young men should not practise it; I hold the contrary. Furthermore he preaches chastity to them. Both precepts are equally harmful. Have you ever seen chastity of any use to anyone? Answer and try to confute me.

JUST DISCOURSE: To many; for instance, Peleus won a sword thereby.[91]

UNJUST DISCOURSE: A sword! Ah! what a fine present to make him! Poor wretch! Hyperbolus, the lamp-seller, thanks to his villainy, has gained more than. . . I do not know how many talents, but certainly no sword.

JUST DISCOURSE: Peleus owed it to his chastity that he became the husband of Thetis.[92]

UNJUST DISCOURSE: . . . who left him in the lurch, for he was not the most ardent; in those nocturnal sports between two sheets, which so please women, he possessed but little merit. Get you gone, you are but an old fool. But you, young man, just consider a little what this temperance means and the delights of which it deprives you—young fellows, women, play, dainty dishes, wine, boisterous laughter. And what is life worth without these? Then, if you happen to commit one of these faults inherent in human weakness, some seduction or adultery, and you are caught in the act, you are lost, if you cannot speak. But follow my teaching and you will be able to satisfy your passions, to dance, to laugh, to blush at nothing. Are you surprised in adultery? Then up and tell the husband you are not guilty, and recall to him the example of Zeus, who allowed himself to be conquered by love and by women. Being but a mortal, can you be stronger than a god?

---

90. King of Pylos, according to Homer, the wisest of all the Greeks.
91. Peleus, son of Aeacus, having resisted the appeals of Astydamia, the wife of Acastus, King of Iolchos, was denounced to her husband by her as having wished to seduce her, so that she might be avenged for his disdain. Acastus in his anger took Peleus to hunt with him on Mount Pelion, there deprived him of his weapons and left him a prey to wild animals. He was about to die, when Hermes brought him a sword forged by Hephaestus.
92. Thetis, to escape the solicitations of Peleus, assumed in turn the form of a bird, of a tree, and finally of a tigress; but Peleus learnt of Proteus the way of compelling Thetis to yield to his wishes. The gods were present at his nuptials and made the pair rich presents.

JUST DISCOURSE: And if your pupil gets impaled, his hairs plucked out, and he is seared with a hot ember,[93] how are you going to prove to him that he is not a filthy debauchee?

UNJUST DISCOURSE: And wherein lies the harm of being so?

JUST DISCOURSE: Is there anything worse than to have such a character?

UNJUST DISCOURSE: Now what will you say, if I beat you even on this point?

JUST DISCOURSE: I should certainly have to be silent then.

UNJUST DISCOURSE: Well then, reply! Our advocates, what are they?

JUST DISCOURSE: Low scum.

UNJUST DISCOURSE: Nothing is more true. And our tragic poets?

JUST DISCOURSE: Low scum.

UNJUST DISCOURSE: Well said again. And our demagogues?

JUST DISCOURSE: Low scum.

UNJUST DISCOURSE: You admit that you have spoken nonsense. And the spectators, what are they for the most part? Look at them.

JUST DISCOURSE: I am looking at them.

UNJUST DISCOURSE: Well! What do you see?

JUST DISCOURSE: By the gods, they are nearly all low scum. See, this one I know to be such and that one and that other with the long hair.

UNJUST DISCOURSE: What have you to say, then?

JUST DISCOURSE: I am beaten. Debauchees! in the name of the gods, receive my cloak;[94] I pass over to your ranks.

SOCRATES: Well then! do you take away your son or do you wish me to teach him how to speak?

STREPSIADES: Teach him, chastise him and do not fail to sharpen his tongue well, on one side for petty law-suits and on the other for important cases.

SOCRATES: Make yourself easy, I shall return to you an accomplished sophist.

PHIDIPPIDES: Very pale then and thoroughly hang-dog-looking.

STREPSIADES: Take him with you.

PHIDIPPIDES: I do assure you, you will repent it.

---

93. According to the scholiast, an adulterer was punished in the following manner: a radish was forced up his rectum, then every hair was torn out round that region, and the portion so treated was then covered with burning embers.

94. Having said this, Just Discourse threw his cloak into the amphitheatre and took a seat with the spectators.

CHORUS: Judges, we are all about to tell you what you will gain by awarding us the crown as equity requires of you. In spring, when you wish to give your fields the first dressing, we will rain upon you first; the others shall wait. Then we will watch over your corn and over your vine-stocks; they will have no excess to fear, neither of heat nor of wet. But if a mortal dares to insult the goddesses of the Clouds, let him think of the ills we shall pour upon him. For him neither wine nor any harvest at all! Our terrible slings will mow down his young olive plants and his vines. If he is making bricks, it will rain, and our round hailstones will break the tiles of his roof. If he himself marries or any of his relations or friends, we shall cause rain to fall the whole night long. Verily, he would prefer to live in Egypt[95] than to have given this iniquitous verdict.

STREPSIADES: Another four, three, two days, then the eve, then the day, the fatal day of payment! I tremble, I quake, I shudder, for 'tis the day of the old moon and the new.[96] Then all my creditors take the oath, pay their deposits,[97] swear my downfall and my ruin. As for me, I beseech them to be reasonable, to be just, "My friend, do not demand this sum, wait a little for this other and give me time for this third one." Then they will pretend that at this rate they will never be repaid, will accuse me of bad faith and will threaten me with the law. Well then, let them sue me! I care nothing for that, if only Phidippides has learnt to speak fluently. I go to find out, let me knock at the door of the school. . . Ho! slave, slave!

SOCRATES: Welcome! Strepsiades!

STREPSIADES: Welcome! Socrates! But first take this sack (*offers him a sack of flour*); it is right to reward the master with some present. And my son, whom you took off lately, has he learnt this famous reasoning, tell me.

SOCRATES: He has learnt it.

STREPSIADES: What a good thing! Oh! thou divine Knavery!

SOCRATES: You will win just as many causes as you choose.

STREPSIADES: Even if I have borrowed before witnesses?

SOCRATES: So much the better, even if there are a thousand of 'em!

---

95. Because it never rains there; for all other reasons residence in Egypt was looked upon as undesirable.
96. That is, the last day of the month.
97. By Athenian law, if anyone summoned another to appear before the Courts, he was obliged to deposit a sum sufficient to cover the costs of procedure.

STREPSIADES: Then I am going to shout with all my might. "Woe to the usurers, woe to their capital and their interest and their compound interest! You shall play me no more bad turns. My son is being taught there, his tongue is being sharpened into a double-edged weapon; he is my defender, the saviour of my house, the ruin of my foes! His poor father was crushed down with misfortune and he delivers him." Go and call him to me quickly. Oh! my child! my dear little one! run forward to your father's voice!

SOCRATES: Here he is.

STREPSIADES: Oh, my friend, my dearest friend!

SOCRATES: Take your son, and get you gone.

STREPSIADES: Oh, my son! oh! oh! what a pleasure to see your pallor! You are ready first to deny and then to contradict; 'tis as clear as noon. What a child of your country you are! How your lips quiver with the famous, "What have you to say now?" How well you know, I am certain, to put on the look of a victim, when it is you who are making both victims and dupes! and what a truly Attic glance! Come, 'tis for you to save me, seeing it is you who have ruined me.

PHIDIPPIDES: What is it you fear then?

STREPSIADES: The day of the old and the new.

PHIDIPPIDES: Is there then a day of the old and the new?

STREPSIADES: The day on which they threaten to pay deposit against me.

PHIDIPPIDES: Then so much the worse for those who have deposited! for 'tis not possible for one day to be two.

STREPSIADES: What?

PHIDIPPIDES: Why, undoubtedly, unless a woman can be both old and young at the same time.

STREPSIADES: But so runs the law.

PHIDIPPIDES: I think the meaning of the law is quite misunderstood.

STREPSIADES: What does it mean?

PHIDIPPIDES: Old Solon loved the people.

STREPSIADES: What has that to do with the old day and the new?

PHIDIPPIDES: He has fixed two days for the summons, the last day of the old moon and the first day of the new; but the deposits must only be paid on the first day of the new moon.

STREPSIADES: And why did he also name the last day of the old?

PHIDIPPIDES: So, my dear sir, that the debtors, being there the day before, might free themselves by mutual agreement, or that else, if not, the creditor might begin his action on the morning of the new moon.

STREPSIADES: Why then do the magistrates have the deposits paid on the last of the month and not the next day?

PHIDIPPIDES: I think they do as the gluttons do, who are the first to pounce upon the dishes. Being eager to carry off these deposits, they have them paid in a day too soon.

STREPSIADES: Splendid! Ah! poor brutes,[98] who serve for food to us clever folk! You are only down here to swell the number, true blockheads, sheep for shearing, heap of empty pots! Hence I will sound the note of victory for my son and myself. "Oh! happy, Strepsiades! what cleverness is thine! and what a son thou hast here!" Thus my friends and my neighbours will say, jealous at seeing me gain all my suits. But come in, I wish to regale you first.

PASIAS (*to his witness*): A man should never lend a single obolus. 'Twould be better to put on a brazen face at the outset than to get entangled in such matters. I want to see my money again and I bring you here to-day to attest the loan. I am going to make a foe of a neighbour; but, as long as I live, I do not wish my country to have to blush for me. Come, I am going to summon Strepsiades.

STREPSIADES: Who is this?

PASIAS: . . . for the old day and the new.

STREPSIADES: I call you to witness, that he has named two days. What do you want of me?

PASIAS: I claim of you the twelve minae, which you borrowed from me to buy the dapple-grey horse.

STREPSIADES: A horse! do you hear him? I, who detest horses, as is well known.

PASIAS: I call Zeus to witness, that you swore by the gods to return them to me.

STREPSIADES: Because at that time, by Zeus! Phidippides did not yet know the irrefutable argument.

PASIAS: Would you deny the debt on that account?

STREPSIADES: If not, what use is his science to me?

PASIAS: Will you dare to swear by the gods that you owe me nothing?

---

98. He points to an earthenware sphere, placed at the entrance of Socrates' dwelling, and which was intended to represent the Whirlwind, the deity of the philosophers. This sphere took the place of the column which the Athenians generally dedicated to Apollo, and which stood in the vestibule of their houses.

STREPSIADES: By which gods?

PASIAS: By Zeus, Hermes and Posidon!

STREPSIADES: Why, I would give three obols for the pleasure of swearing by them.

PASIAS: Woe upon you, impudent knave!

STREPSIADES: Oh! what a fine wine-skin you would make if flayed!

PASIAS: Heaven! he jeers at me!

STREPSIADES: It would hold six gallons easily.

PASIAS: By great Zeus! by all the gods! you shall not scoff at me with impunity.

STREPSIADES: Ah! how you amuse me with your gods! how ridiculous it seems to a sage to hear Zeus invoked.

PASIAS: Your blasphemies will one day meet their reward. But, come, will you repay me my money, yes or no? Answer me, that I may go.

STREPSIADES: Wait a moment, I am going to give you a distinct answer. (*Goes indoors and returns immediately with a kneading-trough*)

PASIAS: What do you think he will do?

WITNESS: He will pay the debt.

STREPSIADES: Where is the man who demands money? Tell me, what is this?

PASIAS: Him? Why he is your kneading-trough.

STREPSIADES: And you dare to demand money of me, when you are so ignorant? I will not return an obolus to anyone who says *him* instead of *her* for a kneading-trough.

PASIAS: You will not repay?

STREPSIADES: Not if I know it. Come, an end to this, pack off as quick as you can.

PASIAS: I go, but, may I die, if it be not to pay my deposit for a summons.

STREPSIADES: Very well! 'Twill be so much more to the bad to add to the twelve minae. But truly it makes me sad, for I do pity a poor simpleton who says *him* for a kneading-trough.

AMYNIAS: Woe! ah woe is me!

STREPSIADES: Hold! who is this whining fellow? Can it be one of the gods of Carcinus?[99]

---

99. An Athenian poet, who is said to have left one hundred and sixty tragedies behind him; he only once carried off the prize. Doubtless he had introduced gods or demi-gods bewailing themselves into one of his tragedies.

AMYNIAS: Do you want to know who I am? I am a man of misfortune!

STREPSIADES: Get on your way then.

AMYNIAS: Oh! cruel god! Oh Fate, who hath broken the wheels of my chariot! Oh, Pallas, thou hast undone me![100]

STREPSIADES: What ill has Tlepolemus done you?

AMYNIAS: Instead of jeering me, friend, make your son return me the money he has had of me; I am already unfortunate enough.

STREPSIADES: What money?

AMYNIAS: The money he borrowed of me.

STREPSIADES: You have indeed had misfortune, it seems to me.

AMYNIAS: Yes, by the gods! I have been thrown from a chariot.

STREPSIADES: Why then drivel as if you had fallen from an ass?[101]

AMYNIAS: Am I drivelling because I demand my money?

STREPSIADES: No, no, you cannot be in your right senses.

AMYNIAS: Why?

STREPSIADES: No doubt your poor wits have had a shake.

AMYNIAS: But by Hermes! I will sue you at law, if you do not pay me.

STREPSIADES: Just tell me; do you think it is always fresh water that Zeus lets fall every time it rains, or is it always the same water that the sun pumps over the earth?

AMYNIAS: I neither know, nor care.

STREPSIADES: And actually you would claim the right to demand your money, when you know not a syllable of these celestial phenomena?

AMYNIAS: If you are short, pay me the interest, at any rate.

STREPSIADES: What kind of animal is interest?

AMYNIAS: What? Does not the sum borrowed go on growing, growing every month, each day as the time slips by?

STREPSIADES: Well put. But do you believe there is more water in the sea now than there was formerly?

AMYNIAS: No, 'tis just the same quantity. It cannot increase.

STREPSIADES: Thus, poor fool, the sea, that receives the rivers, never grows, and yet you would have your money grow? Get you gone, away with you, quick! Ho! bring me the ox-goad!

AMYNIAS: Hither! you witnesses there!

---

100. This exclamation, "Oh! Pallas, thou hast undone me!" and the reply of Strepsiades are borrowed, says the scholiast, from a tragedy by Xenocles, the son of Carcinus. Alcmena is groaning over the death of her brother, Licymnius, who had been killed by Tlepolemus.
101. A proverb, applied to foolish people.

ARISTOPHANES

STREPSIADES: Come, what are you waiting for? Will you not budge, old nag!

AMYNIAS: What an insult!

STREPSIADES: Unless you get a-trotting, I shall catch you and prick up your behind, you sorry packhorse! Ah! you start, do you? I was about to drive you pretty fast, I tell you—you and your wheels and your chariot!

CHORUS: Whither does the passion of evil lead! here is a perverse old man, who wants to cheat his creditors; but some mishap, which will speedily punish this rogue for his shameful schemings, cannot fail to overtake him from to-day. For a long time he has been burning to have his son know how to fight against all justice and right and to gain even the most iniquitous causes against his adversaries every one. I think this wish is going to be fulfilled. But mayhap, mayhap, he will soon wish his son were dumb rather!

STREPSIADES: Oh! oh! neighbours, kinsmen, fellow-citizens, help! help! to the rescue, I am being beaten! Oh! my head! oh! my jaw! Scoundrel! do you beat your own father!

PHIDIPPIDES: Yes, father, I do.

STREPSIADES: See! he admits he is beating me.

PHIDIPPIDES: Undoubtedly I do.

STREPSIADES: You villain, you parricide, you gallows-bird!

PHIDIPPIDES: Go on, repeat your epithets, call me a thousand other names, an it please you. The more you curse, the greater my amusement!

STREPSIADES: Oh! you infamous cynic!

PHIDIPPIDES: How fragrant the perfume breathed forth in your words.

STREPSIADES: Do you beat your own father?

PHIDIPPIDES: Aye, by Zeus! and I am going to show you that I do right in beating you.

STREPSIADES: Oh, wretch! can it be right to beat a father?

PHIDIPPIDES: I will prove it to you, and you shall own yourself vanquished.

STREPSIADES: Own myself vanquished on a point like this?

PHIDIPPIDES: 'Tis the easiest thing in the world. Choose whichever of the two reasonings you like.

STREPSIADES: Of which reasonings?

PHIDIPPIDES: The Stronger and the Weaker.

STREPSIADES: Miserable fellow! Why, 'tis I who had you taught how to refute what is right, and now you would persuade me it is right a son should beat his father.

PHIDIPPIDES: I think I shall convince you so thoroughly that, when you have heard me, you will not have a word to say.

STREPSIADES: Well, I am curious to hear what you have to say.

CHORUS: Consider well, old man, how you can best triumph over him. His brazenness shows me that he thinks himself sure of his case; he has some argument which gives him nerve. Note the confidence in his look! But how did the fight begin? tell the Chorus; you cannot help doing that much.

STREPSIADES: I will tell you what was the start of the quarrel. At the end of the meal you wot of, I bade him take his lyre and sing me the air of Simonides, which tells of the fleece of the ram.[102] He replied bluntly, that it was stupid, while drinking, to play the lyre and sing, like a woman when she is grinding barley.

PHIDIPPIDES: Why, by rights I ought to have beaten and kicked you the very moment you told me to sing!

STREPSIADES: That is just how he spoke to me in the house, furthermore he added, that Simonides was a detestable poet. However, I mastered myself and for a while said nothing. Then I said to him, 'At least, take a myrtle branch and recite a passage from Aeschylus to me.'—'For my own part,' he at once replied, 'I look upon Aeschylus as the first of poets, for his verses roll superbly; 'tis nothing but incoherence, bombast and turgidness.' Yet still I smothered my wrath and said, 'Then recite one of the famous pieces from the modern poets.' Then he commenced a piece in which Euripides shows, oh! horror! a brother, who violates his own uterine sister.[103] Then I could no longer restrain myself, and attacked him with the most injurious abuse; naturally he retorted; hard words were hurled on both sides, and finally he sprang at me, broke my bones, bore me to earth, strangled and started killing me!

PHIDIPPIDES: I was right. What! not praise Euripides, the greatest of our poets!

102. The ram of Phryxus, the golden fleece of which was hung up on a beech tree in a field dedicated to Ares in Colchis.

103. The subject of Euripides' 'Aeolus.' Since among the Athenians it was lawful to marry a half-sister, if not born of the same mother, Strepsiades mentions here that it was his *uterine* sister, whom Macareus dishonoured, thus committing both rape and incest.

STREPSIADES: He the greatest of our poets! Ah! if I but dared to speak! but the blows would rain upon me harder than ever.

PHIDIPPIDES: Undoubtedly, and rightly too.

STREPSIADES: Rightly! oh! what impudence! to me, who brought you up! when you could hardly lisp, I guessed what you wanted. If you said *broo, broo*, well, I brought you your milk; if you asked for *mam mam*, I gave you bread; and you had no sooner said, *caca*, than I took you outside and held you out. And just now, when you were strangling me, I shouted, I bellowed that I would let all go; and you, you scoundrel, had not the heart to take me outside, so that here, though almost choking, I was compelled to ease myself.

CHORUS: Young men, your hearts must be panting with impatience. What is Phidippides going to say? If, after such conduct, he proves he has done well, I would not give an obolus for the hide of old men. Come, you, who know how to brandish and hurl the keen shafts of the new science, find a way to convince us, give your language an appearance of truth.

PHIDIPPIDES: How pleasant it is to know these clever new inventions and to be able to defy the established laws! When I thought only about horses, I was not able to string three words together without a mistake, but now that the master has altered and improved me and that I live in this world of subtle thought, of reasoning and of meditation, I count on being able to prove satisfactorily that I have done well to thrash my father.

STREPSIADES: Mount your horse! By Zeus! I would rather defray the keep of a four-in-hand team than be battered with blows.

PHIDIPPIDES: I revert to what I was saying when you interrupted me. And first, answer me, did you beat me in my childhood?

STREPSIADES: Why, assuredly, for your good and in your own best interest.

PHIDIPPIDES: Tell me, is it not right, that in turn I should beat you for your good? since it is for a man's own best interest to be beaten. What! must your body be free of blows, and not mine? am I not free-born too? the children are to weep and the fathers go free?

STREPSIADES: But. . .

PHIDIPPIDES: You will tell me, that according to the law, 'tis the lot of children to be beaten. But I reply that the old men are children twice over and that it is far more fitting to chastise them than the young, for there is less excuse for their faults.

STREPSIADES: But the law nowhere admits that fathers should be treated thus.

PHIDIPPIDES: Was not the legislator who carried this law a man like you and me? In those days he got men to believe him; then why should not I too have the right to establish for the future a new law, allowing children to beat their fathers in turn? We make you a present of all the blows which were received before this law, and admit that you thrashed us with impunity. But look how the cocks and other animals fight with their fathers; and yet what difference is there betwixt them and ourselves, unless it be that they do not propose decrees?

STREPSIADES: But if you imitate the cocks in all things, why don't you scratch up the dunghill, why don't you sleep on a perch?

PHIDIPPIDES: That has no bearing on the case, good sir; Socrates would find no connection, I assure you.

STREPSIADES: Then do not beat at all, for otherwise you have only yourself to blame afterwards.

PHIDIPPIDES: What for?

STREPSIADES: I have the right to chastise you, and you to chastise your son, if you have one.

PHIDIPPIDES: And if I have not, I shall have cried in vain, and you will die laughing in my face.

STREPSIADES: What say you, all here present? It seems to me that he is right, and I am of opinion that they should be accorded their right. If we think wrongly, 'tis but just we should be beaten.

PHIDIPPIDES: Again, consider this other point.

STREPSIADES: 'Twill be the death of me.

PHIDIPPIDES: But you will certainly feel no more anger because of the blows I have given you.

STREPSIADES: Come, show me what profit I shall gain from it.

PHIDIPPIDES: I shall beat my mother just as I have you.

STREPSIADES: What do you say? what's that you say? Hah! this is far worse still.

PHIDIPPIDES: And what if I prove to you by our school reasoning, that one ought to beat one's mother?

STREPSIADES: Ah! if you do that, then you will only have to throw yourself along with Socrates and his reasoning, into the

Barathrum.[104] Oh! Clouds! all our troubles emanate from you, from you, to whom I entrusted myself, body and soul.

CHORUS: No, you alone are the cause, because you have pursued the path of evil.

STREPSIADES: Why did you not say so then, instead of egging on a poor ignorant old man?

CHORUS: We always act thus, when we see a man conceive a passion for what is evil; we strike him with some terrible disgrace, so that he may learn to fear the gods.

STREPSIADES: Alas! oh Clouds! 'tis hard indeed, but 'tis just! I ought not to have cheated my creditors. . . But come, my dear son, come with me to take vengeance on this wretched Chaerephon and on Socrates, who have deceived us both.

PHIDIPPIDES: I shall do nothing against our masters.

STREPSIADES: Oh! show some reverence for ancestral Zeus!

PHIDIPPIDES: Mark him and his ancestral Zeus! What a fool you are! Does any such being as Zeus exist?

STREPSIADES: Why, assuredly.

PHIDIPPIDES: No, a thousand times no! The ruler of the world is the Whirlwind, that has unseated Zeus.

STREPSIADES: He has not dethroned him. I believed it, because of this whirligig here. Unhappy wretch that I am! I have taken a piece of clay to be a god.

PHIDIPPIDES: Very well! Keep your stupid nonsense for your own consumption. (*Exit*)

STREPSIADES: Oh! what madness! I had lost my reason when I threw over the gods through Socrates' seductive phrases. Oh! good Hermes, do not destroy me in your wrath. Forgive me; their babbling had driven me crazy. Be my councillor. Shall I pursue them at law or shall I. . . ? Order and I obey.—You are right, no law-suit; but up! let us burn down the home of those praters. Here, Xanthias, here! take a ladder, come forth and arm yourself with an axe; now mount upon the school, demolish the roof, if you love your master, and may the house fall in upon them, Ho! bring me a blazing torch! There is more than one of them, arch-impostors as they are, on whom I am determined to have vengeance.

---

104. A cleft in the rocks at the back of the Acropolis at Athens, into which criminals were hurled.

A Disciple: Oh! oh!

Strepsiades: Come, torch, do your duty! Burst into full flame!

Disciple: What are you up to?

Strepsiades: What am I up to? Why, I am entering upon a subtle argument with the beams of the house.

Second Disciple: Hullo! hullo! who is burning down our house?

Strepsiades: The man whose cloak you have appropriated.

Second Disciple: But we are dead men, dead men!

Strepsiades: That is just exactly what I hope, unless my axe plays me false, or I fall and break my neck.

Socrates: Hi! you fellow on the roof, what are you doing up there?

Strepsiades: I traverse the air and contemplate the sun.[105]

Socrates: Ah! ah! woe is upon me! I am suffocating!

Chaerephon: Ah! you insulted the gods! Ah! you studied the face of the moon! Chase them, strike and beat them down! Forward! they have richly deserved their fate—above all, by reason of their blasphemies.

Chorus: So let the Chorus file off the stage. Its part is played.

FINIS OF "THE CLOUDS"

---

105. He repeats the words of Socrates at their first interview, in mockery.

THE WASPS

INTRODUCTION

This Comedy, which was produced by its Author the year after the performance of 'The Clouds,' may be taken as in some sort a companion picture to that piece. Here the satire is directed against the passion of the Athenians for the excitement of the law-courts, as in the former its object was the new philosophy. And as the younger generation—the modern school of thought—were there the subjects of the caricature, so here the older citizens, who took their seats in court as jurymen day by day, to the neglect of their private affairs and the encouragement of a litigious disposition, appear in their turn in the mirror which the satirist holds up."

There are only two characters of any importance to the action—Philocleon ('friend of Cleon') and his son Bdelycleon ('enemy of Cleon'). The plot is soon told. Philocleon is a bigoted devotee of the malady of litigiousness so typical of his countrymen and an enthusiastic attendant at the Courts in his capacity of 'dicast' or juryman. Bdelycleon endeavours to persuade his father by every means in his power to change this unsatisfactory manner of life for something nobler and more profitable; but all in vain. As a last resource he keeps his father a prisoner indoors, so that he cannot attend the tribunals.

The old man tries to escape, and these attempts are conceived in the wildest vein of extravaganza. He endeavours to get out by the chimney, pretending he is "only the smoke"; and all hands rush to clap a cover on the chimney-top, and a big stone on that. He slips through a hole in the tiles, and sits on the roof, pretending to be "only a sparrow"; and they have to set a net to catch him. Then the Chorus of Wasps, representing Philocleon's fellow 'dicasts,' appear on the scene to rescue him. A battle royale takes place on the stage; the Wasps, with their formidable stings, trying to storm the house, while the son and his retainers defend their position with desperate courage. Finally the assailants are repulsed, and father and son agree upon a compromise. Bdelycleon promises, on condition that his father gives up attending the public trails, to set up a mock tribunal for him in his own house.

Presently the theft of a Sicilian cheese by the house-dog Labes gives the old fellow an opportunity of exercising his judicial functions. Labes is duly arraigned and witnesses examines. But alas! Philocleon inadvertently casts his vote for the defendant's *acquittal*, the first time in his life "such a thing has ever occurred," and the old man nearly dies of vexation.

At this point follows the 'Parabasis,' or Author's personal address to the audience, after which the concluding portion of the play has little connection with the main theme. This is a fault, according to modern ideas, common to many of these Comedies, but it is especially marked in this particular instance. The final part might almost be a separate play, under the title perhaps of 'The dicast turned gentleman,' and relates various ridiculous mistakes and laughable blunders committed by Philocleon, who, having given up his attendance on the law-courts, has set up for playing a part in polite society.

The drama, as was very often the case, takes its title from the Chorus—a band of old men dressed up as wasps, who acrimonious, stinging, exasperated temper is meant to typify the character fostered among Athenian citizens by excessive addiction to forensic business.

Racine, in the only comedy he attempted, 'Les Plaideurs,' borrows the incident of the mock trial of the house-dog, amplifying and adding further diverting features.

Perhaps 'The Wasps' is the least amusing of all our Author's pieces which have come down to us—at any rate to a modern reader. The theme of its satire, the litigious spirit of the Athenians, is after all purely local and temporary, while the fun often strikes us as thin and forced. Schlegel writes in his 'Dramatic Literature': "The subject is too limited, the folly it ridicules appears a disease of too singular a description, without a sufficient universality of application, and the action is too much drawn out."

Dramatis Personae

Philocleon, a Dicast.
Bdelycleon, his Son.
Sosias, House-servant of Philocleon.
Xanthias, House-servant of Philocleon.
Boys.
A Dog.
A Baker's Wife.
Accuser.
Chorus of Elders, costumed as Wasps.

Scene: *Philocleon's house at Athens.*

Sosias: Why, Xanthias! what are you doing, wretched man?

Xanthias: I am teaching myself how to rest; I have been awake and on watch the whole night.

Sosias: So you want to earn trouble for your ribs,[1] eh? Don't you know what sort of an animal we are guarding here?

Xanthias: Aye indeed! but I want to put my cares to sleep for a while.

Sosias: Beware what you do. I too feel soft sleep spreading over my eyes. Resist it, for you must be as mad as a Corybant if you fall asleep.[2]

Xanthias: No! 'Tis Bacchus who lulls me off.

Sosias: Then you serve the same god as myself. Just now a heavy slumber settled on my eyelids like a hostile Mede; A nodded and, faith! I had a wondrous dream.

Xanthias: Indeed! and so had I. A dream such as I never had before. But first tell me yours.

Sosias: Methinks I saw an eagle, a gigantic bird, descend upon the market-place; it seized a brazen buckler with its talons and bore it away into the highest heavens; then I saw 'twas Cleonymus had thrown it away.

Xanthias: This Cleonymus is a riddle worth propounding among guests. How can one and the same animal have cast away his buckler both on land, in the sky and at sea?[3]

Sosias: Alas! what ill does such a dream portend for me?

Xanthias: Rest undisturbed! An it please the gods, no evil will befall you.

Sosias: Nevertheless, 'tis a fatal omen when a man throws away his weapons. But what was your dream? Let me hear.

Xanthias: Oh! it is a dream of high import. It has reference to the hull of the State; to nothing less.

Sosias: Tell it me quickly; show me its very keel.

Xanthias: In my first slumber I thought I saw sheep, wearing cloaks and carrying staves,[4] met in assembly on the Pnyx; a rapacious whale was haranguing them and screaming like a pig that is being grilled.

---

1. Meaning, Bdelycleon will thrash you if you do not keep a good watch on his father.
2. The Corybantes, priests of Cybelé, comported themselves like madmen in the celebration of their mysteries and made the air resound with the the noise of their drums.
3. Cleonymus had shown himself equally cowardly on all occasions; he is frequently referred to by Aristophanes, both in this and other comedies.
4. The cloak and the staff were the insignia of the dicasts; the poet describes them as sheep, because they were Cleon's servile tools.

SOSIAS: Faugh! faugh!

XANTHIAS: What's the matter?

SOSIAS: Enough, enough, spare me. Your dream stinks vilely of old leather.[5]

XANTHIAS: Then this scoundrelly whale seized a balance and set to weighing ox-fat.[6]

SOSIAS: Alas! 'tis our poor Athenian people, whom this accursed beast wished to cut up and despoil of their fat.

XANTHIAS: Seated on the ground close to it, I saw Theorus,[7] who had the head of a crow. The Alcibiades said to me in his lisping way, "Do you thee? Theoruth hath a crow'th head."[8]

SOSIAS: Ah! 'twas very well lisped indeed!

XANTHIAS: This is might strange; Theorus turning into a crow!

SOSIAS: No, it is glorious.

XANTHIAS: Why?

SOSIAS: Why? He was a man and now he has suddenly become a crow; does it not foretoken that he will take his flight from here and go to the crows?[9]

XANTHIAS: Interpreting dreams so aptly certainly deserves two obols.[10]

SOSIAS: Come, I must explain the matter to the spectators. But first a few words of preamble: expect nothing very high-flown from us, nor any jests stolen from Megara;[11] we have no slaves, who throw baskets of nuts[12] to the spectators, nor any Heracles to be robbed of his dinner,[13] nor is Euripides loaded with contumely; and despite the happy chance that gave Cleon his fame[14] we shall not

---

5. An allusion to Cleon, who was a tanner.

6. In Greek, (Greek: d emos) ([Greek: d emós], *fat*; [Greek: d êmos], *people*) means both *fat* and *people*.

7. A tool of Cleon's; he had been sent on an embassy to Persia (*vide* 'The Acharnians'). The crow is a thief and rapacious, just as Theorus was.

8. In his life of Alcibiades, Plutarch mentions this defect in his speech; or it may have been a 'fine gentleman' affectation.

9. Among the Greeks, *going to the crows* was equivalent to our *going to the devil*.

10. No doubt the fee generally given to the street diviners who were wont to interpret dreams.

11. Coarse buffoonery was welcomed at Megara, where, by the by, it is said that Comedy had its birth.

12. To gain the favour of the audience, the Comic poets often caused fruit and cakes to be thrown to them.

13. The gluttony of Heracles was a constant subject of jest with the Comic poets.

14. The incident of Pylos (see 'The Knights').

go out of our way to belabour him again. Our little subject is not wanting in sense; it is well within your capacity and at the same time cleverer than many vulgar Comedies.—We have a master of great renown, who is now sleeping up there on the other story. He has bidden us keep guard over his father, whom he has locked in, so that he may not go out. This father has a curious complaint; not one of you could hit upon or guess it, if I did not tell you.—Well then, try! I hear Amynias, the son of Pronapus, over there, saying, "He is addicted to gambling."

XANTHIAS: He's wrong! He is imputing his own malady to others.

SOSIAS: No, yet love is indeed the principal part of his disease. Ah! here is Sosias telling Dercylus, "He loves drinking."

XANTHIAS: Not at all! The love of wine is the complaint of good men.

SOSIAS: "Well then," says Nicostratus of the Scambonian deme, "he either loves sacrifices or else strangers."

XANTHIAS: Ah! great gods! no, he is not fond of strangers, Nicostratus, for he who says "Philoxenus" means a dirty fellow.[15]

SOSIAS: 'Tis mere waste of time, you will not find it out. If you want to know it, keep silence! I will tell you our master's complaint: of all men, it is he who is fondest of the Heliaea.[16] Thus, to be judging is his hobby, and he groans if he is not sitting on the first seat. He does not close an eye at night, and if he dozes off for an instant his mind flies instantly to the clepsydra.[17] He is so accustomed to hold the balloting pebble, that he awakes with his three fingers pinched together[18] as if he were offering incense to the new moon. If he sees scribbled on some doorway, "How charming is Demos,[19] the son of Pyrilampes!" he will write beneath it, "How charming is Cemos!"[20]

---

15. The Greek word for *friend of strangers* is (Greek: philoxenos), which happened also to be the name of one of the vilest debauchees in Athens.

16. The tribunal of the Heliasts came next in dignity only to the Areopagus. The dicasts, or jurymen, generally numbered 500; at times it would call in the assistance of one or two other tribunals, and the number of judges would then rise to 1000 or even 1500.

17. A water-clock, used in the courts for limiting the time of the pleaders.

18. The pebble was held between the thumb and two fingers, in the same way as one would hold a pinch of incense.

19. A young Athenian of great beauty, also mentioned by Plato in his 'Gorgias.' Lovers were font of writing the name of the object of their adoration on the walls (see 'The Acharnians').

20. (Greek: K emos), the Greek term for the funnel-shaped top of the voting urn, into which the judges dropped their voting pebbles.

His cock crowed one evening; said he, "He has had money from the accused to awaken me too late."[21] As soon as he rises from supper he bawls for his shoes and away he rushes down there before dawn to sleep beforehand, glued fast to the column like an oyster.[22] He is a merciless judge, never failing to draw the convicting line[23] and return home with his nails full of wax like a bumble-bee. Fearing he might run short of pebbles[24] he keeps enough at home to cover a sea-beach, so that he may have the means of recording his sentence. Such is his madness, and all advice is useless; he only judges the more each day. So we keep him under lock and key, to prevent his going out; for his son is broken-hearted over this mania. At first he tried him with gentleness, wanted to persuade him to wear the cloak no longer,[25] to go out no more; unable to convince him, he had him bathed and purified according to the ritual[26] without any greater success, and then handed him over the the Corybantes;[27] but the old man escaped them, and carrying off the kettle-drum,[28] rushed right into the midst of the Heliasts. As Cybelé could do nothing with her rites, his son took him again to Aegina and forcibly made him lie one night in the temple of Asclepius, the God of Healing, but before daylight there he was to be seen at the gate of the tribunal. Since then we let him go out no more, but he escaped us by the drains or by the skylights, so we stuffed up every opening with old rags and made all secure; then he drove short sticks into the wall and sprang from rung to rung like a magpie. Now we have stretched nets all round the court and we keep watch and ward. The old man's name is Philocleon,[29] 'tis the best name he could have, and the son is called Bdelycleon,[30] for he is a man very fit to cure an insolent fellow of his boasting.

21. Racine has introduced this incident with some modification into his 'Plaideurs.'
22. Although called *Heliasts* ([Greek: H elios], the sun), the judges sat under cover. One of the columns that supported the roof is here referred to.
23. The juryman gave his vote for condemnation by tracing a line horizontally across a waxed tablet. This was one method in use; another was by means of pebbles placed in one or other of two voting urns.
24. Used for the purpose of voting. There were two urns, one for each of the two opinions, and each heliast placed a pebble in one of them.
25. The Heliast's badge of office.
26. To prepare him for initiation into the mysteries of the Corybantes.
27. Who pretended to cure madness; they were priests of Cybelé.
28. The sacred instrument of the Corybantes.
29. *Friend of Cleon,* who had raised the daily salary of the Heliasts to three obols.
30. *Enemy of Cleon.*

BDELYCLEON: Xanthias! Sosias! Are you asleep?

XANTHIAS: Oh! oh!

SOSIAS: What is the matter?

XANTHIAS: Why, Bdelycleon is rising.

BDELYCLEON: Will neither of you come here? My father has got into the stove-chamber and is ferreting about like a rat in his hole. Take care he does not escape through the bath drain. You there, put all your weight against the door.

SOSIAS: Aye, aye, master.

BDELYCLEON: By Zeus! what is that noise in the chimney? Hullo! who are you?

PHILOCLEON: I am the smoke going up.

BDELYCLEON: Smoke? smoke of what wood?

PHILOCLEON: Of fig-wood.[31]

BDELYCLEON: Ah! 'this the most acrid of all. But you shall not get out. Where is the chimney cover?[32] Come down again. Now, up with another cross-bar. Now look out some fresh dodge. But am I not the most unfortunate of men? Henceforward, I shall only be called the son of the smoky old man. Slave, hold the door stoutly, throw your weight upon it, come, put heart into the work. I will come and help you. Watch both lock and bolt. Take care he does not gnaw through the peg.

PHILOCLEON: What are you dong, you wretches? Let me go out; it is imperative that I go and judge, or Dracontides will be acquitted.

BDELYCLEON: What a dreadful calamity for you!

PHILOCLEON: Once at Delphi, the god, whom I was consulting, foretold, that if an accused man escaped me, I should die of consumption.

BDELYCLEON: Apollo, the Saviour, what a prophecy!

PHILOCLEON: Ah! I beseech you, if you do not want my death, let me go.

BDELYCLEON: No, Philocleon, no never, by Posidon!

PHILOCLEON: Well then, I shall gnaw through the net[33] with my teeth.

BDELYCLEON: But you have no teeth.

PHILOCLEON: Oh! you rascal, how can I kill you? How? Give me a sword, quick, or a conviction tablet.

---

31. The smoke of fig-wood is very acrid, like the character of the Heliasts.
32. Used for closing the chimney, when needed.
33. Which had been stretched all round the courtyard to prevent his escape.

BDELYCLEON: Our friend is planning some great crime.

PHILOCLEON: No, by Zeus! but I want to go and sell my ass and its panniers, for 'this the first of the month.[34]

BDELYCLEON: Could I not sell it just as well?

PHILOCLEON: Not as well as I could.

BDELYCLEON: No, but better. Come, bring it here, bring it here by all means—if you can.

XANTHIAS: What a clever excuse he has found now! What cunning to get you to let him go out!

BDELYCLEON: Yes, but I have not swallowed the hook; I scented the trick. I will go in and fetch the ass, so that the old man may not point his weapons that way again. . .[35] Stupid old ass, are you weeping because you are going to be sold? Come, go a bit quicker. Why, what are you moaning and groaning for? You might be carrying another Odysseus.[36]

XANTHIAS: Why, certainly, so he is! someone has crept beneath his belly.

BDELYCLEON: Who, who? Let us see.

XANTHIAS: 'Tis he.

BDELYCLEON: What does this mean? Who are you? Come, speak!

PHILOCLEON: I am Nobody.

BDELYCLEON: Nobody? Of what country?

PHILOCLEON: Of Ithaca, son of Apodrasippides.[37]

BDELYCLEON: Ha! Mister Nobody, you will not laugh presently. Pull him out quick! Ah! the wretch, where has be crept to? Does he not resemble a she-ass to the life?

PHILOCLEON: If you do not leave me in peace, I shall commence proceedings.

BDELYCLEON: And what will the suit be about?

PHILOCLEON: The shade of an ass.[38]

---

34. Market-day.

35. He enters the courtyard, returning with the ass, under whose belly Philocleon is clinging.

36. In the Odyssey (Bk. IX) Homer makes his hero, 'the wily' Odysseus, escape from the Cyclops' cave by clinging on under a ram's belly, which slips past its blinded master without noticing the trick played on him. Odysseus, when asked his name by the Cyclops, replies, *Outis*, Nobody.

37. A name formed out of two Greek words, meaning, *running away on a horse*.

38. The story goes that a traveller who had hired an ass, having placed himself in its shadow to escape the heat of the sun, was sued by the driver, who had pretended that he

BDELYCLEON: You are a poor man of very little wit, but thoroughly brazen.

PHILOCLEON: A poor man! Ah! by Zeus! you know not now what I am worth; but you will know when you disembowel the old Heliast's money bag.[39]

BDELYCLEON: Come, get back indoors, both you and your ass.

PHILOCLEON: Oh! my brethren of the tribunal! oh! Cleon! to the rescue!

BDELYCLEON: Go and bawl in there under lock and key. And you there, pile plenty of stones against the door, thrust the bolt home into the staple, and to keep this beam in its place roll that great mortar against it. Quick's the word.

SOSIAS: Oh! my god! whence did this brick fall on me?

XANTHIAS: Perhaps a rat loosened it.

SOSIAS: A rat? 'tis surely our gutter-judge,[40] who has crept beneath the tiles of the roof.

XANTHIAS: Ah! woe to us! there he is, he has turned into a sparrow; he will be flying off. Where is the net? where? pschit! pschit! get back!

BDELYCLEON: Ah! by Zeus! I would rather have to guard Scioné[41] than such a father.

SOSIAS: And how that we have driven him in thoroughly and he can no longer escape without our knowledge, can we not have a few winks of sleep, no matter how few?

BDELYCLEON: Why, wretch! the other jurymen will be here almost directly to summon my father!

SOSIAS: Why, 'tis scarcely dawn yet!

BDELYCLEON: Ah, they must have risen late to-day. Generally it is the middle of the night when they come to fetch him. They arrive here, carrying lanterns in their hands and singing the charming old verses of Phrynichus' "Sidonian Women";[42] 'tis their way of calling him.

---

had let the ass, not but its shadow; hence the Greek proverb, *to quarrel about the shade of an ass*, i.e. about nothing at all.

39. When you inherit from me.

40. There is a similar incident in the 'Plaideurs.'

41. A Macedonian town in the peninsula of Pallené; it had shaken off the Athenian yoke and was not retaken for two years.

42. A disciple of Thespis, who even in his infancy devoted himself to the dramatic art. He was the first to introduce female characters on the stage. He flourished about 500 B.C., having won his first prize for Tragedy in 511 B.C., twelve years before Aeschylus.

SOSIAS: Well, if need be, we will chase them off with stones.

BDELYCLEON: What! you dare to speak so? Why, this class of old men, if irritated, becomes as terrible as a swarm of wasps. They carry below their loins the sharpest of stings, with which to sting their foe; they shout and leap and their stings burn like so many sparks.

SOSIAS: Have no fear! If I can find stones to throw into this nest of jurymen-wasps, I shall soon have them cleared off.

CHORUS: March on, advance boldly and bravely! Comias, your feet are dragging; once you were as tough as a dog-skin strap and now even Charinades walks better than you. Ha! Strymodorus of Conthylé, you best of mates, where is Euergides and where is Chales of Phyla? Ha, ha, bravo! there you are, the last of the lads with whom we mounted guard together at Byzantium.[43] Do you remember how, one night, prowling round, we noiselessly stole the kneading-trough of a baker's-wife; we split it in two and cooked our green-stuff with it.—But let us hasten, for the case of the Laches[44] comes on to-day, and they all say he has embezzled a pot of money. Hence Cleon, our protector, advised us yesterday to come early and with a three days' stock of fiery rage so as to chastise him for his crimes. Let us hurry, comrades, before it is light; come, let us search every nook with our lanterns to see whether those who wish us ill have not set us some trap.

BOY: Ah! here is mud! Father, take care!

CHORUS: Pick up a blade of straw and trim the lamp of your lantern.

BOY: No, I can trim it quite well with my finger.

CHORUS: Why do you pull out the wick, you little dolt? Oil is scarce, and 'tis not you who suffer when it has to be paid for. (*Strikes him*)

BOY: If you teach us again with your fists, we shall put out the lamps and go home; then you will have no light and will squatter about in the mud like ducks in the dark.

CHORUS: I know how to punish other offenders bigger than you. But I think I am treading in some mud. Oh! 'tis certain it will rain in torrents for four days at least; look, what thieves are in our lamps; that is always a sign of heavy rain; but the rain and the north wind will be good for the crops that are still standing. . . Why, what

43. Originally subjected to Sparta by Pausanias in 478 B.C., it was retaken by Cimon in 471, or forty-eight years previous to the production of 'The Wasps.' The old Heliasts refer to this latter event.

44. An Athenian general, who had been defeated when sent to Sicily with a fleet to the succour of Leontini; no doubt Cleon had charged him with treachery.

ARISTOPHANES

can have happened to our mate, who lives here? Why does he not come to join our party? There used to be no need to haul him in our wake, for he would march at our head singing the verses of Phrynichus; he was a lover of singing. Should we not, friends, make a halt here and sign to call him out? The charm of my voice will fetch him out, if he hears it.

Why does the old man not show himself before the door? why does he not answer? Has he lost his shoes? has he stubbed his toe in the dark and thus got a swollen ankle? Perhaps he has a tumour in his groin. He was the hardest of us all; he alone *never* allowed himself to be moved. If anyone tried to move him, he would lower his head, saying, "You might just as well try to boil a stone." But I bethink me, an accused ma escaped us yesterday through his false pretence that he loved Athens and had been the first to unfold the Samian plot.[45] Perhaps his acquittal has so distressed Philocleon that he is abed with fever—he is quite capable of such a thing.— Friend, arise, do not thus vex your heart, but forget your wrath. Today we have to judge a man made wealthy by treason, one of those who set Thrace free;[46] we have to prepare him a funeral urn. . . so march on, my boy, get a-going.

BOY: Father, would you give me something if I asked for it?

CHORUS: Assuredly, my child, but tell me what nice thing do you want me to buy you? A set of knuckle-bones, I suppose.

BOY: No, dad, I prefer figs; they are better.

CHORUS: No, by Zeus! even if you were to hang yourself with vexation.

BOY: Well then, I will lead you no father.

CHORUS: With my small pay, I am obliged to buy bread, wood, stew; and now you ask me for figs!

BOY: But, father, if the Archon[47] should not form a court to-day, how are we to buy our dinner? Have you some good hope to offer us or merely "Hellé's sacred waves"?[48]

---

45. The Samians were in league with the Persians, but a certain Carystion betrayed the plot, and thanks to this the Athenians were able to retake Samos before the island had obtained help from Asia.

46. The towns of Thrace, up to that time the faithful allies of Athens, were beginning to throw off her yoke.

47. Who fulfilled the office of president.

48. Meaning, "Will it only remain for us to throw ourselves into the water?" Hellé, taken by a ram across the narrow strait, called the Hellespont after her name, fell into the waves and was drowned.

CHORUS: Alas! alas! I have not a notion how we shall dine.

BOY: Oh! my poor mother! why did you let me see this day?

CHORUS: Oh! my little wallet! you seem like to be a mere useless ornament!

BOY: 'Tis our destiny to groan.

PHILOCLEON:[49] My friends, I have long been pining away while listening to you from my window, but I absolutely know not what do do. I am detained here, because I have long wanted to go with you to the law court and do all the harm I can. Oh! Zeus! cause the peals of they thunder to roll, change me quickly into smoke or make me into a Proxenides, a perfect braggart, like the son of Sellus. Oh, King of Heaven! hesitate not to grant me this favour, pity my misfortune or else may thy dazzling lightning instantly reduce me to ashes; then carry me hence, and may thy breath hurl me into some burning pickle[50] or turn me into one of the stones on which the votes are counted.

CHORUS: Who is it detains you and shuts you in? Speak, for you are talking to friends.

PHILOCLEON: 'Tis my son. But no bawling, he is there in front asleep; lower your voice.

CHORUS: But, poor fellow, what is his aim? what is his object?

PHILOCLEON: My friends, he will not have me judge nor do anyone any ill, but he wants me to stay at home and enjoy myself, and I will not.

CHORUS: This wretch, this Demolochocleon[51] dares to say such odious things, just because you tell the truth about our navy!

PHILOCLEON: He would not have dared, had he not been a conspirator.

CHORUS: Meanwhile, you must devise some new dodge, so that you can come down here without his knowledge.

PHILOCLEON: But what? Try to find some way. For myself, I am ready for anything, so much do I burn to run along the tiers of the tribunal with my voting-pebble in my hand.

CHORUS: There is surely some hole through which you could manage to squeeze from within, and escape dressed in rags, like the crafty Odysseus.[52]

---

49. He is a prisoner inside, and speaks through the closed doors.

50. This boiling, acid pickle reminds him of the fiery, acrid temper of the heliasts.

51. A name invented for the occasion; it really means, *Cleon who holds the people in his snares.*

52. When he entered Troy as a spy.

PHILOCLEON: Everything is sealed fast; not so much as a gnat could get through. Think of some other plan; there is no possible hold of escape.

CHORUS: Do you recall how, when you were with the army at the taking of Naxos,[53] you descended so readily from the top of the wall by means of the spits you have stolen?

PHILOCLEON: I remember that well enough, but what connection is there with present circumstances? I was young, clever at thieving, I had all my strength, none watched over me, and I could run off without fear. But to-day men-at-arms are placed at every outlet to watch me, and two of them are lying in wait for me at this very door armed with spits, just as folk lie in wait for a cat that has stolen a piece of meat.

CHORUS: Come, discover some way as quick as possible. Here is the dawn come, my dear little friend.

PHILOCLEON: The best way is to gnaw through the net. Oh! goddess, who watches over the nets,[54] forgive me for making a hole in this one.

CHORUS: 'Tis acting like a man eager for his safety. Get your jaws to work!

PHILOCLEON: There! 'tis gnawed through! But no shouting! let Bdelycleon notice nothing!

CHORUS: Have no fear, have no fear! if he breathes a syllable, 'twill be to bruise his own knuckles; he will have to fight to defend his own head. We shall teach him not to insult the mysteries of the goddesses.[55] But fasten a rope to the window, tie it around your body and let yourself down to the ground, with your heart bursting with the fury of Diopithes.[56]

PHILOCLEON: But if these notice it and want to fish me up and drag me back into the house, what will you do? Tell me that.

CHORUS: We shall call up the full strength of out courage to your aid. That is what we will do.

---

53. The island of Naxos was taken by Cimon, in consequence of sedition in the town of Naxos, about fifty years before the production of 'The Wasps.'

54. One of the titles under which Artemis, the goddess of the chase, was worshipped.

55. Demeter and Persephone. This was an accusation frequently brought against people in Athens.

56. An orator of great violence of speech and gesture.

PHILOCLEON: I trust myself to you and risk the danger. If misfortune overtakes me, take away my body, bathe it with your tears and bury it beneath the bar of the tribunal.

CHORUS: Nothing will happen to you, rest assured. Come friend, have courage and let yourself slide down while you invoke your country's gods.

PHILOCLEON: Oh! mighty Lycus![57] noble hero and my neighbour, thou, like myself, takest pleasure in the tears and the groans of the accused. If thou art come to live near the tribunal, 'tis with the express design of hearing them incessantly; thou alone of all the heroes hast wished to remain among those who weep. Have pity on me and save him, who lives close to thee; I swear I will never make water, never, nor relieve my belly with a fart against the railing of thy statue.

BDELYCLEON: Ho there! ho! get up!

SOSIAS: What's the matter?

BDELYCLEON: Methought I heard talking close to me.

SOSIAS: Is the old man at it again, escaping through some loophole?

BDELYCLEON: No, by Zeus! no, but he is letting himself down by a rope.

SOSIAS: Ha, rascal! what are you doing there? You shall not descend.

BDELYCLEON: Mount quick to the other window, strike him with the boughs that hang over the entrance; perchance he will turn back when he feels himself being thrashed.

PHILOCLEON: To the rescue! all you, who are going to have lawsuits this year—Smicythion, Tisiades, Chremon and Pheredipnus. 'Tis now or never, before they force me to return, that you must help.

CHORUS: Why do we delay to let loose that fury, that is so terrible, when our nests are attacked? I feel my angry sting is stiffening, that sharp sting, with which we punish our enemies. Come, children, cast your cloaks to the winds, run, shout, tell Cleon what is happening, that he may march against this foe to our city, who deserves death, since he proposes to prevent the trial of lawsuits.

BDELYCLEON: Friends, listen to the truth, instead of bawling.

CHORUS: By Zeus! we will shout to heaven and never forsake our friend. Why, this is intolerable, 'tis manifest tyranny. Oh! citizens,

---

57. For Philocleon, the titulary god was Lycus, the son of Pandion, the King of Athens, because a statue stood erected to him close to the spot where the tribunals sat, and because he recognized no other fatherland but the tribunals.

oh! Theorus,[58] the enemy of the gods! and all you flatterers, who rule us! come to our aid.

XANTHIAS: By Heracles! they have stings. Do you see them, master?

BDELYCLEON: 'Twas with these weapons that they killed Philippus the son of Gorgias[59] when he was put on trial.

CHORUS: And you too shall die. Turn yourselves this way, all, with your stings out for attack and throw yourselves upon him in good and serried order, and swelled up with wrath and rage. Let him learn to know the sort of foes he has dared to irritate.

XANTHIAS: The fight will be fast and furious, by great Zeus! I tremble at the sight of their stings.

CHORUS: Let this man go, unless you want to envy the tortoise his hard shell.

PHILOCLEON: Come, my dear companions, wasps with relentless hearts, fly against him, animated with your fury. Sting him in the back, in his eyes and on his fingers.

BDELYCLEON: Midas, Phryx, Masyntias, here! Come and help. Seize this man and hand him over to no one, otherwise you shall starve to death in chains. Fear nothing, I have often heard the crackling of fig-leaves in the fire.[60]

CHORUS: If you won't let him go, I shall bury this sting in your body.

PHILOCLEON: Oh, Cecrops, mighty hero with the tail of a dragon! Seest thou how these barbarians ill-use me—me, who have many a time made them weep a full bushel of tears?

CHORUS: Is not old age filled with cruel ills? What violence these two slaves offer to their old master! they have forgotten all bygones, the fur-coats and the jackets and the caps he bought for them; in winter he watched that their feet should not get frozen. And only see them now; there is no gentleness in their look nor any recollection of the slippers of other days.

PHILOCLEON: Will you let me go, you accursed animal? Don't you remember the day when I surprised you stealing the grapes; I tied you to an olive-tree and I cut open your bottom with such vigorous lashes that folks thought you had been pedicated. Get away, you are ungrateful. But let go of me, and you too, before my son comes up.

---

58. A debauchee and an embezzler of public funds, already mentioned a little above.
59. Aristophanes speaks of him in 'The Birds' as a traitor and as an alien who usurped the rights of the city.
60. A Greek proverb signifying "Much ado about nothing."

CHORUS: You shall repay us for all this and 'twill not be long first. Tremble at our ferocious glance; you shall taste our just anger.

BDELYCLEON: Strike! strike, Xanthias! Drive these wasps away from the house.

XANTHIAS: That's just what I am doing; but do you smoke them out thoroughly too.

SOSIAS: You will not go? The plague seize you! Will you not clear off? Xanthias, strike them with your stick!

XANTHIAS: And you, to smoke them out better, throw Aeschinus, the son of Selartius, on the fire. Ah! we were bound to drive you off in the end.

BDELYCLEON: Eh! by Zeus! you would not have put them to flight so easily if they had fed on the verses of Philocles.

CHORUS: It is clear to all the poor that tyranny has attacked us sorely. Proud emulator of Amynias, you, who only take pleasure in doing ill, see how you are preventing us from obeying the laws of the city; you do not even seek a pretext or any plausible excuse, but claim to rule alone.

BDELYCLEON: Hold! A truce to all blows and brawling! Had we not better confer together and come to some understanding?

CHORUS: Confer with you, the people's foe! with you, a royalist, the accomplice of Brasidas![61] with you, who wear woollen fringes on your cloak and let your beard grow!

BDELYCLEON: Ah! it were better to separate altogether from my father than to steer my boat daily through such stormy seas!

CHORUS: Oh! you have but reached the parsley and the rue, to use the common saying.[62] What you are suffering is nothing! but welcome the hour when the advocate shall adduce all these same arguments against you and shall summon your accomplices to give witness.

BDELYCLEON: In the name of the gods! withdraw or we shall fight you the whole day long.

CHORUS: No, not as long as I retain an atom of breath. Ha! your desire is to tyrannize over us!

BDELYCLEON: Everything is now tyranny with us, no matter what is concerned, whether it be large or small. Tyranny! I have not

---

61. A Spartan general, who perished in the same battle as Cleon, before Amphipolis, in 422 B.C.

62. Meaning, the mere beginnings of any matter.

heard the word mentioned once in fifty years, and now it is more common than salt-fish, the word is even current on the market. If you are buying gurnards and don't want anchovies, the huckster next door, who is selling the latter, at once exclaims, "That is a man, whose kitchen savours of tyranny!" If you ask for onions to season your fish, the green-stuff woman winks one eye and asks, "Ha! you ask for onions! are you seeking to tyrannize, or do you think that Athens must pay you your seasonings as a tribute?"

XANTHIAS: Yesterday I went to see a gay girl about noon and suggested she should mount and ride me; she flew into a rage, pretending I wanted to restore the tyranny of Hippias.[63]

BDELYCLEON: That's the talk that pleases the people! As for myself, I want my father to lead a joyous life like Morychus[64] instead of going away before dawn to basely calumniate and condemn; and for this I am accused of conspiracy and tyrannical practice!

PHILOCLEON: And quite right too, by Zeus! The most exquisite dishes do not make up to me for the life of which you deprive me. I scorn your red mullet and your eels, and would far rather eat a nice little law suitlet cooked in the pot.

BDELYCLEON: 'Tis because you have got used to seeking your pleasure in it; but if you will agree to keep silence and hear me, I think I could persuade you that you deceive yourself altogether.

PHILOCLEON: *I* deceive myself, when I am judging?

BDELYCLEON: You do not see that you are the laughing-stock of these men, whom you are ready to worship. You are their slave and do not know it.

PHILOCLEON: *I* a slave, I, who lord it over all!

BDELYCLEON: Not at all, you think you are ruling when you are only obeying. Tell me, father, what do you get out of the tribute paid by so many Greek towns?

PHILOCLEON: Much, and I appoint my colleagues jurymen.

BDELYCLEON: And I also. Release him, all of you, and bring me a sword. If my arguments do not prevail I will fall upon this blade. As for you, tell me whether you accept the verdict of the Court.

---

63. This 'figure of love'—woman atop of the man—is known in Greek as (Greek: hippos) (Latin *equus*, 'the horse'); note the play upon words with the name Hippias.
64. A tragic poet, who was a great lover of good cheer, it appears.

PHILOCLEON: May I never drink my Heliast's pay in honour of the good Genius, if I do not.

CHORUS: Tis now we have to draw upon our arsenal for some fresh weapon; above all do not side with this youth in his opinions. You see how serious the question has become; 'twill be all over with us, which the gods forfend, if he should prevail.

BDELYCLEON: Let someone bring me my tablets with all speed!

CHORUS: Your tablets? Ha, ha! what an importance you would fain assume!

BDELYCLEON: I merely wish to note down my father's points.

PHILOCLEON: But what will you say of it, if he should triumph in the debate?

CHORUS: That old men are no longer good for anything; we shall be perpetually laughed at in the streets, shall be called thallophores,[65] mere brief-bags. You are to be the champion of all our rights and sovereignty. Come, take courage! Bring into action all the resources of your wit.

PHILOCLEON: At the outset I will prove to you that there exists no king whose might is greater than ours. Is there a pleasure, a blessing comparable with that of a juryman? Is there a being who lives more in the midst of delights, who is more feared, aged though he be? From the moment I leave my bed, men of power, the most illustrious in the city, await me at the bar of the tribunal; the moment I am seen from the greatest distance, they come forward to offer me a gentle hand,—that has pilfered the public funds; they entreat me, bowing right low and with a piteous voice, "Oh! father," they say, "pity me, I adjure you by the profit *you* were able to make in the public service or in the army, when dealing with the victuals." Why, the man who thus speaks would not know of my existence, had I not let him off on some former occasion.

BDELYCLEON: Let us note this first point, the supplicants.

PHILOCLEON: These entreaties have appeased my wrath, and I enter—firmly resolved to do nothing that I have promised. Nevertheless I listen to the accused. Oh! what tricks to secure acquittal! Ah! there is no form of flattery that is not addressed to the heliast!

---

65. Old men, who carried olive branches in the processions of the Panathenaea. Those whose great age or infirmity forbade their being used for any other purpose were thus employed.

Some groan over their poverty and they exaggerate the truth in order to make their troubles equal to my own. Others tell us anecdotes or some comic story from Aesop. Others, again, cut jokes; they fancy I shall be appeased if I laugh. If we are not even then won over, why, then they drag forward their young children by the hand, both boys and girls, who prostrate themselves and whine with one accord, and then the father, trembling as if before a god, beseeches me not to condemn him out of pity for them, "If you love the voice of the lamb, have pity on my son's"; and because I am fond of little sows,[66] I must yield to his daughter's prayers. Then we relax the heat of our wrath a little for him. Is not this great power indeed, which allows even wealth to be disdained?

BDELYCLEON: A second point to note, the disdain of wealth. And now recall to me what are the advantages you enjoy, you, who pretend to rule over Greece?

PHILOCLEON: Being entrusted with the inspection of the young men, we have a right to examine their organs. Is Aeagrus[67] accused, he is not acquitted before he has recited a passage from 'Niobe'[68] and he chooses the finest. If a flute-player gains his case, he adjusts his mouth-strap[69] in return and plays us the final air while we are leaving. A father on his death-bed names some husband for his daughter, who is his sole heir; but we care little for his will or for the shell so solemnly placed over the seal;[70] we give the young maiden to him who has best known how to secure our favour. Name me another duty that is so important and so irresponsible.

BDELYCLEON: Aye, 'tis a fine privilege, and the only one on which I can congratulate you; but surely to violate the will is to act badly towards the heiress.

PHILOCLEON: And if the Senate and the people have trouble in deciding some important case, it is decreed to send the culprits before the heliasts; then Euathlus[71] and the illustrious

---

66. An obscene pun. (Greek: Choiros) means both *a sow* and the female organ.

67. A celebrated actor.

68. There were two tragedies named 'Niobé,' one by Aeschylus and the other by Sophocles, both now lost.

69. A double strap, which flute-players applied to their lips and was said to give softness to the tones.

70. The shell was fixed over the seal to protect it.

71. A calumniator and a traitor (see 'The Acharnians').

Colaconymus,[72] who cast away his shield, swear not to betray us and to fight for the people. Did ever an orator carry the day with his opinion if he had not first declared that the jury should be dismissed for the day as soon as they had given their first verdict? We are the only ones whom Cleon, the great bawler, does not badger. On the contrary, he protects and caresses us; he keeps off the flies, which is what you have never done for your father. Theorus, who is a man not less illustrious than Euphemius,[73] takes the sponge out of the pot and blacks our shoes. See then what good things you deprive and despoil me of. Pray, is this obeying or being a slave, as you pretended to be able to prove?

BDELYCLEON: Talk away to your heart's content; you must come to a stop at last and then you shall see that this grand power only resembles one of those things that, wash 'em as you will, remain as foul as ever.

PHILOCLEON: But I am forgetting the most pleasing thing of all. When I return home with my pay, everyone runs to greet me because of my money. First my daughter bathes me, anoints my feet, stoops to kiss me and, while she is calling me "her dearest father," fishes out my triobolus with her tongue;[74] then my little wife comes to wheedle me and brings a nice light cake; she sits beside me and entreats me in a thousand ways, "Do take this now; do have some more." All this delights me hugely, and I have no need to turn towards you or the steward to know when it shall please him to serve my dinner, all the while cursing and grumbling. But if he does not quickly knead my cake, I have this,[75] which is my defence, my shield against all ills. If you do not pour me out drink, I have brought this long-eared jar[76] full of wine. How it brays, when I bend back and bury its neck in my mouth! What terrible and noisy gurglings, and how I laugh at your wine-skins. As to power, am I not equal to the king of the gods? If our assembly is noisy, all say as they pass, "Great gods! the tribunal is rolling out its thunder!"

---

72. Cleonymus, whose name the poet modifies, so as to introduce the idea of a flatterer ([Greek: kolax]).

73. Another flatterer, a creature of Cleon's.

74. Athenian poor, having no purse, would put small coins into mouth for safety. We know that the triobolus was the daily of the judges. Its value was about 4-1/2 d.

75. A jar of wine, which he had bought with his pay.

76. A jar with two long ears or handles, in this way resembling an ass.

If I let loose the lightning, the richest, aye, the noblest are half dead with fright and shit themselves with terror. You yourself are afraid of me, yea, by Demeter! you are afraid.

BDELYCLEON: May I die if you frighten me.

CHORUS: Never have I heard speech so elegant or so sensible.

PHILOCLEON: Ah! he thought he had only to turn me round his finger; he should, however, have known the vigour of my eloquence.

CHORUS: He has said everything without omission. I felt myself grow taller while I listened to him. Methought myself meting out justice in the Islands of the Blest, so much was I taken with the charm of his words.

BDELYCLEON: How overjoyed they are! What extravagant delight! Ah! ah! you are going to get a thrashing to-day.

CHORUS: Come, plot everything you can to beat him; 'tis not easy to soften me if you do not talk on my side, and if you have nothing but nonsense to spout, 'tis time to buy a good millstone, freshly cut withal, to crush my anger.

BDELYCLEON: The cure of a disease, so inveterate and so widespread in Athens, is a difficult task and of too great importance for the scope of Comedy. Nevertheless, my old father. . .

PHILOCLEON: Cease to call me by that name, for, if you do not prove me a slave and that quickly too, you must die by my hand, even if I must be deprived of my share in the sacred feasts.

BDELYCLEON: Listen to me, dear little father, unruffle that frowning brow and reckon, you can do so without trouble, not with pebbles, but on your fingers, what is the sum-total of the tribute paid by the allied towns; besides this we have the direct imposts, a mass of percentage dues, the fees of the courts of justice, the produce from the mines, the markets, the harbours, the public lands and the confiscations. All these together amount to close on two thousand talents. Take from this sum the annual pay of the dicasts; they number six thousand, and there have never been more in this town; so therefore it is one hundred and fifty talents that come to you.

PHILOCLEON: What! our pay is not even a tithe of the State revenue?

BDELYCLEON: Why no, certainly not.

PHILOCLEON: And where does the rest go then?

BDELYCLEON: To those who say: "I shall never betray the interests of the masses; I shall always fight for the people." And 'tis you, father, who let yourself be caught with their fine talk, who give them all power over yourself. They are the men who extort fifty talents at a time by threat and intimidation from the allies. "Pay tribute to me," they say, "or I shall loose the lightning on your town and destroy it." And you, you are content to gnaw the crumbs of your own might. What do the allies do? They see that the Athenian mob lives on the tribunal in niggard and miserable fashion, and they count you for nothing, for not more than the vote of Connus;[77] 'tis on those wretches that they lavish everything, dishes of salt fish, wine, tapestries, cheese, honey, sesame-fruit, cushions, flagons, rich clothing, chaplets, necklets, drinking-cups, all that yields pleasure and health. And you, their master, to you as a reward for all your toil both on land and sea, nothing is given, not even a clove of garlic to eat with your little fish.

PHILOCLEON: No, undoubtedly not; I have had to send and buy some from Eucharides. But you told me I was a slave. Prove it then, for I am dying with impatience.

BDELYCLEON: Is it not the worst of all slaveries to see all these wretches and their flatterers, whom they gorge with gold, at the head of affairs? As for you, you are content with the three obols they give you and which you have so painfully earned in the galleys, in battles and sieges. But what I stomach least is that you go to sit on the tribunal by order. Some lewd stripling, the son of Chereas, to wit, enters your house balancing his body, rotten with debauchery, on his straddling legs and charges you to come and judge at daybreak, and precisely to the minute. "He who only presents himself after the opening of the Court," says he, "will not get the triobolus." But he himself, though he arrives late, will nevertheless get his drachma as a public advocate. If an accused man makes him some present, he shares it with a colleague and the pair agree to arrange the matter like two sawyers, one of whom pulls and the other pushes. As for you, you have only eyes for the public pay-clerk, and you see nothing.

PHILOCLEON: Can it be I am treated thus? Oh! what is it you are saying? You stir me to the bottom of my heart! I am all ears! I cannot syllable what I feel.

BDELYCLEON: Consider then; you might be rich, both you and all the others; I know not why you let yourself be fooled by these folk who

---

77. A well-known flute-player.

ARISTOPHANES

call themselves the people's friends. A myriad of towns obey you, from the Euxine to Sardis. What do you gain thereby? Nothing but this miserable pay, and even that is like the oil with which the flock of wool is impregnated and is doled to you drop by drop, just enough to keep you from dying of hunger. They want you to be poor, and I will tell you why. 'Tis so that you may know only those who nourish you, and so that, if it pleases them to loose you against one of their foes, you shall leap upon him with fury. If they wished to assure the well-being of the people, nothing would be easier for them. We have now a thousand towns that pay us tribute; let them command each of these to feed twenty Athenians; then twenty thousand of our citizens would be eating nothing but hare, would drink nothing but the purest of milk, and always crowned with garlands, would be enjoying the delights to which the great name of their country and the trophies of Marathon give them the right; whereas to-day you are like the hired labourers who gather the olives; you follow him who pays you.

PHILOCLEON: Alas! my hand is benumbed; I can no longer draw my sword.[78] What has become of my strength?

BDELYCLEON: When they are afraid, they promise to divide Euboea[79] among you and to give each fifty bushels of wheat, but what have they given you? Nothing excepting, quite recently, five bushels of barley, and even these you have only obtained with great difficulty, on proving you were not aliens, and then choenix by choenix.[80] That is why I always kept you shut in; I wanted you to be fed by me and no longer at the beck of these blustering braggarts. Even now I am ready to let you have all you want, provided you no longer let yourself be suckled by the pay-clerk.

CHORUS: He was right who said, "Decide nothing till you have heard both sides," for it seems to me, that 'tis you who now gain the complete victory. My wrath is appeased, I throw away my sticks. Come, comrade, our contemporary, let yourself be gained over by his words; come, do not be too obstinate or too perverse. Why

---

78. We have already seen that when accepting his son's challenge he swore to fall upon his sword if defeated in the debate.
79. Pericles had first introduced the custom of sending poor citizens, among whom the land was divided, into the conquered countries. The island of Aegina had been mainly divided in this way among Athenian colonists.
80. The choenix was a measure corresponding to our quart.

have I no relation, no ally to speak to me like this? Do not doubt it, 'tis a god who is now protecting you and loading you with his benefits. Accept them.

BDELYCLEON: I will feed him, I will give him everything that is suitable for an old man, oatmeal gruel, a cloak, soft furs and a maid to rub his loins and play with his tool. But he is silent and utters not a word; 'tis a bad sign.

CHORUS: He has thought the thing over and has recognized his folly; he reproaches himself for not having followed your advice always. But there he is, converted by your words, and has no doubt become wiser to alter his ways in future and to believe in none but you.

PHILOCLEON: Alas! alas!

BDELYCLEON: Now why this lamentation?

PHILOCLEON: A truce to your promises! What I love is down there, 'tis down there I want to be, there, where the herald cries, "Who has not yet voted? Let him rise!" I want to be the last to leave the urn of all. Oh, my soul, my soul! where art thou? come! oh! dark shadows, make way for me![81] By Heracles, may I reach the Court in time to convict Cleon of theft.

BDELYCLEON: Come, father, in the name of the gods, believe me!

PHILOCLEON: Believe you! Ask me anything, anything, except one.

BDELYCLEON: What is it? Let us hear.

PHILOCLEON: Not to judge any more! Before I consent, I shall have appeared before Pluto.

BDELYCLEON: Very well then, since you find so much pleasure in it, go down there no more, but stay here and deal out justice to your slaves.

PHILOCLEON: But what is there to judge? Are you mad?

BDELYCLEON: Everything as in a tribunal. If a servant opens a door secretly, you inflict upon him a simple fine; 'tis what you have repeatedly done down there. Everything can be arranged to suit you. If it is warm in the morning, you can judge in the sunlight; if it is snowing, then seated at your fire; if it rains, you go indoors; and if you only rise at noon, there will be no Thesmothetes[82] to exclude you from the precincts.

---

81. A verse borrowed from Euripides' 'Bellerophon.'

82. I.e. a legislator. The name given in Athens to the last six of the nine Archons, because it was their special duty to see the laws respected.

PHILOCLEON: The notion pleases me.

BDELYCLEON: Moreover, if a pleader is long-winded, you will not be fasting and chafing and seeking vengeance on the accused.

PHILOCLEON: But could I judge as well with my mouth full?

BDELYCLEON: Much better. Is it not said, that the dicasts, when deceived by lying witnesses, have need to ruminate well in order to arrive at the truth?

PHILOCLEON: Well said, but you have not told me yet who will pay salary.

BDELYCLEON: I will.

PHILOCLEON: So much the better; in this way I shall be paid by myself. Because that cursed jester, Lysistratus,[83] played me an infamous trick the other day. He received a drachma for the two of us[84] and went on the fish-market to get it changed and then brought me back three mullet scales. I took them for obols and crammed them into my mouth;[85] but the smell choked me and I quickly spat them out. So I dragged him before the Court.

BDELYCLEON: And what did he say to that?

PHILOCLEON: Well, he pretended I had the stomach of a cock. "You have soon digested the money," he said with a laugh.

BDELYCLEON: You see, that is yet another advantage.

PHILOCLEON: And no small one either. Come, do as you will.

BDELYCLEON: Wait! I will bring everything here.

PHILOCLEON: You see, the oracles are coming true; I have heard it foretold, that one day the Athenians would dispense justice in their own houses, that each citizen would have himself a little tribunal constructed in his porch similar to the altars of Hecaté,[86] and that there would be such before every door.

BDELYCLEON: Hold! what do you say? I have brought you everything needful and much more into the bargain. See, here is an *article*, should you want to piss; it shall be hung beside you on a nail.

PHILOCLEON: Good idea! Right useful at my age. You have found the true preventive of bladder troubles.

---

83. Mentioned both in 'The Acharnians' and 'The Knights.'

84. The drachma was worth six obols, or twice the pay of a heliast.

85. We have already seen that the Athenians sometimes kept their small money in their mouth.

86. Which were placed in the courts; dogs were sacrificed on them.

BDELYCLEON: Here is fire, and near to it are lentils, should you want to take a snack.

PHILOCLEON: 'Tis admirably arranged. For thus, even when feverish, I shall nevertheless receive my pay; and besides, I could eat my lentils without quitting my seat. But why this cock?

BDELYCLEON: So that, should you doze during some pleading, he may awaken you by crowing up there.

PHILOCLEON: I want only for one thing more; all the rest is as good as can be.

BDELYCLEON: What is that?

PHILOCLEON: If only they could bring me an image of the hero Lycus.[87]

BDELYCLEON: Here it is! Why, you might think it was the god himself!

PHILOCLEON: Oh! hero, my master! how repulsive you are to look at! 'Tis an exact portrait of Cleonymus!

SOSIAS: That is why, hero though he be, he has no weapon.

BDELYCLEON: The sooner you take your seat, the sooner I shall call a case.

PHILOCLEON: Call it, for I have been seated ever so long.

BDELYCLEON: Let us see. What case shall we bring up first? Is there a slave who has done something wrong? Ah! you Thracian there, who burnt the stew-pot t'other day.

PHILOCLEON: Hold, hold! Here is a fine state of things! you had almost made me judge without a bar,[88] and that is the thing of all others most sacred among us.

BDELYCLEON: By Zeus! I had forgotten it, but I will run indoors and bring you one immediately. What is this after all, though, but mere force of habit!

XANTHIAS: Plague take the brute! Can anyone keep such a dog?

BDELYCLEON: Hullo! what's the matter?

XANTHIAS: Why, 'tis Labes,[89] who has just rushed into the kitchen and has seized a whole Sicilian cheese and gobbled it up.

BDELYCLEON: Good! this will be the first offence I shall make my father try. (*To Xanthias*) Come along and lay your accusation.

---

87. As already stated, the statue of Lycus stood close to the place where the tribunals sat.
88. The barrier in the Heliaea, which separated the heliasts from the public.
89. The whole of this comic trial of the dog Labes is an allusion to the general Laches, already mentioned, who had failed in Sicily. He was accused of taking bribes of money from the Sicilians.

XANTHIAS: No, not I; the other dog vows he will be accuser, if the matter is set down for trial.

BDELYCLEON: Well then, bring them both along.

XANTHIAS: I am coming.

PHILOCLEON: What is this?

BDELYCLEON: 'Tis the pig-trough[90] of the swine dedicated to Hestia.

PHILOCLEON: But it's sacrilege to bring it here.

BDELYCLEON: No, no, by addressing Hestia first,[91] I might, thanks to her, crush an adversary.

PHILOCLEON: Put an end to delay by calling up the case. My verdict is already settled.

BDELYCLEON: Wait! I must yet bring out the tablets[92] and the scrolls.[93]

PHILOCLEON: Oh! I am boiling, I am dying with impatience at your delays. I could have traced the sentence in the dust.

BDELYCLEON: There you are.

PHILOCLEON: Then call the case.

BDELYCLEON: I am here.

PHILOCLEON: Firstly, who is this?

BDELYCLEON: Ah! my god! why, this is unbearable! I have forgotten the urns.

PHILOCLEON: Well now! where are you off to?

BDELYCLEON: To look for the urns.

PHILOCLEON: Unnecessary, I shall use these vases.[94]

BDELYCLEON: Very well, then we have all we need, except the clepsydra.

PHILOCLEON: Well then! and this? what is it if not a clepsydra?[95]

BDELYCLEON: True again! 'Tis calling things by their right name! Let fire be brought quickly from the house with myrtle boughs and incense, and let us invoke the gods before opening the sitting.

CHORUS: Offer them libations and your vows and we will thank them that a noble agreement has put an end to your bickerings and strife.

---

90. To serve for a bar.

91. This was a customary formula, (Greek: aph' Estias archou), "begin from Hestia," first adore Vesta, the god of the family hearth. In similar fashion, the Romans said, *ab Jove principium*.

92. For conviction and acquittal.

93. On which the sentence was entered.

94. No doubt the stew-pot and the wine-jar.

95. The *article* Bdelycleon had brought.—The clepsydra was a kind of water-clock; the other vessel is compared to it, because of the liquid in it.

BDELYCLEON: And first let there be a sacred silence.

CHORUS: Oh! god of Delphi! oh! Phoebus Apollo! convert into the greatest blessing for us all what is now happening before this house, and cure us of our error, oh, Paean,[96] our helper!

BDELYCLEON: Oh! Powerful god, Apollo Aguieus,[97] who watchest at the door of my entrance hall, accept this fresh sacrifice; I offer it that you may deign to soften my father's excessive severity; he is as hard as iron, his heart is like sour wine; do thou pour into it a little honey. Let him become gentle like other men, let him take more interest in the accused than in the accusers, may he allow himself to be softened by entreaties; calm his acrid humour and deprive his irritable mind of all sting.

CHORUS: We unite our vows and chants to those of this new magistrate.[98] His words have won our favour and we are convinced that he loves the people more than any of the young men of the present day.

BDELYCLEON: If there be any judge near at hand, let him enter; once the proceedings have opened, we shall admit him no more.[99]

PHILOCLEON: Who is the defendant? Ha! what a sentence he will get!

XANTHIAS (*Prosecuting Council*): Listen to the indictment. A dog of Cydathenea doth hereby charge Labes of Aexonia with having devoured a Sicilian cheese by himself without accomplices. Penalty demanded, a collar of fig-tree wood.[100]

PHILOCLEON: Nay, a dog's death, if convicted.

BDELYCLEON: This is Labes, the defendant.

PHILOCLEON: Oh! what a wretched brute! how entirely he looks the rogue! He thinks to deceive me by keeping his jaws closed. Where is the plaintiff, the dog of Cydathenea?

DOG: Bow wow! bow wow!

BDELYCLEON: Here he is.

PHILOCLEON: Why, 'tis a second Labes, a great barker and a licker of dishes.

---

96. A title of Apollo, worshipped as the god of healing.
97. A title of Apollo, because of the sacrifices, which the Athenians offered him in the streets, from (Greek: aguia), a street.
98. Bdelycleon.
99. The formula used by the president before declaring the sitting of the Court opened.
100. That is, by way of fine.

SOSIAS (*Herald*): Silence! Keep your seats! (*To Xanthias*) And you, up on your feet and accuse him.

PHILOCLEON: Go on, and I will help myself and eat these lentils.

XANTHIAS: Men of the jury, listen to this indictment I have drawn up. He has committed the blackest of crimes, both against me and the seamen.[101] He sought refuge in a dark corner to glutton on a big Sicilian cheese, with which he sated his hunger.

PHILOCLEON: Why, the crime is clear; the foul brute this very moment belched forth a horrible odour of cheese right under my nose.

XANTHIAS: And he refused to share with me. And yet can anyone style himself your benefactor, when he does not cast a morsel to your poor dog?

PHILOCLEON: Then he has not shared?

XANTHIAS: Not with me, his comrade.

PHILOCLEON: Then his madness is as hot as my lentils.

BDELYCLEON: In the name of the gods, father! No hurried verdict without hearing the other side!

PHILOCLEON: But the evidence is plain; the fact speaks for itself.

XANTHIAS: Then beware of acquitting the most selfish of canine gluttons, who has devoured the whole cheese, rind and all, prowling round the platter.

PHILOCLEON: There is not even enough left for me to fill up the chinks in my pitcher.

XANTHIAS: Besides, you *must* punish him, because the same house cannot keep two thieves. Let me not have barked in vain, else I shall never bark again.

PHILOCLEON: Oh! the black deeds he has just denounced! What a shameless thief! Say, cock, is not that your opinion too? Ha, ha! He thinks as I do. Here, Thesmothetes![102] where are you? Hand me the vessel.

SOSIAS (*Thesmothetes*): Take it yourself. I go to call the witnesses; these are a plate, a pestle, a cheese knife, a brazier, a stew-pot and other half-burnt utensils. (*To Philocleon*) But you have not finished? you are piddling away still! Have done and be seated.

---

101. A reference to the peculations Laches was supposed to have practised in keeping back part of the pay of the Athenian sailors engaged in the Sicilian Expedition.
102. The (Greek: Thesmothetai) at Athens were the six junior Archons, who judged cases assigned to no special Court, presided at the allotment of magistrates, etc.

PHILOCLEON: Ha, ha! I reckon I know somebody who will shit himself with fright today.

BDELYCLEON: Will you never cease showing yourself hard and intractable, and especially to the accused? You tear them to pieces tooth and nail.

PHILOCLEON: Come forward and defend yourself. What means this silence? Answer.

SOSIAS: No doubt he has nothing to say.

BDELYCLEON: Not so, but I think he has got what happened once to Thucydides, when accused;[103] his jaws suddenly set fast. Get away! I will undertake your defence.—Gentlemen of the jury, 'tis a difficult thing to speak for a dog who has been calumniated, but nevertheless I will try. 'Tis a good dog, and he chivies the wolves finely.

PHILOCLEON: He! that thief and conspirator!

BDELYCLEON: But 'tis the best of all our dogs; he is capable of guarding a whole flock.

PHILOCLEON: And what good is that, if he eats the cheese?

BDELYCLEON: What? he fights for you, he guards your door; 'tis an excellent dog in every respect. Forgive him his larceny; he is wretchedly ignorant, he cannot play the lyre.

PHILOCLEON: I wish he did not know how to write either; then the rascal would not have drawn up his pleadings.

BDELYCLEON: Witnesses, I pray you, listen. Come forward, grafting-knife, and speak up; answer me clearly. You were paymaster at the time. Did you grate out to the soldiers what was given you?—He says he did so.

PHILOCLEON: But, by Zeus! he lies.

BDELYCLEON: Oh! have patience. Take pity on the unfortunate. Labes feeds only on fish-bones and fishes' heads and has not an instant of peace. The other is good only to guard the house; he never moves from here, but demands his share of all that is brought in and bites those who refuse.

PHILOCLEON: Oh! Heaven! have I fallen ill? I feel my anger cooling! Woe to me! I am softening!

---

103. Thucydides, son of Milesias, when accused by Pericles, could not say a word in his own defence. One would have said his tongue was paralysed. He was banished.—He must not be confounded with Thucydides the historian, whose exile took place after the production of 'The Wasps.'

BDELYCLEON: Have pity, father, pity, I adjure you; you would not have him dead. Where are his puppies? Come, poor little beasties, yap, up on your haunches, beg and whine!

PHILOCLEON: Descend, descend, descend, descend![104]

BDELYCLEON: I will descend, although that word, "descend," has too often raised false hope. None the less, I will descend.

PHILOCLEON: Plague seize it! Have I then done wrong to eat! What! I to be crying! Ah! I certainly should not be weeping, if I were not blown out with lentils.

BDELYCLEON: Then he is acquitted?

PHILOCLEON: I did not say so.

BDELYCLEON: Ah! my dear father, be good! be humane! Take this voting pebble and rush with your eyes closed to that second urn[105] and, father, acquit him.

PHILOCLEON: No, I know no more how to acquit than to play the lyre.

BDELYCLEON: Come quickly, I will show you the way.

PHILOCLEON: Is this the first urn?

BDELYCLEON: Yes.

PHILOCLEON: Then I have voted.

BDELYCLEON (*aside*): I have fooled him and he has acquitted in spite of himself.

PHILOCLEON: Come, I will turn out the urns. What is the result?

BDELYCLEON: We shall see.—Labes, you stand acquitted.—Eh! father, what's the matter, what is it?

PHILOCLEON: Ah me! ah me! water! water!

BDELYCLEON: Pull yourself together, sir!

PHILOCLEON: Tell me! Is he really acquitted?

BDELYCLEON: Yes, certainly.

PHILOCLEON: Then it's all over with me!

BDELYCLEON: Courage, dear father, don't let this afflict you so terribly.

PHILOCLEON: And so I have charged my conscience with the acquittal of an accused being! What will become of me? Sacred gods! forgive me. I did it despite myself; it is not in my character.

BDELYCLEON: Do not vex yourself, father; I will feed you well, will take you everywhere to eat and drink with me; you shall go to

---

104. When the judges were touched by the pleading of the orator and were decided on acquittal, they said to the defending advocate, "*Cease speaking, descend from the rostrum.*"
105. There were two urns, one called that of Conviction, the other of Acquittal.

every feast; henceforth your life shall be nothing but pleasure, and Hyperbolus shall no longer have you for a tool. But come, let us go in.

PHILOCLEON: So be it; if you will, let us go in.

CHORUS (*Parabasis*): Go where it pleases you and may your happiness be great. You meanwhile, oh! countless myriads, listen to the sound counsels I am going to give you and take care they are not lost upon you. 'Twould be the fate of vulgar spectators, not that of such an audience. Hence, people, lend me your ear, if you love frank speaking. The poet has a reproach to make against his audience; he says you have ill-treated him in return for the many services he has rendered you. At first he kept himself in the background and lent help secretly to other poets,[106] and like the prophetic Genius, who hid himself in the belly of Eurycles,[107] slipped within the spirit of another and whispered to him many a comic hit. Later he ran the risks of the theatre on his own account, with his face uncovered, and dared to guide his Muse unaided. Though overladen with success and honours more than any of your poets, indeed despite all his glory, he does not yet believe he has attained his goal; his heart is not swollen with pride and he does not seek to seduce the young folk in the wrestling school.[108] If any lover runs up to him to complain because he is furious at seeing the object of his passion derided on the stage, he takes no heed of such reproaches, for he is only inspired with honest motives and his Muse is no go-between. From the very outset of his dramatic career he has disdained to assail those who were men, but with a courage worthy of Heracles himself he attacked the most formidable monsters, and at the beginning went straight for that beast[109] with the sharp teeth, with the terrible eyes that flashed lambent fire like those of Cynna,[110] surrounded by a hundred lewd flatterers who spittle-licked him to

---

106. Meaning, that he had at first produced pieces under the name of other poets, such as Callistrates and Phidonides.

107. Eurycles, an Athenian diviner, surnamed the Engastromythes ([Greek: muthos], speech, [Greek: en gastri], in the belly), because he was believed to be inspired by a genius within him.—The same name was also given to the priestesses of Apollo, who spoke their oracles without moving their lips.

108. Some poets misused their renown as a means of seduction among young men.

109. Cleon, whom he attacked in 'The Knights,' the first Comedy that Aristophanes had produced in his own name.

110. Cynna, like Salabaccha, was a shameless courtesan of the day.

his heart's content; it had a voice like a roaring torrent, the stench of a seal, a foul Lamia's testicles,[111] and the rump of a camel. Our poet did not tremble at the sight of this horrible monster, nor did he dream of gaining him over; and again this very day he is fighting for your good. Last year besides, he attacked those pale, shivering and feverish beings[112] who strangled your fathers in the dark, throttled your grandfathers,[113] and who, lying in the beds of the most inoffensive, piled up against them lawsuits, summonses and witnesses to such an extent, that many of them flew in terror to the Polemarch for refuge.[114] Such is the champion you have found to purify your country of all its evil, and last year you betrayed him,[115] when he sowed the most novel ideas, which, however, did not strike root, because you did not understand their value; notwithstanding this, he swears by Bacchus, the while offering him libations, that none ever heard better comic verses. 'Tis a disgrace to you not to have caught their drift at once; as for the poet, he is none the less appreciated by the enlightened judges. He shivered his oars in rushing boldly forward to board his foe.[116] But in future, my dear fellow-citizens, love and honour more those of your poets who seek to imagine and express some new thought. Make their ideas your own, keep them in your caskets like sweet-scented fruit.[117] If you do, your clothing will emit an odour of wisdom the whole year through.

Formerly we were untiring, especially in *other* exercises,[118] but 'tis over now; our brow is crowned with hair whiter than the swan. We must, however, rekindle a youthful ardour in these remnants of

---

111. The lamiae were mysterious monsters, to whom the ancients ascribed the most varied forms. They were depicted most frequently with the face and bosom of a woman and the body of a serpent. Here Aristophanes endows them with organs of virility. It was said that the blood of young men had a special attraction for them. These lines, abusive of Cleon, occur again in the 'Peace,' ll. 738-42.
112. Socrates and the sophists, with whom the poet confounds him in his attacks.
113. He likens them to vampires.
114. The third Archon, whose duty was the protection of strangers. All cases involving the rights of citizenship were tried before him. These were a frequent cause of lawsuit at Athens.
115. 'The Clouds' had not been well received.
116. Aristophanes lets it be understood that the refusal to crown him arose from the fact that he had been too bold in his attack.
117. To perfume their caskets, etc., the Ancients placed scented fruit, especially oranges, in them.
118. The pastimes of love.

what was, and for myself, I prefer my old age to the curly hair and the finery of all these lewd striplings.

Should any among you spectators look upon me with wonder, because of this wasp waist, or not know the meaning of this sting, I will soon dispel his ignorance. We, who wear this appendage, are the true Attic men, who alone are noble and native to the soil, the bravest of all people. 'Tis we who, weapon in hand, have done so much for the country, when the Barbarian shed torrents of fire and smoke over our city in his relentless desire to seize our nests by force. At once we ran up, armed with lance and buckler, and, drunk with the bitter wine of anger, we gave them battle, man standing to man and rage distorting our lips.[119] A hail of arrows hid the sky. However, by the help of the gods, we drove off the foe towards evening. Before the battle an owl had flown over our army.[120] Then we pursued them with our lance point in their loins as one hunts the tunny-fish; they fled and we stung them in the jaw and in the eyes, so that even now the barbarians tell each other that there is nothing in the world more to be feared than the Attic wasp.

Oh! at that time I was terrible, I feared nothing; forth on my galleys I went in search of my foe and subjected him.[121] Then we never thought of rounding fine phrases, we never dreamt of calumny; 'twas who should prove the strongest rower. And thus we took many a town from the Medes,[122] and 'tis to us that Athens owes the tributes that our young men thieve to-day.

Look well at us, and you will see that we have all the character and habits of the wasp. Firstly, if roused, no beings are more irascible, more relentless than we are. In all other things, too, we act like wasps. We collect in swarms, in a kind of nests,[123] and some go a-judging with the Archon,[124] some with the Eleven,[125]

---

119. At Marathon, where the Athenians defeated the Persian invaders, 490 B.C. The battle-field is a plain on the north-east coast of Attica, about twenty-seven miles from Athens.
120. A favourable omen, of course. The owl was the bird of Athené.
121. An allusion to Cimon's naval victories.
122. The Cyclades islands and many towns on the coast of Asia Minor.
123. The tribunals.
124. The six last Archons presided over the civil courts and were styled Thesmothetae (see above).
125. Magistrates, who had charge of criminal cases.

others at the Odeon;[126] there are yet others, who hardly move at all, like the grubs in the cells, but remain glued to the walls[127] and bent double to the ground. We also pay full attention to the discovery of all sorts of means of existing and sting the first who comes, so as to live at his expense. Finally, we have among us drones,[128] who have no sting and who, without giving themselves the least trouble, seize on our revenues as they flow past them and devour them. 'Tis this that grieves us most of all, to see men who have never served or held either lance or oar in defence of their country, enriching themselves at our expense without ever raising a blister on their hands. In short, I give it as my deliberate opinion that in future every citizen not possessed of a sting shall not receive the triobolus.

PHILOCLEON: As long as I live, I will never give up this cloak; 'tis the one I wore in that battle[129] when Boreas delivered us from such fierce attacks,

BDELYCLEON: You do not know what is good for you.

PHILOCLEON: Ah! I know not how to use fine clothing! T'other day, when cramming myself with fried fish, I dropped so many grease spots that I had to pay three obols to the cleaner.

BDELYCLEON: At least have a try, since you have once for all handed the care for your well-being over to me.

PHILOCLEON: Very well then! what must I do?

BDELYCLEON: Take off your cloak, and put on this tunic in its stead.

PHILOCLEON: 'Twas well worth while to beget and bring up children, so that this one should now wish to choke me.

BDELYCLEON: Come, take this tunic and put it on without so much talk.

PHILOCLEON: Great gods! what sort of a cursed garment is this?

BDELYCLEON: Some call it a pelisse, others a Persian cloak.[130]

PHILOCLEON: Ah! I thought it was a wraprascal like those made at Thymaetia.[131]

---

126. Built by Pericles. Musical contests were held there. Here also took place distributions of flour, and the presence of the magistrates was no doubt necessary to decide on the spot any disputes that might arise regarding this.

127. This, says the Scholiast, refers to magistrates appointed for the upkeep of the walls. They were selected by ballot from amongst the general body of Heliasts.

128. The demagogues and their flatterers.

129. The battle of Artemisium on the Euboean coast; a terrible storm arose and almost destroyed the barbarian fleet, while sparing that of the Athenians.

130. A mantle trimmed with fur.

131. A rural deme of Attica. Rough coats were made there, formed of skins sewn together.

BDELYCLEON: Pray, how should you know such garments? 'Tis only at Sardis you could have seen them, and you have never been there.

PHILOCLEON: I' faith, no! but it seems to me exactly like the mantle Morychus[132] sports.

BDELYCLEON: Not at all; I tell you they are woven at Ecbatana.

PHILOCLEON: What! are there woollen ox-guts[133] then at Ecbatana?

BDELYCLEON: Whatever are you talking about? These are woven by the Barbarians at great cost. I am certain this pelisse has consumed more than a talent of wool.[134]

PHILOCLEON: It should be called wool-waster then instead of pelisse.

BDELYCLEON: Come, father, just hold still for a moment and put it on.

PHILOCLEON: Oh! horrors! what a waft of heat the hussy wafts up my nose!

BDELYCLEON: Will you have done with this fooling?

PHILOCLEON: No, by Zeus! if need be, I prefer you should put me in the oven.

BDELYCLEON: Come! I will put it round you. There!

PHILOCLEON: At all events, bring out a crook.

BDELYCLEON: Why, whatever for?

PHILOCLEON: To drag me out of it before I am quite melted.

BDELYCLEON: Now take off those wretched clogs and put on these nice Laconian slippers.

PHILOCLEON: I put on odious slippers made by our foes! Never!

BDELYCLEON: Come! put your foot in and push hard. Quick!

PHILOCLEON: 'Tis ill done of you. You want me to put my foot on Laconian ground.

BDELYCLEON: Now the other.

PHILOCLEON: Ah! no, not that one; one of its toes holds the Laconians in horror.

BDELYCLEON: Positively you must.

PHILOCLEON: Alas! alas! Then I shall have no chilblains in my old age.[135]

BDELYCLEON: Now, hurry up and get them on; and now imitate the easy effeminate gait of the rich. See, like this.

---

132. An effeminate poet.

133. He compares the thick, shaggy stuff of the pelisse to the intestines of a bullock, which have a sort of crimped and curled look.

134. An Attic talent was equal to about fifty-seven pounds avoirdupois.

135. He grumbles over his own good fortune, as old men will.

PHILOCLEON: There! . . . Look at my get-up and tell me which rich man I most resemble in my walk.

BDELYCLEON: Why, you look like a garlic plaster on a boil.

PHILOCLEON: Ah! I am longing to swagger and sway my rump about.

BDELYCLEON: Now, will you know how to talk gravely with well-informed men of good class?

PHILOCLEON: Undoubtedly.

BDELYCLEON: What will you say to them?

PHILOCLEON: Oh, lots of things. First of all I shall say, that Lamia,[136] seeing herself caught, let fly a fart; then, that Cardopion and her mother. . .

BDELYCLEON: Come, no fabulous tales, pray! talk of realities, of domestic facts, as is usually done.

PHILOCLEON: Ah! I know something that is indeed most domestic. Once upon a time there was a rat and a cat. . .

BDELYCLEON: "Oh, you ignorant fool," as Theagenes said[137] to the scavenger in a rage. Are you going to talk of cats and rats among high-class people?

PHILOCLEON: Then what should I talk about?

BDELYCLEON: Tell some dignified story. Relate how you were sent on a solemn mission with Androcles and Clisthenes.

PHILOCLEON: On a mission! never in my life, except once to Paros,[138] a job which brought me in two obols a day.

BDELYCLEON: At least say, that you have just seen Ephudion making good play in the pancratium[139] with Ascondas and, that despite his age and his white hair, he is still robust in loin and arm and flank and that his chest is a very breastplate.

PHILOCLEON: Stop! stop! what nonsense! Who ever contested at the pancratium with a breast-plate on?

---

136. Lamia, the daughter of Belus and Libya, was loved by Zeus. Heré deprived her of her beauty and instilled her with a passion for blood; she is said to have plucked babes from their mothers' breast to devour them. Weary of her crimes, the gods turned her into a beast of prey.

137. Theagenes, of the Acharnian deme, was afflicted with a weakness which caused him to be constantly letting off loud, stinking farts, even in public—the cause of many gibes on the part of the Comic poets and his contemporaries.

138. He had been sent on a mission as an armed ambassador, i.e. as a common soldier, whose pay was two obols.

139. The (Greek: pankration) was a combined exercise, including both wrestling and boxing.

BDELYCLEON: That is how well-behaved folk like to talk. But another thing. When at wine, it would be fitting to relate some good story of your youthful days. What is your most brilliant feat?

PHILOCLEON: My best feat? Ah! 'twas when I stole Ergasion's vine-props.

BDELYCLEON: You and your vine-props! you'll be the death of me! Tell of one of your boar-hunts or of when you coursed the hare. Talk about some torch-race you were in; tell of some deed of daring.

PHILOCLEON: Ah! my most daring deed was when, quite a young man still, I prosecuted Phayllus, the runner, for defamation, and he was condemned by a majority of two votes.

BDELYCLEON: Enough of that! Now recline there, and practise the bearing that is fitting at table in society.

PHILOCLEON: How must I recline? Tell me quick!

BDELYCLEON: In an elegant style.

PHILOCLEON: Like this?

BDELYCLEON: Not at all.

PHILOCLEON: How then?

BDELYCLEON: Spread your knees on the tapestries and give your body the most easy curves, like those taught in the gymnasium. Then praise some bronze vase, survey the ceiling, admire the awning stretched over the court. Water is poured over our hands; the tables are spread; we sup and, after ablution, we now offer libations to the gods.

PHILOCLEON: But, by Zeus! this supper is but a dream, it appears!

BDELYCLEON: The flute-player has finished the prelude. The guests are Theorus, Aeschines, Phanus, Cleon, Acestor;[140] and beside this last, I don't know who else. You are with them. Shall you know exactly how to take up the songs that are started?

PHILOCLEON: Better than any born mountaineer of Attica.

BDELYCLEON: That we shall see. Suppose me to be Cleon. I am the first to begin the song of Harmodius, and you take it up: "There never was yet seen in Athens. . .

PHILOCLEON: . . . such a rogue or such a thief."[141]

---

140. All these names have been already mentioned.
141. Each time Philocleon takes up the song with words that are a satire on the guest who begins the strain.

BDELYCLEON: Why, you wretched man, 'twill be the end of you if you sing that. He will vow your ruin, your destruction, to chase you out of the country.

PHILOCLEON: Well! then I shall answer his threats with another song: "With your madness for supreme power, you will end by overthrowing the city, which even now totters towards ruin."

BDELYCLEON: And when Theorus, prone at Cleon's feet, takes his hand and sings, "Like Admetus, love those who are brave,"[142] what reply will you make him?

PHILOCLEON: I shall sing, "I know not how to play the fox, nor call myself the friend of both parties."

BDELYCLEON: Then comes the turn of Aeschines, the son of Sellus, and a well-trained and clever musician, who will sing, "Good things and riches for Clitagoras and me and eke for the Thessalians!"

PHILOCLEON: "The two of us have squandered a deal between us."

BDELYCLEON: At this game you seem at home. But come, we will go and dine with Philoctemon.—Slave! slave! place our dinner in a basket, and let us go for a good long drinking bout.

PHILOCLEON: By no means, it is too dangerous; for after drinking, one breaks in doors, one comes to blows, one batters everything. Anon, when the wine is slept off, one is forced to pay.

BDELYCLEON: Not if you are with decent people. Either they undertake to appease the offended person or, better still, you say something witty, you tell some comic story, perhaps one of those you have yourself heard at table, either in Aesop's style or in that of Sybaris; all laugh and the trouble is ended.

PHILOCLEON: Faith! 'tis worth while learning many stories then, if you are thus not punished for the ill you do. But come, no more delay!

CHORUS: More than once have I given proof of cunning and never of stupidity, but how much more clever is Amynias, the son of Sellus and of the race of forelock-wearers; him we saw one day coming to dine with Leogaras,[143] bringing as his share one apple and a pomegranate, and bear in mind he was as hungry as Antiphon.[144]

---

142. King Admetus (Euripides' 'Alcestis') had suffered his devoted wife Alcestis to die to save his life when ill to death. Heracles, however, to repay former benefits received, descended into Hades and rescued Alcestis from Pluto's clutches.

143. A famous epicure, the Lucullus of Athens (see 'The Acharnians').

144. A parasite renowned for his gluttony.

He went on an embassy to Pharsalus,[145] and there he lived solely among the Thessalian mercenaries;[146] indeed, is he not the vilest of mercenaries himself?

Oh! blessed, oh! fortunate Automenes, how enviable is your fortune! You have three sons, the most industrious in the world; one is the friend of all, a very able man, the first among the lyre-players, the favourite of the Graces. The second is an actor, and his talent is beyond all praise. As for Ariphrades, he is by far the most gifted; his father would swear to me, that without any master whatever and solely through the spontaneous effort of his happy nature, he taught himself the use of his tongue in the lewd places[147] where he spends the whole of his time.

Some have said that I and Cleon were reconciled. This is the truth of the matter: Cleon was harassing me, persecuting and belabouring me in every way; and, when I was being fleeced, the public laughed at seeing me uttering such loud cries; not that they cared about me, but simply curious to know whether, when trodden down by my enemy, I would not hurl at him some taunt. Noticing this, I have played the wheedler a bit; but now, look! the prop is deceiving the vine![148]

XANTHIAS: Oh! tortoises! happy to have so hard a skin, thrice happy to carry this roof that protects your backs! Oh! creatures full of sense! what a happy thought to cover your bodies with this shell, which shields it from blows! As for me, I can no longer move; the stick has so belaboured my body.

CHORUS: Eh, what's the matter, child? for, old as he may be, one has the right to call anyone a child who has let himself be beaten.

XANTHIAS: Alas! my master is really the worst of all plagues. He was the most drunk of all the guests, and yet among them were Hippyllus, Antiphon, Lycon, Lysistratus, Theophrastus and Phrynichus. But he was a hundred times more insolent than any. As soon as he had stuffed himself with a host of good dishes, he began to leap and spring, to laugh and to let wind like a little ass well blown out with barley. Then he set to a-beating me with all his heart, shouting, "Slave! slave!" Lysistratus, as soon as he saw him,

---

145. A town in Thessaly.
146. Because of his poverty.
147. Four lines in 'The Knights' describe the infamous habits of Ariphrades in detail.
148. That is, it ceases to support it; Aristophanes does the same to Cleon.

let fly this comparison at him. "Old fellow," said he, "you resemble one of the scum assuming the airs of a rich man or a stupid ass that has broken loose from its stable." "As for you," bawled the other at the top of his voice, "you are like a grasshopper,[149] whose cloak is worn to the thread, or like Sthenelus[150] after his clothes had been sold." All applauded excepting Theophrastus, who made a grimace as behoved a well-bred man like him. The old man called to him, "Hi! tell me then what you have to be proud of? Not so much mouthing, you, who so well know how to play the buffoon and to lick-spittle the rich!"'Twas thus he insulted each in turn with the grossest of jests, and he reeled off a thousand of the most absurd and ridiculous speeches. At last, when he was thoroughly drunk, he started towards here, striking everyone he met. Hold, here he comes reeling along. I will be off for fear of his blows.

PHILOCLEON:[151] Halt! and let everyone begone, or I shall do an evil turn to some of those who insist on following me. Clear off, rascals, or I shall roast you with this torch!

BDELYCLEON: We shall all make you smart to-morrow for your youthful pranks. We shall come in a body to summon you to justice.

PHILOCLEON: Ho! ho! summon me! what old women's babble! Know that I can no longer bear to hear even the name of suits. Ha! ha! ha! this is what pleases *me*, "Down with the urns!" Won't you begone? Down with the dicasts! away with them, away with them! (*To the flute-girl*) Mount up there, my little gilded cock-chafer; seize hold of this rope's end in your hand.[152] Hold it tight, but have a care; the rope's a bit old and worn, but it loves a nice rubbing still. Do you see how opportunely I got you away from the solicitations of those fellows, who wanted to make you work their tools in your mouth? You therefore owe me this return to gratify mine by masturbating it. But will you pay the debt? Oh! I know well you will not even try; you will play with me, you will laugh heartily at my poor old weapon as you have done at many another man's. And yet, if you would not be a naughty girl, I would redeem you,

149. Referring to Lysistratus' leanness.
150. A tragic actor, whose wardrobe had been sold up, so the story went, by his creditors.
151. He enters, followed closely by the persons he has ill-used, and leading a flute-girl by the hand.
152. Meaning his penis.

when my son is dead, and you should be my concubine, my little cuntling. At present I am not my own master; I am very young and am watched very closely. My dear son never lets me out of his sight; 'tis an unbearable creature, who would quarter a thread and skin a flint; he is afraid I should get lost, for I am his only father. But here he comes running towards us. But be quick, don't stir, hold these torches. I am going to play him a young man's trick, the same as he played me before I was initiated into the mysteries.

BDELYCLEON: Oh! oh! you debauched old dotard! you desire and, meseems, you love pretty baggages; but, by Apollo, it shall not be with impunity!

PHILOCLEON: Ah! you would be very glad to eat a lawsuit in vinegar, you would.

BDELYCLEON: 'Tis a rascally trick to steal the flute-girl away from the other guests.

PHILOCLEON: What flute-girl? Are you distraught, as if you had just returned from Pluto?

BDELYCLEON: By Zeus! But here is the Dardanian wench in person.[153]

PHILOCLEON: Nonsense. This is a torch that I have lit in the public square in honour of the gods.

BDELYCLEON: Is this a torch?

PHILOCLEON: A torch? Certainly. Do you not see it is of several different colours?

BDELYCLEON: And what is that black part in the middle?[154]

PHILOCLEON: 'Tis the pitch running out while it burns.

BDELYCLEON: And there, on the other side, surely that is a girl's bottom?

PHILOCLEON: No. 'Tis a small bit of the torch, that projects.

BDELYCLEON: What do you mean? what bit? Hi! you woman! come here!

PHILOCLEON: Ah! ah! What do you want to do?

BDELYCLEON: To take her from you and lead her away. You are too much worn out and can do nothing.

PHILOCLEON: Hear me! One day, at Olympia, I saw Euphudion boxing bravely against Ascondas;[155] he was already aged, and yet

---

153. Dardanus, a district of Asia Minor, north of the Troad, supplied many flute-girls to the cities of Greece.
154. Pointing to the flute-girl's *motte*.
155. He tells his son the very story the latter had taught him.

with a blow from his fist he knocked down his young opponent. So beware lest I blacken *your* eyes.

BDELYCLEON: By Zeus! you have Olympia at your finger-ends!

A BAKER'S WIFE (*to Bdelycleon*): Come to my help, I beg you, in the name of the gods! This cursed man, when striking out right and left with his torch, knocked over ten loaves worth an obolus apiece, and then, to cap the deal, four others.

BDELYCLEON: Do you see what lawsuits you are drawing upon yourself with your drunkenness? You will have to plead.

PHILOCLEON: Oh, no, no! a little pretty talk and pleasant tales will soon settle the matter and reconcile her with me.

BAKER'S WIFE: Not so, by the goddesses twain! It shall not be said that you have with impunity spoilt the wares of Myrtia,[156] the daughter of Ancylion and Sostraté.

PHILOCLEON: Listen, woman, I wish to tell you a lovely anecdote.

BAKER'S WIFE: Oh! friend, no anecdotes for me, thank you.

PHILOCLEON: One night Aesop was going out to supper. A drunken bitch had the impudence to bark near him. Aesop said to her, "Oh, bitch, bitch! you would do well to sell your wicked tongue and buy some wheat."

BAKER'S WIFE: You make a mock of me! Very well! Be you who you like, I shall summons you before the market inspectors[157] for damage done to my business. Chaerephon[158] here shall be my witness.

PHILOCLEON: But just listen, here's another will perhaps please you better. Lasus and Simonides[159] were contesting against each other for the singing prize. Lasus said, "Damn me if I care."

BAKER'S WIFE: Ah! really, did he now!

PHILOCLEON: As for you, Chaerephon, *can* you be witness to this woman, who looks as pale and tragic as Ino when she throws herself from her rock[160] . . . at the feet of Euripides?

---

156. The name of the baker's wife.
157. Or Agoranomi, who numbered ten at Athens.
158. The disciple of Socrates.
159. Lasus, a musician and dithyrambic poet, born about 500 B.C. in Argolis, was the rival of Simonides and thought himself his superior.
160. Ino, the daughter of Cadmus and Harmonia. Being pursued by her husband, Athamas, whom the Fury Tisiphoné had driven mad, she threw herself into the sea with Melicerta, whereupon they were both changed into sea-goddesses.—This is the subject of one of Euripides' tragedies.

BDELYCLEON: Here, methinks, comes another to summons you; *he* has his witness too. Ah! unhappy indeed we are!

ACCUSER: I summons you, old man, for outrage.

BDELYCLEON: For outrage? Oh! in the name of the gods, do not summons him! I will be answerable for him; name the penalty and I will be more grateful still.

PHILOCLEON: I ask for nothing better than to be reconciled with him; for I admit I struck him and threw stones at him. So, first come here. Will you leave it in my hands to name the indemnity I must pay, if I promise you my friendship as well, or will you fix it yourself?

ACCUSER: Fix it; I like neither lawsuits nor disputes.

PHILOCLEON: A man of Sybaris[161] fell from his chariot and wounded his head most severely; he was a very poor driver. One of his friends came up to him and said, "Every man to his trade." Well then, go you to Pittalus[162] to get mended.

BDELYCLEON: You are incorrigible.

ACCUSER (*to his witness*): At all events, make a note of his reply.

PHILOCLEON: Listen, instead of going off so abruptly. A woman at Sybaris broke a box.

ACCUSER (*to his witness*): I again ask you to witness this.

PHILOCLEON: The box therefore had the fact attested, but the woman said, "Never worry about witnessing the matter, but hurry off to buy a cord to tie it together with; 'twill be the more sensible course."

ACCUSER: Oh! go on with your ribaldry until the Archon calls the case.

BDELYCLEON (*to Philocleon*): No, by Demeter! you stay here no longer! I take you and carry you off.

PHILOCLEON: And what for?

BDELYCLEON: What for? I shall carry you to the house; else there would not be enough witnesses for the accusers.

PHILOCLEON: One day at Delphi, Aesop. . .

BDELYCLEON: I don't care a fig for that.

PHILOCLEON: . . . was accused of having stolen a sacred vase. But he replied, that the horn beetle. . . (*Philocleon goes on with his fable while Bdelycleon is carrying him off the scene by main force*)

---

161. A famous town in Magna Graecia, south coast of Italy.
162. A celebrated physician.—Philocleon means, "Instead of starting an action, go and have yourself cared for; that is better worth your while."

BDELYCLEON: Oh, dear, dear! You drive me crazy with your horn-beetle.

CHORUS: I envy you your happiness, old man. What a contrast to his former frugal habits and his very hard life! Taught now in quite another school, he will know nothing but the pleasures of ease. Perhaps he will jib at it, for indeed 'tis difficult to renounce what has become one's second nature. However, many have done it, and adopting the ideas of others, have changed their use and wont. As for Philocleon's son, I, like all wise and judicious men, cannot sufficiently praise his filial tenderness and his tact. Never have I met a more amiable nature, and I have conceived the greatest fondness for him. How he triumphed on every point in his discussion with his father, when he wanted to bring him back to more worthy and honourable tastes!

XANTHIAS: By Bacchus! 'Tis some Evil Genius has brought this unbearable disorder into our house. The old man, full up with wine and excited by the sound of the flute, is so delighted, so enraptured, that he spends the night executing the old dances that Thespis first produced on the stage,[163] and just now he offered to prove to the modern tragedians, by disputing with them for the dancing prize, that they are nothing but a lot of old dotards.

PHILOCLEON: "Who loiters at the door of the vestibule?"[164]

XANTHIAS: Here comes our pest, our plague!

PHILOCLEON: Let down the barriers.[165] The dance is now to begin.

XANTHIAS: Or rather the madness.

PHILOCLEON: Impetuous movement already twists and racks my sides. How my nostrils wheeze! how my back cracks!

XANTHIAS: Go and fill yourself with hellebore.[166]

PHILOCLEON: Phrynichus is as bold as a cock and terrifies his rivals.

XANTHIAS: Oh! oh! have a care he does not kick you.

PHILOCLEON: His leg kicks out sky-high, and his arse gapes open.[167]

XANTHIAS: Do have a care.

PHILOCLEON: Look how easily my leg-joints move.

---

163. The dances that Thespis, the originator of Tragedy, interspersed with the speaking parts of his plays.
164. A verse borrowed from an unknown Tragedy.
165. As was done in the stadia when the races were to be started.
166. The ancients considered it a specific against madness.
167. Phrynichus, like all the ancient tragic writers, mingled many dances with his pieces.

BDELYCLEON: Great gods! What does all this mean? Is it actual, downright madness?

PHILOCLEON: And now I summon and challenge my rivals. If there be a tragic poet who pretends to be a skilful dancer, let him come and contest the matter with me. Is there one? Is there *not* one?

BDELYCLEON: Here comes one, and one only.

PHILOCLEON: Who is the wretch?

BDELYCLEON: 'Tis the younger son of Carcinus.[168]

PHILOCLEON: I will crush him to nothing; in point of keeping time, I will knock him out, for he knows nothing of rhythm.

BDELYCLEON: Ah! ah! here comes his brother too, another tragedian, and another son of Carcinus.

PHILOCLEON: Him I will devour for my dinner.

BDELYCLEON: Oh! ye gods! I see nothing but crabs.[169] Here is yet another son of Carcinus.

PHILOCLEON: What is't comes here? A shrimp or a spider?[170]

BDELYCLEON: 'Tis a crab,[171]—a crabkin, the smallest of its kind; he writes tragedies.

PHILOCLEON: Oh! Carcinus, how proud you should be of your brood! What a crowd of kinglets have come swooping down here!

BDELYCLEON: Come, come, my poor father, you will have to measure yourself against them.

PHILOCLEON: Have pickle prepared for seasoning them, if I am bound to prove the victor.

CHORUS: Let us stand out of the way a little, so that they may twirl at their ease. Come, illustrious children of this inhabitant of the briny, brothers of the shrimps, skip on the sand and the shore of the barren sea; show us the lightning whirls and twirls of your nimble limbs. Glorious offspring of Phrynichus,[172] let fly your kicks, so that the spectators may be overjoyed at seeing your legs so high in air. Twist, twirl, tap your bellies, kick your legs to the sky.

---

168. Tragic poet. His three sons had also written tragedies and were dancers into the bargain.

169. Carcinus, by a mere transposition of the accent ([Greek: karkívos]), means *crab* in Greek; hence the pun.

170. Carcinus' sons were small and thin.

171. The third son of Carcinus.

172. Meaning, the three sons of Carcinus, the dancers, because, as mentioned before, Phrynichus often introduced a chorus of dancers into his Tragedies.

Here comes your famous father, the ruler of the sea,[173] delighted to see his three lecherous kinglets.[174] Go on with your dancing, if it pleases you, but as for us, we shall not join you. Lead us promptly off the stage, for never a Comedy yet was seen where the Chorus finished off with a dance.

FINIS OF "THE WASPS"

---

173. Carcinus himself.
174. The Greek word is (Greek: triorchoi)—possessed of three testicles, of three-testicle power, inordinately lecherous; with the change of a letter ([Greek: triarchoi]) it means 'three rulers,' 'three kinglets.'

PEACE

Introduction

T he 'Peace' was brought out four years after 'The Acharnians' (422 B.C.), when the War had already lasted ten years. The leading motive is the same as in the former play—the intense desire of the less excitable and more moderate-minded citizens for relief from the miseries of war.

Trygaeus, a rustic patriot, finding no help in men, resolves to ascend to heaven to expostulate personally with Zeus for allowing this wretched state of things to continue. With this object he has fed and trained a gigantic dung-beetle, which he mounts, and is carried, like Bellerophon on Pegasus, on an aerial journey. Eventually he reaches Olympus, only to find that the gods have gone elsewhere, and that the heavenly abode is occupied solely by the demon of War, who is busy pounding up the Greek States in a huge mortar. However, his benevolent purpose is not in vain; for learning from Hermes that the goddess Peace has been cast into a pit, where she is kept a fast prisoner, he calls upon the different peoples of Hellas to make a united effort and rescue her, and with their help drags her out and brings her back in triumph to earth. The play concludes with the restoration of the goddess to her ancient honours, the festivities of the rustic population and the nuptials of Trygaeus with Opora (Harvest), handmaiden of Peace, represented as a pretty courtesan.

Such references as there are to Cleon in this play are noteworthy. The great Demagogue was now dead, having fallen in the same action as the rival Spartan general, the renowned Brasidas, before Amphipolis, and whatever Aristophanes says here of his old enemy is conceived in the spirit of 'de mortuis nil nisi bonum.' In one scene Hermes is descanting on the evils which had nearly ruined Athens and declares that 'The Tanner' was the cause of them all. But Trygaeus interrupts him with the words:

> *"Hold—say not so, good master Hermes;*
> *Let the man rest in peace where now he lies.*
> *He is no longer of our world, but yours."*

Here surely we have a trait of magnanimity on the author's part as admirable in its way as the wit and boldness of his former attacks had been in theirs.

Dramatis Personae

Trygaeus.
Two Servants of Trygaeus.
Maidens, Daughters of Trygaeus.
Hermes.
War.
Tumult.
Hierocles, a Soothsayer.
A Sickle-Maker.
A Crest-Maker.
A Trumpet-Maker.
A Helmet-Maker.
A Spear-Maker.
Son of Lamachus.
Son of Cleonymus.
Chorus of Husbandmen.

Scene: *A farmyard, two slaves busy beside a dungheap; afterwards, in Olympus.*

FIRST SERVANT: Quick, quick, bring the dung-beetle his cake.

SECOND SERVANT: Coming, coming.

FIRST SERVANT: Give it to him, and may it kill him!

SECOND SERVANT: May he never eat a better.

FIRST SERVANT: Now give him this other one kneaded up with ass's dung.

SECOND SERVANT: There! I've done that too.

FIRST SERVANT: And where's what you gave him just now; surely he can't have devoured it yet!

SECOND SERVANT: Indeed he has; he snatched it, rolled it between his feet and boiled it.

FIRST SERVANT: Come, hurry up, knead up a lot and knead them stiffly.

SECOND SERVANT: Oh, scavengers, help me in the name of the gods, if you do not wish to see me fall down choked.

FIRST SERVANT: Come, come, another made of the stool of a young scapegrace catamite. 'Twill be to the beetle's taste; he likes it well ground.[1]

SECOND SERVANT: There! I am free at least from suspicion; none will accuse me of tasting what I mix.

FIRST SERVANT: Faugh! come, now another! keep on mixing with all your might.

SECOND SERVANT: I' faith, no. I can stand this awful cesspool stench no longer, so I bring you the whole ill-smelling gear.

FIRST SERVANT: Pitch it down the sewer sooner, and yourself with it.

SECOND SERVANT: Maybe, one of you can tell me where I can buy a stopped-up nose, for there is no work more disgusting than to mix food for a beetle and to carry it to him. A pig or a dog will at least pounce upon our excrement without more ado, but this foul wretch affects the disdainful, the spoilt mistress, and won't eat unless I offer him a cake that has been kneaded for an entire day. . . But let us open the door a bit ajar without his seeing it. Has he done eating? Come, pluck up courage, cram yourself till you burst! The cursed creature! It wallows in its food! It grips it between its claws like a wrestler clutching his opponent, and with head and feet together rolls up its paste like a ropemaker twisting a hawser.

---

1. An obscene allusion, the faeces of catamites being 'well ground' from the treatment they are in the habit of submitting to.

What an indecent, stinking, gluttonous beast! I know not what angry god let this monster loose upon us, but of a certainty it was neither Aphrodité nor the Graces.

FIRST SERVANT: Who was it then?

SECOND SERVANT: No doubt the Thunderer, Zeus.

FIRST SERVANT: But perhaps some spectator, some beardless youth, who thinks himself a sage, will say, "What is this? What does the beetle mean?" And then an Ionian,[2] sitting next him, will add, "I think 'tis an allusion to Cleon, who so shamelessly feeds on filth all by himself."—But now I'm going indoors to fetch the beetle a drink.

SECOND SERVANT: As for me, I will explain the matter to you all, children, youths, grown-ups and old men, aye, even to the decrepit dotards. My master is mad, not as you are, but with another sort of madness, quite a new kind. The livelong day he looks open-mouthed towards heaven and never stops addressing Zeus. "Ah! Zeus," he cries, "what are thy intentions? Lay aside thy besom; do not sweep Greece away!"

TRYGAEUS: Ah! ah! ah!

FIRST SERVANT: Hush, hush! Methinks I hear his voice!

TRYGAEUS: Oh! Zeus, what art thou going to do for our people? Dost thou not see this, that our cities will soon be but empty husks?

FIRST SLAVE: As I told you, that is his form of madness. There you have a sample of his follies. When his trouble first began to seize him, he said to himself, "By what means could I go straight to Zeus?" Then he made himself very slender little ladders and so clambered up towards heaven; but he soon came hurtling down again and broke his head. Yesterday, to our misfortune, he went out and brought us back this thoroughbred, but from where I know not, this great beetle, whose groom he has forced me to become. He himself caresses it as though it were a horse, saying, "Oh! my little Pegasus,[3] my noble aerial steed, may your wings soon bear me straight to Zeus!" But what is my master doing? I must stoop down to look through this hole. Oh! great gods! Here! neighbours, run here quick! here is my master flying off mounted on his beetle as if on horseback.

---

2. 'Peace' was no doubt produced at the festival of the Apaturia, which was kept at the end of October, a period when strangers were numerous in Athens.

3. The winged steed of Perseus—an allusion to a lost tragedy of Euripides, in which Bellerophon was introduced riding on Pegasus.

TRYGAEUS: Gently, gently, go easy, beetle; don't start off so proudly, or trust at first too greatly to your powers; wait till you have sweated, till the beating of your wings shall make your limb joints supple. Above all things, don't let off some foul smell, I adjure you; else I would rather have you stop in the stable altogether.

SECOND SERVANT: Poor master! Is he crazy?

TRYGAEUS: Silence! silence!

SECOND SERVANT (to Trygaeus): But why start up into the air on chance?

TRYGAEUS: 'Tis for the weal of all the Greeks; I am attempting a daring and novel feat.

SECOND SERVANT: But what is your purpose? What useless folly!

TRYGAEUS: No words of ill omen! Give vent to joy and command all men to keep silence, to close down their drains and privies with new tiles and to stop their own vent-holes.[4]

FIRST SERVANT: No, I shall not be silent, unless you tell me where you are going.

TRYGAEUS: Why, where am I likely to be going across the sky, if it be not to visit Zeus?

FIRST SERVANT: For what purpose?

TRYGAEUS: I want to ask him what he reckons to do for all the Greeks.

SECOND SERVANT: And if he doesn't tell you?

TRYGAEUS: I shall pursue him at law as a traitor who sells Greece to the Medes.[5]

SECOND SERVANT: Death seize me, if I let you go.

TRYGAEUS: It is absolutely necessary.

SECOND SERVANT: Alas! alas! dear little girls, your father is deserting you secretly to go to heaven. Ah! poor orphans, entreat him, beseech him.

LITTLE DAUGHTER: Father! father! what is this I hear? Is it true? What! you would leave me, you would vanish into the sky, you would go to the crows?[6] 'Tis impossible! Answer, father, an you love me.

---

4. Fearing that if it caught a whiff from earth to its liking, the beetle might descend from the highest heaven to satisfy itself.

5. The Persians and the Spartans were not then allied as the Scholiast states, since a treaty between them was only concluded in 412 B.C., i.e. eight years after the production of 'Peace'; the great king, however, was trying to derive advantages out of the dissensions in Greece.

6. *Go to the crows*, a proverbial expression equivalent to our *Go to the devil*.

TRYGAEUS: Yes, I am going. You hurt me too sorely, my daughters, when you ask me for bread, calling me your daddy, and there is not the ghost of an obolus in the house; if I succeed and come back, you will have a barley loaf every morning—and a punch in the eye for sauce!

LITTLE DAUGHTER: But how will you make the journey? 'Tis not a ship that will carry you thither.

TRYGAEUS: No, but this winged steed will.

LITTLE DAUGHTER: But what an idea, daddy, to harness a beetle, on which to fly to the gods.

TRYGAEUS: We see from Aesop's fables that they alone can fly to the abode of the Immortals.[7]

LITTLE DAUGHTER: Father, father, 'tis a tale nobody can believe! that such a stinking creature can have gone to the gods.

TRYGAEUS: It went to have vengeance on the eagle and break its eggs.

LITTLE DAUGHTER: Why not saddle Pegasus? you would have a more *tragic*[8] appearance in the eyes of the gods.

TRYGAEUS: Eh! don't you see, little fool, that then twice the food would be wanted? Whereas my beetle devours again as filth what I have eaten myself.

LITTLE DAUGHTER: And if it fell into the watery depths of the sea, could it escape with its wings?

TRYGAEUS (*showing his penis*): I am fitted with a rudder in case of need, and my Naxos beetle will serve me as a boat.[9]

LITTLE DAUGHTER: And what harbour will you put in at?

TRYGAEUS: Why, is there not the harbour of Cantharos at the Piraeus?[10]

LITTLE DAUGHTER: Take care not to knock against anything and so fall off into space; once a cripple, you would be a fit subject for Euripides, who would put you into a tragedy.[11]

---

7. Aesop tells us that the eagle and the beetle were at war; the eagle devoured the beetle's young and the latter got into its nest and tumbled out its eggs. On this the eagle complained to Zeus, who advised it to lay its eggs in his bosom; but the beetle flew up to the abode of Zeus, who, forgetful of the eagle's eggs, at once rose to chase off the objectionable insect. The eggs fell to earth and were smashed to bits.

8. Pegasus is introduced by Euripides both in his 'Andromeda' and his 'Bellerophon.'

9. Boats, called 'beetles,' doubtless because in form they resembled these insects, were built at Naxos.

10. Nature had divided the Piraeus into three basins—Cantharos, Aphrodisium and Zea; (Greek: kántharos) is Greek for a dung-beetle.

11. In allusion to Euripides' fondness for introducing lame heroes in his plays.

TRYGAEUS: I'll see to it. Good-bye! (*To the Athenians*) You, for love of whom I brave these dangers, do ye neither let wind nor go to stool for the space of three days, for, if, while cleaving the air, my steed should scent anything, he would fling me head foremost from the summit of my hopes. Now come, my Pegasus, get a-going with up-pricked ears and make your golden bridle resound gaily. Eh! what are you doing? What are you up to? Do you turn your nose towards the cesspools? Come, pluck up a spirit; rush upwards from the earth, stretch out your speedy wings and make straight for the palace of Zeus; for once give up foraging in your daily food.—Hi! you down there, what are you after now? Oh! my god! 'tis a man emptying his belly in the Piraeus, close to the house where the bad girls are. But is it my death you seek then, my death? Will you not bury that right away and pile a great heap of earth upon it and plant wild thyme therein and pour perfumes on it? If I were to fall from up here and misfortune happened to me, the town of Chios[12] would owe a fine of five talents for my death, all along of your cursed rump. Alas! how frightened I am! oh! I have no heart for jests. Ah! machinist, take great care of me. There is already a wind whirling round my navel; take great care or, from sheer fright, I shall form food for my beetle. . . But I think I am no longer far from the gods; aye, that is the dwelling of Zeus, I perceive. Hullo! Hi! where is the doorkeeper? Will no one open?

The scene changes and heaven is presented.

HERMES: Meseems I can sniff a man. (*He perceives Trygaeus astride his beetle*) Why, what plague is this?

TRYGAEUS: A horse-beetle.

HERMES: Oh! impudent, shameless rascal! oh! scoundrel! triple scoundrel! the greatest scoundrel in the world! how did you come here? Oh! scoundrel of all scoundrels! your name? Reply.

TRYGAEUS: Triple scoundrel.

HERMES: Your country?

TRYGAEUS: Triple scoundrel.

---

12. An allusion to the proverbial nickname applied to the Chians—(Greek: Chios apopat on), "shitting Chian." On account of their notoriously pederastic habits, the inhabitants of this island were known throughout Greece as '*loose-arsed*' Chians, and therefore always on the point of voiding their faeces. There is a further joke, of course, in connection with the hundred and one frivolous pretexts which the Athenians invented for exacting contributions from the maritime allies.

HERMES: Your father?

TRYGAEUS: My father? Triple scoundrel.

HERMES: By the Earth, you shall die, unless you tell me your name.

TRYGAEUS: I am Trygaeus of the Athmonian deme, a good vine-dresser, little addicted to quibbling and not at all an informer.

HERMES: Why do you come?

TRYGAEUS: I come to bring you this meat.

HERMES: Ah! my good friend, did you have a good journey?

TRYGAEUS: Glutton, be off! I no longer seem a triple scoundrel to you. Come, call Zeus.

HERMES: Ah! ah! you are a long way yet from reaching the gods, for they moved yesterday.

TRYGAEUS: To what part of the earth?

HERMES: Eh! of the earth, did you say?

TRYGAEUS: In short, where are they then?

HERMES: Very far, very far, right at the furthest end of the dome of heaven.

TRYGAEUS: But why have they left you all alone here?

HERMES: I am watching what remains of the furniture, the little pots and pans, the bits of chairs and tables, and odd wine-jars.

TRYGAEUS: And why have the gods moved away?

HERMES: Because of their wrath against the Greeks. They have located War in the house they occupied themselves and have given him full power to do with you exactly as he pleases; then they went as high up as ever they could, so as to see no more of your fights and to hear no more of your prayers.

TRYGAEUS: What reason have they for treating us so?

HERMES: Because they have afforded you an opportunity for peace more than once, but you have always preferred war. If the Laconians got the very slightest advantage, they would exclaim, "By the Twin Brethren! the Athenians shall smart for this." If, on the contrary, the latter triumphed and the Laconians came with peace proposals, you would say, "By Demeter, they want to deceive us. No, by Zeus, we will not hear a word; they will always be coming as long as we hold Pylos."[13]

---

13. Masters of Pylos and Sphacteria, the Athenians had brought home the three hundred prisoners taken in the latter place in 425 B.C.; the Spartans had several times sent envoys to offer peace and to demand back both Pylos and the prisoners, but the Athenian pride

ARISTOPHANES

TRYGAEUS: Yes, that is quite the style our folk do talk in.

HERMES: So that I don't know whether you will ever see Peace again.

TRYGAEUS: Why, where has she gone to then?

HERMES: War has cast her into a deep pit.

TRYGAEUS: Where?

HERMES: Down there, at the very bottom. And you see what heaps of stones he has piled over the top, so that you should never pull her out again.

TRYGAEUS: Tell me, what is War preparing against us?

HERMES: All I know is that last evening he brought along a huge mortar.

TRYGAEUS: And what is he going to do with his mortar?

HERMES: He wants to pound up all the cities of Greece in it. . . But I must say good-bye, for I think he is coming out; what an uproar he is making!

TRYGAEUS: Ah! great gods! let us seek safety; meseems I already hear the noise of this fearful war mortar.

WAR (*enters carrying a mortar*): Oh! mortals, mortals, wretched mortals, how your jaws will snap!

TRYGAEUS: Oh! divine Apollo! what a prodigious big mortar! Oh, what misery the very sight of War causes me! This then is the foe from whom I fly, who is so cruel, so formidable, so stalwart, so solid on his legs!

WAR: Oh! Prasiae![14] thrice wretched, five times, aye, a thousand times wretched! for thou shalt be destroyed this day.

TRYGAEUS: This does not yet concern us over much; 'tis only so much the worse for the Laconians.

WAR: Oh! Megara! Megara! how utterly are you going to be ground up! what fine mincemeat[15] are you to be made into!

TRYGAEUS: Alas! alas! what bitter tears there will be among the Megarians![16]

---

had caused these proposals to be long refused. Finally the prisoners had been given up in 423 B.C., but the War was continued nevertheless.

14. An important town in Eastern Laconia on the Argolic gulf, celebrated for a temple where a festival was held annually in honour of Achilles. It had been taken and pillaged by the Athenians in the second year of the Peloponnesian War, 430 B.C. As he utters this imprecation, War throws some leeks, (Greek: prasa), the root-word of the name Prasiae, into his mortar.

15. War throws some garlic into his mortar as emblematical of the city of Megara, where it was grown in abundance.

16. Because the smell of bruised garlic causes the eyes to water.

War: Oh, Sicily! you too must perish! Your wretched towns shall be grated like this cheese.[17] Now let us pour some Attic honey[18] into the mortar.

Trygaeus: Oh! I beseech you! use some other honey; this kind is worth four obols; be careful, oh! be careful of our Attic honey.

War: Hi! Tumult, you slave there!

Tumult: What do you want?

War: Out upon you! You stand there with folded arms. Take this cuff o' the head for your pains.

Tumult: Oh! how it stings! Master, have you got garlic in your fist, I wonder?

War: Run and fetch me a pestle.

Tumult: But we haven't got one; 'twas only yesterday we moved.

War: Go and fetch me one from Athens, and hurry, hurry!

Tumult: Aye, I hasten there; if I return without one, I shall have no cause for laughing. (*Exit*)

Trygaeus: Ah! what is to become of us, wretched mortals that we are? See the danger that threatens if he returns with the pestle, for War will quietly amuse himself with pounding all the towns of Hellas to pieces. Ah! Bacchus! cause this herald of evil to perish on his road!

War: Well!

Tumult (*who has returned*): Well, what?

War: You have brought back nothing?

Tumult: Alas! the Athenians have lost their pestle—the tanner, who ground Greece to powder.[19]

Trygaeus: Oh! Athené, venerable mistress! 'tis well for our city he is dead, and before he could serve us with this hash.

War: Then go and seek one at Sparta and have done with it!

Tumult: Aye, aye, master!

War: Be back as quick as ever you can.

Trygaeus (*to the audience*): What is going to happen, friends? 'Tis a critical hour. Ah! if there is some initiate of Samothrace[20] among

---

17. He throws cheese into the mortar as emblematical of Sicily, on account of its rich pastures.
18. Emblematical of Athens. The honey of Mount Hymettus was famous.
19. Cleon, who had lately fallen before Amphipolis, in 422 B.C.
20. An island in the Aegean Sea, on the coast of Thrace and opposite the mouth of the Hebrus; the Mysteries are said to have found their first home in this island, where the

you, 'tis surely the moment to wish this messenger some accident—some sprain or strain.

TUMULT (*who returns*): Alas! alas! thrice again, alas!

WAR: What is it? Again you come back without it?

TUMULT: The Spartans too have lost their pestle.

WAR: How, varlet?

TUMULT: They had lent it to their allies in Thrace,[21] who have lost it for them.

TRYGAEUS: Long life to you, Thracians! My hopes revive, pluck up courage, mortals!

WAR: Take all this stuff away; I am going in to make a pestle for myself.

TRYGAEUS: 'Tis now the time to sing as Datis did, as he masturbated himself at high noon, "Oh pleasure! oh enjoyment! oh delights!"'Tis now, oh Greeks! the moment when freed of quarrels and fighting, we should rescue sweet Peace and draw her out of this pit, before some other pestle prevents us. Come, labourers, merchants, workmen, artisans, strangers, whether you be domiciled or not, islanders, come here, Greeks of all countries, come hurrying here with picks and levers and ropes! 'Tis the moment to drain a cup in honour of the Good Genius.

CHORUS: Come hither, all! quick, quick, hasten to the rescue! All peoples of Greece, now is the time or never, for you to help each other. You see yourselves freed from battles and all their horrors of bloodshed. The day, hateful to Lamachus,[22] has come. Come then, what must be done? Give your orders, direct us, for I swear to work this day without ceasing, until with the help of our levers and our engines we have drawn back into light the greatest of all goddesses, her to whom the olive is so dear.

TRYGAEUS: Silence! if War should hear your shouts of joy he would bound forth from his retreat in fury.

Cabirian gods were worshipped; this cult, shrouded in deep mystery to even the initiates themselves, has remained an almost insoluble problem for the modern critic. It was said that the wishes of the initiates were always granted, and they were feared as to-day the *jettatori* (spell-throwers, casters of the evil eye) in Sicily are feared.

21. Brasidas perished in Thrace in the same battle as Cleon at Amphipolis, 422 B.C.

22. An Athenian general as ambitious as he was brave. In 423 B.C. he had failed in an enterprise against Heraclea, a storm having destroyed his fleet. Since then he had distinguished himself in several actions, and was destined, some years later, to share the command of the expedition to Sicily with Alcibiades and Nicias.

CHORUS: Such a decree overwhelms us with joy; how different to the edict, which bade us muster with provisions for three days.[23]

TRYGAEUS: Let us beware lest the cursed Cerberus[24] prevent us even from the nethermost hell from delivering the goddess by his furious howling, just as he did when on earth.

CHORUS: Once we have hold of her, none in the world will be able to take her from us. Huzza! huzza![25]

TRYGAEUS: You will work my death if you don't subdue your shouts. War will come running out and trample everything beneath his feet.

CHORUS: Well then! *Let* him confound, let him trample, let him overturn everything! We cannot help giving vent to our joy.

TRYGAEUS: Oh! cruel fate! My friends! in the name of the gods, what possesses you? Your dancing will wreck the success of a fine undertaking.

CHORUS: 'Tis not I who want to dance; 'tis my legs that bound with delight.

TRYGAEUS: Enough, an you love me, cease your gambols.

CHORUS: There! 'Tis over.

TRYGAEUS: You say so, and nevertheless you go on.

CHORUS: Yet one more figure and 'tis done.

TRYGAEUS: Well, just this one; then you must dance no more.

CHORUS: No, no more dancing, if we can help you.

TRYGAEUS: But look, you are not stopping even now.

CHORUS: By Zeus, I am only throwing up my right leg, that's all.

TRYGAEUS: Come, I grant you that, but pray, annoy me no further.

CHORUS: Ah! the left leg too will have its fling; well, 'tis but its right. I am so happy, so delighted at not having to carry my buckler any more. I sing and I laugh more than if I had cast my old age, as a serpent does its skin.

TRYGAEUS: No, 'tis no time for joy yet, for you are not sure of success. But when you have got the goddess, then rejoice, shout and laugh; thenceforward you will be able to sail or stay at home, to make love or sleep, to attend festivals and processions, to play at cottabos,[26] live like true Sybarites and to shout, Io, io!

---

23. Meaning, to start on a military expedition.
24. Cleon.
25. The Chorus insist on the conventional choric dance.
26. One of the most favourite games with the Greeks. A stick was set upright in the ground and to this the beam of a balance was attached by its centre. Two vessels were

CHORUS: Ah! God grant we may see the blessed day. I have suffered so much; have so oft slept with Phormio[27] on hard beds. You will no longer find me an acid, angry, hard judge as heretofore, but will find me turned indulgent and grown younger by twenty years through happiness. We have been killing ourselves long enough, tiring ourselves out with going to the Lyceum[28] and returning laden with spear and buckler.—But what can we do to please you? Come, speak; for 'tis a good Fate, that has named you our leader.

TRYGAEUS: How shall we set about removing these stones?

HERMES: Rash reprobate, what do you propose doing?

TRYGAEUS: Nothing bad, as Cillicon said.[29]

HERMES: You are undone, you wretch.

TRYGAEUS: Yes, if the lot had to decide my life, for Hermes would know how to turn the chance.[30]

HERMES: You are lost, you are dead.

TRYGAEUS: On what day?

HERMES: This instant.

TRYGAEUS: But I have not provided myself with flour and cheese yet[31] to start for death.

HERMES: You *are* kneaded and ground already, I tell you.[32]

TRYGAEUS: Hah! I have not yet tasted that gentle pleasure.

HERMES: Don't you know that Zeus has decreed death for him who is surprised exhuming Peace?

TRYGAEUS: What! must I really and truly die?

HERMES: You must.

---

hung from the extremities of the beam so as to balance; beneath these two other and larger dishes were placed and filled with water, and in the middle of each a brazen figure, called Manes, was stood. The game consisted in throwing drops of wine from an agreed distance into one or the other vessel, so that, dragged downwards by the weight of the liquor, it bumped against Manes.

27. A general of austere habits; he disposed of all his property to pay the cost of a naval expedition, in which he beat the fleet of the foe off the promontory of Rhium in 429 B.C.

28. The Lyceum was a portico ornamented with paintings and surrounded with gardens, in which military exercises took place.

29. A citizen of Miletus, who betrayed his country to the people of Priené. When asked what he purposed, he replied, "Nothing bad," which expression had therefore passed into a proverb.

30. Hermes was the god of chance.

31. As the soldiers had to do when starting on an expedition.

32. That is, you are pedicated.

TRYGAEUS: Well then, lend me three drachmae to buy a young pig; I wish to have myself initiated before I die.[33]

HERMES: Oh! Zeus, the Thunderer![34]

TRYGAEUS: I adjure you in the name of the gods, master, don't denounce us!

HERMES: I may not, I cannot keep silent.

TRYGAEUS: In the name of the meats which I brought you so good-naturedly.

HERMES: Why, wretched man, Zeus will annihilate me, if I do not shout out at the top of my voice, to inform him what you are plotting.

TRYGAEUS: Oh, no! don't shout, I beg you, dear little Hermes. . . And what are you doing, comrades? You stand there as though you were stocks and stones. Wretched men, speak, entreat him at once; otherwise he will be shouting.

CHORUS: Oh! mighty Hermes! don't do it; no, don't do it! If ever you have eaten some young pig, sacrificed by us on your altars, with pleasure, may this offering not be without value in your sight to-day.

TRYGAEUS: Do you not hear them wheedling you, mighty god?

CHORUS: Be not pitiless toward our prayers; permit us to deliver the goddess. Oh! the most human, the most generous of the gods, be favourable toward us, if it be true that you detest the haughty crests and proud brows of Pisander;[35] we shall never cease, oh master, offering you sacred victims and solemn prayers.

TRYGAEUS: Have mercy, mercy, let yourself be touched by their words; never was your worship so dear to them as to-day.

HERMES: I' truth, never have you been greater thieves.[36]

TRYGAEUS: I will reveal a great, a terrible conspiracy against the gods to you.

HERMES: Hah! speak and perchance I shall let myself be softened.

TRYGAEUS: Know then, that the Moon and that infamous Sun are plotting against you, and want to deliver Greece into the hands of the Barbarians.

---

33. The initiated were thought to enjoy greater happiness after death.
34. He summons Zeus to reveal Trygaeus' conspiracy.
35. An Athenian captain, who later had the recall of Alcibiades decreed by the Athenian people; in 'The Birds' Aristophanes represents him as a cowardly braggart. He was the reactionary leader who established the Oligarchical Government of the Four Hundred, 411 B.C., after the failure of the Syracusan expedition.
36. Among other attributes, Hermes was the god of thieves.

HERMES: What for?

TRYGAEUS: Because it is to you that we sacrifice, whereas the barbarians worship them; hence they would like to see you destroyed, that they alone might receive the offerings.

HERMES: 'Tis then for this reason that these untrustworthy charioteers have for so long been defrauding us, one of them robbing us of daylight and the other nibbling away at the other's disk.[37]

TRYGAEUS: Yes, certainly. So therefore, Hermes, my friend, help us with your whole heart to find and deliver the captive and we will celebrate the great Panathenaea[38] in your honour as well as all the festivals of the other gods; for Hermes shall be the Mysteries, the Dipolia, the Adonia; everywhere the towns, freed from their miseries, will sacrifice to Hermes, the Liberator; you will be loaded with benefits of every kind, and to start with, I offer you this cup for libations as your first present.

HERMES: Ah! how golden cups do influence me! Come, friends, get to work. To the pit quickly, pick in hand and drag away the stones.

CHORUS: We go, but you, the cleverest of all the gods, supervise our labours; tell us, good workman as you are, what we must do; we shall obey your orders with alacrity.

TRYGAEUS: Quick, reach me your cup, and let us preface our work by addressing prayers to the gods.

HERMES: Oh! sacred, sacred libations! Keep silence, oh! ye people! keep silence!

TRYGAEUS: Let us offer our libations and our prayers, so that this day may begin an era of unalloyed happiness for Greece and that he who has bravely pulled at the rope with us may never resume his buckler.

CHORUS: Aye, may we pass our lives in peace, caressing our mistresses and poking the fire.

TRYGAEUS: May he who would prefer the war, oh Dionysus, be ever drawing barbed arrows out of his elbows.

CHORUS: If there be a citizen, greedy for military rank and honours, who refuses, oh, divine Peace! to restore you to daylight, may he behave as cowardly as Cleonymus on the battlefield.

---

37. Alluding to the eclipses of the sun and the moon.
38. The Panathenaea were dedicated to Athené, the Mysteries to Demeter, the Dipolia to Zeus, the Adonia to Aphrodité and Adonis. Trygaeus promises Hermes that he shall be worshipped in the place of all the other gods.

TRYGAEUS: If a lance-maker or a dealer in shields desires war for the sake of better trade, may he be taken by pirates and eat nothing but barley.

CHORUS: If some ambitious man does not help us, because he wants to become a General, or if a slave is plotting to pass over to the enemy, let his limbs be broken on the wheel, may he be beaten to death with rods! As for us, may Fortune favour us! Io! Paean, Io!

TRYGAEUS: Don't say Paean,[39] but simply, Io.

CHORUS: Very well, then! Io! Io! I'll simply say, Io!

TRYGAEUS: To Hermes, the Graces, Hora, Aphrodité, Eros!

CHORUS: And not to Ares?

TRYGAEUS: No.

CHORUS: Nor doubtless to Enyalius?

TRYGAEUS: No.

CHORUS: Come, all strain at the ropes to tear away the stones. Pull!

HERMES: Heave away, heave, heave, oh!

CHORUS: Come, pull harder, harder.

HERMES: Heave away, heave, heave, oh!

CHORUS: Still harder, harder still.

HERMES: Heave away, heave! Heave away, heave, heave, oh!

TRYGAEUS: Come, come, there is no working together. Come! all pull at the same instant! you Boeotians are only pretending. Beware!

HERMES: Come, heave away, heave!

CHORUS: Hi! you two pull as well.

TRYGAEUS: Why, I am pulling, I am hanging on to the rope and straining till I am almost off my feet; I am working with all my might.

HERMES: Why does not the work advance then?

TRYGAEUS: Lamachus, this is too bad! You are in the way, sitting there. We have no use for your Medusa's head, friend.[40]

HERMES: But hold, the Argives have not pulled the least bit; they have done nothing but laugh at us for our pains while they were getting gain with both hands.[41]

TRYGAEUS: Ah! my dear sir, the Laconians at all events pull with vigour.

---

39. The pun here cannot be kept. The word (Greek: paian), Paean, resembles (Greek: paiein), to strike; hence the word, as recalling the blows and wounds of the war, seems of ill omen to Trygaeus.

40. The device on his shield was a Gorgon's head. (*See* 'The Acharnians.')

41. Both Sparta and Athens had sought the alliance of the Argives; they had kept themselves strictly neutral and had received pay from both sides. But, the year after the

CHORUS: But look! only those among them who generally hold the plough-tail show any zeal,[42] while the armourers impede them in their efforts.

HERMES: And the Megarians too are doing nothing, yet look how they are pulling and showing their teeth like famished curs; the poor wretches are dying of hunger![43]

TRYGAEUS: This won't do, friends. Come! all together! Everyone to the work and with a good heart for the business.

HERMES: Heave away, heave!

TRYGAEUS: Harder!

HERMES: Heave away, heave!

TRYGAEUS: Come on then, by heaven.

HERMES: Heave away, heave! Heave away, heave!

CHORUS: This will never do.

TRYGAEUS: Is it not a shame? some pull one way and others another. You, Argives there, beware of a thrashing!

HERMES: Come, put your strength into it.

TRYGAEUS: Heave away, heave!

CHORUS: There are many ill-disposed folk among us.

TRYGAEUS: Do you at least, who long for peace, pull heartily.

CHORUS: But there are some who prevent us.

HERMES: Off to the Devil with you, Megarians! The goddess hates you. She recollects that you were the first to rub her the wrong way. Athenians, you are not well placed for pulling. There you are too busy with law-suits; if you really want to free the goddess, get down a little towards the sea.[44]

CHORUS: Come, friends, none but husbandmen on the rope.

HERMES: Ah! that will do ever so much better.

CHORUS: He says the thing is going well. Come, all of you, together and with a will.

TRYGAEUS: 'Tis the husbandmen who are doing all the work.

---

production of 'The Wasps,' they openly joined Athens, had attacked Epidaurus and got cut to pieces by the Spartans.

42. These are the Spartan prisoners from Sphacteria, who were lying in gaol at Athens. They were chained fast to large beams of wood.

43. 'Twas want of force, not want of will. They had suffered more than any other people from the war. (*See* 'The Acharnians.')

44. Meaning, look chiefly to your fleet. This was the counsel that Themistocles frequently gave the Athenians.

CHORUS: Come then, come, and all together! Hah! hah! at last there is some unanimity in the work. Don't let us give up, let us redouble our efforts. There! now we have it! Come then, all together! Heave away, heave! Heave away, heave! Heave away, heave! Heave away, heave! Heave away, heave! All together! (*Peace is drawn out of the pit*)

TRYGAEUS: Oh! venerated goddess, who givest us our grapes, where am I to find the ten-thousand-gallon words[45] wherewith to greet thee? I have none such at home. Oh! hail to thee, Opora,[46] and thou, Theoria![47] How beautiful is thy face! How sweet thy breath! What gentle fragrance comes from thy bosom, gentle as freedom from military duty, as the most dainty perfumes!

HERMES: Is it then a smell like a soldier's knapsack?

CHORUS: Oh! hateful soldier! your hideous satchel makes me sick! it stinks like the belching of onions, whereas this lovable deity has the odour of sweet fruits, of festivals, of the Dionysia, of the harmony of flutes, of the comic poets, of the verses of Sophocles, of the phrases of Euripides. . .

TRYGAEUS: That's a foul calumny, you wretch! She detests that framer of subtleties and quibbles.

CHORUS: . . . of ivy, of straining-bags for wine, of bleating ewes, of provision-laden women hastening to the kitchen, of the tipsy servant wench, of the upturned wine-jar, and of a whole heap of other good things.

HERMES: Then look how the reconciled towns chat pleasantly together, how they laugh; and yet they are all cruelly mishandled; their wounds are bleeding still.

TRYGAEUS: But let us also scan the mien of the spectators; we shall thus find out the trade of each.

HERMES: Ah! good gods! look at that poor crest-maker, tearing at his hair,[48] and at that pike-maker, who has just broken wind in yon sword-cutler's face.

---

45. A metaphor referring to the abundant vintages that peace would assure.
46. The goddess of fruits.
47. Aristophanes personifies under this name the sacred ceremonies in general which peace would allow to be celebrated with due pomp. Opora and Theoria come on the stage in the wake of Peace, clothed and decked out as courtesans.
48. Aristophanes has already shown us the husbandmen and workers in peaceful trades pulling at the rope to extricate Peace, while the armourers hindered them by pulling the other way.

TRYGAEUS: And do you see with what pleasure this sickle-maker is making long noses at the spear-maker?

HERMES: Now ask the husbandmen to be off.

TRYGAEUS: Listen, good folk! Let the husbandmen take their farming tools and return to their fields as quick as possible, but without either sword, spear or javelin. All is as quiet as if Peace had been reigning for a century. Come, let everyone go till the earth, singing the Paean.

CHORUS: Oh, thou, whom men of standing desired and who art good to husbandmen, I have gazed upon thee with delight; and now I go to greet my vines, to caress after so long an absence the fig trees I planted in my youth.

TRYGAEUS: Friends, let us first adore the goddess, who has delivered us from crests and Gorgons;[49] then let us hurry to our farms, having first bought a nice little piece of salt fish to eat in the fields.

HERMES: By Posidon! what a fine crew they make and dense as the crust of a cake; they are as nimble as guests on their way to a feast.

TRYGAEUS: See, how their iron spades glitter and how beautifully their three-pronged mattocks glisten in the sun! How regularly they will align the plants! I also burn myself to go into the country and to turn over the earth I have so long neglected.—Friends, do you remember the happy life that peace afforded us formerly; can you recall the splendid baskets of figs, both fresh and dried, the myrtles, the sweet wine, the violets blooming near the spring, and the olives, for which we have wept so much? Worship, adore the goddess for restoring you so many blessings.

CHORUS: Hail! hail! thou beloved divinity! thy return overwhelms us with joy. When far from thee, my ardent wish to see my fields again made me pine with regret. From thee came all blessings. Oh! much desired Peace! thou art the sole support of those who spend their lives tilling the earth. Under thy rule we had a thousand delicious enjoyments at our beck; thou wert the husbandman's wheaten cake and his safeguard. So that our vineyards, our young fig-tree woods and all our plantations hail thee with delight and smile at thy coming. But where was she then, I wonder, all the long time she spent away from us? Hermes, thou benevolent god, tell us!

---

49. An allusion to Lamachus' shield.

HERMES: Wise husbandmen, hearken to my words, if you want to know why she was lost to you. The start of our misfortunes was the exile of Phidias;[50] Pericles feared he might share his ill-luck, he mistrusted your peevish nature and, to prevent all danger to himself, he threw out that little spark, the Megarian decree,[51] set the city aflame, and blew up the conflagration with a hurricane of war, so that the smoke drew tears from all Greeks both here and over there. At the very outset of this fire our vines were a-crackle, our casks knocked together;[52] it was beyond the power of any man to stop the disaster, and Peace disappeared.

TRYGAEUS: That, by Apollo! is what no one ever told me; I could not think what connection there could be between Phidias and Peace.

CHORUS: Nor I; I know it now. This accounts for her beauty, if she is related to him. There are so many things that escape us.

HERMES: Then, when the towns subject to you saw that you were angered one against the other and were showing each other your teeth like dogs, they hatched a thousand plots to pay you no more dues and gained over the chief citizens of Sparta at the price of gold. They, being as shamelessly greedy as they were faithless in diplomacy, chased off Peace with ignominy to let loose War. Though this was profitable to them, 'twas the ruin of the husbandmen, who were innocent of all blame; for, in revenge, your galleys went out to devour their figs.

TRYGAEUS: And 'twas with justice too; did they not break down my black fig tree, which I had planted and dunged with my own hands?

CHORUS: Yes, by Zeus! yes, 'twas well done; the wretches broke a chest for me with stones, which held six medimni of corn.

HERMES: Then the rural labourers flocked into the city[53] and let themselves be bought over like the others. Not having even a

---

50. Having been commissioned to execute a statue of Athené, Phidias was accused of having stolen part of the gold given him out of the public treasury for its decoration. Rewarded for his work by calumny and banishment, he resolved to make a finer statue than his Athené, and executed one for the temple of Elis, that of the Olympian Zeus, which was considered one of the wonders of the world.

51. He had issued a decree, which forbade the admission of any Megarian on Attic soil, and also all trade with that people. The Megarians, who obtained all their provisions from Athens, were thus almost reduced to starvation.

52. That is, the vineyards were ravaged from the very outset of the war, and this increased the animosity.

53. Driven in from the country parts by the Lacedaemonian invaders.

grape-stone to munch and longing after their figs, they looked towards the orators.[54] These well knew that the poor were driven to extremity and lacked even bread; but they nevertheless drove away the Goddess each time she reappeared in answer to the wish of the country with their loud shrieks, that were as sharp as pitchforks; furthermore, they attacked the well-filled purses of the richest among our allies on the pretence that they belonged to Brasidas' party.[55] And then you would tear the poor accused wretch to pieces with your teeth; for the city, all pale with hunger and cowed with terror, gladly snapped up any calumny that was thrown it to devour. So the strangers, seeing what terrible blows the informers dealt, sealed their lips with gold. They grew rich, while you, alas! you could only see that Greece was going to ruin. 'Twas the tanner who was the author of all this woe.[56]

TRYGAEUS: Enough said, Hermes, leave that man in Hades, whither he has gone; he no longer belongs to us, but rather to yourself.[57] That he was a cheat, a braggart, a calumniator when alive, why, nothing could be truer; but anything you might say now would be an insult to one of your own folk. Oh! venerated Goddess! why art thou silent?

HERMES: And how could she speak to the spectators? She is too angry at all that they have made her suffer.

TRYGAEUS: At least let her speak a little to you, Hermes.

HERMES: Tell me, my dear, what are your feelings with regard to them? Come, you relentless foe of all bucklers, speak; I am listening to you. (*Peace whispers into Hermes' ear*) Is that your grievance against them? Yes, yes, I understand. Hearken, you folk, this is her complaint. She says, that after the affair of Pylos[58] she came to you unbidden to bring you a basket full of truces and that you thrice repulsed her by your votes in the assembly.

TRYGAEUS: Yes, we did wrong, but forgive us, for our mind was then entirely absorbed in leather.[59]

---

54. The demagogues, who distributed the slender dole given to the poor, and by that means exercised undue power over them.
55. Meaning, the side of the Spartans.
56. Cleon.
57. It was Hermes who conducted the souls of the dead down to the lower regions.
58. The Spartans had thrice offered to make peace after the Pylos disaster.
59. I.e. dominated by Cleon.

HERMES: Listen again to what she has just asked me. Who was her greatest foe here? and furthermore, had she a friend who exerted himself to put an end to the fighting?

TRYGAEUS: Her most devoted friend was Cleonymus; it is undisputed.

HERMES: How then did Cleonymus behave in fights?

TRYGAEUS: Oh! the bravest of warriors! Only he was not born of the father he claims; he showed it quick enough in the army by throwing away his weapons.[60]

HERMES: There is yet another question she has just put to me. Who rules now in the rostrum?

TRYGAEUS: 'Tis Hyperbolus, who now holds empire on the Pnyx. (*To Peace*) What now? you turn away your head!

HERMES: She is vexed, that the people should give themselves a wretch of that kind for their chief.

TRYGAEUS: Oh! we shall not employ him again; but the people, seeing themselves without a leader, took him haphazard, just as a man, who is naked, springs upon the first cloak he sees.

HERMES: She asks, what will be the result of such a choice of the city?

TRYGAEUS: We shall be more far-seeing in consequence.

HERMES: And why?

TRYGAEUS: Because he is a lamp-maker. Formerly we only directed our business by groping in the dark; now we shall only deliberate by lamplight.

HERMES: Oh! oh! what questions she does order me to put to you!

TRYGAEUS: What are they?

HERMES: She wants to have news of a whole heap of old-fashioned things she left here. First of all, how is Sophocles?

TRYGAEUS: Very well; but something very strange has happened to him.

HERMES: What then?

TRYGAEUS: He has turned from Sophocles into Simonides.[61]

HERMES: Into Simonides? How so?

TRYGAEUS: Because, though old and broken-down as he is, he would put to sea on a hurdle to gain an obolus.[62]

---

60. There is a pun here, that cannot be rendered, between (Greek: apobolimaios), which means, *one who throws away his weapons*, and (Greek: upobolimaios), which signifies, *a supposititious child*.

61. Simonides was very avaricious, and sold his pen to the highest bidder. It seems that Sophocles had also started writing for gain.

62. I.e. he would recoil from no risk to turn an honest penny.

ARISTOPHANES

HERMES: And wise Cratinus, is he still alive?[63]

TRYGAEUS: He died about the time of the Laconian invasion.

HERMES: How?

TRYGAEUS: Of a swoon. He could not bear the shock of seeing one of his casks full of wine broken. Ah! what a number of other misfortunes our city has suffered! So, dearest mistress, nothing can now separate us from thee.

HERMES: If that be so, receive Opora here for a wife; take her to the country, live with her, and grow fine grapes together.[64]

TRYGAEUS: Come, my dear friend, come and accept my kisses. Tell me, Hermes, my master, do you think it would hurt me to fuck her a little, after so long an abstinence?

HERMES: No, not if you swallow a potion of penny-royal afterwards.[65] But hasten to lead Theoria[66] to the Senate; 'twas there she lodged before.

TRYGAEUS: Oh! fortunate Senate! Thanks to Theoria, what soups you will swallow for the space of three days![67] how you will devour meats and cooked tripe! Come, farewell, friend Hermes!

HERMES: And to you also, my dear sir, may you have much happiness, and don't forget me.

TRYGAEUS: Come, beetle, home, home, and let us fly on a swift wing.

HERMES: Oh! he is no longer here.

TRYGAEUS: Where has he gone to then?

HERMES: He is harnessed to the chariot of Zeus and bears the thunderbolts.

TRYGAEUS: But where will the poor wretch get his food?

HERMES: He will eat Ganymede's ambrosia.

TRYGAEUS: Very well then, but how am I going to descend?

---

63. A comic poet as well known for his love of wine as for his writings; he died in 431 B.C., the first year of the war, at the age of ninety-seven.

64. Opora was the goddess of fruits.

65. The Scholiast says fruit may be eaten with impunity in great quantities if care is taken to drink a decoction of this herb afterwards.

66. Theoria is confided to the care of the Senate, because it was this body who named the (Greek: The orhoi), deputies appointed to go and consult the oracles beyond the Attic borders or to be present at feasts and games.

67. The great festivals, e.g. the Dionysia, lasted three days. Those in honour of the return of Peace, which was so much desired, could not last a shorter time.

HERMES: Oh! never fear, there is nothing simpler; place yourself beside the goddess.

TRYGAEUS: Come, my pretty maidens, follow me quickly; there are plenty of folk awaiting you with standing tools.

CHORUS: Farewell and good luck be yours! Let us begin by handing over all this gear to the care of our servants, for no place is less safe than a theatre; there is always a crowd of thieves prowling around it, seeking to find some mischief to do. Come, keep a good watch over all this. As for ourselves, let us explain to the spectators what we have in our minds, the purpose of our play.

Undoubtedly the comic poet who mounted the stage to praise himself in the parabasis would deserve to be handed over to the sticks of the beadles. Nevertheless, oh Muse, if it be right to esteem the most honest and illustrious of our comic writers at his proper value, permit our poet to say that he thinks he has deserved a glorious renown. First of all, 'tis he who has compelled his rivals no longer to scoff at rags or to war with lice; and as for those Heracles, always chewing and ever hungry, those poltroons and cheats who allow themselves to be beaten at will, he was the first to cover them with ridicule and to chase them from the stage;[68] he has also dismissed that slave, whom one never failed to set a-weeping before you, so that his comrade might have the chance of jeering at his stripes and might ask, "Wretch, what has happened to your hide? Has the lash rained an army of its thongs on you and laid your back waste?" After having delivered us from all these wearisome ineptitudes and these low buffooneries, he has built up for us a great art, like a palace with high towers, constructed of fine phrases, great thoughts and of jokes not common on the streets. Moreover 'tis not obscure private persons or women that he stages in his comedies; but, bold as Heracles, 'tis the very greatest whom he attacks, undeterred by the fetid stink of leather or the threats of hearts of mud. He has the right to say, "I am the first ever dared to go straight for that beast with the sharp teeth and the terrible eyes that flashed lambent fire like those of Cynna,[69] surrounded by a hundred lewd flatterers, who spittle-licked him to his heart's content; it had

---

68. In spite of what he says, Aristophanes has not always disdained this sort of low comedy—for instance, his Heracles in 'The Birds.'

69. A celebrated Athenian courtesan of Aristophanes' day.

a voice like a roaring torrent, the stench of a seal, a foul Lamia's testicles and the rump of a camel."[70]

I did not recoil in horror at the sight of such a monster, but fought him relentlessly to win your deliverance and that of the Islanders. Such are the services which should be graven in your recollection and entitle me to your thanks. Yet I have not been seen frequenting the wrestling school intoxicated with success and trying to tamper with young boys;[71] but I took all my theatrical gear[72] and returned straight home. I pained folk but little and caused them much amusement; my conscience rebuked me for nothing. Hence both grown men and youths should be on my side and I likewise invite the bald[73] to give me their votes; for, if I triumph, everyone will say, both at table and at festivals, "Carry this to the bald man, give these cakes to the bald one, do not grudge the poet whose talent shines as bright as his own bare skull the share he deserves."

Oh, Muse! drive the War far from our city and come to preside over our dances, if you love me; come and celebrate the nuptials of the gods, the banquets of us mortals and the festivals of the fortunate; these are the themes that inspire thy most poetic songs. And should Carcinus come to beg thee for admission with his sons to thy chorus, refuse all traffic with them; remember they are but gelded birds, stork-necked dancers, mannikins about as tall as a pat of goat's dung, in fact machine-made poets.[74] Contrary to all expectation, the father has at last managed to finish a piece, but he owns himself a cat strangled it one fine evening.[75]

Such are the songs[76] with which the Muse with the glorious hair inspires the able poet and which enchant the assembled populace,

---

70. Cleon. These four verses are here repeated from the parabasis of 'The Wasps,' produced 423 B.C., the year before this play.
71. Shafts aimed at certain poets, who used their renown as a means of seducing young men to grant them pederastic favours.
72. The poet supplied everything needful for the production of his piece—vases, dresses, masks, etc.
73. Aristophanes was bald himself, it would seem.
74. Carcinus and his three sons were both poets and dancers. (*See* the closing scene of 'The Wasps.') Perhaps relying little on the literary value of their work, it seems that they sought to please the people by the magnificence of its staging.
75. He had written a piece called 'The Mice,' which he succeeded with great difficulty in getting played, but it met with no success.
76. This passage really follows on the invocation, "*Oh, Muse! drive the War*," etc., from which indeed it is only divided by the interpolated criticism aimed at Carcinus.

when the spring swallow twitters beneath the foliage;[77] but the god spare us from the chorus of Morsimus and that of Melanthius![78] Oh! what a bitter discordancy grated upon my ears that day when the tragic chorus was directed by this same Melanthius and his brother, these two Gorgons,[79] these two harpies, the plague of the seas, whose gluttonous bellies devour the entire race of fishes, these followers of old women, these goats with their stinking arm-pits. Oh! Muse, spit upon them abundantly and keep the feast gaily with me.

TRYGAEUS: Ah! 'tis a rough job getting to the gods! my legs are as good as broken through it. How small you were, to be sure, when seen from heaven! you had all the appearance too of being great rascals; but seen close, you look even worse.

SERVANT: Is that you, master?

TRYGAEUS: So I have been told.

SERVANT: What has happened to you?

TRYGAEUS: My legs pain me; it is such a plaguey long journey.

SERVANT: Oh! do tell me. . .

TRYGAEUS: What?

SERVANT: Did you see any other man besides yourself strolling about in heaven?

TRYGAEUS: No, only the souls of two or three dithyrambic poets.

SERVANT: What were they doing up there?

TRYGAEUS: They were seeking to catch some lyric exordia as they flew by immersed in the billows of the air.

SERVANT: Is it true, what they tell us, that men are turned into stars after death?

TRYGAEUS: Quite true.

SERVANT: Then who is that star I see over yonder?

TRYGAEUS: That is Ion of Chios,[80] the author of an ode beginning "Morning"; as soon as ever he got to heaven, they called him "the Morning Star."

---

77. The Scholiast informs us that these verses are borrowed from a poet of the sixth century B.C.

78. Sons of Philocles, of the family of Aeschylus, tragic writers, derided by Aristophanes as bad poets and notorious gluttons.

79. The Gorgons were represented with great teeth, and therefore the same name was given to gluttons. The Harpies, to whom the two voracious poets are also compared, were monsters with the face of a woman, the body of a vulture and hooked beak and claws.

80. A tragic and dithyrambic poet, who had written many pieces, which had met with great success at Athens.

SERVANT: And those stars like sparks, that plough up the air as they dart across the sky?[81]

TRYGAEUS: They are the rich leaving the feast with a lantern and a light inside it. But hurry up, show this young girl into my house, clean out the bath, heat some water and prepare the nuptial couch for herself and me. When 'tis done, come back here; meanwhile I am off to present this one to the Senate.

SERVANT: But where then did you get these pretty chattels?

TRYGAEUS: Where? why in heaven.

SERVANT: I would not give more than an obolus for gods who have got to keeping brothels like us mere mortals.

TRYGAEUS: They are not all so, but there are some up there too who live by this trade.

SERVANT: Come, that's rich! But I bethink me, shall I give her something to eat?

TRYGAEUS: No, for she would neither touch bread nor cake; she is used to licking ambrosia at the table of the gods.

SERVANT: Well, we can give her something to lick down here too.[82]

CHORUS: Here is a truly happy old man, as far as I can judge.

TRYGAEUS: Ah! but what shall I be, when you see me presently dressed for the wedding?

CHORUS: Made young again by love and scented with perfumes, your lot will be one we all shall envy.

TRYGAEUS: And when I lie beside her and caress her bosoms?

CHORUS: Oh! then you will be happier than those spinning-tops who call Carcinus their father.[83]

TRYGAEUS: And I well deserve it; have I not bestridden a beetle to save the Greeks, who now, thanks to me, can make love at their ease and sleep peacefully on their farms?

SERVANT: The girl has quitted the bath; she is charming from head to foot, both belly and buttocks; the cake is baked and they are kneading the sesame-biscuit;[84] nothing is lacking but the bridegroom's penis.

TRYGAEUS: Let us first hasten to lodge Theoria in the hands of the Senate.

---

81. The shooting stars.
82. That is, men's tools;—we can set her to 'fellate.'
83. It has already been mentioned that the sons of Carcinus were dancers.
84. It was customary at weddings, says Menander, to give the bride a sesame-cake as an emblem of fruitfulness, because sesame is the most fruitful of all seeds.

SERVANT: But tell me, who is this woman?

TRYGAEUS: Why, 'tis Theoria, with whom we used formerly to go to Brauron,[85] to get tipsy and frolic. I had the greatest trouble to get hold of her.

SERVANT: Ah! you charmer! what pleasure your pretty bottom will afford me every four years!

TRYGAEUS: Let us see, who of you is steady enough to be trusted by the Senate with the care of this charming wench? Hi! you, friend! what are you drawing there?

SERVANT: I am drawing the plan of the tent I wish to erect for myself on the isthmus.[86]

TRYGAEUS: Come, who wishes to take the charge of her? No one? Come, Theoria, I am going to lead you into the midst of the spectators and confide you to their care.

SERVANT: Ah! there is one who makes a sign to you.

TRYGAEUS: Who is it?

SERVANT: 'Tis Ariphrades. He wishes to take her home at once.

TRYGAEUS: No, I'm sure he shan't. He would soon have her done for, licking up all her life juice.[87] Come, Theoria, put down all this gear.[88]—Senate, Prytanes, look upon Theoria and see what precious blessings I place in your hands.[89] Hasten to raise its limbs and to immolate the victim. Admire the fine chimney,[90] it is quite black with smoke, for 'twas here that the Senate did their cooking before

---

85. An Attic town on the east coast, noted for a magnificent temple, in which stood the statue of Artemis, which Orestes and Iphigenia had brought from the Tauric Chersonese and also for the Brauronia, festivals that were celebrated every four years in honour of the goddess. This was one of the festivals which the Attic people kept with the greatest pomp, and was an occasion for debauchery.

86. Competitors intending to take part in the great Olympic, Isthmian and other games took with them a tent, wherein to camp in the open. Further, there is an obscene allusion which the actor indicates by gesture, pointing to the girl's privates, signifying there is the lodging where he would fain find a delightful abode. The 'Isthmus' is the perineum, the narrow space betwixt *anus* and *cunnus*.

87. He was a 'cunnilingue,' as we gather also from what Aristophanes says of his infamous habits in the 'Knights.'

88. Doubtless the vessels and other sacrificial objects and implements with which Theoria was laden in her character of presiding deity at religious ceremonies.

89. The whole passage is full of obscene *double entendres*. Theoria throughout is spoken of in words applicable to either of her twofold character—as a sacred, religious feast, and as a lady of pleasure.

90. Where the meats were cooked after sacrifice; Trygaeus points to Theoria's privates, marking the secondary obscene sense he means to convey.

ARISTOPHANES

the War. Now that you have found Theoria again, you can start the most charming games from to-morrow, wrestling with her on the ground, either on your hands and feet, or you can lay her on her side, or stand before her with bent knees, or, well rubbed with oil, you can boldly enter the lists, as in the Pancratium, belabouring your foe with blows from your fist or otherwise.[91] The next day you will celebrate equestrian games, in which the riders will ride side by side, or else the chariot teams, thrown one on top of another, panting and whinnying, will roll and knock against each other on the ground, while other rivals, thrown out of their seats, will fall before reaching the goal, utterly exhausted by their efforts.—Come, Prytanes, take Theoria. Oh! look how graciously yonder fellow has received her; you would not have been in such a hurry to introduce her to the Senate, if nothing were coming to you through it;[92] you would not have failed to plead some holiday as an excuse.

CHORUS: Such a man as you assures the happiness of all his fellow-citizens.

TRYGAEUS: When you are gathering your vintages you will prize me even better.

CHORUS: E'en from to-day we hail you as the deliverer of mankind.

TRYGAEUS: Wait until you have drunk a beaker of new wine, before you appraise my true merits.

CHORUS: Excepting the gods, there is none greater than yourself, and that will ever be our opinion.

TRYGAEUS: Yea, Trygaeus of Athmonia has deserved well of you, he has freed both husbandman and craftsman from the most cruel ills; he has vanquished Hyperbolus.

CHORUS: Well then, what must we do now?

TRYGAEUS: You must offer pots of green-stuff to the goddess to consecrate her altars.

---

91. "Or otherwise"—that is, with the standing penis. The whole sentence contains a series of allusions to different 'modes of love.'

92. One of the offices of the Prytanes was to introduce those who asked admission to the Senate, but it would seem that none could obtain this favour without payment. Without this, a thousand excuses would be made; for instance, it would be a public holiday, and consequently the Senate could receive no one. As there was some festival nearly every day, he whose purse would not open might have to wait a very long while.

CHORUS: Pots of green-stuff[93] as we do to poor Hermes—and even he thinks the fare but mean?

TRYGAEUS: What will you offer then? A fatted bull?

CHORUS: Oh, no! I don't want to start bellowing the battle-cry.[94]

TRYGAEUS: A great fat swine then?

CHORUS: No, no.

TRYGAEUS: Why not?

CHORUS: We don't want any of the swinishness of Theagenes.[95]

TRYGAEUS: What other victim do you prefer then?

CHORUS: A sheep.

TRYGAEUS: A sheep?

CHORUS: Yes.

TRYGAEUS: But you must give the word the Ionic form.

CHORUS: Purposely. So that if anyone in the assembly says, "We must go to war," all may start bleating in alarm, "Oï, oï."[96]

TRYGAEUS: A brilliant idea.

CHORUS: And we shall all be lambs one toward the other, yea, and milder still toward the allies.

TRYGAEUS: Then go for the sheep and haste to bring it back with you; I will prepare the altar for the sacrifice.

CHORUS: How everything succeeds to our wish, when the gods are willing and Fortune favours us! how opportunely everything falls out.

TRYGAEUS: Nothing could be truer, for look! here stands the altar all ready at my door.

CHORUS: Hurry, hurry, for the winds are fickle; make haste, while the divine will is set on stopping this cruel war and is showering on us the most striking benefits.

TRYGAEUS: Here is the basket of barley-seed mingled with salt, the chaplet and the sacred knife; and there is the fire; so we are only waiting for the sheep.

CHORUS: Hasten, hasten, for, if Chaeris sees you, he will come without bidding, he and his flute; and when you see him

---

93. This was only offered to lesser deities.

94. In the Greek we have a play upon the similarity of the words, (Greek: bous), a bull, and (Greek: boan), to shout the battle cry.

95. Theagenes, of the Piraeus, a hideous, coarse, debauched and evil-living character of the day.

96. That is the vocative of (Greek: oïs), (Greek: oïos), the Ionic form of the word; in Attic Greek it is contracted throughout—(Greek: ois), (Greek: oios), etc.

puffing and panting and out of breath, you will have to give him something.

TRYGAEUS: Come, seize the basket and take the lustral water and hurry to circle round the altar to the right.

SERVANT: There! 'tis done. What is your next bidding?

TRYGAEUS: Hold! I take this fire-brand first and plunge it into the water.

SERVANT: Be quick! be quick! Sprinkle the altar.

TRYGAEUS: Give me some barley-seed, purify yourself and hand me the basin; then scatter the rest of the barley among the audience.

SERVANT: 'Tis done.

TRYGAEUS: You have thrown it?

SERVANT: Yes, by Hermes! and all the spectators have had their share.

TRYGAEUS: But not the women?

SERVANT: Oh! their husbands will give it them this evening.[97]

TRYGAEUS: Let us pray! Who is here? Are there any good men?[98]

SERVANT: Come, give, so that I may sprinkle these. Faith! they are indeed good, brave men.

TRYGAEUS: You believe so?

SERVANT: I am sure, and the proof of it is that we have flooded them with lustral water and they have not budged an inch.[99]

TRYGAEUS: Come then, to prayers; to prayers, quick!—Oh! Peace, mighty queen, venerated goddess, thou, who presidest over choruses and at nuptials, deign to accept the sacrifices we offer thee.

SERVANT: Receive it, greatly honoured mistress, and behave not like the coquettes, who half open the door to entice the gallants, draw back when they are stared at, to return once more if a man passes on. But do not act like this to us.

TRYGAEUS: No, but like an honest woman, show thyself to thy worshippers, who are worn with regretting thee all these thirteen years. Hush the noise of battle, be a true Lysimacha to us.[100] Put an end to this tittle-tattle, to this idle babble, that set us defying

---

97. An obscene jest. The Greek word, says the Scholiast, means both barley and the male organ.

98. Before sacrificing, the officiating person asked, "*Who is here?*" and those present answered, "*Many good men.*"

99. The actors forming the chorus are meant here.

100. Lysimacha is derived from (Greek: luein), to put an end to, and (Greek: mach e), fight.

one another. Cause the Greeks once more to taste the pleasant beverage of friendship and temper all hearts with the gentle feeling of forgiveness. Make excellent commodities flow to our markets, fine heads of garlic, early cucumbers, apples, pomegranates and nice little cloaks for the slaves; make them bring geese, ducks, pigeons and larks from Boeotia and baskets of eels from Lake Copaïs; we shall all rush to buy them, disputing their possession with Morychus, Teleas, Glaucetes and every other glutton. Melanthius[101] will arrive on the market last of all; 'twill be, "no more eels, all sold!" and then he'll start a-groaning and exclaiming as in his monologue of Medea,[102] "I am dying, I am dying! Alas! I have let those hidden in the beet escape me!"[103] And won't we laugh? These are the wishes, mighty goddess, which we pray thee to grant.

SERVANT: Take the knife and slaughter the sheep like a finished cook.

TRYGAEUS: No, the goddess does not wish it.[104]

SERVANT: And why not?

TRYGAEUS: Blood cannot please Peace, so let us spill none upon her altar. Therefore go and sacrifice the sheep in the house, cut off the legs and bring them here; thus the carcase will be saved for the choragus.

CHORUS: You, who remain here, get chopped wood and everything needed for the sacrifice ready.

TRYGAEUS: Don't I look like a diviner preparing his mystic fire?

CHORUS: Undoubtedly. Will anything that it behoves a wise man to know escape you? Don't you know all that a man should know, who is distinguished for his wisdom and inventive daring?

TRYGAEUS: There! the wood catches. Its smoke blinds poor Stilbides.[105] I am now going to bring the table and thus be my own slave.

CHORUS: You have braved a thousand dangers to save your sacred town. All honour to you! your glory will be ever envied.

---

101. A tragic poet, reputed a great gourmand.
102. A tragedy by Melanthius.
103. Eels were cooked with beet.—A parody on some verses in the 'Medea' of Melanthius.
104. As a matter of fact, the Sicyonians, who celebrated the festival of Peace on the sixteenth day of the month of hecatombeon (July), spilled no blood upon her altar.
105. A celebrated diviner, who had accompanied the Athenians on their expedition to Sicily. Thus the War was necessary to make his calling pay and the smoke of the sacrifice offered to Peace must therefore be unpleasant to him.

SERVANT: Hold! here are the legs, place them upon the altar. For myself, I mean to go back to the entrails and the cakes.

TRYGAEUS: I'll see to those; I want you here.

SERVANT: Well then, here I am. Do you think I have been long?

TRYGAEUS: Just get this roasted. Ah! who is this man, crowned with laurel, who is coming to me?

SERVANT: He has a self-important look; is he some diviner?

TRYGAEUS: No, i' faith! 'tis Hierocles.

SERVANT: Ah! that oracle-monger from Oreus.[106] What is he going to tell us?

TRYGAEUS: Evidently he is coming to oppose the peace.

SERVANT: No, 'tis the odour of the fat that attracts him.

TRYGAEUS: Let us appear not to see him.

SERVANT: Very well.

HIEROCLES: What sacrifice is this? to what god are you offering it?

TRYGAEUS (*to the servant*): Silence!—(*Aloud*) Look after the roasting and keep your hands off the meat.

HIEROCLES: To whom are you sacrificing? Answer me. Ah! the tail[107] is showing favourable omens.

SERVANT: Aye, very favourable, oh, loved and mighty Peace!

HIEROCLES: Come, cut off the first offering[108] and make the oblation.

TRYGAEUS: 'Tis not roasted enough.

HIEROCLES: Yea, truly, 'tis done to a turn.

TRYGAEUS: Mind your own business, friend! (*To the servant*) Cut away. Where is the table? Bring the libations.

HIEROCLES: The tongue is cut separately.

TRYGAEUS: We know all that. But just listen to one piece of advice.

HIEROCLES: And that is?

TRYGAEUS: Don't talk, for 'tis divine Peace to whom we are sacrificing.

HIEROCLES: Oh! wretched mortals, oh, you idiots!

TRYGAEUS: Keep such ugly terms for yourself.

---

106. A town in Euboea on the channel which separated that island from Thessaly.

107. When sacrificing, the tail was cut off the victim and thrown into the fire. From the way in which it burnt the inference was drawn as to whether or not the sacrifice was agreeable to the deity.

108. This was the part that belonged to the priests and diviners. As one of the latter class, Hierocles is in haste to see this piece cut off.

HIEROCLES: What! you are so ignorant you don't understand the will of the gods and you make a treaty, you, who are men, with apes, who are full of malice![109]

TRYGAEUS: Ha, ha, ha!

HIEROCLES: What are you laughing at?

TRYGAEUS: Ha, ha! your apes amuse me!

HIEROCLES: You simple pigeons, you trust yourselves to foxes, who are all craft, both in mind and heart.

TRYGAEUS: Oh, you trouble-maker! may your lungs get as hot as this meat!

HIEROCLES: Nay, nay! if only the Nymphs had not fooled Bacis, and Bacis mortal men; and if the Nymphs had not tricked Bacis a second time[110] . . .

TRYGAEUS: May the plague seize you, if you won't stop wearying us with your Bacis!

HIEROCLES: . . . it would not have been written in the book of Fate that the bonds of Peace must be broken; but first. . .

TRYGAEUS: The meat must be dusted with salt.

HIEROCLES: . . . it does not please the blessed gods that we should stop the War until the wolf uniteth with the sheep.

TRYGAEUS: How, you cursed animal, could the wolf ever unite with the sheep?

HIEROCLES: As long as the wood-bug gives off a fetid odour, when it flies; as long as the noisy bitch is forced by nature to litter blind pups, so long shall peace be forbidden.

TRYGAEUS: Then what should be done? Not to stop the War would be to leave it to the decision of chance which of the two people should suffer the most, whereas by uniting under a treaty, we share the empire of Greece.

HIEROCLES: You will never make the crab walk straight.

TRYGAEUS: You shall no longer be fed at the Prytaneum; the war done, oracles are not wanted.

HIEROCLES: You will never smooth the rough spikes of the hedgehog.

TRYGAEUS: Will you never stop fooling the Athenians?

---

109. The Spartans.
110. Emphatic pathos, incomprehensible even to the diviner himself; this is a satire on the obscure style of the oracles. Bacis was a famous Boeotian diviner.

ARISTOPHANES

HIEROCLES: What oracle ordered you to burn these joints of mutton in honour of the gods?

TRYGAEUS: This grand oracle of Homer's: "Thus vanished the dark war-clouds and we offered a sacrifice to new-born Peace. When the flame had consumed the thighs of the victim and its inwards had appeased our hunger, we poured out the libations of wine.""Twas I who arranged the sacred rites, but none offered the shining cup to the diviner.[111]

HIEROCLES: I care little for that. 'Tis not the Sibyl who spoke it.[112]

TRYGAEUS: Wise Homer has also said: "He who delights in the horrors of civil war has neither country nor laws nor home." What noble words!

HIEROCLES: Beware lest the kite turn your brain and rob. . .

TRYGAEUS: Look out, slave! This oracle threatens our meat. Quick, pour the libation, and give me some of the inwards.

HIEROCLES: I too will help myself to a bit, if you like.

TRYGAEUS: The libation! the libation!

HIEROCLES: Pour out also for me and give me some of this meat.

TRYGAEUS: No, the blessed gods won't allow it yet; let us drink; and as for you, get you gone, for 'tis their will. Mighty Peace! stay ever in our midst.

HIEROCLES: Bring the tongue hither.

TRYGAEUS: Relieve us of your own.

HIEROCLES: The libation.

TRYGAEUS: Here! and this into the bargain (*strikes him*).

HIEROCLES: You will not give me any meat?

TRYGAEUS: We cannot give you any until the wolf unites with the sheep.

HIEROCLES: I will embrace your knees.

TRYGAEUS: 'Tis lost labour, good fellow; you will never smooth the rough spikes of the hedgehog. . . Come, spectators, join us in our feast.

HIEROCLES: And what am I to do?

TRYGAEUS: You? go and eat the Sibyl.

HIEROCLES: No, by the Earth! no, you shall not eat without me; if you do not give, I take; 'tis common property.

---

111. Of course this is not a *bona fide* quotation, but a whimsical adaptation of various Homeric verses; the last is a coinage of his own, and means, that he is to have no part, either in the flesh of the victim or in the wine of the libations.
112. Probably the Sibyl of Delphi is meant.

TRYGAEUS (*to the servant*): Strike, strike this Bacis, this humbugging soothsayer.

HIEROCLES: I take to witness. . .

TRYGAEUS: And I also, that you are a glutton and an impostor. Hold him tight and beat the impostor with a stick.

SERVANT: You look to that; I will snatch the skin from him, which he has stolen from us.[113] Are you going to let go that skin, you priest from hell! do you hear! Oh! what a fine crow has come from Oreus! Stretch your wings quickly for Elymnium.[114]

CHORUS: Oh! joy, joy! no more helmet, no more cheese nor onions![115] No, I have no passion for battles; what I love, is to drink with good comrades in the corner by the fire when good dry wood, cut in the height of the summer, is crackling; it is to cook pease on the coals and beechnuts among the embers; 'tis to kiss our pretty Thracian[116] while my wife is at the bath. Nothing is more pleasing, when the rain is sprouting our sowings, than to chat with some friend, saying, "Tell me, Comarchides, what shall we do? I would willingly drink myself, while the heavens are watering our fields. Come, wife, cook three measures of beans, adding to them a little wheat, and give us some figs. Syra! call Manes off the fields, 'tis impossible to prune the vine or to align the ridges, for the ground is too wet to-day. Let someone bring me the thrush and those two chaffinches; there were also some curds and four pieces of hare, unless the cat stole them last evening, for I know not what the infernal noise was that I heard in the house. Serve up three of the pieces for me, slave, and give the fourth to my father. Go and ask Aeschinades for some myrtle branches with berries on them, and then, for 'tis the same road, you will invite Charinades to come and drink with me to the honour of the gods who watch over our crops."

When the grasshopper sings its dulcet tune, I love to see the Lemnian vines beginning to ripen, for 'tis the earliest plant of all. I love likewise to watch the fig filling out, and when it has reached maturity I eat with appreciation and exclaim, "Oh! delightful

---

113. The skin of the victim, that is to say.

114. A temple of Euboea, close to Oreus. The servant means, "Return where you came from."

115. This was the soldier's usual ration when on duty.

116. Slaves often bore the name of the country of their birth.

ARISTOPHANES

season!" Then too I bruise some thyme and infuse it in water. Indeed I grow a great deal fatter passing the summer this way than in watching a cursed captain with his three plumes and his military cloak of a startling crimson (*he calls it true Sardian purple*), which he takes care to dye himself with Cyzicus saffron in a battle; then he is the first to run away, shaking his plumes like a great yellow prancing cock,[117] while I am left to watch the nets.[118] Once back again in Athens, these brave fellows behave abominably; they write down these, they scratch through others, and this backwards and forwards two or three times at random. The departure is set for to-morrow, and some citizen has brought no provisions, because he didn't know he had to go; he stops in front of the statue of Pandion,[119] reads his name, is dumbfounded and starts away at a run, weeping bitter tears. The townsfolk are less ill-used, but that is how the husbandmen are treated by these men of war, the hated of the gods and of men, who know nothing but how to throw away their shield. For this reason, if it please heaven, I propose to call these rascals to account, for they are lions in times of peace, but sneaking foxes when it comes to fighting.

TRYGAEUS: Oh! oh! what a crowd for the nuptial feast! Here! dust the tables with this crest, which is good for nothing else now. Halloa! produce the cakes, the thrushes, plenty of good jugged hare and the little loaves.

A SICKLE-MAKER: Trygaeus, where is Trygaeus?

TRYGAEUS: I am cooking the thrushes.

SICKLE-MAKER: Trygaeus, my best of friends, what a fine stroke of business you have done for me by bringing back Peace! Formerly my sickles would not have sold at an obolus apiece, to-day I am being paid fifty drachmas for every one. And here is a neighbour who is selling his casks for the country at three drachmae each. So come, Trygaeus, take as many sickles and casks as you will for nothing. Accept them for nothing; 'tis because of our handsome profits on our sales that we offer you these wedding presents.

---

117. Because of the new colour which fear had lent his chlamys.
118. Meaning, that he deserts his men in mid-campaign, leaving them to look after the enemy.
119. Ancient King of Athens. This was one of the twelve statues, on the pedestals of which the names of the soldiers chosen for departure on service were written. The decrees were also placarded on them.

TRYGAEUS: Thanks. Put them all down inside there, and come along quick to the banquet. Ah! do you see that armourer yonder coming with a wry face?

A CREST-MAKER: Alas! alas! Trygaeus, you have ruined me utterly.

TRYGAEUS: What! won't the crests go any more, friend?

CREST-MAKER: You have killed my business, my livelihood, and that of this poor lance-maker too.

TRYGAEUS: Come, come, what are you asking for these two crests?

CREST-MAKER: What do you bid for them?

TRYGAEUS: What do I bid? Oh! I am ashamed to say. Still, as the clasp is of good workmanship, I would give two, even three measures of dried figs; I could use 'em for dusting the table.

CREST-MAKER: All right, tell them to bring me the dried figs; 'tis always better than nothing.

TRYGAEUS: Take them away, be off with your crests and get you gone; they are moulting, they are losing all their hair; I would not give a single fig for them.

A BREASTPLATE-MAKER: Good gods, what am I going to do with this fine ten-minae breast-plate, which is so splendidly made?

TRYGAEUS: Oh, you will lose nothing over it.

BREASTPLATE-MAKER: I will sell it you at cost price.

TRYGAEUS: 'Twould be very useful as a night-stool. . .

BREASTPLATE-MAKER: Cease your insults, both to me and my wares.

TRYGAEUS: . . . if propped on three stones. Look, 'tis admirable.

BREASTPLATE-MAKER: But how can you wipe, idiot?

TRYGAEUS: I can pass one hand through here, and the other there, and so. . .

BREASTPLATE-MAKER: What! do you wipe with both hands?

TRYGAEUS: Aye, so that I may not be accused of robbing the State, by blocking up an oar-hole in the galley.[120]

BREASTPLATE-MAKER: So you would pay ten minae[121] for a night-stool?

TRYGAEUS: Undoubtedly, you rascal. Do you think I would sell my rump for a thousand drachmae?[122]

---

120. The trierarchs stopped up some of the holes made for the oars, in order to reduce the number of rowers they had to supply for the galleys; they thus saved the wages of the rowers they dispensed with.

121. The mina was equivalent to about £3 10s.

122. Which is the same thing, since a mina was worth a hundred drachmae.

BREASTPLATE-MAKER: Come, have the money paid over to me.

TRYGAEUS: No, friend; I find it hurts me to sit on. Take it away, I won't buy.

A TRUMPET-MAKER: What is to be done with this trumpet, for which I gave sixty drachmae the other day?

TRYGAEUS: Pour lead into the hollow and fit a good, long stick to the top; and you will have a balanced cottabos.[123]

TRUMPET-MAKER: Ha! would you mock me?

TRYGAEUS: Well, here's another notion. Pour in lead as I said, add here a dish hung on strings, and you will have a balance for weighing the figs which you give your slaves in the fields.

A HELMET-MAKER: Cursed fate! I am ruined. Here are helmets, for which I gave a mina each. What am I to do with them? who will buy them?

TRYGAEUS: Go and sell them to the Egyptians; they will do for measuring loosening medicines.[124]

A SPEAR-MAKER: Ah! poor helmet-maker, things are indeed in a bad way.

TRYGAEUS: That man has no cause for complaint.

SPEAR-MAKER: But helmets will be no more used.

TRYGAEUS: Let him learn to fit a handle to them and he can sell them for more money.[125]

SPEAR-MAKER: Let us be off, comrade.

TRYGAEUS: No, I want to buy these spears.

SPEAR-MAKER: What will you give?

TRYGAEUS: If they could be split in two, I would take them at a drachma per hundred to use as vine-props.

SPEAR-MAKER: The insolent dog! Let us go, friend.

TRYGAEUS: Ah! here come the guests, children from the table to relieve themselves; I fancy they also want to hum over what they will be singing presently. Hi! child! what do you reckon to sing? Stand there and give me the opening line.

THE SON OF LAMACHUS: "Glory to the young warriors. . ."

TRYGAEUS: Oh! leave off about your young warriors, you little wretch; we are at peace and you are an idiot and a rascal.

---

123. For *cottabos* see note above, p. 177. (Footnote 287. Transcriber.)

124. *Syrmaea*, a kind of purgative syrup much used by the Egyptians, made of antiscorbutic herbs, such as mustard, horse-radish, etc.

125. As wine-pots or similar vessels.

Son of Lamachus: "The skirmish begins, the hollow bucklers clash against each other."[126]

Trygaeus: Bucklers! Leave me in peace with your bucklers.

Son of Lamachus: "And then there came groanings and shouts of victory."

Trygaeus: Groanings! ah! by Bacchus! look out for yourself, you cursed squaller, if you start wearying us again with your groanings and hollow bucklers.

Son of Lamachus: Then what should I sing? Tell me what pleases you.

Trygaeus: "'Tis thus they feasted on the flesh of oxen," or something similar, as, for instance, "Everything that could tickle the palate was placed on the table."

Son of Lamachus: "'Tis thus they feasted on the flesh of oxen and, tired of warfare, unharnessed their foaming steeds."

Trygaeus: That's splendid; tired of warfare, they seat themselves at table; sing, sing to us how they still go on eating after they are satiated.

Son of Lamachus: "The meal over, they girded themselves. . ."

Trygaeus: With good wine, no doubt?

Son of Lamachus: ". . . with armour and rushed forth from the towers, and a terrible shout arose."

Trygaeus: Get you gone, you little scapegrace, you and your battles! You sing of nothing but warfare. Who is your father then?

Son of Lamachus: My father?

Trygaeus: Why yes, your father.

Son of Lamachus: I am Lamachus' son.

Trygaeus: Oh! oh! I could indeed have sworn, when I was listening to you, that you were the son of some warrior who dreams of nothing but wounds and bruises, of some Boulomachus or Clausimachus;[127] go and sing your plaguey songs to the spearmen. . . Where is the son of Cleonymus? Sing me something before going back to the feast. I am at least certain he will not sing of battles, for his father is far too careful a man.

---

126. These verses and those which both Trygaeus and the son of Lamachus quote afterwards are borrowed from the 'Iliad.'

127. Boulomachus is derived from (Greek: boulesthai) and (Greek: mach e) to wish for battle; Clausimachus from (Greek: klaein) and (Greek: mach e), the tears that battles cost. The same root, (Greek: mach e), battle, is also contained in the name Lamachus.

SON OF CLEONYMUS: "An inhabitant of Saïs is parading with the spotless shield which I regret to say I have thrown into a thicket."[128]

TRYGAEUS: Tell me, you little good-for-nothing, are you singing that for your father?

SON OF CLEONYMUS: "But I saved my life."

TRYGAEUS: And dishonoured your family. But let us go in; I am very certain, that being the son of such a father, you will never forget this song of the buckler. You, who remain to the feast, 'tis your duty to devour dish after dish and not to ply empty jaws. Come, put heart into the work and eat with your mouths full. For, believe me, poor friends, white teeth are useless furniture, if they chew nothing.

CHORUS: Never fear; thanks all the same for your good advice.

TRYGAEUS: You, who yesterday were dying of hunger, come, stuff yourselves with this fine hare-stew; 'tis not every day that we find cakes lying neglected. Eat, eat, or I predict you will soon regret it.

CHORUS: Silence! Keep silence! Here is the bride about to appear! Take nuptial torches and let all rejoice and join in our songs. Then, when we have danced, clinked our cups and thrown Hyperbolus through the doorway, we will carry back all our farming tools to the fields and shall pray the gods to give wealth to the Greeks and to cause us all to gather in an abundant barley harvest, enjoy a noble vintage, to grant that we may choke with good figs, that our wives may prove fruitful, that in fact we may recover all our lost blessings, and that the sparkling fire may be restored to the hearth.

TRYGAEUS: Come, wife, to the fields and seek, my beauty, to brighten and enliven my nights. Oh! Hymen! oh! Hymenaeus!

CHORUS: Oh! Hymen! oh! Hymenaeus! oh! thrice happy man, who so well deserve your good fortune!

TRYGAEUS: Oh! Hymen! oh! Hymenaeus!

CHORUS: Oh! Hymen! oh! Hymenaeus!

FIRST SEMI-CHORUS: What shall we do to her?

SECOND SEMI-CHORUS: What shall we do to her?

FIRST SEMI-CHORUS: We will gather her kisses.

---

128. A distich borrowed from Archilochus, a celebrated poet of the seventh century B.C., born at Paros, and the author of odes, satires, epigrams and elegies. He sang his own shame. 'Twas in an expedition against Saïs, not the town in Egypt as the similarity in name might lead one to believe, but in Thrace, that he had cast away his buckler. "A mighty calamity truly!" he says without shame. "I shall buy another."

SECOND SEMI-CHORUS: We will gather her kisses.

CHORUS: Come, comrades, we who are in the first row, let us pick up the bridegroom and carry him in triumph. Oh! Hymen! oh! Hymenaeus!

TRYGAEUS: Oh! Hymen! oh! Hymenaeus!

CHORUS: You shall have a fine house, no cares and the finest of figs. Oh! Hymen! oh! Hymenaeus!

TRYGAEUS: Oh! Hymen! oh! Hymenaeus!

CHORUS: The bridegroom's fig is great and thick; the bride's is very soft and tender.

TRYGAEUS: While eating and drinking deep draughts of wine, continue to repeat: Oh! Hymen! oh! Hymenaeus!

CHORUS: Oh! Hymen! oh! Hymenaeus!

TRYGAEUS: Farewell, farewell, my friends. All who come with me shall have cakes galore.

FINIS OF "PEACE"

THE BIRDS

INTRODUCTION

The Birds' differs markedly from all the other Comedies of Aristophanes which have come down to us in subject and general conception. It is just an extravaganza pure and simple—a graceful, whimsical theme chosen expressly for the sake of the opportunities it afforded of bright, amusing dialogue, pleasing lyrical interludes, and charming displays of brilliant stage effects and pretty dresses. Unlike other plays of the same Author, there is here apparently no serious political *motif* underlying the surface burlesque and buffoonery.

Some critics, it is true, profess to find in it a reference to the unfortunate Sicilian Expedition, then in progress, and a prophecy of its failure and the political downfall of Alcibiades. But as a matter of fact, the whole thing seems rather an attempt on the dramatist's part to relieve the overwrought minds of his fellow-citizens, anxious and discouraged at the unsatisfactory reports from before Syracuse, by a work conceived in a lighter vein than usual and mainly unconnected with contemporary realities.

The play was produced in the year 414 B.C., just when success or failure in Sicily hung in the balance, though already the outlook was gloomy, and many circumstances pointed to impending disaster. Moreover, the public conscience was still shocked and perturbed over the mysterious affair of the mutilation of the Hermae, which had occurred immediately before the sailing of the fleet, and strongly suspicious of Alcibiades' participation in the outrage. In spite of the inherent charm of the subject, the splendid outbursts of lyrical poetry in some of the choruses and the beauty of the scenery and costumes, 'The Birds' failed to win the first prize. This was acclaimed to a play of Aristophanes' rival, Amipsias, the title of which, 'The Comastae,' *or* 'Revellers,' "seems to imply that the chief interest was derived from direct allusions to the outrage above mentioned and to the individuals suspected to have been engaged in it."

For this reason, which militated against its immediate success, viz. the absence of direct allusion to contemporary politics—there are, of course, incidental references here and there to topics and personages of the day—the play appeals perhaps more than any other of our Author's productions to the modern reader. Sparkling wit, whimsical fancy, poetic charm, are of all ages, and can be appreciated as readily by ourselves as by an Athenian audience of two thousand years ago, though, of course, much is inevitably lost "without the important adjuncts of music, scenery, dresses and what we may call 'spectacle' generally, which we know in this instance to have been on the most magnificent scale."

"The plot is this. Euelpides and Pisthetaerus, two old Athenians, disgusted with the litigiousness, wrangling and sycophancy of their countrymen, resolve upon quitting Attica. Having heard of the fame of Epops (the hoopoe), sometime called Tereus, and now King of the Birds, they determine, under the direction of a raven and a jackdaw, to seek from him and his subject birds a city free from all care and strife." Arrived at the Palace of Epops, they knock, and Trochilus (the wren), in a state of great flutter, as he mistakes them for fowlers, opens the door and informs them that his Majesty is asleep. When he awakes, the strangers appear before him, and after listening to a long and eloquent harangue on the superior attractions of a residence among the birds, they propose a notable scheme of their own to further enhance its advantages and definitely secure the sovereignty of the universe now exercised by the gods of Olympus.

The birds are summoned to meet in general council. They come flying up from all quarters of the heavens, and after a brief misunderstanding, during which they come near tearing the two human envoys to pieces, they listen to the exposition of the latters' plan. This is nothing less than the building of a new city, to be called Nephelococcygia, or 'Cloud-cuckoo-town,' between earth and heaven, to be garrisoned and guarded by the birds in such a way as to intercept all communication of the gods with their worshippers on earth. All steam of sacrifice will be prevented from rising to Olympus, and the Immortals will very soon be starved into an acceptance of any terms proposed.

The new Utopia is duly constructed, and the daring plan to secure the sovereignty is in a fair way to succeed. Meantime various quacks and charlatans, each with a special scheme for improving things, arrive from earth, and are one after the other exposed and dismissed. Presently arrives Prometheus, who informs Epops of the desperate straits to which the gods are by this time reduced, and advises him to push his claims and demand the hand of Basileia (Dominion), the handmaid of Zeus. Next an embassy from the Olympians appears on the scene, consisting of Heracles, Posidon and a god from the savage regions of the Triballians. After some disputation, it is agreed that all reasonable demands of the birds are to be granted, while Pisthetaerus is to have Basileia as his bride. The comedy winds up with the epithalamium in honour of the nuptials.

Dramatis Personae

EUELPIDES.
PISTHETAERUS.
EPOPS (the Hoopoe).
TROCHILUS, Servant to Epops.
PHOENICOPTERUS.
HERALDS.
A PRIEST.
A POET.
A PROPHET.
METON, a Geometrician.
A COMMISSIONER.
A DEALER IN DECREES.
IRIS.
A PARRICIDE.
CINESIAS, a Dithyrambic Bard.
AN INFORMER.
PROMETHEUS.
POSIDON.
TRIBALLUS.
HERACLES.
SERVANT of PISTHETAERUS.
MESSENGERS.
CHORUS OF BIRDS.

SCENE: *A wild, desolate tract of open country; broken rocks and brushwood occupy the centre of the stage.*

EUELPIDES (*to his jay*):[1] Do you think I should walk straight for yon tree?

PISTHETAERUS (*to his crow*): Cursed beast, what are you croaking to me? . . . to retrace my steps?

EUELPIDES: Why, you wretch, we are wandering at random, we are exerting ourselves only to return to the same spot; 'tis labour lost.

PISTHETAERUS: To think that I should trust to this crow, which has made me cover more than a thousand furlongs!

EUELPIDES: And I to this jay, who has torn every nail from my fingers!

PISTHETAERUS: If only I knew where we were. . .

EUELPIDES: Could you find your country again from here?

PISTHETAERUS: No, I feel quite sure I could not, any more than could Execestides[2] find his.

EUELPIDES: Oh dear! oh dear!

PISTHETAERUS: Aye, aye, my friend, 'tis indeed the road of "oh dears" we are following.

EUELPIDES: That Philocrates, the bird-seller, played us a scurvy trick, when he pretended these two guides could help us to find Tereus,[3] the Epops, who is a bird, without being born of one. He has indeed sold us this jay, a true son of Tharelides,[4] for an obolus, and this crow for three, but what can they do? Why, nothing whatever but bite and scratch!—What's the matter with you then, that you keep opening your beak? Do you want us to fling ourselves headlong down these rocks? There is no road that way.

PISTHETAERUS: Not even the vestige of a track in any direction.

EUELPIDES: And what does the crow say about the road to follow?

---

1. Euelpides is holding a jay and Pisthetaerus a crow; they are the guides who are to lead them to the kingdom of the birds.
2. A stranger, who wanted to pass as an Athenian, although coming originally from a far-away barbarian country.
3. A king of Thrace, a son of Ares, who married Procné, the daughter of Pandion, King of Athens, whom he had assisted against the Megarians. He violated his sister-in-law, Philomela, and then cut out her tongue; she nevertheless managed to convey to her sister how she had been treated. They both agreed to kill Itys, whom Procné had born to Tereus, and dished up the limbs of his own son to the father; at the end of the meal Philomela appeared and threw the child's head upon the table. Tereus rushed with drawn sword upon the princesses, but all the actors in this terrible scene were metamorphised. Tereus became an Epops (hoopoe), Procné a swallow, Philomela a nightingale, and Itys a goldfinch. According to Anacreon and Apollodorus it was Procné who became the nightingale and Philomela the swallow, and this is the version of the tradition followed by Aristophanes.
4. An Athenian who had some resemblance to a jay—so says the Scholiast, at any rate.

PISTHETAERUS: By Zeus, it no longer croaks the same thing it did.

EUELPIDES: And which way does it tell us to go now?

PISTHETAERUS: It says that, by dint of gnawing, it will devour my fingers.

EUELPIDES: What misfortune is ours! we strain every nerve to get to the birds,[5] do everything we can to that end, and we cannot find our way! Yes, spectators, our madness is quite different to that of Sacas. He is not a citizen, and would fain be one at any cost; we, on the contrary, born of an honourable tribe and family and living in the midst of our fellow-citizens, we have fled from our country as hard as ever we could go. 'Tis not that we hate it; we recognize it to be great and rich, likewise that everyone has the right to ruin himself; but the crickets only chirrup among the fig-trees for a month or two, whereas the Athenians spend their whole lives in chanting forth judgments from their law courts.[6] That is why we started off with a basket, a stew-pot and some myrtle boughs[7] and have come to seek a quiet country in which to settle. We are going to Tereus, the Epops, to learn from him, whether, in his aerial flights, he has noticed some town of this kind.

PISTHETAERUS: Here! look!

EUELPIDES: What's the matter?

PISTHETAERUS: Why, the crow has been pointing me to something up there for some time now.

EUELPIDES: And the jay is also opening its beak and craning its neck to show me I know not what. Clearly, there are some birds about here. We shall soon know, if we kick up a noise to start them.

PISTHETAERUS: Do you know what to do? Knock your leg against this rock.

EUELPIDES: And you your head to double the noise.

PISTHETAERUS: Well then use a stone instead; take one and hammer with it.

EUELPIDES: Good idea! Ho there, within! Slave! slave!

PISTHETAERUS: What's that, friend! You say, "slave," to summon Epops! 'Twould be much better to shout, "Epops, Epops!"

EUELPIDES: Well then, Epops! Must I knock again? Epops!

---

5. Literally, *to go to the crows*, a proverbial expression equivalent to our *going to the devil*.

6. They leave Athens because of their hatred of lawsuits and informers; this is the especial failing of the Athenians satirized in 'The Wasps.'

7. Myrtle boughs were used in sacrifices, and the founding of every colony was started by a sacrifice.

TROCHILUS: Who's there? Who calls my master?

EUELPIDES: Apollo the Deliverer! what an enormous beak![8]

TROCHILUS: Good god! they are bird-catchers.

EUELPIDES: The mere sight of him petrifies me with terror. What a horrible monster!

TROCHILUS: Woe to you!

EUELPIDES: But we are not men.

TROCHILUS: What are you, then?

EUELPIDES: I am the Fearling, an African bird.

TROCHILUS: You talk nonsense.

EUELPIDES: Well, then, just ask it of my feet.[9]

TROCHILUS: And this other one, what bird is it?

PISTHETAERUS: I? I am a Cackling,[10] from the land of the pheasants.

EUELPIDES: But you yourself, in the name of the gods! what animal are you?

TROCHILUS: Why, I am a slave-bird.

EUELPIDES: Why, have you been conquered by a cock?

TROCHILUS: No, but when my master was turned into a peewit, he begged me to become a bird too, to follow and to serve him.

EUELPIDES: Does a bird need a servant, then?

TROCHILUS: 'Tis no doubt because he was a man. At times he wants to eat a dish of loach from Phalerum; I seize my dish and fly to fetch him some. Again he wants some pea-soup; I seize a ladle and a pot and run to get it.

EUELPIDES: This is, then, truly a running-bird.[11] Come, Trochilus, do us the kindness to call your master.

TROCHILUS: Why, he has just fallen asleep after a feed of myrtle-berries and a few grubs.

EUELPIDES: Never mind; wake him up.

TROCHILUS: I am certain he will be angry. However, I will wake him to please you.

PISTHETAERUS: You cursed brute! why, I am almost dead with terror!

EUELPIDES: Oh! my god! 'twas sheer fear that made me lose my jay.

---

8. The actors wore masks made to resemble the birds they were supposed to represent.
9. Fear had had disastrous effects upon Euelpides' internal economy, this his feet evidenced.
10. The same mishap had occurred to Pisthetaerus.
11. The Greek word for a wren, (Greek: trochilos), is derived from the same root as (Greek: trechein), to run.

PISTHETAERUS: Ah! you great coward! were you so frightened that you let go your jay?

EUELPIDES: And did you not lose your crow, when you fell sprawling on the ground? Pray tell me that.

PISTHETAERUS: No, no.

EUELPIDES: Where is it, then?

PISTHETAERUS: It has flown away.

EUELPIDES: Then you did not let it go! Oh! you brave fellow!

EPOPS: Open the forest,[12] that I may go out!

EUELPIDES: By Heracles! what a creature! what plumage! What means this triple crest?

EPOPS: Who wants me?

EUELPIDES: The twelve great gods have used you ill, meseems.

EPOPS: Are you chaffing me about my feathers? I have been a man, strangers.

EUELPIDES: 'Tis not you we are jeering at.

EPOPS: At what, then?

EUELPIDES: Why, 'tis your beak that looks so odd to us.

EPOPS: This is how Sophocles outrages me in his tragedies. Know, I once was Tereus.[13]

EUELPIDES: You were Tereus, and what are you now? a bird or a peacock?[14]

EPOPS: I am a bird.

EUELPIDES: Then where are your feathers? For I don't see them.

EPOPS: They have fallen off.

EUELPIDES: Through illness.

EPOPS: No. All birds moult their feathers, you know, every winter, and others grow in their place. But tell me, who are you?

EUELPIDES: We? We are mortals.

EPOPS: From what country?

EUELPIDES: From the land of the beautiful galleys.[15]

---

12. No doubt there was some scenery to represent a forest. Besides, there is a pun intended. The words answering for *forest* and *door* ([Greek: hul e and thura]) in Greek only differ slightly in sound.

13. Sophocles had written a tragedy about Tereus, in which, no doubt, the king finally appears as a hoopoe.

14. A (Greek: para prosdokian); one would expect the question to be "bird or man."—Are you a peacock? The hoopoe resembles the peacock inasmuch as both have crests.

15. Athens.

Epops: Are you dicasts?[16]

Euelpides: No, if anything, we are anti-dicasts.

Epops: Is that kind of seed sown among you?[17]

Euelpides: You have to look hard to find even a little in our fields.

Epops: What brings you here?

Euelpides: We wish to pay you a visit.

Epops: What for?

Euelpides: Because you formerly were a man, like we are, formerly you had debts, as we have, formerly you did not want to pay them, like ourselves; furthermore, being turned into a bird, you have when flying seen all lands and seas. Thus you have all human knowledge as well as that of birds. And hence we have come to you to beg you to direct us to some cosy town, in which one can repose as if on thick coverlets.

Epops: And are you looking for a greater city than Athens?

Euelpides: No, not a greater, but one more pleasant to dwell in.

Epops: Then you are looking for an aristocratic country.

Euelpides: I? Not at all! I hold the son of Scellias in horror.[18]

Epops: But, after all, what sort of city would please you best?

Euelpides: A place where the following would be the most important business transacted.—Some friend would come knocking at the door quite early in the morning saying, "By Olympian Zeus, be at my house early, as soon as you have bathed, and bring your children too. I am giving a nuptial feast, so don't fail, or else don't cross my threshold when I am in distress."

Epops: Ah! that's what may be called being fond of hardships. And what say you?

Pisthetaerus: My tastes are similar.

Epops: And they are?

Pisthetaerus: I want a town where the father of a handsome lad will stop in the street and say to me reproachfully as if I had failed him, "Ah! Is this well done, Stilbonides! You met my son coming from the bath after the gymnasium and you neither spoke to him, nor

---

16. The Athenians were madly addicted to lawsuits. (*Vide* 'The Wasps.')

17. As much as to say, *Then you have such things as anti-dicasts?* And Euelpides practically replies, *Very few.*

18. His name was Aristocrates; he was a general and commanded a fleet sent in aid of Corcyra.

embraced him, nor took him with you, nor ever once twitched his testicles. Would anyone call you an old friend of mine?"

EPOPS: Ah! wag, I see you are fond of suffering. But there is a city of delights, such as you want. 'Tis on the Red Sea.

EUELPIDES: Oh, no. Not a sea-port, where some fine morning the Salaminian[19] galley can appear, bringing a writ-server along. Have you no Greek town you can propose to us?

EPOPS: Why not choose Lepreum in Elis for your settlement?

EUELPIDES: By Zeus! I could not look at Lepreum without disgust, because of Melanthius.[20]

EPOPS: Then, again, there is the Opuntian, where you could live.

EUELPIDES: I would not be Opuntian[21] for a talent. But come, what is it like to live with the birds? You should know pretty well.

EPOPS: Why, 'tis not a disagreeable life. In the first place, one has no purse.

EUELPIDES: That does away with much roguery.

EPOPS: For food the gardens yield us white sesame, myrtle-berries, poppies and mint.

EUELPIDES: Why, 'tis the life of the newly-wed indeed.[22]

PISTHETAERUS: Ha! I am beginning to see a great plan, which will transfer the supreme power to the birds, if you will but take my advice.

EPOPS: Take your advice? In what way?

PISTHETAERUS: In what way? Well, firstly, do not fly in all directions with open beak; it is not dignified. Among us, when we see a thoughtless man, we ask, "What sort of bird is this?" and Teleas answers, "'Tis a man who has no brain, a bird that has lost his head, a creature you cannot catch, for it never remains in any one place."

EPOPS: By Zeus himself! your jest hits the mark. What then is to be done?

PISTHETAERUS: Found a city.

EPOPS: We birds? But what sort of city should we build?

---

19. The State galley, which carried the officials of the Athenian republic to their several departments and brought back those whose time had expired; it was this galley that was sent to Sicily to fetch back Alcibiades, who was accused of sacrilege.

20. A tragic poet, who was a leper; there is a play, of course, on the Lepreum.

21. An allusion to Opuntius, who was one-eyed.

22. The newly-married ate a sesame cake, decorated with garlands of myrtle, poppies, and mint.

PISTHETAERUS: Oh, really, really! 'tis spoken like a fool! Look down.

EPOPS: I am looking.

PISTHETAERUS: Now look upwards.

EPOPS: I am looking.

PISTHETAERUS: Turn your head round.

EPOPS: Ah! 'twill be pleasant for me, if I end in twisting my neck!

PISTHETAERUS: What have you seen?

EPOPS: The clouds and the sky.

PISTHETAERUS: Very well! is not this the pole of the birds then?

EPOPS: How their pole?

PISTHETAERUS: Or, if you like it, the land. And since it turns and passes through the whole universe, it is called, 'pole.'[23] If you build and fortify it, you will turn your pole into a fortified city.[24] In this way you will reign over mankind as you do over the grasshoppers and cause the gods to die of rabid hunger.

EPOPS: How so?

PISTHETAERUS: The air is 'twixt earth and heaven. When we want to go to Delphi, we ask the Boeotians[25] for leave of passage; in the same way, when men sacrifice to the gods, unless the latter pay you tribute, you exercise the right of every nation towards strangers and don't allow the smoke of the sacrifices to pass through your city and territory.

EPOPS: By earth! by snares! by network![26] I never heard of anything more cleverly conceived; and, if the other birds approve, I am going to build the city along with you.

PISTHETAERUS: Who will explain the matter to them?

EPOPS: You must yourself. Before I came they were quite ignorant, but since I have lived with them I have taught them to speak.

PISTHETAERUS: But how can they be gathered together?

EPOPS: Easily. I will hasten down to the coppice to waken my dear Procné;[27] as soon as they hear our voices, they will come to us hot wing.

---

23. From (Greek: polein), to turn.

24. The Greek words for *pole* and *city* ([Greek: polos] and [Greek: polis]) only differ by a single letter.

25. Boeotia separated Attica from Phocis.

26. He swears by the powers that are to him dreadful.

27. As already stated, according to the legend, accepted by Aristophanes, it was Procné who was turned into the nightingale.

PISTHETAERUS: My dear bird, lose no time, I beg. Fly at once into the coppice and awaken Procné.

EPOPS: Chase off drowsy sleep, dear companion. Let the sacred hymn gush from thy divine throat in melodious strains; roll forth in soft cadence your refreshing melodies to bewail the fate of Itys,[28] which has been the cause of so many tears to us both. Your pure notes rise through the thick leaves of the yew-tree right up to the throne of Zeus, where Phoebus listens to you, Phoebus with his golden hair. And his ivory lyre responds to your plaintive accents; he gathers the choir of the gods and from their immortal lips rushes a sacred chant of blessed voices. (*The flute is played behind the scene*)

PISTHETAERUS: Oh! by Zeus! what a throat that little bird possesses. He has filled the whole coppice with honey-sweet melody!

EUELPIDES: Hush!

PISTHETAERUS: What's the matter?

EUELPIDES: Will you keep silence?

PISTHETAERUS: What for?

EUELPIDES: Epops is going to sing again.

EPOPS (*in the coppice*): Epopoi, poi, popoi, epopoi, popoi, here, here, quick, quick, quick, my comrades in the air; all you, who pillage the fertile lands of the husbandmen, the numberless tribes who gather and devour the barley seeds, the swift flying race who sing so sweetly. And you whose gentle twitter resounds through the fields with the little cry of tio, tio, tio, tio, tio, tio, tio, tio; and you who hop about the branches of the ivy in the gardens; the mountain birds, who feed on the wild olive berries or the arbutus, hurry to come at my call, trioto, trioto, totobrix; you also, who snap up the sharp-stinging gnats in the marshy vales, and you who dwell in the fine plain of Marathon, all damp with dew, and you, the francolin with speckled wings; you too, the halcyons, who flit over the swelling waves of the sea, come hither to hear the tidings; let all the tribes of long-necked birds assemble here; know that a clever old man has come to us, bringing an entirely new idea and proposing great reforms. Let all come to the debate here, here, here, here. Torotorotorotorotix, kikkobau, kikkobau, torotorotorotorolililix.

---

28. The son of Tereus and Procné.

PISTHETAERUS: Can you see any bird?

EUELPIDES: By Phoebus, no! and yet I am straining my eyesight to scan the sky.

PISTHETAERUS: 'Twas really not worth Epops' while to go and bury himself in the thicket like a plover when a-hatching.

PHOENICOPTERUS: Torotina, torotina.

PISTHETAERUS: Hold, friend, here is another bird.

EUELPIDES: I' faith, yes! 'tis a bird, but of what kind? Isn't it a peacock?

PISTHETAERUS: Epops will tell us. What is this bird?

EPOPS: 'Tis not one of those you are used to seeing; 'tis a bird from the marshes.

PISTHETAERUS: Oh! oh! but he is very handsome with his wings as crimson as flame.

EPOPS: Undoubtedly; indeed he is called flamingo.[29]

EUELPIDES: Hi! I say! You!

PISTHETAERUS: What are you shouting for?

EUELPIDES: Why, here's another bird.

PISTHETAERUS: Aye, indeed; 'tis a foreign bird too. What is this bird from beyond the mountains with a look as solemn as it is stupid?

EPOPS: He is called the Mede.[30]

PISTHETAERUS: The Mede! But, by Heracles! how, if a Mede, has he flown here without a camel?

EUELPIDES: Here's another bird with a crest.

PISTHETAERUS: Ah! that's curious. I say, Epops, you are not the only one of your kind then?

EPOPS: This bird is the son of Philocles, who is the son of Epops;[31] so that, you see, I am his grandfather; just as one might say, Hipponicus,[32] the son of Callias, who is the son of Hipponicus.

---

29. An African bird, that comes to the southern countries of Europe, to Greece, Italy, and Spain; it is even seen in Provence.

30. Aristophanes amusingly mixes up real birds with people and individuals, whom he represents in the form of birds; he is personifying the Medians here.

31. Philocles, a tragic poet, had written a tragedy on Tereus, which was simply a plagiarism of the play of the same name by Sophocles. Philocles is the son of Epops, because he got his inspiration from Sophocles' Tereus, and at the same time is father to Epops, since he himself produced another Tereus.

32. This Hipponicus is probably the orator whose ears Alcibiades boxed to gain a bet; he was a descendant of Callias, who was famous for his hatred of Pisistratus.

PISTHETAERUS: Then this bird is Callias! Why, what a lot of his feathers he has lost![33]

EPOPS: That's because he is honest; so the informers set upon him and the women too pluck out his feathers.

PISTHETAERUS: By Posidon, do you see that many-coloured bird? What is his name?

EPOPS: This one? 'Tis the glutton.

PISTHETAERUS: Is there another glutton besides Cleonymus? But why, if he is Cleonymus, has he not thrown away his crest?[34] But what is the meaning of all these crests? Have these birds come to contend for the double stadium prize?[35]

EPOPS: They are like the Carians, who cling to the crests of their mountains for greater safety.[36]

PISTHETAERUS: Oh, Posidon! do you see what swarms of birds are gathering here?

EUELPIDES: By Phoebus! what a cloud! The entrance to the stage is no longer visible, so closely do they fly together.

PISTHETAERUS: Here is the partridge.

EUELPIDES: Faith! there is the francolin.

PISTHETAERUS: There is the poachard.

EUELPIDES: Here is the kingfisher. And over yonder?

EPOPS: 'Tis the barber.

EUELPIDES: What? a bird a barber?

PISTHETAERUS: Why, Sporgilus is one.[37] Here comes the owl.

EUELPIDES: And who is it brings an owl to Athens?[38]

PISTHETAERUS: Here is the magpie, the turtle-dove, the swallow, the horned owl, the buzzard, the pigeon, the falcon, the ring-dove, the cuckoo, the red-foot, the red-cap, the purple-cap, the kestrel, the diver, the ousel, the osprey, the wood-pecker.

EUELPIDES: Oh! oh! what a lot of birds! what a quantity of blackbirds! how they scold, how they come rushing up! What a noise! what a

---

33. This Callias, who must not be confounded with the foe of Pisistratus, had ruined himself.

34. Cleonymus had cast away his shield; he was as great a glutton as he was a coward.

35. A race in which the track had to be circled twice.

36. A people of Asia Minor; when pursued by the Ionians they took refuge in the mountains.

37. An Athenian barber.

38. The owl was dedicated to Athené, and being respected at Athens, it had greatly multiplied. Hence the proverb, *taking owls to Athens*, similar to our English *taking coals to Newcastle*.

noise! Can they be bearing us ill-will? Oh! there! there! they are opening their beaks and staring at us.

PISTHETAERUS: Why, so they are.

CHORUS: Popopopopopopopoi. Where is he who called me? Where am I to find him?

EPOPS: I have been waiting for you this long while; I never fail in my word to my friends.

CHORUS: Tititititititi. What good thing have you to tell me?

EPOPS: Something that concerns our common safety, and that is just as pleasant as it is to the purpose. Two men, who are subtle reasoners, have come here to seek me.

CHORUS: Where? What? What are you saying?

EPOPS: I say, two old men have come from the abode of men to propose a vast and splendid scheme to us.

CHORUS: Oh! 'tis a horrible, unheard-of crime! What are you saying?

EPOPS: Nay! never let my words scare you.

CHORUS: What have you done then?

EPOPS: I have welcomed two men, who wish to live with us.

CHORUS: And you have dared to do that!

EPOPS: Aye, and am delighted at having done so.

CHORUS: Where are they?

EPOPS: In your midst, as I am.

CHORUS: Ah! ah! we are betrayed; 'tis sacrilege! Our friend, he who picked up corn-seeds in the same plains as ourselves, has violated our ancient laws; he has broken the oaths that bind all birds; he has laid a snare for me, he has handed us over to the attacks of that impious race which, throughout all time, has never ceased to war against us. As for this traitorous bird, we will decide his case later, but the two old men shall be punished forthwith; we are going to tear them to pieces.

PISTHETAERUS: 'Tis all over with us.

EUELPIDES: You are the sole cause of all our trouble. Why did you bring me from down yonder?

PISTHETAERUS: To have you with me.

EUELPIDES: Say rather to have me melt into tears.

PISTHETAERUS: Go to! you are talking nonsense.

EUELPIDES: How so?

PISTHETAERUS: How will you be able to cry when once your eyes are pecked out?

CHORUS: Io! io! forward to the attack, throw yourselves upon the foe, spill his blood; take to your wings and surround them on all sides. Woe to them! let us get to work with our beaks, let us devour them. Nothing can save them from our wrath, neither the mountain forests, nor the clouds that float in the sky, nor the foaming deep. Come, peck, tear to ribbons. Where is the chief of the cohort? Let him engage the right wing.

EUELPIDES: This is the fatal moment. Where shall I fly to, unfortunate wretch that I am?

PISTHETAERUS: Stay! stop here!

EUELPIDES: That they may tear me to pieces?

PISTHETAERUS: And how do you think to escape them?

EUELPIDES: I don't know at all.

PISTHETAERUS: Come, I will tell you. We must stop and fight them. Let us arm ourselves with these stew-pots.

EUELPIDES: Why with the stew-pots?

PISTHETAERUS: The owl will not attack us.[39]

EUELPIDES: But do you see all those hooked claws?

PISTHETAERUS: Seize the spit and pierce the foe on your side.

EUELPIDES: And how about my eyes?

PISTHETAERUS: Protect them with this dish or this vinegar-pot.

EUELPIDES: Oh! what cleverness! what inventive genius! You are a great general, even greater than Nicias,[40] where stratagem is concerned.

CHORUS: Forward, forward, charge with your beaks! Come, no delay. Tear, pluck, strike, flay them, and first of all smash the stew-pot.

EPOPS: Oh, most cruel of all animals, why tear these two men to pieces, why kill them? What have they done to you? They belong to the same tribe, to the same family as my wife.[41]

CHORUS: Are wolves to be spared? Are they not our most mortal foes? So let us punish them.

---

39. An allusion to the Feast of Pots; it was kept at Athens on the third day of the Anthesteria, when all sorts of vegetables were stewed together and offered for the dead to Bacchus and Athené. This Feast was peculiar to Athens.—Hence Pisthetaerus thinks that the owl will recognize they are Athenians by seeing the stew-pots, and as he is an Athenian bird, he will not attack them.

40. Nicias, the famous Athenian general.—The siege of Melos in 417 B.C., or two years previous to the production of 'The Birds,' had especially done him great credit. He was joint commander of the Sicilian expedition.

41. Procné, the daughter of Pandion, King of Athens.

EPOPS: If they are your foes by nature, they are your friends in heart, and they come here to give you useful advice.

CHORUS: Advice or a useful word from their lips, from them, the enemies of my forbears!

EPOPS: The wise can often profit by the lessons of a foe, for caution is the mother of safety. 'Tis just such a thing as one will not learn from a friend and which an enemy compels you to know. To begin with, 'tis the foe and not the friend that taught cities to build high walls, to equip long vessels of war; and 'tis this knowledge that protects our children, our slaves and our wealth.

CHORUS: Well then, I agree, let us first hear them, for 'tis best; one can even learn something in an enemy's school.

PISTHETAERUS: Their wrath seems to cool. Draw back a little.

EPOPS: 'Tis only justice, and you will thank me later.

CHORUS: Never have we opposed your advice up to now.

PISTHETAERUS: They are in a more peaceful mood; put down your stew-pot and your two dishes; spit in hand, doing duty for a spear, let us mount guard inside the camp close to the pot and watch in our arsenal closely; for we must not fly.

EUELPIDES: You are right. But where shall we be buried, if we die?

PISTHETAERUS: In the Ceramicus;[42] for, to get a public funeral, we shall tell the Strategi that we fell at Orneae,[43] fighting the country's foes.

CHORUS: Return to your ranks and lay down your courage beside your wrath as the Hoplites do. Then let us ask these men who they are, whence they come, and with what intent. Here, Epops, answer me.

EPOPS: Are you calling me? What do you want of me?

CHORUS: Who are they? From what country?

EPOPS: Strangers, who have come from Greece, the land of the wise.

CHORUS: And what fate has led them hither to the land of the birds?

EPOPS: Their love for you and their wish to share your kind of life; to dwell and remain with you always.

CHORUS: Indeed, and what are their plans?

EPOPS: They are wonderful, incredible, unheard of.

---

42. A space beyond the walls of Athens which contained the gardens of the Academy and the graves of citizens who had died for their country.
43. A town in Western Argolis, where the Athenians had been recently defeated. The somewhat similar word in Greek, (Greek: ornithes), signifies *birds*.

CHORUS: Why, do they think to see some advantage that determines them to settle here? Are they hoping with our help to triumph over their foes or to be useful to their friends?

EPOPS: They speak of benefits so great it is impossible either to describe or conceive them; all shall be yours, all that we see here, there, above and below us; this they vouch for.

CHORUS: Are they mad?

EPOPS: They are the sanest people in the world.

CHORUS: Clever men?

EPOPS: The slyest of foxes, cleverness its very self, men of the world, cunning, the cream of knowing folk.

CHORUS: Tell them to speak and speak quickly; why, as I listen to you, I am beside myself with delight.

EPOPS: Here, you there, take all these weapons and hang them up inside close to the fire, near the figure of the god who presides there and under his protection;[44] as for you, address the birds, tell them why I have gathered them together.

PISTHETAERUS: Not I, by Apollo, unless they agree with me as the little ape of an armourer agreed with his wife, not to bite me, nor pull me by the testicles, nor shove things up my. . .

CHORUS: You mean the. . . (*Puts finger to bottom*) Oh! be quite at ease.

PISTHETAERUS: No, I mean my eyes.

CHORUS: Agreed.

PISTHETAERUS: Swear it.

CHORUS: I swear it and, if I keep my promise, let judges and spectators give me the victory unanimously.

PISTHETAERUS: It is a bargain.

CHORUS: And if I break my word, may I succeed by one vote only.

HERALD: Hearken, ye people! Hoplites, pick up your weapons and return to your firesides; do not fail to read the decrees of dismissal we have posted.

CHORUS: Man is a truly cunning creature, but nevertheless explain. Perhaps you are going to show me some good way to extend my power, some way that I have not had the wit to find out and which you have discovered. Speak! 'tis to your own interest as well as to mine, for if you secure me some advantage, I will surely share it

---

44. Epops is addressing the two slaves, no doubt Xanthias and Manes, who are mentioned later on.

ARISTOPHANES

with you. But what object can have induced you to come among us? Speak boldly, for I shall not break the truce,—until you have told us all.

PISTHETAERUS: I am bursting with desire to speak; I have already mixed the dough of my address and nothing prevents me from kneading it. . . Slave! bring the chaplet and water, which you must pour over my hands. Be quick![45]

EUELPIDES: Is it a question of feasting? What does it all mean?

PISTHETAERUS: By Zeus, no! but I am hunting for fine, tasty words to break down the hardness of their hearts.—I grieve so much for you, who at one time were kings. . .

CHORUS: We kings! Over whom?

PISTHETAERUS: . . . of all that exists, firstly of me and of this man, even of Zeus himself. Your race is older than Saturn, the Titans and the Earth.

CHORUS: What, older than the Earth!

PISTHETAERUS: By Phoebus, yes.

CHORUS: By Zeus, but I never knew that before!

PISTHETAERUS: 'Tis because you are ignorant and heedless, and have never read your Aesop. 'Tis he who tells us that the lark was born before all other creatures, indeed before the Earth; his father died of sickness, but the Earth did not exist then; he remained unburied for five days, when the bird in its dilemma decided, for want of a better place, to entomb its father in its own head.

EUELPIDES: So that the lark's father is buried at Cephalae.[46]

EPOPS: Hence, if we existed before the Earth, before the gods, the kingship belongs to us by right of priority.

EUELPIDES: Undoubtedly, but sharpen your beak well; Zeus won't be in a hurry to hand over his sceptre to the woodpecker.

PISTHETAERUS: It was not the gods, but the birds, who were formerly the masters and kings over men; of this I have a thousand proofs. First of all, I will point you to the cock, who governed the

---

45. It was customary, when speaking in public and also at feasts, to wear a chaplet; hence the question Euelpides puts. The guests wore chaplets of flowers, herbs, and leaves, which had the property of being refreshing.

46. A deme of Attica. In Greek the word ([Greek: kephalai]) also means *heads*, and hence the pun.

Persians before all other monarchs, before Darius and Megabyzus.[47] 'Tis in memory of his reign that he is called the Persian bird.

EUELPIDES: For this reason also, even to-day, he alone of all the birds wears his tiara straight on his head, like the Great King.[48]

PISTHETAERUS: He was so strong, so great, so feared, that even now, on account of his ancient power, everyone jumps out of bed as soon as ever he crows at daybreak. Blacksmiths, potters, tanners, shoemakers, bathmen, corn-dealers, lyre-makers and armourers, all put on their shoes and go to work before it is daylight.

EUELPIDES: I can tell you something anent that. 'Twas the cock's fault that I lost a splendid tunic of Phrygian wool. I was at a feast in town, given to celebrate the birth of a child; I had drunk pretty freely and had just fallen asleep, when a cock, I suppose in a greater hurry than the rest, began to crow. I thought it was dawn and set out for Alimos.[49] I had hardly got beyond the walls, when a footpad struck me in the back with his bludgeon; down I went and wanted to shout, but he had already made off with my mantle.

PISTHETAERUS: Formerly also the kite was ruler and king over the Greeks.

EPOPS: The Greeks?

PISTHETAERUS: And when he was king, 'twas he who first taught them to fall on their knees before the kites.[50]

EUELPIDES: By Zeus! 'tis what I did myself one day on seeing a kite; but at the moment I was on my knees, and leaning backwards[51] with mouth agape, I bolted an obolus and was forced to carry my bag home empty.[52]

---

47. One of Darius' best generals. After his expedition against the Scythians, this prince gave him the command of the army which he left in Europe. Megabyzus took Perinthos (afterwards called Heraclea) and conquered Thrace.

48. All Persians wore the tiara, but always on one side; the Great King alone wore it straight on his head.

49. Noted as the birthplace of Thucydides, a deme of Attica of the tribe of Leontis. Demosthenes tells us it was thirty-five stadia from Athens.

50. The appearance of the kite in Greece betokened the return of springtime; it was therefore worshipped as a symbol of that season.

51. To look at the kite, who no doubt was flying high in the sky.

52. As already shown, the Athenians were addicted to carrying small coins in their mouths.—This obolus was for the purpose of buying flour to fill the bag he was carrying.

PISTHETAERUS: The cuckoo was king of Egypt and of the whole of Phoenicia. When he called out "cuckoo," all the Phoenicians hurried to the fields to reap their wheat and their barley.[53]

EUELPIDES: Hence no doubt the proverb, "Cuckoo! cuckoo! go to the fields, ye circumcised."[54]

PISTHETAERUS: So powerful were the birds, that the kings of Grecian cities, Agamemnon, Menelaus, for instance, carried a bird on the tip of their sceptres, who had his share of all presents.[55]

EUELPIDES: That I didn't know and was much astonished when I saw Priam come upon the stage in the tragedies with a bird, which kept watching Lysicrates[56] to see if he got any present.

PISTHETAERUS: But the strongest proof of all is, that Zeus, who now reigns, is represented as standing with an eagle on his head as a symbol of his royalty;[57] his daughter has an owl, and Phoebus, as his servant, has a hawk.

EUELPIDES: By Demeter, 'tis well spoken. But what are all these birds doing in heaven?

PISTHETAERUS: When anyone sacrifices and, according to the rite, offers the entrails to the gods, these birds take their share before Zeus. Formerly the men always swore by birds and never by the gods; even now Lampon[58] swears by the goose, when he wants to lie. . . Thus 'tis clear that you were great and sacred, but now you are looked upon as slaves, as fools, as Helots; stones are thrown at you as at raving madmen, even in holy places. A crowd of bird-catchers sets snares, traps, limed-twigs and nets of all sorts for you; you are caught, you are sold in heaps and the buyers finger you over to be certain you are fat. Again, if they would but serve you up simply roasted; but they rasp cheese into a mixture of oil, vinegar and laserwort, to which another sweet and greasy sauce is added,

---

53. In Phoenicia and Egypt the cuckoo makes its appearance about harvest-time.
54. This was an Egyptian proverb, meaning, *When the cuckoo sings we go harvesting*. Both the Phoenicians and the Egyptians practised circumcision.
55. The staff, called a sceptre, generally terminated in a piece of carved work, representing a flower, a fruit, and most often a bird.
56. A general accused of treachery. The bird watches Lysicrates, because, according to Pisthetaerus, he had a right to a share of the presents.
57. It is thus that Phidias represents his Olympian Zeus.
58. One of the diviners sent to Sybaris (in Magna Graecia, S. Italy) with the Athenian colonists, who rebuilt the town under the new name of Thurium.

and the whole is poured scalding hot over your back, for all the world as if you were diseased meat.

CHORUS: Man, your words have made my heart bleed; I have groaned over the treachery of our fathers, who knew not how to transmit to us the high rank they held from their forefathers. But 'tis a benevolent Genius, a happy Fate, that sends you to us; you shall be our deliverer and I place the destiny of my little ones and my own in your hands with every confidence. But hasten to tell me what must be done; we should not be worthy to live, if we did not seek to regain our royalty by every possible means,

PISTHETAERUS: First I advise that the birds gather together in one city and that they build a wall of great bricks, like that at Babylon, round the plains of the air and the whole region of space that divides earth from heaven.

EPOPS: Oh, Cebriones! oh, Porphyrion![59] what a terribly strong place!

PISTHETAERUS: This, this being well done and completed, you demand back the empire from Zeus; if he will not agree, if he refuses and does not at once confess himself beaten, you declare a sacred war against him and forbid the gods henceforward to pass through your country with standing organ, as hitherto, for the purpose of fondling their Alcmenas, their Alopés, or their Semelés;[60] if they try to pass through, you infibulate them with rings so that they can fuck no longer. You send another messenger to mankind, who will proclaim to them that the birds are kings, that for the future they must first of all sacrifice to them, and only afterwards to the gods; that it is fitting to appoint to each deity the bird that has most in common with it. For instance, are they sacrificing to Aphrodité, let them at the same time offer barley to the coot;[61] are they immolating a sheep to Posidon, let them consecrate wheat in honour of the duck;[62] is a steer being offered to

---

59. As if he were saying, "Oh, gods!" Like Lampon, he swears by the birds, instead of swearing by the gods.—The names of these birds are those of two of the Titans.

60. Alcmena, wife of Amphitryon, King of Thebes and mother of Heracles.—Semelé, the daughter of Cadmus and Hermioné and mother of Bacchus; both seduced by Zeus.—Alopé, daughter of Cercyon, a robber, who reigned at Eleusis and was conquered by Perseus. Alopé was honoured with Posidon's caresses; by him she had a son named Hippothous, at first brought up by shepherds but who afterwards was restored to the throne of his grandfather by Theseus.

61. Because the bald patch on the coot's head resembles the shaven and depilated 'motte.'

62. Because water is the duck's domain, as it is that of Posidon.

Heracles, let honey-cakes be dedicated to the gull;[63] is a goat being slain for King Zeus, there is a King-Bird, the wren,[64] to whom the sacrifice of a male gnat is due before Zeus himself even.

EUELPIDES: This notion of an immolated gnat delights me! And now let the great Zeus thunder!

EPOPS: But how will mankind recognize us as gods and not as jays? Us, who have wings and fly?

PISTHETAERUS: You talk rubbish! Hermes is a god and has wings and flies, and so do many other gods. First of all, Victory flies with golden wings, Eros is undoubtedly winged too, and Iris is compared by Homer to a timorous dove.[65] If men in their blindness do not recognize you as gods and continue to worship the dwellers in Olympus, then a cloud of sparrows greedy for corn must descend upon their fields and eat up all their seeds; we shall see then if Demeter will mete them out any wheat.

EUELPIDES: By Zeus, she'll take good care she does not, and you will see her inventing a thousand excuses.

PISTHETAERUS: The crows too will prove your divinity to them by pecking out the eyes of their flocks and of their draught-oxen; and then let Apollo cure them, since he is a physician and is paid for the purpose.[66]

EUELPIDES: Oh! don't do that! Wait first until I have sold my two young bullocks.

PISTHETAERUS: If on the other hand they recognize that you are God, the principle of life, that you are Earth, Saturn, Posidon, they shall be loaded with benefits.

EPOPS: Name me one of these then.

PISTHETAERUS: Firstly, the locusts shall not eat up their vine-blossoms; a legion of owls and kestrels will devour them. Moreover, the gnats and the gall-bugs shall no longer ravage the figs; a flock of thrushes shall swallow the whole host down to the very last.

---

63. Because the gull, like Heracles, is voracious.
64. The Germans still call it *Zaunkönig* and the French *roitelet*, both names thus containing the idea of *king*.
65. The Scholiast draws our attention to the fact that Homer says this of Heré and not of Iris (Iliad, V. 778); it is only another proof that the text of Homer has reached us in a corrupted form, or it may be that Aristophanes was liable, like other people, to occasional mistakes of quotation.
66. In sacrifices.

Epops: And how shall we give wealth to mankind? This is their strongest passion.

Pisthetaerus: When they consult the omens, you will point them to the richest mines, you will reveal the paying ventures to the diviner, and not another shipwreck will happen or sailor perish.

Epops: No more shall perish? How is that?

Pisthetaerus: When the auguries are examined before starting on a voyage, some bird will not fail to say, "Don't start! there will be a storm," or else, "Go! you will make a most profitable venture."

Euelpides: I shall buy a trading-vessel and go to sea. I will not stay with you.

Pisthetaerus: You will discover treasures to them, which were buried in former times, for you know them. Do not all men say, "None know where my treasure lies, unless perchance it be some bird."[67]

Euelpides: I shall sell my boat and buy a spade to unearth the vessels.

Epops: And how are we to give them health, which belongs to the gods?

Pisthetaerus: If they are happy, is not that the chief thing towards health? The miserable man is never well.

Epops: Old Age also dwells in Olympus. How will they get at it? Must they die in early youth?

Pisthetaerus: Why, the birds, by Zeus, will add three hundred years to their life.

Epops: From whom will they take them?

Pisthetaerus: From whom? Why, from themselves. Don't you know the cawing crow lives five times as long as a man?

Euelpides: Ah! ah! these are far better kings for us than Zeus!

Pisthetaerus: Far better, are they not? And firstly, we shall not have to build them temples of hewn stone, closed with gates of gold; they will dwell amongst the bushes and in the thickets of green oak; the most venerated of birds will have no other temple than the foliage of the olive tree; we shall not go to Delphi or to Ammon to sacrifice;[68] but standing erect in the midst of arbutus and wild olives and holding forth our hands filled with wheat and barley, we

---

67. An Athenian proverb.
68. A celebrated temple to Zeus in an oasis of Libya.

shall pray them to admit us to a share of the blessings they enjoy
and shall at once obtain them for a few grains of wheat.

CHORUS: Old man, whom I detested, you are now to me the dearest
of all; never shall I, if I can help it, fail to follow your advice.
Inspirited by your words, I threaten my rivals the gods, and I swear
that if you march in alliance with me against the gods and are
faithful to our just, loyal and sacred bond, we shall soon have
shattered their sceptre. 'Tis our part to undertake the toil, 'tis yours
to advise.

EPOPS: By Zeus! 'tis no longer the time to delay and loiter like
Nicias;[69] let us act as promptly as possible. . . In the first place,
come, enter my nest built of brushwood and blades of straw, and
tell me your names.

PISTHETAERUS: That is soon done; my name is Pisthetaerus.

EPOPS: And his?

PISTHETAERUS: Euelpides, of the deme of Thria.

EPOPS: Good! and good luck to you.

PISTHETAERUS: We accept the omen.

EPOPS: Come in here.

PISTHETAERUS: Very well, 'tis you who lead us and must introduce us.

EPOPS: Come then.

PISTHETAERUS: Oh! my god! do come back here. Hi! tell us how we
are to follow you. You can fly, but we cannot.

EPOPS: Well, well.

PISTHETAERUS: Remember Aesop's fables. It is told there, that the fox
fared very ill, because he had made an alliance with the eagle.

EPOPS: Be at ease. You shall eat a certain root and wings will grow on
your shoulders.

PISTHETAERUS: Then let us enter. Xanthias and Manes,[70] pick up our
baggage.

CHORUS: Hi! Epops! do you hear me?

EPOPS: What's the matter?

CHORUS: Take them off to dine well and call your mate, the melodious
Procné, whose songs are worthy of the Muses; she will delight our
leisure moments.

---

69. Nicias was commander, along with Demosthenes, and later on Alcibiades, of the
Athenian forces before Syracuse, in the ill-fated Sicilian Expedition, 415–413 B.C. He
was much blamed for dilatoriness and indecision.
70. Servants of Pisthetaerus and Euelpides.

PISTHETAERUS: Oh! I conjure you, accede to their wish; for this delightful bird will leave her rushes at the sound of your voice; for the sake of the gods, let her come here, so that we may contemplate the nightingale.[71]

EPOPS: Let it be as you desire. Come forth, Procné, show yourself to these strangers.

PISTHETAERUS: Oh! great Zeus! what a beautiful little bird! what a dainty form! what brilliant plumage![72]

EUELPIDES: Do you know how dearly I should like to split her legs for her?

PISTHETAERUS: She is dazzling all over with gold, like a young girl.[73]

EUELPIDES: Oh! how I should like to kiss her!

PISTHETAERUS: Why, wretched man, she has two little sharp points on her beak.

EUELPIDES: I would treat her like an egg, the shell of which we remove before eating it; I would take off her mask and then kiss her pretty face.

EPOPS: Let us go in.

PISTHETAERUS: Lead the way, and may success attend us.

CHORUS: Lovable golden bird, whom I cherish above all others, you, whom I associate with all my songs, nightingale, you have come, you have come, to show yourself to me and to charm me with your notes. Come, you, who play spring melodies upon the harmonious flute,[74] lead off our anapaests.[75]

Weak mortals, chained to the earth, creatures of clay as frail as the foliage of the woods, you unfortunate race, whose life is but darkness, as unreal as a shadow, the illusion of a dream, hearken to us, who are immortal beings, ethereal, ever young and occupied with eternal thoughts, for we shall teach you about all celestial matters; you shall know thoroughly what is the nature of the birds,

---

71. It has already been mentioned that, according to the legend followed by Aristophanes, Procné had been changed into a nightingale and Philomela into a swallow.

72. The actor, representing Procné, was dressed out as a courtesan, but wore the mask of a bird.

73. Young unmarried girls wore golden ornaments; the apparel of married women was much simpler.

74. The actor, representing Procné, was a flute-player.

75. The parabasis.

what the origin of the gods, of the rivers, of Erebus, and Chaos; thanks to us, Prodicus[76] will envy you your knowledge.

At the beginning there was only Chaos, Night, dark Erebus, and deep Tartarus. Earth, the air and heaven had no existence. Firstly, black-winged Night laid a germless egg in the bosom of the infinite deeps of Erebus, and from this, after the revolution of long ages, sprang the graceful Eros with his glittering golden wings, swift as the whirlwinds of the tempest. He mated in deep Tartarus with dark Chaos, winged like himself, and thus hatched forth our race, which was the first to see the light. That of the Immortals did not exist until Eros had brought together all the ingredients of the world, and from their marriage Heaven, Ocean, Earth and the imperishable race of blessed gods sprang into being. Thus our origin is very much older than that of the dwellers in Olympus. We are the offspring of Eros; there are a thousand proofs to show it. We have wings and we lend assistance to lovers. How many handsome youths, who had sworn to remain insensible, have not been vanquished by our power and have yielded themselves to their lovers when almost at the end of their youth, being led away by the gift of a quail, a waterfowl, a goose, or a cock.[77]

And what important services do not the birds render to mortals! First of all, they mark the seasons for them, springtime, winter, and autumn. Does the screaming crane migrate to Libya,—it warns the husbandman to sow, the pilot to take his ease beside his tiller hung up in his dwelling,[78] and Orestes[79] to weave a tunic, so that the rigorous cold may not drive him any more to strip other folk. When the kite reappears, he tells of the return of spring and of the period when the fleece of the sheep must be clipped. Is the swallow in sight? All hasten to sell their warm tunic and to buy some light clothing. We are your Ammon,

---

76. A sophist of the island of Ceos, a disciple of Protagoras, as celebrated for his knowledge as for his eloquence. The Athenians condemned him to death as a corrupter of youth in 396 B.C.

77. Lovers were wont to make each other presents of birds. The cock and the goose are mentioned, of course, in jest.

78. I.e. that it gave notice of the approach of winter, during which season the Ancients did not venture to sea.

79. A notorious robber.

Delphi, Dodona, your Phoebus Apollo.[80] Before undertaking anything, whether a business transaction, a marriage, or the purchase of food, you consult the birds by reading the omens, and you give this name of omen[81] to all signs that tell of the future. With you a word is an omen, you call a sneeze an omen, a meeting an omen, an unknown sound an omen, a slave or an ass an omen.[82] Is it not clear that we are a prophetic Apollo to you? If you recognize us as gods, we shall be your divining Muses, through us you will know the winds and the seasons, summer, winter, and the temperate months. We shall not withdraw ourselves to the highest clouds like Zeus, but shall be among you and shall give to you and to your children and the children of your children, health and wealth, long life, peace, youth, laughter, songs and feasts; in short, you will all be so well off, that you will be weary and satiated with enjoyment.

Oh, rustic Muse of such varied note, tio, tio, tio, tiotinx, I sing with you in the groves and on the mountain tops, tio, tio, tio, tio, tiotinx.[83] I pour forth sacred strains from my golden throat in honour of the god Pan,[84] tio, tio, tio, tiotinx, from the top of the thickly leaved ash, and my voice mingles with the mighty choirs who extol Cybelé on the mountain tops,[85] totototototototinx. 'Tis to our concerts that Phrynicus comes to pillage like a bee the ambrosia of his songs, the sweetness of which so charms the ear, tio, tio, tio, tio, tinx.

If there be one of you spectators who wishes to spend the rest of his life quietly among the birds, let him come to us. All that is disgraceful and forbidden by law on earth is on the contrary honourable among us, the birds. For instance, among you 'tis a crime to beat your father, but with us 'tis an estimable deed; it's considered fine to run straight at your father and hit him, saying,

---

80. Meaning, *"We are your oracles."*—Dodona was an oracle in Epirus.—The temple of Zeus there was surrounded by a dense forest, all the trees of which were endowed with the gift of prophecy; both the sacred oaks and the pigeons that lived in them answered the questions of those who came to consult the oracle in pure Greek.
81. The Greek word for *omen* is the same as that for *bird*—(Greek: ornis).
82. A satire on the passion of the Greeks for seeing an omen in everything.
83. An imitation of the nightingale's song.
84. God of the groves and wilds.
85. The 'Mother of the Gods'; roaming the mountains, she held dances, always attended by Pan and his accompanying rout of Fauns and Satyrs.

ARISTOPHANES

"Come, lift your spur if you want to fight."[86] The runaway slave, whom you brand, is only a spotted francolin with us.[87] Are you Phrygian like Spintharus?[88] Among us you would be the Phrygian bird, the goldfinch, of the race of Philemon.[89] Are you a slave and a Carian like Execestides? Among us you can create yourself forefathers;[90] you can always find relations. Does the son of Pisias want to betray the gates of the city to the foe? Let him become a partridge, the fitting offspring of his father; among us there is no shame in escaping as cleverly as a partridge.

So the swans on the banks of the Hebrus, tio, tio, tio, tio, tiotinx, mingle their voices to serenade Apollo, tio, tio, tio, tio, tiotinx, flapping their wings the while, tio, tio, tio, tio, tiotinx; their notes reach beyond the clouds of heaven; all the dwellers in the forests stand still with astonishment and delight; a calm rests upon the waters, and the Graces and the choirs in Olympus catch up the strain, tio, tio, tio, tio, tiotinx.

There is nothing more useful nor more pleasant than to have wings. To begin with, just let us suppose a spectator to be dying with hunger and to be weary of the choruses of the tragic poets; if he were winged, he would fly off, go home to dine and come back with his stomach filled. Some Patroclides in urgent need would not have to soil his cloak, but could fly off, satisfy his requirements, and, having recovered his breath, return. If one of you, it matters not who, had adulterous relations and saw the husband of his mistress in the seats of the senators, he might stretch his wings, fly thither, and, having appeased his craving, resume his place. Is it not the most priceless gift of all, to be winged? Look at Diitrephes![91] His wings were only wicker-work ones, and yet he got himself chosen Phylarch and then Hipparch; from being

---

86. An allusion to cock-fighting; the birds are armed with brazen spurs.
87. An allusion to the spots on this bird, which resemble the scars left by a branding iron.
88. He was of Asiatic origin, but wished to pass for an Athenian.
89. Or Philamnon, King of Thrace; the Scholiast remarks that the Phrygians and the Thracians had a common origin.
90. The Greek word here, (Greek: pappos), is also the name of a little bird.
91. A basket-maker who had become rich.—The Phylarchs were the headmen of the tribes, (Greek: Phulai). They presided at the private assemblies and were charged with the management of the treasury.—The Hipparchs, as the name implies, were the leaders of the cavalry; there were only two of these in the Athenian army.

nobody, he has risen to be famous; 'tis now the finest gilded cock of his tribe.[92]

PISTHETAERUS: Halloa! What's this? By Zeus! I never saw anything so funny in all my life.[93]

EUELPIDES: What makes you laugh?

PISTHETAERUS: 'Tis your bits of wings. D'you know what you look like? Like a goose painted by some dauber-fellow.

EUELPIDES: And you look like a close-shaven blackbird.

PISTHETAERUS: 'Tis ourselves asked for this transformation, and, as Aeschylus has it, "These are no borrowed feathers, but truly our own."[94]

EPOPS: Come now, what must be done?

PISTHETAERUS: First give our city a great and famous name, then sacrifice to the gods.

EUELPIDES: I think so too.

EPOPS: Let's see. What shall our city be called?

PISTHETAERUS: Will you have a high-sounding Laconian name? Shall we call it Sparta?

EUELPIDES: What! call my town Sparta? Why, I would not use esparto for my bed,[95] even though I had nothing but bands of rushes.

PISTHETAERUS: Well then, what name can you suggest?

EUELPIDES: Some name borrowed from the clouds, from these lofty regions in which we dwell—in short, some well-known name.

PISTHETAERUS: Do you like Nephelococcygia?[96]

EPOPS: Oh! capital! truly 'tis a brilliant thought!

EUELPIDES: Is it in Nephelococcygia that all the wealth of Theogenes[97] and most of Aeschines'[98] is?

---

92. He had now become a senator, member of the (Greek: Boul e).
93. Pisthetaerus and Euelpides now both return with wings.
94. Meaning, 'tis we who wanted to have these wings.—The verse from Aeschylus, quoted here, is taken from 'The Myrmidons,' a tragedy of which only a few fragments remain.
95. The Greek word signified the city of Sparta, and also a kind of broom used for weaving rough matting, which served for the beds of the very poor.
96. A fanciful name constructed from (Greek: nephel e), a cloud, and (Greek: kokkux), a cuckoo; thus a city of clouds and cuckoos.—*Wolkenkukelheim** is a clever approximation in German. Cloud-cuckoo-town, perhaps, is the best English equivalent.

* Transcriber's note: So in original. The correct German word is *Wolkenkuckucksheim*.
97. He was a boaster nicknamed (Greek: Kapnos), *smoke*, because he promised a great deal and never kept his word.
98. Also mentioned in 'The Wasps.'

PISTHETAERUS: No, 'tis rather the plain of Phlegra,[99] where the gods withered the pride of the sons of the Earth with their shafts.

EUELPIDES: Oh! what a splendid city! But what god shall be its patron? for whom shall we weave the peplus?[100]

PISTHETAERUS: Why not choose Athené Polias?[101]

EUELPIDES: Oh! what a well-ordered town 'twould be to have a female deity armed from head to foot, while Clisthenes[102] was spinning!

PISTHETAERUS: Who then shall guard the Pelargicon?[103]

EPOPS: One of ourselves, a bird of Persian strain, who is everywhere proclaimed to be the bravest of all, a true chick of Ares.[104]

EUELPIDES: Oh! noble chick! what a well-chosen god for a rocky home!

PISTHETAERUS: Come! into the air with you to help the workers, who are building the wall; carry up rubble, strip yourself to mix the mortar, take up the hod, tumble down the ladder, an you like, post sentinels, keep the fire smouldering beneath the ashes, go round the walls, bell in hand,[105] and go to sleep up there yourself; then despatch two heralds, one to the gods above, the other to mankind on earth and come back here.

EUELPIDES: As for yourself, remain here, and may the plague take you for a troublesome fellow!

PISTHETAERUS: Go, friend, go where I send you, for without you my orders cannot be obeyed. For myself, I want to sacrifice to the new god, and I am going to summon the priest who must preside at the ceremony. Slaves! slaves! bring forward the basket and the lustral water.

CHORUS: I do as you do, and I wish as you wish, and I implore you to address powerful and solemn prayers to the gods, and in addition to immolate a sheep as a token of our gratitude. Let us sing the Pythian chant in honour of the god, and let Chaeris accompany our voices.

---

99. Because the war of the Titans against the gods was only a fiction of the poets.

100. A sacred cloth, with which the statue of Athené in the Acropolis was draped.

101. Meaning, to be patron-goddess of the city. Athené had a temple of this name.

102. An Athenian effeminate, frequently ridiculed by Aristophanes.

103. This was the name of the wall surrounding the Acropolis.

104. I.e. the fighting-cock.

105. To waken the sentinels, who might else have fallen asleep.—There are several merry contradictions in the various parts of this list of injunctions.

PISTHETAERUS (*to the flute-player*): Enough! but, by Heracles! what is this? Great gods! I have seen many prodigious things, but I never saw a muzzled raven.[106]

EPOPS: Priest! 'tis high time! Sacrifice to the new gods.

PRIEST: I begin, but where is he with the basket? Pray to the Vesta of the birds, to the kite, who presides over the hearth, and to all the god and goddess-birds who dwell in Olympus.

CHORUS: Oh! Hawk, the sacred guardian of Sunium, oh, god of the storks!

PRIEST: Pray to the swan of Delos, to Latona the mother of the quails, and to Artemis, the goldfinch.

PISTHETAERUS: 'Tis no longer Artemis Colaenis, but Artemis the goldfinch.[107]

PRIEST: And to Bacchus, the finch and Cybelé, the ostrich and mother of the gods and mankind.

CHORUS: Oh! sovereign ostrich, Cybelé, the mother of Cleocritus,[108] grant health and safety to the Nephelococcygians as well as to the dwellers in Chios. . .

PISTHETAERUS: The dwellers in Chios! Ah! I am delighted they should be thus mentioned on all occasions.[109]

CHORUS: . . . to the heroes, the birds, to the sons of heroes, to the porphyrion, the pelican, the spoon-bill, the redbreast, the grouse, the peacock, the horned-owl, the teal, the bittern, the heron, the stormy petrel, the fig-pecker, the titmouse. . .

PISTHETAERUS: Stop! stop! you drive me crazy with your endless list. Why, wretch, to what sacred feast are you inviting the vultures and the sea-eagles? Don't you see that a single kite could easily carry off the lot at once? Begone, you and your fillets and all; I shall know how to complete the sacrifice by myself.

PRIEST: It is imperative that I sing another sacred chant for the rite of the lustral water, and that I invoke the immortals, or at least one

---

106. In allusion to the leather strap which flute-players wore to constrict the cheeks and add to the power of the breath. The performer here no doubt wore a raven's mask.

107. Hellanicus, the Mitylenian historian, tells that this surname of Artemis is derived from Colaenus, King of Athens before Cecrops and a descendant of Hermes. In obedience to an oracle he erected a temple to the goddess, invoking her as Artemis Colaenis (the Artemis of Colaenus).

108. This Cleocritus, says the Scholiast, was long-necked and strutted like an ostrich.

109. The Chians were the most faithful allies of Athens, and hence their name was always mentioned in prayers, decrees, etc.

ARISTOPHANES

of them, provided always that you have some suitable food to offer him; from what I see here, in the shape of gifts, there is naught whatever but horn and hair.

PISTHETAERUS: Let us address our sacrifices and our prayers to the winged gods.

A POET: Oh, Muse! celebrate happy Nephelococcygia in your hymns.

PISTHETAERUS: What have we here? Where do you come from, tell me? Who are you?

POET: I am he whose language is sweeter than honey, the zealous slave of the Muses, as Homer has it.

PISTHETAERUS: You a slave! and yet you wear your hair long?

POET: No, but the fact is all we poets are the assiduous slaves of the Muses according to Homer.

PISTHETAERUS: In truth your little cloak is quite holy too through zeal! But, poet, what ill wind drove you here?

POET: I have composed verses in honour of your Nephelococcygia, a host of splendid dithyrambs and parthenians,[110] worthy of Simonides himself.

PISTHETAERUS: And when did you compose them? How long since?

POET: Oh! 'tis long, aye, very long, that I have sung in honour of this city.

PISTHETAERUS: But I am only celebrating its foundation with this sacrifice;[111] I have only just named it, as is done with little babies.

POET: "Just as the chargers fly with the speed of the wind, so does the voice of the Muses take its flight. Oh! thou noble founder of the town of Aetna,[112] thou, whose name recalls the holy sacrifices,[113] make us such gift as thy generous heart shall suggest."

PISTHETAERUS: He will drive us silly if we do not get rid of him by some present. Here! you, who have a fur as well as your tunic, take it off and give it to this clever poet. Come, take this fur; you look to me to be shivering with cold.

POET: My Muse will gladly accept this gift; but engrave these verses of Pindar's on your mind.

PISTHETAERUS: Oh! what a pest! 'Tis impossible then to be rid of him.

---

110. Verses sung by maidens.
111. This ceremony took place on the tenth day after birth, and may be styled the pagan baptism.
112. Hiero, tyrant of Syracuse.—This passage is borrowed from Pindar.
113. (Greek: Hierón) in Greek means sacrifice.

POET: "Straton wanders among the Scythian nomads, but has no linen garment. He is sad at only wearing an animal's pelt and no tunic." Do you conceive my bent?

PISTHETAERUS: I understand that you want me to offer you a tunic. Hi! you (*to Euelpides*), take off yours; we must help the poet. . . Come, you, take it and begone.

POET: I am going, and these are the verses that I address to this city: "Phoebus of the golden throne, celebrate this shivery, freezing city; I have travelled through fruitful and snow-covered plains. Tralala! Tralala!"[114]

PISTHETAERUS: What are you chanting us about frosts? Thanks to the tunic, you no longer fear them. Ah! by Zeus! I could not have believed this cursed fellow could so soon have learnt the way to our city. Come, priest, take the lustral water and circle the altar.

PRIEST: Let all keep silence!

A PROPHET: Let not the goat be sacrificed.[115]

PISTHETAERUS: Who are you?

PROPHET: Who am I? A prophet.

PISTHETAERUS: Get you gone.

PROPHET: Wretched man, insult not sacred things. For there is an oracle of Bacis, which exactly applies to Nephelococcygia.

PISTHETAERUS: Why did you not reveal it to me before I founded my city?

PROPHET: The divine spirit was against it.

PISTHETAERUS: Well, 'tis best to know the terms of the oracle.

PROPHET: "But when the wolves and the white crows shall dwell together between Corinth and Sicyon. . ."[116]

PISTHETAERUS: But how do the Corinthians concern me?

PROPHET: 'Tis the regions of the air that Bacis indicated in this manner. "They must first sacrifice a white-fleeced goat to Pandora, and give the prophet, who first reveals my words, a good cloak and new sandals."

PISTHETAERUS: Are the sandals there?

PROPHET: Read. "And besides this a goblet of wine and a good share of the entrails of the victim."

---

114. A parody of poetic pathos, not to say bathos.
115. Which the priest was preparing to sacrifice.
116. Orneae, a city in Argolis ([Greek: ornis] in Greek means a bird). It was because of this similarity in sound that the prophet alludes to Orneae.

PISTHETAERUS: Of the entrails—is it so written?

PROPHET: Read. "If you do as I command, divine youth, you shall be an eagle among the clouds; if not, you shall be neither turtle-dove, nor eagle, nor woodpecker."

PISTHETAERUS: Is all that there?

PROPHET: Read.

PISTHETAERUS: This oracle in no sort of way resembles the one Apollo dictated to me: "If an impostor comes without invitation to annoy you during the sacrifice and to demand a share of the victim, apply a stout stick to his ribs."

PROPHET: You are drivelling.

PISTHETAERUS: "And don't spare him, were he an eagle from out of the clouds, were it Lampon himself[117] or the great Diopithes."[118]

PROPHET: Is all that there?

PISTHETAERUS: Here, read it yourself, and go and hang yourself.

PROPHET: Oh! unfortunate wretch that I am.

PISTHETAERUS: Away with you, and take your prophecies elsewhere.

METON:[119] I have come to you.

PISTHETAERUS: Yet another pest. What have you come to do? What's your plan? What's the purpose of your journey? Why these splendid buskins?

METON: I want to survey the plains of the air for you and to parcel them into lots.

PISTHETAERUS: In the name of the gods, who are you?

METON: Who am I? Meton, known throughout Greece and at Colonus.[120]

PISTHETAERUS: What are these things?

METON: Tools for measuring the air. In truth, the spaces in the air have precisely the form of a furnace. With this bent ruler I draw a line from top to bottom; from one of its points I describe a circle with the compass. Do you understand?

---

117. Noted Athenian diviner, who, when the power was still shared between Thucydides and Pericles, predicted that it would soon be centred in the hands of the latter; his ground for this prophecy was the sight of a ram with a single horn.

118. No doubt another Athenian diviner, and possibly the same person whom Aristophanes names in 'The Knights' and 'The Wasps' as being a thief.

119. A celebrated geometrician and astronomer.

120. A deme contiguous to Athens. It is as though he said, "Well known throughout all England and at Croydon."

PISTHETAERUS: Not the very least.

METON: With the straight ruler I set to work to inscribe a square within this circle; in its centre will be the marketplace, into which all the straight streets will lead, converging to this centre like a star, which, although only orbicular, sends forth its rays in a straight line from all sides.

PISTHETAERUS: Meton, you new Thales. . .[121]

METON: What d'you want with me?

PISTHETAERUS: I want to give you a proof of my friendship. Use your legs.

METON: Why, what have I to fear?

PISTHETAERUS: 'Tis the same here as in Sparta. Strangers are driven away, and blows rain down as thick as hail.

METON: Is there sedition in your city?

PISTHETAERUS: No, certainly not.

METON: What's wrong then?

PISTHETAERUS: We are agreed to sweep all quacks and impostors far from our borders.

METON: Then I'm off.

PISTHETAERUS: I fear me 'tis too late. The thunder growls already. (*Beats him*)

METON: Oh, woe! oh, woe!

PISTHETAERUS: I warned you. Now, be off, and do your surveying somewhere else. (*Meton takes to his heels*)

AN INSPECTOR: Where are the Proxeni?[122]

PISTHETAERUS: Who is this Sardanapalus?[123]

INSPECTOR: I have been appointed by lot to come to Nephelococcygia as inspector.[124]

PISTHETAERUS: An inspector! and who sends you here, you rascal?

INSPECTOR: A decree of Taleas.[125]

PISTHETAERUS: Will you just pocket your salary, do nothing, and be off?

---

121. Thales was no less famous as a geometrician than he was as a sage.
122. Officers of Athens, whose duty was to protect strangers who came on political or other business, and see to their interests generally.
123. He addresses the inspector thus because of the royal and magnificent manners he assumes.
124. Magistrates appointed to inspect the tributary towns.
125. A much-despised citizen, already mentioned. He ironically supposes him invested with the powers of an Archon, which ordinarily were entrusted only to men of good repute.

ARISTOPHANES

INSPECTOR: I' faith! that I will; I am urgently needed to be at Athens to attend the assembly; for I am charged with the interests of Pharnaces.[126]

PISTHETAERUS: Take it then, and be off. See, here is your salary. (*Beats him*)

INSPECTOR: What does this mean?

PISTHETAERUS: 'Tis the assembly where you have to defend Pharnaces.

INSPECTOR: You shall testify that they dare to strike me, the inspector.

PISTHETAERUS: Are you not going to clear out with your urns. 'Tis not to be believed; they send us inspectors before we have so much as paid sacrifice to the gods.

A DEALER IN DECREES: "If the Nephelococcygian does wrong to the Athenian. . ."

PISTHETAERUS: Now whatever are these cursed parchments?

DEALER IN DECREES: I am a dealer in decrees, and I have come here to sell you the new laws.

PISTHETAERUS: Which?

DEALER IN DECREES: "The Nephelococcygians shall adopt the same weights, measures and decrees as the Olophyxians."[127]

PISTHETAERUS: And you shall soon be imitating the Ototyxians. (*Beats him*)

DEALER IN DECREES: Hullo! what are you doing?

PISTHETAERUS: Now will you be off with your decrees? For I am going to let *you* see some severe ones.

INSPECTOR (*returning*): I summon Pisthetaerus for outrage for the month of Munychion.[128]

PISTHETAERUS: Ha! my friend! are you still there?

DEALER IN DECREES: "Should anyone drive away the magistrates and not receive them, according to the decree duly posted. . ."

PISTHETAERUS: What! rascal! you are there too?

---

126. A Persian satrap.—An allusion to certain orators, who, bribed with Asiatic gold, had often defended the interests of the foe in the Public Assembly.

127. A Macedonian people in the peninsula of Chalcidicé. This name is chosen because of its similarity to the Greek word (Greek: olophuresthai), *to groan*. It is from another verb, (Greek: ototuzein), meaning the same thing, that Pisthetaerus coins the name of Ototyxians, i.e. groaners, because he is about to beat the dealer.—The mother-country had the right to impose any law it chose upon its colonies.

128. Corresponding to our month of April.

INSPECTOR: Woe to you! I'll have you condemned to a fine of ten thousand drachmae.

PISTHETAERUS: And I'll smash your urns.[129]

INSPECTOR: Do you recall that evening when you stooled against the column where the decrees are posted?

PISTHETAERUS: Here! here! let him be seized. (*The inspectors run off*) Well! don't you want to stop any longer?

PRIEST: Let us get indoors as quick as possible; we will sacrifice the goat inside.[130]

CHORUS: Henceforth it is to me that mortals must address their sacrifices and their prayers. Nothing escapes my sight nor my might. My glance embraces the universe, I preserve the fruit in the flower by destroying the thousand kinds of voracious insects the soil produces, which attack the trees and feed on the germ when it has scarcely formed in the calyx; I destroy those who ravage the balmy terrace gardens like a deadly plague; all these gnawing crawling creatures perish beneath the lash of my wing. I hear it proclaimed everywhere: "A talent for him who shall kill Diagoras of Melos,[131] and a talent for him who destroys one of the dead tyrants."[132] We likewise wish to make our proclamation: "A talent to him among you who shall kill Philocrates, the Strouthian;[133] four, if he brings him to us alive. For this Philocrates skewers the finches together and sells them at the rate of an obolus for seven. He tortures the thrushes by blowing them out, so that they may look bigger, sticks their own feathers into the nostrils of blackbirds, and collects pigeons, which he shuts up and forces them, fastened in a net, to decoy others." That is what we wish to proclaim. And

---

129. Which the inspector had brought with him for the purpose of inaugurating the assemblies of the people or some tribunal.

130. So that the sacrifices might no longer be interrupted.

131. A disciple of Democrites; he passed over from superstition to atheism. The injustice and perversity of mankind led him to deny the existence of the gods, to lay bare the mysteries and to break the idols. The Athenians had put a price on his head, so he left Greece and perished soon afterwards in a storm at sea.

132. By this jest Aristophanes means to imply that tyranny is dead, and that no one aspires to despotic power, though this silly accusation was constantly being raised by the demagogues and always favourably received by the populace.

133. A poulterer.—Strouthian, used in joke to designate him, as if from the name of his 'deme,' is derived from (Greek: strouthos), *a sparrow*. The birds' foe is thus grotesquely furnished with an ornithological surname.

ARISTOPHANES

if anyone is keeping birds shut up in his yard, let him hasten to let them loose; those who disobey shall be seized by the birds and we shall put them in chains, so that in their turn they may decoy other men.

Happy indeed is the race of winged birds who need no cloak in winter! Neither do I fear the relentless rays of the fiery dog-days; when the divine grasshopper, intoxicated with the sunlight, when noon is burning the ground, is breaking out into shrill melody, my home is beneath the foliage in the flowery meadows. I winter in deep caverns, where I frolic with the mountain nymphs, while in spring I despoil the gardens of the Graces and gather the white, virgin berry on the myrtle bushes.

I want now to speak to the judges about the prize they are going to award; if they are favourable to us, we will load them with benefits far greater than those Paris[134] received. Firstly, the owls of Laurium,[135] which every judge desires above all things, shall never be wanting to you; you shall see them homing with you, building their nests in your money-bags and laying coins. Besides, you shall be housed like the gods, for we shall erect gables[136] over your dwellings; if you hold some public post and want to do a little pilfering, we will give you the sharp claws of a hawk. Are you dining in town, we will provide you with crops.[137] But, if your award is against us, don't fail to have metal covers fashioned for yourselves, like those they place over statues;[138] else, look out! for the day you wear a white tunic all the birds will soil it with their droppings.

PISTHETAERUS: Birds! the sacrifice is propitious. But I see no messenger coming from the wall to tell us what is happening. Ah!

---

134. From Aphrodité (Venus), to whom he had awarded the apple, prize of beauty, in the contest of the "goddesses three."

135. Laurium was an Athenian deme at the extremity of the Attic peninsula containing valuable silver mines, the revenues of which were largely employed in the maintenance of the fleet and payment of the crews. The "owls of Laurium," of course, mean pieces of money; the Athenian coinage was stamped with a representation of an owl, the bird of Athené.

136. A pun impossible to keep in English, on the two meanings of the word (Greek: aetos), which signifies both an eagle and the gable of a house or pediment of a temple.

137. That is, birds' crops, into which they could stow away plenty of good things.

138. The Ancients appear to have placed metal discs over statues standing in the open air, to save them from injury from the weather, etc.

here comes one running himself out of breath as though he were running the Olympic stadium.

MESSENGER: Where, where is he? Where, where, where is he? Where, where, where is he? Where is Pisthetaerus, our leader?

PISTHETAERUS: Here am I.

MESSENGER: The wall is finished.

PISTHETAERUS: That's good news.

MESSENGER: 'Tis a most beautiful, a most magnificent work of art. The wall is so broad, that Proxenides, the Braggartian, and Theogenes could pass each other in their chariots, even if they were drawn by steeds as big as the Trojan horse.

PISTHETAERUS: 'Tis wonderful!

MESSENGER: Its length is one hundred stadia; I measured it myself.

PISTHETAERUS: A decent length, by Posidon! And who built such a wall?

MESSENGER: Birds—birds only; they had neither Egyptian brickmaker, nor stonemason, nor carpenter; the birds did it all themselves, I could hardly believe my eyes. Thirty thousand cranes came from Libya with a supply of stones,[139] intended for the foundations. The water-rails chiselled them with their beaks. Ten thousand storks were busy making bricks; plovers and other water fowl carried water into the air.

PISTHETAERUS: And who carried the mortar?

MESSENGER: Herons, in hods.

PISTHETAERUS: But how could they put the mortar into hods?

MESSENGER: Oh! 'twas a truly clever invention; the geese used their feet like spades; they buried them in the pile of mortar and then emptied them into the hods.

PISTHETAERUS: Ah! to what use cannot feet be put?[140]

MESSENGER: You should have seen how eagerly the ducks carried bricks. To complete the tale, the swallows came flying to the work, their beaks full of mortar and their trowel on their back, just the way little children are carried.

PISTHETAERUS: Who would want paid servants after this? But, tell me, who did the woodwork?

---

139. So as not to be carried away by the wind when crossing the sea, cranes are popularly supposed to ballast themselves with stones, which they carry in their beaks.

140. Pisthetaerus modifies the Greek proverbial saying, "To what use cannot hands be put?"

MESSENGER: Birds again, and clever carpenters too, the pelicans, for they squared up the gates with their beaks in such a fashion that one would have thought they were using axes; the noise was just like a dockyard. Now the whole wall is tight everywhere, securely bolted and well guarded; it is patrolled, bell in hand; the sentinels stand everywhere and beacons burn on the towers. But I must run off to clean myself; the rest is your business.

CHORUS: Well! what do you say to it? Are you not astonished at the wall being completed so quickly?

PISTHETAERUS: By the gods, yes, and with good reason. 'Tis really not to be believed. But here comes another messenger from the wall to bring us some further news! What a fighting look he has!

SECOND MESSENGER: Oh! oh! oh! oh! oh! oh!

PISTHETAERUS: What's the matter?

SECOND MESSENGER: A horrible outrage has occurred; a god sent by Zeus has passed through our gates and has penetrated the realms of the air without the knowledge of the jays, who are on guard in the daytime.

PISTHETAERUS: Tis an unworthy and criminal deed. What god was it?

SECOND MESSENGER: We don't know that. All we know is, that he has got wings.

PISTHETAERUS: Why were not guards sent against him at once?

SECOND MESSENGER: We have despatched thirty thousand hawks of the legion of mounted archers.[141] All the hook-clawed birds are moving against him, the kestrel, the buzzard, the vulture, the great-horned owl; they cleave the air, so that it resounds with the flapping of their wings; they are looking everywhere for the god, who cannot be far away; indeed, if I mistake not, he is coming from yonder side.

PISTHETAERUS: All arm themselves with slings and bows! This way, all our soldiers; shoot and strike! Some one give me a sling!

CHORUS: War, a terrible war is breaking out between us and the gods! Come, let each one guard the Air, the son of Erebus,[142] in which the clouds float. Take care no immortal enters it without your

---

141. A corps of Athenian cavalry was so named.
142. Chaos, Night, Tartarus, and Erebus alone existed in the beginning; Eros was born from Night and Erebus, and he wedded Chaos and begot Earth, Air, and Heaven; so runs the fable.

knowledge. Scan all sides with your glance. Hark! methinks I can hear the rustle of the swift wings of a god from heaven.

PISTHETAERUS: Hi! you woman! where are you flying to? Halt, don't stir! keep motionless! not a beat of your wing!—Who are you and from what country? You must say whence you come.[143]

IRIS: I come from the abode of the Olympian gods.

PISTHETAERUS: What's your name, ship or cap?[144]

IRIS: I am swift Iris.

PISTHETAERUS: Paralus or Salaminia?[145]

IRIS: What do you mean?

PISTHETAERUS: Let a buzzard rush at her and seize her.[146]

IRIS: Seize me! But what do all these insults betoken?

PISTHETAERUS: Woe to you!

IRIS: 'Tis incomprehensible.

PISTHETAERUS: By which gate did you pass through the wall, wretched woman?

IRIS: By which gate? Why, great gods, I don't know.

PISTHETAERUS: You hear how she holds us in derision. Did you present yourself to the officers in command of the jays? You don't answer. Have you a permit, bearing the seal of the storks?

IRIS: Am I awake?

PISTHETAERUS: Did you get one?

IRIS: Are you mad?

PISTHETAERUS: No head-bird gave you a safe-conduct?

IRIS: A safe-conduct to me, you poor fool!

PISTHETAERUS: Ah! and so you slipped into this city on the sly and into these realms of air-land that don't belong to you.

IRIS: And what other road can the gods travel?

PISTHETAERUS: By Zeus! I know nothing about that, not I. But they won't pass this way. And you still dare to complain! Iris would ever have more justly suffered death.

IRIS: I am immortal.

---

143. Iris appears from the top of the stage and arrests her flight in mid-career.

144. Ship, because of her wings, which resemble oars; cap, because she no doubt wore the head-dress (as a messenger of the gods) with which Hermes is generally depicted.

145. The names of the two sacred galleys which carried Athenian officials on State business.

146. A buzzard is named in order to raise a laugh, the Greek name (Greek: triorchos) also meaning, etymologically, provided with three testicles, vigorous in love.

PISTHETAERUS: You would have died nevertheless.—Oh! 'twould be truly intolerable! What! should the universe obey us and the gods alone continue their insolence and not understand that they must submit to the law of the strongest in their due turn? But tell me, where are you flying to?

IRIS: I? The messenger of Zeus to mankind, I am going to tell them to sacrifice sheep and oxen on the altars and to fill their streets with the rich smoke of burning fat.

PISTHETAERUS: Of which gods are you speaking?

IRIS: Of which? Why, of ourselves, the gods of heaven.

PISTHETAERUS: You, gods?

IRIS: Are there others then?

PISTHETAERUS: Men now adore the birds as gods, and 'tis to them, by Zeus, that they must offer sacrifices, and not to Zeus at all!

IRIS: Oh! fool! fool! Rouse not the wrath of the gods, for 'tis terrible indeed. Armed with the brand of Zeus, Justice would annihilate your race; the lightning would strike you as it did Lycimnius and consume both your body and the porticos of your palace.[147]

PISTHETAERUS: Here! that's enough tall talk. Just you listen and keep quiet! Do you take me for a Lydian or a Phrygian[148] and think to frighten me with your big words? Know, that if Zeus worries me again, I shall go at the head of my eagles, who are armed with lightning, and reduce his dwelling and that of Amphion to cinders.[149] I shall send more than six hundred porphyrions clothed in leopards' skins[150] up to heaven against him; and formerly a single Porphyrion gave him enough to do. As for you, his messenger, if you annoy me, I shall begin by stretching your legs asunder and so conduct myself, Iris though you be, that despite my age, you will be astonished. I will show you a fine long tool that will fuck you three times over.

IRIS: May you perish, you wretch, you and your infamous words!

PISTHETAERUS: Won't you be off quickly? Come, stretch your wings or look out for squalls!

---

147. Iris' reply is a parody of the tragic style.—'Lycimnius' is, according to the Scholiast, the title of a tragedy by Euripides, which is about a ship that is struck by lightning.
148. I.e. for a poltroon, like the slaves, most of whom came to Athens from these countries.
149. A parody of a passage in the lost tragedy of 'Niobe' of Aeschylus.
150. Because this bird has a spotted plumage.—Porphyrion is also the name of one of the Titans who tried to storm heaven.

IRIS: If my father does not punish you for your insults. . .

PISTHETAERUS: Ha! . . . but just you be off elsewhere to roast younger folk than us with your lightning.

CHORUS: We forbid the gods, the sons of Zeus, to pass through our city and the mortals to send them the smoke of their sacrifices by this road.

PISTHETAERUS: 'Tis odd that the messenger we sent to the mortals has never returned.

HERALD: Oh! blessed Pisthetaerus, very wise, very illustrious, very gracious, thrice happy, very. . . Come, prompt me, somebody, do.

PISTHETAERUS: Get to your story!

HERALD: All peoples are filled with admiration for your wisdom, and they award you this golden crown.

PISTHETAERUS: I accept it. But tell me, why do the people admire me?

HERALD: Oh you, who have founded so illustrious a city in the air, you know not in what esteem men hold you and how many there are who burn with desire to dwell in it. Before your city was built, all men had a mania for Sparta; long hair and fasting were held in honour, men went dirty like Socrates and carried staves. Now all is changed. Firstly, as soon as 'tis dawn, they all spring out of bed together to go and seek their food, the same as you do; then they fly off towards the notices and finally devour the decrees. The bird-madness is so clear, that many actually bear the names of birds. There is a halting victualler, who styles himself the partridge; Menippus calls himself the swallow; Opontius the one-eyed crow; Philocles the lark; Theogenes the fox-goose; Lycurgus the ibis; Chaerephon the bat; Syracosius the magpie; Midias the quail;[151] indeed he looks like a quail that has been hit heavily over the head. Out of love for the birds they repeat all the songs which concern the swallow, the teal, the goose or the pigeon; in each verse you see wings, or at all events a few feathers. This is what is happening down there. Finally, there are more than ten thousand folk who are coming here from earth to ask you for feathers and hooked claws; so, mind you supply yourself with wings for the immigrants.

---

151. All these surnames bore some relation to the character or the build of the individual to whom the poet applies them.—Chaerephon, Socrates' disciple, was of white and ashen hue.—Opontius was one-eyed.—Syracosius was a braggart.—Midias had a passion for quail-fights, and, besides, resembled that bird physically.

PISTHETAERUS: Ah! by Zeus, 'tis not the time for idling. Go as quick as possible and fill every hamper, every basket you can find with wings. Manes[152] will bring them to me outside the walls, where I will welcome those who present themselves.

CHORUS: This town will soon be inhabited by a crowd of men.

PISTHETAERUS: If fortune favours us.

CHORUS: Folk are more and more delighted with it.

PISTHETAERUS: Come, hurry up and bring them along.

CHORUS: Will not man find here everything that can please him— wisdom, love, the divine Graces, the sweet face of gentle peace?

PISTHETAERUS: Oh! you lazy servant! won't you hurry yourself?

CHORUS: Let a basket of wings be brought speedily. Come, beat him as I do, and put some life into him; he is as lazy as an ass.

PISTHETAERUS: Aye, Manes is a great craven.

CHORUS: Begin by putting this heap of wings in order; divide them in three parts according to the birds from whom they came; the singing, the prophetic[153] and the aquatic birds; then you must take care to distribute them to the men according to their character.

PISTHETAERUS (*to Manes*): Oh! by the kestrels! I can keep my hands off you no longer; you are too slow and lazy altogether.

A PARRICIDE:[154] Oh! might I but become an eagle, who soars in the skies! Oh! might I fly above the azure waves of the barren sea![155]

PISTHETAERUS: Ha! 'twould seem the news was true; I hear someone coming who talks of wings.

PARRICIDE: Nothing is more charming than to fly; I burn with desire to live under the same laws as the birds; I am bird-mad and fly towards you, for I want to live with you and to obey your laws.

PISTHETAERUS: Which laws? The birds have many laws.

PARRICIDE: All of them; but the one that pleases me most is, that among the birds it is considered a fine thing to peck and strangle one's father.

PISTHETAERUS: Aye, by Zeus! according to us, he who dares to strike his father, while still a chick, is a brave fellow.

---

152. Pisthetaerus' servant, already mentioned.
153. From the inspection of which auguries were taken, e.g. the eagles, the vultures, the crows.
154. Or rather, a young man who contemplated parricide.
155. A parody of verses in Sophocles' 'Oenomaus.'

PARRICIDE: And therefore I want to dwell here, for I want to strangle my father and inherit his wealth.

PISTHETAERUS: But we have also an ancient law written in the code of the storks, which runs thus, "When the stork father has reared his young and has taught them to fly, the young must in their turn support the father."

PARRICIDE: 'Tis hardly worth while coming all this distance to be compelled to keep my father!

PISTHETAERUS: No, no, young friend, since you have come to us with such willingness, I am going to give you these black wings, as though you were an orphan bird; furthermore, some good advice, that I received myself in infancy. Don't strike your father, but take these wings in one hand and these spurs in the other; imagine you have a cock's crest on your head and go and mount guard and fight; live on your pay and respect your father's life. You're a gallant fellow! Very well, then! Fly to Thrace and fight.[156]

PARRICIDE: By Bacchus! 'Tis well spoken; I will follow your counsel.

PISTHETAERUS: 'Tis acting wisely, by Zeus.

CINESIAS:[157] "On my light pinions I soar off to Olympus; in its capricious flight my Muse flutters along the thousand paths of poetry in turn. . ."

PISTHETAERUS: This is a fellow will need a whole shipload of wings.

CINESIAS: . . . it is seeking fresh outlet."

PISTHETAERUS: Welcome, Cinesias, you lime-wood man![158] Why have you come here a-twisting your game leg in circles?

CINESIAS: "I want to become a bird, a tuneful nightingale."

PISTHETAERUS: Enough of that sort of ditty. Tell me what you want.

CINESIAS: Give me wings and I will fly into the topmost airs to gather fresh songs in the clouds, in the midst of the vapours and the fleecy snow.

PISTHETAERUS: Gather songs in the clouds?

CINESIAS: 'Tis on them the whole of our latter-day art depends. The most brilliant dithyrambs are those that flap their wings in void space and are clothed in mist and dense obscurity. To appreciate this, just listen.

---

156. The Athenians were then besieging Amphipolis in the Thracian Chalcidicé.

157. There was a real Cinesias—a dithyrambic poet, born at Thebes.

158. The Scholiast thinks that Cinesias, who was tall and slight of build, wore a kind of corset of lime-wood to support his waist—surely rather a far-fetched interpretation!

PISTHETAERUS: Oh! no, no, no!

CINESIAS: By Hermes! but indeed you shall. "I shall travel through thine ethereal empire like a winged bird, who cleaveth space with his long neck. . ."

PISTHETAERUS: Stop! easy all, I say![159]

CINESIAS: . . . as I soar over the seas, carried by the breath of the winds. . .

PISTHETAERUS: By Zeus! but I'll cut your breath short.

CINESIAS: . . . now rushing along the tracks of Notus, now nearing Boreas across the infinite wastes of the ether." (*Pisthetaerus beats him*) Ah! old man, that's a pretty and clever idea truly!

PISTHETAERUS: What! are you not delighted to be cleaving the air?[160]

CINESIAS: To treat a dithyrambic poet, for whom the tribes dispute with each other, in this style![161]

PISTHETAERUS: Will you stay with us and form a chorus of winged birds as slender as Leotrophides[162] for the Cecropid tribe?

CINESIAS: You are making game of me, 'tis clear; but know that I shall never leave you in peace if I do not have wings wherewith to traverse the air.

AN INFORMER: What are these birds with downy feathers, who look so pitiable to me? Tell me, oh swallow with the long dappled wings.[163]

PISTHETAERUS: Oh! but 'tis a perfect invasion that threatens us. Here comes another of them, humming along.

INFORMER: Swallow with the long dappled wings, once more I summon you.

PISTHETAERUS: It's his cloak I believe he's addressing; 'faith, it stands in great need of the swallows' return.[164]

---

159. The Greek word used here was the word of command employed to stop the rowers.

160. Cinesias makes a bound each time that Pisthetaerus struck him.

161. The tribes of Athens, or rather the rich citizens belonging to them, were wont on feast-days to give representations of dithyrambic choruses as well as of tragedies and comedies.

162. Another dithyrambic poet, a man of extreme leanness.

163. A parody of a hemistich from 'Alcaeus.'—The informer is dissatisfied at only seeing birds of sombre plumage and poor appearance. He would have preferred to denounce the rich.

164. The informer, says the Scholiast, was clothed with a ragged cloak, the tatters of which hung down like wings, in fact, a cloak that could not protect him from the cold and must have made him long for the swallows' return, i.e. the spring.

INFORMER: Where is he who gives out wings to all comers?

PISTHETAERUS: 'Tis I, but you must tell me for what purpose you want them.

INFORMER: Ask no questions. I want wings, and wings I must have.

PISTHETAERUS: Do you want to fly straight to Pellené?[165]

INFORMER: I? Why, I am an accuser of the islands,[166] an informer. . .

PISTHETAERUS: A fine trade, truly!

INFORMER: . . . a hatcher of lawsuits. Hence I have great need of wings to prowl round the cities and drag them before justice.

PISTHETAERUS: Would you do this better if you had wings?

INFORMER: No, but I should no longer fear the pirates; I should return with the cranes, loaded with a supply of lawsuits by way of ballast.

PISTHETAERUS: So it seems, despite all your youthful vigour, you make it your trade to denounce strangers?

INFORMER: Well, and why not? I don't know how to dig.

PISTHETAERUS: But, by Zeus! there are honest ways of gaining a living at your age without all this infamous trickery.

INFORMER: My friend, I am asking you for wings, not for words.

PISTHETAERUS: 'Tis just my words that give you wings.

INFORMER: And how can you give a man wings with your words?

PISTHETAERUS: 'Tis thus that all first start.

INFORMER: All?

PISTHETAERUS: Have you not often heard the father say to young men in the barbers' shops, "It's astonishing how Diitrephes' advice has made my son fly to horse-riding."—"Mine," says another, "has flown towards tragic poetry on the wings of his imagination."

INFORMER: So that words give wings?

PISTHETAERUS: Undoubtedly; words give wings to the mind and make a man soar to heaven. Thus I hope that my wise words will give you wings to fly to some less degrading trade.

INFORMER: But I do not want to.

PISTHETAERUS: What do you reckon on doing then?

INFORMER: I won't belie my breeding; from generation to generation we have lived by informing. Quick, therefore, give me quickly some light, swift hawk or kestrel wings, so that I may summon the

---

165. A town in Achaia, where woollen cloaks were made.
166. His trade was to accuse the rich citizens of the subject islands, and drag them before the Athenian courts; he explains later the special advantages of this branch of the informer's business.

islanders, sustain the accusation here, and haste back there again on flying pinions.

PISTHETAERUS: I see. In this way the stranger will be condemned even before he appears.

INFORMER: That's just it.

PISTHETAERUS: And while he is on his way here by sea, you will be flying to the islands to despoil him of his property.

INFORMER: You've hit it, precisely; I must whirl hither and thither like a perfect humming-top.

PISTHETAERUS: I catch the idea. Wait, i' faith, I've got some fine Corcyraean wings.[167] How do you like them?

INFORMER: Oh! woe is me! Why, 'tis a whip!

PISTHETAERUS: No, no; these are the wings, I tell you, that set the top a-spinning.

INFORMER: Oh! oh! oh!

PISTHETAERUS: Take your flight, clear off, you miserable cur, or you will soon see what comes of quibbling and lying. Come, let us gather up our wings and withdraw.

CHORUS: In my ethereal nights I have seen many things new and strange and wondrous beyond belief. There is a tree called Cleonymus belonging to an unknown species; it has no heart, is good for nothing and is as tall as it is cowardly. In springtime it shoots forth calumnies instead of buds and in autumn it strews the ground with bucklers in place of leaves.[168]

Far away in the regions of darkness, where no ray of light ever enters, there is a country, where men sit at the table of the heroes and dwell with them always—save always in the evening. Should any mortal meet the hero Orestes at night, he would soon be stripped and covered with blows from head to foot.[169]

PROMETHEUS: Ah! by the gods! if only Zeus does not espy me! Where is Pisthetaerus?

PISTHETAERUS: Ha! what is this? A masked man!

PROMETHEUS: Can you see any god behind me?

PISTHETAERUS: No, none. But who are you, pray?

---

167. That is, whips—Corcyra being famous for these articles.
168. Cleonymus is a standing butt of Aristophanes' wit, both as an informer and a notorious poltroon.
169. In allusion to the cave of the bandit Orestes; the poet terms him a hero only because of his heroic name Orestes.

PROMETHEUS: What's the time, please?

PISTHETAERUS: The time? Why, it's past noon. Who are you?

PROMETHEUS: Is it the fall of day? Is it no later than that?[170]

PISTHETAERUS: Oh! 'pon my word! but you grow tiresome!

PROMETHEUS: What is Zeus doing? Is he dispersing the clouds or gathering them?[171]

PISTHETAERUS: Take care, lest I lose all patience.

PROMETHEUS: Come, I will raise my mask.

PISTHETAERUS: Ah! my dear Prometheus!

PROMETHEUS: Stop! stop! speak lower!

PISTHETAERUS: Why, what's the matter, Prometheus?

PROMETHEUS: H'sh, h'sh! Don't call me by my name; you will be my ruin, if Zeus should see me here. But, if you want me to tell you how things are going in heaven, take this umbrella and shield me, so that the gods don't see me.

PISTHETAERUS: I can recognize Prometheus in this cunning trick. Come, quick then, and fear nothing; speak on.

PROMETHEUS: Then listen.

PISTHETAERUS: I am listening, proceed!

PROMETHEUS: It's all over with Zeus.

PISTHETAERUS: Ah! and since when, pray?

PROMETHEUS: Since you founded this city in the air. There is not a man who now sacrifices to the gods; the smoke of the victims no longer reaches us. Not the smallest offering comes! We fast as though it were the festival of Demeter.[172] The barbarian gods, who are dying of hunger, are bawling like Illyrians[173] and threaten to make an armed descent upon Zeus, if he does not open markets where joints of the victims are sold.

PISTHETAERUS: What! there are other gods besides you, barbarian gods who dwell above Olympus?

PROMETHEUS: If there were no barbarian gods, who would be the patron of Execestides?[174]

PISTHETAERUS: And what is the name of these gods?

---

170. Prometheus wants night to come and so reduce the risk of being seen from Olympus.
171. The clouds would prevent Zeus seeing what was happening below him.
172. The third day of the festival of Demeter was a fast.
173. A semi-savage people, addicted to violence and brigandage.
174. Who, being reputed a stranger despite his pretension to the title of a citizen, could only have a strange god for his patron or tutelary deity.

PROMETHEUS: Their name? Why, the Triballi.[175]

PISTHETAERUS: Ah, indeed! 'tis from that no doubt that we derive the word 'tribulation.'[176]

PROMETHEUS: Most likely. But one thing I can tell you for certain, namely, that Zeus and the celestial Triballi are going to send deputies here to sue for peace. Now don't you treat, unless Zeus restores the sceptre to the birds and gives you Basileia[177] in marriage.

PISTHETAERUS: Who is this Basileia?

PROMETHEUS: A very fine young damsel, who makes the lightning for Zeus; all things come from her, wisdom, good laws, virtue, the fleet, calumnies, the public paymaster and the triobolus.

PISTHETAERUS: Ah! then she is a sort of general manageress to the god.

PROMETHEUS: Yes, precisely. If he gives you her for your wife, yours will be the almighty power. That is what I have come to tell you; for you know my constant and habitual goodwill towards men.

PISTHETAERUS: Oh, yes! 'tis thanks to you that we roast our meat.[178]

PROMETHEUS: I hate the gods, as you know.

PISTHETAERUS: Aye, by Zeus, you have always detested them.

PROMETHEUS: Towards them I am a veritable Timon;[179] but I must return in all haste, so give me the umbrella; if Zeus should see me from up there, he would think I was escorting one of the Canephori.[180]

PISTHETAERUS: Wait, take this stool as well.

CHORUS: Near by the land of the Sciapodes[181] there is a marsh, from the borders whereof the odious Socrates evokes the souls of men.

---

175. The Triballi were a Thracian people; it was a term commonly used in Athens to describe coarse men, obscene debauchees and greedy parasites.

176. There is a similar pun in the Greek.

177. I.e. the *supremacy* of Greece, the real object of the war.

178. Prometheus had stolen the fire from the gods to gratify mankind.

179. A celebrated misanthrope, contemporary to Aristophanes. Hating the society of men, he had only a single friend, Apimantus, to whom he was attached, because of their similarity of character; he also liked Alcibiades, because he foresaw that this young man would be the ruin of his country.

180. The Canephori were young maidens, chosen from the first families of the city, who carried baskets wreathed with myrtle at the feast of Athené, while at those of Bacchus and Demeter they appeared with gilded baskets.—The daughters of 'Metics,' or resident aliens, walked behind them, carrying an umbrella and a stool.

181. According to Ctesias, the Sciapodes were a people who dwelt on the borders of the Atlantic. Their feet were larger than the rest of their bodies, and to shield themselves

Pisander[182] came one day to see his soul, which he had left there when still alive. He offered a little victim, a camel,[183] slit his throat and, following the example of Ulysses, stepped one pace backwards.[184] Then that bat of a Chaerephon[185] came up from hell to drink the camel's blood.

POSIDON:[186] This is the city of Nephelococcygia, Cloud-cuckoo-town, whither we come as ambassadors. (*To Triballus*) Hi! what are you up to? you are throwing your cloak over the left shoulder. Come, fling it quick over the right! And why, pray, does it draggle this fashion? Have you ulcers to hide like Laespodias?[187] Oh! democracy![188] whither, oh! whither are you leading us? Is it possible that the gods have chosen such an envoy?

TRIBALLUS: Leave me alone.

POSIDON: Ugh! the cursed savage! you are by far the most barbarous of all the gods.—Tell me, Heracles, what are we going to do?

HERACLES: I have already told you that I want to strangle the fellow who has dared to block us in.

POSIDON: But, my friend, we are envoys of peace.

HERACLES: All the more reason why I wish to strangle him.

PISTHETAERUS: Hand me the cheese-grater; bring me the silphium for sauce; pass me the cheese and watch the coals.[189]

HERACLES: Mortal! we who greet you are three gods.

PISTHETAERUS: Wait a bit till I have prepared my silphium pickle.

HERACLES: What are these meats?[190]

---

from the sun's rays they held up one of their feet as an umbrella.—By giving the Socratic philosophers the name of Sciapodes here ([Greek: podes], feet, and [Greek: skia], shadow) Aristophanes wishes to convey that they are walking in the dark and busying themselves with the greatest nonsense.

182. This Pisander was a notorious coward; for this reason the poet jestingly supposes that he had lost his soul, the seat of courage.

183. A (Greek: para prosdokian), considering the shape and height of the camel, which can certainly not be included in the list of *small* victims, e.g. the sheep and the goat.

184. In the evocation of the dead, Book XI of the Odyssey.

185. Chaerephon was given this same title by the Herald earlier in this comedy.—Aristophanes supposes him to have come from hell because he is lean and pallid.

186. Posidon appears on the stage accompanied by Heracles and a Triballian god.

187. An Athenian general.—Neptune is trying to give Triballus some notions of elegance and good behaviour.

188. Aristophanes supposes that democracy is in the ascendant in Olympus as it is in Athens.

189. He is addressing his servant, Manes.

190. Heracles softens at sight of the food.—Heracles is the glutton of the comic poets.

PISTHETAERUS: These are birds that have been punished with death for attacking the people's friends.

HERACLES: And you are seasoning them before answering us?

PISTHETAERUS: Ah! Heracles! welcome, welcome! What's the matter?[191]

HERACLES: The gods have sent us here as ambassadors to treat for peace.

A SERVANT: There's no more oil in the flask.

PISTHETAERUS: And yet the birds must be thoroughly basted with it.[192]

HERACLES: We have no interest to serve in fighting you; as for you, be friends and we promise that you shall always have rain-water in your pools and the warmest of warm weather. So far as these points go we are armed with plenary authority.

PISTHETAERUS: We have never been the aggressors, and even now we are as well disposed for peace as yourselves, provided you agree to one equitable condition, namely, that Zeus yield his sceptre to the birds. If only this is agreed to, I invite the ambassadors to dinner.

HERACLES: That's good enough for me. I vote for peace.

POSIDON: You wretch! you are nothing but a fool and a glutton. Do you want to dethrone your own father?

PISTHETAERUS: What an error! Why, the gods will be much more powerful if the birds govern the earth. At present the mortals are hidden beneath the clouds, escape your observation, and commit perjury in your name; but if you had the birds for your allies, and a man, after having sworn by the crow and Zeus, should fail to keep his oath, the crow would dive down upon him unawares and pluck out his eye.

POSIDON: Well thought of, by Posidon![193]

HERACLES: My notion too.

PISTHETAERUS (*to the Triballian*): And you, what's your opinion?

TRIBALLUS: Nabaisatreu.[194]

PISTHETAERUS: D'you see? he also approves. But hear another thing in which we can serve you. If a man vows to offer a sacrifice to some god and then procrastinates, pretending that the gods can wait, and thus does not keep his word, we shall punish his stinginess.

---

191. He pretends not to have seen them at first, being so much engaged with his cookery.

192. He pretends to forget the presence of the ambassadors.

193. Posidon jestingly swears by himself.

194. The barbarian god utters some gibberish which Pisthetaerus interprets into consent.

POSIDON: Ah! ah! and how?

PISTHETAERUS: While he is counting his money or is in the bath, a kite will relieve him, before he knows it, either in coin or in clothes, of the value of a couple of sheep, and carry it to the god.

HERACLES: I vote for restoring them the sceptre.

POSIDON: Ask the Triballian.

HERACLES: Hi! Triballian, do you want a thrashing?

TRIBALLUS: Saunaka baktarikrousa.

HERACLES: He says, "Right willingly."

POSIDON: If that be the opinion of both of you, why, I consent too.

HERACLES: Very well! we accord the sceptre.

PISTHETAERUS: Ah! I was nearly forgetting another condition. I will leave Heré to Zeus, but only if the young Basileia is given me in marriage.

POSIDON: Then you don't want peace. Let us withdraw.

PISTHETAERUS: It matters mighty little to me. Cook, look to the gravy.

HERACLES: What an odd fellow this Posidon is! Where are you off to? Are we going to war about a woman?

POSIDON: What else is there to do?

HERACLES: What else? Why, conclude peace.

POSIDON: Oh! the ninny! do you always want to be fooled? Why, you are seeking your own downfall. If Zeus were to die, after having yielded them the sovereignty, you would be ruined, for you are the heir of all the wealth he will leave behind.

PISTHETAERUS: Oh! by the gods! how he is cajoling you. Step aside, that I may have a word with you. Your uncle is getting the better of you, my poor friend.[195] The law will not allow you an obolus of the paternal property, for you are a bastard and not a legitimate child.

HERACLES: I a bastard! What's that you tell me?

PISTHETAERUS: Why, certainly; are you not born of a stranger woman?[196] Besides, is not Athené recognized as Zeus' sole heiress? And no daughter would be that, if she had a legitimate brother.

HERACLES: But what if my father wished to give me his property on his death-bed, even though I be a bastard?

PISTHETAERUS: The law forbids it, and this same Posidon would be the first to lay claim to his wealth, in virtue of being his legitimate

195. Heracles, the god of strength, was far from being remarkable in the way of cleverness.
196. This was Athenian law.

ARISTOPHANES

brother. Listen; thus runs Solon's law: "A bastard shall not inherit, if there are legitimate children; and if there are no legitimate children, the property shall pass to the nearest kin."

HERACLES: And I get nothing whatever of the paternal property?

PISTHETAERUS: Absolutely nothing. But tell me, has your father had you entered on the registers of his phratria?[197]

HERACLES: No, and I have long been surprised at the omission.

PISTHETAERUS: What ails you, that you should shake your fist at heaven? Do you want to fight it? Why, be on my side, I will make you a king and will feed you on bird's milk and honey.

HERACLES: Your further condition seems fair to me. I cede you the young damsel.

POSIDON: But I, I vote against this opinion.

PISTHETAERUS: Then all depends on the Triballian. (*To the Triballian*) What do you say?

TRIBALLUS: Big bird give daughter pretty and queen.

HERACLES: You say that you give her?

POSIDON: Why no, he does not say anything of the sort, that he gives her; else I cannot understand any better than the swallows.

PISTHETAERUS: Exactly so. Does he not say she must be given to the swallows?

POSIDON: Very well! you two arrange the matter; make peace, since you wish it so; I'll hold my tongue.

HERACLES: We are of a mind to grant you all that you ask. But come up there with us to receive Basileia and the celestial bounty.

PISTHETAERUS: Here are birds already cut up, and very suitable for a nuptial feast.

HERACLES: You go and, if you like, I will stay here to roast them.

PISTHETAERUS: You to roast them! you are too much the glutton; come along with us.

HERACLES: Ah! how well I would have treated myself!

PISTHETAERUS: Let some bring me a beautiful and magnificent tunic for the wedding.

---

197. The poet attributes to the gods the same customs as those which governed Athens, and according to which no child was looked upon as legitimate unless his father had entered him on the registers of his phratria. The phratria was a division of the tribe and consisted of thirty families.

CHORUS:[198] At Phanae,[199] near the Clepsydra,[200] there dwells a people who have neither faith nor law, the Englottogastors,[201] who reap, sow, pluck the vines and the figs[202] with their tongues; they belong to a barbaric race, and among them the Philippi and the Gorgiases[203] are to be found; 'tis these Englottogastorian Phillippi who introduced the custom all over Attica of cutting out the tongue separately at sacrifices.[204]

A MESSENGER: Oh, you, whose unbounded happiness I cannot express in words, thrice happy race of airy birds, receive your king in your fortunate dwellings. More brilliant than the brightest star that illumes the earth, he is approaching his glittering golden palace; the sun itself does not shine with more dazzling glory. He is entering with his bride at his side[205] whose beauty no human tongue can express; in his hand he brandishes the lightning, the winged shaft of Zeus; perfumes of unspeakable sweetness pervade the ethereal realms. 'Tis a glorious spectacle to see the clouds of incense wafting in light whirlwinds before the breath of the Zephyr! But here he is himself. Divine Muse! let thy sacred lips begin with songs of happy omen.

CHORUS: Fall back! to the right! to the left! advance![206] Fly around this happy mortal, whom Fortune loads with her blessings. Oh! oh! what grace! what beauty! Oh, marriage so auspicious for our city! All honour to this man! 'tis through him that the birds are called to such glorious destinies. Let your nuptial hymns, your nuptial songs, greet him and his Basileia! 'Twas in the midst of such festivities that the Fates formerly united Olympian Here to

---

198. The chorus continues to tell what it has seen on its flights.
199. The harbour of the island of Chios; but this name is here used in the sense of being the land of informers ([Greek: phainein], to denounce).
200. I.e. near the orators' platform, or (Greek: B ema), in the Public Assembly, or (Greek: Ekkl esia), because there stood the (Greek: klepsudra), or water-clock, by which speeches were limited.
201. A coined name, made up of (Greek: gl otta), the tongue, and (Greek: Gast er), the stomach, and meaning those who fill their stomach with what they gain with their tongues, to wit, the orators.
202. (Greek: Sukon) a fig, forms part of the word, (Greek: Sukophant es), which in Greek means an informer.
203. Both rhetoricians.
204. Because they consecrated it specially to the god of eloquence.
205. Basileia, whom he brings back from heaven.
206. Terms used in regulating a dance.

the King who governs the gods from the summit of his inaccessible throne. Oh! Hymen! oh! Hymenaeus! Rosy Eros with the golden wings held the reins and guided the chariot; 'twas he, who presided over the union of Zeus and the fortunate Heré. Oh! Hymen! oh! Hymenaeus!

PISTHETAERUS: I am delighted with your songs, I applaud your verses. Now celebrate the thunder that shakes the earth, the flaming lightning of Zeus and the terrible flashing thunderbolt.

CHORUS: Oh, thou golden flash of the lightning! oh, ye divine shafts of flame, that Zeus has hitherto shot forth! Oh, ye rolling thunders, that bring down the rain! 'Tis by the order of our king that ye shall now stagger the earth! Oh, Hymen! 'tis through thee that he commands the universe and that he makes Basileia, whom he has robbed from Zeus, take her seat at his side. Oh! Hymen! oh! Hymenaeus!

PISTHETAERUS: Let all the winged tribes of our fellow-citizens follow the bridal couple to the palace of Zeus[207] and to the nuptial couch! Stretch forth your hands, my dear wife! Take hold of me by my wings and let us dance; I am going to lift you up and carry you through the air.

CHORUS: Oh, joy! Io Paean! Tralala! victory is thine, oh, thou greatest of the gods!

FINIS OF "THE BIRDS"

---

207. Where Pisthetaerus is henceforth to reign.

LYSISTRATA

Introduction

The 'Lysistrata,' the third and concluding play of the War and Peace series, was not produced till ten years later than its predecessor, the 'Peace,' viz. in 411 B.C. It is now the twenty-first year of the War, and there seems as little prospect of peace as ever. A desperate state of things demands a desperate remedy, and the Poet proceeds to suggest a burlesque solution of the difficulty.

The women of Athens, led by Lysistrata and supported by female delegates from the other states of Hellas, determine to take matters into their own hands and force the men to stop the War. They meet in solemn conclave, and Lysistrata expounds her scheme, the rigorous application to husbands and lovers of a self-denying ordinance—"we must refrain from the male organ altogether." Every wife and mistress is to refuse all sexual favours whatsoever, till the men have come to terms of peace. In cases where the women *must* yield 'par force majeure,' then it is to be with an ill grace and in such a way as to afford the minimum of gratification to their partner; they are to lie passive and take no more part in the amorous game than they are absolutely obliged to. By these means Lysistrata assures them they will very soon gain their end. "If we sit indoors prettily dressed out in our best transparent silks and prettiest gewgaws, and with our 'mottes' all nicely depilated, their tools will stand up so stiff that they will be able to deny us nothing." Such is the burden of her advice.

After no little demur, this plan of campaign is adopted, and the assembled women take a solemn oath to observe the compact faithfully. Meantime as a precautionary measure they seize the Acropolis, where the State treasure is kept; the old men of the city assault the doors, but are repulsed by "the terrible regiment" of women. Before long the device of the bold Lysistrata proves entirely effective, Peace is concluded, and the play ends with the hilarious festivities of the Athenian and Spartan plenipotentiaries in celebration of the event.

This drama has a double Chorus—of women and of old men, and much excellent fooling is got out of the fight for possession of the citadel between the two hostile bands; while the broad jokes and decidedly suggestive situations arising out of the general idea of the plot outlined above may be "better imagined than described."

Dramatis Personae

Lysistrata.
Calonicé.
Myrrhiné.
Lampito.
Stratyllis.
A Magistrate.
Cinesias.
A Child.
Herald of the Lacedaemonians.
Envoys of the Lacedaemonians.
Polycharides.
Market Loungers.
A Servant.
An Athenian Citizen.
Chorus of Old Men.
Chorus of Women.

Scene: *In a public square at Athens; afterwards before the gates of the Acropolis, and finally within the precincts of the citadel.*

LYSISTRATA (*alone*): Ah! if only they had been invited to a Bacchic revelling, or a feast of Pan or Aphrodité or Genetyllis,[1] why! the streets would have been impassable for the thronging tambourines! Now there's never a woman here-ah! except my neighbour Calonicé, whom I see approaching yonder. . . Good day, Calonicé.

CALONICÉ: Good day, Lysistrata; but pray, why this dark, forbidding face, my dear? Believe me, you don't look a bit pretty with those black lowering brows.

LYSISTRATA: Oh! Calonicé, my heart is on fire; I blush for our sex. Men *will* have it we are tricky and sly. . .

CALONICÉ: And they are quite right, upon my word!

LYSISTRATA: Yet, look you, when the women are summoned to meet for a matter of the last importance, they lie abed instead of coming.

CALONICÉ: Oh! they will come, my dear; but 'tis not easy, you know, for women to leave the house. One is busy pottering about her husband; another is getting the servant up; a third is putting her child asleep, or washing the brat or feeding it.

LYSISTRATA: But I tell you, the business that calls them here is far and away more urgent.

CALONICÉ: And why *do* you summon us, dear Lysistrata? What is it all about?

LYSISTRATA: About a big affair.[2]

CALONICÉ: And is it thick too?

LYSISTRATA: Yes indeed, both big and great.

CALONICÉ: And we are not all on the spot!

---

1. At Athens more than anywhere the festivals of Bacchus (Dionysus) were celebrated with the utmost pomp—and also with the utmost licence, not to say licentiousness.

Pan—the rustic god and king of the Satyrs; his feast was similarly an occasion of much coarse self-indulgence.

Aphrodité Colias—under this name the goddess was invoked by courtesans as patroness of sensual, physical love. She had a temple on the promontory of Colias, on the Attic coast—whence the surname.

The Genetyllides were minor deities, presiding over the act of generation, as the name indicates. Dogs were offered in sacrifice to them—presumably because of the lubricity of that animal.

At the festivals of Dionysus, Pan and Aphrodité women used to perform lascivious dances to the accompaniment of the beating of tambourines. Lysistrata implies that the women she had summoned to council cared really for nothing but wanton pleasures.

2. An obscene *double entendre*; Calonicé understands, or pretends to understand, Lysistrata as meaning a long and thick "membrum virile"!

LYSISTRATA: Oh! if it were what you suppose, there would be never an absentee. No, no, it concerns a thing I have turned about and about this way and that of many sleepless nights.

CALONICÉ: It must be something mighty fine and subtle for you to have turned it about so!

LYSISTRATA: So fine, it means just this, Greece saved by the women!

CALONICÉ: By women! Why, its salvation hangs on a poor thread then!

LYSISTRATA: Our country's fortunes depend on us—it is with us to undo utterly the Peloponnesians. . .

CALONICÉ: That would be a noble deed truly!

LYSISTRATA: To exterminate the Boeotians to a man!

CALONICÉ: But surely you would spare the eels.[3]

LYSISTRATA: For Athens' sake I will never threaten so fell a doom; trust me for that. However, if the Boeotian and Peloponnesian women join us, Greece is saved.

CALONICÉ: But how should women perform so wise and glorious an achievement, we women who dwell in the retirement of the household, clad in diaphanous garments of yellow silk and long flowing gowns, decked out with flowers and shod with dainty little slippers?

LYSISTRATA: Nay, but those are the very sheet-anchors of our salvation—those yellow tunics, those scents and slippers, those cosmetics and transparent robes.

CALONICÉ: How so, pray?

LYSISTRATA: There is not a man will wield a lance against another. . .

CALONICÉ: Quick, I will get me a yellow tunic from the dyer's.

LYSISTRATA: . . . or want a shield.

CALONICÉ: I'll run and put on a flowing gown.

LYSISTRATA: . . . or draw a sword.

CALONICÉ: I'll haste and buy a pair of slippers this instant.

LYSISTRATA: Now tell me, would not the women have done best to come?

CALONICÉ: Why, they should have *flown* here!

---

3. The eels from Lake Copaïs in Boeotia were esteemed highly by epicures.

LYSISTRATA: Ah! my dear, you'll see that like true Athenians, they will do everything too late⁴ . . . Why, there's not a woman come from the shoreward parts, not one from Salamis.⁵

CALONICÉ: But I know for certain they embarked at daybreak.

LYSISTRATA: And the dames from Acharnae!⁶ why, I thought they would have been the very first to arrive.

CALONICÉ: Theagenes wife⁷ at any rate is sure to come; she has actually been to consult Hecaté. . . But look! here are some arrivals—and there are more behind. Ah! ha! now what countrywomen may they be?

LYSISTRATA: They are from Anagyra.⁸

CALONICÉ: Yes! upon my word, 'tis a levy *en masse* of all the female population of Anagyra!

MYRRHINÉ: Are we late, Lysistrata? Tell us, pray; what, not a word?

LYSISTRATA: I cannot say much for you, Myrrhiné! you have not bestirred yourself overmuch for an affair of such urgency.

MYRRHINÉ: I could not find my girdle in the dark. However, if the matter is so pressing, here we are; so speak.

LYSISTRATA: No, but let us wait a moment more, till the women of Boeotia arrive and those from the Peloponnese.

MYRRHINÉ: Yes, that is best. . . Ah! here comes Lampito.

LYSISTRATA: Good day, Lampito, dear friend from Lacedaemon. How well and handsome you look! what a rosy complexion! and how strong you seem; why, you could strangle a bull surely!

LAMPITO: Yes, indeed, I really think I could. 'Tis because I do gymnastics and practise the kick dance.⁹

---

4. This is the reproach Demosthenes constantly levelled against his Athenian fellow-countrymen—their failure to seize opportunity.

5. An island of the Saronic Gulf, lying between Magara and Attica. It was separated by a narrow strait—scene of the naval battle of Salamis, in which the Athenians defeated Xerxes—only from the Attic coast, and was subject to Athens.

6. A deme, or township, of Attica, lying five or six miles north of Athens. The Acharnians were throughout the most extreme partisans of the warlike party during the Peloponnesian struggle. See 'The Acharnians.'

7. The precise reference is uncertain, and where the joke exactly comes in. The Scholiast says Theagenes was a rich, miserly and superstitious citizen, who never undertook any enterprise without first consulting an image of Hecaté, the distributor of honour and wealth according to popular belief; and his wife would naturally follow her husband's example.

8. A deme of Attica, a small and insignificant community—a 'Little Pedlington' in fact.

9. In allusion to the gymnastic training which was *de rigueur* at Sparta for the women no less than the men, and in particular to the dance of the Lacedaemonian girls, in which

LYSISTRATA: And what superb bosoms!

LAMPITO: La! you are feeling me as if I were a beast for sacrifice.

LYSISTRATA: And this young woman, what countrywoman is she?

LAMPITO: She is a noble lady from Boeotia.

LYSISTRATA: Ah! my pretty Boeotian friend, you are as blooming as a garden.

CALONICÉ: Yes, on my word! and the garden is so prettily weeded too![10]

LYSISTRATA: And who is this?

LAMPITO: 'Tis an honest woman, by my faith! she comes from Corinth.

LYSISTRATA: Oh! honest, no doubt then—as honesty goes at Corinth.[11]

LAMPITO: But who has called together this council of women, pray?

LYSISTRATA: I have.

LAMPITO: Well then, tell us what you want of us.

LYSISTRATA: With pleasure, my dear.

MYRRHINÉ: What is the most important business you wish to inform us about?

LYSISTRATA: I will tell you. But first answer me one question.

MYRRHINÉ: What is that?

LYSISTRATA: Don't you feel sad and sorry because the fathers of your children are far away from you with the army? For I'll undertake, there is not one of you whose husband is not abroad at this moment.

CALONICÉ: Mine has been the last five months in Thrace—looking after Eucrates.[12]

LYSISTRATA: 'Tis seven long months since mine left me for Pylos.[13]

---

the performer was expected to kick the fundament with the heels—always a standing joke among the Athenians against their rivals and enemies the Spartans.

10. The allusion, of course, is to the 'garden of love,' the female parts, which it was the custom with the Greek women, as it is with the ladies of the harem in Turkey to this day, to depilate scrupulously, with the idea of making themselves more attractive to men.

11. Corinth was notorious in the Ancient world for its prostitutes and general dissoluteness.

12. An Athenian general strongly suspected of treachery; Aristophanes pretends his own soldiers have to see that he does not desert to the enemy.

13. A town and fortress on the west coast of Messenia, south-east part of Peloponnese, at the northern extremity of the bay of Sphacteria—the scene by the by of the modern naval battle of Navarino—in Lacedaemonian territory; it had been seized by the Athenian

LAMPITO: As for mine, if he ever does return from service, he's no sooner back than he takes down his shield again and flies back to the wars.

LYSISTRATA: And not so much as the shadow of a lover! Since the day the Milesians betrayed us, I have never once seen an eight-inch-long *godemiche* even, to be a leathern consolation to us poor widows. . . Now tell me, if I have discovered a means of ending the war, will you all second me?

MYRRHINÉ: Yes verily, by all the goddesses, I swear I will, though I have to put my gown in pawn, and drink the money the same day.[14]

CALONICÉ: And so will I, though I must be split in two like a flat-fish, and have half myself removed.

LAMPITO: And I too; why, to secure Peace, I would climb to the top of Mount Taygetus.[15]

LYSISTRATA: Then I will out with it at last, my mighty secret! Oh! sister women, if we would compel our husbands to make peace, we must refrain. . .

MYRRHINÉ: Refrain from what? tell us, tell us!

LYSISTRATA: But will you do it?

MYRRHINÉ: We will, we will, though we should die of it.

LYSISTRATA: We must refrain from the male organ altogether. . . Nay, why do you turn your backs on me? Where are you going? So, you bite your lips, and shake your heads, eh? Why these pale, sad looks? why these tears? Come, will you do it—yes or no? Do you hesitate?

MYRRHINÉ: No, I will not do it; let the War go on.

LYSISTRATA: And you, my pretty flat-fish, who declared just now they might split you in two?

CALONICÉ: Anything, anything but that! Bid me go through the fire, if you will; but to rob us of the sweetest thing in all the world, my dear, dear Lysistrata!

LYSISTRATA: And you?

---

fleet, and was still in their possession at the date, 412 B.C., of the representation of the 'Lysistrata,' though two years later, in the twenty-second year of the War, it was recovered by Sparta.

14. The Athenian women, rightly or wrongly, had the reputation of being over fond of wine. Aristophanes, here and elsewhere, makes many jests on this weakness of theirs.

15. The lofty range of hills overlooking Sparta from the west.

MYRRHINÉ: Yes, I agree with the others; I too would sooner go through the fire.

LYSISTRATA: Oh, wanton, vicious sex! the poets have done well to make tragedies upon us; we are good for nothing then but love and lewdness![16] But you, my dear, you from hardy Sparta, if *you* join me, all may yet be well; help me, second me, I conjure you.

LAMPITO: 'Tis a hard thing, by the two goddesses[17] it is! for a woman to sleep alone without ever a standing weapon in her bed. But there, Peace must come first.

LYSISTRATA: Oh, my dear, my dearest, best friend, you are the only one deserving the name of woman!

CALONICÉ: But if—which the gods forbid—we do refrain altogether from what you say, should we get peace any sooner?

LYSISTRATA: Of course we should, by the goddesses twain! We need only sit indoors with painted cheeks, and meet our mates lightly clad in transparent gowns of Amorgos[18] silk, and with our "mottes" nicely plucked smooth; then their tools will stand like mad and they will be wild to lie with us. That will be the time to refuse, and they will hasten to make peace, I am convinced of that!

LAMPITO: Yes, just as Menelaus, when he saw Helen's naked bosom, threw away his sword, they say.

CALONICÉ: But, poor devils, suppose our husbands go away and leave us.

LYSISTRATA: Then, as Pherecrates says, we must "flay a skinned dog,"[19] that's all.

CALONICÉ: Bah! these proverbs are all idle talk. . . But if our husbands drag us by main force into the bedchamber?

---

16. In the original "we are nothing but Poseidon and a boat"; the allusion is to a play of Sophocles, now lost, but familiar to Aristophanes' audience, entitled 'Tyro,' in which the heroine, Tyro, appears with Poseidon, the sea-god, at the beginning of the tragedy, and at the close with the two boys she had had by him, whom she exposes in an open boat.

17. "By the two goddesses,"—a woman's oath, which recurs constantly in this play; the two goddesses are always Demeter and Proserpine.

18. One of the Cyclades, between Naxos and Cos, celebrated, like the latter, for its manufacture of fine, almost transparent silks, worn in Greece, and later at Rome, by women of loose character.

19. The proverb, quoted by Pherecrates, is properly spoken of those who go out of their way to do a thing already done—"to kill a dead horse," but here apparently is twisted by Aristophanes into an allusion to the leathern 'godemiche' mentioned a little above; if the worst comes to the worst, we must use artificial means. Pherecrates was a comic playwright, a contemporary of Aristophanes.

LYSISTRATA: Hold on to the door posts.

CALONICÉ: But if they beat us?

LYSISTRATA: Then yield to their wishes, but with a bad grace; there is no pleasure for them, when they do it by force. Besides, there are a thousand ways of tormenting them. Never fear, they'll soon tire of the game; there's no satisfaction for a man, unless the woman shares it.

CALONICÉ: Very well, if you *will* have it so, we agree.

LAMPITO: For ourselves, no doubt we shall persuade our husbands to conclude a fair and honest peace; but there is the Athenian populace, how are we to cure these folk of their warlike frenzy?

LYSISTRATA: Have no fear; we undertake to make our own people hear reason.

LAMPITO: Nay, impossible, so long as they have their trusty ships and the vast treasures stored in the temple of Athené.

LYSISTRATA: Ah! but we have seen to that; this very day the Acropolis will be in our hands. That is the task assigned to the older women; while we are here in council, they are going, under pretence of offering sacrifice, to seize the citadel.

LAMPITO: Well said indeed! so everything is going for the best.

LYSISTRATA: Come, quick, Lampito, and let us bind ourselves by an inviolable oath.

LAMPITO: Recite the terms; we will swear to them.

LYSISTRATA: With pleasure. Where is our Usheress?[20] Now, what are you staring at, pray? Lay this shield on the earth before us, its hollow upwards, and someone bring me the victim's inwards.

CALONICÉ: Lysistrata, say, what oath are we to swear?

LYSISTRATA: What oath? Why, in Aeschylus, they sacrifice a sheep, and swear over a buckler;[21] we will do the same.

CALONICÉ: No, Lysistrata, one cannot swear peace over a buckler, surely.

LYSISTRATA: What other oath do you prefer?

CALONICÉ: Let's take a white horse, and sacrifice it, and swear on its entrails.

LYSISTRATA: But where get a white horse from?

---

20. Literally "our Scythian woman." At Athens, policemen and ushers in the courts were generally Scythians; so the revolting women must have *their* Scythian "Usheress" too.
21. In allusion to the oath which the seven allied champions before Thebes take upon a buckler, in Aeschylus' tragedy of 'The Seven against Thebes,' v. 42.

CALONICÉ: Well, what oath shall we take then?

LYSISTRATA: Listen to me. Let's set a great black bowl on the ground; let's sacrifice a skin of Thasian[22] wine into it, and take oath not to add one single drop of water.

LAMPITO: Ah! that's an oath pleases me more than I can say.

LYSISTRATA: Let them bring me a bowl and a skin of wine.

CALONICÉ: Ah! my dears, what a noble big bowl! what a delight 'twill be to empty it!

LYSISTRATA: Set the bowl down on the ground, and lay your hands on the victim. . . Almighty goddess, Persuasion, and thou, bowl, boon comrade of joy and merriment, receive this our sacrifice, and be propitious to us poor women!

CALONICÉ: Oh! the fine red blood! how well it flows!

LAMPITO: And what a delicious savour, by the goddesses twain!

LYSISTRATA: Now, my dears, let me swear first, if you please.

CALONICÉ: No, by the goddess of love, let us decide that by lot.

LYSISTRATA: Come then, Lampito, and all of you, put your hands to the bowl; and do you, Calonicé, repeat in the name of all the solemn terms I am going to recite. Then you must all swear, and pledge yourselves by the same promises.—*"I will have naught to do whether with lover or husband. . ."*

CALONICÉ: *I will have naught to do whether with lover or husband. . .*

LYSISTRATA: *Albeit he come to me with stiff and standing tool. . .*

CALONICÉ: *Albeit he come to me with stiff and standing tool. . .* Oh! Lysistrata, I cannot bear it!

LYSISTRATA: *I will live at home in perfect chastity. . .*

CALONICÉ: *I will live at home in perfect chastity. . .*

LYSISTRATA: *Beautifully dressed and wearing a saffron-coloured gown. . .*

CALONICÉ: *Beautifully dressed and wearing a saffron-coloured gown. . .*

LYSISTRATA: *To the end I may inspire my husband with the most ardent longings.*

CALONICÉ: *To the end I may inspire my husband with the most ardent longings.*

LYSISTRATA: *Never will I give myself voluntarily. . .*

CALONICÉ: *Never will I give myself voluntarily. . .*

LYSISTRATA: *And if he has me by force. . .*

CALONICÉ: *And if he has me by force. . .*

---

22. A volcanic island in the northern part of the Aegaean, celebrated for its vineyards.

LYSISTRATA: *I will be cold as ice, and never stir a limb. . .*

CALONICÉ: *I will be cold as ice, and never stir a limb. . .*

LYSISTRATA: *I will not lift my legs in air. . .*

CALONICÉ: *I will not lift my legs in air. . .*

LYSISTRATA: *Nor will I crouch with bottom upraised, like carven lions on a knife-handle.*

CALONICÉ: *Nor will I crouch with bottom upraised, like carven lions on a knife-handle.*

LYSISTRATA: *An if I keep my oath, may I be suffered to drink of this wine.*

CALONICÉ: *An if I keep my oath, may I be suffered to drink of this wine.*

LYSISTRATA: *But if I break it, let my bowl be filled with water.*

CALONICÉ: *But if I break it, let my bowl be filled with water.*

LYSISTRATA: Will ye all take this oath?

MYRRHINÉ: Yes, yes!

LYSISTRATA: Then lo! I immolate the victim. (*She drinks*)

CALONICÉ: Enough, enough, my dear; now let us all drink in turn to cement our friendship.

LAMPITO: Hark! what do those cries mean?

LYSISTRATA: 'Tis what I was telling you; the women have just occupied the Acropolis. So now, Lampito, do you return to Sparta to organize the plot, while your comrades here remain as hostages. For ourselves, let us away to join the rest in the citadel, and let us push the bolts well home.

CALONICÉ: But don't you think the men will march up against us?

LYSISTRATA: I laugh at them. Neither threats nor flames shall force our doors; they shall open only on the conditions I have named.

CALONICÉ: Yes, yes, by the goddess of love! let us keep up our old-time repute for obstinacy and spite.

CHORUS OF OLD MEN:[23] Go easy, Draces, go easy; why, your shoulder is all chafed by these plaguey heavy olive stocks. But forward still, forward, man, as needs must. What unlooked-for things do happen, to be sure, in a long life! Ah! Strymodorus, who would ever have thought it? Here we have the women, who used, for our misfortune, to eat our bread and live in our houses, daring nowadays to lay hands on the holy image of the goddess, to seize the Acropolis and draw bars and bolts to keep any from entering!

---

23. The old men are carrying faggots and fire to burn down the gates of the Acropolis, and supply comic material by their panting and wheezing as they climb the steep approaches

Come, Philurgus man, let's hurry thither; let's lay our faggots all about the citadel, and on the blazing pile burn with our hands these vile conspiratresses, one and all—and Lycon's wife, Lysistrata, first and foremost! Nay, by Demeter, never will I let 'em laugh at me, whiles I have a breath left in my body. Cleomenes himself,[24] the first who ever seized our citadel, had to quit it to his sore dishonour; spite his Lacedaemonian pride, he had to deliver me up his arms and slink off with a single garment to his back. My word! but he was filthy and ragged! and what an unkempt beard, to be sure! He had not had a bath for six long years! Oh! but that was a mighty siege! Our men were ranged seventeen deep before the gate, and never left their posts, even to sleep. These women, these enemies of Euripides and all the gods, shall I do nothing to hinder their inordinate insolence? else let them tear down my trophies of Marathon. But look ye, to finish our toilsome climb, we have only this last steep bit left to mount. Verily 'tis no easy job without beasts of burden, and how these logs do bruise my shoulder! Still let us on, and blow up our fire and see it does not go out just as we reach our destination. Phew! phew! (*blows the fire*) Oh! dear! what a dreadful smoke! it bites my eyes like a mad dog. It is Lemnos[25] fire for sure, or it would never devour my eyelids like this. Come on, Laches, let's hurry, let's bring succour to the goddess; it's now or never! Phew! phew! (*blows the fire*) Oh! dear! what a confounded smoke!—There now, there's our fire all bright and burning, thank the gods! Now, why not first put down our loads here, then take a vine-branch, light it at the brazier and hurl it at the gate by way of battering-ram? If they don't answer our summons by pulling back the bolts, then we set fire to the woodwork, and the smoke will choke 'em. Ye gods! what a smoke! Pfaugh! Is there never a Samos general will help me unload my burden?[26]—Ah! it shall not gall my

---

to the fortress and puff and blow at their fires. Aristophanes gives them names, purely fancy ones—Draces, Strymodorus, Philurgus, Laches.

24. Cleomenes, King of Sparta, had in the preceding century commanded a Lacedaemonian expedition against Athens. At the invitation of the Alcmaeonidae, enemies of the sons of Peisistratus, he seized the Acropolis, but after an obstinately contested siege was forced to capitulate and retire.

25. Lemnos was proverbial with the Greeks for chronic misfortune and a succession of horrors and disasters. Can any good thing come out of *Lemnos*?

26. That is, a friend of the Athenian people; Samos had just before the date of the play re-established the democracy and renewed the old alliance with Athens.

ARISTOPHANES

shoulder any more. (*Tosses down his wood*) Come, brazier, do your
duty, make the embers flare, that I may kindle a brand; I want to
be the first to hurl one. Aid me, heavenly Victory; let us punish for
their insolent audacity the women who have seized our citadel, and
may we raise a trophy of triumph for success!

CHORUS OF WOMEN:[27] Oh! my dears, methinks I see fire and smoke;
can it be a conflagration? Let us hurry all we can. Fly, fly, Nicodicé,
ere Calycé and Crityllé perish in the fire, or are stifled in the smoke
raised by these accursed old men and their pitiless laws. But, great
gods, can it be I come too late? Rising at dawn, I had the utmost
trouble to fill this vessel at the fountain. Oh! what a crowd there
was, and what a din! What a rattling of water-pots! Servants and
slave-girls pushed and thronged me! However, here I have it full at
last; and I am running to carry the water to my fellow townswomen,
whom our foes are plotting to burn alive. News has been brought
us that a company of old, doddering greybeards, loaded with
enormous faggots, as if they wanted to heat a furnace, have taken
the field, vomiting dreadful threats, crying that they must reduce
to ashes these horrible women. Suffer them not, oh! goddess, but,
of thy grace, may I see Athens and Greece cured of their warlike
folly. 'Tis to this end, oh! thou guardian deity of our city, goddess
of the golden crest, that they have seized thy sanctuary. Be their
friend and ally, Athené, and if any man hurl against them lighted
firebrands, aid us to carry water to extinguish them.

STRATYLLIS: Let me be, I say. Oh! oh! (*She calls for help*)

CHORUS OF WOMEN: What is this I see, ye wretched old men? Honest
and pious folk ye cannot be who act so vilely.

CHORUS OF OLD MEN: Ah, ha! here's something new! a swarm of
women stand posted outside to defend the gates!

CHORUS OF WOMEN: Ah! ah! we frighten you, do we; we seem a
mighty host, yet you do not see the ten-thousandth part of our sex.

CHORUS OF OLD MEN: Ho, Phaedrias! shall we stop their cackle?
Suppose one of us were to break a stick across their backs, eh?

CHORUS OF WOMEN: Let us set down our water-pots on the ground,
to be out of the way, if they should dare to offer us violence.

---

27. A second Chorus enters—of women who are hurrying up with water to extinguish
the fire just started by the Chorus of old men. Nicodicé, Calycé, Crityllé, Rhodippé, are
fancy names the poet gives to different members of the band. Another, Stratyllis, has been
stopped by the old men on her way to rejoin her companions.

CHORUS OF OLD MEN: Let someone knock out two or three teeth for them, as they did to Bupalus;[28] they won't talk so loud then.

CHORUS OF WOMEN: Come on then; I wait you with unflinching foot, and I will snap off your testicles like a bitch.

CHORUS OF OLD MEN: Silence! ere my stick has cut short your days.

CHORUS OF WOMEN: Now, just you dare to touch Stratyllis with the tip of your finger!

CHORUS OF OLD MEN: And if I batter you to pieces with my fists, what will you do?

CHORUS OF WOMEN: I will tear out your lungs and entrails with my teeth.

CHORUS OF OLD MEN: Oh! what a clever poet is Euripides! how well he says that woman is the most shameless of animals.

CHORUS OF WOMEN: Let's pick up our water-jars again, Rhodippé.

CHORUS OF OLD MEN: Ah! accursed harlot, what do you mean to do here with your water?

CHORUS OF WOMEN: And you, old death-in-life, with your fire? Is it to cremate yourself?

CHORUS OF OLD MEN: I am going to build you a pyre to roast your female friends upon.

CHORUS OF WOMEN: And I,—I am going to put out your fire.

CHORUS OF OLD MEN: You put out my fire—you!

CHORUS OF WOMEN: Yes, you shall soon see.

CHORUS OF OLD MEN: I don't know what prevents me from roasting you with this torch.

CHORUS OF WOMEN: I am getting you a bath ready to clean off the filth.

CHORUS OF OLD MEN: A bath for me, you dirty slut, you!

CHORUS OF WOMEN: Yes, indeed, a nuptial bath—he, he!

CHORUS OF OLD MEN: Do you hear that? What insolence!

CHORUS OF WOMEN: I am a free woman, I tell you.

CHORUS OF OLD MEN: I will make you hold your tongue, never fear!

---

28. Bupalus was a celebrated contemporary sculptor, a native of Clazomenae. The satiric poet Hipponax, who was extremely ugly, having been portrayed by Bupalus as even more unsightly-looking than the reality, composed against the artist so scurrilous an invective that the latter hung himself in despair. Apparently Aristophanes alludes here to a verse in which Hipponax threatened to beat Bupalus.

CHORUS OF WOMEN: Ah, ha! you shall never sit more amongst the heliasts.[29]

CHORUS OF OLD MEN: Burn off her hair for her!

CHORUS OF WOMEN: Water, do your office! (*The women pitch the water in their water-pots over the old men*)

CHORUS OF OLD MEN: Oh, dear! oh, dear! oh, dear!

CHORUS OF WOMEN: Was it hot?

CHORUS OF OLD MEN: Hot, great gods! Enough, enough!

CHORUS OF WOMEN: I'm watering you, to make you bloom afresh.

CHORUS OF OLD MEN: Alas! I am too dry! Ah, me! how I am trembling with cold!

MAGISTRATE: These women, have they made din enough, I wonder, with their tambourines? bewept Adonis enough upon their terraces?[30] I was listening to the speeches last assembly day,[31] and Demostratus,[32] whom heaven confound! was saying we must all go over to Sicily—and lo! his wife was dancing round repeating: Alas! alas! Adonis, woe is me for Adonis!

Demostratus was saying we must levy hoplites at Zacynthus[33]— and lo! his wife, more than half drunk, was screaming on the house-roof: "Weep, weep for Adonis!"—while that infamous *Mad Ox* [34] was bellowing away on his side.—Do ye not blush, ye women, for your wild and uproarious doings?

CHORUS OF OLD MEN: But you don't know all their effrontery yet! They abused and insulted us; then soused us with the water in their

---

29. The Heliasts at Athens were the body of citizens chosen by lot to act as jurymen (or, more strictly speaking, as judges and jurymen, the Dicast, or so-called Judge, being merely President of the Court, the majority of the Heliasts pronouncing sentence) in the Heliaia, or High Court, where all offences liable to public prosecution were tried. They were 6000 in number, divided into ten panels of 500 each, a thousand being held in reserve to supply occasional vacancies. Each Heliast was paid three obols for each day's attendance in court.

30. Women only celebrated the festivals of Adonis. These rites were not performed in public, but on the terraces and flat roofs of the houses.

31. The Assembly, or Ecclesia, was the General Parliament of the Athenian people, in which every adult citizen had a vote. It met on the Pnyx hill, where the assembled Ecclesiasts were addressed from the Bema, or speaking-block.

32. An orator and statesman who had first proposed the disastrous Sicilian Expedition, of 415–413 B.C. This was on the first day of the festival of Adonis—ever afterwards regarded by the Athenians as a day of ill omen.

33. An island in the Ionian Sea, on the west of Greece, near Cephalenia, and an ally of Athens during the Peloponnesian War.

34. Cholozyges, a nickname for Demostratus.

water-pots, and have set us wringing out our clothes, for all the world as if we had bepissed ourselves.

MAGISTRATE: And 'tis well done too, by Poseidon! We men must share the blame of their ill conduct; it is we who teach them to love riot and dissoluteness and sow the seeds of wickedness in their hearts. You see a husband go into a shop: "Look you, jeweller," says he, "you remember the necklace you made for my wife. Well, t'other evening, when she was dancing, the catch came open. Now, I am bound to start for Salamis; will you make it convenient to go up to-night to make her fastening secure?" Another will go to a cobbler, a great, strong fellow, with a great, long tool, and tell him: "The strap of one of my wife's sandals presses her little toe, which is extremely sensitive; come in about midday to supple the thing and stretch it." Now see the results. Take my own case—as a Magistrate I have enlisted rowers; I want money to pay 'em, and lo! the women clap to the door in my face.[35] But why do we stand here with arms crossed? Bring me a crowbar; I'll chastise their insolence!—Ho! there, my fine fellow! (*addressing one of his attendant officers*) what are you gaping at the crows about? looking for a tavern, I suppose, eh? Come, crowbars here, and force open the gates. I will put a hand to the work myself.

LYSISTRATA: No need to force the gates; I am coming out—here I am. And why bolts and bars? What we want here is not bolts and bars and locks, but common sense.

MAGISTRATE: Really, my fine lady! Where is my officer? I want him to tie that woman's hands behind her back.

LYSISTRATA: By Artemis, the virgin goddess! if he touches me with the tip of his finger, officer of the public peace though he be, let him look out for himself!

MAGISTRATE (*to the officer*): How now, are you afraid? Seize her, I tell you, round the body. Two of you at her, and have done with it!

FIRST WOMAN: By Pandrosos! if you lay a hand on her, I'll trample you underfoot till you shit your guts!

MAGISTRATE: Oh, there! my guts! Where is my other officer? Bind that minx first, who speaks so prettily!

SECOND WOMAN: By Phoebé, if you touch her with one finger, you'd better call quick for a surgeon!

---

35. The State treasure was kept in the Acropolis, which the women had seized.

MAGISTRATE: What do you mean? Officer, where are you got to? Lay hold of her. Oh! but I'm going to stop your foolishness for you all!

THIRD WOMAN: By the Tauric Artemis, if you go near her, I'll pull out your hair, scream as you like.

MAGISTRATE: Ah! miserable man that I am! My own officers desert me. What ho! are we to let ourselves be bested by a mob of women? Ho! Scythians mine, close up your ranks, and forward!

LYSISTRATA: By the holy goddesses! you'll have to make acquaintance with four companies of women, ready for the fray and well armed to boot.

MAGISTRATE: Forward, Scythians, and bind them!

LYSISTRATA: Forward, my gallant companions; march forth, ye vendors of grain and eggs, garlic and vegetables, keepers of taverns and bakeries, wrench and strike and tear; come, a torrent of invective and insult! (*They beat the officers*) Enough, enough! now retire, never rob the vanquished!

MAGISTRATE: Here's a fine exploit for my officers!

LYSISTRATA: Ah, ha! so you thought you had only to do with a set of slave-women! you did not know the ardour that fills the bosom of free-born dames.

MAGISTRATE: Ardour! yes, by Apollo, ardour enough—especially for the wine-cup!

CHORUS OF OLD MEN: Sir, sir! what use of words? they are of no avail with wild beasts of this sort. Don't you know how they have just washed us down—and with no very fragrant soap!

CHORUS OF WOMEN: What would you have? You should never have laid rash hands on us. If you start afresh, I'll knock your eyes out. My delight is to stay at home as coy as a young maid, without hurting anybody or moving any more than a milestone; but 'ware the wasps, if you go stirring up the wasps' nest!

CHORUS OF OLD MEN: Ah! great gods! how get the better of these ferocious creatures? 'tis past all bearing! But come, let us try to find out the reason of the dreadful scourge. With what end in view have they seized the citadel of Cranaus,[36] the sacred shrine that is raised upon the inaccessible rock of the Acropolis? Question them; be cautious and not too credulous. 'Twould be culpable negligence not to pierce the mystery, if we may.

---

36. The second (mythical) king of Athens, successor of Cecrops.

MAGISTRATE (*addressing the women*): I would ask you first why ye have barred our gates.

LYSISTRATA: To seize the treasury; no more money, no more war.

MAGISTRATE: Then money is the cause of the War?

LYSISTRATA: And of all our troubles. 'Twas to find occasion to steal that Pisander[37] and all the other agitators were for ever raising revolutions. Well and good! but they'll never get another drachma here.

MAGISTRATE: What do you propose to do then, pray?

LYSISTRATA: You ask me that! Why, we propose to administer the treasury ourselves.

MAGISTRATE: *You* do?

LYSISTRATA: What is there in that to surprise you? Do we not administer the budget of household expenses?

MAGISTRATE: But that is not the same thing.

LYSISTRATA: How so—not the same thing?

MAGISTRATE: It is the treasury supplies the expenses of the War.

LYSISTRATA: That's our first principle—no War!

MAGISTRATE: What! and the safety of the city?

LYSISTRATA: We will provide for that.

MAGISTRATE: You?

LYSISTRATA: Yes, just we.

MAGISTRATE: What a sorry business!

LYSISTRATA: Yes, we're going to save you, whether you will or no.

MAGISTRATE: Oh! the impudence of the creatures!

LYSISTRATA: You seem annoyed! but there, you've got to come to it.

MAGISTRATE: But 'tis the very height of iniquity!

LYSISTRATA: We're going to save you, my man.

MAGISTRATE: But if I don't want to be saved?

LYSISTRATA: Why, all the more reason!

MAGISTRATE: But what a notion, to concern yourselves with questions of Peace and War!

LYSISTRATA: We will explain our idea.

MAGISTRATE: Out with it then; quick, or. . . (*threatening her*)

LYSISTRATA: Listen, and never a movement, please!

---

37. The leader of the Revolution which resulted in the temporary overthrow of the Democracy at Athens (413, 412 B.C.), and the establishment of the Oligarchy of the Four Hundred.

ARISTOPHANES

MAGISTRATE: Oh! it is too much for me! I cannot keep my temper!

A WOMAN: Then look out for yourself; you have more to fear than we have.

MAGISTRATE: Stop your croaking, old crow, you! (*To Lysistrata*) Now you, say your say.

LYSISTRATA: Willingly. All the long time the War has lasted, we have endured in modest silence all you men did; we never allowed ourselves to open our lips. We were far from satisfied, for we knew how things were going; often in our homes we would hear you discussing, upside down and inside out, some important turn of affairs. Then with sad hearts, but smiling lips, we would ask you: Well, in to-day's Assembly did they vote Peace?—But, "Mind your own business!" the husband would growl, "Hold your tongue, do!" And I would say no more.

A WOMAN: I would not have held my tongue though, not I!

MAGISTRATE: You would have been reduced to silence by blows then.

LYSISTRATA: Well, for my part, I would say no more. But presently I would come to know you had arrived at some fresh decision more fatally foolish than ever. "Ah! my dear man," I would say, "what madness next!" But he would only look at me askance and say: "Just weave your web, do; else your cheeks will smart for hours. War is men's business!"

MAGISTRATE: Bravo! well said indeed!

LYSISTRATA: How now, wretched man? not to let us contend against your follies, was bad enough! But presently we heard you asking out loud in the open street: "Is there never a man left in Athens?" and, "No, not one, not one," you were assured in reply. Then, then we made up our minds without more delay to make common cause to save Greece. Open your ears to our wise counsels and hold your tongues, and we may yet put things on a better footing.

MAGISTRATE: *You* put things indeed! Oh! 'tis too much! The insolence of the creatures! Silence, I say.

LYSISTRATA: Silence yourself!

MAGISTRATE: May I die a thousand deaths ere I obey one who wears a veil!

LYSISTRATA: If that's all that troubles you, here, take my veil, wrap it round your head, and hold your tongue. Then take this basket; put on a girdle, card wool, munch beans. The War shall be women's business.

CHORUS OF WOMEN: Lay aside your water-pots, we will guard them, we will help our friends and companions. For myself, I will never weary of the dance; my knees will never grow stiff with fatigue. I will brave everything with my dear allies, on whom Nature has lavished virtue, grace, boldness, cleverness, and whose wisely directed energy is going to save the State. Oh! my good, gallant Lysistrata, and all my friends, be ever like a bundle of nettles; never let your anger slacken; the winds of fortune blow our way.

LYSISTRATA: May gentle Love and the sweet Cyprian Queen shower seductive charms on our bosoms and all our person. If only we may stir so amorous a lust among the men that their tools stand stiff as sticks, we shall indeed deserve the name of peace-makers among the Greeks.

MAGISTRATE: How will that be, pray?

LYSISTRATA: To begin with, we shall not see you any more running like mad fellows to the Market holding lance in fist.

A WOMAN: That will be something gained, anyway, by the Paphian goddess, it will!

LYSISTRATA: Now we see 'em, mixed up with saucepans and kitchen stuff, armed to the teeth, looking like wild Corybantes![38]

MAGISTRATE: Why, of course; that's how brave men should do.

LYSISTRATA: Oh! but what a funny sight, to behold a man wearing a Gorgon's-head buckler coming along to buy fish!

A WOMAN: 'Tother day in the Market I saw a phylarch[39] with flowing ringlets; he was a-horseback, and was pouring into his helmet the broth he had just bought at an old dame's stall. There was a Thracian warrior too, who was brandishing his lance like Tereus in the play;[40] he had scared a good woman selling figs into a perfect panic, and was gobbling up all her ripest fruit.

MAGISTRATE: And how, pray, would you propose to restore peace and order in all the countries of Greece?

LYSISTRATA: 'Tis the easiest thing in the world!

MAGISTRATE: Come, tell us how; I am curious to know.

---

38. Priests of Cybelé, who indulged in wild, frenzied dances, to the accompaniment of the clashing of cymbals, in their celebrations in honour of the goddess.

39. Captain of a cavalry division; they were chosen from amongst the *Hippeis*, or 'Knights' at Athens.

40. In allusion to a play of Euripides, now lost, with this title. Tereus was son of Ares and king of the Thracians in Daulis.

LYSISTRATA: When we are winding thread, and it is tangled, we pass
the spool across and through the skein, now this way, now that
way; even so, to finish off the War, we shall send embassies hither
and thither and everywhere, to disentangle matters.

MAGISTRATE: And 'tis with your yarn, and your skeins, and your
spools, you think to appease so many bitter enmities, you silly
women?

LYSISTRATA: If only you had common sense, you would always do in
politics the same as we do with our yarn.

MAGISTRATE: Come, how is that, eh?

LYSISTRATA: First we wash the yarn to separate the grease and filth;
do the same with all bad citizens, sort them out and drive them
forth with rods—'tis the refuse of the city. Then for all such as
come crowding up in search of employments and offices, we
must card them thoroughly; then, to bring them all to the same
standard, pitch them pell-mell into the same basket, resident aliens
or no, allies, debtors to the State, all mixed up together. Then as for
our Colonies, you must think of them as so many isolated hanks;
find the ends of the separate threads, draw them to a centre here,
wind them into one, make one great hank of the lot, out of which
the Public can weave itself a good, stout tunic.

MAGISTRATE: Is it not a sin and a shame to see them carding and
winding the State, these women who have neither art nor part in
the burdens of the War?

LYSISTRATA: What! wretched man! why, 'tis a far heavier burden to us
than to you. In the first place, we bear sons who go off to fight far
away from Athens.

MAGISTRATE: Enough said! do not recall sad and sorry memories![41]

LYSISTRATA: Then secondly, instead of enjoying the pleasures of
love and making the best of our youth and beauty, we are left to
languish far from our husbands, who are all with the army. But say
no more of ourselves; what afflicts me is to see our girls growing
old in lonely grief.

MAGISTRATE: Don't the men grow old too?

LYSISTRATA: That is not the same thing. When the soldier returns
from the wars, even though he has white hair, he very soon finds

---

41. An allusion to the disastrous Sicilian Expedition (415–413 B.C.), in which many
thousands of Athenian citizens perished.

a young wife. But a woman has only one summer; if she does not make hay while the sun shines, no one will afterwards have anything to say to her, and she spends her days consulting oracles, that never send her a husband.

MAGISTRATE: But the old man who can still erect his organ. . .

LYSISTRATA: But you, why don't you get done with it and die? You are rich; go buy yourself a bier, and I will knead you a honey-cake for Cerberus. Here, take this garland. (*Drenching him with water*)

FIRST WOMAN: And this one too. (*Drenching him with water*)

SECOND WOMAN: And these fillets. (*Drenching him with water*)

LYSISTRATA: What do you lack more? Step aboard the boat; Charon is waiting for you, you're keeping him from pushing off.

MAGISTRATE: To treat me so scurvily! What an insult! I will go show myself to my fellow-magistrates just as I am.

LYSISTRATA: What! are you blaming us for not having exposed you according to custom?[42] Nay, console yourself; we will not fail to offer up the third-day sacrifice for you, first thing in the morning.[43]

CHORUS OF OLD MEN: Awake, friends of freedom; let us hold ourselves aye ready to act. I suspect a mighty peril; I foresee another Tyranny like Hippias'.[44] I am sore afraid the Laconians assembled here with Cleisthenes have, by a stratagem of war, stirred up these women, enemies of the gods, to seize upon our treasury and the funds whereby I lived.[45] Is it not a sin and a shame for them to interfere in advising the citizens, to prate of shields and lances, and to ally themselves with Laconians, fellows I trust no more than I would so many famished wolves? The whole thing, my friends, is nothing else but an attempt to re-establish Tyranny. But I will never submit; I will be on my guard for the future; I will always carry a blade hidden under myrtle boughs; I will post myself in the Public Square under arms, shoulder to shoulder with

---

42. The dead were laid out at Athens before the house door.

43. An offering made to the Manes of the deceased on the third day after the funeral.

44. Hippias and Hipparchus, the two sons of Pisistratus, known as the Pisistratidae, became Tyrants of Athens upon their father's death in 527 B.C. In 514 the latter was assassinated by the conspirators, Harmodius and Aristogiton, who took the opportunity of the Panathenaic festival and concealed their daggers in myrtle wreaths. They were put to death, but four years later the surviving Tyrant Hippias was expelled, and the young and noble martyrs to liberty were ever after held in the highest honour by their fellow-citizens. Their statues stood in the Agora or Public Market-Square.

45. That is, the three obols paid for attendance as a Heliast at the High Court.

Aristogiton;[46] and now, to make a start, I must just break a few of that cursed old jade's teeth yonder.

CHORUS OF WOMEN: Nay, never play the brave man, else when you go back home, your own mother won't know you. But, dear friends and allies, first let us lay our burdens down; then, citizens all, hear what I have to say. I have useful counsel to give our city, which deserves it well at my hands for the brilliant distinctions it has lavished on my girlhood. At seven years of age, I was bearer of the sacred vessels; at ten, I pounded barley for the altar of Athené; next, clad in a robe of yellow silk, I was *little bear* to Artemis at the Brauronia;[47] presently, grown a tall, handsome maiden, they put a necklace of dried figs about my neck, and I was Basket-Bearer.[48] So surely I am bound to give my best advice to Athens. What matters that I was born a woman, if I can cure your misfortunes? I pay my share of tolls and taxes, by giving men to the State. But you, you miserable greybeards, you contribute nothing to the public charges; on the contrary, you have wasted the treasure of our forefathers, as it was called, the treasure amassed in the days of the Persian Wars.[49] You pay nothing at all in return; and into the bargain you endanger our lives and liberties by your mistakes. Have you one word to say for yourselves? . . . Ah! don't irritate me, you there, or I'll lay my slipper across your jaws; and it's pretty heavy.

CHORUS OF OLD MEN: Outrage upon outrage! things are going from bad to worse. Let us punish the minxes, every one of us that has a man's appendages to boast of. Come, off with our tunics, for a man must savour of manhood; come, my friends, let us strip naked from head to foot. Courage, I say, we who in our day garrisoned

---

46. See above, under note 3 (433. Transcriber.).

47. The origin of the name was this: in ancient days a tame bear consecrated to Artemis, the huntress goddess, it seems, devoured a young girl, whose brothers killed the offender. Artemis was angered and sent a terrible pestilence upon the city, which only ceased when, by direction of the oracle, a company of maidens was dedicated to the deity, to act the part of she-bears in the festivities held annually in her honour at the *Brauronia*, her festival so named from the deme of Brauron in Attica.

48. The Basket-Bearers, Canephoroi, at Athens were the maidens who, clad in flowing robes, carried in baskets on their heads the sacred implements and paraphernalia in procession at the celebrations in honour of Demeter, Dionysus and Athené.

49. A treasure formed by voluntary contributions at the time of the Persian Wars; by Aristophanes' day it had all been dissipated, through the influence of successive demagogues, in distributions and gifts to the public under various pretexts.

Lipsydrion;[50] let us be young again, and shake off eld. If we give them the least hold over us, 'tis all up! their audacity will know no bounds! We shall see them building ships, and fighting sea-fights, like Artemisia;[51] nay, if they want to mount and ride as cavalry, we had best cashier the knights, for indeed women excel in riding, and have a fine, firm seat for the gallop.[52] Just think of all those squadrons of Amazons Micon has painted for us engaged in hand-to-hand combat with men.[53] Come then, we must e'en fit collars to all these willing necks.

CHORUS OF WOMEN: By the blessed goddesses, if you anger me, I will let loose the beast of my evil passions, and a very hailstorm of blows will set you yelling for help. Come, dames, off tunics, and quick's the word; women must scent the savour of women in the throes of passion. . . Now just you dare to measure strength with me, old greybeard, and I warrant you you'll never eat garlic or black beans more. No, not a word! my anger is at boiling point, and I'll do with you what the beetle did with the eagle's eggs.[54] I laugh at your threats, so long as I have on my side Lampito here, and the noble Theban, my dear Ismenia. . . Pass decree on decree, you can do us no hurt, you wretch abhorred of all your fellows. Why, only yesterday, on occasion of the feast of Hecaté, I asked my neighbours of Boeotia for one of their daughters for whom my girls have a lively liking—a fine, fat eel to wit; and if they did not refuse, all along of your silly decrees! We shall never cease to suffer the like, till someone gives you a neat trip-up and breaks your neck for you!

---

50. A town and fortress of Southern Attica, in the neighbourhood of Marathon, occupied by the Alcmaeonidae—the noble family or clan at Athens banished from the city in 595 B.C., restored 560, but again expelled by Pisistratus—in the course of their contest with that Tyrant. Returning to Athens on the death of Hippias (510 B.C.), they united with the democracy, and the then head of the family, Cleisthenes, gave a new constitution to the city.

51. Queen of Halicarnassus, in Caria; an ally of the Persian King Xerxes in his invasion of Greece; she fought gallantly at the battle of Salamis.

52. A *double entendre*—with allusion to the posture in sexual intercourse known among the Greeks as (Greek: hippos), in Latin 'equus,' the horse, where the woman mounts the man in reversal of the ordinary position.

53. Micon, a famous Athenian painter, decorated the walls of the Poecilé Stoa, or Painted Porch, at Athens with a series of frescoes representing the battles of the Amazons with Theseus and the Athenians.

54. To avenge itself on the eagle, the beetle threw the former's eggs out of the nest and broke them. See the Fables of Aesop.

CHORUS OF WOMEN (*addressing Lysistrata*): You, Lysistrata, you who are leader of our glorious enterprise, why do I see you coming towards me with so gloomy an air?

LYSISTRATA: 'Tis the behaviour of these naughty women, 'tis the female heart and female weakness so discourages me.

CHORUS OF WOMEN: Tell us, tell us, what is it?

LYSISTRATA: I only tell the simple truth.

CHORUS OF WOMEN: What has happened so disconcerting; come, tell your friends.

LYSISTRATA: Oh! the thing is so hard to tell—yet so impossible to conceal.

CHORUS OF WOMEN: Nay, never seek to hide any ill that has befallen our cause.

LYSISTRATA: To blurt it out in a word—we are in heat!

CHORUS OF WOMEN: Oh! Zeus, oh! Zeus!

LYSISTRATA: What use calling upon Zeus? The thing is even as I say. I cannot stop them any longer from lusting after the men. They are all for deserting. The first I caught was slipping out by the postern gate near the cave of Pan; another was letting herself down by a rope and pulley; a third was busy preparing her escape; while a fourth, perched on a bird's back, was just taking wing for Orsilochus' house,[55] when I seized her by the hair. One and all, they are inventing excuses to be off home. Look! there goes one, trying to get out! Halloa there! whither away so fast?

FIRST WOMAN: I want to go home; I have some Miletus wool in the house, which is getting all eaten up by the worms.

LYSISTRATA: Bah! you and your worms! go back, I say!

FIRST WOMAN: I will return immediately, I swear I will by the two goddesses! I only have just to spread it out on the bed.

LYSISTRATA: You shall not do anything of the kind! I say, you shall not go.

FIRST WOMAN: Must I leave my wool to spoil then?

LYSISTRATA: Yes, if need be.

SECOND WOMAN: Unhappy woman that I am! Alas for my flax! I've left it at home unstript!

LYSISTRATA: So, here's another trying to escape to go home and strip her flax forsooth!

---

55. Keeper of a house of ill fame apparently.

SECOND WOMAN: Oh! I swear by the goddess of light, the instant I have put it in condition I will come straight back.

LYSISTRATA: You shall do nothing of the kind! If once you began, others would want to follow suit.

THIRD WOMAN: Oh! goddess divine, Ilithyia, patroness of women in labour, stay, stay the birth, till I have reached a spot less hallowed than Athene's Mount!

LYSISTRATA: What mean you by these silly tales?

THIRD WOMAN: I am going to have a child—now, this minute.

LYSISTRATA: But you were not pregnant yesterday!

THIRD WOMAN: Well, I am to-day. Oh! let me go in search of the midwife, Lysistrata, quick, quick!

LYSISTRATA: What is this fable you are telling me? Ah! what have you got there so hard?

THIRD WOMAN: A male child.

LYSISTRATA: No, no, by Aphrodité! nothing of the sort! Why, it feels like something hollow—a pot or a kettle. Oh! you baggage, if you have not got the sacred helmet of Pallas—and you said you were with child!

THIRD WOMAN: And so I am, by Zeus, I am!

LYSISTRATA: Then why this helmet, pray?

THIRD WOMAN: For fear my pains should seize me in the Acropolis; I mean to lay my eggs in this helmet, as the doves do.

LYSISTRATA: Excuses and pretences every word! the thing's as clear as daylight. Anyway, you must stay here now till the fifth day, your day of purification.

THIRD WOMAN: I cannot sleep any more in the Acropolis, now I have seen the snake that guards the Temple.

FOURTH WOMAN: Ah! and those confounded owls with their dismal hooting! I cannot get a wink of rest, and I'm just dying of fatigue.

LYSISTRATA: You wicked women, have done with your falsehoods! You want your husbands, that's plain enough. But don't you think they want you just as badly? They are spending dreadful nights, oh! I know that well enough. But hold out, my dears, hold out! A little more patience, and the victory will be ours. An Oracle promises us success, if only we remain united. Shall I repeat the words?

FIRST WOMAN: Yes, tell us what the Oracle declares.

LYSISTRATA: Silence then! Now—"Whenas the swallows, fleeing before the hoopoes, shall have all flocked together in one place, and shall refrain them from all amorous commerce, then will be the end of all the ills of life; yea, and Zeus, which doth thunder in the skies, shall set above what was erst below. . ."

CHORUS OF WOMEN: What! shall the men be underneath?

LYSISTRATA: "But if dissension do arise among the swallows, and they take wing from the holy Temple, 'twill be said there is never a more wanton bird in all the world."

CHORUS OF WOMEN: Ye gods! the prophecy is clear. Nay, never let us be cast down by calamity! let us be brave to bear, and go back to our posts. 'Twere shameful indeed not to trust the promises of the Oracle.

CHORUS OF OLD MEN: I want to tell you a fable they used to relate to me when I was a little boy. This is it: Once upon a time there was a young man called Melanion, who hated the thought of marriage so sorely that he fled away to the wilds. So he dwelt in the mountains, wove himself nets, kept a dog and caught hares. He never, never came back, he had such a horror of women. As chaste as Melanion,[56] we loathe the jades just as much as he did.

AN OLD MAN: You dear old woman, I would fain kiss you.

A WOMAN: I will set you crying without onions.

OLD MAN: . . . And give you a sound kicking.

OLD WOMAN: Ah, ha! what a dense forest you have there! (*Pointing*)

OLD MAN: So was Myronides one of the best-bearded of men o' this side; his backside was all black, and he terrified his enemies as much as Phormio.[57]

CHORUS OF WOMEN: I want to tell you a fable too, to match yours about Melanion. Once there was a certain man called Timon,[58] a tough customer, and a whimsical, a true son of the Furies, with a face that seemed to glare out of a thorn-bush. He withdrew from the world because he couldn't abide bad men, after vomiting a

---

56. "As chaste as Melanion" was a Greek proverb. Who Melanion was is unknown.

57. Myronides and Phormio were famous Athenian generals. The former was celebrated for his conquest of all Boeotia, except Thebes, in 458 B.C.; the latter, with a fleet of twenty triremes, equipped at his own cost, defeated a Lacedaemonian fleet of forty-seven sail, in 429.

58. Timon, the misanthrope; he was an Athenian and a contemporary of Aristophanes. Disgusted by the ingratitude of his fellow-citizens and sickened with repeated disappointments, he retired altogether from society, admitting no one, it is said, to his intimacy except the brilliant young statesman Alcibiades.

thousand curses at 'em. He had a holy horror of ill-conditioned fellows, but he was mighty tender towards women.

A WOMAN: Suppose I up and broke your jaw for you!

AN OLD MAN: I am not a bit afraid of you.

A WOMAN: Suppose I let fly a good kick at you?

OLD MAN: I should see your backside then.

WOMAN: You would see that, for all my age, it is very well attended to, and all fresh singed smooth.

LYSISTRATA: Ho there! come quick, come quick!

FIRST WOMAN: What is it? Why these cries?

LYSISTRATA: A man! a man! I see him approaching all afire with the flames of love. Oh! divine Queen of Cyprus, Paphos and Cythera, I pray you still be propitious to our emprise.

FIRST WOMAN: Where is he, this unknown foe?

LYSISTRATA: Yonder—beside the Temple of Demeter.

FIRST WOMAN: Yes, indeed, I see him; but who is it?

LYSISTRATA: Look, look! does any of you recognize him?

FIRST WOMAN: I do, I do! 'tis my husband Cinesias.

LYSISTRATA: To work then! Be it your task to inflame and torture and torment him. Seductions, caresses, provocations, refusals, try every means! Grant every favour,—always excepting what is forbidden by our oath on the wine-bowl.

MYRRHINÉ: Have no fear, I undertake the work.

LYSISTRATA: Well, I will stay here to help you cajole the man and set his passions aflame. The rest of you, withdraw.

CINESIAS: Alas! alas! how I am tortured by spasm and rigid convulsion! Oh! I am racked on the wheel!

LYSISTRATA: Who is this that dares to pass our lines?

CINESIAS: It is I.

LYSISTRATA: What, a man?

CINESIAS: Yes, no doubt about it, a man!

LYSISTRATA: Begone!

CINESIAS: But who are you that thus repulses me?

LYSISTRATA: The sentinel of the day.

CINESIAS: By all the gods, call Myrrhiné hither.

LYSISTRATA: Call Myrrhiné hither, quotha? And pray, who are you?

CINESIAS: I am her husband, Cinesias, son of Peon.

LYSISTRATA: Ah! good day, my dear friend. Your name is not unknown amongst us. Your wife has it for ever on her lips; and she never touches an egg or an apple without saying: "'Twill be for Cinesias."

CINESIAS: Really and truly?

LYSISTRATA: Yes, indeed, by Aphrodité! And if we fall to talking of men, quick your wife declares: "Oh! all the rest, they're good for nothing compared with Cinesias."

CINESIAS: Oh! I beseech you, go and call her to me.

LYSISTRATA: And what will you give me for my trouble?

CINESIAS: This, if you like (*handling his tool*) I will give you what I have there!

LYSISTRATA: Well, well, I will tell her to come.

CINESIAS: Quick, oh! be quick! Life has no more charms for me since she left my house. I am sad, sad, when I go indoors; it all seems so empty; my victuals have lost their savour. Desire is eating out my heart!

MYRRHINÉ: I love him, oh! I love him; but he won't let himself be loved. No! I shall not come.

CINESIAS: Myrrhiné, my little darling Myrrhiné, what are you saying? Come down to me quick.

MYRRHINÉ: No indeed, not I.

CINESIAS: I call you, Myrrhiné, Myrrhiné; will you not come?

MYRRHINÉ: Why should you call me? You do not want me.

CINESIAS: Not want you! Why, my weapon stands stiff with desire!

MYRRHINÉ: Good-bye.

CINESIAS: Oh! Myrrhiné, Myrrhiné, in our child's name, hear me; at any rate hear the child! Little lad, call your mother.

CHILD: Mammy, mammy, mammy!

CINESIAS: There, listen! Don't you pity the poor child? It's six days now you've never washed and never fed the child.

MYRRHINÉ: Poor darling, your father takes mighty little care of you!

CINESIAS: Come down, dearest, come down for the child's sake.

MYRRHINÉ: Ah! what a thing it is to be a mother! Well, well, we must come down, I suppose.

CINESIAS: Why, how much younger and prettier she looks! And how she looks at me so lovingly! Her cruelty and scorn only redouble my passion.

MYRRHINÉ: You are as sweet as your father is provoking! Let me kiss you, my treasure, mother's darling!

CINESIAS: Ah! what a bad thing it is to let yourself be led away by other women! Why give me such pain and suffering, and yourself into the bargain?

MYRRHINÉ: Hands off, sir!

CINESIAS: Everything is going to rack and ruin in the house.

MYRRHINÉ: I don't care.

CINESIAS: But your web that's all being pecked to pieces by the cocks and hens, don't you care for that?

MYRRHINÉ: Precious little.

CINESIAS: And Aphrodite, whose mysteries you have not celebrated for so long? Oh! won't you come back home?

MYRRHINÉ: No, at least, not till a sound Treaty put an end to the War.

CINESIAS: Well, if you wish it so much, why, we'll make it, your Treaty.

MYRRHINÉ: Well and good! When that's done, I will come home. Till then, I am bound by an oath.

CINESIAS: At any rate, let's have a short time together.

MYRRHINÉ: No, no, no! . . . all the same I cannot say I don't love you.

CINESIAS: You love me? Then why refuse what I ask, my little girl, my sweet Myrrhiné.

MYRRHINÉ: You must be joking! What, before the child!

CINESIAS: Manes, carry the lad home. There, you see, the child is gone; there's nothing to hinder us; let us to work!

MYRRHINÉ: But, miserable man, where, where are we to do it?

CINESIAS: In the cave of Pan; nothing could be better.

MYRRHINÉ: But how to purify myself, before going back into the citadel?

CINESIAS: Nothing easier! you can wash at the Clepsydra.[59]

MYRRHINÉ: But my oath? Do you want me to perjure myself?

CINESIAS: I take all responsibility; never make yourself anxious.

MYRRHINÉ: Well, I'll be off, then, and find a bed for us.

CINESIAS: Oh! 'tis not worth while; we can lie on the ground surely.

MYRRHINÉ: No, no! bad man as you are, I don't like your lying on the bare earth.

CINESIAS: Ah! how the dear girl loves me!

MYRRHINÉ (coming back with a bed): Come, get to bed quick; I am going to undress. But, plague take it, we must get a mattress.

CINESIAS: A mattress! Oh! no, never mind!

---

59. A spring so named within the precincts of the Acropolis.

MYRRHINÉ: No, by Artemis! lie on the bare sacking, never! That were too squalid.

CINESIAS: A kiss!

MYRRHINÉ: Wait a minute!

CINESIAS: Oh! by the great gods, be quick back!

MYRRHINÉ (*coming back with a mattress*): Here is a mattress. Lie down, I am just going to undress. But, but you've got no pillow.

CINESIAS: I don't want one, no, no.

MYRRHINÉ: But *I* do.

CINESIAS: Oh! dear, oh, dear! they treat my poor penis for all the world like Heracles.[60]

MYRRHINÉ (*coming back with a pillow*): There, lift your head, dear!

CINESIAS: That's really everything.

MYRRHINÉ: Is it everything, I wonder.

CINESIAS: Come, my treasure.

MYRRHINÉ: I am just unfastening my girdle. But remember what you promised me about making Peace; mind you keep your word.

CINESIAS: Yes, yes, upon my life I will.

MYRRHINÉ: Why, you have no blanket.

CINESIAS: Great Zeus! what matter of that? 'tis you I want to fuck.

MYRRHINÉ: Never fear—directly, directly! I'll be back in no time.

CINESIAS: The woman will kill me with her blankets!

MYRRHINÉ (*coming back with a blanket*): Now, get up for one moment.

CINESIAS: But I tell you, our friend here is up—all stiff and ready!

MYRRHINÉ: Would you like me to scent you?

CINESIAS: No, by Apollo, no, please!

MYRRHINÉ: Yes, by Aphrodité, but I will, whether you wish it or no.

CINESIAS: Ah! great Zeus, may she soon be done!

MYRRHINÉ (*coming back with a flask of perfume*): Hold out your hand; now rub it in.

CINESIAS: Oh! in Apollo's name, I don't much like the smell of it; but perhaps 'twill improve when it's well rubbed in. It does not somehow smack of the marriage bed!

MYRRHINÉ: There, what a scatterbrain I am; if I have not brought Rhodian perfumes![61]

---

60. The comic poets delighted in introducing Heracles (Hercules) on the stage as an insatiable glutton, whom the other characters were for ever tantalizing by promising toothsome dishes and then making him wait indefinitely for their arrival.

61. The Rhodian perfumes and unguents were less esteemed than the Syrian.

CINESIAS: Never mind, dearest, let be now.

MYRRHINÉ: You are joking!

CINESIAS: Deuce take the man who first invented perfumes, say I!

MYRRHINÉ (*coming back with another flask*): Here, take this bottle.

CINESIAS: I have a better all ready for your service, darling. Come, you provoking creature, to bed with you, and don't bring another thing.

MYRRHINÉ: Coming, coming; I'm just slipping off my shoes. Dear boy, will you vote for peace?

CINESIAS: I'll think about it. (*Myrrhiné runs away*) I'm a dead man, she is killing me! She has gone, and left me in torment! I must have someone to fuck, I must! Ah me! the loveliest of women has choused and cheated me. Poor little lad (*addressing his penis*), how am I to give you what you want so badly? Where is Cynalopex? quick, man, get him a nurse, do![62]

CHORUS OF OLD MEN: Poor, miserable wretch, baulked in your amorousness! what tortures are yours! Ah! you fill me with pity. Could any man's back and loins stand such a strain? His organ stands stiff and rigid, and there's never a wench to help him!

CINESIAS: Ye gods in heaven, what pains I suffer!

CHORUS OF OLD MEN: Well, there it is; 'tis her doing, that abandoned hussy!

CINESIAS: Nay, nay! rather say that sweetest, dearest darling.

CHORUS OF OLD MEN: That dearest darling? no, no, that hussy, say I! Zeus, thou god of the skies, canst not let loose a hurricane, to sweep them all up into the air, and whirl 'em round, then drop 'em down crash! and impale them on the point of his weapon!

A HERALD: Say, where shall I find the Senate and the Prytanes? I am bearer of despatches.

MAGISTRATE: But are you a man or a Priapus, pray?[63]

HERALD: Oh! but he's mighty simple. I am a herald, of course, I swear I am, and I come from Sparta about making peace.

MAGISTRATE: But look, you are hiding a lance under your clothes, surely.

HERALD: No, nothing of the sort.

---

62. 'Dog-fox,' nickname of a certain notorious Philostratus, keeper of an Athenian brothel of note in Aristophanes' day.

63. The god of gardens—and of lubricity; represented by a grotesque figure with an enormous penis.

MAGISTRATE: Then why do you turn away like that, and hold your cloak out from your body? Have you gotten swellings in the groin with your journey?

HERALD: By the twin brethren! the man's an old maniac.

MAGISTRATE: Ah, ha! my fine lad, why I can see it standing, oh fie!

HERALD: I tell you no! but enough of this foolery.

MAGISTRATE: Well, what is it you have there then?

HERALD: A Lacedaemonian 'skytalé.'[64]

MAGISTRATE: Oh, indeed, a 'skytalé,' is it? Well, well, speak out frankly; I know all about these matters. How are things going at Sparta now?

HERALD: Why, everything is turned upside down at Sparta; and all the allies are half dead with lusting. We simply must have Pellené.[65]

MAGISTRATE: What is the reason of it all? Is it the god Pan's doing?

HERALD: No, but Lampito's and the Spartan women's, acting at her instigation; they have denied the men all access to their cunts.

MAGISTRATE: But whatever do you do?

HERALD: We are at our wits' end; we walk bent double, just as if we were carrying lanterns in a wind. The jades have sworn we shall not so much as touch their cunts till we have all agreed to conclude peace.

MAGISTRATE: Ha, ha! So I see now, 'tis a general conspiracy embracing all Greece. Go you back to Sparta and bid them send Envoys with plenary powers to treat for peace. I will urge our Senators myself to name Plenipotentiaries from us; and to persuade them, why, I will show them this. (*Pointing to his erect penis*)

HERALD: What could be better? I fly at your command.

CHORUS OF OLD MEN: No wild beast is there, no flame of fire, more fierce and untameable than woman; the panther is less savage and shameless.

---

64. A staff in use among the Lacedaemonians for writing cipher despatches. A strip of leather or paper was wound round the 'skytalé,' on which the required message was written lengthwise, so that when unrolled it became unintelligible; the recipient abroad had a staff of the same thickness and pattern, and so was enabled by rewinding the document to decipher the words.

65. A city of Achaia, the acquisition of which had long been an object of Lacedaemonian ambition. To make the joke intelligible here, we must suppose Pellené was also the name of some notorious courtesan of the day.

CHORUS OF WOMEN: And yet you dare to make war upon me, wretch, when you might have me for your most faithful friend and ally.

CHORUS OF OLD MEN: Never, never can my hatred cease towards women.

CHORUS OF WOMEN: Well, please yourself. Still I cannot bear to leave you all naked as you are; folks would laugh at me. Come, I am going to put this tunic on you.

CHORUS OF OLD MEN: You are right, upon my word! it was only in my confounded fit of rage I took it off.

CHORUS OF WOMEN: Now at any rate you look like a man, and they won't make fun of you. Ah! if you had not offended me so badly, I would take out that nasty insect you have in your eye for you.

CHORUS OF OLD MEN: Ah! so that's what was annoying me so! Look, here's a ring, just remove the insect, and show it me. By Zeus! it has been hurting my eye this ever so long.

CHORUS OF WOMEN: Well, I agree, though your manners are not over and above pleasant. Oh! what a huge great gnat! just look! It's from Tricorysus, for sure.[66]

CHORUS OF OLD MEN: A thousand thanks! the creature was digging a regular well in my eye; now it's gone, my tears flow freely.

CHORUS OF WOMEN: I will wipe them for you—bad, naughty man though you are. Now, just one kiss.

CHORUS OF OLD MEN: No—a kiss, certainly not!

CHORUS OF WOMEN: Just one, whether you like it or not.

CHORUS OF OLD MEN: Oh! those confounded women! how they do cajole us! How true the saying: "'Tis impossible to live with the baggages, impossible to live without 'em"! Come, let us agree for the future not to regard each other any more as enemies; and to clinch the bargain, let us sing a choric song.

CHORUS OF WOMEN: We desire, Athenians, to speak ill of no man; but on the contrary to say much good of everyone, and to *do* the like. We have had enough of misfortunes and calamities. Is there any, man or woman, wants a bit of money—two or three minas or so;[67] well, our purse is full. If only peace is concluded, the borrower will not have to pay back. Also I'm inviting to supper a few

---

66. A deme of Attica, abounding in woods and marshes, where the gnats were particularly troublesome. There is very likely also an allusion to the spiteful, teasing character of its inhabitants.

67. A mina was a little over £4; 60 minas made a talent.

Carystian friends,[68] who are excellently well qualified. I have still a drop of good soup left, and a young porker I'm going to kill, and the flesh will be sweet and tender. I shall expect you at my house to-day; but first away to the baths with you, you and your children; then come all of you, ask no one's leave, but walk straight up, as if you were at home; never fear, the door will be. . . shut in your faces![69]

CHORUS OF OLD MEN: Ah! here come the Envoys from Sparta with their long flowing beards; why, you would think they wore a cage[70] between their thighs. (*Enter the Lacedaemonian Envoys*) Hail to you, first of all, Laconians; then tell us how you fare.

A LACONIAN: No need for many words; you see what a state we are in.

CHORUS OF OLD MEN: Alas! the situation grows more and more strained! the intensity of the thing is just frightful.

LACONIAN: 'Tis beyond belief. But to work! summon your Commissioners, and let us patch up the best peace we may.

CHORUS OF OLD MEN: Ah! our men too, like wrestlers in the arena, cannot endure a rag over their bellies; 'tis an athlete's malady, which only exercise can remedy.

AN ATHENIAN: Can anybody tell us where Lysistrata is? Surely she will have some compassion on our condition.

CHORUS OF OLD MEN: Look! 'tis the very same complaint. (*Addressing the Athenian*) Don't you feel of mornings a strong nervous tension?

ATHENIAN: Yes, and a dreadful, dreadful torture it is! Unless peace is made very soon, we shall find no resource but to fuck Clisthenes.[71]

CHORUS OF OLD MEN: Take my advice, and put on your clothes again; one of the fellows who mutilated the Hermae[72] might see you.

ATHENIAN: You are right.

---

68. Carystus was a city of Euboea notorious for the dissoluteness of its inhabitants; hence the inclusion of these Carystian youths in the women's invitation.

69. A (Greek: para prosdokian); i.e. exactly the opposite of the word expected is used to conclude the sentence—to move the sudden hilarity of the audience as a finale to the scene.

70. A wattled cage or pen for pigs.

71. An effeminate, a pathic; failing women, they will have to resort to pederasty.

72. These *Hermae* were half-length figures of the god Hermes, which stood at the corners of streets and in public places at Athens. One night, just before the sailing of the Sicilian Expedition, they were all mutilated—to the consternation of the inhabitants. Alcibiades and his wild companions were suspected of the outrage.

LACONIAN: Quite right. There, I will slip on my tunic.

ATHENIAN: Oh! what a terrible state we are in! Greeting to you, Laconian fellow-sufferers.

LACONIAN (*addressing one of his countrymen*): Ah! my boy, what a thing it would have been if these fellows had seen us just now when our tools were on full stand!

ATHENIAN: Speak out, Laconians, what is it brings you here?

LACONIAN: We have come to treat for peace.

ATHENIAN: Well said; we are of the same mind. Better call Lysistrata then; she is the only person will bring us to terms.

LACONIAN: Yes, yes—and Lysistratus into the bargain, if you will.

CHORUS OF OLD MEN: Needless to call her; she has heard your voices, and here she comes.

ATHENIAN: Hail, boldest and bravest of womankind! The time is come to show yourself in turn uncompromising and conciliatory, exacting and yielding, haughty and condescending. Call up all your skill and artfulness. Lo! the foremost men in Hellas, seduced by your fascinations, are agreed to entrust you with the task of ending their quarrels.

LYSISTRATA: 'Twill be an easy task—if only they refrain from mutual indulgence in masculine love; if they do, I shall know the fact at once. Now, where is the gentle goddess Peace? Lead hither the Laconian Envoys. But, look you, no roughness or violence; our husbands always behaved so boorishly.[73] Bring them to me with smiles, as women should. If any refuse to give you his hand, then catch him by the penis and draw him politely forward. Bring up the Athenians too; you may take them just how you will. Laconians, approach; and you, Athenians, on my other side. Now hearken all! I am but a woman; but I have good common sense; Nature has dowered me with discriminating judgment, which I have yet further developed, thanks to the wise teachings of my father and the elders of the city. First I must bring a reproach against you that applies equally to both sides. At Olympia, and Thermopylae, and Delphi, and a score of other places too numerous to mention, you celebrate before the same

---

73. They had repeatedly dismissed with scant courtesy successive Lacedaemonian embassies coming to propose terms of peace after the notable Athenian successes at Pylos, when the Island of Sphacteria was captured and 600 Spartan citizens brought prisoners to Athens. This was in 425 B.C., the seventh year of the War.

altars ceremonies common to all Hellenes; yet you go cutting each other's throats, and sacking Hellenic cities, when all the while the Barbarian is yonder threatening you! That is my first point.

ATHENIAN: Ah, ah! concupiscence is killing me!

LYSISTRATA: Now 'tis to you I address myself, Laconians. Have you forgotten how Periclides,[74] your own countryman, sat a suppliant before our altars? How pale he was in his purple robes! He had come to crave an army of us; 'twas the time when Messenia was pressing you sore, and the Sea-god was shaking the earth. Cimon marched to your aid at the head of four thousand hoplites, and saved Lacedaemon. And, after such a service as that, you ravage the soil of your benefactors!

ATHENIAN: They do wrong, very wrong, Lysistrata.

LACONIAN: We do wrong, very wrong. Ah! great gods! what lovely thighs she has!

LYSISTRATA: And now a word to the Athenians. Have you no memory left of how, in the days when ye wore the tunic of slaves, the Laconians came, spear in hand, and slew a host of Thessalians and partisans of Hippias the Tyrant? They, and they only, fought on your side on that eventful day; they delivered you from despotism, and thanks to them our Nation could change the short tunic of the slave for the long cloak of the free man.

LACONIAN: I have never seen a woman of more gracious dignity.

ATHENIAN: I have never seen a woman with a finer cunt!

LYSISTRATA: Bound by such ties of mutual kindness, how can you bear to be at war? Stop, stay the hateful strife, be reconciled; what hinders you?

LACONIAN: We are quite ready, if they will give us back our rampart.

LYSISTRATA: What rampart, my dear man?

LACONIAN: Pylos, which we have been asking for and craving for ever so long.

ATHENIAN: In the Sea-god's name, you shall never have it!

LYSISTRATA: Agree, my friends, agree.

ATHENIAN: But then what city shall we be able to stir up trouble in?

LYSISTRATA: Ask for another place in exchange.

---

74. Chief of the Lacedaemonian embassy which came to Athens, after the earthquake of 464 B.C., which almost annihilated the town of Sparta, to invoke the help of the Athenians against the revolted Messenians and helots.

ATHENIAN: Ah! that's the ticket! Well, to begin with, give us Echinus, the Maliac gulf adjoining, and the two legs of Megara.[75]

LACONIAN: Oh! surely, surely not all that, my dear sir.

LYSISTRATA: Come to terms; never make a difficulty of two legs more or less!

ATHENIAN: Well, I'm ready now to off coat and cultivate my land.

LACONIAN: And I too, to dung it to start with.

LYSISTRATA: That's just what you shall do, once peace is signed. So, if you really want to make it, go consult your allies about the matter.

ATHENIAN: What allies, I should like to know? Why, we are *all* on the stand; not one but is mad to be fucking. What we all want, is to be abed with our wives; how should our allies fail to second our project?

LACONIAN: And ours the same, for certain sure!

ATHENIANS: The Carystians first and foremost, by the gods!

LYSISTRATA: Well said, indeed! Now be off to purify yourselves for entering the Acropolis, where the women invite you to supper; we will empty our provision baskets to do you honour. At table, you will exchange oaths and pledges; then each man will go home with his wife.

ATHENIAN: Come along then, and as quick as may be.

LACONIAN: Lead on; I'm your man.

ATHENIAN: Quick, quick's the word, say I.

CHORUS OF WOMEN: Embroidered stuffs, and dainty tunics, and flowing gowns, and golden ornaments, everything I have, I offer them you with all my heart; take them all for your children, for your girls, against they are chosen "basket-bearers" to the goddess. I invite you every one to enter, come in and choose whatever you will; there is nothing so well fastened, you cannot break the seals, and carry away the contents. Look about you everywhere. . . you won't find a blessed thing, unless you have sharper eyes than mine.[76] And if any of you lacks corn to feed his slaves and his young and numerous family, why, I have a few grains of wheat at home; let him take what I have to give, a big twelve-pound loaf included. So

---

75. Echinus was a town on the Thessalian coast, at the entrance to the Maliac Gulf, near Thermopylae and opposite the northern end of the Athenian island of Euboea. By the "legs of Megara" are meant the two "long walls" or lines of fortification connecting the city of Megara with its seaport Nisaea—in the same way as Piraeus was joined to Athens.
76. Examples of (Greek: para prosdokian) again; see above.

let my poorer neighbours all come with bags and wallets; my man, Manes, shall give them corn; but I warn them not to come near my door, or—beware the dog!

A MARKET-LOUNGER: I say, you, open the door!

A SLAVE: Go your way, I tell you. Why, bless me, they're sitting down now; I shall have to singe 'em with my torch to make 'em stir! What an impudent lot of fellows!

MARKET-LOUNGER: I don't mean to budge.

SLAVE: Well, as you *must* stop, and I don't want to offend you—but you'll see some queer sights.

MARKET-LOUNGER: Well and good, I've no objection.

SLAVE: No, no, you must be off—or I'll tear your hair out, I will; be off, I say, and don't annoy the Laconian Envoys; they're just coming out from the banquet-hall.

AN ATHENIAN: Such a merry banquet I've never seen before! The Laconians were simply charming. After the drink is in, why, we're all wise men, all. It's only natural, to be sure, for sober, we're all fools. Take my advice, my fellow-countrymen, our Envoys should always be drunk. We go to Sparta; we enter the city sober; why, we must be picking a quarrel directly. We don't understand what they say to us, we imagine a lot they don't say at all, and we report home all wrong, all topsy-turvy. But, look you, to-day it's quite different; we're enchanted whatever happens; instead of Clitagoras, they might sing us Telamon,[77] and we should clap our hands just the same. A perjury or two into the bargain, la! what does that matter to merry companions in their cups?

SLAVE: But here they are back again! Will you begone, you loafing scoundrels.

MARKET-LOUNGER: Ah ha! here's the company coming out already.

A LACONIAN: My dear, sweet friend, come, take your flute in hand; I would fain dance and sing my best in honour of the Athenians and our noble selves.

AN ATHENIAN: Yes, take your flute, i' the gods' name. What a delight to see him dance!

CHORUS OF LACONIANS: Oh Mnemosyné! inspire these men, inspire my muse who knows our exploits and those of the Athenians.

---

77. Clitagoras was a composer of drinking songs, Telamon of war songs.

With what a godlike ardour did they swoop down at Artemisium[78] on the ships of the Medes! What a glorious victory was that! For the soldiers of Leonidas,[79] they were like fierce wild-boars whetting their tushes. The sweat ran down their faces, and drenched all their limbs, for verily the Persians were as many as the sands of the seashore. Oh! Artemis, huntress queen, whose arrows pierce the denizens of the woods, virgin goddess, be thou favourable to the Peace we here conclude; through thee may our hearts be long united! May this treaty draw close for ever the bonds of a happy friendship! No more wiles and stratagems! Aid us, oh! aid us, maiden huntress!

LYSISTRATA: All is for the best; and now, Laconians, take your wives away home with you, and you, Athenians, yours. May husband live happily with wife, and wife with husband. Dance, dance, to celebrate our bliss, and let us be heedful to avoid like mistakes for the future.

CHORUS OF ATHENIANS: Appear, appear, dancers, and the Graces with you! Let us invoke, one and all, Artemis, and her heavenly brother, gracious Apollo, patron of the dance, and Dionysus, whose eye darts flame, as he steps forward surrounded by the Maenad maids, and Zeus, who wields the flashing lightning, and his august, thrice-blessed spouse, the Queen of Heaven! These let us invoke, and all the other gods, calling all the inhabitants of the skies to witness the noble Peace now concluded under the fond auspices of Aphrodité. Io Paean! Io Paean! dance, leap, as in honour of a victory won. Evoé! Evoé! And you, our Laconian guests, sing us a new and inspiring strain!

CHORUS OF LACONIANS: Leave once more, oh! leave once more the noble height of Taygetus, oh! Muse of Lacedaemon, and join us in singing the praises of Apollo of Amyclae, and Athena of the Brazen House, and the gallant twin sons of Tyndarus, who practise arms on the banks of Eurotas river.[80] Haste, haste hither

---

78. Here, off the north coast of Euboea, the Greeks defeated the Persians in a naval battle, 480 B.C.

79. The hero of Thermopylae, where the 300 Athenians arrested the advance of the invading hosts of Xerxes in the same year.

80. Amyclae, an ancient town on the Eurotas within two or three miles of Sparta, the traditional birthplace of Castor and Pollux; here stood a famous and magnificent Temple of Apollo.

with nimble-footed pace, let us sing Sparta, the city that delights in choruses divinely sweet and graceful dances, when our maidens bound lightly by the river side, like frolicsome fillies, beating the ground with rapid steps and shaking their long locks in the wind, as Bacchantes wave their wands in the wild revels of the Wine-god. At their head, oh! chaste and beauteous goddess, daughter of Latona, Artemis, do thou lead the song and dance. A fillet binding thy waving tresses, appear in thy loveliness; leap like a fawn; strike thy divine hands together to animate the dance, and aid us to renown the valiant goddess of battles, great Athené of the Brazen House!

F<small>INIS OF</small> "L<small>YSISTRATA</small>"

"Of the Brazen House," a surname of Athené, from the Temple dedicated to her worship at Chalcis in Euboea, the walls of which were covered with plates of brass.

Sons of Tyndarus, that is, Castor and Pollux, "the great twin brethren," held in peculiar reverence at Sparta.

THESMOPHORIAZUSAE OR, THE WOMEN
CELEBRATING THE THESMOPHORIA

INTRODUCTION

L ike the 'Lysistrata,' the 'Thesmophoriazusae, or Women's Festival,' and the next following play, the 'Ecclesiazusae, or Women in Council' are comedies in which the fair sex play a great part, and also resemble that extremely *scabreux* production in the plentiful crop of doubtful 'double entendres' and highly suggestive situations they contain.

The play has more of a proper intrigue and formal dénouement than is general with our Author's pieces, which, like modern extravaganzas and musical comedies, are often strung on a very slender thread of plot. The idea of the 'Thesmophoriazusae' is as follows.

Euripides is summoned as a notorious woman-hater and detractor of the female sex to appear for trial and judgment before the women of Athens assembled to celebrate the Thesmophoria, a festival held in honour of the goddesses Demeter and Persephone, from which men were rigidly excluded. The poet is terror-stricken, and endeavours to persuade his confrère, the tragedian Agathon, to attend the meeting in the guise of a woman to plead his cause, Agathon's notorious effeminacy of costume and way of life lending itself to the deception; but the latter refuses point-blank. He then prevails on his father-in-law, Mnesilochus, to do him this favour, and shaves, depilates, and dresses him up accordingly. But so far from throwing oil on the troubled waters, Mnesilochus indulges in a long harangue full of violent abuse of the whole sex, and relates some scandalous stories of the naughty ways of peccant wives. The assembly suspects at once there is a man amongst them, and on examination of the old fellow's person, this is proved to be the case. He flies for sanctuary to the altar, snatching a child from the arms of one of the women as a hostage, vowing to kill it if they molest him further. On investigation, however, the infant turns out to be a wine-skin dressed in baby's clothes.

In despair Mnesilochus sends urgent messages to Euripides to come and rescue him from his perilous predicament. The latter then appears, and in successive characters selected from his different Tragedies—now Menelaus meeting Helen again in Egypt, now Echo sympathising with the chained Andromeda, presently Perseus about to release the heroine from her rock—pleads for his unhappy father-in-law. At length he succeeds in getting him away in the temporary absence of the guard, a Scythian archer, whom he entices from his post by the charms of a dancing-girl.

As may be supposed, the appearance of Mnesilochus among the women dressed in women's clothes, the examination of his person to discover his true sex and his final detection, afford fine opportunities for a display of the broadest Aristophanic humour. The latter part of the play also, where various pieces of Euripides are burlesqued, is extremely funny; and must have been still more so when represented before an audience familiar with every piece and almost every line parodied, and played by actors trained and got up to imitate every trick and mannerism of appearance and delivery of the tragic actors who originally took the parts.

The 'Thesmophoriazusae' was produced in the year 412 B.C., six years before the death of Euripides, who is held up to ridicule in it, as he is in 'The Wasps' and several other of our Author's comedies.

Dramatis Personae

Euripides.

Mnesilochus, Father-in-law of Euripides.

Agathon.

Servant of Agathon.

Chorus attending Agathon.

Herald.

Women.

Clisthenes.

A Prytanis or Member of the Council.

A Scythian or Police Officer.

Chorus of Thesmophoriazusae—women keeping the Feast of Demeter.

Scene: *In front of Agathon's house; afterwards in the precincts of the Temple of Demeter.*

MNESILOCHUS: Great Zeus! will the swallow never appear to end the winter of my discontent? Why the fellow has kept me on the run ever since early this morning; he wants to kill me, that's certain. Before I lose my spleen entirely, Euripides, can you at least tell me whither you are leading me?

EURIPIDES: What need for you to hear what you are going to see?

MNESILOCHUS: How is that? Repeat it. No need for me to hear. . .

EURIPIDES: What you are going to see.

MNESILOCHUS: Nor consequently to see. . .

EURIPIDES: What you have to hear.[1]

MNESILOCHUS: What is this wiseacre stuff you are telling me? I must neither see nor hear.

EURIPIDES: Ah! but you have two things there that are essentially distinct.

MNESILOCHUS: Seeing and hearing.

EURIPIDES: Undoubtedly.

MNESILOCHUS: In what way distinct?

EURIPIDES: In this way. Formerly, when Ether separated the elements and bore the animals that were moving in her bosom, she wished to endow them with sight, and so made the eye round like the sun's disc and bored ears in the form of a funnel.

MNESILOCHUS: And because of this funnel I neither see nor hear. Ah! great gods! I am delighted to know it. What a fine thing it is to talk with wise men!

EURIPIDES: I will teach you many another thing of the sort.

MNESILOCHUS: That's well to know; but first of all I should like to find out how to grow lame, so that I need not have to follow you all about.

EURIPIDES: Come, hear and give heed!

MNESILOCHUS: I'm here and waiting.

EURIPIDES: Do you see that little door?

MNESILOCHUS: Yes, certainly.

EURIPIDES: Silence!

MNESILOCHUS: Silence about what? About the door?

EURIPIDES: Pay attention!

MNESILOCHUS: Pay attention and be silent about the door? Very well.

EURIPIDES: 'Tis there that Agathon, the celebrated tragic poet, dwells.[2]

---

1. Aristophanes parodies Euripides' language, which is occasionally sillily sententious.

2. He flourished about 420 B.C. and composed many tragedies, such as 'Telephus,' 'Thyestes,' which are lost. Some fragments of his work are to be found in Aristotle and

MNESILOCHUS: Who is this Agathon?

EURIPIDES: 'Tis a certain Agathon. . .

MNESILOCHUS: Swarthy, robust of build?

EURIPIDES: No, another. You have never seen him?

MNESILOCHUS: He has a big beard?

EURIPIDES: No, no, evidently you have never seen him.

MNESILOCHUS: Never, so far as I know.

EURIPIDES: And yet you have pedicated him. Well, it must have been without knowing who he was. Ah! let us step aside; here is one of his slaves bringing a brazier and some myrtle branches; no doubt he is going to offer a sacrifice and pray for a happy poetical inspiration for Agathon.

SERVANT OF AGATHON: Silence! oh, people! keep your mouths sedately shut! The chorus of the Muses is moulding songs at my master's hearth. Let the winds hold their breath in the silent Ether! Let the azure waves cease murmuring on the shore! . . .

MNESILOCHUS: Brouuouou! brouuouou! (*Imitates the buzzing of a fly*)

EURIPIDES: Keep quiet! what are you saying there?

SERVANT: . . . Take your rest, ye winged races, and you, ye savage inhabitants of the woods, cease from your erratic wandering. . .

MNESILOCHUS: Broum, broum, brouuouou.

SERVANT: . . . for Agathon, our master, the sweet-voiced poet, is going. . .

MNESILOCHUS: . . . to be pedicated?

SERVANT: Whose voice is that?

MNESILOCHUS: 'Tis the silent Ether.

SERVANT: . . . is going to construct the framework of a drama. He is rounding fresh poetical forms, he is polishing them in the lathe and is welding them; he is hammering out sentences and metaphors; he is working up his subject like soft wax. First he models it and then he casts it in bronze. . .

MNESILOCHUS: . . . and sways his buttocks amorously.

SERVANT: Who is the rustic who approaches this sacred enclosure?

MNESILOCHUS: Take care of yourself and of your sweet-voiced poet! I have a strong instrument here both well rounded and well polished, which will pierce your enclosure and penetrate your bottom.

---

in Athenaeus; he also distinguished himself as a musician. The banquet, which gave his name to one of Plato's dialogues, is supposed to have taken place at his house.

SERVANT: Old man, you must have been a very insolent fellow in your youth!

EURIPIDES (*to the servant*): Let him be, friend, and, quick, go and call Agathon to me.

SERVANT: 'Tis not worth the trouble, for he will soon be here himself. He has started to compose, and in winter[3] it is never possible to round off strophes without coming to the sun to excite the imagination. (*He departs*)

MNESILOCHUS: And what am I to do?

EURIPIDES: Wait till he comes. . . Oh, Zeus! what hast thou in store for me to-day?

MNESILOCHUS: But, great gods, what is the matter then? What are you grumbling and groaning for? Tell me; you must not conceal anything from your father-in-law.

EURIPIDES: Some great misfortune is brewing against me.

MNESILOCHUS: What is it?

EURIPIDES: This day will decide whether it is all over with Euripides or not.

MNESILOCHUS: But how? Neither the tribunals nor the Senate are sitting, for it is the third of the five days consecrated to Demeter.[4]

EURIPIDES: That is precisely what makes me tremble; the women have plotted my ruin, and to-day they are to gather in the Temple of Demeter to execute their decision.

MNESILOCHUS: Why are they against you?

EURIPIDES: Because I mishandle them in my tragedies.

MNESILOCHUS: By Posidon, you would seem to have thoroughly deserved your fate. But how are you going to get out of the mess?

EURIPIDES: I am going to beg Agathon, the tragic poet, to go to the Thesmophoria.

MNESILOCHUS: And what is he to do there?

---

3. The Thesmophoria were celebrated in the month of Pyanepsion, or November.

4. The Thesmophoria lasted five days; they were dedicated to Demeter Thesmophoros, or Legislatress, in recognition of the wise laws she had given mankind. For many days before the solemn event, the women of high birth (who alone were entitled to celebrate it) had to abstain from all pleasures that appealed to the senses, even the most legitimate, and to live with the greatest sobriety. The presiding priest at the Thesmophoria was always chosen from the sacerdotal family of the Eumolpidae, the descendants of Eumolpus, the son of Posidon. At these feasts, the worship of Persephoné was associated with that of Demeter.

EURIPIDES: He would mingle with the women, and stand up for me, if needful.

MNESILOCHUS: Would he be openly present or secretly?

EURIPIDES: Secretly, dressed in woman's clothes.

MNESILOCHUS: That's a clever notion, thoroughly worthy of you. The prize for trickery is ours.

EURIPIDES: Silence!

MNESILOCHUS: What's the matter?

EURIPIDES: Here comes Agathon.

MNESILOCHUS: Where, where?

EURIPIDES: That's the man they are bringing out yonder on the machine.[5]

MNESILOCHUS: I am blind then! I see no man here, I only see Cyrené.[6]

EURIPIDES: Be still! He is getting ready to sing.

MNESILOCHUS: What subtle trill, I wonder, is he going to warble to us?

AGATHON: Damsels, with the sacred torch[7] in hand, unite your dance to shouts of joy in honour of the nether goddesses; celebrate the freedom of your country.

CHORUS: To what divinity is your homage addressed? I wish to mingle mine with it.

AGATHON: Oh! Muse! glorify Phoebus with his golden bow, who erected the walls of the city of the Simois.[8]

CHORUS: To thee, oh Phoebus, I dedicate my most beauteous songs; to thee, the sacred victor in the poetical contests.

AGATHON: And praise Artemis too, the maiden huntress, who wanders on the mountains and through the woods. . .

CHORUS: I, in my turn, celebrate the everlasting happiness of the chaste Artemis, the mighty daughter of Latona!

AGATHON: . . . and Latona and the tones of the Asiatic lyre, which wed so well with the dances of the Phrygian Graces.[9]

---

5. Refers presumably to the (Greek: ekkukl ema), a piece of machinery by means of which interiors were represented on the Greek stage—room and occupant being in some way wheeled out into view of the spectators bodily.

6. A celebrated 'lady of pleasure'; Agathon is like her by reason of his effeminate, wanton looks and dissolute habits.

7. Demeter is represented wandering, torch in hand, about the universe looking for her lost child Proserpine (Persephoné).

8. Troy.

9. Agathon, in accordance with his character, voluptuousness, is represented as preferring the effeminate music and lascivious dances of Asia.

CHORUS: I do honour to the divine Latona and to the lyre, the mother of songs of male and noble strains. The eyes of the goddess sparkle while listening to our enthusiastic chants. Honour to the powerful Phoebus! Hail! thou blessed son of Latona!

MNESILOCHUS: Oh! ye venerable Genetyllides,[10] what tender and voluptuous songs! They surpass the most lascivious kisses in sweetness; I feel a thrill of delight pass up my rectum as I listen to them. Young man, whoever you are, answer my questions, which I am borrowing from Aeschylus' 'Lycurgeia.'[11] Whence comes this effeminate? What is his country? his dress? What contradictions his life shows! A lyre and a hair-net! A wrestling school oil flask and a girdle![12] What could be more contradictory? What relation has a mirror to a sword? And you yourself, who are you? Do you pretend to be a man? Where is the sign of your manhood, your penis, pray? Where is the cloak, the footgear that belong to that sex? Are you a woman? Then where are your breasts? Answer me. But you keep silent. Oh! just as you choose; your songs display your character quite sufficiently.

AGATHON: Old man, old man, I hear the shafts of jealousy whistling by my ears, but they do not hit me. My dress is in harmony with my thoughts. A poet must adopt the nature of his characters. Thus, if he is placing women on the stage, he must contract all their habits in his own person.

MNESILOCHUS: Then you ride the high horse[13] when you are composing a Phaedra.

AGATHON: If the heroes are men, everything in him will be manly. What we don't possess by nature, we must acquire by imitation.

MNESILOCHUS: When you are staging Satyrs, call me; I will do my best to help you from behind with standing tool.

---

10. Goddesses who presided over generation; see also the 'Lysistrata.'

11. A tetralogy, a series of four dramas connected by subject, of which the principal character was Lycurgus, king of the Thracians. When Bacchus returned to Thrace as conqueror of the Indies he dared to deride the god, and was punished by him in consequence. All four plays are lost.

12. That is, the attributes of a man and those of a woman combined.

13. That is, you make love in the posture known as 'the horse,' *equus*, in other words the woman atop of the man. There is a further joke intended here, inasmuch as Euripides, in his 'Phaedra,' represents the heroine as being passionately addicted to hunting and horses.

AGATHON: Besides, it is bad taste for a poet to be coarse and hairy. Look at the famous Ibycus, at Anacreon of Teos, and at Alcaeus,[14] who handled music so well; they wore headbands and found pleasure in the lascivious dances of Ionia. And have you not heard what a dandy Phrynichus was[15] and how careful in his dress? For this reason his pieces were also beautiful, for the works of a poet are copied from himself.

MNESILOCHUS: Ah! so it is for this reason that Philocles, who is so hideous, writes hideous pieces; Xenocles, who is malicious, malicious ones, and Theognis,[16] who is cold, such cold ones?

AGATHON: Yes, necessarily and unavoidably; and 'tis because I knew this that I have so well cared for my person.

MNESILOCHUS: How, in the gods' name?

EURIPIDES: Come, leave off badgering him; I was just the same at his age, when I began to write.

MNESILOCHUS: At! then, by Zeus! I don't envy you your fine manners.

EURIPIDES (*to Agathon*): But listen to the cause that brings me here.

AGATHON: Say on.

EURIPIDES: Agathon, wise is he who can compress many thoughts into few words.[17] Struck by a most cruel misfortune, I come to you as a suppliant.

AGATHON: What are you asking?

EURIPIDES: The women purpose killing me to-day during the Thesmophoria, because I have dared to speak ill of them.

AGATHON: And what can I do for you in the matter?

EURIPIDES: Everything. Mingle secretly with the women by making yourself pass as one of themselves; then do you plead my cause

---

14. Ibycus, a lyric poet of the sixth century, originally from Rhegium in Magna Graecia.—Anacreon, a celebrated erotic poet of the beginning of the fifth century.—Alcaeus, a lyric poet, born about 600 B.C. at Mytilené, in the island of Lesbos, was driven out of his country by a tyrant and sang of his loves, his services as a warrior, his travels and the miseries of his exile. He was a contemporary of Sappho, and conceived a passion for her, which she only rewarded with disdain.

15. Phrynichus, a disciple of Thespis, improved the dramatic art, when still no more than a child; it was he who first introduced female characters upon the stage and made use of the iambic of six feet in tragedies. He flourished about 500 B.C.

16. Philocles, Xenocles, and Theognis were dramatic poets and contemporaries of Aristophanes. The two first were sons of Carcinus, the poet and dancer.

17. Fragment of Euripides' 'Aeolus,' a lost drama.

with your own lips, and I am saved. You, and you alone, are capable of speaking of me worthily.

AGATHON: But why not go and defend yourself?

EURIPIDES: 'Tis impossible. First of all, I am known; further, I have white hair and a long beard; whereas you, you are good-looking, charming, and are close-shaven; you are fair, delicate, and have a woman's voice.

AGATHON: Euripides!

EURIPIDES: Well?

AGATHON: Have you not said in one of your pieces, "You love to see the light, and don't you believe your father loves it too?"[18]

EURIPIDES: Yes.

AGATHON: Then never you think I am going to expose myself in your stead; 'twould be madness. 'Tis for you to submit to the fate that overtakes you; one must not try to trick misfortune, but resign oneself to it with good grace.

MNESILOCHUS: This is why you, you wretch, offer your posterior with a good grace to lovers, not in words, but in actual fact.

EURIPIDES: But what prevents your going there?

AGATHON: I should run more risk than you would.

EURIPIDES: Why?

AGATHON: Why? I should look as if I were wanting to trespass on secret nightly pleasures of the women and to ravish their Aphrodité.[19]

MNESILOCHUS: Of wanting to ravish indeed! you mean wanting to be ravished—in the rearward mode. Ah! great gods! a fine excuse truly!

EURIPIDES: Well then, do you agree?

AGATHON: Don't count upon it.

EURIPIDES: Oh! I am unfortunate indeed! I am undone!

MNESILOCHUS: Euripides, my friend, my son-in-law, never despair.

EURIPIDES: What can be done?

MNESILOCHUS: Send him to the devil and do with me as you like.

EURIPIDES: Very well then, since you devote yourself to my safety, take off your cloak first.

MNESILOCHUS: There, it lies on the ground. But what do you want to do with me?

---

18. Fragment of Euripides' well-known play, the 'Alcestis.'
19. An allusion to the secret practices of mutual love which the women assembled for the Thesmophoria were credited by popular repute with indulging in.

EURIPIDES: To shave off this beard of yours, and to remove your hair below as well.

MNESILOCHUS: Do what you think fit; I yield myself entirely to you.

EURIPIDES: Agathon, you have always razors about you; lend me one.

AGATHON: Take if yourself, there, out of that case.

EURIPIDES: Thanks. Sit down and puff out the right cheek.

MNESILOCHUS: Oh! oh! oh!

EURIPIDES: What are you shouting for? I'll cram a spit down your gullet, if you're not quiet.

MNESILOCHUS: Oh! oh! oh! oh! oh! oh! (*He springs up and starts running away*)

EURIPIDES: Where are you running to now?

MNESILOCHUS: To the temple of the Eumenides.[20] No, by Demeter I won't let myself be gashed like that.

EURIPIDES: But you will get laughed at, with your face half-shaven like that.

MNESILOCHUS: Little care I.

EURIPIDES: In the gods' names, don't leave me in the lurch. Come here.

MNESILOCHUS: Oh! by the gods! (*Resumes his seat*)

EURIPIDES: Keep still and hold up your head. Why do you want to fidget about like this?

MNESILOCHUS: Mu, mu.

EURIPIDES: Well! why, mu, mu? There! 'tis done and well done too!

MNESILOCHUS: Ah! great god! It makes me feel quite light.

EURIPIDES: Don't worry yourself; you look charming. Do you want to see yourself?

MNESILOCHUS: Aye, that I do; hand the mirror here.

EURIPIDES: Do you see yourself?

MNESILOCHUS: But this is not I, it is Clisthenes![21]

EURIPIDES: Stand up; I am now going to remove your hair. Bend down.

MNESILOCHUS: Alas! alas! they are going to grill me like a pig.

EURIPIDES: Come now, a torch or a lamp! Bend down and take care of the tender end of your tail!

MNESILOCHUS: Aye, aye! but I'm afire! oh! oh! Water, water, neighbour, or my rump will be alight!

EURIPIDES: Keep up your courage!

---

20. That is, to sanctuary.
21. An effeminate often mentioned by Aristophanes.

MNESILOCHUS: Keep my courage, when I'm being burnt up?

EURIPIDES: Come, cease your whining, the worst is over.

MNESILOCHUS: Oh! it's quite black, all burnt below there all about the hole!

EURIPIDES: Don't worry! that will be washed off with a sponge.

MNESILOCHUS: Woe to him who dares to wash my rump!

EURIPIDES: Agathon, you refuse to devote yourself to helping me; but at any rate lend me a tunic and a belt. You cannot say you have not got them.

AGATHON: Take them and use them as you like; I consent.

MNESILOCHUS: What must be taken?

EURIPIDES: What must be taken? First put on this long saffron-coloured robe.

MNESILOCHUS: By Aphrodité! what a sweet odour! how it smells of a man's genitals![22] Hand it me quickly. And the belt?

EURIPIDES: Here it is.

MNESILOCHUS: Now some rings for my legs.

EURIPIDES: You still want a hair-net and a head-dress.

AGATHON: Here is my night-cap.

EURIPIDES: Ah! that's capital.

MNESILOCHUS: Does it suit me?

AGATHON: It could not be better.

EURIPIDES: And a short mantle?

AGATHON: There's one on the couch; take it.

EURIPIDES: He wants slippers.

AGATHON: Here are mine.

MNESILOCHUS: Will they fit me? You like a loose fit.[23]

AGATHON: Try them on. Now that you have all you need, let me be taken inside.[24]

EURIPIDES: You look for all the world like a woman. But when you talk, take good care to give your voice a woman's tone.

MNESILOCHUS: I'll try my best.

EURIPIDES: Come, get yourself to the temple.

MNESILOCHUS: No, by Apollo, not unless you swear to me. . .

EURIPIDES: What?

---

22. An allusion to the pederastic habits which the poet attributes to Agathon.
23. An obscene allusion.
24. On the machine upon which he is perched.

MNESILOCHUS: . . . that, if anything untoward happen to me, you will leave nothing undone to save me.

EURIPIDES: Very well! I swear it by the Ether, the dwelling-place of the king of the gods.[25]

MNESILOCHUS: Why not rather swear it by the disciples of Hippocrates?[26]

EURIPIDES: Come, I swear it by all the gods, both great and small.

MNESILOCHUS: Remember, 'tis the heart, and not the tongue, that has sworn;[27] for the oaths of the tongue concern me but little.

EURIPIDES: Hurry yourself! The signal for the meeting has just been displayed on the Temple of Demeter. Farewell. (*Exit*)

MNESILOCHUS: Here, Thratta, follow me.[28] Look, Thratta, at the cloud of smoke that arises from all these lighted torches. Ah! beautiful Thesmophorae![29] grant me your favours, protect me, both within the temple and on my way back! Come, Thratta, put down the basket and take out the cake, which I wish to offer to the two goddesses. Mighty divinity, oh, Demeter, and thou, Persephoné, grant that I may be able to offer you many sacrifices; above all things, grant that I may not be recognized. Would that my young daughter might marry a man as rich as he is foolish and silly, so that she may have nothing to do but amuse herself. But where can a place be found for hearing well? Be off, Thratta, be off; slaves have no right to be present at this gathering.[30]

HERALD: Silence! Silence! Pray to the Thesmophorae, Demeter and Cora; pray to Plutus,[31] Calligenia,[32] Curotrophos,[33] the Earth,

---

25. A fragment of the 'Menalippé' of Euripides.

26. The ether played an important part in the physical theories of Hippocrates, the celebrated physician.

27. An allusion to a verse in his 'Hippolytus,' where Euripides says, "*The tongue has sworn, but the heart is unsworn.*" See also 'The Frogs.'

28. The name of a slave; being disguised as a woman, Mnesilochus has himself followed by a female servant, a Thracian slave-woman.

29. Demeter and Cora (or Persephoné), who were adored together during the Thesmophoria.

30. Women slaves were forbidden by law to be present at the Thesmophoria; they remained at the door of the temple and there waited for the orders of their mistresses.

31. The god of riches.

32. The nurse of Demeter. According to another version, Calligenia was a surname of Demeter herself, who was adored as presiding over the growth of a child at its mother's breast.

33. A surname of Demeter, who, by means of the food she produces as goddess of abundance, presides over the development of the bodies of children and young people. Curotrophos is derived from (Greek: trephein), to nourish, and (Greek: kouros), young boy.

Hermes and the Graces, that all may happen for the best at this gathering, both for the greatest advantage of Athens and for our own personal happiness! May the award be given her, who, by both deeds and words, has most deserved it from the Athenian people and from the women! Address these prayers to heaven and demand happiness for yourselves. Io Paean! Io Paean! Let us rejoice!

CHORUS: May the gods deign to accept our vows and our prayers! Oh! almighty Zeus, and thou, god with the golden lyre,[34] who reignest on sacred Delos, and thou, oh, invincible virgin, Pallas, with the eyes of azure and the spear of gold, who protectest our illustrious city, and thou, the daughter of the beautiful Latona, the queen of the forests,[35] who art adored under many names, hasten hither at my call. Come, thou mighty Posidon, king of the Ocean, leave thy stormy whirlpools of Nereus; come goddesses of the seas, come, ye nymphs, who wander on the mountains. Let us unite our voices to the sounds of the golden lyre, and may wisdom preside at the gathering of the noble matrons of Athens.

HERALD: Address your prayers to the gods and goddesses of Olympus, of Delphi, Delos and all other places; if there be a man who is plotting against the womenfolk or who, to injure them, is proposing peace to Euripides and the Medes, or who aspires to usurping the tyranny, plots the return of a tyrant, or unmasks a supposititious child; or if there be a slave who, a confidential party to a wife's intrigues, reveals them secretly to her husband, or who, entrusted with a message, does not deliver the same faithfully; if there be a lover who fulfils naught of what he has promised a woman, whom he has abused on the strength of his lies, if there be an old woman who seduces the lover of a maiden by dint of her presents and treacherously receives him in her house; if there be a host or hostess who sells false measure, pray the gods that they will overwhelm them with their wrath, both them and their families, and that they may reserve all their favours for you.

CHORUS: Let us ask the fulfilment of these wishes both for the city and for the people, and may the wisest of us cause her opinion to be accepted. But woe to those women who break their oaths, who speculate on the public misfortune, who seek to alter the laws and

---

34. Apollo.
35. Artemis.

the decrees, who reveal our secrets to the foe and admit the Medes into our territory so that they may devastate it! I declare them both impious and criminal. Oh! almighty Zeus! see to it that the gods protect us, albeit we are but women!

HERALD: Hearken, all of you! this is the decree passed by the Senate of the Women under the presidency of Timoclea and at the suggestion of Sostrata; it is signed by Lysilla, the secretary: "There will be a gathering of the people on the morning of the third day of the Thesmophoria, which is a day of rest for us; the principal business there shall be the punishment that it is meet to inflict upon Euripides for the insults with which he has loaded us." Now who asks to speak?

FIRST WOMAN: I do.

HERALD: First put on this garland, and then speak. Silence! let all be quiet! Pay attention! for here she is spitting as orators generally do before they begin; no doubt she has much to say.

FIRST WOMAN: If I have asked to speak, may the goddesses bear me witness, it was not for sake of ostentation. But I have long been pained to see us women insulted by this Euripides, this son of the green-stuff woman,[36] who loads us with every kind of indignity. Has he not hit us enough, calumniated us sufficiently, wherever there are spectators, tragedians, and a chorus? Does he not style us gay, lecherous, drunken, traitorous, boastful? Does he not repeat that we are all vice, that we are the curse of our husbands? So that, directly they come back from the theatre, they look at us doubtfully and go searching every nook, fearing there may be some hidden lover. We can do nothing as we used to, so many are the false ideas which he has instilled into our husbands. Is a woman weaving a garland for herself? 'Tis because she is in love.[37] Does she let some vase drop while going or returning to the house? her husband asks her in whose honour she has broken it, "It can only be for that Corinthian stranger."[38] Is a maiden unwell? Straightway her brother says, "That is a colour that does not please me."[39] And

---

36. An insult which Aristophanes constantly repeats in every way he can; as we have seen before, Euripides' mother was, or was commonly said to be, a market-woman.

37. Lovers sent each other chaplets and flowers.

38. In parody of a passage in the 'Sthenoboea' of Euripides, which is preserved in Athenaeus.

39. He believes her pregnant.

ARISTOPHANES

if a childless woman wishes to substitute one, the deceit can no longer be a secret, for the neighbours will insist on being present at her delivery. Formerly the old men married young girls, but they have been so calumniated that none think of them now, thanks to the verse: "A woman is the tyrant of the old man who marries her."[40] Again, it is because of Euripides that we are incessantly watched, that we are shut up behind bolts and bars, and that dogs are kept to frighten off the gallants. Let that pass; but formerly it was we who had the care of the food, who fetched the flour from the storeroom, the oil and the wine; we can do it no more. Our husbands now carry little Spartan keys on their persons, made with three notches and full of malice and spite.[41] Formerly it sufficed to purchase a ring marked with the same sign for three obols, to open the most securely sealed-up door;[42] but now this pestilent Euripides has taught men to hang seals of worm-eaten wood about their necks.[43] My opinion, therefore, is that we should rid ourselves of our enemy by poison or by any other means, provided he dies. That is what I announce publicly; as to certain points, which I wish to keep secret, I propose to record them on the secretary's minutes.

CHORUS: Never have I listened to a cleverer or more eloquent woman. Everything she says is true; she has examined the matter from all sides and has weighed up every detail. Her arguments are close, varied, and happily chosen. I believe that Xenocles himself, the son of Carcinus, would seem to talk mere nonsense, if placed beside her.

SECOND WOMAN: I have only a very few words to add, for the last speaker has covered the various points of the indictment; allow me only to tell you what happened to me. My husband died at Cyprus, leaving me five children, whom I had great trouble to bring up by weaving chaplets on the myrtle market. Anyhow, I lived as well as I could until this wretch had persuaded the spectators by his tragedies that there were no gods; since then I have not sold as many chaplets by half. I charge you therefore and exhort you all to punish him, for does he not deserve it in a thousand respects, he who loads you with troubles, who is as coarse toward you as the

---

40. A fragment from the 'Phoenix,' by Euripides.
41. It seems that the Spartan locksmiths were famous for their skill.
42. The women broke the seals their husbands had affixed, and then, with the aid of their ring bearing the same device, they replaced them as before.
43. The impression of which was too complicated and therefore could not be imitated.

green-stuff upon which his mother reared him? But I must back to the market to weave my chaplets; I have twenty to deliver yet.

CHORUS: This is even more animated and more trenchant than the first speech; all she has just said is full of good sense and to the point; it is clever, clear and well calculated to convince. Yes! we must have striking vengeance on the insults of Euripides.

MNESILOCHUS: Oh, women! I am not astonished at these outbursts of fiery rage; how could your bile not get inflamed against Euripides, who has spoken so ill of you? As for myself, I hate the man, I swear it by my children; 'twould be madness not to hate him! Yet, let us reflect a little; we are alone and our words will not be repeated outside. Why be so bent on his ruin? Because he has known and shown up two or three of our faults, when we have a thousand? As for myself, not to speak of other women, I have more than one great sin upon my conscience, but this is the blackest of them. I had been married three days and my husband was asleep by my side; I had a lover, who had seduced me when I was seven years old; impelled by his passion, he came scratching at the door; I understood at once he was there and was going down noiselessly. "Where are you going?" asked my husband. "I am suffering terribly with colic," I told him, "and am going to the closet." "Go," he replied, and started pounding together juniper berries, aniseed, and sage.[44] As for myself, I moistened the door-hinge[45] and went to find my lover, who embraced me, half-reclining upon Apollo's altar[46] and holding on to the sacred laurel with one hand. Well now! Consider! that is a thing of which Euripides has never spoken. And when we bestow our favours on slaves and muleteers for want of better, does he mention this? And when we eat garlic early in the morning after a night of wantonness, so that our husband, who has been keeping guard upon the city wall, may be reassured by the smell and suspect nothing,[47] has Euripides ever breathed a word of this? Tell me. Neither has he spoken of the woman who spreads open a large cloak before her husband's eyes to make him admire it in full daylight to conceal her lover by so

---

44. As a remedy against the colic.
45. So that it might not creak when opened.
46. An altar in the form of a column in the front vestibule of houses and dedicated to Apollo.
47. Because the smell of garlic is not inviting to gallants.

doing and afford him the means of making his escape. I know another, who for ten whole days pretended to be suffering the pains of labour until she had secured a child; the husband hurried in all directions to buy drugs to hasten her deliverance, and meanwhile an old woman brought the infant in a stew-pot; to prevent its crying she had stopped up its mouth with honey. With a sign she told the wife that she was bringing a child for her, who at once began exclaiming, "Go away, friend, go away, I think I am going to be delivered; I can feel him kicking his heels in the belly. . . of the stew-pot."[48] The husband goes off full of joy, and the old wretch quickly picks the honey out of the child's mouth, which sets a-crying; then she seizes the babe, runs to the father and tells him with a smile on her face, "'Tis a lion, a lion, that is born to you; 'tis your very image. Everything about it is like you, even to its little tool, which is all twisty like a fir-cone." Are these not our everyday tricks? Why certainly, by Artemis, and we are angry with Euripides, who assuredly treats us no worse than we deserve!

CHORUS: Great gods! where has she unearthed all that? What country gave birth to such an audacious woman? Oh! you wretch! I should not have thought ever a one of us could have spoken in public with such impudence. 'Tis clear, however, that we must expect everything and, as the old proverb says, must look beneath every stone, lest it conceal some orator[49] ready to sting us. There is but one thing in the world worse than a shameless woman, and that's another woman.

THIRD WOMAN: By Aglaurus![50] you have lost your wits, friends! You must be bewitched to suffer this plague to belch forth insults against us all. Is there no one has any spirit at all? If not, we and our maid-servants will punish her. Run and fetch coals and let's

---

48. The last words are the thoughts of the woman, who pretends to be in child-bed; she is, however, careful not to utter them to her husband.

49. The proverb runs, "*There is a scorpion beneath every stone.*" By substituting *orator* for *scorpion*, Aristophanes means it to be understood that one is no less venomous than the other.

50. There were two women named Aglaurus. One, the daughter of Actaeus, King of Attica, married Cecrops and brought him the kingship as her dowry; the other was the daughter of Cecrops, and was turned into stone for having interfered from jealousy with Hermes' courtship of Hersé her sister. It was this second Aglaurus the Athenian women were in the habit of invoking; they often associated with her her sister Pandrosus.

depilate her cunt in proper style, to teach her not to speak ill of her sex.

MNESILOCHUS: Oh! no! have mercy, friends. Have we not the right to speak frankly at this gathering? And because I have uttered what I thought right in favour of Euripides, do you want to depilate me for my trouble?

THIRD WOMAN: What! we ought not to punish you, who alone have dared to defend the man who has done us so much harm, whom it pleases to put all the vile women that ever were upon the stage, who only shows us Melanippés Phaedras? But of Penelopé he has never said a word, because she was reputed chaste and good.

MNESILOCHUS: I know the reason. 'Tis because not a single Penelopé exists among the women of to-day, but all without exception are Phaedras.

THIRD WOMAN: Women, you hear how this creature still dares to speak of us all.

MNESILOCHUS: And, 'faith, I have not said all that I know. Do you want any more?

THIRD WOMAN: You cannot tell us any more; you have emptied your bag.

MNESILOCHUS: Why, I have not told the thousandth part of what we women do. Have I said how we use the hollow handles of our brooms to draw up wine unbeknown to our husbands.

THIRD WOMAN: The cursed jade!

MNESILOCHUS: And how we give meats to our lovers at the feast of the Apaturia and then accuse the cat. . .

THIRD WOMAN: She's mad!

MNESILOCHUS: . . . Have I mentioned the woman who killed her husband with a hatchet? Of another, who caused hers to lose his reason with her potions? And of the Acharnian woman. . .

THIRD WOMAN: Die, you bitch!

MNESILOCHUS: . . . who buried her father beneath the bath?[51]

THIRD WOMAN: And yet we listen to such things?

MNESILOCHUS: Have I told how you attributed to yourself the male child your slave had just borne and gave her your little daughter?

THIRD WOMAN: This insult calls for vengeance. Look out for your hair!

---

51. Underneath the baths were large hollow chambers filled with steam to maintain the temperature of the water.

MNESILOCHUS: By Zeus! don't touch me.

THIRD WOMAN: There!

MNESILOCHUS: There! tit for tat! (*They exchange blows*)

THIRD WOMAN: Hold my cloak, Philista!

MNESILOCHUS: Come on then, and by Demeter. . .

THIRD WOMAN: Well! what?

MNESILOCHUS: . . . I'll make you disgorge the sesame-cake you have eaten.[52]

CHORUS: Cease wrangling! I see a woman[53] running here in hot haste. Keep silent, so that we may hear the better what she has to say.

CLISTHENES: Friends, whom I copy in all things, my hairless chin sufficiently evidences how dear you are to me; I am women-mad and make myself their champion wherever I am. Just now on the market-place I heard mention of a thing that is of the greatest importance to you; I come to tell it you, to let you know it, so that you may watch carefully and be on your guard against the danger which threatens you.

CHORUS: What is it, my child? I can well call you child, for you have so smooth a skin.

CLISTHENES: 'Tis said that Euripides has sent an old man here to-day, one of his relations. . .

CHORUS: With what object? What is his purpose?

CLISTHENES: . . . so that he may hear your speeches and inform him of your deliberations and intentions.

CHORUS: But how would a man fail to be recognized amongst women?

CLISTHENES: Euripides singed and depilated him and disguised him as a woman.

MNESILOCHUS: This is pure invention! What man is fool enough to let himself be depilated? As for myself, I don't believe a word of it.

CLISTHENES: Are you mad? I should not have come here to tell you, if I did not know it on indisputable authority.

CHORUS: Great gods! what is it you tell us! Come, women, let us not lose a moment; let us search and rummage everywhere! Where can

---

52. By kicking her in the stomach.
53. Clisthenes is always represented by Aristophanes as effeminate in the extreme in dress and habits.

this man have hidden himself escape our notice? Help us to look, Clisthenes; we shall thus owe you double thanks, dear friend.

CLISTHENES (*to a fourth woman*): Well then! let us see. To begin with you; who are you?

MNESILOCHUS (*aside*): Wherever am I to stow myself?

CLISTHENES: Each and every one must pass the scrutiny.

MNESILOCHUS (*aside*): Oh! great gods!

FOURTH WOMAN: You ask me who I am? I am the wife of Cleonymus.[54]

CLISTHENES: Do you know this woman?

CHORUS: Yes, yes, pass on to the rest.

CLISTHENES: And she who carries the child?

MNESILOCHUS (*aside*): I'm a dead man. (*He runs off*)

CLISTHENES (*to Mnesilochus*): Hi! you there! where are you off to? Stop there. What are you running away for?

MNESILOCHUS: I want to relieve myself.

CLISTHENES: The shameless thing! Come, hurry yourself; I will wait here for you.

CHORUS: Wait for her and examine her closely; 'tis the only one we do not know.

CLISTHENES: You are a long time about your business.

MNESILOCHUS: Aye, my god, yes; 'tis because I am unwell, for I ate cress yesterday.[55]

CLISTHENES: What are you chattering about cress? Come here and be quick.

MNESILOCHUS: Oh! don't pull a poor sick woman about like that.

CLISTHENES: Tell me, who is your husband?

MNESILOCHUS: My husband? Do you know a certain individual at Cothocidae[56] . . . ?

CLISTHENES: Whom do you mean? Give his name.

MNESILOCHUS: 'Tis an individual to whom the son of a certain individual one day. . .

CLISTHENES: You are drivelling! Let's see, have you ever been here before?

MNESILOCHUS: Why certainly, every year.

---

54. The coward, often mentioned with contempt by Aristophanes, had thrown away his shield.

55. The ancients believed that cress reduced the natural secretions.

56. A deme of Attica.

CLISTHENES: Who is your tent companion?[57]

MNESILOCHUS: 'Tis a certain. . . Oh! my god!

CLISTHENES: You don't answer.

FIFTH WOMAN: Withdraw, all of you; I am going to examine her thoroughly about last year's mysteries. But move away, Clisthenes, for no man may hear what is going to be said. Now answer my questions! What was done first?

MNESILOCHUS: Let's see then. What was done first? Oh! we drank.

FIFTH WOMAN: And then?

MNESILOCHUS: We drank to our healths.

FIFTH WOMAN: You will have heard that from someone. And then?

MNESILOCHUS: Xenylla relieved herself in a cup, for there was no other vessel.

FIFTH WOMAN: You trifle. Here, Clisthenes, here! This is the man of whom you spoke.

CLISTHENES: What is to be done then?

FIFTH WOMAN: Take off his clothes, I can get nothing out of him.

MNESILOCHUS: What! are you going to strip a mother of nine children naked?

CLISTHENES: Come, undo your girdle, you shameless thing.

FIFTH WOMAN: Ah! what a sturdy frame! but she has no breasts like we have.

MNESILOCHUS: That's because I'm barren. I never had any children.

FIFTH WOMAN: Oh! indeed! just now you were the mother of nine.

CLISTHENES: Stand up straight. Hullo! what do I see there? Why, a penis sticking out behind.

FIFTH WOMAN: There's no mistaking it; you can see it projecting, and a fine red it is.

CLISTHENES: Where has it gone to now?

FIFTH WOMAN: To the front.

CLISTHENES: No.

FIFTH WOMAN: Ah! 'tis behind now.

CLISTHENES: Why, friend, 'tis for all the world like the Isthmus; you keep pulling your tool backwards and forwards just as the Corinthians do their ships.[58]

---

57. The women lodged in pairs during the Thesmophoria in tents erected near the Temple of Demeter.

58. The Corinthians were constantly passing their vessels across the isthmus from one sea to the other; we know that the Grecian ships were of very small dimensions.

FIFTH WOMAN: Ah! the wretch! this is why he insulted us and defended Euripides.

MNESILOCHUS: Aye, wretch indeed, what troubles have I not got into now!

FIFTH WOMAN: What shall we do?

CLISTHENES: Watch him closely, so that he does not escape. As for me, I go to report the matter to the magistrates, the Prytanes.

CHORUS: Let us kindle our lamps; let us go firmly to work and with courage, let us take off our cloaks and search whether some other man has not come here too; let us pass round the whole Pnyx,[59] examine the tents and the passages.[60] Come, be quick, let us start off on a light toe[61] and rummage all round in silence. Let us hasten, let us finish our round as soon as possible. Look quickly for the traces that might show you a man hidden here, let your glance fall on every side; look well to the right and to the left. If we seize some impious fellow, woe to him! He will know how we punish the outrage, the crime, the sacrilege. The criminal will then acknowledge at last that gods exist; his fate will teach all men that the deities must be revered, that justice must be observed and that they must submit to the sacred laws. If not, then woe to them! Heaven itself will punish sacrilege; being aflame with fury and mad with frenzy, all their deeds will prove to mortals, both men and women, that the deity punishes injustice and impiety, and that she is not slow to strike. But I think I have now searched everywhere and that no other man is hidden among us.

SIXTH WOMAN: Where is he flying to? Stop him! stop him! Ah! miserable woman that I am, he has torn my child from my breast and has disappeared with it.

MNESILOCHUS: Scream as loud as you will, but he shall never suck your bosom more. If you do not let me go this very instant, I am going to cut open the veins of his thighs with this cutlass and his blood shall flow over the altar.

---

59. This was the name of the place where the Ecclesia, the public meeting of the people, took place; the chorus gives this name here to Demeter's temple, because the women are gathered there.
60. The spaces left free between the tents, and which served as passage-ways.
61. A choric dance began here.

SIXTH WOMAN: Oh! great gods! oh! friends, help me! terrify him with your shrieks, triumph over this monster, permit him not to rob me of my only child.

CHORUS: Oh! oh! venerable Parcae, what fresh attack is this? 'Tis the crowning act of audacity and shamelessness! What has he done now, friends, what has he done?

MNESILOCHUS: Ah! this insolence passes all bounds, but I shall know how to curb it.

CHORUS: What a shameful deed! the measure of his iniquities is full!

SIXTH WOMAN: Aye, 'tis shameful that he should have robbed me of my child.

CHORUS: 'Tis past belief to be so criminal and so impudent!

MNESILOCHUS: Ah! you're not near the end of it yet.

SIXTH WOMAN: Little I care whence you come; you shall not return to boast of having acted so odiously with impunity, for you shall be punished.

MNESILOCHUS: You won't do it, by the gods!

CHORUS: And what immortal would protect you for your crime?

MNESILOCHUS: 'Tis in vain you talk! I shall not let go the child.

CHORUS: By the goddesses, you will not laugh presently over your crime and your impious speech. For with impiety, as 'tis meet, shall we reply to your impiety. Soon fortune will turn round and overwhelm you. Come! bring wood along. Let us burn the wretch, let us roast him as quickly as possible.

SIXTH WOMAN: Bring faggots, Mania! (*To Mnesilochus*) You will be mere charcoal soon.

CHORUS: Grill away, roast me, but you, my child, take off this Cretan robe and blame no one but your mother for your death. But what does this mean? The little girl is nothing but a skin filled with wine and shod with Persian slippers.[62] Oh! you wanton, you tippling woman, who think of nothing but wine; you are a fortune to the drinking-shops and are our ruin; for the sake of drink, you neglect both your household and your shuttle!

SIXTH WOMAN: Faggots, Mania, plenty of them.

MNESILOCHUS: Bring as many as you like. But answer me; are you the mother of this brat?

---

62. A woman's footgear.—On undressing the supposed child, Mnesilochus perceives that it is nothing but a skin of wine.

SixtH Woman: I carried it ten months.[63]

Mnesilochus: You carried it?

SixtH Woman: I swear it by Artemis.

Mnesilochus: How much does it hold? Three cotylae?[64] Tell me.

SixtH Woman: Oh! what have you done? You have stripped the poor child quite naked, and it is so small, so small.

Mnesilochus: So small?

SixtH Woman: Yes, quite small, to be sure.

Mnesilochus: How old is it? Has it seen the feast of cups thrice or four times?

SixtH Woman: It was born about the time of the last Dionysia.[65] But give it back to me.

Mnesilochus: No, may Apollo bear me witness.

SixtH Woman: Well, then we are going to burn him.

Mnesilochus: Burn me, but then I shall rip this open instantly.

SixtH Woman: No, no, I adjure you, don't; do anything you like to me rather than that.

Mnesilochus: What a tender mother you are; but nevertheless I shall rip it open. (*Tears open the wine-skin*)

SixtH Woman: Oh, my beloved daughter! Mania, hand me the sacred cup, that I may at least catch the blood of my child.

Mnesilochus: Hold it below; 'tis the sole favour I grant you.

SixtH Woman: Out upon you, you pitiless monster!

Mnesilochus: This robe belongs to the priestess.[66]

SixtH Woman: What belongs to the priestess?

Mnesilochus: Here, take it. (*Throws her the Cretan robe*)

Seventh Woman: Ah! unfortunate Mica! who has robbed you of your daughter, your beloved child?

SixtH Woman: That wretch. But as you are here, watch him well, while I go with Clisthenes to the Prytanes and denounce him for his crimes.

Mnesilochus: Ah! how can I secure safety? what device can I hit on? what can I think of? He whose fault it is, he who hurried

---

63. Dr. P. Menier repeatedly points out in his "La médecine et les poètes latins," that the ancient writers constantly spoke of ten months as being a woman's period of gestation.

64. A cotyla contained nearly half a pint.

65. Both the Feast of Cups and the Dionysia were dedicated to Bacchus, the god of wine; it is for this reason that Mnesilochus refers to the former when guessing the wine-skin's age.

66. The Cretan robe that had covered the wine-skin.

me into this trouble, will not come to my rescue. Let me see, whom could I best send to him? Ha! I know a means taken from Palamedes; like him, I will write my misfortune on some oars, which I will cast into the sea. But there are no oars here. Where might I find some?[67] Where indeed? Bah! what if I took these statues[68] instead of oars, wrote upon them and then threw them towards this side and that. 'Tis the best thing to do. Besides, like oars they are of wood. Oh! my hands, keep up your courage, for my safety is at stake. Come, my beautiful tablets, receive the traces of my stylus and be the messengers of my sorry fate. Oh! oh! this B looks miserable enough! Where is it running to then? Come, off with you in all directions, to the right and to the left; and hurry yourselves, for there's much need indeed!

CHORUS: Let us address ourselves to the spectators to sing our praises, despite the fact that each one says much ill of women. If the men are to be believed, we are a plague to them; through us come all their troubles, quarrels, disputes, sedition, griefs and wars. But if we are truly such a pest, why marry us? Why forbid us to go out or show ourselves at the window? You want to keep this pest, and take a thousand cares to do it. If your wife goes out and you meet her away from the house, you fly into a fury. Ought you not rather to rejoice and give thanks to the gods? for if the pest has disappeared, you will no longer find it at home. If we fall asleep at friends' houses from the fatigue of playing and sporting, each of you comes prowling round the bed to contemplate the features of this pest. If we seat ourselves at the window, each one wants to see the pest, and if we withdraw through modesty, each wants all the more to see the pest perch herself there again. It is thus clear that we are better than you, and the proof of this is easy. Let us find out which is worse of the two sexes. We say, "'Tis you," while you aver, 'tis we. Come, let us compare them in detail, each individual man

---

67. An allusion to the tragedy by Euripides called 'Palamedes,' which belonged to the tetralogy of the Troades, and was produced in 414 B.C. Aristophanes is railing at the strange device which the poet makes Oeax resort to. Oeax was Palamedes' brother, and he is represented as inscribing the death of the latter on a number of oars with the hope that at least one would reach the shores of Euboea and thus inform his father, Nauplias, the king of the fact.
68. The images of the various gods which were invoked at the Thesmophoria, and the enumeration of which we have already had.

with a woman. Charminus is not equal to Nausimaché,[69] that's certain. Cleophon[70] is in every respect inferior to Salabaccho.[71] 'Tis long now since any of you has dared to contest the prize with Aristomaché, the heroine of Marathon, or with Stratonicé.[72]

Among the last year's Senators, who have just yielded their office to other citizens, is there one who equals Eubulé?[73] Therefore we maintain that men are greatly our inferiors. You see no woman who has robbed the State of fifty talents rushing about the city in a magnificent chariot; our greatest peculations are a measure of corn, which we steal from our husbands, and even then we return it them the very same day. But we could name many amongst you who do quite as much, and who are, even more than ourselves, gluttons, parasites, cheats and kidnappers of slaves. We know how to keep our property better than you. We still have our cylinders, our beams,[74] our baskets and our sunshades; whereas many among you have lost the wood of your spears as well as the iron, and many others have cast away their bucklers on the battlefield.

There are many reproaches we have the right to bring against men. The most serious is this, that the woman, who has given birth to a useful citizen, whether taxiarch or strategus[75] should receive some distinction; a place of honour should be reserved for her at the Sthenia, the Scirophoria,[76] and the other festivals that we keep. On the other hand, she of whom a coward was born or a worthless

---

69. Charminus, an Athenian general, who had recently been defeated at sea by the Spartans.—Nausimaché was a courtesan, but her name is purposely chosen because of its derivation ([Greek: naus], ship, and [Greek: mach e], fight), so as to point more strongly to Charminus' disgrace.

70. A general and an Athenian orator.

71. A courtesan.

72. Aristomaché ([Greek: mach e], fight, and [Greek: arist e], excellent) and Stratonicé ([Greek: stratos], army, and [Greek: nik e], victory) are imaginary names, invented to show the decadence of the Athenian armies.

73. Eubulé ([Greek: eu], well, and [Greek: bouleuesthai], to deliberate) is also an imaginary name. The poet wishes to say that in that year wisdom had not ruled the decisions of the Senate; they had allowed themselves to be humbled by the tyranny of the Four Hundred.

74. The cylinder and the beams were the chief tools of the weaver. It was the women who did this work.

75. The taxiarch had the command of 128 men; the strategus had the direction of an army.

76. The Sthenia were celebrated in honour of Athené Sthenias, or the goddess of force; the women were then wont to attack each other with bitter sarcasms.—During the Scirophoria ([Greek: skiron], canopy) the statues of Athené, Demeter, Persephone, the Sun and Posidon were carried in procession under canopies with great pomp.

man, a bad trierarch[77] or an unskilful pilot, should sit with shaven head, behind her sister who had borne a brave man. Oh! citizens! is it just, that the mother of Hyperbolus should sit dressed in white and with loosened tresses beside that of Lamachus[78] and lend out money on usury? He, who may have done a deal of this nature with her, so far from paying her interest, should not even repay the capital, saying, "What, pay you interest? after you have given us this delightful son?"

MNESILOCHUS: I have contracted quite a squint by looking round for him, and yet Euripides does not come. Who is keeping him? No doubt he is ashamed of his cold Palamedes.[79] What will attract him? Let us see! By which of his pieces does he set most store? Ah! I'll imitate his Helen,[80] his lastborn. I just happen to have a complete woman's outfit.

SEVENTH WOMAN: What are you ruminating over now again? Why are you rolling up your eyes? You'll have no reason to be proud of your Helen, if you don't keep quiet until one of the Prytanes arrives.

MNESILOCHUS (as Helen): "These shores are those of the Nile with the beautiful nymphs, these waters take the place of heaven's rain and fertilize the white earth, that produces the black syrmea."[81]

SEVENTH WOMAN: By bright Hecaté, you're a cunning varlet.

MNESILOCHUS: "Glorious Sparta is my country and Tyndareus is my father."[82]

SEVENTH WOMAN: He your father, you rascal! Why, 'tis Phrynondas.[83]

---

77. The trierarchs were rich citizens, whose duty it was to maintain the galleys or triremes of the fleet.

78. Hyperbolus is incessantly railed at by Aristophanes as a traitor and an informer. Lamachus, although our poet does not always spare him, was a brave general; he had been one of the commanders of the Sicilian Expedition.

79. It will be remembered that Mnesilochus had employed a similar device to one imputed to Oeax by Euripides in his 'Palamedes,' in order to inform his father-in-law of his predicament.

80. A tragedy, in which Menelaus is seen in Egypt, whither he has gone to seek Helen, who is detained there.

81. These are the opening verses of Euripides' 'Helen,' with the exception of the last words, which are a parody.—Syrmea is a purgative plant very common in Egypt. Aristophanes speaks jestingly of the white soil of Egypt, because the slime of the Nile is very black.

82. This reply and those that follow are fragments from 'Helen.'

83. An infamous Athenian, whose name had become a byword for everything that was vile.

MNESILOCHUS: "I was given the name of Helen."

SEVENTH WOMAN: What! you are again becoming a woman, before we have punished you for having pretended it a first time!

MNESILOCHUS: "A thousand warriors have died on my account on the banks of the Scamander."

SEVENTH WOMAN: Why have you not done the same?

MNESILOCHUS: "And here I am upon these shores; Menelaus, my unhappy husband, does not yet come. Ah! how life weighs upon me! Oh! ye cruel crows, who have not devoured my body! But what sweet hope is this that sets my heart a-throb? Oh, Zeus! grant it may not prove a lying one!"

EURIPIDES (as Menelaus): "To what master does this splendid palace belong? Will he welcome strangers who have been tried on the billows of the sea by storm and shipwreck?"[84]

MNESILOCHUS: "This is the palace of Proteus."[85]

EURIPIDES: "Of what Proteus?"

SEVENTH WOMAN: Oh! the thrice cursed rascal! how he lies! By the goddesses, 'tis ten years since Proteas[86] died.

EURIPIDES: "What is this shore whither the wind has driven our boat?"

MNESILOCHUS: "It's Egypt."

EURIPIDES: "Alas! how far we are from our own country!"

SEVENTH WOMAN: But don't believe that cursed fool. This is Demeter's Temple.

EURIPIDES: "Is Proteus in these parts?"

SEVENTH WOMAN: Ah, now, stranger, it must be sea-sickness that makes you so distraught! You have been told that Proteas is dead, and yet you ask if he is in these parts.

EURIPIDES: "He is no more! Oh! woe! where lie his ashes?"

MNESILOCHUS: 'Tis on his tomb you see me sitting.

SEVENTH WOMAN: You call an altar a tomb! Beware of the rope!

EURIPIDES: "And why remain sitting on this tomb, wrapped in this long veil, oh, stranger lady?"[87]

MNESILOCHUS: "They want to force me to marry a son of Proteus."

---

84. The whole of this dialogue between Mnesilochus and Euripides is composed of fragments taken from 'Helen,' slightly parodied at times.

85. King of Egypt.

86. Son of Epicles, and mentioned by Thucydides.

87. Aristophanes invents this in order to give coherence to what follows.

SEVENTH WOMAN: Ah! wretch, why tell such shameful lies? Stranger, this is a rascal who has slipped in amongst us women to rob us of our trinkets.

MNESILOCHUS (*to Seventh Woman*): "Shout! load me with your insults, for little care I."

EURIPIDES: "Who is the old woman who reviles you, stranger lady?"

MNESILOCHUS: "'Tis Theonoé, the daughter of Proteus."

SEVENTH WOMAN: I! Why, my name's Critylla, the daughter of Antitheus,[88] of the deme of Gargettus;[89] as for you, you are a rogue.

MNESILOCHUS: "Your entreaties are vain. Never shall I wed your brother; never shall I betray the faith I owe my husband Menelaus, who is fighting before Troy."

EURIPIDES: "What are you saying? Turn your face towards me."

MNESILOCHUS: "I dare not; my cheeks show the marks of the insults I have been forced to suffer."

EURIPIDES: "Oh! great gods! I cannot speak, for very emotion. . . Ah! what do I see? Who are you?"

MNESILOCHUS: "And you, what is your name? for my surprise is as great as yours."

EURIPIDES: "Are you Grecian or born in this country?"

MNESILOCHUS: "I am Grecian. But now your name, what is it?"

EURIPIDES: "Oh! how you resemble Helen!"

MNESILOCHUS: And you Menelaus, if I can judge by those pot-herbs.[90]

EURIPIDES: "You are not mistaken, 'tis that unfortunate mortal who stands before you."

MNESILOCHUS: "Ah! how you have delayed coming to your wife's arms! Press me to your heart, throw your arms about me, for I wish to cover you with kisses. Carry me away, carry me away, quick, quick, far, very far from here."

SEVENTH WOMAN: By the goddesses, woe to him who would carry you away! I should thrash him with my torch.

EURIPIDES: "Do you propose to prevent me from taking my wife, the daughter of Tyndareus, to Sparta?"

---

88. An Athenian general whom Thucydides mentions.
89. A deme of Attica.
90. No doubt Euripides appeared on the stage carrying some herbs in his hand or wearing them in his belt, so as to recall his mother's calling. If the gibes of Aristophanes can be believed, she dealt in vegetables, as we have noted repeatedly.

Seventh Woman: You seem to me to be a cunning rascal too; you are in collusion with this man, and 'twas not for nothing that you kept babbling about Egypt. But the hour for punishment has come; here is the magistrate come with his archer.

Euripides: This grows awkward. Let me hide myself.

Mnesilochus: And what is to become of me, poor unfortunate man?

Euripides: Be at ease. I shall never abandon you, as long as I draw breath and one of my numberless artifices remains untried.

Mnesilochus: The fish has not bitten this time.

The Prytanis: Is this the rascal of whom Clisthenes told us? Why are you trying to make yourself so small? Archer, arrest him, fasten him to the post, then take up your position there and keep guard over him. Let none approach him. A sound lash with your whip for him who attempts to break the order.

Seventh Woman: Excellent, for just now a rogue almost took him from me.

Mnesilochus: Prytanis, in the name of that hand which you know so well how to bend, when money is placed in it, grant me a slight favour before I die.

Prytanis: What favour?

Mnesilochus: Order the archer to strip me before lashing me to the post; the crows, when they make their meal on the poor old man, would laugh too much at this robe and head-dress.

Prytanis: 'Tis in that gear that you must be exposed by order of the Senate, so that your crime may be patent to the passers-by.

Mnesilochus: Oh! cursed robe, the cause of all my misfortune! My last hope is thus destroyed!

Chorus: Let us now devote ourselves to the sports which the women are accustomed to celebrate here, when time has again brought round the mighty Mysteries of the great goddesses, the sacred days which Pauson[91] himself honours by fasting and would wish feast to succeed feast, that he might keep them all holy. Spring forward with a light step, whirling in mazy circles; let your hands interlace, let the eager and rapid dancers sway to the music and glance on every side as they move. Let the chorus sing likewise and praise the Olympian gods in their pious transport.

---

91. A ruined man, living in penury, presumably well known to the audience.

'Tis wrong to suppose that, because I am a woman and in this Temple, I am going to speak ill of men; but since we want something fresh, we are going through the rhythmic steps of the round dance for the first time.

Start off while you sing to the god of the lyre and to the chaste goddess armed with the bow. Hail! thou god who flingest thy darts so far,[92] grant us the victory! The homage of our song is also due to Heré, the goddess of marriage, who interests herself in every chorus and guards the approach to the nuptial couch. I also pray Hermes, the god of the shepherds, and Pan and the beloved Graces to bestow a benevolent smile upon our songs.

Let us lead off anew, let us double our zeal during our solemn days, and especially let us observe a close fast; let us form fresh measures that keep good time, and may our songs resound to the very heavens. Do thou, oh divine Bacchus, who art crowned with ivy, direct our chorus; 'tis to thee that both my hymns and my dances are dedicated; oh, Evius, oh, Bromius,[93] oh, thou son of Semelé, oh, Bacchus, who delightest to mingle with the dear choruses of the nymphs upon the mountains, and who repeatest, while dancing with them, the sacred hymn, Evius, Evius, Evoe. Echo, the nymph of Cithaeron returns thy words, which resound beneath the dark vaults of the thick foliage and in the midst of the rocks of the forest; the ivy enlaces thy brow with its tendrils charged with flowers.

SCYTHIAN ARCHER:[94] You shall stay here in the open air to wail.

MNESILOCHUS: Archer, I adjure you.

SCYTHIAN: 'Tis labour lost.

MNESILOCHUS: Loosen the wedge a little.[95]

SCYTHIAN: Aye, certainly.

MNESILOCHUS: Oh! by the gods! why, you are driving it in tighter.

SCYTHIAN: Is that enough?

MNESILOCHUS: Oh! la, la! oh! la, la! May the plague take you!

---

92. Apollo.

93. Surnames of Bacchus.

94. The archers, or the police officers, at Athens were mostly Scythians. If not from that country always, they were known generally by that name.

95. Which the archer had driven in to tighten up the rope binding the prison to the pillory.

SCYTHIAN: Silence! you cursed old wretch! I am going to get a mat to lie upon, so as to watch you close at hand at my ease.

MNESILOCHUS: Ah! what exquisite pleasures Euripides is securing for me! But, oh, ye gods! oh, Zeus the Deliverer, all is not yet lost! I don't believe him the man to break his word; I just caught sight of him appearing in the form of Perseus, and he told me with a mysterious sign to turn myself into Andromeda. And in truth am I not really bound? 'Tis certain, then, that he is coming to my rescue; for otherwise he would not have steered his flight this way.[96]

EURIPIDES (*as Perseus*): Oh Nymphs, ye virgins who are dear to me, how am I to approach him? how can I escape the sight of this Scythian? And Echo, thou who reignest in the inmost recesses of the caves, oh! favour my cause and permit me to approach my spouse.

MNESILOCHUS (*as Andromeda*):[97] A pitiless ruffian has chained up the most unfortunate of mortal maids. Alas! I had barely escaped the filthy claws of an old fury, when another mischance overtook me! This Scythian does not take his eye off me and he has exposed me as food for the crows. Alas! what is to become of me, alone here and without friends! I am not seen mingling in the dances nor in the games of my companions, but heavily loaded with fetters I am given over to the voracity of a Glaucetes.[98] Sing no bridal hymn for me, oh women, but rather the hymn of captivity, and in tears. Ah! how I suffer! great gods! how I suffer! Alas! alas! and through my own relatives too![99] My misery would make Tartarus dissolve into tears! Alas! in my terrible distress, I implore the mortal who first shaved me and depilated me, then dressed me in this long robe, and then sent me to this Temple into the midst of the women, to save me. Oh, thou pitiless Fate! I am then accursed, great gods! Ah! who would not be moved at the sight of the appalling tortures under which I succumb? Would that the blazing shaft of the lightning would wither. . . this barbarian for me! (*pointing to the*

---

96. Perseus was returning from the land of the Gorgons mounted upon Pegasus, when, while high up in the air, he saw Andromeda bound to a rock and exposed to the lusts and voracity of a sea monster. Touched by the misfortune and the beauty of the princess, he turned the monster to stone by showing him the head of Medusa, released Andromeda and married her.—Euripides had just produced a tragedy on this subject.

97. Mnesilochus speaks alternately in his own person and as though he were Andromeda, the effect being comical in the extreme.

98. A notorious glutton, mentioned also in the 'Peace.'

99. Through Euripides, his father-in-law.

ARISTOPHANES

Scythian archer) for the immortal light has no further charm for my eyes since I have been descending the shortest path to the dead, tied up, strangled, and maddened with pain.

EURIPIDES (*as Echo*): Hail! beloved girl. As for your father, Cepheus, who has exposed you in this guise, may the gods annihilate him.

MNESILOCHUS (*as Andromeda*): And who are you whom my misfortunes have moved to pity?

EURIPIDES: I am Echo, the nymph who repeats all she hears. 'Tis I, who last year lent my help to Euripides in this very place.[100] But, my child, give yourself up to the sad laments that belong to your pitiful condition.

MNESILOCHUS: And you will repeat them?

EURIPIDES: I will not fail you. Begin.

MNESILOCHUS: "Oh! thou divine Night! how slowly thy chariot threads its way through the starry vault, across the sacred realms of the Air and mighty Olympus."

EURIPIDES: Mighty Olympus.

MNESILOCHUS: "Why is it necessary that Andromeda should have all the woes for her share?"

EURIPIDES: For her share.

MNESILOCHUS: "Sad death!"

EURIPIDES: Sad death!

MNESILOCHUS: You weary me, old babbler.

EURIPIDES: Old babbler.

MNESILOCHUS: Oh! you are too unbearable.

EURIPIDES: Unbearable.

MNESILOCHUS: Friend, let me talk by myself. Do please let me. Come, that's enough.

EURIPIDES: That's enough.

MNESILOCHUS: Go and hang yourself!

EURIPIDES: Go and hang yourself!

MNESILOCHUS: What a plague!

EURIPIDES: What a plague!

MNESILOCHUS: Cursed brute!

EURIPIDES: Cursed brute!

MNESILOCHUS: Beware of blows!

---

100. On the occasion of the presentation of the tragedy of 'Andromeda,' in which the nymph Echo plays an important part.

EURIPIDES: Beware of blows!

SCYTHIAN: Hullo! what are you jabbering about?

EURIPIDES: What are you jabbering about?

SCYTHIAN: I go to call the Prytanes.

EURIPIDES: I go to call the Prytanes.

SCYTHIAN: This is odd!

EURIPIDES: This is odd!

SCYTHIAN: Whence comes this voice?

EURIPIDES: Whence comes this voice.

SCYTHIAN: Ah! beware!

EURIPIDES: Ah! beware!

SCYTHIAN (*to Mnesilochus*): Are you mocking me?

EURIPIDES: Are you mocking me?

MNESILOCHUS: No, 'tis this woman, who stands near you.

EURIPIDES: Who stands near you.

SCYTHIAN: Where is the hussy? Ah! she is escaping! Whither, whither are you escaping?

EURIPIDES: Whither, whither are you escaping?

SCYTHIAN: You shall not get away.

EURIPIDES: You shall not get away.

SCYTHIAN: You are chattering still?

EURIPIDES: You are chattering still?

SCYTHIAN: Stop the hussy.

EURIPIDES: Stop the hussy.

SCYTHIAN: What a babbling, cursed woman!

EURIPIDES (*as Perseus*): "Oh! ye gods! to what barbarian land has my swift flight taken me? I am Perseus, who cleaves the plains of the air with my winged feet, and I am carrying the Gorgon's head to Argos."

SCYTHIAN: What, are you talking about the head of Gorgos,[101] the scribe?

EURIPIDES: No, I am speaking of the head of the Gorgon.

SCYTHIAN: Why, yes! of Gorgus!

EURIPIDES: "But what do I behold? A young maiden, beautiful as the immortals, chained to this rock like a vessel in port?"

MNESILOCHUS: Take pity on me, oh, stranger! I am so unhappy and distraught! Free me from these bonds.

---

101. Unknown; Aristophanes plays upon the similarity of name.

SCYTHIAN: Don't you talk! a curse upon your impudence! you are going to die, and yet you will be chattering!

EURIPIDES: "Oh! virgin! I take pity on your chains."

SCYTHIAN: But this is no virgin; 'tis an old rogue, a cheat and a thief.

EURIPIDES: You have lost your wits, Scythian. This is Andromeda, the daughter of Cepheus.

SCYTHIAN: But just look at this tool; is that like a woman?

EURIPIDES: Give me your hand, that I may descend near this young maiden. Each man has his own particular weakness; as for me I am aflame with love for this virgin.

SCYTHIAN: Oh! I'm not jealous; and as he has his back turned this way, why, I make no objection to your pedicating him.

EURIPIDES: "Ah! let me release her, and hasten to join her on the bridal couch."

SCYTHIAN: If this old man instils you with such ardent concupiscence, why, you can bore through the plank, and so get at his behind.

EURIPIDES: No, I will break his bonds.

SCYTHIAN: Beware of my lash!

EURIPIDES: No matter.

SCYTHIAN: This blade shall cut off your head.

EURIPIDES: "Ah! what can be done? what arguments can I use? This savage will understand nothing! The newest and most cunning fancies are a dead letter to the ignorant. Let us invent some artifice to fit in with his coarse nature."

SCYTHIAN: I can see the rascal is trying to outwit me.

MNESILOCHUS: Ah! Perseus! remember in what condition you are leaving me.

SCYTHIAN: Are you wanting to feel my lash again!

CHORUS: Oh! Pallas, who art fond of dances, hasten hither at my call. Oh! thou chaste virgin, the protectress of Athens, I call thee in accordance with the sacred rites, thee, whose evident protection we adore and who keepest the keys of our city in thy hands. Do thou appear, thou whose just hatred has overturned our tyrants. The womenfolk are calling thee; hasten hither at their bidding along with Peace, who shall restore the festivals. And ye, august goddesses,[102] display a smiling and propitious countenance to our gaze; come into your sacred grove, the entry to which is forbidden

---

102. That is, the Thesmophoriae, viz. Demeter and Persephoné.

to men; 'tis there in the midst of sacred orgies that we contemplate your divine features. Come, appear, we pray it of you, oh, venerable Thesmophoriae! If you have ever answered our appeal, oh! come into our midst.

EURIPIDES: Women, if you will be reconciled with me, I am willing, and I undertake never to say anything ill of you in future. Those are my proposals for peace.

CHORUS: And what impels you to make these overtures?

EURIPIDES: This unfortunate man, who is chained to the post, is my father-in-law; if you will restore him to me, you will have no more cause to complain of me; but if not, I shall reveal your pranks to your husbands when they return from the war.

CHORUS: We accept peace, but there is this barbarian whom you must buy over.

EURIPIDES: That's my business. (*He returns as an old woman and is accompanied by a dancing-girl and a flute-girl*) Come, my little wench, bear in mind what I told you on the road and do it well. Come, go past him and gird up your robe. And you, you little dear, play us the air of a Persian dance.

SCYTHIAN: What is this music that makes me so blithe?

EURIPIDES (*as an old woman*): Scythian, this young girl is going to practise some dances, which she has to perform at a feast presently.

SCYTHIAN: Very well! let her dance and practise; I won't hinder her. How nimbly she bounds! one might think her a flea on a fleece.

EURIPIDES: Come, my dear, off with your robe and seat yourself on the Scythian's knee; stretch forth your feet to me, that I may take off your slippers.

SCYTHIAN: Ah! yes, seat yourself, my little girl, ah! yes, to be sure. What a firm little bosom! 'tis just like a turnip.

EURIPIDES (*to the flute-girl*): An air on the flute, quick! (*To the dancing-girl*) Well! are you still afraid of the Scythian?

SCYTHIAN: What beautiful thighs!

EURIPIDES: Come! keep still, can't you?

SCYTHIAN: 'Tis altogether a very fine morsel to make a man's cock stand.

EURIPIDES: That's so! (*To the dancing-girl*) Resume your dress, it is time to be going.

SCYTHIAN: Give me a kiss.

EURIPIDES (*to the dancing-girl*): Come, give him a kiss.

SCYTHIAN: Oh! oh! oh! my goodness, what soft lips! 'tis like Attic honey. But might she not stop with me?

EURIPIDES: Impossible, archer; good evening.

SCYTHIAN: Oh! oh! old woman, do me this pleasure.

EURIPIDES: Will you give a drachma?

SCYTHIAN: Aye, that I will.

EURIPIDES: Hand over the money.

SCYTHIAN: I have not got it, but take my quiver in pledge.

EURIPIDES: You will bring her back?

SCYTHIAN: Follow me, my beautiful child. And you, old woman, just keep guard over this man. But what is your name?

EURIPIDES: Artemisia. Can you remember that name?

SCYTHIAN: Artemuxia.[103] Good!

EURIPIDES (*aside*): Hermes, god of cunning, receive my thanks! everything is turning out for the best. (*To the Scythian*) As for you, friend, take away this girl, quick. (*Exit the Scythian with the dancing-girl*) Now let me loose his bonds. (*To Mnesilochus*) And you, directly I have released you, take to your legs and run off full tilt to your home to find your wife and children.

MNESILOCHUS: I shall not fail in that as soon as I am free.

EURIPIDES (*releases Mnesilochus*): There! 'Tis done. Come, fly, before the archer lays his hand on you again.

MNESILOCHUS: That's just what I am doing. (*Exit with Euripides*)

SCYTHIAN: Ah! old woman! what a charming little girl! Not at all the prude, and so obliging! Eh! where is the old woman? Ah! I am undone! And the old man, where is he? Hi! old woman! old woman! Ah! but this is a dirty trick! Artemuxia! she has tricked me, that's what the little old woman has done! Get clean out of my sight, you cursed quiver! (*Picks it up and throws it across the stage*) Ha! you are well named quiver, for you have made me quiver indeed.[104] Oh! what's to be done? Where is the old woman then? Artemuxia!

CHORUS: Are you asking for the old woman who carried the lyre?

SCYTHIAN: Yes, yes; have you seen her?

CHORUS: She has gone that way along with an old man.

---

103. Throughout the whole scene the Scythian speaks with a grotesque barbarian accent.
104. The pun depends in the Greek on the similarity of the final syllables of (Greek: subin e), and (Greek: katabin esi). It can be given literally in English.

Scythian: Dressed in a long robe?

Chorus: Yes; run quick, and you will overtake them.

Scythian: Ah! rascally old woman! Which way has she fled? Artemuxia!

Chorus: Straight on; follow your nose. But, hi! where are you running to now? Come back, you are going exactly the wrong way.

Scythian: Ye gods! ye gods! and all this while Artemuxia is escaping. (*Exit running*)

Chorus: Go your way! and a pleasant journey to you! But our sports have lasted long enough; it is time for each of us to be off home; and may the two goddesses reward us for our labours!

Finis of "The Thesmophoriazusae"

THE FROGS

INTRODUCTION

Like 'The Birds' this play rather avoids politics than otherwise, its leading *motif*, over and above the pure fun and farce for their own sake of the burlesque descent into the infernal regions, being a literary one, an onslaught on Euripides the Tragedian and all his works and ways.

It was produced in the year 405 B.C., the year after 'The Birds,' and only one year before the Peloponnesian War ended disastrously for the Athenian cause in the capture of the city by Lysander. First brought out at the Lenaean festival in January, it was played a second time at the Dionysia in March of the same year—a far from common honour. The drama was not staged in the Author's own name, we do not know for what reasons, but it won the first prize, Phrynichus' 'Muses' being second.

The plot is as follows. The God Dionysus, patron of the Drama, is dissatisfied with the condition of the Art of Tragedy at Athens, and resolves to descend to Hades in order to bring back again to earth one of the old tragedians—Euripides, he thinks, for choice. Dressing himself up, lion's skin and club complete, as Heracles, who has performed the same perilous journey before, and accompanied by his slave Xanthias (a sort of classical Sancho Panza) with the baggage, he starts on the fearful expedition.

Coming to the shores of Acheron, he is ferried over in Charon's boat—Xanthias has to walk round—the First Chorus of Marsh Frogs (from which the play takes its title) greeting him with prolonged croakings. Approaching Pluto's Palace in fear and trembling, he knocks timidly at the gate. Being presently admitted, he finds a contest on the point of being held before the King of Hades and the Initiates of the Eleusinian Mysteries, who form the Second Chorus, between Aeschylus, the present occupant of the throne of tragic excellence in hell, and the pushing, self-satisfied, upstart Euripides, who is for ousting him from his pride of place.

Each poet quotes in turn from his Dramas, and the indignant Aeschylus makes fine fun of his rival's verses, and shows him up in the usual Aristophanic style as a corrupter of morals, a contemptible casuist, and a professor of the dangerous new learning of the Sophists, so justly held in suspicion by true-blue Athenian Conservatives. Eventually a pair of scales is brought in, and verses alternately spouted by the two candidates are weighed against each other, the mighty lines of the Father of Tragedy making his flippant, finickin little rival's scale kick the beam every time.

Dionysus becomes a convert to the superior merits of the old school of tragedy, and contemptuously dismisses Euripides, to take Aeschylus back with him to the upper world instead, leaving Sophocles meantime in occupation of the coveted throne of tragedy in the nether regions.

Needless to say, the various scenes of the journey to Hades, the crossing of Acheron, the Frogs' choric songs, and the trial before Pluto, afford opportunities for much excellent fooling in our Author's very finest vein of drollery, and "seem to have supplied the original idea for those modern burlesques upon the Olympian and Tartarian deities which were at one time so popular."

Dramatis Personae

Dionysus.
Xanthias, his Servant.
Heracles.
A Dead Man.
Charon.
Aeacus.
Female Attendant of Persephoné.
Inkeepers' Wives.
Euripides.
Aeschylus.
Pluto.
Chorus of Frogs.
Chorus of Initiates.

Scene: *In front of the temple of Heracles, and on the banks of Acheron in the Infernal Regions.*

XANTHIAS: Now am I to make one of those jokes that have the knack
of always making the spectators laugh?

DIONYSUS: Aye, certainly, any one you like, excepting "I am worn out."
Take care you don't say that, for it gets on my nerves.

XANTHIAS: Do you want some other drollery?

DIONYSUS: Yes, only not, "I am quite broken up."

XANTHIAS: Then what witty thing shall I say?

DIONYSUS: Come, take courage; only. . .

XANTHIAS: Only what?

DIONYSUS: . . . don't start saying as you shift your package from
shoulder to shoulder, "Ah! that's a relief!"

XANTHIAS: May I not at least say, that unless I am relieved of this
cursed load I shall let wind?

DIONYSUS: Oh! for pity's sake, no! you don't want to make me spew.

XANTHIAS: What need then had I to take this luggage, if I must not
copy the porters that Phrynichus, Lycis and Amipsias[1] never fail to
put on the stage?

DIONYSUS: Do nothing of the kind. Whenever I chance to see one
of these stage tricks, I always leave the theatre feeling a good year
older.

XANTHIAS: Oh! my poor back! you are broken and I am not allowed
to make a single joke.

DIONYSUS: Just mark the insolence of this Sybarite! I, Dionysus, the
son of a. . . wine-jar,[2] I walk, I tire myself, and I set yonder rascal
upon an ass, that he may not have the burden of carrying his load.

XANTHIAS: But am I not carrying it?

DIONYSUS: No, since you are on your beast.

XANTHIAS: Nevertheless I am carrying this. . .

DIONYSUS: What?

XANTHIAS: . . . and it is very heavy.

DIONYSUS: But this burden you carry is borne by the ass.

XANTHIAS: What I have here, 'tis certainly I who bear it, and not the
ass, no, by all the gods, most certainly not!

---

1. These were comic poets contemporary with Aristophanes. Phrynichus, the best known,
gained the second prize with his 'Muses' when the present comedy was put upon the
stage. Amipsias had gained the first prize over our author's first edition of 'The Clouds'
and again over his 'Birds.' Aristophanes is ridiculing vulgar and coarse jests, which,
however, he does not always avoid himself.

2. Instead of the expected "son of Zeus," he calls himself the "son of a wine-jar."

DIONYSUS: How can you claim to be carrying it, when you are carried?

XANTHIAS: That I can't say; but this shoulder is broken, anyhow.

DIONYSUS: Well then, since you say that the ass is no good to you, pick her up in your turn and carry her.

XANTHIAS: What a pity I did not fight at sea;[3] I would baste your ribs for that joke.

DIONYSUS: Dismount, you clown! Here is a door,[4] at which I want to make my first stop. Hi! slave! hi! hi! slave!

HERACLES (*from inside the Temple*): Do you want to beat in the door? He knocks like a Centaur.[5] Why, what's the matter?

DIONYSUS: Xanthias!

XANTHIAS: Well?

DIONYSUS: Did you notice?

XANTHIAS: What?

DIONYSUS: How I frightened him?

XANTHIAS: Bah! you're mad!

HERACLES: Ho, by Demeter! I cannot help laughing; it's no use biting my lips, I must laugh.

DIONYSUS: Come out, friend; I have need of you.

HERACLES: Oh! 'tis enough to make a fellow hold his sides to see this lion's-skin over a saffron robe![6] What does this mean? Buskins[7] and a bludgeon! What connection have they? Where are you off to in this rig?

DIONYSUS: When I went aboard Clisthenes[8] . . .

HERACLES: Did you fight?

DIONYSUS: We sank twelve or thirteen ships of the enemy.

HERACLES: You?

---

3. At the sea-fight at Arginusae the slaves who had distinguished themselves by their bravery were presented with their freedom. This battle had taken place only a few months before the production of 'The Frogs.' Had Xanthias been one of these slaves he could then have treated his master as he says, for he would have been his equal.

4. The door of the Temple of Heracles, situated in the deme of Melité, close to Athens. This temple contained a very remarkable statue of the god, the work of Eleas, the master of Phidias.

5. A fabulous monster, half man and half horse.

6. So also, in 'The Thesmophoriazusae,' Agathon is described as wearing a saffron robe, which was a mark of effeminacy.

7. A woman's foot-gear.

8. He speaks of him as though he were a vessel. Clisthenes, who was scoffed at for his ugliness, was completely beardless, which fact gave him the look of a eunuch. He was accused of prostituting himself.

DIONYSUS: Aye, by Apollo!

HERACLES: You have dreamt it.[9]

DIONYSUS: As I was reading the 'Andromeda'[10] on the ship, I suddenly felt my heart afire with a wish so violent. . .

HERACLES: A wish! of what nature?

DIONYSUS: Oh, quite small, like Molon.[11]

HERACLES: You wished for a woman?

DIONYSUS: No.

HERACLES: A young boy, then?

DIONYSUS: Nothing of the kind.

HERACLES: A man?

DIONYSUS: Faugh!

HERACLES: Might you then have had dealings with Clisthenes?

DIONYSUS: Have mercy, brother; no mockery! I am quite ill, so greatly does my desire torment me!

HERACLES: And what desire is it, little brother?

DIONYSUS: I cannot disclose it, but I will convey it to you by hints. Have you ever been suddenly seized with a desire for pea-soup?

HERACLES: For pea-soup! oh! oh! yes, a thousand times in my life.[12]

DIONYSUS: Do you take me or shall I explain myself in some other way?

HERACLES: Oh! as far as the pea-soup is concerned, I understand marvellously well.

DIONYSUS: So great is the desire, which devours me, for Euripides.

HERACLES: But he is dead.[13]

DIONYSUS: There is no human power can prevent my going to him.

HERACLES: To the bottom of Hades?

DIONYSUS: Aye, and further than the bottom, an it need.

HERACLES: And what do you want with him?

---

9. Heracles cannot believe it. Dionysus had no repute for bravery. His cowardice is one of the subjects for jesting which we shall most often come upon in 'The Frogs.'

10. A tragedy by Euripides, produced some years earlier, some fragments of which are quoted by Aristophanes in his 'Thesmophoriazusae.'

11. An actor of immense stature.

12. The gluttony of Heracles was a byword. See 'The Birds.'

13. Euripides, weary, it is said, of the ridicule and envy with which he was assailed in Athens, had retired in his old age to the court of Archelaus, King of Macedonia, where he had met with the utmost hospitality. We are assured that he perished through being torn to pieces by dogs, which set upon him in a lonely spot. His death occurred in 407 B.C., the year before the production of 'The Frogs.'

DIONYSUS: I want a master poet; "some are dead and gone, and others are good for nothing."[14]

HERACLES: Is Iophon[15] dead then?

DIONYSUS: He is the only good one left me, and even of him I don't know quite what to think.

HERACLES: Then there's Sophocles, who is greater than Euripides; if you must absolutely bring someone back from Hades, why not make him live again?

DIONYSUS: No, not until I have taken Iophon by himself and tested him for what he is worth. Besides, Euripides is very artful and won't leave a stone unturned to get away with me, whereas Sophocles is as easy-going with Pluto as he was when on earth.

HERACLES: And Agathon? Where is he?[16]

DIONYSUS: He has left me; 'twas a good poet and his friends regret him.

HERACLES: And whither has the poor fellow gone?

DIONYSUS: To the banquet of the blest.

HERACLES: And Xenocles?[17]

DIONYSUS: May the plague seize him!

HERACLES: And Pythangelus?[18]

XANTHIAS: They don't say ever a word of poor me, whose shoulder is quite shattered.

HERACLES: Is there not a crowd of other little lads, who produce tragedies by the thousand and are a thousand times more loquacious than Euripides?

DIONYSUS: They are little sapless twigs, chatterboxes, who twitter like the swallows, destroyers of the art, whose aptitude is withered with a single piece and who sputter forth all their talent to the tragic

---

14. This is a hemistich, the Scholiast says, from Euripides.

15. The son of Sophocles. Once, during his father's lifetime, he gained the prize for tragedy, but it was suspected that the piece itself was largely the work of Sophocles himself. It is for this reason that Dionysus wishes to try him when he is dependent on his own resources, now that his father is dead. The death of the latter was quite recent at the time of the production of 'The Frogs,' and the fact lent all the greater interest to this piece.

16. Agathon was a contemporary of Euripides, and is mentioned in terms of praise by Aristotle for his delineation of the character of Achilles, presumably in his tragedy of 'Telephus.' From the fragments which remain of this author it appears that his style was replete with ornament, particularly antithesis.

17. Son of Caminus, an inferior poet, often made the butt of Aristophanes' jeers.

18. A poet apparently, unknown.

Muse at their first attempt. But look where you will, you will not find a creative poet who gives vent to a noble thought.

HERACLES: How creative?

DIONYSUS: Aye, creative, who dares to risk "the ethereal dwellings of Zeus," or "the wing of Time," or "a heart that is above swearing by the sacred emblems," and "a tongue that takes an oath, while yet the soul is unpledged."[19]

HERACLES: Is that the kind of thing that pleases you?

DIONYSUS: I'm more than madly fond of it.

HERACLES: But such things are simply idiotic, you feel it yourself.

DIONYSUS: "Don't come trespassing on my mind; you have a brain of your own to keep thoughts in."[20]

HERACLES: But nothing could be more detestable.

DIONYSUS: Where cookery is concerned, you can be my master.[21]

XANTHIAS: They don't say a thing about me!

DIONYSUS: If I have decked myself out according to your pattern, 'tis that you may tell me, in case I should need them, all about the hosts who received you, when you journeyed to Cerberus; tell me of them as well as of the harbours, the bakeries, the brothels, the drinking-shops, the fountains, the roads, the eating-houses and of the hostels where there are the fewest bugs.

XANTHIAS: They never speak of me.[22]

HERACLES: Go down to hell? Will you be ready to dare that, you madman?

DIONYSUS: Enough of that; but tell me the shortest road, that is neither too hot nor too cold, to get down to Pluto.

HERACLES: Let me see, what is the best road to show you? Aye, which? Ah! there's the road of the gibbet and the rope. Go and hang yourself.

DIONYSUS: Be silent! your road is choking me.

HERACLES: There is another path, both very short and well-trodden; the one that goes through the mortar.[23]

---

19. Expressions used by Euripides in different tragedies.
20. Parody of a verse in Euripides' 'Andromeda,' a lost play.
21. Heracles, being such a glutton, must be a past master in matters of cookery, but this does not justify him in posing as a dramatic critic.
22. Xanthias, bent double beneath his load, gets more and more out of patience with his master's endless talk with Heracles.
23. The mortar in which hemlock was pounded.

DIONYSUS: 'Tis hemlock you mean to say.

HERACLES: Precisely so.

DIONYSUS: That road is both cold and icy. Your legs get frozen at once.[24]

HERACLES: Do you want me to tell you a very steep road, one that descends very quickly?

DIONYSUS: Ah! with all my heart; I don't like long walks.

HERACLES: Go to the Ceramicus.[25]

DIONYSUS: And then?

HERACLES: Mount to the top of the highest tower. . .

DIONYSUS: To do what?

HERACLES: . . . and there keep your eye on the torch, which is to be the signal. When the spectators demand it to be flung, fling yourself. . .

DIONYSUS: Where?

HERACLES: . . . down.

DIONYSUS: But I should break the two hemispheres of my brain. Thanks for your road, but I don't want it.

HERACLES: But which one then?

DIONYSUS: The one you once travelled yourself.

HERACLES: Ah! that's a long journey. First you will reach the edge of the vast, deep mere of Acheron.

DIONYSUS: And how is that to be crossed?

HERACLES: There is an ancient ferryman, Charon by name, who will pass you over in his little boat for a diobolus.

DIONYSUS: Oh! what might the diobolus has everywhere! But however has it got as far as that?

HERACLES: 'Twas Theseus who introduced its vogue.[26] After that you will see snakes and all sorts of fearful monsters. . .

---

24. An allusion to the effect of hemlock.

25. A quarter of Athens where the Lampadephoria was held in honour of Athené, Hephaestus, and Prometheus, because the first had given the mortals oil, the second had invented the lamp, and the third had stolen fire from heaven. The principal part of this festival consisted in the *lampadedromia*, or torch-race. This name was given to a race in which the competitors for the prize ran with a torch in their hand; it was essential that the goal should be reached with the torch still alight. The signal for starting was given by throwing a torch from the top of the tower mentioned a few verses later on.

26. Theseus had descended into Hades with Pirithous to fetch away Persephoné. Aristophanes doubtless wishes to say that in consequence of this descent Pluto established

DIONYSUS: Oh! don't try to frighten me and make me afraid, for I am quite decided.

HERACLES: . . . then a great slough with an eternal stench, a veritable cesspool, into which those are plunged who have wronged a guest, cheated a young boy out of the fee for his complaisance, beaten their mother, boxed their father's ears, taken a false oath or transcribed some tirade of Morsimus.[27]

DIONYSUS: For mercy's sake, add likewise—or learnt the Pyrrhic dance of Cinesias.[28]

HERACLES: Further on 'twill be a gentle concert of flutes on every side, a brilliant light, just as there is here, myrtle groves, bands of happy men and women and noisy plaudits.

DIONYSUS: Who are these happy folk?

HERACLES: The initiate.[29]

XANTHIAS: And I am the ass that carries the Mysteries;[30] but I've had enough of it.

HERACLES: They will give you all the information you will need, for they live close to Pluto's palace, indeed on the road that leads to it. Farewell, brother, and an agreeable journey to you. (*He returns into his Temple*)

DIONYSUS: And you, good health. Slave! take up your load again.

XANTHIAS: Before having laid it down?

DIONYSUS: And be quick about it too.

XANTHIAS: Oh, no, I adjure you! Rather hire one of the dead, who is going to Hades.

DIONYSUS: And should I not find one. . .

XANTHIAS: Then you can take me.

---

a toll across Acheron, in order to render access to his kingdom less easy, and so that the poor and the greedy, who could not or would not pay, might be kept out.

27. Morsimus was a minor poet, who is also mentioned with disdain in 'The Knights,' and is there called the son of Philocles. Aristophanes jestingly likens anyone who helps to disseminate his verses to the worst of criminals.

28. The Pyrrhic dance was a lively and quick-step dance. Cinesias was not a dancer, but a dithyrambic poet, who declaimed with much gesticulation and movement that one might almost think he was performing this dance.

29. Those initiated into the Mysteries of Demeter, who, according to the belief of the ancients, enjoyed a kind of beatitude after death.

30. Xanthias, his strength exhausted and his patience gone, prepares to lay down his load. Asses were used for the conveyance from Athens to Eleusis of everything that was necessary for the celebration of the Mysteries. They were often overladen, and from this fact arose the proverb here used by Xanthias, as indicating any heavy burden.

DIONYSUS: You talk sense. Ah! here they are just bringing a dead man along. Hi! man, 'tis you I'm addressing, you, dead fellow there! Will you carry a package to Pluto for me?

DEAD MAN: Is't very heavy?

DIONYSUS: This. (*He shows him the baggage, which Xanthias has laid on the ground*)

DEAD MAN: You will pay me two drachmae.

DIONYSUS: Oh! that's too dear.

DEAD MAN: Well then, bearers, move on.

DIONYSUS: Stay, friend, so that I may bargain with you.

DEAD MAN: Give me two drachmae, or it's no deal.

DIONYSUS: Hold! here are nine obols.

DEAD MAN: I would sooner go back to earth again.

XANTHIAS: Is that cursed rascal putting on airs? Come, then, I'll go.

DIONYSUS: You're a good and noble fellow. Let us make the best of our way to the boat.

CHARON: Ahoy, ahoy! put ashore.

XANTHIAS: What's that?

DIONYSUS: Why, by Zeus, 'tis the mere of which Heracles spoke, and I see the boat.

XANTHIAS: Ah! there's Charon.

DIONYSUS: Hail! Charon.

DEAD MAN: Hail! Charon.

CHARON: Who comes hither from the home of cares and misfortunes to rest on the banks of Lethé? Who comes to the ass's fleece, who is for the land of the Cerberians, or the crows, or Taenarus?

DIONYSUS: I am.

CHARON: Get aboard quick then.

DIONYSUS: Where will you ferry me to? Where are you going to land me?

CHARON: In hell, if you wish. But step in, do.

DIONYSUS: Come here, slave.

CHARON: I carry no slave, unless he has fought at sea to save his skin.

XANTHIAS: But I could not, for my eyes were bad.

CHARON: Well then! be off and walk round the mere.

XANTHIAS: Where shall I come to a halt?

CHARON: At the stone of Auaenus, near the drinking-shop.

DIONYSUS: Do you understand?

XANTHIAS: Perfectly. Oh! unhappy wretch that I am, surely, surely
I must have met something of evil omen as I came out of the
house?[31]

CHARON: Come, sit to your oar. If there be anyone else who wants to
cross, let him hurry. Hullo! what are you doing?

DIONYSUS: What am I doing? I am sitting on the oar[32] as you told me.

CHARON: Will you please have the goodness to place yourself there,
pot-belly?

DIONYSUS: There.

CHARON: Put out your hands, stretch your arms.

DIONYSUS: There.

CHARON: No tomfoolery! row hard, and put some heart into the work!

DIONYSUS: Row! and how can I? I, who have never set foot on a ship?

CHARON: There's nothing easier; and once you're at work, you will
hear some enchanting singers.

DIONYSUS: Who are they?

CHARON: Frogs with the voices of swans; 'tis most delightful.

DIONYSUS: Come, set the stroke.

CHARON: Yo ho! yo ho!

FROGS: Brekekekex, coax, coax, brekekekex, coax. Slimy offspring
of the marshland, let our harmonious voices mingle with the
sounds of the flute, coax, coax! let us repeat the songs that we sing
in honour of the Nysaean Dionysus[33] on the day of the feast of
pots,[34] when the drunken throng reels towards our temple in the
Limnae.[35] Brekekekex, coax, coax.

DIONYSUS: I am beginning to feel my bottom getting very sore, my
dear little coax, coax.

FROGS: Brekekekex, coax, coax.

DIONYSUS: But doubtless you don't care.

FROGS: Brekekekex, coax, coax.

---

31. The Ancients believed that meeting this or that person or thing at the outset of a
journey was of good or bad omen. The superstition is not entirely dead even to-day.

32. Dionysus had seated himself *on* instead of *at* the oar.

33. One of the titles given to Dionysus, because of the worship accorded him at Nysa, a
town in Ethiopia, where he was brought up by the nymphs.

34. This was the third day of the Anthesteria or feasts of Dionysus. All kinds of vegetables
were cooked in pots and offered to Dionysus and Athené. It was also the day of the
dramatic contests.

35. Dionysus' temple, the Lenaeum, was situated in the district of Athens known as the
Linnae, or Marshes, on the south side of the Acropolis.

DIONYSUS: May you perish with your coax, your endless coax!

FROGS: And why change it, you great fool? I am beloved by the Muses with the melodious lyre, by the goat-footed Pan, who draws soft tones out of his reed; I am the delight of Apollo, the god of the lyre, because I make the rushes, which are used for the bridge of the lyre, grow in my marshes. Brekekekex, coax, coax.

DIONYSUS: I have got blisters and my behind is all of a sweat; by dint of constant movement, it will soon be saying. . .

FROGS: Brekekekex, coax, coax.

DIONYSUS: Come, race of croakers, be quiet.

FROGS: Not we; we shall only cry the louder. On fine sunny days, it pleases us to hop through galingale and sedge and to sing while we swim; and when Zeus is pouring down his rain, we join our lively voices to the rustle of the drops. Brekekekex, coax, coax.

DIONYSUS: I forbid you to do it.

FROGS: Oh! that would be too hard!

DIONYSUS: And is it not harder for me to wear myself out with rowing?

FROGS: Brekekekex, coax, coax.

DIONYSUS: May you perish! I don't care.

FROGS: And from morning till night we will shriek with the whole width of our gullets, "Brekekekex, coax, coax."

DIONYSUS: I will cry louder than you all.

FROGS: Oh! don't do that!

DIONYSUS: Oh, yes, I will. I shall cry the whole day, if necessary, until I no longer hear your coax. (*He begins to cry against the frogs, who finally stop*) Ah! I knew I would soon put an end to your coax.

CHARON: Enough, enough, a last pull, ship oars, step ashore and pay your passage money.

DIONYSUS: Look! here are my two obols. . . Xanthias! where is Xanthias? Hi! Xanthias!

XANTHIAS (*from a distance*): Hullo!

DIONYSUS: Come here.

XANTHIAS: I greet you, master.

DIONYSUS: What is there that way?

XANTHIAS: Darkness and mud!

DIONYSUS: Did you see the parricides and the perjured he told us of?

XANTHIAS: Did you?

DIONYSUS: Ha! by Posidon! I see some of them now.[36] Well, what are
we going to do?

XANTHIAS: The best is to go on, for 'tis here that the horrible monsters
are, Heracles told us of.

DIONYSUS: Ah! the wag! He spun yarns to frighten me, but I am
a brave fellow and he is jealous of me. There exists no greater
braggart than Heracles. Ah! I wish I might meet some monster,
so as to distinguish myself by some deed of daring worthy of my
daring journey.

XANTHIAS: Ah! hark! I hear a noise.

DIONYSUS (*all of a tremble*): Where then, where?

XANTHIAS: Behind you.

DIONYSUS: Place yourself behind me.

XANTHIAS: Ah! 'tis in front now.

DIONYSUS: Then pass to the front.

XANTHIAS: Oh! what a monster I can see!

DIONYSUS: What's it like?

XANTHIAS: Dreadful, terrible! it assumes every shape; now 'tis a bull,
then a mule; again it is a most beautiful woman.

DIONYSUS: Where is she that I may run toward her?

XANTHIAS: The monster is no longer a woman; 'tis now a dog.

DIONYSUS: Then it is the Empusa.[37]

XANTHIAS: Its whole face is ablaze.

DIONYSUS: And it has a brazen leg?

XANTHIAS: Aye, i' faith! and the other is an ass's leg,[38] rest well
assured of that.

DIONYSUS: Where shall I fly to?

XANTHIAS: And I?

DIONYSUS: Priest,[39] save me, that I may drink with you.

XANTHIAS: Oh! mighty Heracles! we are dead men.

DIONYSUS: Silence! I adjure you. Don't utter that name.

XANTHIAS: Well then, we are dead men, Dionysus!

DIONYSUS: That still less than the other.

---

36. He points to the audience.
37. A spectre, which Hecaté sent to frighten men. It took all kinds of hideous shapes. It
was exorcised by abuse.
38. This was one of the monstrosities which credulity attributed to the Empusa.
39. He is addressing a priest of Bacchus, who occupied a seat reserved for him in the first
row of the audience.

XANTHIAS: Keep straight on, master, here, here, this way.

DIONYSUS: Well?

XANTHIAS: Be at ease, all goes well and we can say with Hegelochus, "After the storm, I see the return of the *cat*."[40] The Empusa has gone.

DIONYSUS: Swear it to me.

XANTHIAS: By Zeus!

DIONYSUS: Swear it again.

XANTHIAS: By Zeus!

DIONYSUS: Once more.

XANTHIAS: By Zeus!

DIONYSUS: Oh! my god! how white I went at the sight of the Empusa! But yonder fellow got red instead, so horribly afraid was he![41] Alas! to whom do I owe this terrible meeting? What god shall I accuse of having sought my death? Might it be "the Aether, the dwelling of Zeus," or "the wing of Time"?[42]

XANTHIAS: Hist!

DIONYSUS: What's the matter?

XANTHIAS: Don't you hear?

DIONYSUS: What then?

XANTHIAS: The sound of flutes.

DIONYSUS: Aye, certainly, and the wind wafts a smell of torches hither, which bespeaks the Mysteries a league away. But make no noise; let us hide ourselves and listen.

CHORUS:[43] Iacchus, oh! Iacchus! Iacchus, oh! Iacchus!

XANTHIAS: Master, these are the initiates, of whom Heracles spoke and who are here at their sports; they are incessantly singing of Iacchus, just like Diagoras.[44]

DIONYSUS: I believe you are right, but 'tis best to keep ourselves quiet till we get better information.

---

40. A verse from the Orestes of Euripides.—Hegelochus was an actor who, in a recent representation, had spoken the line in such a manner as to lend it an absurd meaning; instead of saying, (Greek: gal en en), which means *calm*, he had pronounced it (Greek: gal en), which means *a cat*.

41. The priest of Bacchus, mentioned several verses back.

42. High-flown expressions from Euripides' Tragedies.

43. A second Chorus, comprised of Initiates into the Mysteries of Demeter and Dionysus.

44. A philosopher, a native of Melos, and originally a dithyrambic poet. He was prosecuted on a charge of atheism.

CHORUS: Iacchus, venerated god, hasten at our call. Iacchus, oh! Iacchus! come into this meadow, thy favourite resting-place; come to direct the sacred choirs of the Initiate; may a thick crown of fruit-laden myrtle branches rest on thy head and may thy bold foot step this free and joyful dance, taught us by the Graces—this pure, religious measure, that our sacred choirs rehearse.

XANTHIAS: Oh! thou daughter of Demeter, both mighty and revered, what a delicious odour of pork!

DIONYSUS: Cannot you keep still then, fellow, once you get a whiff of a bit of tripe?

CHORUS: Brandish the flaming torches and so revive their brilliancy. Iacchus, oh! Iacchus! bright luminary of our nocturnal Mysteries. The meadow sparkles with a thousand fires; the aged shake off the weight of cares and years; they have once more found limbs of steel, wherewith to take part in thy sacred measures; and do thou, blessed deity, lead the dances of youth upon this dewy carpet of flowers with a torch in thine hand.

Silence, make way for our choirs, you profane and impure souls, who have neither been present at the festivals of the noble Muses, nor ever footed a dance in their honour, and who are not initiated into the mysterious language of the dithyrambs of the voracious Cratinus;[45] away from here he who applauds misplaced buffoonery. Away from here the bad citizen, who for his private ends fans and nurses the flame of sedition, the chief who sells himself, when his country is weathering the storms, and surrenders either fortresses or ships; who, like Thorycion,[46] the wretched collector of tolls, sends prohibited goods from Aegina to Epidaurus, such as oar-leathers, sailcloth and pitch, and who secures a subsidy for a hostile fleet,[47] or soils the statues of Hecaté,[48] while he is humming some dithyramb. Away from here, the orator who nibbles at the salary of

---

45. A comic and dithyrambic poet.
46. This Thorycion, a toll collector at Aegina, which then belonged to Athens, had taken advantage of his position to send goods to Epidaurus, an Argolian town, thereby defrauding the treasury of the duty of 5 per cent, which was levied on every import and export.
47. An allusion to Alcibiades, who is said to have obtained a subsidy for the Spartan fleet from Cyrus, satrap of Asia Minor.
48. An allusion to the dithyrambic poet, Cinesias, who was accused of having sullied, by stooling against it, the pedestal of a statue of Hecaté at one of the street corners of Athens.

the poets, because he has been scouted in the ancient solemnities of Dionysus; to all such I say, and I repeat, and I say it again for the third time, "Make way for the choruses of the Initiate." But you, raise you your voice anew; resume your nocturnal hymns as it is meet to do at this festival.

Let each one advance boldly into the retreats of our flowery meads, let him mingle in our dances, let him give vent to jesting, to wit and to satire. Enough of junketing, lead forward! let our voices praise the divine protectress[49] with ardent love, yea! praise her, who promises to assure the welfare of this country for ever, in spite of Thorycion.

Let our hymns now be addressed to Demeter, the Queen of Harvest, the goddess crowned with ears of corn; to her be dedicated the strains of our divine concerts. Oh! Demeter, who presidest over the pure mysteries, help us and protect thy choruses; far from all danger, may I continually yield myself to sports and dancing, mingle laughter with seriousness, as is fitting at thy festivals, and as the reward for my biting sarcasms may I wreathe my head with the triumphal fillets. And now let our songs summon hither the lovable goddess, who so often joins in our dances.

Oh, venerated Dionysus, who hast created such soft melodies for this festival, come to accompany us to the goddess, show that you can traverse a long journey without wearying.[50] Dionysus, the king of the dance, guide my steps. 'Tis thou who, to raise a laugh and for the sake of economy,[51] hast torn our sandals and our garments; let us bound, let us dance at our pleasure, for we have nothing to spoil. Dionysus, king of the dance, guide my steps. Just now I saw through a corner of my eye a ravishing young girl, the companion of our sports; I saw the nipple of her bosom peeping through a rent in her tunic. Dionysus, king of the dance, guide my steps.

DIONYSUS: Aye, I like to mingle with these choruses; I would fain dance and sport with that young girl.

XANTHIAS: And I too.

---

49. Athené.

50. The route of the procession of the Initiate was from the Ceramicus (a district of Athens) to Eleusis, a distance of twenty-five stadia.

51. A shaft shot at the *choragi* by the poet, because they had failed to have new dresses made for the actors on this occasion.

CHORUS: Would you like us to mock together at Archidemus? He is still awaiting his seven-year teeth to have himself entered as a citizen;[52] but he is none the less a chief of the people among the Athenians and the greatest rascal of 'em all. I am told that Clisthenes is tearing the hair out of his rump and lacerating his cheeks on the tomb of Sebinus, the Anaphlystian;[53] with his forehead against the ground, he is beating his bosom and groaning and calling him by name. As for Callias,[54] the illustrious son of Hippobinus, the new Heracles, he is fighting a terrible battle of love on his galleys; dressed up in a lion's skin, he fights a fierce naval battle—with the girls' cunts.

DIONYSUS: Could you tell us where Pluto dwells? We are strangers and have just arrived.

CHORUS: Go no farther, and know without further question that you are at his gates.

DIONYSUS: Slave, pick up your baggage.

XANTHIAS: This wretched baggage, 'tis like Corinth, the daughter of Zeus, for it's always in his mouth.[55]

CHORUS: And now do ye, who take part in this religious festival, dance a gladsome round in the flowery grove in honour of the goddess.[56]

DIONYSUS: As for myself, I will go with the young girls and the women into the enclosure, where the nocturnal ceremonies are held; 'tis I will bear the sacred torch.

---

52. It was at the age of seven that children were entered on the registers of their father's tribe. Aristophanes is accusing Archidemus, who at that time was the head of the popular party, of being no citizen, because his name is not entered upon the registers of any tribe.
53. At funerals women tore their hair, rent their garments, and beat their bosoms. Aristophanes parodies these demonstrations of grief and attributes them to the effeminate Clisthenes. Sebinus the Anaphlystian is a coined name containing an obscene allusion, implying he was in the habit of allowing connexion with himself a posteriori, and being masturbated by the other in turn.
54. Callias, the son of Hipponicus, which the poet turns into Hippobinus, i.e. one who treads a mare, was an Athenian general, who had distinguished himself at the battle of Arginusae; he was notorious for his debauched habits, which he doubtless practised even on board his galleys. He is called a new Heracles, because of the legend that Heracles triumphed over fifty virgins in a single night; no doubt the poet alludes to some exploit of the kind here.
55. A proverb applied to silly boasters. The Corinthians had sent an envoy to Megara, who, in order to enhance the importance of his city, incessantly repeated the phrase, "*The Corinth of Zeus*."
56. Demeter.

CHORUS: Let us go into the meadows, that are sprinkled with roses, to form, according to our rites, the graceful choirs, over which the blessed Fates preside. 'Tis for us alone that the sun doth shine; his glorious rays illumine the Initiate, who have led the pious life, that is equally dear to strangers and citizens.

DIONYSUS: Come now! how should we knock at this door? How do the dwellers in these parts knock?

XANTHIAS: Lose no time and attack the door with vigour, if you have the courage of Heracles as well as his costume.

DIONYSUS: Ho! there! Slave!

AEACUS: Who's there?

DIONYSUS: Heracles, the bold.

AEACUS: Ah! wretched, impudent, shameless, threefold rascal, the most rascally of rascals. Ah! 'tis you who hunted out our dog Cerberus, whose keeper I was! But I have got you to-day; and the black stones of Styx, the rocks of Acheron, from which the blood is dripping, and the roaming dogs of Cocytus shall account to me for you; the hundred-headed Hydra shall tear your sides to pieces; the Tartessian Muraena[57] shall fasten itself on your lungs and the Tithrasian[58] Gorgons shall tear your kidneys and your gory entrails to shreds; I will go and fetch them as quickly as possible.

XANTHIAS: Eh! what are you doing there?

DIONYSUS (*stooping down*): I have just shit myself! Invoke the god.[59]

XANTHIAS: Get up at once. How a stranger would laugh, if he saw you.

DIONYSUS: Ah! I'm fainting. Place a sponge on my heart.

XANTHIAS: Here, take it.

DIONYSUS: Place it yourself.

XANTHIAS: But where? Good gods, where *is* your heart?

DIONYSUS: It has sunk into my shoes with fear. (*Takes his slave's hand holding the sponge, and applies it to his bottom*)

XANTHIAS: Oh! you most cowardly of gods and men!

DIONYSUS: What! I cowardly? I, who have asked you for a sponge! 'Tis what no one else would have done.

---

57. Tartessus was an Iberian town, near the Avernian marshes, which were said to be tenanted by reptiles, the progeny of vipers and muraenae, a kind of fish.

58. Tithrasios was a part of Libya, fabled to be peopled by Gorgons.

59. "Invoke the god" was the usual formula which immediately followed the offering of the libation in the festival of Dionysus. Here he uses the words after a libation of a new kind and induced by fear.

XANTHIAS: How so?

DIONYSUS: A poltroon would have fallen backwards, being overcome with the fumes; as for me, I got up and moreover I wiped myself clean.

XANTHIAS: Ah! by Posidon! a wonderful feat of intrepidity!

DIONYSUS: Aye, certainly. And you did not tremble at the sound of his threatening words?

XANTHIAS: They never troubled me.

DIONYSUS: Well then, since you are so brave and fearless, become what I am, take this bludgeon and this lion's hide, you, whose heart has no knowledge of fear; I, in return, will carry the baggage.

XANTHIAS: Here, take it, take it quick! 'this my duty to obey you, and behold, Heracles-Xanthias! Do I look like a coward of your kidney?

DIONYSUS: No. You are the exact image of the god of Melité,[60] dressed up as a rascal. Come, I will take the baggage.

FEMALE ATTENDANT OF PERSEPHONÉ: Ah! is it you then, beloved Heracles? Come in. As soon as ever the goddess, my mistress Persephoné, knew of your arrival, she quickly had the bread into the oven and clapped two or three pots of bruised peas upon the fire; she has had a whole bullock roasted and both cakes and rolled backed. Come in quick!

XANTHIAS: No, thank you.

ATTENDANT: Oh! by Apollo! I shall not let you off. She has also had poultry boiled for you, sweetmeats makes, and has prepared you some delicious wine. Come then, enter with me.

XANTHIAS: I am much obliged.

ATTENDANT: Are you mad? I will not let you go. There is likewise and enchanted flute-girl specially for you, and two or three dancing wenches.

XANTHIAS: What do you say? Dancing wenches?

ATTENDANT: In the prime of their life and all freshly depilated. Come, enter, for the cook was going to take the fish off the fire and the table was being spread.

XANTHIAS: Very well then! Run in quickly and tell the dancing-girls I am coming. Slave! pick up the baggage and follow me.

---

60. That is, Heracles, whose temple was at Melité, a suburban deme of Athens.

DIONYSUS: Not so fast! Oh! indeed! I disguise you as Heracles for a joke and you take the thing seriously! None of your nonsense, Xanthias! Take back the baggage.

XANTHIAS: What? You are not thinking of taking back what you gave me yourself?

DIONYSUS: No, I don't think about it; I do it. Off with that skin!

XANTHIAS: Witness how i am treated, ye great dogs, and be my judges!

DIONYSUS: What gods? Are you so stupid, such a fool? How can you, a slave and a mortal, be the son of Alcmena?

XANTHIAS: Come then! 'tis well! take them. But perhaps you will be needing me one day, an it please the gods.

CHORUS: 'Tis the act of a wise and sensible man, who has done much sailing, always to trim his sail towards the quarter whence the fair wind wafts, rather than stand stiff and motionless like a god Terminus.[61] To change your part to serve your own interest is to act like a clever man, a true Theramenes.[62]

DIONYSUS: Faith! 'twould be funny indeed if Xanthias, a slave, were indolently stretched out on purple cushions and fucking the dancing-girl; if he were then to ask me for a pot, while I, looking on, would be rubbing my tool, and this master rogue, on seeing it, were to know out my front teeth with a blow of his fist.

FIRST INKEEPER'S WIFE: Here! Plathané, Plathané! do come! here is the rascal who once came into our shop and ate up sixteen loaves for us.

SECOND INKEEPER'S WIFE: Aye, truly, 'tis he himself!

XANTHIAS: This is turning out rough for somebody.

FIRST WIFE: And besides that, twenty pieces of boiled meat at half an obolus apiece.

XANTHIAS: There's someone going to get punished.

FIRST WIFE: And I don't know how many cloves of garlic.

DIONYSUS: You are rambling, my dear, you don't know what you are saying.

FIRST WIFE: Hah! you thought I should not know you, because of your buskins! And then all the salt fish, I had forgotten that!

---

61. Whose statues were placed to make the boundaries of land.
62. One of the Thirty Tyrants, noted for his versatility.

SECOND WIFE: And then, alas! the fresh cheese that he devoured, osier baskets and all! Ten, when I asked for my money, he started to roar and shoot terrible looks at me.

XANTHIAS: As! I recognize him well by that token; 'tis just his way.

SECOND WIFE: And he drew out his sword like a madman.

FIRST WIFE: By the gods, yes.

SECOND WIFE: Terrified to death, we clambered up to the upper storey, and he fled at top speed, carrying off our baskets with him.

XANTHIAS: Ah! this is again his style! But you ought to take action.

FIRST WIFE: Run quick and call Cleon, my patron.

SECOND WIFE: And you, should you run against Hyperbolus,[63] bring him to me; we will knock the life out of our robber.

FIRST WIFE: Oh! you miserable glutton! how I should delight in breaking those grinders of yours, which devoured my goods!

SECOND WIFE: And I in hurling you into the malefactor's pit.

FIRST WIFE: And I in slitting with one stroke of the sickle that gullet that bolted down the tripe. But I am going to fetch Cleon; he shall summon you before the court this very day and force you to disgorge.

DIONYSUS: May I die, if Xanthias is not my dearest friend.

XANTHIAS: Can I be the son of Alcmena, I, a slave and a mortal?

DIONYSUS: I know, I know, that you are in a fury and you have the right to be; you can even beat me and I will not reply. But if I ever take this costume from you again, may I die of the most fearful torture—I, my wife, my children, all those who belong to me, down to the very last, and blear-eyed Archidemus[64] into the bargain.

XANTHIAS: I accept your oath, and on those terms I agree.

CHORUS: 'Tis now your cue, since you have resumed the dress, to act the brave and to throw terror into your glance, thus recalling the god whom you represent. But if you play your part badly, if you yield to any weakness, you will again have to load your shoulders with the baggage.

XANTHIAS: Friends, your advice is good, but I was thinking the same myself; if there is any good to be got, my master will again want to

---

63. Celon and Hyperbolus were both dead, and are therefore supposed to have become the leaders and patrons of the populace in Hades, the same as they had been on earth.

64. Already mentioned; one of the chiefs of the popular party in 406 B.C.

despoil me of this costume, of that I am quite certain. Ne'ertheless, I am going to show a fearless heart and shoot forth ferocious looks. And lo! the time for it has come, for I hear a noise at the door.

AEACUS (*to his slaves*): Bind me this dog-thief,[65] that he may be punished. Hurry yourselves, hurry!

DIONYSUS: This is going to turn out badly for someone.

XANTHIAS: Look to yourselves and don't come near me.

AEACUS: Hah! you would show fight! Ditylas, Sceblyas, Pardocas,[66] come here and have at him!

DIONYSUS: Ah! you would strike him because he has stolen!

XANTHIAS: 'Tis horrible!

DIONYSUS: 'Tis a revolting cruelty!

XANTHIAS: By Zeus! may I die, if I ever came here or stole from you the value of a pin! But I will act nobly; take this slave, put him to the question, and if you obtain the proof of my guilt, put me to death.

AEACUS: In what manner shall I put him to the question?

XANTHIAS: In every manner; you may lash him to the wooden horse, hang him, cut him open with scourging, flay him, twist his limbs, pour vinegar down his nostrils, load him with bricks, anything you like; only don't beat him with leeks or fresh garlic.[67]

AEACUS: 'Tis well conceived; but if the blows maim your slave, you will be claiming damages from me.

XANTHIAS: No, certainly not! set about putting him to the question.

AEACUS: It shall be done here, for I wish him to speak in your presence. Come, put down your pack, and be careful not to lie.

DIONYSUS: I forbid you to torture me, for I am immortal; if you dare it, woe to you!

AEACUS: What say you?

DIONYSUS: I say that I am an immortal, Dionysus, the son of Zeus, and that this fellow is only a slave.

AEACUS (*to Xanthias*): D'you hear him?

XANTHIAS: Yes. 'Tis all the better reason for beating him with rods, for, if he is a god, he will not feel the blows.

---

65. Heracles had carried of Cerberus.

66. Names of Thracian slaves.

67. As was done to unruly children; he allows every kind of torture with the exception of the mildest.

DIONYSUS (*to Xanthias*): But why, pray, since you also claim to be a god, should you not be beaten like myself?

XANTHIAS (*to Aeacus*): That's fair. Very well then, whichever of us two you first see crying and caring for the blows, him believe not to be a god.

AEACUS: 'Tis spoken like a brave fellow; you don't refuse what is right. Strip yourselves.

XANTHIAS: To do the thing fairly, how do you propose to act?

AEACUS: Oh! that's easy. I shall hit you one after the other.

XANTHIAS: Well thought of.

AEACUS: There! (*He strikes Xanthias*)

XANTHIAS: Watch if you see me flinch.

AEACUS: I have already struck you.

XANTHIAS: No, you haven't.

AEACUS: Why, you have not felt it at all, I think. Now for t'other one.

DIONYSUS: Be quick about it.

AEACUS: But I have struck you.

DIONYSUS: Ah! I did not even sneeze. How is that?

AEACUS: I don't know; come, I will return to the first one.

XANTHIAS: Get it over. Oh, oh!

AEACUS: What does that "oh, oh!" mean? Did it hurt you?

XANTHIAS: Oh, no! but I was thinking of the feasts of Heracles, which are being held at Diomeia.[68]

AEACUS: Oh! what a pious fellow! I pass on to the other again.

DIONYSUS: Oh! oh!

AEACUS: What's wrong?

DIONYSUS: I see some knights.[69]

AEACUS: Why are you weeping?

DIONYSUS: Because I can smell onions.

AEACUS: Ha! so you don't care a fig for the blows?

DIONYSUS: Not the least bit in the world.

AEACUS: Well, let us proceed. Your turn now.

XANTHIAS: Oh, I say!

AEACUS: What's the matter?

XANTHIAS: Pull out this thorn.[70]

---

68. A deme of Attica, where there was a temple to Heracles. No doubt those present uttered the cry "Oh! oh!" in honour of the god.
69. He pretends it was not a cry of pain at all, but of astonishment and admiration.
70. Pretending that it was the thorn causing him pain, and not the lash of the whip.

AEACUS: What? Now the other one again.

DIONYSUS: "Oh, Apollo! . . . King of Delos and Delphi!"

XANTHIAS: He felt that. Do you hear?

DIONYSUS: Why, no! I was quoting an iambic of Hipponax.

XANTHIAS: 'Tis labour in vain. Come, smite his flanks.

AEACUS: No, present your belly.

DIONYSUS: Oh, Posidon. . .

XANTHIAS: Ah! here's someone who's feeling it.

DIONYSUS: . . . who reignest on the Aegean headland and in the depths of the azure sea.[71]

AEACUS: By Demeter, I cannot find out which of you is the god. But come in; the master and Persephoné will soon tell you, for they are gods themselves.

DIONYSUS: You are quite right; but you should have thought of that before you beat us.

CHORUS: Oh! Muse, take part in our sacred choruses; our songs will enchant you and you shall see a people of wise men, eager for a nobler glory than that of Cleophon,[72] the braggart, the swallow, who deafens us with his hoarse cries, while perched upon a Thracian tree. He whines in his barbarian tongue and repeats the lament of Philomela with good reason, for even if the votes were equally divided, he would have to perish.[73]

The sacred chorus owes the city its opinion and its wise lessons. First I demand that equality be restored among the citizens, so that none may be disquieted. If there be any whom the artifices of Phrynichus have drawn into any error,[74] let us allow them to offer their excuses and let us forget these old mistakes. Furthermore, that there be not a single citizen in Athens who is deprived of his rights; otherwise would it not be shameful to see slaves become masters and treated as honourably as Plataeans, because they

---

71. According to the Scholiast this is a quotation from the 'Laocoon,' a lost play of Sophocles.

72. A general known for his cowardice; he was accused of not being a citizen, but of Thracian origin; in 406 B.C. he was in disfavour, and he perished shortly after in a popular tumult.

73. According to Athenian law, the accused was acquitted when the voting was equal.

74. He had helped to establish the oligarchical government of the Four Hundred, who had just been overthrown.

helped in a single naval fight?[75] Not that I censure this step, for, on the contrary I approve it; 'tis the sole thing you have done that is sensible. But those citizens, both they and their fathers, have so often fought with you and are allied to you by ties of blood, so ought you not to listen to their prayers and pardon them their single fault? Nature has given you wisdom, therefore let your anger cool and let all those who have fought together on Athenian galleys live in brotherhood and as fellow-citizens, enjoying the same equal rights; to show ourselves proud and intractable about granting the rights of the city, especially at a time when we are riding at the mercy of the waves,[76] is a folly, of which we shall later repent.

If I am adept at reading the destiny or the soul of a man, the fatal hour for little Cligenes is near, that unbearable ape, the greatest rogue of all the washermen, who use a mixture of ashes and Cimolian earth and call it potash.[77] He knows it; hence he is always armed for war; for he fears, if he ventures forth without his bludgeon, he would be stripped of his clothes when he is drunk.

I have often noticed that there are good and honest citizens in Athens, who are as old gold is to new money. The ancient coins are excellent in point of standard; they are assuredly the best of all moneys; they alone are well struck and give a pure ring; everywhere they obtain currency, both in Greece and in strange lands; yet we make no use of them and prefer those bad copper pieces quite recently issued and so wretchedly struck. Exactly in the same way do we deal with our citizens. If we know them to be well-born, sober, brave, honest, adepts in the exercises of the gymnasium and in the liberal arts, they are the butts of our contumely and we have only a use for the petty rubbish, consisting of strangers, slaves and low-born folk not worth a whit more, mushrooms of yesterday, whom formerly Athens would not have even wanted as scapegoats. Madmen, do change your ways at last; employ the honest men

---

75. The fight of Arginusae; the slaves who had fought there had been accorded their freedom.—The Plataeans had had the title of citizens since the battle of Marathon.
76. Things were not going well for Athens at the time; it was only two years later, 404 B.C., that Lysander took the city.
77. A demagogue; because he deceived the people, Aristophanes compares him with the washermen who cheated their clients by using some mixture that was cheaper than potash.

afresh; if you are fortunate through doing this, 'twill be but right, and if Fate betrays you, the wise will at least praise you for having fallen honourably.

AEACUS: By Zeus, the Deliverer! what a brave man your master is.

XANTHIAS: A brave man! I should think so indeed, for he only knows how to drink and to make love!

AEACUS: He has convicted you of lying and did not thrash the impudent rascal who had dared to call himself the master.

XANTHIAS: Ah! he would have rued it if he had.

AEACUS: Well spoken! that's a reply that does a slave credit; 'tis thus that I like to act too.

XANTHIAS: How, pray?

AEACUS: I am beside myself with joy, when I can curse my master in secret.

XANTHIAS: And when you go off grumbling, after having been well thrashed?

AEACUS: I am delighted.

XANTHIAS: And when you make yourself important?

AEACUS: I know of nothing sweeter.

XANTHIAS: Ah! by Zeus! we are brothers. And when you are listening to what your masters are saying?

AEACUS: 'Tis a pleasure that drives me to distraction.

XANTHIAS: And when you repeat it to strangers?

AEACUS: Oh! I feel as happy as if I were emitting semen.

XANTHIAS: By Phoebus Apollo! reach me your hand; come hither, that I may embrace you; and, in the name of Zeus, the Thrashed one, tell me what all this noise means, these shouts, these quarrels, that I can hear going on inside yonder.

AEACUS: 'Tis Aeschylus and Euripides.

XANTHIAS: What do you mean?

AEACUS: The matter is serious, very serious indeed; all Hades is in commotion.

XANTHIAS: What's it all about?

AEACUS: We have a law here, according to which, whoever in each of the great sciences and liberal arts beats all his rivals, is fed at the Prytaneum and sits at Pluto's side. . .

XANTHIAS: I know that.

AEACUS: . . . until someone cleverer than he in the same style of thing comes along; then he has to give way to him.

XANTHIAS: And how has this law disturbed Aeschylus?

AEACUS: He held the chair for tragedy, as being the greatest in his art.

XANTHIAS: And who has it now?

AEACUS: When Euripides descended here, he started reciting his verses to the cheats, cut-purses, parricides, and brigands, who abound in Hades; his supple and tortuous reasonings filled them with enthusiasm, and they pronounced him the cleverest by far. So Euripides, elated with pride, took possession of the throne on which Aeschylus was installed.

XANTHIAS: And did he not get stoned?

AEACUS: No, but the folk demanded loudly that a regular trial should decide to which of the two the highest place belonged.

XANTHIAS: What folk? this mob of rascals? (*Points to the spectators*)

AEACUS: Their clamour reached right up to heaven.

XANTHIAS: And had Aeschylus not his friends too?

AEACUS: Good people are very scarce here, just the same as on earth.

XANTHIAS: What does Pluto reckon to do?

AEACUS: To open a contest as soon as possible; the two rivals will show their skill, and finally a verdict will be given.

XANTHIAS: What! has not Sophocles also claimed the chair then?

AEACUS: No, no! he embraced Aeschylus and shook his hand, when he came down; he could have taken the seat, for Aeschylus vacated it for him; but according to Clidemides,[78] he prefers to act as his second; if Aeschylus triumphs, he will stay modestly where he is, but if not, he has declared that he will contest the prize with Euripides.

XANTHIAS: When is the contest to begin?

AEACUS: Directly! the battle royal is to take place on this very spot. Poetry is to be weighed in the scales.

XANTHIAS: What? How can tragedy be weighed?

AEACUS: They will bring rulers and compasses to measure the words, and those forms which are used for moulding bricks, also diameter measures and wedges, for Euripides says he wishes to torture every verse of his rival's tragedies.

XANTHIAS: If I mistake not, Aeschylus must be in a rage.

AEACUS: With lowered head he glares fiercely like a bull.

---

78. Callistrates says that Clidemides was one of Sophocles' sons; Apollonius states him to have been an actor.

XANTHIAS: And who will be the judge?

AEACUS: The choice was difficult; it was seen that there was a dearth of able men. Aeschylus took exception to the Athenians. . .

XANTHIAS: No doubt he thought there were too many thieves among them.

AEACUS: . . . and moreover believed them too light-minded to judge of a poet's merits. Finally they fell back upon your master, because he understands tragic poetry.[79] But let us go in; when the masters are busy, we must look out for blows!

CHORUS: Ah! what fearful wrath will be surging in his heart! what a roar there'll be when he sees the babbler who challenges him sharpening his teeth! how savagely his eyes will roll! What a battle of words like plumed helmets and waving crests hurling themselves against fragile outbursts and wretched parings! We shall see the ingenious architect of style defending himself against immense periods. Then, the close hairs of his thick mane all a-bristle, the giant will knit his terrible brow; he will pull out verses as solidly bolted together as the framework of a ship and will hurl them forth with a roar, while the pretty speaker with the supple and sharpened tongue, who weighs each syllable and submits everything to the lash of his envy, will cut this grand style to mincemeat and reduce to ruins this edifice erected by one good sturdy puff of breath.[80]

EURIPIDES (*to Dionysus*): Your advice is in vain, I shall not vacate the chair, for I contend I am superior to him.

DIONYSUS: Aeschylus, why do you keep silent? You understand what he says.

EURIPIDES: He is going to stand on his dignity first; 'tis a trick he never failed to use in his tragedies.

DIONYSUS: My dear fellow, a little less arrogance, please.

EURIPIDES: Oh! I know him for many a day. I have long had a thorough hold of his ferocious heroes, for his high-flown language and of the monstrous blustering words which his great, gaping mouth hurls forth thick and close without curb or measure.

AESCHYLUS: It is indeed you, the son of a rustic goddess,[81] who dare to treat me thus, you, who only know how to collect together stupid

---

79. Dionysus was, of course, the patron god of the drama and dramatic contests.

80. The majestic grandeur of Aeschylus' periods, coupled with a touch of parody, is to be recognized in this piece.

81. It is said that Euripides was the son of a fruit-seller.

sayings and to stitch the rags of your beggars?[82] I shall make you rue your insults.

DIONYSUS: Enough said, Aeschylus, calm the wild wrath that is turning your heart into a furnace.

AESCHYLUS: No, not until I have clearly shown the true value of this impudent fellow with his lame men.[83]

DIONYSUS: A lamb, a black lamb! Slaves, bring it quickly, the storm-cloud is about to burst.[84]

AESCHYLUS: Shame on your Cretan monologues![85] Shame on the infamous nuptials[86] that you introduce into the tragic art!

DIONYSUS: Curb yourself, noble Aeschylus, and as for you, my poor Euripides, be prudent, protect yourself from this hailstorm, or he may easily in his rage hit you full in the temple with some terrible word, that would let out your Telephus.[87] Come, Aeschylus, no flying into a temper! discuss the question coolly; poets must not revile each other like market wenches. Why, you shout at the very outset and burst out like a pine that catches fire in the forest.

EURIPIDES: I am ready for the contest and don't flinch; let him choose the attack or the defence; let him discuss everything, the dialogue, the choruses, the tragic genius, Peleus, Aeolus, Meleager[88] and especially Telephus.

DIONYSUS: And what do you propose to do, Aeschylus? Speak!

AESCHYLUS: I should have wished not to maintain a contest that is not equal or fair.

DIONYSUS: Why not fair?

AESCHYLUS: Because my poetry has outlived me, whilst his died with him and he can use it against me. However, I submit to your ruling.

DIONYSUS: Let incense and a brazier be brought, for I want to offer a prayer to the gods. Thanks to their favour, may I be able to decide

---

82. Euripides is constantly twitted by Aristophanes with his predilection for ragged beggars and vagabonds as characters in his plays.

83. Bellerophon, Philoctetes, and Telephus, were all characters in different Tragedies of Euripides.

84. Sailors, when in danger, sacrificed a black lamb to Typhon, the god of storms.

85. An allusion to a long monologue of Icarus in the tragedy called 'The Cretans.'

86. In 'Aeolus,' Macareus violates his own sister; in 'The Clouds,' this incest, which Euripides introduced upon the stage, is also mentioned.

87. The title of one of Euripides' pieces.

88. The titles of three lost Tragedies of Euripides.

between these ingenious rivals as a clever expert should! And do you sing a hymn in honour of the Muses.

CHORUS: Oh! ye chaste Muses, the daughters of Zeus, you who read the fine and subtle minds of thought-makers when they enter upon a contest of quibbles and tricks, look down on these two powerful athletes; inspire them, one with mighty words and the other with odds and ends of verses. Now the great mind contest is beginning.

DIONYSUS: And do you likewise make supplication to the gods before entering the lists.

AESCHYLUS: Oh, Demeter! who hast formed my mind, may I be able to prove myself worthy of thy Mysteries![89]

DIONYSUS: And you, Euripides, prove yourself meet to sprinkle incense on the brazier.

EURIPIDES: Thanks, but I sacrifice to other gods.[90]

DIONYSUS: To private gods of your own, which you have made after your own image?

EURIPIDES: Why, certainly!

DIONYSUS: Well then, invoke your gods.

EURIPIDES: Oh! thou Aether, on which I feed, oh! thou Volubility of Speech, oh! Craftiness, oh! Subtle Scent! enable me to crush the arguments of my opponent.

CHORUS: We are curious to see upon what ground these clever tilters are going to measure each other. Their tongue is keen, their wit is ready, their heart is full of audacity. From the one we must expect both elegance and polish of language, whereas the other, armed with his ponderous words, will fall hip and thigh upon his foe and with a single blow tear down and scatter all his vain devices.

DIONYSUS: Come, be quick and speak and let your words be elegant, but without false imagery or platitude.

EURIPIDES: I shall speak later of my poetry, but I want first to prove that Aeschylus is merely a wretched impostor; I shall relate by what means he tricked a coarse audience, trained in the school of Phrynichus.[91] First one saw some seated figure, who was veiled,

---

89. A verse from one of the lost Tragedies of Euripides; the poet was born at Eleusis.
90. Aristophanes often makes this accusation of religious heterodoxy against Euripides.
91. A dramatic poet, who lived about the end of the sixth century B.C., and a disciple of Thespis; the scenic art was then comparatively in its infancy.

some Achilles or Niobé,[92] who then strutted about the stage, but neither uncovered their face nor uttered a syllable.

DIONYSUS: I' faith! that's true!

EURIPIDES: Meanwhile, the Chorus would pour forth as many as four tirades one after the other, without stopping, and the characters would still maintain their stony silence.

DIONYSUS: I liked their silence, and these mutes pleased me no less than those characters that have such a heap to say nowadays.

EURIPIDES: 'Tis because you were a fool, understand that well.

DIONYSUS: Possibly; but what was his object?

EURIPIDES: 'Twas pure quackery; in this way the spectator would sit motionless, waiting, waiting for Niobé to say something, and the piece would go running on.

DIONYSUS: Oh! the rogue! how he deceived me! Well, Aeschylus, why are you so restless? Why this impatience, eh?

EURIPIDES: 'Tis because he sees himself beaten. Then when he had rambled on well, and got half-way through the piece, he would spout some dozen big, blustering, winged words, tall as mountains, terrible scarers, which the spectator admired without understanding what they meant.

DIONYSUS: Oh! great gods!

AESCHYLUS: Silence!

EURIPIDES: There was no comprehending one word.

DIONYSUS (*to Aeschylus*): Don't grind your teeth.

EURIPIDES: There were Scamanders, abysses, griffins with eagles' beaks chiselled upon brazen bucklers, all words with frowning crests and hard, hard to understand.

DIONYSUS: 'Faith, I was kept awake almost an entire night, trying to think out his yellow bird, half cock and half horse.[93]

AESCHYLUS: Why, fool, 'tis a device that is painted on the prow of a vessel.

DIONYSUS: Ah! I actually thought 'twas Eryxis, the son of Philoxenus.[94]

---

92. The Scholiast tells us that Achilles remained mute in the tragedy entitled 'The Phrygians' or 'The Ransom of Hector,' and that his face was veiled; he only spoke a few words at the beginning of the drama during a dialogue with Hermes.—We have no information about the Niobé mentioned here.

93. The Scholiast tells us that this expression ([Greek: Hippalektru on]) was used in 'The Myrmidons' of Aeschylus; Aristophanes ridicules it again both in the 'Peace' and in 'The Birds.'

94. An individual apparently noted for his uncouth ugliness.

EURIPIDES: But what did you want with a cock in tragedy?

AESCHYLUS: But you, you foe of the gods, what have you done that is so good?

EURIPIDES: Oh! I have not made horses with cocks' heads like you, nor goats with deer's horns, as you may see 'em on Persian tapestries; but, when I received tragedy from your hands, it was quite bloated with enormous, ponderous words, and I began by lightening it of its heavy baggage and treated it with little verses, with subtle arguments, with the sap of white beet and decoctions of philosophical folly, the whole being well filtered together;[95] then I fed it with monologues, mixing in some Cephisophon;[96] but I did not chatter at random nor mix in any ingredients that first came to hand; from the outset I made my subject clear, and told the origin of the piece.

AESCHYLUS: Well, that was better than telling your own.[97]

EURIPIDES: Then, starting with the very first verse, each character played his part; all spoke, both woman and slave and master, young girl and old hag.[98]

AESCHYLUS: And was not such daring deserving of death?

EURIPIDES: No, by Apollo! 'twas to please the people.

DIONYSUS: Oh! leave that alone, do; 'tis not the best side of your case.

EURIPIDES: Furthermore, I taught the spectators the art of speech. . .

AESCHYLUS: 'Tis true indeed! Would that you had burst before you did it!

EURIPIDES: . . . the use of the straight lines and of the corners of language, the science of thinking, of reading, of understanding, plotting, loving deceit, of suspecting evil, of thinking of everything. . .

AESCHYLUS: Oh! true, true again!

EURIPIDES: I introduced our private life upon the stage, our common habits; and 'twas bold of me, for everyone was at home with these and could be my critic; I did not burst out into big noisy words

---

95. The beet and the decoctions are intended to indicate the insipidity of Euripides' style.

96. An intimate friend of Euripides, who is said to have worked with him on his Tragedies, to have been 'ghost' to him in fact.

97. An allusion to Euripides' obscure birth; his mother had been, so it was said, a vegetable-seller in the public market.

98. Euripides had introduced every variety of character into his pieces, whereas Aeschylus only staged divinities or heroes.

to prevent their comprehension; nor did I terrify the audience by showing them Cycni[99] and Memnons[100] on chariots harnessed with steeds and jingling bells. Look at his disciples and look at mine. His are Phormisius and Megaenetus of Magnesia[101], all a-bristle with long beards, spears and trumpets, and grinning with sardonic and ferocious laughter, while my disciples are Clitophon and the graceful Theramenes.[102]

DIONYSUS: Theramenes? An able man and ready for anything; a man, who in imminent dangers knew well how to get out of the scrape by saying he was from Chios and not from Ceos.[103]

EURIPIDES: 'Tis thus that I taught my audience how to judge, namely, by introducing the art of reasoning and considering into tragedy. Thanks to me, they understand everything, discern all things, conduct their households better and ask themselves, "What is to be thought of this? Where is that? Who has taken the other thing?"

DIONYSUS: Yes, certainly, and now every Athenian who returns home, bawls to his slaves, "Where is the stew-pot? Who has eaten off the sprat's head? Where is the clove of garlic that was left over from yesterday? Who has been nibbling at my olives?" Whereas formerly they kept their seats with mouths agape like fools and idiots.

CHORUS: You hear him, illustrious Achilles,[104] and what are you going to reply? Only take care that your rage does not lead you astray, for he has handled you brutally. My noble friend, don't get carried away; furl all your sails, except the top-gallants, so that your ship may only advance slowly, until you feel yourself driven forward by a soft and favourable wind. Come then, you who were the first of the Greeks to construct imposing monuments of words and to

---

99. There are two Cycni, one, the son of Ares, was killed by Heracles according to the testimony of Hesiod in his description of the "Shield of Heracles"; the other, the son of Posidon, who, according to Pindar, perished under the blows of Achilles. It is not known in which Tragedy of Aeschylus this character was introduced.
100. Memnon, the son of Aurora, was killed by Achilles; in the list of the Tragedies of Aeschylus there is one entitled 'Memnon.'
101. These two were not poets, but Euripides supposes them disciples of Aeschylus, because of their rude and antiquated manners.
102. Clitophon and Theramenes were elegants of effeminate habits and adept talkers.
103. A proverb which was applied to versatile people; the two Greek names (Greek: Chios) and (Greek: Keios) might easily be mistaken for one another. Both, of course, are islands of the Cyclades.
104. A verse from the 'Myrmidons' of Aeschylus; here Achilles is Aeschylus himself.

raise the old tragedy above childish trifling, open a free course to the torrent of your words.

AESCHYLUS: This contest rouses my gall; my heart is boiling over with wrath. Am I bound to dispute with this fellow? But I will not let him think me unarmed and helpless. So, answer me! what is it in a poet one admires?

EURIPIDES: Wise counsels, which make the citizens better.

AESCHYLUS: And if you have failed in this duty, if out of honest and pure-minded men you have made rogues, what punishment do you think is your meet?

DIONYSUS: Death. I will reply for him.

AESCHYLUS: Behold then what great and brave men I bequeathed to him! They did not shirk the public burdens; they were not idlers, rogues and cheats, as they are to-day; their very breath was spears, pikes, helmets with white crests, breastplates and greaves; they were gallant souls encased in seven folds of ox-leather.

EURIPIDES: I must beware! he will crush me beneath the sheer weight of his hail of armour.

DIONYSUS: And how did you teach them this bravery? Speak, Aeschylus, and don't display so much haughty swagger.

AESCHYLUS: By composing a drama full of the spirit of Ares.

DIONYSUS: Which one?

AESCHYLUS: The Seven Chiefs before Thebes. Every man who had once seen it longed to be marching to battle.

DIONYSUS: And you did very wrongly; through you the Thebans have become more warlike; for this misdeed you deserve to be well beaten.

AESCHYLUS: You too might have trained yourself, but you were not willing. Then, by producing 'The Persae,' I have taught you to conquer all your enemies; 'twas my greatest work.

DIONYSUS: Aye, I shook with joy at the announcement of the death of Darius; and the Chorus immediately clapped their hands and shouted, "Triumph!"[105]

AESCHYLUS: Those are the subjects that poets should use. Note how useful, even from remotest times, the poets of noble thought have

---

105. The 'Persae' of Aeschylus (produced 472 B.C.) was received with transports of enthusiasm, reviving as it did memories of the glorious defeat of Xerxes at Salamis, where the poet had fought, only a few years before, 480 B.C.

been! Orpheus taught us the mystic rites and the horrid nature of murder; Musaeus, the healing of ailments and the oracles; Hesiod, the tilling of the soil and the times for delving and harvest. And does not divine Homer owe his immortal glory to his noble teachings? Is it not he who taught the warlike virtues, the art of fighting and of carrying arms?

DIONYSUS: At all events he has not taught it to Pantacles,[106] the most awkward of all men; t'other day, when he was directing a procession, 'twas only after he had put on his helmet that he thought of fixing in the crest.

AESCHYLUS: But he has taught a crowd of brave warriors, such as Lamachus,[107] the hero of Athens. 'Tis from Homer that I borrowed the Patrocli and the lion-hearted Teucers,[108] whom I revived to the citizens, to incite them to show themselves worthy of these illustrious examples when the trumpets sounded. But I showed them neither Sthenoboea[109] nor shameless Phaedra; and I don't remember ever having placed an amorous woman on the stage.

EURIPIDES: No, no, you have never known Aphrodité.

AESCHYLUS: And I am proud of it. Whereas with you and those like you, she appears everywhere and in every shape; so that even you yourself were ruined and undone by her.[110]

DIONYSUS: That's true; the crimes you imputed to the wives of others, you suffered from in turn.

EURIPIDES: But, cursed man, what harm have my Sthenoboeas done to Athens?

AESCHYLUS: You are the cause of honest wives of honest citizens drinking hemlock, so greatly have your Bellerophons made them blush.[111]

---

106. Nothing is known of this Pantacles, whom Eupolis, in his 'Golden Age,' also describes as awkward ([Greek: skaios]).

107. Aristophanes had by this time modified his opinion of this general, whom he had so flouted in 'The Acharnians.'

108. Son of Telamon, the King of Salamis and brother of Ajax.

109. The wife of Proetus, King of Argos. Bellerophon, who had sought refuge at the court of this king after the accidental murder of his brother Bellerus, had disdained her amorous overtures. Therefore she denounced him to her husband as having wanted to attempt her virtue and urged him to cause his death. She killed herself immediately after the departure of the young hero.

110. Cephisophon, Euripides' friend, is said to have seduced his wife.

111. Meaning, they have imitated Sthenoboea in everything; like her, they have conceived adulterous passions and, again like her, they have poisoned themselves.

EURIPIDES: Why, did I invent the story of Phaedra?

AESCHYLUS: No, the story is true enough; but the poet should hide what is vile and not produce nor represent it on the stage. The schoolmaster teaches little children and the poet men of riper age. We must only display what is good.

EURIPIDES: And when you talk to us of towering mountains— Lycabettus and of the frowning Parnes[112]—is that teaching us what is good? Why not use human language?

AESCHYLUS: Why, miserable man, the expression must always rise to the height of great maxims and of noble thoughts. Thus as the garment of the demi-gods is more magnificent, so also is their language more sublime. I ennobled the stage, while you have degraded it.

EURIPIDES: And how so, pray?

AESCHYLUS: Firstly you have dressed the kings in rags,[113] so that they might inspire pity.

EURIPIDES: Where's the harm?

AESCHYLUS: You are the cause why no rich man will now equip the galleys, they dress themselves in tatters, groan and say they are poor.

DIONYSUS: Aye, by Demeter! and he wears a tunic of fine wool underneath; and when he has deceived us with his lies, he may be seen turning up on the fish-market.[114]

AESCHYLUS: Moreover, you have taught boasting and quibbling; the wrestling schools are deserted and the young fellows have submitted their arses to outrage,[115] in order that they might learn to reel off idle chatter, and the sailors have dared to bandy words with their officers.[116] In my day they only knew how to ask for their ship's-biscuit and to shout "Yo ho! heave ho!"

---

112. Lycabettus, a mountain of Attica, just outside the walls of Athens, the "Arthur's Seat" of the city. Parnassus, the famous mountain of Phocis, the seat of the temple and oracle of Delphi and the home of the Muses. The whole passage is, of course, in parody of the grandiloquent style of Aeschylus.

113. An allusion to Oeneus, King of Aetolia, and to Telephus, King of Mysia; characters put upon the stage by Euripides.

114. It was only the rich Athenians who could afford fresh fish, because of their high price; we know how highly the gourmands prized the eels from the Copaic lake.

115. If Aristophanes is to be believed, the orators were of depraved habits, and exacted infamous complaisances as payment for their lessons in rhetoric.

116. Aristophanes attributes the general dissoluteness to the influence of Euripides; he suggests that the subtlety of his poetry, by sharpening the wits of the vulgar and even of the coarsest, has instigated them to insubordination.

DIONYSUS: . . . and to let wind under the nose of the rower below
them, to befoul their mate with filth and to steal when they went
ashore. Nowadays they argue instead of rowing and the ship can
travel as slow as she likes.

AESCHYLUS: Of what crimes is he not the author? Has he not shown
us procurers, women who get delivered in the temples, have traffic
with their brothers,[117] and say that life is not life.[118] 'Tis thanks
to him that our city is full of scribes and buffoons, veritable apes,
whose grimaces are incessantly deceiving the people; but there
is no one left who knows how to carry a torch,[119] so little is it
practised.

DIONYSUS: I' faith, that's true! I almost died of laughter at the last
Panathenaea at seeing a slow, fat, pale-faced fellow, who ran
well behind all the rest, bent completely double and evidently in
horrible pain. At the gate of the Ceramicus the spectators started
beating his belly, sides, flanks and thighs; these slaps knocked
so much wind out of him that it extinguished his torch and he
hurried away.

CHORUS: 'Tis a serious issue and an important debate; the fight is
proceeding hotly and its decision will be difficult; for, as violently
as the one attacks, as cleverly and as subtly does the other reply.
But don't keep always to the same ground; you are not at the end
of your specious artifices. Make use of every trick you have, no
matter whether it be old or new! Out with everything boldly,
blunt though it be; risk anything—that is smart and to the point.
Perchance you fear that the audience is too stupid to grasp your
subtleties, but be reassured, for that is no longer the case. They are
all well-trained folk; each has his book, from which he learns the
art of quibbling; such wits as they are happily endowed with have
been rendered still keener through study. So have no fear! Attack
everything, for you face an enlightened audience.

---

117. Augé, who was seduced by Heracles, was delivered in the temple of Athené
(Scholiast); it is unknown in what piece this fact is mentioned.—Macareus violates his
sister Canacé in the 'Aeolus.'

118. I.e. they busy themselves with philosophic subtleties. This line is taken from 'The
Phryxus,' of which some fragments have come down to us.

119. In the torch-race the victor was the runner who attained the goal first without having
allowed his torch to go out. This race was a very ancient institution. Aristophanes means
to say that the old habits had fallen into disuse.

EURIPIDES: Let's take your prologues; 'tis the beginnings of this able poet's tragedies that I wish to examine at the outset. He was obscure in the description of his subjects.

DIONYSUS: And which prologue are you going to examine?

EURIPIDES: A lot of them. Give me first of all that of the 'Orestes.'[120]

DIONYSUS: All keep silent, Aeschylus, recite.

AESCHYLUS: "Oh! Hermes of the nether world, whose watchful power executes the paternal bidding, be my deliverer, assist me, I pray thee. I come, I return to this land."[121]

DIONYSUS: Is there a single word to condemn in that?

EURIPIDES: More than a dozen.

DIONYSUS: But there are but three verses in all.

EURIPIDES: And there are twenty faults in each.

DIONYSUS: Aeschylus, I beg you to keep silent; otherwise, besides these three iambics, there will be many more attacked.

AESCHYLUS: What? Keep silent before this fellow?

DIONYSUS: If you will take my advice.

EURIPIDES: He begins with a fearful blunder. Do you see the stupid thing?

DIONYSUS: Faith! I don't care if I don't.

AESCHYLUS: A blunder? In what way?

EURIPIDES: Repeat the first verse.

AESCHYLUS: "Oh! Hermes of the nether world, whose watchful power executes the paternal bidding."

EURIPIDES: Is not Orestes speaking in this fashion before his father's tomb?

AESCHYLUS: Agreed.

EURIPIDES: Does he mean to say that Hermes had watched, only that Agamemnon should perish at the hands of a woman and be the victim of a criminal intrigue?

AESCHYLUS: 'Tis not to the god of trickery, but to Hermes the benevolent, that he gives the name of god of the nether world, and this he proves by adding that Hermes is accomplishing the mission given him by his father.

---

120. A tetralogy composed of three tragedies, the 'Agamemnon,' the 'Choëphorae,' the 'Eumenides,' together with a satirical drama, the 'Proteus.'

121. This is the opening of the 'Choëphorae.' Aeschylus puts the words in the mouth of Orestes, who is returning to his native land and visiting his father's tomb.

EURIPIDES: The blunder is even worse than I had thought to make it out; for if he holds his office in the nether world from his father. . .

DIONYSUS: It means his father has made him a grave-digger.

AESCHYLUS: Dionysus, your wine is not redolent of perfume.[122]

DIONYSUS: Continue, Aeschylus, and you, Euripides, spy out the faults as he proceeds.

AESCHYLUS: "Be my deliverer, assist me, I pray thee. I come, I return to this land."

EURIPIDES: Our clever Aeschylus says the very same thing twice over.

AESCHYLUS: How twice over?

EURIPIDES: Examine your expressions, for I am going to show you the repetition. "I come, I return to this land." But I *come* is the same thing as I *return*.

DIONYSUS: Undoubtedly. 'Tis as though I said to my neighbour, "Lend me either your kneading-trough or your trough to knead in."

AESCHYLUS: No, you babbler, no, 'tis not the same thing, and the verse is excellent.

DIONYSUS: Indeed! then prove it.

AESCHYLUS: To come is the act of a citizen who has suffered no misfortune; but the exile both comes and returns.

DIONYSUS: Excellent! by Apollo! What do you say to that, Euripides?

EURIPIDES: I say that Orestes did not return to his country, for he came there secretly, without the consent of those in power.

DIONYSUS: Very good indeed! by Hermes! only I have not a notion what it is you mean.

EURIPIDES: Go on.

DIONYSUS: Come, be quick, Aeschylus, continue; and you look out for the faults.

AESCHYLUS: "At the foot of this tomb I invoke my father and beseech him to hearken to me and to hear."

EURIPIDES: Again a repetition, to hearken and to hear are obviously the same thing.

DIONYSUS: Why, wretched man, he's addressing the dead, whom to call thrice even is not sufficient.

AESCHYLUS: And you, how do you form your prologues?

EURIPIDES: I am going to tell you, and if you find a repetition, an idle word or inappropriate, let me be scouted!

---

122. I.e. your jokes are very coarse.

DIONYSUS: Come, speak; 'tis my turn to listen. Let us hear the beauty of your prologues,

EURIPIDES: "Oedipus was a fortunate man at first. . ."

AESCHYLUS: Not at all; he was destined to misfortune before he even existed, since Apollo predicted he would kill his father before ever he was born. How can one say he was fortunate at first?

EURIPIDES: " . . . and he became the most unfortunate of mortals afterwards."

AESCHYLUS: No, he did not become so, for he never ceased being so. Look at the facts! First of all, when scarcely born, he is exposed in the middle of winter in an earthenware vessel, for fear he might become the murderer of his father, if brought up; then he came to Polybus with his feet swollen; furthermore, while young, he marries an old woman, who is also his mother, and finally he blinds himself.

DIONYSUS: 'Faith! I think he could not have done worse to have been a colleague of Erasinidas.[123]

EURIPIDES: You can chatter as you will, my prologues are very fine.

AESCHYLUS: I will take care not to carp at them verse by verse and word for word;[124] but, an it please the gods, a simple little bottle will suffice me for withering every one of your prologues.

EURIPIDES: You will wither my prologues with a little bottle?[125]

AESCHYLUS: With only one. You make verses of such a kind, that one can adapt what one will to your iambics: a little bit of fluff, a little bottle, a little bag. I am going to prove it.

EURIPIDES: You will prove it?

AESCHYLUS: Yes.

DIONYSUS: Come, recite.

---

123. He was one of the Athenian generals in command at Arginusae; he and his colleagues were condemned to death for not having given burial to the men who fell in that naval fight.

124. As Euripides had done to those of Aeschylus; that sort of criticism was too low for him.

125. (Greek: D ekuthion ap olesa), *oleum perdidi,* I have lost my labour, was a proverbial expression, which was also possibly the refrain of some song. Aeschylus means to say that all Euripides' phrases are cast in the same mould, and that his style is so poor and insipid that one can adapt to it any foolery one wishes; as for the phrase he adds to every one of the phrases his rival recites, he chooses it to insinuate that the work of Euripides is *labour lost*, and that he would have done just as well not to meddle with tragedy. The joke is mediocre at its best and is kept up far too long.

EURIPIDES: "Aegyptus, according to the most widely spread reports, having landed at Argos with his fifty daughters[126] . . ."

AESCHYLUS: . . . lost his little bottle.

EURIPIDES: What little bottle? May the plague seize you!

DIONYSUS: Recite another prologue to him. We shall see.

EURIPIDES: "Dionysus, who leads the choral dance on Parnassus with the thyrsus in his hand and clothed in skins of fawns[127] . . ."

AESCHYLUS: . . . lost his little bottle.

DIONYSUS: There again his little bottle upsets us.

EURIPIDES: He won't bother us much longer. I have a certain prologue to which he cannot adapt his tag: "There is no perfect happiness; this one is of noble origin, but poor; another of humble birth[128] . . ."

AESCHYLUS: . . . lost his little bottle.

DIONYSUS: Euripides!

EURIPIDES: What's the matter?

DIONYSUS: Clue up your sails, for this damned little bottle is going to blow a gale.

EURIPIDES: Little I care, by Demeter! I am going to make it burst in his hands.

DIONYSUS: Then out with it; recite another prologue, but beware, beware of the little bottle.

EURIPIDES: "Cadmus, the son of Agenor, while leaving the city of Sidon[129] . . ."

AESCHYLUS: . . . lost his little bottle.

DIONYSUS: Oh! my poor friend; buy that bottle, do, for it is going to tear all your prologues to ribbons.

EURIPIDES: What? Am I to buy it of him?

DIONYSUS: If you take my advice.

EURIPIDES: No, not I, for I have many prologues to which he cannot possibly fit his catchword: "Pelops, the son of Tantalus, having started for Pisa on his swift chariot[130] . . ."

AESCHYLUS: . . . lost his little bottle.

---

126. Prologue of the 'Archelaus' of Euripides, a tragedy now lost.
127. From prologue of the 'Hypsipilé' of Euripides, a play now lost.
128. From prologue of the 'Sthenoboea' of Euripides, a play now lost.
129. From prologue of the 'Phryxus' of Euripides, a play now lost.
130. From prologue of the 'Iphigeneia in Tauris' of Euripides.

Dionysus: D'ye see? Again he has popped in his little bottle. Come, Aeschylus, he is going to buy it of you at any price, and you can have a splendid one for an obolus.

Euripides: By Zeus, no, not yet! I have plenty of other prologues. "Oeneus in the fields one day[131] . . ."

Aeschylus: . . . lost his little bottle.

Euripides: Let me first finish the opening verse: "Oeneus in the fields one day, having made an abundant harvest and sacrificed the first-fruits to the gods. . ."

Aeschylus: . . . lost his little bottle.

Dionysus: During the sacrifice? And who was the thief?

Euripides: Allow him to try with this one: "Zeus, as even Truth has said[132] . . ."

Dionysus (*to Euripides*): You have lost again; he is going to say, "lost his little bottle," for that bottle sticks to your prologues like a ringworm. But, in the name of the gods, turn now to his choruses.

Euripides: I will prove that he knows nothing of lyric poetry, and that he repeats himself incessantly.

Chorus: What's he going to say now? I am itching to know what criticisms he is going to make on the poet, whose sublime songs so far outclass those of his contemporaries. I cannot imagine with what he is going to reproach the king of the Dionysia, and I tremble for the aggressor.

Euripides: Oh! those wonderful songs! But watch carefully, for I am going to condense them all into a single one.

Dionysus: And I am going to take pebbles to count the fragments.

Euripides: "Oh, Achilles, King of Phthiotis, hearken to the shout of the conquering foe and haste to sustain the assault. We dwellers in the marshes do honour to Hermes, the author of our race. Haste to sustain the assault."

Dionysus: There, Aeschylus, you have already two assaults against you.

Euripides: "Oh, son of Atreus, the most illustrious of the Greeks, thou, who rulest so many nations, hearken to me. Haste to the assault."

Dionysus: A third assault. Beware, Aeschylus.

---

131. Prologue of 'The Meleager' by Euripides, lost.
132. Prologue of 'The Menalippé Sapiens,' by Euripides, lost.

EURIPIDES: "Keep silent, for the inspired priestesses are opening the temple of Artemis. Haste to sustain the assault. I have the right to proclaim that our warriors are leaving under propitious auspices. Haste to sustain the assault."[133]

DIONYSUS: Great gods, what a number of assaults! my kidneys are quite swollen with fatigue; I shall have to go to the bath after all these assaults.

EURIPIDES: Not before you have heard this other song arranged for the music of the cithara.

DIONYSUS: Come then, continue; but, prithee, no more "assaults."

EURIPIDES: "What! the two powerful monarchs, who reign over the Grecian youth, phlattothrattophlattothrat, are sending the Sphinx, that terrible harbinger of death, phlattothrattophlattothrat. With his avenging arm bearing a spear, phlattothrattophlattothrat, the impetuous bird delivers those who lean to the side of Ajax, phlattothrattophlattothrat, to the dogs who roam in the clouds, phlattothrattophlattothrat."[134]

DIONYSUS (*to Aeschylus*): What is this 'phlattothrat'? Does it come from Marathon or have you picked it out of some labourer's chanty?

AESCHYLUS: I took what was good and improved it still more, so that I might not be accused of gathering the same flowers as Phrynichus in the meadow of the Muse. But this man borrows from everybody, from the suggestions of prostitutes, from the sons of Melitus,[135] from the Carian flute-music, from wailing women, from dancing-girls. I am going to prove it, so let a lyre be brought. But what need of a lyre in his case? Where is the girl with the castanets? Come, thou Muse of Euripides; 'tis quite thy business to accompany songs of this sort.

---

133. The whole of these fragments are quoted at random and have no meaning. Euripides, no doubt, wants to show that the choruses of Aeschylus are void of interest or coherence. As to the refrain, "haste to sustain the assault," Euripides possibly wants to insinuate that Aeschylus incessantly repeats himself and that a wearying monotony pervades his choruses. However, all these criticisms are in the main devoid of foundation.

134. This ridiculous couplet pretends to imitate the redundancy and nonsensicality of Aeschylus' language; it can be seen how superficial and unfair the criticism of Euripides is; probably this is just what Aristophanes wanted to convey by this long and wearisome scene.

135. The Scholiast conjectures this Melitus to be the same individual who later accused Socrates.

DIONYSUS: This Muse has surely done fellation in her day, like a Lesbian wanton.[136]

AESCHYLUS: "Ye halcyons, who twitter over the ever-flowing billows of the sea, the damp dew of the waves glistens on your wings; and you spiders, who we-we-we-we-we-weave the long woofs of your webs in the corners of our houses with your nimble feet like the noisy shuttle, there where the dolphin by bounding in the billows, under the influence of the flute, predicts a favourable voyage; thou glorious ornaments of the vine, the slender tendrils that support the grape. Child, throw thine arms about my neck."[137] Do you note the harmonious rhythm?

DIONYSUS: Yes.

AESCHYLUS: Do you note it?

DIONYSUS: Yes, undoubtedly.

AESCHYLUS: And does the author of such rubbish dare to criticize my songs? he, who imitates the twelve postures of Cyrené in his poetry?[138] There you have his lyric melodies, but I still want to give you a sample of his monologues. "Oh! dark shadows of the night! what horrible dream are you sending me from the depths of your sombre abysses! Oh! dream, thou bondsman of Pluto, thou inanimate soul, child of the dark night, thou dread phantom in long black garments, how bloodthirsty, bloodthirsty is thy glance! how sharp are thy claws! Handmaidens, kindle the lamp, draw up the dew of the rivers in your vases and make the water hot; I wish to purify myself of this dream sent me by the gods. Oh! king of the ocean, that's right, that's right! Oh! my comrades, behold this wonder. Glycé has robbed me of my cock and has fled. Oh, Nymphs of the mountains! oh! Mania! seize her! How unhappy

---

136. The most infamous practices were attributed to the Lesbian women, amongst others, that of *fellation*, that is the vile trick of taking a man's penis in the mouth, to give him gratification by sucking and licking it with the tongue. Dionysus means to say that Euripides takes pleasure in describing shameful passions.

137. Here the criticism only concerns the rhythm and not either the meaning or the style. This passage was sung to one of the airs that Euripides had adopted for his choruses and which have not come down to us; we are therefore absolutely without any data that would enable us to understand and judge a criticism of this kind.

138. A celebrated courtesan, who was skilled in twelve different postures of Venus. Aeschylus returns to his idea, which he has so often indicated, that Euripides' poetry is low and impure; he at the same time scoffs at the artifices to which Euripides had recourse when inspiration and animation failed him.

I am! I was full busy with my work, I was sp-sp-sp-sp-spinning the flax that was on my spindle, I was rounding off the clew that I was to go and sell in the market at dawn; and he flew off, flew off, cleaving the air with his swift wings; he left to me nothing but pain, pain! What tears, tears, poured, poured from my unfortunate eyes! Oh! Cretans, children of Ida, take your bows; help me, haste hither, surround the house. And thou, divine huntress, beautiful Artemis, come with thy hounds and search through the house. And thou also, daughter of Zeus, seize the torches in thy ready hands and go before me to Glycé's home, for I propose to go there and rummage everywhere."[139]

DIONYSUS: That's enough of choruses.

AESCHYLUS: Yes, faith, enough indeed! I wish now to see my verses weighed in the scales; 'tis the only way to end this poetic struggle.

DIONYSUS: Well then, come, I am going to sell the poet's genius the same way cheese is sold in the market.

CHORUS: Truly clever men are possessed of an inventive mind. Here again is a new idea that is marvellous and strange, and which another would not have thought of; as for myself I would not have believed anyone who had told me of it, I would have treated him as a driveller.

DIONYSUS: Come, hither to the scales.

AESCHYLUS AND EURIPIDES: Here we are.

DIONYSUS: Let each one hold one of the scales, recite a verse, and not let go until I have cried, "Cuckoo!"

AESCHYLUS AND EURIPIDES: We understand.

DIONYSUS: Well then, recite and keep your hands on the scales.

EURIPIDES: "Would it had pleased the gods that the vessel Argo had never unfurled the wings of her sails!"[140]

AESCHYLUS: "Oh! river Sperchius! oh! meadows, where the oxen graze!"[141]

DIONYSUS: Cuckoo! let go! Oh! the verse of Aeschylus sinks far the lower of the two.

EURIPIDES: And why?

---

139. No monologue of Euripides that has been preserved bears the faintest resemblance to this specimen which. Aeschylus pretends to be giving here.
140. Beginning of Euripides' 'Medea.'
141. Fragment from Aeschylus 'Philoctetes.' The Sperchius is a river in Thessaly, which has its source in the Pindus range and its mouth in the Maliac gulf.

DIONYSUS: Because, like the wool-merchants, who moisten their wares, he has thrown a river into his verse and has made it quite wet, whereas yours was winged and flew away.

EURIPIDES: Come, another verse! You recite, Aeschylus, and you, weigh.

DIONYSUS: Hold the scales again.

AESCHYLUS AND EURIPIDES: Ready.

DIONYSUS (*to Euripides*): You begin.

EURIPIDES: "Eloquence is Persuasion's only sanctuary."[142]

AESCHYLUS: "Death is the only god whom gifts cannot bribe."[143]

DIONYSUS: Let go! let go! Here again our friend Aeschylus' verse drags down the scale; 'tis because he has thrown in Death, the weightiest of all ills.

EURIPIDES: And I Persuasion; my verse is excellent.

DIONYSUS: Persuasion has both little weight and little sense. But hunt again for a big weighty verse and solid withal, that it may assure you the victory.

EURIPIDES: But where am I to find one—where?

DIONYSUS: I'll tell you one: "Achilles has thrown two and four."[144] Come, recite! 'tis the last trial.

EURIPIDES: "With his arm he seized a mace, studded with iron."[145]

AESCHYLUS: "Chariot upon chariot and corpse upon corpse."[146]

DIONYSUS (*to Euripides*): There you're foiled again.

EURIPIDES: Why?

DIONYSUS: There are two chariots and two corpses in the verse; why, 'tis a weight a hundred Egyptians could not lift.[147]

AESCHYLUS: 'Tis no longer verse against verse that I wish to weigh, but let him clamber into the scale himself, he, his children, his

---

142. A verse from Euripides' 'Antigoné.' Its meaning is, that it is better to speak well than to speak the truth, if you want to persuade.

143. From the 'Niobe,' a lost play, of Aeschylus.

144. From the 'Telephus' of Euripides, in which he introduces Achilles playing at dice. This line was also ridiculed by Eupolis.

145. From Euripides' 'Meleager.' All these plays, with the one exception of the 'Medea,' are lost.

146. From the 'Glaucus Potniensis,' a lost play of Aeschylus.

147. I.e. one hundred porters, either because many of the Athenian porters were Egyptians, or as an allusion to the Pyramids and other great works, which had habituated them to carrying heavy burdens.

ARISTOPHANES

wife, Cephisophon[148] and all his works; against all these I will place but two of my verses on the other side.

DIONYSUS: I will *not* be their umpire, for they are dear to me and I will not have a foe in either of them; meseems the one is mighty clever, while the other simply delights me.

PLUTO: Then you are foiled in the object of your voyage.

DIONYSUS: And if I do decide?

PLUTO: You shall take with you whichever of the twain you declare the victor; thus you will not have come in vain.

DIONYSUS: That's all right! Well then, listen; I have come down to find a poet.

EURIPIDES: And with what intent?

DIONYSUS: So that the city, when once it has escaped the imminent dangers of the war, may have tragedies produced. I have resolved to take back whichever of the two is prepared to give good advice to the citizens. So first of all, what think you of Alcibiades? For the city is in most difficult labour over this question.

EURIPIDES: And what does it think about it?

DIONYSUS: What does it think? It regrets him, hates him, and yet wishes to have him, all at the same time. But tell me your opinion, both of you.

EURIPIDES: I hate the citizen who is slow to serve his country, quick to involve it in the greatest troubles, ever alert to his own interests, and a bungler where those of the State are at stake.

DIONYSUS: That's good, by Posidon! And you, what is your opinion?

AESCHYLUS: A lion's whelp should not be reared within the city. No doubt that's best; but if the lion has been reared, one must submit to his ways.

DIONYSUS: Zeus, the Deliverer! this puzzles me greatly. The one is clever, the other clear and precise. Now each of you tell me your idea of the best way to save the State.

EURIPIDES: If Cinesias were fitted to Cleocritus as a pair of wings, and the wind were to carry the two of them across the waves of the sea. . .

DIONYSUS: 'Twould be funny. But what is he driving at?

---

148. Euripides' friend and collaborator.

EURIPIDES: . . . they could throw vinegar into the eyes of the foe in the event of a sea-fight. But I know something else I want to tell you.

DIONYSUS: Go on.

EURIPIDES: When we put trust in what we mistrust and mistrust what we trust. . .

DIONYSUS: What? I don't understand. Tell us something less profound, but clearer.

EURIPIDES: If we were to mistrust the citizens, whom we trust, and to employ those whom we to-day neglect, we should be saved. Nothing succeeds with us; very well then, let's do the opposite thing, and our deliverance will be assured.

DIONYSUS: Very well spoken. You are the most ingenious of men, a true Palamedes![149] Is this fine idea your own or is it Cephisophon's?

EURIPIDES: My very own,—bar the vinegar, which is Cephisophon's.

DIONYSUS (*to Aeschylus*): And you, what have you to say?

AESCHYLUS: Tell me first who the commonwealth employs. Are they the just?

DIONYSUS: Oh! she holds *them* in abhorrence.

AESCHYLUS: What, are then the wicked those she loves?

DIONYSUS: Not at all, but she employs them against her will.

AESCHYLUS: Then what deliverance can there be for a city that will neither have cape nor cloak?[150]

DIONYSUS: Discover, I adjure you, discover a way to save her from shipwreck.

AESCHYLUS: I will tell you the way on earth, but I won't here.

DIONYSUS: No, send her this blessing from here.

AESCHYLUS: They will be saved when they have learnt that the land of the foe is theirs and their own land belongs to the foe; that their vessels are their true wealth, the only one upon which they can rely.[151]

---

149. The invention of weights and measures, of dice, and of the game of chess are attributed to him, also that of four additional letters of the alphabet.

150. I.e. that cannot decide for either party.

151. I.e. that a country can always be invaded and that the fleet alone is a safe refuge. This is the same advice as that given by Pericles, and which Thucydides expresses thus, "Let your country be devastated, or even devastate it yourself, and set sail for Laconia with your fleet."

DIONYSUS: That's true, but the dicasts devour everything.[152]

PLUTO (*to Dionysus*): Now decide.

DIONYSUS: 'Tis for you to decide, but I choose him whom my heart prefers.

EURIPIDES: You called the gods to witness that you would bear me through; remember your oath and choose your friends.

DIONYSUS: Yes, "my tongue has sworn."[153] . . . But I choose Aeschylus.

EURIPIDES: What have you done, you wretch?

DIONYSUS: I? I have decided that Aeschylus is the victor. What then?

EURIPIDES: And you dare to look me in the face after such a shameful deed?

DIONYSUS: "Why shameful, if the spectators do not think so?"[154]

EURIPIDES: Cruel wretch, will you leave me pitilessly among the dead?

DIONYSUS: "Who knows if living be not dying,[155] if breathing be not feasting, if sleep be not a fleece?"[156]

PLUTO: Enter my halls. Come, Dionysus.

DIONYSUS: What shall we do there?

PLUTO: I want to entertain my guests before they leave.

DIONYSUS: Well said, by Zeus; 'tis the very thing to please me best.

CHORUS: Blessed the man who has perfected wisdom! Everything is happiness for him. Behold Aeschylus; thanks to the talent, to the cleverness he has shown, he returns to his country; and his fellow-citizens, his relations, his friends will all hail his return with joy. Let us beware of jabbering with Socrates and of disdaining the sublime notes of the tragic Muse. To pass an idle life reeling off grandiloquent speeches and foolish quibbles, is the part of a madman.

PLUTO: Farewell, Aeschylus! Go back to earth and may your noble precepts both save our city[157] and cure the mad; there are such, a

---

152. An allusion to the fees of the dicasts, or jurymen; we have already seen that at this period it was two obols, and later three.

153. A half-line from Euripides' 'Hippolytus.' The full line is: (Greek: h e gl ott' om omok', h e de phr en an omotos,) "my tongue has taken an oath, but my mind is unsworn," a bit of casuistry which the critics were never tired of bringing up against the author.

154. A verse from the 'Aeolus' of Euripides, but slightly altered. Euripides said, "Why is is shameful, if the spectators, who enjoy it, do not think so?"

155. A verse from the 'Phrixus' of Euripides; what follows is a parody.

156. We have already seen Aeschylus pretending that it was possible to adapt any foolish expression one liked to the verses of Euripides: "a little bottle, a little bag, a little fleece."

157. Pluto speaks as though he were an Athenian himself.

many of them! Carry this rope from me to Cleophon, this one to Myrmex and Nichomachus, the public receivers, and this other one to Archenomous.[158] Bid them come here at once and without delay; if not, by Apollo, I will brand them with the hot iron.[159] I will make one bundle of them and Adimantus,[160] the son of Leucolophus,[161] and despatch the lot into hell with all possible speed.

AESCHYLUS: I will do your bidding, and do you make Sophocles occupy my seat. Let him take and keep it for me, against I should ever return here. In fact I award him the second place among the tragic poets. As for this impostor, watch that he never usurps my throne, even should he be placed there in spite of himself.

PLUTO (*to the Chorus of the Initiate*): Escort him with your sacred torches, singing to him as you go his own hymns and choruses.

CHORUS: Ye deities of the nether world, grant a pleasant journey to the poet who is leaving us to return to the light of day; grant likewise wise and healthy thoughts to our city. Put an end to the fearful calamities that overwhelm us, to the awful clatter of arms. As for Cleophon and the likes of him, let them go, an it please them, and fight in their own land.[162]

FINIS OF "THE FROGS"

---

158. That they should hang themselves. Cleophon is said to have been an influential alien resident who was opposed to concluding peace; Myrmex and Nicomachus were two officials guilty of peculation of public funds; Archenomus is unknown.

159. He would brand them as fugitive slaves, if, despite his orders, they refused to come down.

160. An Athenian admiral.

161. The real name of the father of Adimantus was Leucolophides, which Aristophanes jestingly turns into Leucolophus, i.e. *White Crest*.

162. I.e. in a foreign country; Cleophon, as we have just seen, was not an Athenian.

ECCLESIAZUSAE OR,
THE ASSEMBLYWOMEN

Introduction

The 'Ecclesiazusae, or Women in Council,' was not produced till twenty years after the preceding play, the 'Thesmophoriazusae' (at the Great Dionysia of 392 B.C.), but is conveniently classed with it as being also largely levelled against the fair sex. "It is a broad, but very amusing, satire upon those ideal republics, founded upon communistic principles, of which Plato's well-known treatise is the best example. His 'Republic' had been written, and probably delivered in the form of oral lectures at Athens, only two or three years before, and had no doubt excited a considerable sensation. But many of its most startling principles had long ago been ventilated in the Schools."

Like the 'Lysistrata,' the play is a picture of woman's ascendancy in the State, and the topsy-turvy consequences resulting from such a reversal of ordinary conditions. The women of Athens, under the leadership of the wise Praxagora, resolve to reform the constitution. To this end they don men's clothes, and taking seats in the Assembly on the Pnyx, command a majority of votes and carry a series of revolutionary proposals—that the government be vested in a committee of women, and further, that property and women be henceforth held in common. The main part of the comedy deals with the many amusing difficulties that arise inevitably from this new state of affairs, the community of women above all necessitating special safeguarding clauses to secure the rights of the less attractive members of the sex to the service of the younger and handsomer men. Community of goods again, private property being abolished, calls for a regulation whereby all citizens are to dine at the public expense in the various public halls of the city, the particular place of each being determined by lot; and the drama winds up with one of these feasts, the elaborate menu of which is given in burlesque, and with the jubilations of the women over their triumph.

"This comedy appears to labour under the very same faults as the 'Peace.' The introduction, the secret assembly of the women, their rehearsal of their parts as men, the description of the popular assembly, are all handled in the most masterly manner; but towards the middle the action stands still. Nothing remains but the representation of the perplexities and confusion which arise from the new arrangements, especially in connection with the community of women, and from the prescribed equality of rights in love both for the old and ugly and for the young and beautiful. These perplexities are pleasant enough, but they turn too much on a repetition of the same joke."

We learn from the text of the play itself that the 'Ecclesiazusae' was drawn by lot for first representation among the comedies offered for competition at the Festival, the Author making a special appeal to his audience not to let themselves be influenced unfavourably by the circumstance; but whether the play was successful in gaining a prize is not recorded.

Dramatis Personae

Praxagora.
Blepyrus, husband of Praxagora.
Women.
A Man.
Chremes.
Two Citizens.
Herald.
An Old Man.
A Girl.
A Young Man.
Three Old Women.
A Servant Maid.
Her Master.
Chorus of Women.

Scene: *Before a house in a Public Square at Athens; a lamp is burning over the door.*
Time: *a little after midnight.*

PRAXAGORA (*enters carrying a lamp in her hand*): Oh! thou shining
light of my earthenware lamp, from this high spot shalt thou look
abroad. Oh! lamp, I will tell thee thine origin and thy future; 'tis
the rapid whirl of the potter's wheel that has lent thee thy shape,
and thy wick counterfeits the glory of the sun;[1] mayst thou send
the agreed signal flashing afar! In thee alone do we confide, and
thou art worthy, for thou art near us when we practise the various
postures in which Aphrodité delights upon our couches, and none
dream even in the midst of her sports of seeking to avoid thine eye
that watches our swaying bodies. Thou alone shinest into the depths
of our most secret charms, and with thy flame dost singe the hairy
growth of our privates. If we open some cellar stored with fruits and
wine, thou art our companion, and never dost thou betray or reveal
to a neighbour the secrets thou hast learned about us. Therefore
thou shalt know likewise the whole of the plot that I have planned
with my friends, the women, at the festival of the Scirophoria.[2]

I see none of those I was expecting, though dawn approaches;
the Assembly is about to gather and we must take our seats in spite
of Phyromachus,[3] who forsooth would say, "It is meet the women
sit apart and hidden from the eyes of the men." Why, have they
not been able then to procure the false beards that they must wear,
or to steal their husbands cloaks? Ah! I see a light approaching; let
us draw somewhat aside, for fear it should be a man.

FIRST WOMAN: Let us start, it is high time; as we left our dwellings,
the cock was crowing for the second time.

PRAXAGORA: And I have spent the whole night waiting for you. But
come, let us call our neighbour by scratching at her door; and
gently too, so that her husband may hear nothing.

SECOND WOMAN: I was putting on my shoes, when I heard you
scratching, for I was not asleep, so there! Oh! my dear, my husband
(*he is a Salaminian*) never left me an instant's peace, but was at
me, for ever at me, all night long, so that it was only just now that
I was able to filch his cloak.

---

1. A parody of the pompous addresses to inanimate objects so frequent in the prologues
and monodies of Euripides.
2. A festival which was kept in Athens in the month of scirophorion (June), whence
its name; the statues of Athené, Demeter, Persephoné, Apollo and Posidon were borne
through the city with great pomp with banners or canopies ([Greek: skira]) over them.
3. Unknown.

FIRST WOMAN: I see Clinareté coming too, along with Sostraté and their next-door neighbour Philaeneté.

PRAXAGORA: Hurry yourselves then, for Glycé has sworn that the last comer shall forfeit three measures of wine and a *choenix* of pease.

FIRST WOMAN: Don't you see Melisticé, the wife of Smicythion, hurrying hither in her great shoes? Methinks she is the only one of us all who has had no trouble in getting rid of her husband.

SECOND WOMAN: And can't you see Gusistraté, the tavern-keeper's wife, with a lamp in her hand, and the wives of Philodoretus and Chaeretades?

PRAXAGORA: I can see many others too, indeed the whole of the flower of Athens.

THIRD WOMAN: Oh! my dear, I have had such trouble in getting away! My husband ate such a surfeit of sprats last evening that he was coughing and choking the whole night long.

PRAXAGORA: Take your seats, and, since you are all gathered here at last, let us see if what we decided on at the feast of the Scirophoria has been duly done.

FOURTH WOMAN: Yes. Firstly, as agreed, I have let the hair under my armpits grow thicker than a bush; furthermore, whilst my husband was at the Assembly, I rubbed myself from head to foot with oil and then stood the whole day long in the sun.[4]

FIFTH WOMAN: So did I. I began by throwing away my razor, so that I might get quite hairy, and no longer resemble a woman.

PRAXAGORA: Have you the beards that we had all to get ourselves for the Assembly?

FOURTH WOMAN: Yea, by Hecaté! Is this not a fine one?

FIFTH WOMAN: Aye, much finer than Epicrates'.[5]

PRAXAGORA (*to the other women*): And you?

FOURTH WOMAN: Yes, yes; look, they all nod assent.

PRAXAGORA: I see that you have got all the rest too, Spartan shoes, staffs and men's cloaks, as 'twas arranged.

SIXTH WOMAN: I have brought Lamias'[6] club, which I stole from him while he slept.

---

4. So as to get sunburnt and thus have a more manly appearance.

5. A demagogue, well known on account of his long flowing beard; he was nicknamed by his fellow-citizens (Greek: Sakesphoros) that is, shield-bearer, because his beard came down to his waist and covered his body like a shield.

6. Unknown.

PRAXAGORA: What, the club that makes him puff and pant with its weight?

SIXTH WOMAN: By Zeus the Deliverer, if he had the skin of Argus, he would know better than any other how to shepherd the popular herd.

PRAXAGORA: But come, let us finish what has yet to be done, while the stars are still shining; the Assembly, at which we mean to be present, will open at dawn.

FIRST WOMAN: Good; you must take up your place at the foot of the platform and facing the Prytanes.

SIXTH WOMAN: I have brought this with me to card during the Assembly. (*She shows some wool*)

PRAXAGORA: During the Assembly, wretched woman?

SIXTH WOMAN: Aye, by Artemis! shall I hear any less well if I am doing a bit of carding? My little ones are all but naked.

PRAXAGORA: Think of her wanting to card! whereas we must not let anyone see the smallest part of our bodies.[7] 'Twould be a fine thing if one of us, in the midst of the discussion, rushed on to the speaker's platform and, flinging her cloak aside, showed her hairy privates. If, on the other hand, we are the first to take our seats closely muffled in our cloaks, none will know us. Let us fix these beards on our chins, so that they spread all over our bosoms. How can we fail then to be mistaken for men? Agyrrhius has deceived everyone, thanks to the beard of Pronomus;[8] yet he was no better than a woman, and you see how he now holds the first position in the city. Thus, I adjure you by this day that is about to dawn, let us dare to copy him and let us be clever enough to possess ourselves of the management of affairs. Let us save the vessel of State, which just at present none seems able either to sail or row.

SIXTH WOMAN: But where shall we find orators in an Assembly of women?

---

7. Whereas the arms must be extended to do carding, and folk could not fail to recognize her as a woman by their shape.

8. Agyrrhius was an Athenian general, who commanded at Lesbos; he was effeminate and of depraved habits. No doubt he had let his beard grow to impose on the masses and to lend himself that dignity which he was naturally wanting in.—Pronomus was a flute-player, who had a fine beard.

PRAXAGORA: Nothing simpler. Is it not said, that the cleverest speakers are those who submit themselves oftenest to men? Well, thanks to the gods, we are that by nature.

SIXTH WOMAN: There's no doubt of that; but the worst of it is our inexperience.

PRAXAGORA: That's the very reason we are gathered here, in order to prepare the speech we must make in the Assembly. Hasten, therefore, all you who know aught of speaking, to fix on your beards.

SEVENTH WOMAN: Oh! you great fool! is there ever a one among us cannot use her tongue?

PRAXAGORA: Come, look sharp, on with your beard and become a man. As for me, I will do the same in case I should have a fancy for getting on to the platform. Here are the chaplets.

SECOND WOMAN: Oh! great gods! my dear Praxagora, do look here! Is it not laughable?

PRAXAGORA: How laughable?

SECOND WOMAN: Our beards look like broiled cuttle-fishes.

PRAXAGORA: The priest is bringing in—the cat.[9] Make ready, make ready! Silence, Ariphrades![10] Go and take your seat. Now, who wishes to speak?

SEVENTH WOMAN: I do.

PRAXAGORA: Then put on this chaplet[11] and success be with you.

SEVENTH WOMAN: There, 'tis done!

PRAXAGORA: Well then! begin.

SEVENTH WOMAN: Before drinking?

PRAXAGORA: Hah! she wants to drink![12]

SEVENTH WOMAN: Why, what else is the meaning of this chaplet?

PRAXAGORA: Get you hence! you would probably have played us this trick also before the people.

SEVENTH WOMAN: Well! don't the men drink then in the Assembly?

---

9. Young pigs were sacrificed at the beginning of the sittings; here the comic writer substitutes a cat for the pig, perhaps because of its lasciviousness.

10. A pathic; Aristophanes classes him with the women, because of his effeminacy.

11. The orators wore green chaplets, generally of olive leaves; guests also wore them at feasts, but then flowers were mingled with the leaves.

12. An allusion to the rapacity of the orators, who only meddled in political discussions with the object of getting some personal gain through their influence; also to the fondness for strong drink we find attributed in so many passages to the Athenian women.

PRAXAGORA: Now she's telling us the men drink!

SEVENTH WOMAN: Aye, by Artemis, and neat wine too. That's why their decrees breathe of drunkenness and madness. And why libations, why so many ceremonies, if wine plays no part in them? Besides, they abuse each other like drunken men, and you can see the archers dragging more than one uproarious drunkard out of the Agora.

PRAXAGORA: Go back to your seat, you are wandering.

SEVENTH WOMAN: Ah! I should have done better not to have muffled myself in this beard; my throat's afire and I feel I shall die of thirst.

PRAXAGORA: Who else wishes to speak?

EIGHTH WOMAN: I do.

PRAXAGORA: Quick then, take the chaplet, for time's running short. Try to speak worthily, let your language be truly manly, and lean on your staff with dignity.

EIGHTH WOMAN: I had rather have seen one of your regular orators giving you wise advice; but, as that is not to be, it behoves me to break silence; I cannot, for my part indeed, allow the tavern-keepers to fill up their wine-pits with water.[13] No, by the two goddesses. . .

PRAXAGORA: What? by the two goddesses![14] Wretched woman, where are your senses?

EIGHTH WOMAN: Eh! what? . . . I have not asked you for a drink!

PRAXAGORA: No, but you want to pass for a man, and you swear by the two goddesses. Otherwise 'twas very well.

EIGHTH WOMAN: Well then. By Apollo. . .

PRAXAGORA: Stop! All these details of language must be adjusted; else it is quite useless to go to the Assembly.

SEVENTH WOMAN: Pass me the chaplet; I wish to speak again, for I think I have got hold of something good. You women who are listening to me. . .

PRAXAGORA: Women again; why, wretched creature, 'tis men that you are addressing.

SEVENTH WOMAN: 'Tis the fault of Epigonus;[15] I caught sight of him over yonder, and I thought I was speaking to women.

---

13. A sort of cistern dug in the ground, in which the ancients kept their wine.
14. This was a form of oath that women made use of; hence it is barred by Praxagora.
15. Another pathic, like Ariphrades, mentioned above.

PRAXAGORA: Come, withdraw and remain seated in future. I am going to take this chaplet myself and speak in your name. May the gods grant success to my plans!

My country is as dear to me as it is to you, and I groan, I am grieved at all that is happening in it. Scarcely one in ten of those who rule it is honest, and all the others are bad. If you appoint fresh chiefs, they will do still worse. It is hard to correct your peevish humour; you fear those who love you and throw yourselves at the feet of those who betray you. There was a time when we had no assemblies, and then we all thought Agyrrhius a dishonest man;[16] now they are established, he who gets money thinks everything is as it should be, and he who does not, declares all who sell their votes to be worthy of death.

FIRST WOMAN: By Aphrodité, that is well spoken.

PRAXAGORA: Why, wretched woman, you have actually called upon Aphrodité. Oh! what a fine thing 'twould have been had you said that in the Assembly!

FIRST WOMAN: I should never have done that!

PRAXAGORA: Well, mind you don't fall into the habit.—When we were discussing the alliance,[17] it seemed as though it were all over with Athens if it fell through. No sooner was it made than we were vexed and angry, and the orator who had caused its adoption was compelled to seek safety in flight.[18] Is there talk of equipping a fleet? The poor man says, yes, but the rich citizen and the countryman say, no. You were angered against the Corinthians and they with you; now they are well disposed towards you, be so towards them. As a rule the Argives are dull, but the Argive Hieronymus[19] is a distinguished chief. Herein lies a spark of

---

16. Before the time of Pericles, when manners had not yet become corrupt, the fame of each citizen was based on fact; worthy men were honoured, and those who resembled Agyrrhius, already mentioned, were detested. For this general, see note a little above.

17. The alliance with Corinth, Boeotia and Argolis against Sparta in 393 B.C.

18. Conon, who went to Asia Minor and was thrown into prison at Sardis by the Persian Satrap.

19. An Argive to whom Conon entrusted the command of his fleet when he went to the court of the King of Persia.—In this passage the poet is warning his fellow-citizens not to alienate the goodwill of the allies by their disdain, but to know how to honour those among them who had distinguished themselves by their talents.

hope; but Thrasybulus is far from Athens[20] and you do not recall him.

FIRST WOMAN: Oh! what a brilliant man!

PRAXAGORA: That's better! that's fitting applause.—Citizens, 'tis you who are the cause of all this trouble. You vote yourselves salaries out of the public funds and care only for your own personal interests; hence the State limps along like Aesimus.[21] But if you hearken to me, you will be saved. I assert that the direction of affairs must be handed over to the women, for 'tis they who have charge and look after our households.

SECOND WOMAN: Very good, very good, 'tis perfect! Say on, say on.

PRAXAGORA: They are worth more than you are, as I shall prove. First of all they wash all their wool in warm water, according to the ancient practice; you will never see them changing their method. Ah! if Athens only acted thus, if it did not take delight in ceaseless innovations, would not its happiness be assured? Then the women sit down to cook, as they always did; they carry things on their head as was their wont; they keep the Thesmophoria, as they have ever done; they knead their cakes just as they used to; they make their husbands angry as they have always done; they receive their lovers in their houses as was their constant custom; they buy dainties as they always did; they love unmixed wine as well as ever; they delight in being loved just as much as they always have. Let us therefore hand Athens over to them without endless discussions, without bothering ourselves about what they will do; let us simply hand them over the power, remembering that they are mothers and will therefore spare the blood of our soldiers; besides, who will know better than a mother how to forward provisions to the front? Woman is adept at getting money for herself and will not easily let herself be deceived; she understands deceit too well herself. I omit

20. The Lacedaemonians, after having recalled their king, Agesilas, who gained the victory of Coronea, were themselves beaten at sea off Cnidus by Conon and Pharnabazus. 'Twas no doubt this victory which gave a *spark of hope* to the Athenians, who had suffered so cruelly during so many years; but Aristophanes declares that, in order to profit by this return of fortune, they must recall Thrasybulus, the deliverer of Athens in 401 B.C. He was then ostensibly employed in getting the islands of the Aegean sea and the towns of the Asiatic coast to return under the Athenian power, but this was really only an honourable excuse for thrusting him aside for reasons of jealousy.

21. Unknown.

a thousand other advantages. Take my advice and you will live in perfect happiness.

FIRST WOMAN: How beautiful this is, my dearest Praxagora, how clever! But where, pray, did you learn all these pretty things?

PRAXAGORA: When the countryfolk were seeking refuge in the city,[22] I lived on the Pnyx with my husband, and there I learnt to speak through listening to the orators.

FIRST WOMAN: Then, dear, 'tis not astonishing that you are so eloquent and clever; henceforward you shall be our leader, so put your great ideas into execution. But if Cephalus[23] belches forth insults against you, what answer will you give him in the Assembly?

PRAXAGORA: I shall say that he drivels.

FIRST WOMAN: But all the world knows that.

PRAXAGORA: I shall furthermore say that he is a raving madman.

FIRST WOMAN: There's nobody who does not know it.

PRAXAGORA: That he, as excellent a statesman as he is, is a clumsy tinker.[24]

FIRST WOMAN: And if the blear-eyed Neoclides[25] comes to insult you?

PRAXAGORA: To him I shall say, "Go and look at a dog's backside".[26]

FIRST WOMAN: And if they fly at you?

PRAXAGORA: Oh! I shall shake them off as best I can; never fear, I know how to use this tool.[27]

FIRST WOMAN: But there is one thing we don't think of. If the archers drag you away, what will you do?

PRAXAGORA: With my arms akimbo like this, I will never, never let myself be taken round the middle.

FIRST WOMAN: If they seize you, we will bid them let you go.

---

22. During the earlier years of the Peloponnesian war, when the annual invasion of Attica by the Lacedaemonians drove the country population into the city.

23. A demagogue, otherwise unknown.

24. Cephalus' father was said to have been a tinker.

25. The comic poets accused him of being an alien by birth and also an informer and a rogue. See the 'Plutus.'

26. There was a Greek saying, "*Look into the backside of a dog and of three foxes*" which, says the Scholiast, used to be addressed to those who had bad eyes. But the precise point of the joke here is difficult to see.

27. An obscene allusion; (Greek: hupokrouein) means both *pulsare* and *subagitare*,—to strike, and also to move to the man in sexual intercourse.

SECOND WOMAN: That's the best way. But how are we going to lift up our arm[28] in the Assembly, we, who only know how to lift our legs in the act of love?

PRAXAGORA: 'Tis difficult; yet it must be done, and the arm shown naked to the shoulder in order to vote. Quick now, put on these tunics and these Laconian shoes, as you see the men do each time they go to the Assembly or for a walk. Then this done, fix on your beards, and when they are arranged in the best way possible, dress yourselves in the cloaks you have abstracted from your husbands; finally start off leaning on your staffs and singing some old man's song as the villagers do.

SECOND WOMAN: Well spoken; and let us hurry to get to the Pnyx before the women from the country, for they will no doubt not fail to come there.

PRAXAGORA: Quick, quick, for 'tis all the custom that those who are not at the Pnyx early in the morning, return home empty-handed.

CHORUS: Move forward, citizens, move forward; let us not forget to give ourselves this name and may that of *woman* never slip out of our mouths; woe to us, if it were discovered that we had laid such a plot in the darkness of night. Let us go to the Assembly then, fellow-citizens; for the Thesmothetae have declared that only those who arrive at daybreak with haggard eye and covered with dust, without having snatched time to eat anything but a snack of garlic-pickle, shall alone receive the triobolus. Walk up smartly, Charitimides,[29] Smicythus and Draces, and do not fail in any point of your part; let us first demand our fee and then vote for all that may perchance be useful for our partisans. . . Ah! what am I saying? I meant to say, for our fellow-citizens. Let us drive away these men of the city,[30] who used to stay at home and chatter round the table in the days when only an obolus was paid, whereas now one is stifled by the crowds at the Pnyx.[31] No! during the

---

28. In order to vote.
29. The Chorus addresses the leaders amongst the women by the names of men. Charitimides was commander of the Athenian navy.
30. The countryfolk affected to despise the townspeople, whom they dubbed idle and lazy.
31. The fee of the citizens who attended the Assembly had varied like that of the dicasts, or jurymen.

Archonship of generous Myronides,[32] none would have dared to let himself be paid for the trouble he spent over public business; each one brought his own meal of bread, a couple of onions, three olives and some wine in a little wine-skin. But nowadays we run here to earn the three obols, for the citizen has become as mercenary as the stonemason. (*The Chorus marches away*)

BLEPYRUS (*husband of Praxagora*): What does this mean? My wife has vanished! it is nearly daybreak and she does not return! Wanting to relieve myself, lo! I awake and hunt in the darkness for my shoes and my cloak; but grope where I will, I cannot find them. Meanwhile my need grew each moment more urgent and I had only just time to seize my wife's little mantle and her Persian slippers. But where shall I find a spot suitable for my purpose. Bah! One place is as good as another at night-time, for no one will see me. Ah! what fatal folly 'twas to take a wife at my age, and how I could thrash myself for having acted so foolishly! 'Tis a certainty she's not gone out for any honest purpose. However, that's not our present business.

A MAN: Who's there? Is that not my neighbour Blepyrus? Why, yes, 'tis himself and no other. Tell me, what's all that yellow about you? Can it be Cinesias[33] who has befouled you so?

BLEPYRUS: No, no, I only slipped on my wife's tunic[34] to come out in.

MAN: And where is your cloak?

BLEPYRUS: I cannot tell you, for I hunted for it vainly on the bed.

MAN: And why did you not ask your wife for it?

BLEPYRUS: Ah! why indeed! because she is not in the house; she has run away, and I greatly fear that she may be doing me an ill turn.

MAN: But, by Posidon, 'tis the same with myself. My wife has disappeared with my cloak, and what is still worse, with my shoes as well, for I cannot find them anywhere.

BLEPYRUS: Nor can I my Laconian shoes; but as I had urgent need, I popped my feet into these slippers, so as not to soil my blanket, which is quite new.

MAN: What does it mean? Can some friend have invited her to a feast?

---

32. An Athenian general, who gained brilliant victories over the Thebans during the period prior to the Peloponnesian war.
33. A dithyrambic poet, and notorious for his dissoluteness; he was accused of having daubed the statues of Hecate at the Athenian cross-roads with ordure.
34. The women wore yellow tunics, called (Greek: krok otoi), because of their colour.

ARISTOPHANES

BLEPYRUS: I expect so, for she does not generally misconduct herself, as far as I know.

MAN: Come, I say, you seem to be making ropes. Are you never going to be done? As for myself, I would like to go to the Assembly, and it is time to start, but the thing is to find my cloak, for I have only one.

BLEPYRUS: I am going to have a look too, when I have done; but I really think there must be a wild pear obstructing my rectum.

MAN: Is it the one which Thrasybulus spoke about to the Lacedaemonians?[35]

BLEPYRUS: Oh! oh! oh! how the obstruction holds! Whatever am I to do? 'Tis not merely for the present that I am frightened; but when I have eaten, where is it to find an outlet now? This cursed Achradusian fellow[36] has bolted the door. Let a doctor be fetched; but which is the cleverest in this branch of the science? Amynon?[37] Perhaps he would not come. Ah! Antithenes![38] Let him be brought to me, cost what it will. To judge by his noisy sighs, that man knows what a rump wants, when in urgent need. Oh! venerated Ilithyia![39] I shall burst unless the door gives way. Have pity! pity! Let me not become the night-stool of the comic poets.[40]

CHREMES: Hi! friend, what are you after there? Easing yourself!

BLEPYRUS: Oh! there! it is over and I can get up again at last.

CHREMES: What's this? You have your wife's tunic on.

BLEPYRUS: Aye, 'twas the first thing that came to my hand in the darkness. But where do you hail from?

CHREMES: From the Assembly.

BLEPYRUS: Is it already over then?

---

35. This Thrasybulus, not to be confounded with the more famous Thrasybulus, restorer of the Athenian democracy, in 403 B.C., had undertaken to speak against the Spartans, who had come with proposals of peace, but afterwards excused himself, pretending to be labouring under a sore throat, brought on by eating wild pears (B.C. 393). The Athenians suspected him of having been bribed by the Spartans.

36. A coined word, derived from (Greek: achras), a wild pear.

37. Amynon was not a physician, according to the Scholiast, but one of those orators called (Greek: europr oktoi) (*laticuli*) 'wide-arsed,' because addicted to habits of pathic vice, and was invoked by Blepyrus for that reason.

38. A doctor notorious for his dissolute life.

39. The Grecian goddess who presided over child-birth.

40. He is afraid lest some comic poet should surprise him in his ridiculous position and might cause a laugh at his expense upon the stage.

CHREMES: Certainly.

BLEPYRUS: Why, it is scarcely daylight.

CHREMES: I did laugh, ye gods, at the vermilion rope-marks that were to be seen all about the Assembly.[41]

BLEPYRUS: Did you get the triobolus?

CHREMES: Would it had so pleased the gods! but I arrived just too late, and am quite ashamed of it; I bring back nothing but this empty wallet.

BLEPYRUS: But why is that?

CHREMES: There was a crowd, such as has never been seen at the Pnyx, and the folk looked pale and wan, like so many shoemakers, so white were they in hue; both I and many another had to go without the triobolus.

BLEPYRUS: Then if I went now, I should get nothing.

CHREMES: No, certainly not, nor even had you gone at the second cock-crow.

BLEPYRUS: Oh! what a misfortune! Oh, Antilochus![42] no triobolus! Even death would be better! I am undone! But what can have attracted such a crowd at that early hour?

CHREMES: The Prytanes started the discussion of measures nearly concerning the safety of the State; immediately, that blear-eyed fellow, the son of Neoclides,[43] was the first to mount the platform. Then the folk shouted with their loudest voice, "What! he dares to speak, and that, too, when the safety of the State is concerned, and he a man who has not known how to save even his own eyebrows!" He, however, shouted louder than they all, and looking at them asked, "Why, what ought I to have done?"

BLEPYRUS: Pound together garlic and laserpitium juice, add to this mixture some Laconian spurge, and rub it well into the eyelids at night. That's what I should have answered, had I been there.

---

41. In accordance with a quaint Athenian custom a rope daubed with vermilion was drawn across from end to end of the Agora (market-place) by officials of the city at the last moment before the Ecclesia, or Public Assembly, was to meet. Any citizen trying to evade his duty to be present was liable to have his white robe streaked red, and so be exposed to general ridicule on finally putting in an appearance on the Pnyx.

42. A parody on a verse in 'The Myrmidons' of Aeschylus.—Antilochus was the son of Nestor; he was killed by Memnon, when defending his father.

43. See above.

CHREMES: After him that clever rascal Evaeon[44] began to speak; he was naked, so far as we all could see, but he declared he had a cloak; he propounded the most popular, the most democratic, doctrines. "You see," he said, "I have the greatest need of sixteen drachmae, the cost of a new cloak, my health demands it; nevertheless I wish first to care for that of my fellow-citizens and of my country. If the fullers were to supply tunics to the indigent at the approach of winter, none would be exposed to pleurisy. Let him who has neither beds nor coverlets go to sleep at the tanners' after taking a bath; and if they shut the door in winter, let them be condemned to give him three goat-skins."

BLEPYRUS: By Dionysus, a fine, a very fine notion! Not a soul will vote against his proposal, especially if he adds that the flour-sellers must supply the poor with three measures of corn, or else suffer the severest penalties of the law; 'tis only in this way that Nausicydes[45] can be of any use to us.

CHREMES: Then we saw a handsome young man rush into the tribune, he was all pink and white like young Nicias,[46] and he began to say that the direction of matters should be entrusted to the women; this the crowd of shoemakers[47] began applauding with all their might, while the country-folk assailed him with groans.

BLEPYRUS: And, 'faith, they did well.

CHREMES: But they were outnumbered, and the orator shouted louder than they, saying much good of the women and much ill of you.

BLEPYRUS: And what did he say?

CHREMES: First he said you were a rogue. . .

BLEPYRUS: And you?

CHREMES: Let me speak. . . and a thief. . .

BLEPYRUS: I alone?

CHREMES: And an informer.

---

44. He was very poor, and his cloak was such a mass of holes that one might doubt his having one at all. This surname, Evaeon ([Greek: eu ai on], delicious life) had doubtless been given him on the 'lucus a non' principle because of his wretchedness.

45. Apparently a wealthy corn-factor.

46. Presumably this refers to the grandson of Nicias, the leader of the expedition to Sicily; he must have been sixteen or seventeen years old about that time, since, according to Lysias, Niceratus, the son of the great Nicias, was killed in 405 B.C. and had left a son of tender age behind him, who bore the name of his grandfather.

47. That is, the pale-faced folk in the Assembly already referred to—really the women there present surreptitiously.

BLEPYRUS: I alone?

CHREMES: Why, no, by the gods! all of us.

BLEPYRUS: And who avers the contrary?

CHREMES: He maintained that women were both clever and thrifty, that they never divulged the Mysteries of Demeter, while you and I go about babbling incessantly about whatever happens at the Senate.

BLEPYRUS: By Hermes, he was not lying!

CHREMES: Then he added, that the women lend each other clothes, trinkets of gold and silver, drinking-cups, and not before witnesses too, but all by themselves, and that they return everything with exactitude without ever cheating each other; whereas, according to him, we are ever ready to deny the loans we have effected.

BLEPYRUS: Aye, by Posidon, and in spite of witnesses.

CHREMES: Again, he said that women were not informers, nor did they bring lawsuits, nor hatch conspiracies; in short, he praised the women in every possible manner.

BLEPYRUS: And what was decided?

CHREMES: To confide the direction of affairs to them; 'tis the one and only innovation that has not yet been tried at Athens.

BLEPYRUS: And it was voted?

CHREMES: Yes.

BLEPYRUS: And everything that used to be the men's concern has been given over to the women?

CHREMES: You express it exactly.

BLEPYRUS: Thus 'twill be my wife who will go to the Courts now in my stead.

CHREMES: And it will be she who will keep your children in your place.

BLEPYRUS: I shall no longer have to tire myself out with work from daybreak onwards?

CHREMES: No, 'twill be the women's business, and you can stop at home and take your ease.

BLEPYRUS: Well, what I fear for us fellows now is, that, holding the reins of government, they will forcibly compel us. . .

CHREMES: To do what?

BLEPYRUS: . . . to work them.

CHREMES: And if we are not able?

BLEPYRUS: They will give us no dinner.

CHREMES: Well then, do your duty; dinner and love form a double enjoyment.

BLEPYRUS: Ah! but I hate compulsion.

CHREMES: But if it be for the public weal, let us resign ourselves. 'Tis an old saying, that our absurdest and maddest decrees always somehow turn out for our good. May it be so in this case, oh gods, oh venerable Pallas! But I must be off; so, good-bye to you!

BLEPYRUS: Good-bye, Chremes.

CHORUS: March along, go forward. Is there some man following us? Turn round, examine everywhere and keep a good look-out; be on your guard against every trick, for they might spy on us from behind. Let us make as much noise as possible as we tramp. It would be a disgrace for all of us if we allowed ourselves to be caught in this deed by the men. Come, wrap yourselves up well, and search both right and left, so that no mischance may happen to us. Let us hasten our steps; here we are close to the meeting-place, whence we started for the Assembly, and here is the house of our leader, the author of this bold scheme, which is now decreed by all the citizens. Let us not lose a moment in taking off our false beards, for we might be recognized and denounced. Let us stand under the shadow of this wall; let us glance round sharply with our eye to beware of surprises, while we quickly resume our ordinary dress. Ah! here is our leader, returning from the Assembly. Hasten to relieve your chins of these flowing manes. Look at your comrades yonder; they have already made themselves women again some while ago.

PRAXAGORA: Friends, success has crowned our plans. But off with these cloaks and these boots quick, before any man sees you; unbuckle the Laconian straps and get rid of your staffs; and do you help them with their toilet. As for myself, I am going to slip quietly into the house and replace my husband's cloak and other gear where I took them from, before he can suspect anything.

CHORUS: There! 'tis done according to your bidding. Now tell us how we can be of service to you, so that we may show you our obedience, for we have never seen a cleverer woman than you.

PRAXAGORA: Wait! I only wish to use the power given me in accordance with your wishes; for, in the market-place, in the midst of the shouts and danger, I appreciated your indomitable courage.

BLEPYRUS: Eh, Praxagora! where do you come from?

PRAXAGORA: How does that concern you, friend?

BLEPYRUS: Why, greatly! what a silly question!

PRAXAGORA: You don't think I have come from a lover's?

BLEPYRUS: No, perhaps not from only one.

PRAXAGORA: You can make yourself sure of that.

BLEPYRUS: And how?

PRAXAGORA: You can see whether my hair smells of perfume.

BLEPYRUS: What? cannot a woman possibly be loved without perfume, eh!

PRAXAGORA: The gods forfend, as far as I am concerned.

BLEPYRUS: Why did you go off at early dawn with my cloak?

PRAXAGORA: A companion, a friend who was in labour, had sent to fetch me.

BLEPYRUS: Could you not have told me?

PRAXAGORA: Oh, my dear, would you have me caring nothing for a poor woman in that plight?

BLEPYRUS: A word would have been enough. There's something behind all this.

PRAXAGORA: No, I call the goddesses to witness! I went running off; the poor woman who summoned me begged me to come, whatever might betide.

BLEPYRUS: And why did you not take your mantle? Instead of that, you carry off mine, you throw your dress upon the bed and you leave me as the dead are left, bar the chaplets and perfumes.

PRAXAGORA: 'Twas cold, and I am frail and delicate; I took your cloak for greater warmth, leaving you thoroughly warm yourself beneath your coverlets.

BLEPYRUS: And my shoes and staff, those too went off with you?

PRAXAGORA: I was afraid they might rob me of the cloak, and so, to look like a man, I put on your shoes and walked with a heavy tread and struck the stones with your staff.

BLEPYRUS: D'you know you have made us lose a *sextary* of wheat, which I should have bought with the *triobolus* of the Assembly?

PRAXAGORA: Be comforted, for she had a boy.

BLEPYRUS: Who? the Assembly?

PRAXAGORA: No, no, the woman I helped. But has the Assembly taken place then?

BLEPYRUS: Did I not tell you of it yesterday?

PRAXAGORA: True; I remember now.

BLEPYRUS: And don't you know the decrees that have been voted?

PRAXAGORA: No indeed.

BLEPYRUS: Go to! you can eat cuttle-fish[48] now, for 'tis said the government is handed over to you.

PRAXAGORA: To do what—to spin?

BLEPYRUS: No, that you may rule. . .

PRAXAGORA: What?

BLEPYRUS: . . . over all public business.

PRAXAGORA: Oh! by Aphrodité! how happy Athens will be!

BLEPYRUS: Why so?

PRAXAGORA: For a thousand reasons. None will dare now to do shameless deeds, to give false testimony or lay informations.

BLEPYRUS: Stop! in the name of the gods! Do you want me to die of hunger?

CHORUS: Good sir, let your wife speak.

PRAXAGORA: There will be no more thieves, nor envious people, no more rags nor misery, no more abuse and no more prosecutions and lawsuits.

BLEPYRUS: By Posidon! 'tis grand, if true.

PRAXAGORA: The results will prove it; you will confess it, and even these good people (*pointing to the spectators*) will not be able to say a word.

CHORUS: You have served your friends, but now it behoves you to apply your ability and your care to the welfare of the people. Devote the fecundity of your mind to the public weal; adorn the citizens' lives with a thousand enjoyments and teach them to seize every favourable opportunity. Devise some ingenious method to secure the much-needed salvation of Athens; but let neither your acts nor your words recall anything of the past, for 'tis only innovations that please. Don't delay the realization of your plans, for speedy execution is greatly esteemed by the public.

PRAXAGORA: I believe my ideas are good, but what I fear is, that the public will cling to the old customs and refuse to accept my reforms.

BLEPYRUS: Have no fear about that. Love of novelty and disdain for the past, these are the dominating principles among us.

PRAXAGORA: Let none contradict nor interrupt me until I have explained my plan. I want all to have a share of everything and all

---

48. To eat cuttle-fish was synonymous with enjoying the highest felicity.

property to be in common; there will no longer be either rich or poor; no longer shall we see one man harvesting vast tracts of land, while another has not ground enough to be buried in, nor one man surround himself with a whole army of slaves, while another has not a single attendant; I intend that there shall only be one and the same condition of life for all.

BLEPYRUS: But how do you mean for all?

PRAXAGORA: Go and eat your excrements![49]

BLEPYRUS: Come, share and share alike!

PRAXAGORA: No, no, but you shall not interrupt me. This is what I was going to say: I shall begin by making land, money, everything that is private property, common to all. Then we shall live on this common wealth, which we shall take care to administer with wise thrift.

BLEPYRUS: And how about the man who has no land, but only gold and silver coins, that cannot be seen?

PRAXAGORA: He must bring them to the common stock, and if he fails he will be a perjured man.

BLEPYRUS: That won't worry him much, for has he not gained them by perjury?

PRAXAGORA: But his riches will no longer be of any use to him.

BLEPYRUS: Why?

PRAXAGORA: The poor will no longer be obliged to work; each will have all that he needs, bread, salt fish, cakes, tunics, wine, chaplets and chick-pease; of what advantage will it be to him not to contribute his share to the common wealth? What do you think of it?

BLEPYRUS: But is it not the folk who rob most that have all these things?

PRAXAGORA: Yes, formerly, under the old order of things; but now that all goods are in common, what will he gain by not bringing his wealth into the general stock?

BLEPYRUS: If someone saw a pretty wench and wished to satisfy his fancy for her, he would take some of his reserve store to make her a present and stay the night with her; this would not prevent him claiming his share of the common property.

---

49. A common vulgar saying, used among the Athenians, as much as to say, *To the devil with interruptions!*

PRAXAGORA: But he can sleep with her for nothing; I intend that women shall belong to all men in common, and each shall beget children by any man that wishes to have her.

BLEPYRUS: But all will go to the prettiest woman and beseech her to go with him.

PRAXAGORA: The ugliest and the most flat-nosed will be side by side with the most charming, and to win the latter's favours, a man will first have to get into the former.

BLEPYRUS: But we old men, shall we have penis enough if we have to satisfy the ugly first?

PRAXAGORA: They will make no resistance.

BLEPYRUS: To what?

PRAXAGORA: Never fear; they will make no resistance.

BLEPYRUS: Resistance to what?

PRAXAGORA: To the pleasure of the thing. 'Tis thus that matters will be ordered for you.

BLEPYRUS: 'Tis right well conceived for you women, for every wench's hole will be occupied; but as regards us poor men, you will leave those who are ugly to run after the handsome fellows.

PRAXAGORA: The ugly will follow the handsomest into the public places after supper and see to it that the law, which forbids the women to sleep with the big, handsome men before having satisfied the ugly shrimps, is complied with.

BLEPYRUS: Thus ugly Lysicrates' nose will be as proud as the handsomest face?

PRAXAGORA: Yes, by Apollo! this is a truly popular decree, and what a set-back 'twill be for one of those elegants with their fingers loaded with rings, when a man with heavy shoes says to him, "Give way to me and wait till I have done; you will pass in after me."

BLEPYRUS: But if we live in this fashion, how will each one know his children?

PRAXAGORA: The youngest will look upon the oldest as their fathers.

BLEPYRUS: Ah! how heartily they will strangle all the old men, since even now, when each one knows his father, they make no bones about strangling him! then, my word! won't they just scorn and shit upon the old folks!

PRAXAGORA: But those around will prevent it. Hitherto, when anyone saw an old man beaten, he would not meddle, because it did not concern him; but now each will fear the sufferer may be his own father and such violence will be stopped.

BLEPYRUS: What you say is not so silly after all; but 'twould be highly unpleasant were Epicurus and Leucolophas to come up and call me father.

PRAXAGORA: But 'twould be far worse, were. . .

BLEPYRUS: Were what?

PRAXAGORA: . . . Aristyllus to embrace you and style you his father.

BLEPYRUS: Ah! let him look to himself if he dares!

PRAXAGORA: For you would smell vilely of mint if he kissed you. But he was born before the decree was carried, so that you have not to fear his kiss.

BLEPYRUS: 'Twould be awful. But who will do the work?

PRAXAGORA: The slaves. Your only cares will be to scent yourself, and to go and dine, when the shadow of the gnomon is ten feet long on the dial.

BLEPYRUS: But how shall we obtain clothing? Tell me that!

PRAXAGORA: You will first wear out those you have, and then we women will weave you others.

BLEPYRUS: Now another point: if the magistrates condemn a citizen to the payment of a fine, how is he going to do it? Out of the public funds? That would not be right surely.

PRAXAGORA: But there will be no more lawsuits.

BLEPYRUS: What a disaster for many people!

PRAXAGORA: I have decreed it. Besides, friend, why should there be lawsuits?

BLEPYRUS: Oh! for a thousand reasons, on my faith! Firstly, because a debtor denies his obligation.

PRAXAGORA: But where will the lender get the money to lend, if all is in common? unless he steals it out of the treasury?

BLEPYRUS: That's true, by Demeter! But then again, tell me this; here are some men who are returning from a feast and are drunk and they strike some passer-by; how are they going to pay the fine? Ah! you are puzzled now!

PRAXAGORA: They will have to take it out of their pittance; and being thus punished through their belly, they will not care to begin again.

BLEPYRUS: There will be no more thieves then, eh?

PRAXAGORA: Why steal, if you have a share of everything?

BLEPYRUS: People will not be robbed any more at night?

PRAXAGORA: No, whether you sleep at home or in the street, there will be no more danger, for all will have the means of living. Besides, if anyone wanted to steal your cloak, you would give it him yourself. Why not? You will only have to go to the common store and be given a better one.

BLEPYRUS: There will be no more playing at dice?

PRAXAGORA: What object will there be in playing?

BLEPYRUS: But what kind of life is it you propose to set up?

PRAXAGORA: The life in common. Athens will become nothing more than a single house, in which everything will belong to everyone; so that everybody will be able to go from one house to the other at pleasure.

BLEPYRUS: And where will the meals be served?

PRAXAGORA: The law-courts and the porticoes will be turned into dining-halls.

BLEPYRUS: And what will the speaker's platform be used for?

PRAXAGORA: I shall place the bowls and the ewers there; and young children will sing the glory of the brave from there, also the infamy of cowards, who out of very shame will no longer dare to come to the public meals.

BLEPYRUS: Well thought of, by Apollo! And what will you do with the urns?

PRAXAGORA: I shall have them taken to the market-place, and standing close to the statue of Harmodius,[50] I shall draw a lot for each citizen, which by its letter will show the place where he must go to dine.[51] Thus, those for whom I have drawn a Beta, will go to the royal portico;[52] if 'tis a Theta, they will go to the portico of Theseus;[53] if 'tis a Kappa, to that of the flour-market.[54]

BLEPYRUS: To cram[55] himself there like a capon?

---

50. This stood in the centre of the market-place.

51. It was the custom at Athens to draw lots to decide in which Court each dicast should serve; Praxagora proposes to apply the same system to decide the dining station for each citizen.

52. In Greek (Greek: h e basileius)([Greek: stoa], understood), the first letter a (Greek: b eta.)

53. Commencing with a (Greek: Th eta).

54. (Greek: Ha alphitop olis stoa); why (Greek: kappa), it is hard to say; from some popular nickname probably, which is unknown to us.

55. The pun cannot be kept in English; it is between (Greek: kaptein), to gobble, to cram oneself, and (Greek: kappa), the designating letter.

PRAXAGORA: No, to dine there.

BLEPYRUS: And the citizen whom the lot has not given a letter showing where he is to dine will be driven off by everyone?

PRAXAGORA: But that will not occur. Each man will have plenty; he will not leave the feast until he is well drunk, and then with a chaplet on his head and a torch in his hand; and then the women running to meet you in the cross-roads will say, "This way, come to our house, you will find a beautiful young girl there."—"And I," another will call from her balcony, "have one so pretty and as white as milk; but before touching her, you must sleep with me." And the ugly men, watching closely after the handsome fellows, will say, "Hi! friend, where are you running to? Go in, but you must do nothing, for 'tis the ugly and the flat-nosed to whom the law gives the first right of admission; amuse yourself in the porch while you wait, in handling your fig-leaves and playing with your tool." Well, tell me, does that picture suit you?

BLEPYRUS: Marvellously well.

PRAXAGORA: I must now go to the market-place to receive the property that is going to be placed in common and to choose a woman with a loud voice as my herald. I have all the cares of State on my shoulders, since the power has been entrusted to me. I must likewise go to busy myself about establishing the common meals, and you will attend your first banquet to-day.

BLEPYRUS: Are we going to banquet?

PRAXAGORA: Why, undoubtedly! Furthermore, I propose abolishing the courtesans.

BLEPYRUS: And what for?

PRAXAGORA: 'Tis clear enough why; so that, instead of them, *we* may have the first-fruits of the young men. It is not meet that tricked-out slaves should rob free-born women of their pleasures. Let the courtesans be free to sleep with the slaves and to depilate their privates for them.

BLEPYRUS: I will march at your side, so that I may be seen and that everyone may say, "Admire our leader's husband!" (*Exeunt Blepyrus and Praxagora*)

(*The Chorus which followed this scene is lost*)

FIRST CITIZEN: Come, let us collect and examine all my belongings before taking them to the market-place. Come hither, my beautiful sieve, I have nothing more precious than you, come, all clotted with the flour of which I have poured so many sacks through you; you shall act the part of Canephoros[56] in the procession of my chattels. Where is the sunshade carrier?[57] Ah! this stew-pot shall take his place. Great gods, how black it is! it could not be more so if Lysicrates[58] had boiled the drugs in it with which he dyes his hair. Hither, my beautiful mirror. And you, my tripod, bear this urn for me; you shall be the waterbearer;[59] and you, cock, whose morning song has so often roused me in the middle of the night to send me hurrying to the Assembly, you shall be my flute-girl. Scaphephoros,[60] do you take the large basin, place in it the honeycombs and twine the olive-branches over them, bring the tripods and the phial of perfume; as for the humble crowd of little pots, I will just leave them behind.

SECOND CITIZEN: What folly to carry one's goods to the common store; I have a little more sense than that. No, no, by Posidon, I want first to ponder and calculate over the thing at leisure. I shall not be fool enough to strip myself of the fruits of my toil and thrift, if it is not for a very good reason; let us see first, which way things turn. Hi! friend, what means this display of goods? Are you moving or are you going to pawn your stuff?

FIRST CITIZEN: Neither.

SECOND CITIZEN: Why then are you setting all these things out in line? Is it a procession that you are starting off to the public crier, Hiero?

FIRST CITIZEN: No, but in accordance with the new law, that has been decreed, I am going to carry all these things to the marketplace to make a gift of them to the State.

SECOND CITIZEN: Oh! bah! you don't mean that.

FIRST CITIZEN: Certainly.

SECOND CITIZEN: Oh! Zeus the Deliverer! you unfortunate man!

FIRST CITIZEN: Why?

---

56. That is, one of the beautiful maidens selected to bear the baskets containing the sacred implements in procession at the Festival of Demeter, Bacchus and Athené.
57. The slave-girl who attended each Canephoros, and sheltered her from the sun's rays.
58. Mentioned a little above for his ugliness; the Scholiast says he was a general.
59. Hydriaphoros; the wives of resident aliens ([Greek: metoikoi]) were allowed to take part in these processions, but in a subordinate position; they carried vessels full of water for the service of the sacrifice.
60. Scaphephoros, bearer of the vases containing the honey required for the sacrifices. The office was assigned to the (Greek: metoikoi) as a recognition of their semi-citizenship.

SECOND CITIZEN: Why? 'Tis as clear as noonday.

FIRST CITIZEN: Must the laws not be obeyed then?

SECOND CITIZEN: What laws, you poor fellow?

FIRST CITIZEN: Those that have been decreed.

SECOND CITIZEN: Decreed! Are you mad, I ask you?

FIRST CITIZEN: Am I mad?

SECOND CITIZEN: Oh! this is the height of folly!

FIRST CITIZEN: Because I obey the law? Is that not the first duty of an honest man?

SECOND CITIZEN: Say rather of a ninny.

FIRST CITIZEN: Don't you propose taking what belongs to you to the common stock?

SECOND CITIZEN: I'll take good care I don't until I see what the majority are doing.

FIRST CITIZEN: There's but one opinion, namely, to contribute every single thing one has.

SECOND CITIZEN: I am waiting to see it, before I believe that.

FIRST CITIZEN: At least, so they say in every street.

SECOND CITIZEN: And they will go on saying so.

FIRST CITIZEN: Everyone talks of contributing all he has.

SECOND CITIZEN: And will go on talking of it.

FIRST CITIZEN: You weary me with your doubts and dubitations.

SECOND CITIZEN: Everybody else will doubt it.

FIRST CITIZEN: The pest seize you!

SECOND CITIZEN: It *will* take you. What? give up your goods! Is there a man of sense who will do such a thing? Giving is not one of our customs. Receiving is another matter; 'tis the way of the gods themselves. Look at the position of their hands on their statues; when we ask a favour, they present their hands turned palm up so as not to give, but to receive.

FIRST CITIZEN: Wretch, let me do what is right. Come, I'll make a bundle of all these things. Where is my strap?

SECOND CITIZEN: Are you really going to carry them in?

FIRST CITIZEN: Undoubtedly, and there are my three tripods strung together already.

SECOND CITIZEN: What folly! Not to wait to see what the others do, and then. . .

FIRST CITIZEN: Well, and then what?

SECOND CITIZEN: . . . wait and put it off again.

FIRST CITIZEN: What for?

SECOND CITIZEN: That an earthquake may come or an ill-omened flash of lightning, that a weasel may run across the street and that none carry in anything more, you fool!

FIRST CITIZEN: 'Twould be a fine matter, were I to find no room left for placing all this.

SECOND CITIZEN: You are much more likely to lose your stuff. As for placing it, you can be at ease, for there will be room enough as long as a month hence.

FIRST CITIZEN: Why?

SECOND CITIZEN: I know these folk; a decree is soon passed, but it is not so easily attended to.

FIRST CITIZEN: All will contribute their property, my friend.

SECOND CITIZEN: But what if they don't?

FIRST CITIZEN: But there is no doubt that they will.

SECOND CITIZEN: But *anyhow*, what if they don't?

FIRST CITIZEN: We shall compel them to do so.

SECOND CITIZEN: And what if they prove the stronger?

FIRST CITIZEN: I shall leave my goods and go off.

SECOND CITIZEN: And what if they sell them for you?

FIRST CITIZEN: The plague take you!

SECOND CITIZEN: And if it does?

FIRST CITIZEN: 'Twill be a good riddance.

SECOND CITIZEN: You are bent on contributing then?

FIRST CITIZEN: 'Pon my soul, yes! Look, there are all my neighbours carrying in all they have.

SECOND CITIZEN: Ha, ha! 'Tis no doubt Antisthenes.[61] He's a fellow who would rather sit on his pot for thirty days than not!

FIRST CITIZEN: The pest seize you!

SECOND CITIZEN: And perhaps Callimachus[62] is going to take in more money than Callias owns? That man want to ruin himself!

FIRST CITIZEN: How you weary me!

SECOND CITIZEN: Ah! I weary you! But, wretch, see what comes of decrees of this kind. Don't you remember the one reducing the price of salt, eh?

FIRST CITIZEN: Why, certainly I do.

---

61. A miser, who, moreover, was obstinately constipated.
62. Presumably a man in extreme poverty.

SECOND CITIZEN: And do you remember that about the copper coinage?

FIRST CITIZEN: Ah! that cursed money did me enough harm. I had sold my grapes and had my mouth stuffed with pieces of copper;[63] indeed I was going to the market to buy flour, and was in the act of holding out my bag wide open, when the herald started shouting, "Let none in future accept pieces of copper; those of silver are alone current."

SECOND CITIZEN: And quite lately, were we not all swearing that the impost of one-fortieth, which Euripides[64] had conceived, would bring five talents to the State, and everyone was vaunting Euripides to the skies? But when the thing was looked at closely, it was seen that this fine decree was mere moonshine and would produce nothing, and you would have willingly burnt this very same Euripides alive.

FIRST CITIZEN: The cases are quite different, my good fellow. We were the rulers then, but now 'tis the women.

SECOND CITIZEN: Whom, by Posidon, I will never allow to piss on my nose.

FIRST CITIZEN: I don't know what the devil you're chattering about. Slave, pick up that bundle.

HERALD: Let all citizens come, let them hasten at our leader's bidding! 'Tis the new law. The lot will teach each citizen where he is to dine; the tables are already laid and loaded with the most exquisite dishes; the couches are covered with the softest of cushions; the wine and water is already being mixed in the ewers; the slaves are standing in a row and waiting to pour scent over the guests; the fish is being grilled, the hares are on the spit and the cakes are being kneaded, chaplets are being plaited and the fritters are frying; the youngest women are watching the pea-soup in the saucepans, and in the midst of them all stands Smaeus,[65] dressed as a knight, washing the crockery. And Geres[66] has come, dressed in a grand tunic and finely shod; he is joking with another young

---

63. The ancients carried small coins in their mouth; this custom still obtains to-day in the East.

64. This Euripides was the son of the tragic poet.

65. This Smaeus was a notorious debauchee; the phrase contains obscene allusions, implying that he was ready both to ride a woman or to lick her privates—(Greek: kel etizein) or (Greek: lesbiazein).

66. Geres, an old fop, who wanted to pass as a young man.

ARISTOPHANES

fellow and has already divested himself of his heavy shoes and his cloak.[67] The pantryman is waiting, so come and use your jaws.

SECOND CITIZEN: Aye, I'll go. Why should I delay, since the Republic commands me?

FIRST CITIZEN: And where are you going to, since you have not deposited your belongings?

SECOND CITIZEN: To the feast.

FIRST CITIZEN: If the women have any wits, they will first insist on your depositing your goods.

SECOND CITIZEN: But I am going to deposit them.

FIRST CITIZEN: When?

SECOND CITIZEN: I am not the man to make delays.

FIRST CITIZEN: How do you mean?

SECOND CITIZEN: There will be many less eager than I.

FIRST CITIZEN: In the meantime you are going to dine.

SECOND CITIZEN: What else should I do? Every sensible man must give his help to the State.

FIRST CITIZEN: But if admission is forbidden you?

SECOND CITIZEN: I shall duck my head and slip in.

FIRST CITIZEN: And if the women have you beaten?

SECOND CITIZEN: I shall summon them.

FIRST CITIZEN: And if they laugh you in the face?

SECOND CITIZEN: I shall stand near the door. . .

FIRST CITIZEN: And then?

SECOND CITIZEN: . . . and seize upon the dishes as they pass.

FIRST CITIZEN: Then go there, but after me. Sicon and Parmeno,[68] pick up all the baggage.

SECOND CITIZEN: Come, I will help you carry it.

FIRST CITIZEN: No, no, I should be afraid of your pretending to the leader that what I am depositing belonged to you.

SECOND CITIZEN: Let me see! let me think of some good trick by which I can keep my goods and yet take my share of the common feast. Ha! that's a good notion! Quick! I'll go and dine, ha, ha! (*Exit laughing*)

FIRST OLD WOMAN: How is this? no men are coming? And yet it must be fully time! 'Tis then for naught that I have painted myself

---

67. According to Greek custom, these were left at the entrance of the banqueting-hall.
68. The names of his slaves.

with white lead, dressed myself in my beautiful yellow robe, and that I am here, frolicking and humming between my teeth to attract some passer-by! Oh, Muses, alight upon my lips, inspire me with some soft Ionian love-song!

A YOUNG GIRL: You rotten old thing, you have placed yourself at the window before me. You were expecting to strip my vines during my absence and to trap some man in your snares with your songs. If you sing, I shall follow suit; all this singing will weary the spectators, but is nevertheless very pleasant and very diverting.

FIRST OLD WOMAN: Ha! here is an old man; take him and lead him away. As for you, you young flute-player, let us hear some airs that are worthy of you and me. Let him who wishes to taste pleasure come to my side. These young things know nothing about it; 'tis only the women of ripe age who understand the art of love, and no one could know how to fondle the lover who possessed me so well as myself; the young girls are all flightiness.

YOUNG GIRL: Don't be jealous of the young girls; voluptuousness resides in the pure outline of their beautiful limbs and blossoms on their rounded bosoms; but you, old woman, you who are tricked out and perfumed as if for your own funeral, are an object of love only for grim Death himself.

FIRST OLD WOMAN: May your hole be stopped; may you be unable to find your couch when you want to be fucked. And on your couch, when your lips seek a lover, may you embrace only a viper!

YOUNG GIRL: Alas! alas! what is to become of me? There is no lover! I am left here alone; my mother has gone out and the rest care little for me. Oh! my dear nurse, I adjure you to call Orthagoras, and may heaven bless you.

FIRST OLD WOMAN: Ah! poor child, desire is consuming you like an Ionian woman; I think you are no stranger to the wanton arts of the Lesbian women, but you shall not rob me of my pleasures; you will not be able to reduce or filch the time that first belongs to me, for your own gain. Sing as much as you please, peep out like a cat lying in wait, but none shall pass through your door without first having been to see me.

YOUNG GIRL: If anyone enter your house, 'twill be to carry out your corpse.

FIRST OLD WOMAN: That's new to me.

YOUNG GIRL: What! you rotten wretch, can anything be new to an old hag like you?

FIRST OLD WOMAN: My old age will not harm you.

YOUNG GIRL: Ah! shame on your painted cheeks!

FIRST OLD WOMAN: Why do you speak to me at all?

YOUNG GIRL: And why do you place yourself at the window?

FIRST OLD WOMAN: I am singing to myself about my lover, Epigenes.

YOUNG GIRL: Can you have any other lover than that old fop Geres?

FIRST OLD WOMAN: Epigenes will show you that himself, for he is coming to me. See, here he is.

YOUNG GIRL: He's not thinking of you in the least, you old witch.

FIRST OLD WOMAN: Aye, but he is, you little pest.

YOUNG GIRL: Let's see what he will do. I will leave my window.

FIRST OLD WOMAN: And I likewise. You will see I am not far wrong.

A YOUNG MAN: Ah! could I but sleep with the young girl without first satisfying the old flat-nose! 'Tis intolerable for a free-born man.

FIRST OLD WOMAN: Willy nilly, you must first gratify my desire. There shall be no nonsense about that, for my authority is the law and the law must be obeyed in a democracy. But come, let me hide, to see what he's going to do.

YOUNG MAN: Ah! ye gods, if I were to find the sweet child alone! for the wine has fired my lust.

YOUNG GIRL: I have tricked that cursed old wretch; she has left her window, thinking I would stay at home.

FIRST OLD WOMAN: Ah! here is the lover we were talking of. This way, my love, this way, come here and haste to rest the whole night in my arms. I worship your lovely curly hair; I am consumed with ardent desire. Oh! Eros, in thy mercy, compel him to my bed.

YOUNG MAN (*standing beneath the young girl's window and singing*):[69] Come down and haste to open the door unless you want to see me fall dead with desire. Dearest treasure, I am burning to yield myself to most voluptuous sport, lying on your bosom, to let my hands play with your buttocks. Aphrodité, why dost thou fire me with such delight in her? Oh! Eros, I beseech thee, have mercy and make her share my couch. Words cannot express the tortures I am suffering. Oh! my adored one, I adjure you, open your door for me and press me to your heart; 'tis for you that I am suffering.

---

69. A specimen of the *serenades* ([Greek: paraklausithura]) of the Greeks.

Oh! my jewel, my idol, you child of Aphrodité, the confidante of the Muses, the sister of the Graces, you living picture of Voluptuousness, oh! open for me, press me to your heart, 'tis for you that I am suffering.

FIRST OLD WOMAN: Are you knocking? Is it I you seek?

YOUNG MAN: What an idea!

FIRST OLD WOMAN: But you were tapping at the door.

YOUNG MAN: Death would be sweeter.

FIRST OLD WOMAN: Why do you come with that torch in your hand?

YOUNG MAN: I am looking for a man from Anaphlystia.[70]

FIRST OLD WOMAN: What's his name?

YOUNG MAN: Oh! 'tis not Sebinus,[71] whom no doubt you are expecting.

FIRST OLD WOMAN: By Aphrodité, you *must*, whether you like it or not.

YOUNG MAN: We are not now concerned with cases dated sixty years back; they are remanded for a later day; we are dealing only with those of less than twenty.[72]

FIRST OLD WOMAN: That was under the old order of things, sweetheart, but now you must first busy yourself with us.

YOUNG MAN: Aye, *if I want to*, according to the rules of draughts, where we may either take or leave.

FIRST OLD WOMAN: But 'tis not according to the rules of draughts that you take your seat at the banquet.[73]

YOUNG MAN: I don't know what you mean; 'tis at this door I want to knock.

FIRST OLD WOMAN: Not before knocking at mine first.

YOUNG MAN: For the moment I really have no need for old leather.

FIRST OLD WOMAN: I know that you love me; perhaps you are surprised to find me at the door. But come, let me kiss you.

YOUNG MAN: No, no, my dear, I am afraid of your lover.

FIRST OLD WOMAN: Of whom?

---

70. An Attic deme. There is an obscene jest here; the word (Greek: anaphlan) means to masturbate.

71. (Greek: Ton Sebinon), a coined name, representing (Greek: ton se binounta), 'the man who is to tread you.'

72. The passage is written in the language of the Bar. It is an allusion to the slowness of justice at Athens.

73. I.e. the new law must be conformed to all round.

ARISTOPHANES

YOUNG MAN: The most gifted of painters.

FIRST OLD WOMAN: Why, whom do you mean to speak of?

YOUNG MAN: The artist who paints the little bottles on coffins.[74] But get you indoors, lest he should find you at the door.

FIRST OLD WOMAN: I know what you want.

YOUNG MAN: I can say as much of you.

FIRST OLD WOMAN: By Aphrodité, who has granted me this good chance, I won't let you go.

YOUNG MAN: You are drivelling, you little old hag.

FIRST OLD WOMAN: Rubbish! I am going to lead you to my couch.

YOUNG MAN: What need for buying hooks? I will let her down to the bottom of the well and pull up the buckets with her old carcase, for she's crooked enough for that.

FIRST OLD WOMAN: A truce to your jeering, poor boy, and follow me.

YOUNG MAN: Nothing compels me to do so, unless you have paid the levy of five hundredths for me.[75]

FIRST OLD WOMAN: Look, by Aphrodité, there is nothing that delights me as much as sleeping with a lad of your years.

YOUNG MAN: And I abhor such as you, and I will never, never consent.

FIRST OLD WOMAN: But, by Zeus, here is something will force you to it.

YOUNG MAN: What's that?

FIRST OLD WOMAN: A decree, which orders you to enter my house.

YOUNG MAN: Read it out then, and let's hear.

FIRST OLD WOMAN: Listen. "The women have decreed, that if a young man desires a young girl, he can only possess her after having satisfied an old woman; and if he refuses and goes to seek the maiden, the old women are authorized to seize him by his privates and so drag him in."

YOUNG MAN: Alas! I shall become a Procrustes.[76]

FIRST OLD WOMAN: Obey the law.

---

74. It was customary to paint phials or little bottles on the coffins of the poor; these emblems took the place of the perfumes that were sprinkled on the bodies of the rich.

75. I.e. unless I am your slave; no doubt this tax of five hundredths was paid by the master on the assumed value of his slave.—We have, however, no historical data to confirm this.

76. Nickname of the notorious brigand. The word means 'one who stretches and tortures,' from (Greek: prokrouein), and refers to his habit of fitting all his captives to the same bedstead—the 'bed of Procrustes'—stretching them if too short to the required length, lopping their limbs as required if they were too long. Here a further pun is involved, (Greek: prokrouein) meaning also 'to go with a woman first.'

YOUNG MAN: But if a fellow-citizen, a friend, came to pay my ransom?

FIRST OLD WOMAN: No man may dispose of anything above a medimnus.[77]

YOUNG MAN: But may I not enter an excuse?

FIRST OLD WOMAN: There's no evasion.

YOUNG MAN: I shall declare myself a merchant and so escape service.[78]

FIRST OLD WOMAN: Beware what you do!

YOUNG MAN: Well! what is to be done?

FIRST OLD WOMAN: Follow me.

YOUNG MAN: Is it absolutely necessary?

FIRST OLD WOMAN: Yes, as surely as if Diomedes had commanded it.[79]

YOUNG MAN: Well then, first spread out a layer of origanum[80] upon four pieces of wood; bind fillets round your head, bring phials of scent and place a bowl filled with lustral water before your door.[81]

FIRST OLD WOMAN: Will you buy a chaplet for me too?

YOUNG MAN: Aye, if you outlast the tapers; for I expect to see you fall down dead as you go in.

YOUNG GIRL: Where are you dragging this unfortunate man to?

FIRST OLD WOMAN: 'Tis my very own property that I am leading in.

YOUNG GIRL: You do ill. A young fellow like him is not of the age to suit you. You ought to be his mother rather than his wife. With these laws in force, the earth will be filled with Oedipuses.[82]

FIRST OLD WOMAN: Oh! you cursed pest! 'tis envy that makes you say this; but I will be revenged.

YOUNG MAN: By Zeus the Deliverer, what a service you have done me, by freeing me of this old wretch! with what ardour I will show you my gratitude in a form both long and thick!

---

77. Athenian law declared it illegal for a woman to contract any debt exceeding the price of a *medimnus* of corn; this law is now supposed to affect the men.

78. Merchants were exempt from military service; in this case, it is another kind of service that the old woman wants to exact from the young man.

79. A Thracian brigand, who forced strangers to share his daughters' bed, or be devoured by his horses.

80. Dead bodies were laid out on a layer of origanum, which is an aromatic plant.

81. The young man is here describing the formalities connected with the laying out of the dead.

82. Who had married his mother Jocasta without knowing it.

SECOND OLD WOMAN: Hi! you there! where are you taking that young man to, in spite of the law? The decree ordains that he must first sleep with me.

YOUNG MAN: Oh! what a misfortune! Where does *this* hag come from? 'Tis a more frightful monster than the other even.

SECOND OLD WOMAN: Come here.

YOUNG MAN (*to the young girl*): Oh! I adjure you, don't let me be led off by her!

SECOND OLD WOMAN: 'Tis not I; 'tis the law that leads you off.

YOUNG MAN: No, 'tis not the law, but an Empusa[83] with a body covered with blemishes and blotches.

SECOND OLD WOMAN: Follow me, my handsome little friend, come along quick without any more ado.

YOUNG MAN: Oh! let me first do the needful, so that I may gather my wits somewhat. Else I should be so terrified that you would see me letting out something yellow.

SECOND OLD WOMAN: Never mind! you can stool, if you want, in my house.

YOUNG MAN: Oh! I fear doing more than I want to; but I offer you two good securities.

SECOND OLD WOMAN: I don't require them.

THIRD OLD WOMAN: Hi! friend, where are you off to with that woman?

YOUNG MAN: I am not going with her, but am being dragged by force. Oh! whoever you are, may heaven bless you for having had pity on me in my dire misfortune. (*Turns round and sees the Third Old Woman*) Oh Heracles! oh Heracles! oh Pan! Oh ye Corybantes! oh ye Dioscuri! Why, she is still more awful! Oh! what a monster! great gods! Are you an ape plastered with white lead, or the ghost of some old hag returned from the dark borderlands of death?

THIRD OLD WOMAN: No jesting! Follow me.

SECOND OLD WOMAN: No, come this way.

THIRD OLD WOMAN: I will never let you go.

SECOND OLD WOMAN: Nor will I.

YOUNG MAN: But you will rend me asunder, you cursed wretches.

SECOND OLD WOMAN: 'Tis I he must go with according to the law.

THIRD OLD WOMAN: Not if an uglier old woman than yourself appears.

---

83. A hideous spectre that Hecaté was supposed to send to frighten men.

YOUNG MAN: But if you kill me at the outset, how shall I afterwards go to find this beautiful girl of mine?

THIRD OLD WOMAN: That's your business. But begin by obeying.

YOUNG MAN: Of which one must I rid myself first?

SECOND OLD WOMAN: Don't you know? Come here.

YOUNG MAN: Then let the other one release me.

THIRD OLD WOMAN: Come to my house.

YOUNG MAN: If this dame will let me go.

SECOND OLD WOMAN: No, by all the gods, I'll not let you go.

THIRD OLD WOMAN: Nor will I.

YOUNG MAN: You would make very bad boatwomen.

SECOND OLD WOMAN: Why?

YOUNG MAN: Because you would tear your passengers to pieces in dragging them on board.

SECOND OLD WOMAN: Then come along, do, and hold your tongue.

THIRD OLD WOMAN: No, by Zeus, come with me.

YOUNG MAN: 'Tis clearly a case of the decree of Cannonus;[84] I must cut myself in two in order to fuck you both. But how am I to work two oars at once?

SECOND OLD WOMAN: Easily enough; you have only to eat a full pot of onions.[85]

YOUNG MAN: Oh! great gods! here I am close to the door and being dragged in!

THIRD OLD WOMAN (*to Second Old Woman*): You will gain nothing by this, for I shall rush into your house with you.

YOUNG MAN: Oh, no! no! 'twould be better to suffer a single misfortune than two.

THIRD OLD WOMAN: Ah! by Hecaté, 'twill be all the same whether you wish it or not.

YOUNG MAN: What a fate is mine, that I must gratify such a stinking harridan the whole night through and all day; then, when I am rid of her, I have still to tackle a hag of brick-colour hue! Am I not truly unfortunate? Ah! by Zeus the Deliverer! under what fatal star must I have been born, that I must sail in company with such monsters! But if my bark sinks in the sewer of these strumpets,

---

84. Which provided that where a number of criminals were charged with the same offence, each must be tried separately.

85. As an aphrodisiac.

may I be buried at the very threshold of the door; let this hag be stood upright on my grave, let her be coated alive with pitch and her legs covered with molten lead up to the ankles, and let her be set alight as a funeral lamp.

A SERVANT-MAID TO PRAXAGORA (*she comes from the banquet*): What happiness is the people's! what joy is mine, and above all that of my mistress! Happy are ye, who form choruses before our house! Happy all ye, both neighbours and fellow-citizens! Happy am I myself! I am but a servant, and yet I have poured on my hair the most exquisite essences. Let thanks be rendered to thee, oh, Zeus! But a still more delicious aroma is that of the wine of Thasos; its sweet bouquet delights the drinker for a long enough, whereas the others lose their bloom and vanish quickly. Therefore, long life to the wine-jars of Thasos! Pour yourselves out unmixed wine, it will cheer you the whole night through, if you choose the liquor that possesses most fragrance. But tell me, friends, where is my mistress's husband?

CHORUS: Wait for him here; he will no doubt pass this way.

MAID-SERVANT: Ah! there he is just going to dinner. Oh! master! what joy! what blessedness is yours!

BLEPYRUS: Ah! d'you think so?

MAID-SERVANT: None can compare his happiness to yours; you have reached its utmost height, you who, alone out of thirty thousand citizens, have not yet dined.

CHORUS: Aye, here is undoubtedly a truly happy man.

MAID-SERVANT: Where are you off to?

BLEPYRUS: I am going to dine.

MAID-SERVANT: By Aphrodité, you will be the last of all, far and away the last. Yet my mistress has bidden me take you and take with you these young girls. Some Chian wine is left and lots of other good things. Therefore hurry, and invite likewise all the spectators whom we have pleased, and such of the judges as are not against us, to follow us; we will offer them everything they can desire. Let our hospitality be large and generous; forget no one, neither old nor young men, nor children. Dinner is ready for them all; they have but to go. . . home.[86]

---

86. We have already seen similar waggish endings to phrases in the 'Lysistrata'; the figure is called (Greek: para prosdokian)—'contrary to expectation.'

CHORUS: I am betaking myself to the banquet with this torch in my hand according to custom. But why do you tarry, Blepyrus? Take these young girls with you and, while you are away a while, I will whet my appetite with some dining-song. I have but a few words to say: let the wise judge me because of whatever is wise in this piece, and those who like a laugh by whatever has made them laugh. In this way I address pretty well everyone. If the lot has assigned my comedy to be played first of all, don't let that be a disadvantage to me; engrave in your memory all that shall have pleased you in it and judge the competitors equitably as you have bound yourselves by oath to do. Don't act like vile courtesans, who never remember any but their last lover. It is time, friends, high time to go to the banquet, if we want to have our share of it. Open your ranks and let the Cretan rhythms regulate your dances.[87]

SEMI-CHORUS: Ready; we are ready!

CHORUS: And you others, let your light steps too keep time. Very soon will be served a very fine menu*—oysters-saltfish-skate-sharks'-heads left-over-vinegar-dressing-laserpitium-leek-with-honey-sauce-thrush blackbird-pigeon-dove-roast-cock's-brains-wagtail-cushat-hare-stewed in-new-wine-gristle-of-veal-pullet's-wings.[88] Come, quick, seize hold of a plate, snatch up a cup, and let's run to secure a place at table. The rest will have their jaws at work by this time.

SEMI-CHORUS: Let up leap and dance, Io! evoë! Let us to dinner, Io! evoë. For victory is ours, victory is ours! Ho! Victory! Io! evoë!

FINIS OF "THE ECCLESIAZUSAE"

---

* Transcriber's note: In the original, all following words until 'wings' are connected with hyphens, i.e. they form *one* word.

87. Nothing is known as to these Cretan rhythms. According to the Scholiast, this is a jest, because the Cretans, who were great eaters, sat down to table early in the morning. This is what the Chorus supposes it is going to do, since 'The Ecclesiazusae' was played first, i.e. during the forenoon.

88. This wonderful word consists, in the original Greek, of seventy-seven syllables. For similar burlesque compounds see the 'Lysistrata,' 457, 458; 'Wasps,' 505 and 520. Compare Shakespeare, 'Love's Labour's Lost,' Act V. sc. 1: "I marvel thy master hath not eaten thee for a word; for thou art not so long by the head as *honorificabilitudinitatibus*." This is outdone by Rabelais' *Antipericatametaanaparbeugedamphicribrationibus*.

PLUTUS OR, WEALTH

Introduction

The 'Plutus' differs widely from all other works of its Author, and, it must be confessed, is the least interesting and diverting of them all. "In its absence of personal interests and personal satire," and its lack of strong comic incidents, "it approximates rather to a whimsical allegory than a comedy properly so called."

The plot is of the simplest. Chremylus, a poor but just man, accompanied by his body-servant Cario—the redeeming feature, by the by, of an otherwise dull play, the original type of the comic valet of the stage of all subsequent periods—consults the Delphic Oracle concerning his son, whether he ought not to be instructed in injustice and knavery and the other arts whereby worldly men acquire riches. By way of answer the god only tells him that he is to follow whomsoever he first meets upon leaving the temple, who proves to be a blind and ragged old man. But this turns out to be no other than Plutus himself, the god of riches, whom Zeus has robbed of his eyesight, so that he may be unable henceforth to distinguish between the just and the unjust. However, succoured by Chremylus and conducted by him to the Temple of Aesculapius, Plutus regains the use of his eyes. Whereupon all just men, including the god's benefactor, are made rich and prosperous, and the unjust reduced to indigence.

The play was, it seems, twice put upon the stage—first in 408 B.C., and again in a revised and reinforced edition, with allusions and innuendoes brought up to date, in 388 B.C., a few years before the Author's death. The text we possess—marred, however, by several considerable lacunae—is now generally allowed to be that of the piece as played at the later date, when it won the prize.

DRAMATIS PERSONAE

CHREMYLUS.
CARIO, Servant of Chremylus.
PLUTUS, God of Riches.
BLEPSIDEMUS, friend of Chremylus.
WIFE OF CHREMYLUS.
POVERTY.
A JUST MAN.
AN INFORMER, or Sycophant.
AN OLD WOMAN.
A YOUTH.
HERMES.
A PRIEST OF ZEUS.
CHORUS OF RUSTICS.

SCENE: *In front of a farmhouse—a road leading up to it.*

CARIO: What an unhappy fate, great gods, to be the slave of a fool!
A servant may give the best of advice, but if his master does not
follow it, the poor slave must inevitably have his share in the
disaster; for fortune does not allow him to dispose of his own body,
it belongs to his master who has bought it. Alas! 'tis the way of the
world. But the god, Apollo, whose oracles the Pythian priestess on
her golden tripod makes known to us, deserves my censure, for 'tis
assured he is a physician and a cunning diviner; and yet my master
is leaving his temple infected with mere madness and insists on
following a blind man. Is this not opposed to all good sense?
'Tis for us, who see clearly, to guide those who don't; whereas he
clings to the trail of a blind fellow and compels me to do the same
without answering my questions with ever a word. (*To Chremylus*)
Aye, master, unless you tell me why we are following this unknown
fellow, I will not be silent, but I will worry and torment you, for
you cannot beat me because of my sacred chaplet of laurel.

CHREMYLUS: No, but if you worry me I will take off your chaplet, and
then you will only get a sounder thrashing.

CARIO: That's an old song! I am going to leave you no peace till you
have told me who this man is; and if I ask it, 'tis entirely because of
my interest in you.

CHREMYLUS: Well, be it so. I will reveal it to you as being the most
faithful and the most rascally of all my servants.[1] I honoured the
gods and did what was right, and yet I was none the less poor and
unfortunate.

CARIO: I know it but too well.

CHREMYLUS: Other amassed wealth—the sacrilegious, the
demagogues, the informers,[2] indeed every sort of rascal.

CARIO: I believe you.

CHREMYLUS: Therefore I came to consult the oracle of the god, not
on my own account, for my unfortunate life is nearing its end, but

---

1. The poet jestingly makes Chremylus attribute two utterly opposed characteristics to
his servant.
2. Literally *sycophants* i.e. denouncers of figs. The Senate, says Plutarch, in very early times
had made a law forbidding the export of figs from Attica; those who were found breaking
the edict were fined to the advantage of the sycophant ([Greek: phainein], to denounce,
and [Greek: sukon], fig). Since the law was abused in order to accuse the innocent, the
name sycophant was given to calumniators and to the too numerous class of informers at
Athens who subsisted on the money their denunciations brought them.

for my only son; I wanted to ask Apollo, if it was necessary for him to become a thorough knave and renounce his virtuous principles, since that seemed to me to be the only way to succeed in life.

CARIO: And with what responding tones did the sacred tripod resound?[3]

CHREMYLUS: You shall know. The god ordered me in plain terms to follow the first man I should meet upon leaving the temple and to persuade him to accompany me home.

CARIO: And who was the first one you met?

CHREMYLUS: This blind man.

CARIO: And you are stupid enough not to understand the meaning of such an answer? Why, the god was advising you thereby, and that in the clearest possible way, to bring up your son according to the fashion of your country.

CHREMYLUS: What makes you think that?

CARIO: Is it not evident to the blind, that nowadays to do nothing that is right is the best way to get on?

CHREMYLUS: No, that is not the meaning of the oracle; there must be another, that is nobler. If this blind man would tell us who he is and why and with what object he has led us here, we should no doubt understand what our oracle really does mean.

CARIO (*to Plutus*): Come, tell us at once who you are, or I give effect to my threat. (*He menaces him*) And quick too, be quick, I say.

PLUTUS: I'll thrash you.

CARIO (*to Chremylus*): Ha! is it thus he tells us his name?

CHREMYLUS: 'Tis to you and not to me that he replies thus; your mode of questioning him was ill-advised. (*To Plutus*) Come, friend, if you care to oblige an honest man, answer me.

PLUTUS: I'll knock you down.

CARIO: Ah! what a pleasant fellow and what a delightful prophecy the god has given you!

CHREMYLUS: By Demeter, you'll have no reason to laugh presently.

CARIO: If you don't speak, you wretch, I will surely do you an ill turn.

PLUTUS: Friends, take yourselves off and leave me.

CHREMYLUS: That we very certainly shan't.

CARIO: This, master, is the best thing to do. I'll undertake to secure him the most frightful death; I will lead him to the verge of a

---

3. A parody of the tragic style.

precipice and then leave him there, so that he'll break his neck when he pitches over.

CHREMYLUS: Well then, I leave him to you, and do the thing quickly.

PLUTUS: Oh, no! Have mercy!

CHREMYLUS: Will you speak then?

PLUTUS: But if you learn who I am, I know well that you will ill-use me and will not let me go again.

CHREMYLUS: I call the gods to witness that you have naught to fear if you will only speak.

PLUTUS: Well then, first unhand me.

CHREMYLUS: There! we set you free.

PLUTUS: Listen then, since I must reveal what I had intended to keep a secret. I am Plutus.[4]

CHREMYLUS: Oh! you wretched rascal! You Plutus all the while, and you never said so!

CARIO: You, Plutus, and in this piteous guise!

CHREMYLUS: Oh, Phoebus Apollo! oh, ye gods of heaven and hell! Oh, Zeus! is it really and truly as you say?

PLUTUS: Aye.

CHREMYLUS: Plutus' very own self?

PLUTUS: His own very self and none other.

CHREMYLUS: But tell me, whence come you to be so squalid?

PLUTUS: I have just left Patrocles' house, who has not had a bath since his birth.[5]

CHREMYLUS: But your infirmity; how did that happen? Tell me.

PLUTUS: Zeus inflicted it on me, because of his jealousy of mankind. When I was young, I threatened him that I would only go to the just, the wise, the men of ordered life; to prevent my distinguishing these, he struck me with blindness! so much does he envy the good!

---

4. Plutus, the god of riches, was included amongst the infernal deities, because riches are extracted from the earth's bosom, which is their dwelling-place. According to Hesiod, he was the son of Demeter; agriculture is in truth the most solid foundation of wealth. He was generally represented as an old blind man, halting in gait and winged, coming with slow steps but going away on a rapid flight and carrying a purse in his hand. At Athens the statue of Peace bore Plutus represented as still a child on her bosom as a symbol of the wealth that peace brings.

5. A rich man, who affected the sordid habits of Lacedaemon, because of his greed. "More sordid than Patrocles" had become a byword at Athens. Even the public baths were too dear for Patrocles, because, in addition to the modest fee that was given to the bath-man, it was necessary to use a little oil for the customary friction after the bath.

CHREMYLUS: And yet, 'tis only the upright and just who honour him.

PLUTUS: Quite true.

CHREMYLUS: Therefore, if ever you recovered your sight, you would shun the wicked?

PLUTUS: Undoubtedly.

CHREMYLUS: You would visit the good?

PLUTUS: Assuredly. It is a very long time since I saw them.

CHREMYLUS: That's not astonishing. I, who see clearly, don't see a single one.

PLUTUS: Now let me leave you, for I have told you everything.

CHREMYLUS: No, certainly not! we shall fasten ourselves on to you faster than ever.

PLUTUS: Did I not tell you, you were going to plague me?

CHREMYLUS: Oh! I adjure you, believe what I say and don't leave me; for you will seek in vain for a more honest man than myself.

CARIO: There is only one man more worthy; and that is I.

PLUTUS: All talk like this, but as soon as they secure my favours and grow rich, their wickedness knows no bounds.

CHREMYLUS: And yet all men are not wicked.

PLUTUS: All. There's no exception.

CARIO: You shall pay for that opinion.

CHREMYLUS: Listen to what happiness there is in store for you, if you but stay with us. I have hope; aye, I have good hope with the god's help to deliver you from that blindness, in fact to restore your sight.

PLUTUS: Oh! do nothing of the kind, for I don't wish to recover it.

CHREMYLUS: What's that you say?

CARIO: This fellow hugs his own misery.

PLUTUS: If you were mad enough to cure me, and Zeus heard of it, he would overwhelm me with his anger.

CHREMYLUS: And is he not doing this now by leaving you to grope your wandering way?

PLUTUS: I don't know; but I'm horribly afraid of him.

CHREMYLUS: Indeed? Ah! you are the biggest poltroon of all the gods! Why, Zeus with his throne and his lightnings would not be worth an obolus if you recovered your sight, were it but for a few instants.

PLUTUS: Impious man, don't talk like that.

CHREMYLUS: Fear nothing! I will prove to you that you are far more powerful and mightier than he.

PLUTUS: I mightier than he?

CHREMYLUS: Aye, by heaven! For instance, what is the origin of the power that Zeus wields over the other gods?[6]

CARIO: 'Tis money; he has so much of it.

CHREMYLUS: And who gives it to him?

CARIO (*pointing to Plutus*): This fellow.

CHREMYLUS: If sacrifices are offered to him, is not Plutus their cause?

CARIO: Undoubtedly, for 'tis wealth that all demand and clamour most loudly for.

CHREMYLUS: Thus 'tis Plutus who is the fount of all the honours rendered to Zeus, whose worship he can wither up at the root, if it so please him.

PLUTUS: And how so?

CHREMYLUS: Not an ox, nor a cake, nor indeed anything at all could be offered, if you did not wish it.

PLUTUS: Why?

CHREMYLUS: Why? but what means are there to buy anything if you are not there to give the money? Hence if Zeus should cause you any trouble, you will destroy his power without other help.

PLUTUS: So 'tis because of me that sacrifices are offered to him?

CHREMYLUS: Most assuredly. Whatever is dazzling, beautiful or charming in the eyes of mankind, comes from you. Does not everything depend on wealth?

CARIO: I myself was bought for a few coins; if I'm a slave, 'tis only because I was not rich.

CHREMYLUS: And what of the Corinthian courtesans?[7] If a poor man offers them proposals, they do not listen; but if it be a rich one, instantly they offer their buttocks for his pleasure.

CARIO: 'Tis the same with the lads; they care not for love, to them money means everything.

CHREMYLUS: You speak of those who accept all comers; yet some of them are honest, and 'tis not money they ask of their patrons.

---

6. This catechizing is completely in the manner of the sophistical teaching of the times, and has its parallel in other comedies. It reminds us in many ways of the Socratic 'Elenchus' as displayed in the Platonic dialogues.

7. Corinth was the most corrupt as well as the most commercial of Greek cities, and held a number of great courtesans, indeed some of the most celebrated, e.g. Laïs, Cyrené, Sinopé, practised their profession there; they, however, set a very high value on their favours, and hence the saying, "*Non cuivis homini contingit adire Corinthum*"—"it is not for every man to go to Corinth."

CARIO: What then?

CHREMYLUS: A fine horse, a pack of hounds.

CARIO: Aye, they would blush to ask for money and cleverly disguise their shame.

CHREMYLUS: 'Tis in you that every art, all human inventions, have had their origin; 'tis through you that one man sits cutting leather in his shop.

CARIO: That another fashions iron or wood.

CHREMYLUS: That yet another chases the gold he has received from you.

CARIO: That one is a fuller.

CHREMYLUS: That t'other washes wool.

CARIO: That this one is a tanner.

CHREMYLUS: And that other sells onions.

CARIO: And if the adulterer, caught red-handed, is depilated,[8] 'tis on account of you.[9]

PLUTUS: Oh! great gods! I knew naught of all this!

CARIO: Is it not he who lends the Great King all his pride?

CHREMYLUS: Is it not he who draws the citizens to the Assembly?[10]

CARIO: And tell me, is it not you who equip the triremes?[11]

CHREMYLUS: And who feed our mercenaries at Corinth?[12]

CARIO: Are not you the cause of Pamphilus' sufferings?[13]

CHREMYLUS: And of the needle-seller's[14] with Pamphilus?

CARIO: Is it not because of you that Agyrrhius[15] lets wind so loudly?

---

8. This was the mild punishment inflicted upon the adulterer by Athenian custom. The laws of Solon were very indulgent to this kind of crime; they only provided that the guilty woman might be repudiated by her husband, but were completely silent concerning her accomplice.

9. Cario means to convey that women often paid their lovers, or at all events made it their business to open up the road to fortune for them.

10. In order to receive the *triobolus,* the fee for attendance.

11. The richest citizens were saddled with this expense and were called trierarchs.

12. Athens had formed an alliance with Corinth and Thebes against Sparta in 393 B.C., a little before the production of the 'Plutus.' Corinth, not feeling itself strong enough to resist the attacks of the Spartans unaided, had demanded the help of an Athenian garrison, and hence Athens maintained some few thousand mercenaries there.

13. A civil servant, who had been exiled for embezzling State funds.

14. No doubt an accomplice of Pamphilus in his misdeeds; the Scholiast says he was one of his parasites.

15. An upstart and, through the favour of the people, an admiral in the year 389 B.C., after Thrasybulus; he had enriched himself through some rather equivocal state employments and was insolent, because of his wealth, 'as a well-fed ass.'

CHREMYLUS: And that Philepsius[16] rolls off his fables?

CARIO: That troops are sent to succour the Egyptians?[17]

CHREMYLUS: And that Laïs is kept by Philonides?[18]

CARIO: That the tower of Timotheus[19] . . .

CHREMYLUS: . . . (*To Cario*) May it fall upon your head! (*To Plutus*) In short, Plutus, 'tis through you that everything is done; be it known to you that you are the sole cause both of good and evil.

CARIO: In war, 'tis the flag under which you serve that victory favours.

PLUTUS: What! I can do so many things by myself and unaided?

CHREMYLUS: And many others besides; wherefore men are never tired of your gifts. They get weary of all else,—of love. . .

CARIO: Of bread.

CHREMYLUS: Of music.

CARIO: Of sweetmeats.

CHREMYLUS: Of honours.

CARIO: Of cakes.

CHREMYLUS: Of battles.

CARIO: Of figs.

CHREMYLUS: Of ambition.

CARIO: Of gruel.

CHREMYLUS: Of military advancement.

CARIO: Of lentils.[20]

CHREMYLUS: But of you they never tire. Has a man got thirteen talents, he has all the greater ardour to possess sixteen; is that wish achieved, he will want forty or will complain that he knows not how to make the two ends meet.

---

16. A buffoon, so the Scholiasts inform us, who was in the habit of visiting the public places of the city in order to make a little money by amusing the crowd with ridiculous stories. Others say he was a statesman of the period, who was condemned for embezzlement of public money; in his defence he may well have invented some fabulous tales to account for the disappearance of the money out of the Treasury.

17. The precise historical reference here is obscure.

18. Laïs, a celebrated courtesan.—Of Philonides little is known, except that he was a native of Melita and a rich and profligate character.

19. The reference is no doubt to a pretentious construction that had been built for the rich and over-proud Timotheus, the son of Conon. He was a clever general of great integrity; when the 'Plutus' was produced, he was still very young.

20. Chremylus rises in a regular climax from love to military glory; the slave in as direct an anti-climax comes from bread, sweetmeats, etc., down to lentils.

PLUTUS: All this, methinks, is very true; there is but one point that makes me feel a bit uneasy.

CHREMYLUS: And that is?

PLUTUS: How could I use this power, which you say I have?

CHREMYLUS: Ah! they were quite right who said, there's nothing more timorous than Plutus.

PLUTUS: No, no; it was a thief who calumniated me. Having broken into a house, he found everything locked up and could take nothing, so he dubbed my prudence fear.

CHREMYLUS: Don't be disturbed; if you support me zealously, I'll make you more sharp-sighted than Lynceus.[21]

PLUTUS: And how should you be able to do that, you, who are but a mortal?

CHREMYLUS: I have great hope, after the answer Apollo gave me, shaking his sacred laurels the while.

PLUTUS: Is *he* in the plot then?

CHREMYLUS: Aye, truly.

PLUTUS: Take care what you say.

CHREMYLUS: Never fear, friend; for, be well assured, that if it has to cost me my life, I will carry out what I have in my head.

CARIO: And I will help you, if you permit it.

CHREMYLUS: We shall have many other helpers as well—all the worthy folk who are wanting for bread.

PLUTUS: Ah! ha! they'll prove sorry helpers.

CHREMYLUS: No, not so, once they've grown rich. But you, Cario, run quick. . .

CARIO: Where?

CHREMYLUS: . . . to call my comrades, the other husbandmen, that each of them may come here to take his share of the gifts of Plutus.

CARIO: I'm off. But let someone come from the house to take this morsel of meat.[22]

---

21. The son of Aphareus, the King of Messenia; according to the legends, he had such piercing sight that he could see through walls, and could even discover what was going on in heaven and in the nether world. He took part in the expedition of the Argonauts.

22. A part of the victim which Cario was bringing back from the Temple; it was customary to present the remains of a sacrifice to friends and relations.

CHREMYLUS: I'll see to that; you run your hardest. As for you, Plutus, the most excellent of all the gods, come in here with me; this is the house you must fill with riches today, by fair means or foul.[23]

PLUTUS: I don't like at all going into other folks' houses in this manner; I have never got any good from it. If I got inside a miser's house, straightway he would bury me deep underground; if some honest fellow among his friends came to ask him for the smallest coin, he would deny ever having seen me. Then if I went to a fool's house, he would sacrifice me as a prey to gaming and to girls, and very soon I should be completely stripped and pitched out of doors.

CHREMYLUS: That's because you have never met a man who knew how to avoid the two extremes; moderation is the strong point in my character. I love saving as much as anybody, and I know how to spend, when 'tis needed. But let us go in; I want to make you known to my wife and to my only son, whom I love most of all after yourself.

PLUTUS: Aye, after myself, I'm very sure of that.

CHREMYLUS: Why should I hide the truth from you?

CARIO: Come, you active workers, who, like my master, eat nothing but garlic and the poorest food, you who are his friends and his neighbours, hasten your steps, hurry yourselves; there's not a moment to lose; this is the critical hour, when your presence and your support is needed by him.

CHORUS: Why, don't you see we are speeding as fast as men can, who are already enfeebled by age? But do you deem it fitting to make us run like this before ever telling us why your master has called us?

CARIO: I've grown hoarse with the telling, but you won't listen. My master is going to drag you all out of the stupid, sapless life you are leading and ensure you one full of all delights.

CHORUS: And how is he going to manage that?

CARIO: My poor friends, he has brought with him a disgusting old fellow, all bent and wrinkled, with a most pitiful appearance, bald and toothless; upon my word, I even believe he is circumcised like some vile barbarian.

CHORUS: These are news worth their weight in gold! What are you saying? Repeat it to me; no doubt it means he is bringing back a heap of wealth.

CARIO: No, but a heap of all the infirmities attendant on old age.

---

23. As soon as Chremylus sees himself assured of wealth he adopts less honest principles.

CHORUS: If you are tricking us, you shall pay us for it. Beware of our sticks!

CARIO: Do you deem me so brazen as all that, and my words mere lies?

CHORUS: What serious airs the rascal puts on! Look! his legs are already shrieking, "oh! oh!" they are asking for the shackles and wedges.

CARIO: 'Tis in the tomb that 'tis your lot to judge. Why don't you go there? Charon has given you your ticket.[24]

CHORUS: Plague take you! you cursed rascal, who rail at us and have not even the heart to tell us why your master has made us come. We were pressed for time and tired out, yet we came with all haste, and in our hurry we have passed by lots of wild onions without even gathering them.

CARIO: I will no longer conceal the truth from you. Friends, 'tis Plutus whom my master brings, Plutus, who will give you riches.

CHORUS: What! we shall really all become rich!

CARIO: Aye, certainly; you will then be Midases, provided you grow ass's ears.

CHORUS: What joy, what happiness! If what you tell me is true, I long to dance with delight.

CARIO: And I too, threttanello![25] I want to imitate Cyclops and lead your troop by stamping like this.[26] Do you, my dear little ones, cry, aye, cry again and bleat forth the plaintive song of the sheep and of the stinking goats; follow me with erected organs like lascivious goats ready for action.

CHORUS: As for us, threttanello! we will seek you, dear Cyclops, bleating, and if we find you with your wallet full of fresh herbs, all disgusting in your filth, sodden with wine and sleeping in the

---

24. The citizens appointed to act as dicasts, or jurymen, drew lots each year to decide in which Court they should sit. There were ten Courts, each of which was indicated by one of the first ten letters of the alphabet, and the urn contained as many tickets marked with these letters as there were dicasts. Cario means to say here that the old men of the Chorus should remember that they have soon to die themselves instead of bothering about punishing him.

25. A word invented to imitate the sound of a lyre.

26. The Cyclops let his flocks graze while he played the lyre; it was thus that Philoxenus had represented him in a piece to which Aristophanes is here alluding.—Cario assumes the part of the Cyclops and leaves that of the flock to the Chorus.

midst of your sheep, we will seize a great flaming stake and burn out your eye.[27]

CARIO: I will copy that Circé of Corinth,[28] whose potent philtres compelled the companions of Philonides to swallow balls of dung, which she herself had kneaded with her hands, as if they were swine; and do you too grunt with joy and follow your mother, my little pigs.

CHORUS: Oh! Circé[29] with the potent philtres, who besmear your companions so filthily, what pleasure I shall have in imitating the son of Laertes! I will hang you up by your testicles,[30] I will rub your nose with dung like a goat, and like Aristyllus[31] you shall say through your half-opened lips, "Follow your mother, my little pigs."

CARIO: Enough of tomfoolery, assume a grave demeanour; unknown to my master I am going to take bread and meat; and when I have fed well, I shall resume my work.

CHREMYLUS: To say, "Hail! my dear neighbours!" is an old form of greeting and well worn with use; so therefore I embrace you, because you have not crept like tortoises, but have come rushing here in all haste. Now help me to watch carefully and closely over the god.

CHORUS: Be at ease. You shall see with what martial zeal I will guard him. What! we jostle each other at the Assembly for three obols, and am I going to let Plutus in person be stolen from me?

CHREMYLUS: But I see Blepsidemus; by his bearing and his haste I can readily see he knows or suspects something.

BLEPSIDEMUS: What has happened then? Whence, how has Chremylus suddenly grown rich? I don't believe a word of it. Nevertheless, nothing but his sudden fortune was being talked about in the barbers' booths. But I am above all surprised that his good fortune has not made him forget his friends; that is not the usual way!

CHREMYLUS: By the gods, Blepsidemus, I will hide nothing from you. To-day things are better than yesterday; let us share, for are you not my friend?

---

27. In allusion to Ulysses' adventures in the cave of Polyphemus.
28. Laïs.
29. I.e. Cario, who is assuming the rôle of Circé of Corinth.
30. This was the torture which Odysseus inflicted on Melanthius, one of the goatherds.
31. A poet of debauched and degraded life, one of those who, like Ariphrades mentioned in 'The Knights,' "defiled his tongue with abominable sensualities," that is to say, was a *fellator* and a *cunnilingue.*

BLEPSIDEMUS: Have you really grown rich as they say?

CHREMYLUS: I shall be soon, if the god agrees to it. But there is still some risk to run.

BLEPSIDEMUS: What risk?

CHREMYLUS: What risk?

BLEPSIDEMUS: What do you mean? Explain.

CHREMYLUS: If we succeed, we are happy for ever, but if we fail, it is all over with us.

BLEPSIDEMUS: 'Tis a bad business, and one that doesn't please me! To grow rich all at once and yet to be fearful! ah! I suspect something that's little good.

CHREMYLUS: What do you mean, that's little good?

BLEPSIDEMUS: No doubt you have just stolen some gold and silver from some temple and are repenting.

CHREMYLUS: Nay! heaven preserve me from that!

BLEPSIDEMUS: A truce to idle phrases! the thing is only too apparent, my friend.

CHREMYLUS: Don't suspect such a thing of me.

BLEPSIDEMUS: Alas! then there is no honest man! not one, that can resist the attraction of gold!

CHREMYLUS: By Demeter, you have no common sense.

BLEPSIDEMUS: To have to persist like this in denial one's whole life long!

CHREMYLUS: But, good gods, you are mad, my dear fellow!

BLEPSIDEMUS: His very look is distraught; he has done some crime!

CHREMYLUS: Ah! I know the tune you are playing now; you think I have stolen, and want your share.

BLEPSIDEMUS: My share of what, pray?

CHREMYLUS: You are beside the mark; the thing is quite otherwise.

BLEPSIDEMUS: 'Tis perhaps not a theft, but some piece of knavery!

CHREMYLUS: You are insane!

BLEPSIDEMUS: What? You have done no man an injury?

CHREMYLUS: No! assuredly not!

BLEPSIDEMUS: But, great gods, what am I to think? You won't tell me the truth.

CHREMYLUS: You accuse me without really knowing anything.

BLEPSIDEMUS: Listen, friend, no doubt the matter can yet be hushed up, before it gets noised abroad, at trifling expense; I will buy the orators' silence.

CHREMYLUS: Aye, you will lay out three minae and, as my friend, you will reckon twelve against me.

BLEPSIDEMUS: I know someone who will come and seat himself at the foot of the tribunal, holding a supplicant's bough in his hand and surrounded by his wife and children, for all the world like the Heraclidae of Pamphilus.[32]

CHREMYLUS: Not at all, poor fool! But, thanks to me, worthy folk, intelligent and moderate men alone shall be rich henceforth.

BLEPSIDEMUS: What are you saying? Have you then stolen so much as all that?

CHREMYLUS: Oh! your insults will be the death of me.

BLEPSIDEMUS: 'Tis rather you yourself who are courting death.

CHREMYLUS: Not so, you wretch, since I have Plutus.

BLEPSIDEMUS: You have Plutus? Which one?

CHREMYLUS: The god himself.

BLEPSIDEMUS: And where is he?

CHREMYLUS: There.

BLEPSIDEMUS: Where?

CHREMYLUS: Indoors.

BLEPSIDEMUS: Indoors?

CHREMYLUS: Aye, certainly.

BLEPSIDEMUS: Get you gone! Plutus in your house?

CHREMYLUS: Yes, by the gods!

BLEPSIDEMUS: Are you telling me the truth?

CHREMYLUS: I am.

BLEPSIDEMUS: Swear it by Hestia.

CHREMYLUS: I swear it by Posidon.

BLEPSIDEMUS: The god of the sea?

CHREMYLUS: Aye, and by all the other Posidons, if such there be.

BLEPSIDEMUS: And you don't send him to us, to your friends?

CHREMYLUS: We've not got to that point yet.

BLEPSIDEMUS: What do you say? Is there no chance of sharing?

CHREMYLUS: Why, no. We must first. . .

BLEPSIDEMUS: Do what?

CHREMYLUS: . . . restore him his sight.

---

32. It is uncertain whether Pamphilus, a tragedian, is meant here, who, like Euripides and Aeschylus, made the Heraclidae the subject of a tragedy, or the painter of that name, so celebrated in later times, who painted that subject in the Poecilé Stoa.

BLEPSIDEMUS: Restore whom his sight? Speak!

CHREMYLUS: Plutus. It must be done, no matter how.

BLEPSIDEMUS: Is he then really blind?

CHREMYLUS: Yes, undoubtedly.

BLEPSIDEMUS: I am no longer surprised he never came to me.

CHREMYLUS: And it please the gods, he'll come there now.

BLEPSIDEMUS: Must we not go and seek a physician?

CHREMYLUS: Seek physicians at Athens? Nay! there's no art where there's no fee.[33]

BLEPSIDEMUS: Let's bethink ourselves well.

CHREMYLUS: There is not one.

BLEPSIDEMUS: 'Tis a positive fact, I don't know of one.

CHREMYLUS: But I have thought the matter well over, and the best thing is to make Plutus lie in the Temple of Aesculapius.[34]

BLEPSIDEMUS: Aye, unquestionably 'tis the very best thing. Be quick and lead him away to the Temple.

CHREMYLUS: I am going there.

BLEPSIDEMUS: Then hurry yourself.

CHREMYLUS: 'Tis just what I am doing.

POVERTY: Unwise, perverse, unholy men! What are you daring to do, you pitiful, wretched mortals? Whither are you flying? Stop! I command it!

BLEPSIDEMUS: Oh! great gods!

POVERTY: My arm shall destroy you, you infamous beings! Such an attempt is not to be borne; neither man nor god has ever dared the like. You shall die!

CHREMYLUS: And who are you? Oh! what a ghastly pallor!

BLEPSIDEMUS: 'Tis perchance some Erinnys, some Fury, from the theatre;[35] there's a kind of wild tragedy look in her eyes.

CHREMYLUS: But she has no torch.

BLEPSIDEMUS: Let's knock her down!

POVERTY: Who do you think I am?

---

33. Physicians at Athens were paid very indifferently, and hence the most skilled sought their practice in other cities.

34. The Temple of Aesculapius stood on the way from the theatre to the citadel and near the tomb of Talos. A large number of invalids were taken there to pass a night; it was believed that the god visited them without being seen himself, because of the darkness, and arranged for their restoration to health.

35. Like the Furies who composed the Chorus in Aeschylus' 'Eumenides.'

ARISTOPHANES

CHREMYLUS: Some wine-shop keeper or egg-woman. Otherwise you would not have shrieked so loud at us, who have done nothing to you.

POVERTY: Indeed? And have you not done me the most deadly injury by seeking to banish me from every country?

CHREMYLUS: Why, have you not got the Barathrum[36] left? But who are you? Answer me quickly!

POVERTY: I am one that will punish you this very day for having wanted to make me disappear from here.

BLEPSIDEMUS: Might it be the tavern-keeper in my neighbourhood, who is always cheating me in measure?

POVERTY: I am Poverty, who have lived with you for so many years.

BLEPSIDEMUS: Oh! great Apollo! oh, ye gods! whither shall I fly?

CHREMYLUS: Now then! what are you doing? You poltroon! Will you kindly stop here?

BLEPSIDEMUS: Not I.

CHREMYLUS: Will you have the goodness to stop. Are two men to fly from a woman?

BLEPSIDEMUS: But, you wretch, 'tis Poverty, the most fearful monster that ever drew breath.

CHREMYLUS: Stay where you are, I beg of you.

BLEPSIDEMUS: No! no! a thousand times, no!

CHREMYLUS: Could we do anything worse than leave the god in the lurch and fly before this woman without so much as ever offering to fight?

BLEPSIDEMUS: But what weapons have we? Are we in a condition to show fight? Where is the breastplate, the buckler, that this wretch has not pledged?

CHREMYLUS: Be at ease. Plutus will readily triumph over her threats unaided.

POVERTY: Dare you reply, you scoundrels, you who are caught red-handed at the most horrible crime?

CHREMYLUS: As for you, you cursed jade, you pursue me with your abuse, though I have never done you the slightest harm.

POVERTY: Do you think it is doing me no harm to restore Plutus to the use of his eyes?

---

36. A ravine into which criminals were hurled at Athens.

CHREMYLUS: Is this doing you harm, that we shower blessings on all men?

POVERTY: And what do you think will ensure their happiness?

CHREMYLUS: Ah! first of all we shall drive you out of Greece.

POVERTY: Drive me out? Could you do mankind a greater harm?

CHREMYLUS: Yes—if I gave up my intention to deliver them from you.

POVERTY: Well, let us discuss this point first. I propose to show that I am the sole cause of all your blessings, and that your safety depends on me alone. If I don't succeed, then do what you like to me.

CHREMYLUS: How dare you talk like this, you impudent hussy?

POVERTY: Agree to hear me and I think it will be very easy for me to prove that you are entirely on the wrong road, when you want to make the just men wealthy.

BLEPSIDEMUS: Oh! cudgel and rope's end, come to my help!

POVERTY: Why such wrath and these shouts, before you hear my arguments?

BLEPSIDEMUS: But who could listen to such words without exclaiming?

POVERTY: Any man of sense.

CHREMYLUS: But if you lose your case, what punishment will you submit to?

POVERTY: Choose what you will.

CHREMYLUS: That's all right.

POVERTY: You shall suffer the same if you are beaten!

CHREMYLUS: Do you think twenty deaths a sufficiently large stake?

BLEPSIDEMUS: Good enough for her, but for us two would suffice.

POVERTY: You won't escape, for is there indeed a single valid argument to oppose me with?

CHORUS: To beat her in this debate, you must call upon all your wits. Make no allowances and show no weakness!

CHREMYLUS: It is right that the good should be happy, that the wicked and the impious, on the other hand, should be miserable; that is a truth, I believe, which no one will gainsay. To realize this condition of things is as great a proposal as it is noble and useful in every respect, and we have found a means of attaining the object of our wishes. If Plutus recovers his sight and ceases from wandering about unseeing and at random, he will go to seek the just men and never leave them again; he will shun the perverse and ungodly; so, thanks to him, all men will become honest, rich and pious. Can anything better be conceived for the public weal?

BLEPSIDEMUS: Of a certainty, no! I bear witness to that. It is not even necessary she should reply.

CHREMYLUS: Does it not seem that everything is extravagance in the world, or rather madness, when you watch the way things go? A crowd of rogues enjoy blessings they have won by sheer injustice, while more honest folks are miserable, die of hunger, and spend their whole lives with you.

CHORUS: Yes, if Plutus became clear-sighted again and drove out Poverty, 'twould be the greatest blessing possible for the human race.

POVERTY: Here are two old men, whose brains are easy to confuse, who assist each other to talk rubbish and drivel to their hearts' content. But if your wishes were realized, your profit would be great! Let Plutus recover his sight and divide his favours out equally to all, and none will ply either trade or art any longer; all toil would be done away with. Who would wish to hammer iron, build ships, sew, turn, cut up leather, bake bricks, bleach linen, tan hides, or break up the soil of the earth with the plough and garner the gifts of Demeter, if he could live in idleness and free from all this work?

CHREMYLUS: What nonsense all this is! All these trades which you just mention will be plied by our slaves.

POVERTY: Your slaves! And by what means will these slaves be got?

CHREMYLUS: We will buy them.

POVERTY: But first say, who will sell them, if everyone is rich?

CHREMYLUS: Some greedy dealer from Thessaly—the land which supplies so many.

POVERTY: But if your system is applied, there won't be a single slave-dealer left. What rich man would risk his life to devote himself to this traffic? You will have to toil, to dig and submit yourself to all kinds of hard labour; so that your life would be more wretched even than it is now.

CHREMYLUS: May this prediction fall upon yourself!

POVERTY: You will not be able to sleep in a bed, for no more will ever be manufactured; nor on carpets, for who would weave them if he had gold? When you bring a young bride to your dwelling, you will have no essences wherewith to perfume her, nor rich embroidered cloaks dyed with dazzling colours in which to clothe her. And yet what is the use of being rich, if you are to be deprived of all these enjoyments? On the other hand, you have all that you need in abundance, thanks to me; to the artisan I am like a severe mistress, who forces him by need and poverty to seek the means of earning his livelihood.

CHREMYLUS: And what good thing can you give us, unless it be burns in the bath,[37] and swarms of brats and old women who cry with hunger, and clouds uncountable of lice, gnats and flies, which hover about the wretch's head, trouble him, awake him and say, "You will be hungry, but get up!" Besides, to possess a rag in place of a mantle, a pallet of rushes swarming with bugs, that do not let you close your eyes for a bed; a rotten piece of matting for a coverlet; a big stone for a pillow, on which to lay your head; to eat mallow roots instead of bread, and leaves of withered radish instead of cake; to have nothing but the cover of a broken jug for a stool, the stave of a cask, and broken at that, for a kneading-trough, that is the life you make for us! Are these the mighty benefits with which you pretend to load mankind?

POVERTY: 'Tis not my life that you describe; you are attacking the existence beggars lead.

CHREMYLUS: Is beggary not Poverty's sister?

POVERTY: Thrasybulus and Dionysius[38] are one and the same according to you. No, my life is not like that and never will be. The beggar, whom you have depicted to us, never possesses anything. The poor man lives thriftily and attentive to his work; he has not got too much, but he does not lack what he really needs.

CHREMYLUS: Oh! what a happy life, by Demeter! to live sparingly, to toil incessantly and not to leave enough to pay for a tomb!

POVERTY: That's it! Jest, jeer, and never talk seriously! But what you don't know is this, that men with me are worth more, both in mind and body, than with Plutus. With him they are gouty, big-bellied, heavy of limb and scandalously stout; with me they are thin, wasp-waisted, and terrible to the foe.

---

37. During the winter the poor went into the public baths for shelter against the cold; they could even stop there all night; sometimes they burnt themselves by getting too near the furnace which heated the water.

38. I.e. the most opposite things; the tyranny of Dionysius of Syracuse and the liberty which Thrasybulus restored to Athens.

CHREMYLUS: 'Tis no doubt by starving them that you give them that waspish waist.

POVERTY: As for behaviour, I will prove to you that modesty dwells with me and insolence with Plutus.

CHREMYLUS: Oh! the sweet modesty of stealing and breaking through walls.[39]

BLEPSIDEMUS: Aye, the thief is truly modest, for he hides himself.

POVERTY: Look at the orators in our republics; as long as they are poor, both State and people can only praise their uprightness; but once they are fattened on the public funds, they conceive a hatred for justice, plan intrigues against the people and attack the democracy.

CHREMYLUS: That is absolutely true, although your tongue is very vile. But it matters not, so don't put on those triumphant airs; you shall not be punished any the less for having tried to persuade me that poverty is worth more than wealth.

POVERTY: Not being able to refute my arguments, you chatter at random and exert yourself to no purpose.

CHREMYLUS: Then tell me this, why does all mankind flee from you?

POVERTY: Because I make them better. Children do the very same; they flee from the wise counsels of their fathers. So difficult is it to see one's true interest.

CHREMYLUS: Will you say that Zeus cannot discern what is best? Well, he takes Plutus to himself. . .

BLEPSIDEMUS: . . . and banishes Poverty to earth.

POVERTY: Ah me! how purblind you are, you old fellows of the days of Saturn! Why, Zeus is poor, and I will clearly prove it to you. In the Olympic games, which he founded, and to which he convokes the whole of Greece every four years, why does he only crown the victorious athletes with wild olive? If he were rich he would give them gold.

CHREMYLUS: 'Tis in that way he shows that he clings to his wealth; he is sparing with it, won't part with any portion of it, only bestows baubles on the victors and keeps his money for himself.

POVERTY: But wealth coupled to such sordid greed is yet more shameful than poverty.

CHREMYLUS: May Zeus destroy you, both you and your chaplet of wild olive!

---

39. Crimes to which men are driven through poverty.

POVERTY: Thus you dare to maintain that poverty is not the fount of all blessings!

CHREMYLUS: Ask Hecaté[40] whether it is better to be rich or starving; she will tell you that the rich send her a meal every month and that the poor make it disappear before it is even served. But go and hang yourself and don't breathe another syllable. I will not be convinced against my will.

POVERTY: "Oh! citizens of Argos! do you hear what he says?"[41]

CHREMYLUS: Invoke Pauson, your boon companion, rather.[42]

POVERTY: Alas! what is to become of me?

CHREMYLUS: Get you gone, be off quick and a pleasant journey to you.

POVERTY: But where shall I go?

CHREMYLUS: To gaol; but hurry up, let us put an end to this.

POVERTY: One day you will recall me.

CHREMYLUS: Then you can return; but disappear for the present. I prefer to be rich; you are free to knock your head against the walls in your rage.

BLEPSIDEMUS: And I too welcome wealth. I want, when I leave the bath all perfumed with essences, to feast bravely with my wife and children and to break wind in the faces of toilers and Poverty.

CHREMYLUS: So that hussy has gone at last! But let us make haste to put Plutus to bed in the Temple of Aesculapius.

BLEPSIDEMUS: Let us make haste; else some bothering fellow may again come to interrupt us.

CHREMYLUS: Cario, bring the coverlets and all that I have got ready from the house; let us conduct the god to the Temple, taking care to observe all the proper rites.

CHORUS: (*Missing*)[43]

---

40. The ancients placed statues of Hecaté at the cross-roads ([Greek: triodoi], places where three roads meet), because of the three names, Artemis, Phoebé and Hecaté, under which the same goddess was worshipped. On the first day of the month the rich had meals served before these statues and invited the poor to them.

41. A verse from Euripides' lost play of 'Telephus.' The same line occurs in 'The Knights.'

42. And not the citizens of Argos, whom agriculture and trade rendered wealthy.— Pauson was an Athenian painter, whose poverty had become a proverb. "Poorer than Pauson" was a common saying.

43. There is here a long interval of time, during which Plutus is taken to the Temple of Aesculapius and cured of his blindness. In the first edition probably the Parabasis came in here; at all events a long choral ode must have intervened.

CARIO: Oh! you old fellows, who used to dip out the broth served
to the poor at the festival of Theseus with little pieces of bread[44]
hollowed like a spoon, how worthy of envy is your fate! How
happy you are, both you and all just men!

CHORUS: My good fellow, what has happened to your friends? You
seem the bearer of good tidings.

CARIO: What joy for my master and even more for Plutus! The god
has regained his sight; his eyes sparkle with the greatest brilliancy,
thanks to the benevolent care of Aesculapius.

CHORUS: Oh! what transports of joy! oh! What shouts of gladness!

CARIO: Aye! one is compelled to rejoice, whether one will or not.

CHORUS: I will sing to the honour of Aesculapius, the son of
illustrious Zeus, with a resounding voice; he is the beneficent star
which men adore.

CHREMYLUS' WIFE: What mean these shouts? Is there good news.
With what impatience have I been waiting in the house, and for so
long too!

CARIO: Quick! quick! some wine, mistress. And drink yourself, for 'tis
much to your taste; I bring you all blessings in a lump.

WIFE: Where are they?

CARIO: In my words, as you are going to see.

WIFE: Have done with trifling! come, speak.

CARIO: Listen, I am going to tell you everything from the feet to the
head.

WIFE: Ah! don't throw anything at my head.

CARIO: Not even the happiness that has come to you?

WIFE: No, no, nothing. . . to annoy me.

CARIO: Having arrived near to the Temple with our patient, then so
unfortunate, but now at the apex of happiness, of blessedness, we
first led him down to the sea to purify him.

WIFE: Ah! what a singular pleasure for an old man to bathe in the cold
sea-water!

CARIO: Then we repaired to the Temple of the god. Once the wafers
and the various offerings had been consecrated upon the altar, and
the cake of wheaten-meal had been handed over to the devouring

---

44. The Athenians had erected a temple to Theseus and instituted feasts in his honour,
which were still kept up in the days of Plutarch and Pausanias. Barley broth and other
coarse foods were distributed among the poor.

Hephaestus, we made Plutus lie on a couch according to the rite, and each of us prepared himself a bed of leaves.

WIFE: Had any other folk come to beseech the deity?

CARIO: Yes. Firstly, Neoclides,[45] who is blind, but steals much better than those who see clearly; then many others attacked by complaints of all kinds. The lights were put out and the priest enjoined us to sleep, especially recommending us to keep silent should we hear any noise. There we were all lying down quite quietly. I could not sleep; I was thinking of a certain stew-pan full of pap placed close to an old woman and just behind her head. I had a furious longing to slip towards that side. But just as I was lifting my head, I noticed the priest, who was sweeping off both the cakes and the figs on the sacred table; then he made the round of the altars and sanctified the cakes that remained, by stowing them away in a bag. I therefore resolved to follow such a pious example and made straight for the pap.

WIFE: You wretch! and had you no fear of the god?

CARIO: Aye, indeed! I feared that the god with his crown on his head might have been near the stew-pan before me. I said to myself, "Like priest, like god." On hearing the noise I made, the old woman put out her hand, but I hissed and bit it, just as a sacred serpent might have done.[46] Quick she drew back her hand, slipped down into the bed with her head beneath the coverlets and never moved again; only she let go some wind in her fear which stunk worse than a weasel. As for myself, I swallowed a goodly portion of the pap and, having made a good feed, went back to bed.

WIFE: And did not the god come?

CAIRO: He did not tarry; and when he was near us, oh! dear! such a good joke happened. My belly was quite blown out, and I let wind with the loudest of noises.

WIFE: Doubtless the god pulled a wry face?

CARIO: No, but Iaso blushed a little and Panacea[47] turned her head away, holding her nose; for my perfume is not that of roses.

---

45. He was an orator, who was accused of theft and extortion, and who, moreover, was said not to be a genuine Athenian citizen.

46. The serpent was sacred to Aesculapius; several of these reptiles lived in the temple of the god.

47. Iaso (from [Greek: iasthai], to heal) and Panacea (from [Greek: pan], everything, and [Greek: akeisthai], to cure) were daughters of Aesculapius.

WIFE: And what did the god do?

CARIO: He paid not the slightest heed.

WIFE: He must then be a pretty coarse kind of god?

CARIO: I don't say that, but he's used to tasting shit.[48]

WIFE: Impudent knave, go on with you!

CARIO: Then I hid myself in my bed all a-tremble. Aesculapius did the round of the patients and examined them all with great attention; then a slave placed beside him a stone mortar, a pestle and a little box.[49]

WIFE: Of stone?

CARIO: No, not of stone.

WIFE: But how could you see all this, you arch-rascal, when you say you were hiding all the time?

CARIO: Why, great gods, through my cloak, for 'tis not without holes! He first prepared an ointment for Neoclides; he threw three heads of Tenian[50] garlic into the mortar, pounded them with an admixture of fig-tree sap and lentisk, moistened the whole with Sphettian[51] vinegar, and, turning back the patient's eyelids, applied his salve to the interior of the eyes, so that the pain might be more excruciating. Neoclides shrieked, howled, sprang towards the foot of his bed and wanted to bolt, but the god laughed and said to him, "Keep where you are with your salve; by doing this you will not go and perjure yourself before the Assembly."

WIFE: What a wise god and what a friend to our city!

CARIO: Thereupon he came and seated himself at the head of Plutus' bed, took a perfectly clean rag and wiped his eye-lids; Panacea covered his head and face with a purple cloth, while the god whistled, and two enormous snakes came rushing from the sanctuary.

WIFE: Great gods!

CARIO: They slipped gently beneath the purple cloth and, as far as I could judge, licked the patient's eyelids; for, in less time than even you need, mistress, to drain down ten beakers of wine, Plutus rose up; he could see. I clapped my hands with joy and awoke my master, and the god immediately disappeared with the serpents into the sanctuary. As for those who were lying near Plutus, you can imagine that they embraced him tenderly. Dawn broke and

---

48. He has to see, examine, and taste pill, potion, urine. . . and worse.

49. An apothecary's outfit.

50. Tenos is one of the Cyclades, near Andros.

51. A deme of Attica, where the strongest vinegar came from.

not one of them had closed an eye. As for myself, I did not cease thanking the god who had so quickly restored to Plutus his sight and had made Neoclides blinder than ever.

WIFE: Oh! thou great Aesculapius! How mighty is thy power! (*To Cario*) But tell me, where is Plutus now?

CARIO: He is approaching, escorted by an immense crowd. The rich, whose wealth is ill-gotten, are knitting their brows and shooting at him looks of fierce hate, while the just folk, who led a wretched existence, embrace him and grasp his hand in the transport of their joy; they follow in his wake, their heads wreathed with garlands, laughing and blessing their deliverer; the old men make the earth resound as they walk together keeping time. Come, all of you, all, down to the very least, dance, leap and form yourselves into a chorus; no longer do you risk being told, when you go home, "There is no meal in the bag."

WIFE: And I, by Hecate! I will string you a garland of cakes for the good tidings you have brought me.

CARIO: Hurry, make haste then; our friends are close at hand.

WIFE: I will go indoors to fetch some gifts of welcome, to celebrate these eyes that have just been opened.

CARIO: Meantime I am going forth to meet them.

CHORUS: (*Missing*)

PLUTUS: I adore thee, oh! thou divine sun, and thee I greet thou city, the beloved of Pallas; be welcome, thou land of Cecrops, which hast received me. Alas! what manner of men I associated with! I blush to think of it. While, on the other hand, I shunned those who deserved my friendship; I knew neither the vices of the ones nor the virtues of the others. A twofold mistake, and in both cases equally fatal! Ah! what a misfortune was mine! But I want to change everything; and in future I mean to prove to mankind that, if I gave to the wicked, 'twas against my will.

CHREMYLUS (*to the crowd who impede him*): Get you gone! Oh! what a lot of friends spring into being when you are fortunate! They dig me with their elbows and bruise my shins to prove their affection. Each one wants to greet me. What a crowd of old fellows thronged round me on the market-place!

WIFE: Oh! thou, who art dearest of all to me, and thou too, be welcome! Allow me, Plutus, to shower these gifts of welcome over you in due accord with custom.

PLUTUS: No. This is the first house I enter after having regained my sight; I shall take nothing from it, for 'tis my place rather to give.

WIFE: Do you refuse these gifts?

PLUTUS: I will accept them at your fireside, as custom requires. Besides, we shall thus avoid a ridiculous scene; it is not meet that the poet should throw dried figs and dainties to the spectators; 'tis a vulgar trick to make 'em laugh.

WIFE: You are right. Look! yonder's Dexinicus, who was already getting to his feet to catch the figs as they flew past him.[52]

CHORUS: (*Missing*)

CARIO: How pleasant it is, friends, to live well, especially when it costs nothing! What a deluge of blessings flood our household, and that too without our having wronged ever a soul! Ah! what a delightful thing is wealth! The bin is full of white flour and the wine-jars run over with fragrant liquor; all the chests are crammed with gold and silver, 'tis a sight to see; the tank is full of oil,[53] the phials with perfumes, and the garret with dried figs. Vinegar flasks, plates, stew-pots and all the platters are of brass; our rotten old wooden trenchers for the fish have to-day become dishes of silver; the very night-commode is of ivory. We others, the slaves, we play at odd and even with gold pieces, and carry luxury so far that we no longer wipe ourselves with stones, but use garlic stalks instead. My master, at this moment, is crowned with flowers and sacrificing a pig, a goat and a ram;[54] 'tis the smoke that has driven me out, for I could no longer endure it, it hurt my eyes so.

A JUST MAN: Come, my child, come with me. Let us go and find the god.

CHREMYLUS: Who comes here?

JUST MAN: A man who was once wretched, but now is happy.

CHREMYLUS: A just man then?

JUST MAN: You have it.

---

52. The Scholiast says that this was an individual as poor as he was greedy, and on the watch for every opportunity to satisfy his voracity.—The comic poets often had nuts, figs and other petty dainties thrown to the audience. It was a fairly good way to secure the favour of a certain section of the public.

53. The ancients used oil in large quantities, whether for rubbing themselves down after bathing or before their exercises in the palaestra, or for the different uses of domestic life. It was kept in a kind of tank, hollowed in the ground and covered with tiles or stones. The wine-sellers had similar tanks, but of larger size, for keeping their wine.

54. This was what was styled the triple or complete sacrifice.

CHREMYLUS: Well! what do you want?

JUST MAN: I come to thank the god for all the blessings he has showered on me. My father had left me a fairly decent fortune, and I helped those of my friends who were in want; 'twas, to my thinking, the most useful thing I could do with my fortune.

CHREMYLUS: And you were quickly ruined?

JUST MAN: Entirely.

CHREMYLUS: Since then you have been living in misery?

JUST MAN: In truth I have; I thought I could count, in case of need, upon the friends whose property I had helped, but they turned their backs upon me and pretended not to see me.

CHREMYLUS: They laughed at you, 'tis evident.

JUST MAN: Just so. With my empty coffers, I had no more friends.

CHREMYLUS: But your lot has changed.

JUST MAN: Yes, and so I come to the god to make him the acts of gratitude that are his due.

CHREMYLUS: But with what object now do you bring this old cloak, which your slave is carrying? Tell me.

JUST MAN: I wish to dedicate it to the god.[55]

CHREMYLUS: Were you initiated into the Great Mysteries in that cloak?[56]

JUST MAN: No, but I shivered in it for thirteen years.

CHREMYLUS: And this footwear?

JUST MAN: These also are my winter companions.

CHREMYLUS: And you wish to dedicate them too?

JUST MAN: Unquestionably.

CHREMYLUS: Fine presents to offer to the god!

AN INFORMER: Alas! alas! I am a lost man. Ah! thrice, four, five, twelve times, or rather ten thousand times unhappy fate! Why, why must fortune deal me such rough blows?

CHREMYLUS: Oh, Apollo, my tutelary! oh! ye favourable gods! what has overtaken this man?

---

55. As evidence of the sorry condition from which he had been raised.

56. The clothes a man wore on the day that he was initiated into the Mysteries of Eleusis had, according to custom, to be dedicated to the gods, but only after they had been worn. Most people only decided to do this when they were full of holes and torn; it is because his visitor's cloak is in such a sorry condition that Chremylus takes it to be the cloak of an Initiate.

INFORMER: Ah! am I not deserving of pity? I have lost everything; this cursed god has stripped me bare. Ah! if there be justice in heaven, he shall be struck blind again.

JUST MAN: Methinks I know what's the matter. If this man is unfortunate, 'tis because he's of little account and small honesty; and i' faith he looks it too.

CHREMYLUS: Then, by Zeus! his plight is but just.

INFORMER: He promised that if he recovered his sight, he would enrich us all unaided; whereas he has ruined more than one.

CHREMYLUS: But whom has he thus ill-used?

INFORMER: Me.

CHREMYLUS: You were doubtless a villainous thief then.

INFORMER (*to Chremylus and Cario*): 'Tis rather you yourselves who were such wretches; I am certain you have got my money.

CHREMYLUS: Ha! by Demeter! 'tis an informer. What impudence!

CARIO: He's ravenously hungry, that's certain.

INFORMER: You shall follow me this very instant to the marketplace, where the torture of the wheel shall force the confession of your misdeeds from you.

CARIO: Ha! look out for yourself!

JUST MAN: By Zeus the Deliverer, what gratitude all Greeks owe to Plutus, if he destroys these vile informers!

INFORMER: You are laughing at me. Ho! ho! I denounce you as their accomplice. Where did you steal that new cloak from? Yesterday I saw you with one utterly worn out.

JUST MAN: I fear you not, thanks to this ring, for which I paid Eudemus[57] a drachma.

CHREMYLUS: Ah! there's no ring to preserve you from the informer's bite.

INFORMER: The insolent wretches! But, my fine jokers, you have not told me what you are up to here. Nothing good, I'll be bound.

CHREMYLUS: Nothing of any good for you, be sure of that.

INFORMER: By Zeus! you're going to dine at my expense!

CHREMYLUS: You vile impostor, may you burst with an empty belly, both you and your witness.

---

57. This Eudemus was a kind of sorcerer, who sold magic rings, to which, among other virtues, he ascribed that of curing, or rather of securing him who wore them, from snake-bites.

INFORMER: You deny it? I reckon, you villians, that there is much salt fish and roast meat in this house. Hu! hu! hu! hu! hu! hu! (*He sniffs*)

CHREMYLUS: Can you smell anything, rascal?

INFORMER: Can such outrages be borne, oh, Zeus! Ye gods! how cruel it is to see me treated thus, when I am such an honest fellow and such a good citizen!

CHREMYLUS: You an honest man! you a good citizen!

INFORMER: A better one than any.

CHREMYLUS: Ah! well then, answer my questions.

INFORMER: Concerning what?

CHREMYLUS: Are you a husbandman?

INFORMER: D'ye take me for a fool?

CHREMYLUS: A merchant?

INFORMER: I assume the title, when it serves me.[58]

CHREMYLUS: Do you ply any trade?

INFORMER: No, most assuredly not!

CHREMYLUS: Then how do you live, if you do nothing?

INFORMER: I superintend public and private business.

CHREMYLUS: You! And by what right, pray?

INFORMER: Because it pleases me to do so.

CHREMYLUS: Like a thief you sneak yourself in where you have no business. You are hated by all and you claim to be an honest man?

INFORMER: What, you fool? I have not the right to dedicate myself entirely to my country's service?

CHREMYLUS: Is the country served by vile intrigue?

INFORMER: It is served by watching that the established law is observed—by allowing no one to violate it.

CHREMYLUS: That's the duty of the tribunals; they are established to that end.

INFORMER: And who is the prosecutor before the dicasts?

CHREMYLUS: Whoever wishes to be.[59]

---

58. The merchants engaged in maritime commerce were absolved from military service; the Scholiast even declares, though it seems highly unlikely, that all merchants were exempt from imposts on their possessions. When it was a question of escaping taxes and military service the informer passed as a merchant.

59. At Athens 'twas only the injured person who could prosecute in private disputes; everyone, however, had this right where wrongs against the State were involved; but if the prosecutor only obtained one-fifth of the votes, he was condemned to a fine of 1000 drachmae or banished the country.

INFORMER: Well then, 'tis I who choose to be prosecutor; and thus all public affairs fall within my province.

CHREMYLUS: I pity Athens for being in such vile clutches. But would you not prefer to live quietly and free from all care and anxiety?

INFORMER: To do nothing is to live an animal's life.

CHREMYLUS: Thus you will not change your mode of life?

INFORMER: No, though they gave me Plutus himself and the *silphium* of Battus.[60]

CHREMYLUS (*to the Informer*): Come, quick, off with your cloak.

CARIO: Hi! friend! 'tis you they are speaking to.

CHREMYLUS: Off with your shoes.

CARIO: All this is addressed to you.

INFORMER: Very well! let one of you come near me, if he dares.

CARIO: I dare.

INFORMER: Alas! I am robbed of my clothes in full daylight.

CARIO: That's what comes of meddling with other folk's business and living at their expense.

INFORMER (*to his witness*): You see what is happening; I call you to witness.

CHREMYLUS: Look how the witness whom you brought is taking to his heels.

INFORMER: Great gods! I am all alone and they assault me.

CARIO: Shout away!

INFORMER: Oh! woe, woe is me!

CARIO: Give me that old ragged cloak, that I may dress out the informer.

JUST MAN: No, no; I have dedicated it to Plutus.

CARIO: And where would your offering be better bestowed than on the shoulders of a rascal and a thief? To Plutus fine, rich cloaks should be given.

JUST MAN: And what then shall be done with these shoes? Tell me.

CARIO: I will nail them to his brow as gifts are nailed to the trunks of the wild olive.

---

60. A proverbial saying, meaning, *the most precious thing*.—Battus, a Lacedaemonian, led out a colony from Thera, an island in the Aegean sea, and, about 630 B.C., founded the city of Cyrené in Africa. He was its first king, and after death was honoured as a god. The inhabitants of that country gathered great quantities of *silphium* or 'laserpitium,' the sap of which plant was the basis of medicaments and sauces that commanded a high price. The coins of Cyrené bore the representation of a stalk of *silphium*.

INFORMER: I'm off, for you are the strongest, I own. But if I find someone to join me, let him be as weak as he will, I will summon this god, who thinks himself so strong, before the Court this very day, and denounce him as manifestly guilty of overturning the democracy by his will alone and without the consent of the Senate or the popular Assembly.

JUST MAN: Now that you are rigged out from head to foot with my old clothes, hasten to the bath and stand there in the front row to warm yourself better; 'tis the place I formerly had.

CHREMYLUS: Ah! the bath-man would grip you by the testicles and fling you through the door; he would only need to see you to appraise you at your true value. . . But let us go in, friend, that you may address your thanksgivings to the god.

CHORUS: (*Missing*)

AN OLD WOMAN: Dear old men, am I near the house where the new god lives, or have I missed the road?

CHORUS: You are at his door, my pretty little maid, who question us so sweetly.[61]

OLD WOMAN: Then I will summon someone in the house.

CHREMYLUS: 'Tis needless! I am here myself. But what matter brings you here?

OLD WOMAN: Ah! a cruel, unjust fate! My dear friend, this god has made life unbearable to me through ceasing to be blind.

CHREMYLUS: What does this mean? Can you be a female informer?

OLD WOMAN: Most certainly not.

CHREMYLUS: Have you not drunk up your money then?

OLD WOMAN: You are mocking me! Nay! I am being devoured with a consuming fire.

CHREMYLUS: Then tell me what is consuming you so fiercely.

OLD WOMAN: Listen! I loved a young man, who was poor, but so handsome, so well-built, so honest! He readily gave way to all I desired and acquitted himself so well! I, for my part, refused him nothing.

CHREMYLUS: And what did he generally ask of you.

OLD WOMAN: Very little; he bore himself towards me with astonishing discretion! perchance twenty drachmae for a cloak or eight for footwear; sometimes he begged me to buy tunics for his

---

61. The old woman had entered dressed as a young girl. Or is it merely said ironically?

sisters or a little mantle for his mother; at times he needed four bushels of corn.

CHREMYLUS: 'Twas very little, in truth; I admire his modesty.

OLD WOMAN: And 'twas not as a reward for his complacency that he ever asked me for anything, but as a matter of pure friendship; a cloak I had given would remind him from whom he had got it.

CHREMYLUS: 'Twas a fellow who loved you madly.

OLD WOMAN: But 'tis no longer so, for the faithless wretch has sadly altered! I had sent him this cake with the sweetmeats you see here on this dish and let him know that I would visit him in the evening. . .

CHREMYLUS: Well?

OLD WOMAN: He sent me back my presents and added this tart to them, on condition that I never set foot in his house again. Besides, he sent me this message, "Once upon a time the Milesians were brave."[62]

CHREMYLUS: An honest lad, indeed! But what would you? When poor, he would devour anything; now he is rich, he no longer cares for lentils.

OLD WOMAN: Formerly he came to me every day.

CHREMYLUS: To see if you were being buried?

OLD WOMAN: No! he longed to hear the sound of my voice.

CHREMYLUS: And to carry off some present.

OLD WOMAN: If I was downcast, he would call me his little duck or his little dove in a most tender manner. . .

CHREMYLUS: And then would ask for the wherewithal to buy a pair of shoes.

OLD WOMAN: When I was at the Mysteries of Eleusis in a carriage,[63] someone looked at me; he was so jealous that he beat me the whole of that day.

CHREMYLUS: 'Twas because he liked to feed alone.

OLD WOMAN: He told me I had very beautiful hands.

---

62. A proverb, meaning, *"All things change with time."* Addressed to the old woman, it meant that she had perhaps been beautiful once, but that the days for love were over for her.—Miletus, the most powerful of the Ionic cities, had a very numerous fleet and founded more than eighty colonies; falling beneath the Persian yoke, the city never succeeded in regaining its independence.

63. Eleusis was some distance from Athens, about seven and a half miles, and the wealthy women drove there. It was an occasion when they vied with each other in the display of luxury.

CHREMYLUS: Aye, no doubt, when they handed him twenty drachmae.

OLD WOMAN: That my whole body breathed a sweet perfume.

CHREMYLUS: Yes, like enough, if you poured him out Thasian wine.

OLD WOMAN: That my glance was gentle and charming.

CHREMYLUS: 'Twas no fool. He knew how to drag drachmae from a hot-blooded old woman.

OLD WOMAN: Ah! the god has done very, very wrong, saying he would support the victims of injustice.

CHREMYLUS: Well, what must he do? Speak, and it shall be done.

OLD WOMAN: 'Tis right to compel him, whom I have loaded with benefits, to repay them in his turn; if not, he does not merit the least of the god's favours.

CHREMYLUS: And did he not do this every night?

OLD WOMAN: He swore he would never leave me, as long as I lived.

CHREMYLUS: Aye, rightly; but he thinks you are no longer alive.[64]

OLD WOMAN: Ah! friend, I am pining away with grief.

CHREMYLUS: You are rotting away, it seems to me.

OLD WOMAN: I have grown so thin, I could slip through a ring.

CHREMYLUS: Yes, if 'twere as large as the hoop of a sieve.

OLD WOMAN: But here is the youth, the cause of my complaint; he looks as though he were going to a festival.

CHREMYLUS: Yes, if his chaplet and his torch are any guides.

YOUTH: Greeting to you.

OLD WOMAN: What does he say?

YOUTH: My ancient old dear, you have grown white very quickly, by heaven!

OLD WOMAN: Oh! what an insult!

CHREMYLUS: It is a long time, then, since he saw you?

OLD WOMAN: A long time? My god! he was with me yesterday.

CHREMYLUS: It must be, then, that, unlike other people, he sees more clearly when he's drunk.

OLD WOMAN: No, but I have always known him for an insolent fellow.

YOUTH: Oh! divine Posidon! Oh, ye gods of old age! what wrinkles she has on her face!

OLD WOMAN: Oh! oh! keep your distance with that torch.

CHREMYLUS: Yes, 'twould be as well; if a single spark were to reach her, she would catch alight like an old olive branch.

---

64. You are so old.

ARISTOPHANES

YOUTH: I propose to have a game with you.

OLD WOMAN: Where, naughty boy?

YOUTH: Here. Take some nuts in your hand.

OLD WOMAN: What game is this?

YOUTH: Let's play at guessing how many teeth you have.

CHREMYLUS: Ah! I'll tell you; she's got three, or perhaps four.

YOUTH: Pay up; you've lost! she has only one single grinder.

OLD WOMAN: You wretch! you're not in your right senses. Do you insult me thus before this crowd?

YOUTH: I am washing you thoroughly; 'tis doing you a service.

CHREMYLUS: No, no! as she is there, she can still deceive; but if this white-lead is washed off, her wrinkles would come out plainly.

OLD WOMAN: You are only an old fool!

YOUTH: Ah! he is playing the gallant, he is fondling your breasts, and thinks I do not see it.

OLD WOMAN: Oh! no, by Aphrodité, no, you naughty jealous fellow.

CHREMYLUS: Oh! most certainly not, by Hecaté![65] Verily and indeed I would need to be mad! But, young man, I cannot forgive you, if you cast off this beautiful child.

YOUTH: Why, I adore her.

CHREMYLUS: But nevertheless she accuses you. . .

YOUTH: Accuses me of what?

CHREMYLUS: . . . of having told her insolently, "Once upon a time the Milesians were brave."

YOUTH: Oh! I shall not dispute with you about her.

CHREMYLUS: Why not?

YOUTH: Out of respect for your age; with anyone but you, I should not be so easy; come, take the girl and be happy.

CHREMYLUS: I see, I see; you don't want her any more.

OLD WOMAN: Nay! this is a thing that cannot be allowed.

YOUTH: I cannot argue with a woman, who has been making love these thirteen thousand years.

CHREMYLUS: Yet, since you liked the wine, you should now consume the lees.

YOUTH: But these lees are quite rancid and fusty.

CHREMYLUS: Pass them through a straining-cloth; they'll clarify.

YOUTH: But I want to go in with you to offer these chaplets to the god.

---

65. The goddess of death and old age.

OLD WOMAN: And I too have something to tell him.

YOUTH: Then I don't enter.

CHREMYLUS: Come, have no fear; she won't harm you.

YOUTH: 'Tis true; I've been managing the old bark long enough.

OLD WOMAN: Go in; I'll follow after you.

CHREMYLUS: Good gods! that old hag has fastened herself to her youth like a limpet to its rock.

CHORUS: (*Missing*)

CARIO (*opening the door*): Who knocks at the door? Halloa! I see no one; 'twas then by chance it gave forth that plaintive tone.

HERMES (*to Carlo, who is about to close the door*): Cario! stop!

CARIO: Eh! friend, was it you who knocked so loudly? Tell me.

HERMES: No, I was going to knock and you forestalled me by opening. Come, call your master quick, then his wife and his children, then his slave and his dog, then thyself and his pig.

CARIO: And what's it all about?

HERMES: It's about this, rascal! Zeus wants to serve you all with the same sauce and hurl the lot of you into the Barathrum.

CARIO: Have a care for your tongue, you bearer of ill tidings! But why does he want to treat us in that scurvy fashion?

HERMES: Because you have committed the most dreadful crime. Since Plutus has recovered his sight, there is nothing for us other gods, neither incense, nor laurels, nor cakes, nor victims, nor anything in the world.

CARIO: And you will never be offered anything more; you governed us too ill.

HERMES: I care nothing at all about the other gods, but 'tis myself. I tell you I am dying of hunger.

CARIO: That's reasoning like a wise fellow.

HERMES: Formerly, from earliest dawn, I was offered all sorts of good things in the wine-shops,—wine-cakes, honey, dried figs, in short, dishes worthy of Hermes. Now, I lie the livelong day on my back, with my legs in the air, famishing.

CARIO: And quite right too, for you often had them punished who treated you so well.[66]

---

66. Wineshop-keepers were often punished for serving false measure. Hermes, who allowed them to be punished although he was the god of cheating and was worshipped as such by the wineshop-keepers, deserved to be neglected by them.

HERMES: Ah! the lovely cake they used to knead for me on the fourth of the month![67]

CARIO: You recall it vainly; your regrets are useless! there'll be no more cake.

HERMES: Ah! the ham I was wont to devour!

CARIO: Well then! make use of your legs and hop on one leg upon the wine-skin,[68] to while away the time.

HERMES: Oh! the grilled entrails I used to swallow down!

CARIO: Your own have got the colic, methinks.

HERMES: Oh! the delicious tipple, half wine, half water!

CARIO: Here, swallow that and be off. (*He discharges a fart*)

HERMES: Would you do a friend a service?

CARIO: Willingly, if I can.

HERMES: Give me some well-baked bread and a big hunk of the victims they are sacrificing in your house.

CARIO: That would be stealing.

HERMES: Do you forget, then, how I used to take care he knew nothing about it when you were stealing something from your master?

CARIO: Because I used to share it with you, you rogue; some cake or other always came your way.

HERMES: Which afterwards you ate up all by yourself.[69]

CARIO: But then you did not share the blows when I was caught.

HERMES: Forget past injuries, now you have taken Phylé.[70] Ah! how I should like to live with you! Take pity and receive me.

CARIO: You would leave the gods to stop here?

HERMES: One is much better off among you.

CARIO: What! you would desert! Do you think that is honest?

---

67. The greater gods had a day in each month specially dedicated to them; thus Hermes had the fourth, Artemis the sixth, Apollo the seventh, etc.

68. This game, which was customary during the feasts of Bacchus' consisted in hopping on one leg upon a wine-skin that was blown out and well greased with oil; the competitor who kept his footing longest on one leg, gained the prize.

69. The cake was placed on the altar, but eaten afterwards by the priest or by him who offered the sacrifice.

70. An allusion to the occupation of Phylé, in Attica on the Boeotian border, by Thrasybulus; this place was the meeting-place of the discontented and the exiled, and it was there that the expulsion of the thirty tyrants was planned. Once victorious, the conspirators proclaimed a general amnesty and swore to forget everything, (Greek: m e mn esikakein), 'to bear no grudge,' hence the proverb which Aristophanes recalls here.

HERMES: "Where I live well, there is my country."[71]

CARIO: But how could we employ you here?

HERMES: Place me near the door; I am the watchman god and would shift off the robbers.

CARIO: Shift off! Ah! but we have no love for shifts.

HERMES: Entrust me with business dealings.

CARIO: But we are rich; why should we keep a haggling Hermes?

HERMES: Let me intrigue for you.[72]

CARIO: No, no, intrigues are forbidden; we believe in good faith.

HERMES: I will work for you as a guide.

CARIO: But the god sees clearly now, so we no longer want a guide.

HERMES: Well then, I will preside over the games. Ah! what can you object to in that? Nothing is fitter for Plutus than to give scenic and gymnastic games.[73]

CARIO: How useful 'tis to have so many names! Here you have found the means of earning your bread. I don't wonder the jurymen so eagerly try to get entered for many tribunals.[74]

HERMES: So then, you admit me on these terms.

CARIO: Go and wash the entrails of the victims at the well, so that you may show yourself serviceable at once.

A PRIEST OF ZEUS: Can anyone direct me where Chremylus is?

CHREMYLUS: What would you with him, friend?

PRIEST: Much ill. Since Plutus has recovered his sight, I am perishing of starvation; I, the priest of Zeus the Deliverer, have nothing to eat!

CHREMYLUS: And what is the cause of that, pray?

PRIEST: No one dreams of offering sacrifices.

CHREMYLUS: Why not?

PRIEST: Because all men are rich. Ah! when they had nothing, the merchant who escaped from shipwreck, the accused who was acquitted, all immolated victims; another would sacrifice for the success of some wish and the priest joined in at the feast; but now there is not the smallest victim, not one of the faithful in the temple, but thousands who come there to ease themselves.

CHREMYLUS: Don't you take your share of those offerings?

---

71. A verse taken from a lost tragedy by Euripides.
72. Hermes runs through the gamut of his different attributes.
73. As the rich citizens were accustomed to do at Athens.
74. This trick was very often practised, its object being to secure the double fee.

ARISTOPHANES

PRIEST: Hence I think I too am going to say good-bye to Zeus the Deliverer, and stop here myself.

CHREMYLUS: Be at ease, all will go well, if it so please the god. Zeus the Deliverer[75] is here; he came of his own accord.

PRIEST: Ha! that's good news.

CHREMYLUS: Wait a little; we are going to install Plutus presently in the place he formerly occupied behind the Temple of Athené;[76] there he will watch over our treasures for ever. But let lighted torches be brought; take these and walk in solemn procession in front of the god.

PRIEST: That's magnificent!

CHREMYLUS: Let Plutus be summoned.

OLD WOMAN: And I, what am I to do?

CHREMYLUS: Take the pots of vegetables which we are going to offer to the god in honour of his installation and carry them on your head; you just happen luckily to be wearing a beautiful embroidered robe.

OLD WOMAN: And what about the object of my coming?

CHREMYLUS: Everything shall be according to your wish. The young man will be with you this evening.

OLD WOMAN: Oh! if you promise me his visit, I will right willingly carry the pots.

CHREMYLUS: Those are strange pots indeed! Generally the scum rises to the top of the pots, but here the pots are raised to the top of the old woman.[77]

CHORUS: Let us withdraw without more tarrying, and follow the others, singing as we go.[78]

FINIS OF "PLUTUS"

---

75. He is giving Plutus this title.

76. Within the precincts of the Acropolis, and behind the Temple of Zeus Polias, there stood a building enclosed with double walls and double gates, where the public Treasury was kept. Plutus had ceased to dwell there, i.e. the Peloponnesian war and its disastrous consequences had emptied the Treasury; however, at the time of the production of the 'Plutus,' Athens had recovered her freedom and a part of her former might, and money was again flowing into her coffers.

77. In the Greek there is a pun on the different significations of (Greek: graus), *an old woman,* and the *scum,* or 'mother,' which forms on the top of boiling milk.

78. In the 'Lysistrata' the Chorus similarly makes its exit singing.

A Note About the Author

Aristophanes (450 b.c.–288 b.c.) was an Ancient Greek playwright. Born in Athens, Aristophanes was a leading playwright and master of comic drama whose contribution to Old Attic Comedy made him both a leading artist of his time and a target of political rebuke. Of the forty plays he wrote, only eleven survive today, including *The Clouds* (423 b.c.), *The Birds* (414 b.c.), *Lysistrata* (411 b.c.) and *The Frogs* (405 b.c.). Noted for his unique use of fantastic and absurd plots, musical elements, and pointed political commentary, Aristophanes changed the course of Western literature and left behind a body of work that would influence such figures as Menander, Goethe, and Percy Bysshe Shelley.

A Note from the Publisher

Spanning many genres, from non-fiction essays to literature classics to children's books and lyric poetry, Mint Edition books showcase the master works of our time in a modern new package. The text is freshly typeset, is clean and easy to read, and features a new note about the author in each volume. Many books also include exclusive new introductory material. Every book boasts a striking new cover, which makes it as appropriate for collecting as it is for gift giving. Mint Edition books are only printed when a reader orders them, so natural resources are not wasted. We're proud that our books are never manufactured in excess and exist only in the exact quantity they need to be read and enjoyed.

bookfinity™

Discover more of your favorite classics with Bookfinity™.

- Track your reading with custom book lists.
- Get great book recommendations for your personalized Reader Type.
- Add reviews for your favorite books.
- AND MUCH MORE!

Visit **bookfinity.com** and take the fun Reader Type quiz to get started.

Enjoy our classic and modern companion pairings!